T0183876

Lecture Notes in Artificial Intelligence 11776

Subseries of Lecture Notes in Computer Science

Series Editors

Randy Goebel
University of Alberta, Edmonton, Canada
Yuzuru Tanaka
Hokkaido University, Sapporo, Japan
Wolfgang Wahlster
DFKI and Saarland University, Saarbrücken, Germany

Founding Editor

Jörg Siekmann
DFKI and Saarland University, Saarbrücken, Germany

More information about this series at http://www.springer.com/series/1244

Christos Douligeris · Dimitris Karagiannis ·
Dimitris Apostolou (Eds.)

Knowledge Science, Engineering and Management

12th International Conference, KSEM 2019
Athens, Greece, August 28–30, 2019
Proceedings, Part II

 Springer

Editors
Christos Douligeris 🆔
University of Piraeus
Piraeus, Greece

Dimitris Karagiannis 🆔
University of Vienna
Vienna, Austria

Dimitris Apostolou
University of Piraeus
Piraeus, Greece

ISSN 0302-9743   ISSN 1611-3349   (electronic)
Lecture Notes in Artificial Intelligence
ISBN 978-3-030-29562-2   ISBN 978-3-030-29563-9   (eBook)
https://doi.org/10.1007/978-3-030-29563-9

LNCS Sublibrary: SL7 – Artificial Intelligence

This Springer imprint is published by the registered company Springer Nature Switzerland AG
The registered company address is: Gewerbestrasse 11, 6330 Cham, Switzerland

Preface

The International Conference on Knowledge Science, Engineering and Management (KSEM) provides a forum for researchers in the broad areas of knowledge science, knowledge engineering, and knowledge management to exchange ideas and to report state-of-the-art research results. KSEM 2019 was the 12th in this series, building on the success of the 11 previous events in Guilin, China (KSEM 2006); Melbourne, Australia (KSEM 2007); Vienna, Austria (KSEM 2009); Belfast, UK (KSEM 2010); Irvine, USA (KSEM 2011); Dalian, China (KSEM 2013); Sibiu, Romania (KSEM 2014); Chongqing, China (KSEM2015); Passau, Germany (KSEM 2016); Melbourne, Australia (KSEM 2017); and Changchun, China (KSEM 2018).

The selection process this year was, as always, very competitive. We received 240 submissions, and each submitted paper was reviewed by at least three members of the Program Committee (PC) (including thorough evaluations by the TPC co-chairs). A total of 77 papers were selected as full papers (32%), and 23 as short papers (10%). 10 posters were also presented at the conference to allow for a more personal and extended dialogue.

Moreover, we were honored to have four prestigious scholars giving keynote speeches at the conference: Prof. Stefanos Kollias (University of Lincoln, UK), Prof. Andrea Passerini (University of Trento, Italy), Prof. Xin Geng (Southeast University, China), and Dr. Dimitrios Tzovaras (Information Technologies Institute and CERTH, Greece).

We would like to thank everyone who participated in the development of the KSEM 2019 program. In particular, we want to give special thanks to the PC, for their diligence and concern for the quality of the program, and, also, for their detailed feedback to the authors.

Moreover, we would like to express our gratitude to the KSEM Steering Committee honorary chair Prof. Ruqian Lu (Chinese Academy of Sciences, China), who provided insight and support during all the stages of this effort. The members of the Steering Committee, who followed the progress of the conference very closely, with sharp comments and helpful suggestions. The KSEM 2019 general co-chairs, Prof. Gang Li (Deakin University, Australia) and Prof. Dimitrios Plexousakis (University of Crete and FORTH, Greece), who were extremely supportive in our efforts and in the general success of the conference.

We would like to thank the members of all the other committees and, in particular, those of the local Organizing Committee, who worked diligently for more than a year to provide a wonderful experience to the KSEM participants. We are also grateful to the team at Springer led by Alfred Hofmann for the publication of this volume, who worked very efficiently and effectively with Lecturer Dimitrios Kallergis, our publication co-chair. Finally, and most importantly, we thank all the authors, who are the primary reason that KSEM 2019 was so exciting and why it remains the premier forum for presentation and discussion of innovative ideas, research results, and experience from around the world.

June 2019

Christos Douligeris
Dimitris Karagiannis
Dimitris Apostolou

Organisation

KSEM Steering Committee

Ruqian Lu (Honorary Chair)	Chinese Academy of Sciences, China
Chengqi Zhang (Past Chair)	University of Technology, Australia
Hui Xiong (Chair)	Rutgers University, USA
Dimitris Karagiannis (Deputy Chair)	University of Vienna, Austria
David Bell	Queen's University, UK
Yaxin Bi	Ulster University, UK
Cungen Cao	Chinese Academy of Sciences, China
Zhi Jin	Peking University, China
Kwok Kee Wei	National University of Singapore, Singapore
Claudiu Kifor	Sibiu University, Romania
Jerome Lang	Paul Sabatier University, France
Gang Li	Deakin University, Australia
Yoshiteru Nakamori	JAIST, Japan
Jorg Siekmann	German Research Centre of Artificial Intelligence, Germany
Eric Tsui	Hong Kong Polytechnic University, SAR China
Zongtuo Wang	Dalian Science and Technology University, China
Martin Wirsing	Ludwig-Maximilians-Universität München, Germany
Bo Yang	Jilin University, China
Mingsheng Ying	Tsinghua University, China
Zili Zhang	Southwest University, China

KSEM 2019 Organising Committee

General Co-chairs

Gang Li	Deakin University, Australia
Dimitrios Plexousakis	University of Crete and FORTH, Greece

Program Committee Co-chairs

Christos Douligeris	University of Piraeus, Greece
Dimitris Karagiannis	University of Vienna, Austria
Dimitris Apostolou	University of Piraeus, Greece

Publication Committee Co-chairs

Dimitrios Kallergis	University of West Attica, Greece
Themistoklis Panayiotopoulos	University of Piraeus, Greece

Publicity Committee Co-chairs

Shaowu Liu	University of Technology, Australia
Yannis Theodoridis	University of Piraeus, Greece
Ergina Kavallieratou	University of the Aegean, Greece
Yonggang Zhang	Jilin University, China

Keynote, Special Sessions and Workshop Co-chairs

Yannis Manolopoulos	Open University of Cyprus, Cyprus and Aristotle University of Thessaloniki, Greece
Vassilis Plagianakos	University of Thessaly, Greece

Program Committee

Salem Benferhat	Université d'Artois, France
Paolo Bouquet	University of Trento, Italy
Remus Brad	Lucian Blaga University of Sibiu, Romania
Robert Andrei Buchmann	Babeş-Bolyai University, Romania
Hechang Chen	Jilin University, China
Paolo Ciancarini	University of Bologna, Italy
Ireneusz Czarnowski	Gdynia Maritime University, Poland
Richard Dapoigny	LISTIC/Polytech'Savoie, France
Yong Deng	Southwest University, China
Josep Domingo-Ferrer	Universitat Rovira i Virgili, Spain
Dieter Fensel	University of Innsbruck, Austria
Hans-Georg Fill	University of Fribourg, Switzerland
Yanjie Fu	Missouri University of Science and Technology, USA
Chiara Ghidini	FBK Trento, Italy
Fausto Giunchiglia	University of Trento, Italy
Knut Hinkelmann	FHNW University of Applied Sciences and Arts, Switzerland
Zhisheng Huang	Vrije Universiteit Amsterdam, The Netherlands
Van Nam Huynh	JAIST, Japan
Tan Jianlong	Institute of Information Engineering, Chinese Academy of Sciences, China
Zhi Jin	Peking University, China
Fang Jin	Texas Tech University, USA
Mouna Kamel	IRIT, Université Paul Sabatier, France
Krzysztof Kluza	AGH UST, Poland
Konstantinos Kotis	University of Piraeus, Greece
Yong Lai	Jilin University, China
Ximing Li	Jilin University, China
Ge Li	Peking University, China
Gang Li	Deakin University, Australia
Li Li	Southwest University, China
Huayu Li	The University of North Carolina at Charlotte, USA

Qian Li	Institute of Information Engineering, Chinese Academy of Sciences, China
Junming Liu	Rutgers University, USA
Shaowu Liu	University of Technology Sydney, Australia
Li Liu	Chongqing University, China
Bin Liu	IBM TJ Watson Research Center, USA
Weiru Liu	University of Bristol, UK
Xudong Luo	Guangxi Normal University, China
Bo Ma	Xinjiang Technical Institute of Physics and Chemistry, Chinese Academy of Sciences, China
Stewart Massie	Robert Gordon University, UK
Maheswari N	VIT University, India
Oleg Okun	Cognizant Technology Solutions GmbH, Germany
Dantong Ouyang	Jilin University, China
Guilin Qi	Southeast University, China
Sven-Volker Rehm	WHU - Otto Beisheim School of Management, Germany
Ulrich Reimer	FHS St. Gallen, University of Applied Sciences, Switzerland
Luciano Serafini	FBK Trento, Italy
Leslie Sikos	University of South Australia, Australia
Leilei Sun	Tsinghua University, China
Yanni Velegrakis	University of Trento, Italy
Lucian Vintan	Lucian Blaga University of Sibiu, Romania
Daniel Volovici	Lucian Blaga University of Sibiu, Romania
Huy Quan Vu	Victoria University, Australia
Hongtao Wang	North China Electric Power University, China
Kewen Wang	Griffith University, Australia
Zhichao Wang	Tsinghua University, China
Martin Wirsing	Ludwig Maximilian University of Munich, Germany
Robert Woitsch	BOC Asset Management GmbH, Austria
Le Wu	University of Science and Technology of China, China
Zhiang Wu	Nanjing University of Finance and Economics, China
Tong Xu	University of Science and Technology of China, China
Ziqi Yan	Beijing Jiaotong University, China
Bo Yang	Jilin University, China
Jingyuan Yang	Rutgers University, USA
Feng Yi	University of Chinese Academy of Sciences, China
Qingtian Zeng	Shandong University of Science and Technology, China
Songmao Zhang	Chinese Academy of Sciences, China
Chunxia Zhang	Beijing Institute of Technology, China
Le Zhang	Sichuan University, China
Zili Zhang	Southwest University, China
Hongke Zhao	University of Science and Technology of China, China
Jiali Zuo	Jiangxi Normal University, China

Finance and Registration Chair

Theodoros Karvounidis   University of Piraeus, Greece

Local Organising Committee

Roza Mavropodi (Chair)   University of Pireaus, Greece
Maria Eftychia Angelaki   University of Pireaus, Greece
Panagiotis Drakoulogkonas   University of Pireaus, Greece
Zacharenia Garofalaki   University of West Attica, Greece
Panos Gotsiopoulos   University of Piraeus, Greece
Apostolos Karalis   University of Piraeus, Greece
Dimitris Kotsifakos   University of Piraeus, Greece
Eleni Seralidou   University of Piraeus, Greece
Dimitra Tzoumpa   University of Piraeus, Greece
Vasilis Vasilakopoulos   University of Piraeus, Greece

Contents – Part II

Network Knowledge Representation and Learning

Contents – Part I

Social Knowledge Analysis and Management

Data Processing and Data Mining

Image and Video Data Analysis

Deep Learning

Knowledge Graph and Knowledge Management

Probabilistic Models and Applications

Improved Text-Independent Speaker Identification and Verification with Gaussian Mixture Models

Rania Chakroun[1,3($\boxtimes$)] and Mondher Frikha[1,2]

[1] Advanced Technologies for Image and Signal Processing (ATISP)
Research Unit, Sfax, Tunisia
chakrounrania@yahoo.fr
[2] National School of Electronics and Telecommunications of Sfax, Sfax, Tunisia
[3] National School of Engineering of Sfax, Sfax, Tunisia

Abstract. Speaker recognition systems proposed in the literature are conditioned by many factors such as the features used, the type of data to be processed, data duration and the approach to be used. This work presents a novel speaker recognition application using a new dimensional cepstral feature vector for building Gaussian Mixture Models (GMM) for speaker identification and verification systems. Recognition results obtained with the proposed system are compared to the state of the art systems requiring high dimensional feature vectors. We experimentally evaluate this work with speakers taken from TIMIT database. The new system gave substantial improvements even when trained with limited data, which explain the effectiveness of the new feature vectors with this approach which can be comparable to the use additional algorithms or approaches.

Keywords: Gaussian Mixture Models · Speaker recognition ·
Speaker verification · Speaker identification

1 Introduction

Over the past decade, technological advances such as remote collaborative data processing through large computer networks and telebanking are among sensitive domains that require improved methods for information security. The ability of verification of the identity of individuals attempting to access to personal information like medical records, bank accounts or credit history still critical. Nowadays, low-cost methods like passwords, magnetic cards, personal identification numbers or PIN codes have been widely used. Since these methods can be easily stolen or forgotten, biometric measures such as finger print analyzers, face recognizers as well as retinal scanners and others have been developed. These measures give a high level of performance. However, the use of these methods has been limited by both cost and also ease of use. Recently, speaker recognition which use the individual's voice as a biometric modality for recognition purposes have received considerable attention. In fact, there are many reasons for this interest. In particular, the speech presents a convenient and natural way of input that conveys an important amount of speaker dependent information [11].

© Springer Nature Switzerland AG 2019
C. Douligeris et al. (Eds.): KSEM 2019, LNAI 11776, pp. 3–10, 2019.
https://doi.org/10.1007/978-3-030-29563-9_1

The speech signal conveys various levels of information to the listener. Indeed, speech conveys a specific message via words. Besides, speech conveys information about the language used, the emotion, gender, and also the identity of the speaker.

While speech recognition applications try to recognize the word spoken in speech, the aim of speaker recognition systems is to extract and recognize the information present in the speech signal which conveying speaker identity.

The broad area of speaker recognition comprehends two more fundamental tasks which are Speaker identification and Speaker verification [3]. Speaker identification corresponds to the task of determining who is talking from a set of known voices taken from known speakers. The unknown individual makes no identity claim and then the system must give a 1:N classification. Speaker verification tries to determine whether a person is the same who he/she claims to be or not.

Speaker recognition applications can be text-dependent or text-independent. In text dependent applications, speaker recognition relies on a specific text being spoken and the system has prior knowledge of the text. In text independent applications, there is not a prior knowledge by the system of the text that can be spoken and the speaker must be recognized independently of what is saying. So, text-independent speaker recognition is more difficult but it provides more flexibility.

Research and development on speaker recognition field is an active area that always looks for improved methods and techniques to reach high recognition rate. Recent Researches use modern statistical pattern recognition approaches like neural networks, Hidden Markov Models (HMMs), Gaussian Mixture Models (GMM) [7, 10–12], etc.

By studying speaker recognition systems, we found that the most important parts of such systems are feature extraction and the classification method. From published results, GMM based systems generally produce the best performances. Extracting vectors of features is a fundamental process to speaker recognition systems which has the aim of capturing the speaker specific characteristics. Cepstral features and especially Mel-Frequency Cepstral Coefficients (MFCCs) give the best performance for speaker recognition applications [3].

Although speaker recognition has reached high performance in literature [3], the performance of the state-of-the-art GMM-based speaker recognition systems when more realistic and challenging conditions are presented such as limited speech data or with computational resource limitation degrades seriously. For that, researches look for additional algorithms, approaches or improving the GMM approach to achieve better performances [13]. In this paper, we look for a suitable solution for text-independent speaker identification and verification systems based on a new low dimensional feature vectors able to improve the GMM system performance.

The rest of the paper is organised as follows. We present in Sect. 2 the proposed approach based on the most popular technique used for speaker recognition applications which is the GMM. Experimental protocol and results compared with the state-of-the-art speaker recognition systems are presented in Sect. 3 and conclusions are drawn in Sect. 4.

2 Proposed Approach

There have been appreciable advancements in the speaker recognition domain over the past few years. The research trend in this field has employed the State-of-the-art speaker recognition systems using the GMM which were successfully evaluated for determining the speaker identity [3].

Recent works assert the increasing adoption of the GMM which are the most popular and effective tools for speaker recognition task [4]. In fact, the GMM is one of the most successful modeling paradigms proposed for speaker recognition which is able to model the speech data from a single speaker from anything the speaker can say, which is required for text-independent speaker recognition systems [6]. The advantages of using GMM are presented on [5].

However, in realistic applications, sufficient data may be available for speaker training. But, the test speech utterances are almost very short during the task of recognition. That's why, speaker recognition systems based on GMM are known to perform significantly worse, when short utterances are encountered [4, 15]. For that, the subsequent research endeavours focused on developing GMM along with new techniques or algorithms [3, 13, 14].

The use of these additional techniques help to reduce the error rate, however the inclusion of more algorithms cannot be efficient with realistic applications which suffer from computational resource limitation. In this work, we search for an optimal solution employing a new low dimensional feature vectors able to ameliorate the task of speaker recognition. The proposed system developed for speaker identification is shown in Fig. 1.

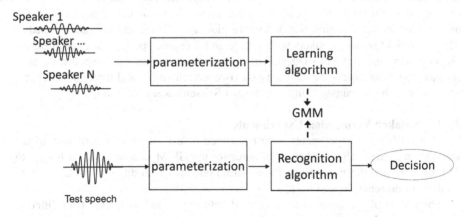

Fig. 1. Automatic speaker identification with the proposed GMM system

This proposed system reduces the error rate while reducing the memory and time complexity required for the system. In fact, it diminish the state of the art dimension of ordinary used feature vectors which leads to lighten the system and at the same time it helps to avoid the use of additional algorithms requiring more computational resources and increase the memory and time complexity of the system.

3 Experimental Results

3.1 Database

The experiments were evaluated using the TIMIT (Texas Instruments Massachusetts Institute of Technology) database. This database consists of 630 speakers as 70% male and 30% female coming from 8 different dialect regions in America. Each speaker speaks approximately 30 s of speech spread over 10 utterances. The speech is recorded using a high quality microphone with a sampling frequency of 16 kHz.

3.2 Experimental Setup

The experiments are evaluated with cepstral features extracted from the speech signal using a 25-ms Hamming window. Each 10 ms, we extract 12 Mel frequency cepstral coefficients (MFCC) together with log energy. This 13-dimensional feature vector was augmented with Delta and double delta coefficients to produce 39-dimensional feature vectors. In fact, this dimension for MFCC vectors presents one of the most widely used vectors up to the present day [3, 5, 14]. The features were extracted with the Hidden Markov Model ToolKit (HTK) [9]. Referring to the investigations in the domain of speaker recognition, we find that speaker verification researches depend on other dimension which is 60 [1, 2]. For that, a second set of experiments is dealt subsequently using 19-dimensional feature vectors together with log energy, Delta and double delta coefficients to give 60-dimensional feature vectors. Afterwards, we decide to use reduced MFCC feature vector dimensions. For that, we eliminate delta and double delta coefficients to evaluate the impact of the number of coefficients of feature vectors on speaker identification and verification systems performance.

For all evaluations, 64 speakers were selected from all the regions of TIMIT database for speaker identification and verification tasks. These speakers are selected as 32 male and 32 female speakers with 4 male and 4 female speakers from each region [3]. Following the protocol suggested in [8], we divide the sentences spoken by each speaker into 8 utterances for the train task (two SA, three SX and three SI sentences) and we keep the remaining 2 utterances (two SX sentences) for testing.

3.2.1 Speaker Verification Experiments

Speaker verification experiments were conducted to examine the performance of the verification system. The number of mixtures for the GMM system is varied from 1 to 256 mixtures and the Equal Error Rates (EER) obtained with different MFCC feature vectors are presented with Fig. 2.

The results of the experiments presented with Fig. 2 and conducted with different feature vectors show that the most significant results are obtained with reduced feature vectors. The use of 39-dimensional feature vectors gives better results than the use of 60-dimensional feature vectors. The inclusion of the delta and double delta coefficients did not ameliorate the system's recognition performance. In fact, we succeed to diminish the EER and we obtain 1.56% of EER with only 12 MFCC together with log energy with 64 mixtures. We achieve a reduction of nearly 11.72% with regard to the

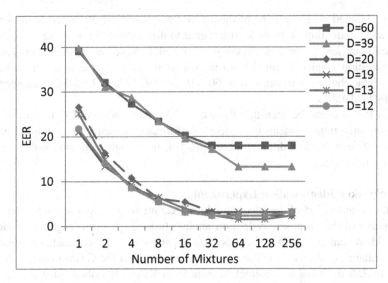

Fig. 2. Speaker EER with different feature vectors for different number of GMM mixtures.

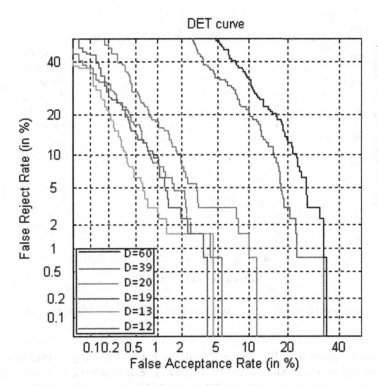

Fig. 3. Detcurves comparison between the different dimensional feature vectors.

EER obtained with the state-of-the-art systems based on 39-dimensional feature vectors and a reduction of 16.41% with regard to the state-of-the-art systems based on 60-dimensional feature vectors. Figure 4 shows DET curves comparison between the best verification results obtained from the different systems evaluated with different feature vectors having a dimension of 60, 39, 20, 19, 13 and 12 MFCC on speakers from TIMIT database.

From Fig. 3 it can be seen that the use of 13-dimensional MFCC feature vectors gives substantial improvements on system's performance which avoid the use of higher dimensional features or additional algorithms that need high computational costs and higher memory space.

3.2.2   Speaker Identification Experiments

For further examination of the effect of reduced feature vectors, we choose to testify the effectiveness of the proposed system on another task of speaker recognition which is speaker identification. Speaker identification experiments were conducted to examine the performance of the system. The number of mixtures for the GMM system is varied from 1 to 256 mixtures and correct Identification Rates (IR) obtained with different MFCC feature vectors are presented with Fig. 4.

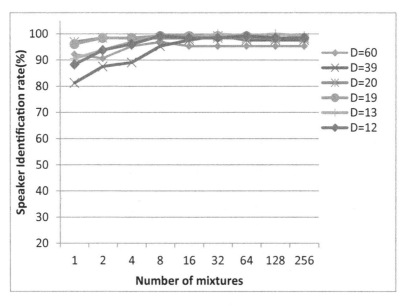

Fig. 4. Speaker identification rate with different feature vectors for different number of GMM mixtures.

The results given with Fig. 3 clearly indicate that the system performance is most significant results with reduced feature vectors. The use of 60 and 39-dimensional feature vectors gives respectively 96,88% and 99,22% of correct Identification rate. The use of more reduced feature vectors such as 13-dimensional feature vectors succeed to reach 100% % of correct Identification rate and there is no need for higher dimensional features or temporal derivates to improve the system's performance.

4 Conclusions and Perspectives

This paper presented a new speaker identification and verification system for which we define new low-dimensional feature vectors able to achieve perfect performance with Gaussian mixture models.

Through the experiments performed on the TIMIT database, we demonstrate that we can ameliorate the systems performance and outperform the standard speaker identification and verification systems using GMM approach in independent mode of the text. We achieve lower error rate and we avoid the use of additional, lengthy and complicated calculations.

This work presents a basic introduction to effective text independent speaker recognition applications that can be used for more investigation concerning the improvement of this technique with harder and realistic conditions such as noise or more reduced amount of speech data.

References

1. Dehak, N., Karam, Z., Reynolds, D., Dehak, R., Campbell, W., Glass, J.: A channel-blind system for speaker verification. In: Proceedings of ICASSP, Prague, Czech Republic, pp. 4536–4539, May 2011
2. Dehak, N., Kenny, P., Dehak, R., Dumouchel, P., Ouellet, P.: Front-end factor analysis for speaker verification. IEEE Trans. Audio Speech Lang. Process. **19**(4), 788–798 (2011)
3. Togneri, R., Pullella, R.: An overview of speaker identification: accuracy and robustness issues. IEEE Circuits Syst. Mag. **11**(2), 23–61 (2011). ISSN: 1531-636X
4. Liu, Z., Wu, Z., Li, T., Li, J., Shen, C.: GMM and CNN hybrid method for short utterance speaker recognition. IEEE Trans. Industr. Inf. **14**(7), 3244–3252 (2018)
5. Kinnunen, T., Li, H.: An overview of text-independent speaker recognition: From features to supervectors. Speech Commun. **52**(1), 12–40 (2010)
6. Bimbot, F., et al.: A tutorial on text-independent speaker verification. EURASIP J. Adv. Signal Process. **2004**(4), 101962 (2004)
7. Reynolds, D.A., Quatieri, T.F., Dunn, R.B.: Speaker verification using adapted Gaussian mixture models. Digit. Signal Process. **10**(1–3), 19–41 (2000)
8. Reynolds, D.A.: Speaker identification and verification using Gaussian mixture speaker models. Speech Commun. **17**(1–2), 91–108 (1995)
9. Young, S., Kershaw, D., Odell, J., Ollason, D., Valtchev, V., Woodland, P.: Hidden Markov model toolkit (htk) version 3.4 user's guide (2002)
10. Campbell, W., Sturim, D., Reynolds, D.: Support vector machines using GMM supervectors for speaker verification. IEEE Signal Process. Lett. **13**(5), 308–311 (2006)
11. Liu, Z., Wu, Z., Li, T., Li, J., Shen, C.: GMM and CNN hybrid method for short utterance speaker recognition. IEEE Trans. Industr. Inf. **14**, 3244–3252 (2018)
12. Jokinen, E., Saeidi, R., Kinnunen, T., Alku, P.: Vocal effort compensation for MFCC feature extraction in a shouted versus normal speaker recognition task. Comput. Speech Lang. **53**, 1–11 (2019)

13. Chettri, B., Sturm, B.L.: A deeper look at Gaussian mixture model based anti-spoofing systems. In: 2018 IEEE International Conference on Acoustics, Speech and Signal Processing (ICASSP), pp. 5159–5163. IEEE, April 2018
14. Venkatesan, R., Ganesh, A.B.: Binaural classification-based speech segregation and robust speaker recognition system. Circuits Syst. Signal Process. **37**(8), 3383–3411 (2018)
15. Hasan, T., Saeidi, R., Hansen, J. H., Van Leeuwen, D.A.: Duration mismatch compensation for i-vector based speaker recognition systems. In: 2013 IEEE International Conference on Acoustics, Speech and Signal Processing, pp. 7663–7667. IEEE, May 2013

TagDeepRec: Tag Recommendation for Software Information Sites Using Attention-Based Bi-LSTM

Can Li[1] , Ling Xu[1(✉)], Meng Yan[2], JianJun He[1], and Zuli Zhang[3]

[1] School of Big Data and Software, Chongqing University, Chongqing, China
{lican96,xuling,hejianjun}@cqu.edu.cn
[2] Zhejiang University, Hangzhou, China
mengy@zju.edu.cn
[3] Chongqing Materials Research Institute Limited Company, Chongqing, China
zuli1973@163.com

Abstract. Software information sites are widely used to help developers to share and communicate their knowledge. Tags in these sites play an important role in facilitating information classification and organization. However, the insufficient understanding of software objects and the lack of relevant knowledge among developers may lead to incorrect tags. Thus, the automatic tag recommendation technique has been proposed. However, tag explosion and tag synonym are two major factors that affect the quality of tag recommendation. Prior studies have found that deep learning techniques are effective for mining software information sites. Inspired by recent deep learning researches, we propose TagDeepRec, a new tag recommendation approach for software information sites using attention-based Bi-LSTM. The attention-based Bi-LSTM model has the advantage of deep potential semantics mining, which can accurately infer tags for new software objects by learning the relationships between historical software objects and their corresponding tags. Given a new software object, TagDeepRec is able to compute the confidence probability of each tag and then recommend top-k tags by ranking the probabilities. We use the dataset from six software information sites with different scales to evaluate our proposed TagDeepRec. The experimental results show that TagDeepRec has achieved better performance compared with the state-of-the-art approaches TagMulRec and FastTagRec in terms of $Recall@k$, $Precision@k$ and $F1 - score@k$.

Keywords: Software information site · Tag recommendation ·
Long short term memory · Attention mechanism ·
Weighted binary cross entropy loss function

1 Introduction

Software information sites (e.g., StackOverflow, AskUbuntu, AskDifferent and Freecode) provide a platform for software developers around the world to share

© Springer Nature Switzerland AG 2019
C. Douligeris et al. (Eds.): KSEM 2019, LNAI 11776, pp. 11–24, 2019.
https://doi.org/10.1007/978-3-030-29563-9_2

and communicate their knowledge [2–5]. These sites enable developers to pose questions, answer questions and search answers they encountered. When posing a new question in the sites, developers need to choose one or more tags from tag repository or create new ones. Tags in these sites play an important role, not only as keywords to summarize the posted content, but also to classify and organize the software objects to improve the performance of various operations [5]. High-quality tags are expected to be concise and accurate, which can capture important features of the software objects. Unfortunately, it is not easy for the developers to choose the appropriate tags to describe the software objects. There are two major factors that affect developers' choices of high-quality tags: tag synonym [7] and tag explosion [6,7]. Tag synonym refers to similar questions may be provided different tags because of insufficient understanding of the problem or lack of relevant expertise. For example, in StackOverflow, we notice that the tag "c#" is usually expressed as "csharp" and "c-sharp", ".net" expressed as "dotnet" and ".net-framework". Some developers may confuse "python2.7" with "python3.5". Tag explosion describes the phenomenon that the number of tags dramatically increases along with continuous additions of software objects. For example, up to now, there are more than 46 thousand tags in StackOverflow. With such huge tags, noise is inevitably introduced and software objects become more poorly classified. This phenomenon has a negative impact on the speed and accuracy of developers' queries.

To address the above issues, several studies on tag recommendation techniques have been proposed in recent years. These approaches can be roughly divided into word similarity-based and semantic similarity-based techniques. word similarity techniques such as TagCombine [2] focus on calculating the similarity based on the textual description. However, the performance of these approaches is limited by the semantic gap because a lot of questions with the same tags have rare common words. Semantic similarity-based techniques (e.g., TagRec [1], EnTagRec++ [25] and TagMulRec [4]) consider text semantic information and always perform significantly better than the approaches that using word similarity calculation. Recently, Liu et al. [5] proposed FastTagRec using neural network classification techniques, which have been proven to improve the accuracy than the comparable state-of-the-art tool TagMulRec. In this work, we compare the effectiveness of our approach with TagMulRec and FastTagRec on six software information sites.

Deep learning has been utilized in other software engineering tasks, such as bug localization [8], code clone detection [9], etc. Inspired by recent Natural Language Processing (NLP) research, in this paper, we proposed a new tag recommendation method called TagDeepRec, a ranking multi-label classification method based on attention-based Bi-LSTM (bidirectional modeling sequence information with long short-term memory). Bi-LSTM has been proven effective in the area of NLP [10–12]. As a deep learning algorithm, Bi-LSTM can capture the deep potential semantic feature by learning the relationships between historical software objects and their corresponding tags. The attention mechanism [13] enables Bi-LSTM model to focus on the key parts of texts associated with tags by attaching more attention weights to the important parts. For a software object, TagDeepRec outputs the confidence probability of each candidate tag by learning from the historical software objects and their corresponding tags, and then k tags with the highest probabilities in the tag candidate set will be recommended to developers as the top-k tags. We evaluate TagDeepRec on six software information sites including StackOverflow@small, Freecode, AskDifferent, AskUbuntu, Unix and StackOverflow@large. StackOverflow@small and StackOverflow@large are divided based on their sizes. Experiments show that TagDeepRec achieves better performance compared with two state-of-the-art approaches: TagMulRec [4] and FastTagRec [5].

Our contributions are as follows:

- We propose an automatic tag recommendation approach for software information sites using attention-based Bi-LSTM model. Experimental results demonstrate that our approach scalable enough to handle both small and very large software information sites.
- We evaluate TagDeepRec on the dataset from six software information sites with different scales. The experiments show that TagDeepRec can achieve high accuracy and outperforms the state-of-the-art approaches TagMulRec and FastTagRec.

The organization of the paper is as follows: In Sect. 2, we give the problem formulation. Section 3 presents our proposed approach. In Sect. 4, we report the results of the experimental evaluation. In Sect. 5, we give the threats to validity of our results. In Sect. 6, we describe the related work. And the conclusion and future work are described in Sect. 7.

2   Problem Formulation

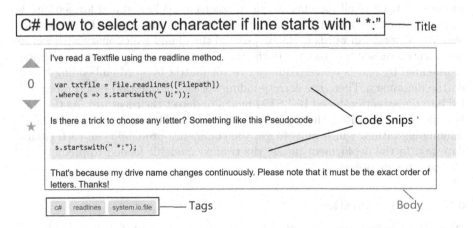

Fig. 1. A software object in StackOverflow

Figure 1 gives a specific example of a software object in StackOverflow. It's observed that this software object consists of a title, a body and three tags. In particular, we can also find code snippets located in the body. Generally, we always treat the combination of a title and a body as a question in a software object.

A software site is a set $S = \{o_1, \cdots, o_n\}$ which is composed of a series of software objects $o_i (1 \leq i \leq n)$. And a software object is also composed of various attributes such as an identifier $o_i.id$, a title $o_i.title$, a body $o_i.body$, several tags $o_i.tags$, etc. We combine the information from title $o_i.title$ and body $o_i.body$ as a new question $o_i.q$. In our method, we assume that each software object contains a question $o_i.q$ and several corresponding tags $o_i.tags$. At the same time, we filter out tags which appear infrequently and define all the remaining tags in a software information site as a candidate tags set $T = \{t_1, \cdots, t_s\}$, where s is the number of remaining tags and $t_i \{1 \leq i \leq n\}$ indicates whether the current tag is selected. The value of t_i is either 0 or 1, where 1 indicates that the current tag is selected and 0 is the opposite phenomenon. Assuming that tags recommended for each software object o_i is a subset of T, given a new software object, the aim of TagDeepRec is to assign several tags from tags candidate set T by learning from existing software objects and their corresponding tags, which can provide great help for developers to choose appropriate tags.

3   Proposed Method

3.1   Approach Overview

Figure 2 presents the overall framework of our TagDeepRec which contains three phases: data preparation, training, and deployment. In the data preparation phase, both the training set and the testing set are derived from the same software information sites. And for a software object, the useful fields including title and body are extracted and further form a question description. After preprocessing, texts of all the question descriptions are collected and formed into a corpus. A word2vec model [15] is used to capture semantic regularities on the corpus. We vectorize all words in the corpus and then build a dictionary with words and their corresponding vectors. In the training phase, each question description represented by text is converted into a vector matrix by word embedding based on the dictionary. Then, the corresponding vectors of question descriptions are fed into the attention-based Bi-LSTM model to detect their features. As the core module of TagDeepRec, the attention-based Bi-LSTM network is a multi-label ranking algorithm, which aims to get the confidence probability of each candidate tag. In the deployment phase, the trained model is loaded to predict tags for the software object.

3.2   Data Preparation

Data Extraction: We first collect historical questions and their tags which are posted on software information sites. For each software object, we only parse out

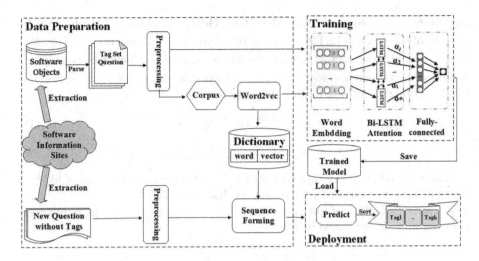

Fig. 2. Overall workflow of TagDeepRec

title, body and tags on the software object and combine the title and the body as a question description. We also remove code snippets in the body, which can easily be located in specific HTML element components ($<code> \cdots <\backslash code>$) [5].

Data Preprocessing: Following previous researches [2–5], we filter out the rare tags whose frequencies of occurrence are less than a predefined threshold θ. And we further remove the software objects if the frequency of all its tags less than θ. These tags rarely appear since few people use them, therefore, they are less useful to be used as representative tags and recommending them provides little help in addressing the tag synonym problem.

For the text information in these software objects, we perform typical preprocessing steps including tokenization, stemming, stop words removal and case conversion by using NLTK (the Natural Language Toolkit) [14]. Stop words removal also deletes some isolated numbers and punctuations.

Matrix Presentation: After preprocessing, all the words in the textual descriptions are made up of the experimental corpus. The word embedding technique (word2vec [15]) with skip-gram model are applied on the corpus to obtain the word vector of each word. Then, we can get a matrix presentation of each question description.

3.3   Attention-Based Bi-LSTM for Tag Recommendation

Given a software object o_i, the matrix presentation of the question $o_i.q = [x_1, \cdots, x_n]$ is fed into attention-based Bi-LSTM model to extract features, where x_i is the vector representation of the $i - th$ word in $o_i.q$. The hidden state $h_i \in \mathbb{R}^d$ denoting the representation of the time step i can be obtained after being processed by the Bi-LSTM layer. Generally, in Bi-LSTM, the hidden state $\overrightarrow{h_i}$ of the forward LSTM is related to its previous memory cell $\overrightarrow{c_{i-1}}$, hidden state $\overrightarrow{h_{i-1}}$ and input vector x_i, while the hidden state $\overleftarrow{h_i}$ of the backward LSTM is related to its next memory cell $\overleftarrow{c_{i+1}}$, hidden state $\overleftarrow{h_{i+1}}$ and input vector x_i, which can be respectively formulated as follows:

$$\overrightarrow{h_i} = f^{(LSTM)}(\overrightarrow{c_{i-1}}, \overrightarrow{h_{i-1}}, x_i) \tag{1}$$

$$\overleftarrow{h_i} = f^{(LSTM)}(\overleftarrow{c_{i+1}}, \overleftarrow{h_{i+1}}, x_i) \tag{2}$$

The final hidden state h_i of time step i $[\overrightarrow{h_i}, \overleftarrow{h_i}]$ is the concatenation of hidden states of both the forward LSTM and the backward LSTM. And we regard H as a matrix consisting of output vectors $[h_1, \cdots, h_n]$, where n is the number of hidden states. H is defined in Eq. (3).

$$H = [h_1, \cdots, h_n] \tag{3}$$

Generally, the tags of a software object are only related to a small portion information of a question. For example, a question like *Binary Data in MySQL, How do I store binary data in MySQL?* Its corresponding tags are {*mysql, binary-data*}. Although there are many words in this question, the words associated with tags are only *mysql, binary* and *data*. In order to capture the key part of software objects, we apply the attention mechanism to pay more attention to the information closely related to tags.

Attention mechanism first attaches weight $\alpha_i\{1 \leqslant i \leqslant n\}$ to the hidden state h_i in our method, which is calculated as follow:

$$M = \tanh(H) \tag{4}$$

$$\alpha_i = Softmax(\omega^T M) \tag{5}$$

where ω is a trained parameter vector and ω^T is a transpose.

Based on the hidden state h_i and its corresponding weight α_i, the context-dependent text representation vector Q of each question is defined as follow:

$$Q = \sum_{i=1}^{n} \alpha_i h_i \tag{6}$$

In the last layer, in order to get a value to represent confidence probability of each tag, we use *Sigmoid* function. Unlike *Softmax*, *Sigmoid* is able to make sure that confidence probability of each tag is independent. Given the input of the fully-connected layer $Q = [q_1, \cdots, q_n]$ and weight vector $W = [w_1, \cdots, w_n]$, the independent probabilities list $TR_i^{predict}$ of candidate tags can be calculated as:

$$TR_i^{predict} = \frac{1}{1 + e^{-(\sum_{i=1}^{n} w_i q_i + b)}} \tag{7}$$

where i is the $i-th$ element of Q, b is the bias vector and n refers to the number of candidate tags.

Considering that the distribution of recommended and not-recommended tags is heavily biased: most of the candidate tags are not be recommended to a software object. Inspired by [16], we set weighted binary cross entropy loss function to balance the loss between positive category and negative category, which is defined as follow:

$$L(TR_i^{predict}, TR_i^{actual}) = -\beta TR_i^{actual} \log TR_i^{predict}$$
$$- (1 - \beta)(1 - TR_i^{actual}) \log (1 - TR_i^{predict}) \tag{8}$$

where TR_i^{actual} is the actual confidence probabilities list, $TR_i^{predict}$ is the predicted confidence probabilities list, and β is the weight attached to the positive samples.

4   Experiments and Results

In this section, we describe the experiments and results to evaluate the performance of the TagDeepRec.

Table 1. Statistics of six software information sites

Site size	Site name	URL	#Software objects	#Tags
Small	StackOverflow@small	www.stackoverflow.com	47836	437
	AskDifferent	www.apple.stackexchange.com	77503	469
	Freecode	www.github.com	43638	427
Medium	Askubuntu	www.askubuntu.com	246138	1146
	Unix	www.unix.stackexchange.com	103243	770
Large	StackOverflow@large	www.stackoverflow.com	10421906	427

4.1   Experimental Settings

We evaluate the effectiveness of TagDeepRec on six software information sites with different scales. We divide our datasets into three categories: one large-scale site StackOverflow@large, two medium-scale sites AskUbuntu and Unix, three small-scale sites Stackoverflow@small, Freecode and AskDifferent. For comparison, we use the same five datasets as FastTagRec [5] including StackOverflow@large, Askubuntu, Unix, Freecode and AskDifferent. StackOverflow@small is the same dataset used in TagCombine [2], EntagRec [3] and TagMulRec [4]. In detail, for Freecode, AskDifferent, AskUbuntu and Unix, we collects the software objects posted on them before Dec 31st, 2016. StackOverflow@small considers the software objects posted from July 1st, 2008 to December 10th, 2008 and StackOverflow@large selects the software objects posted before July 1st, 2014. We choose the relatively old software objects to make sure our data is stable and reliable. The information of our experimental datasets is shown in Table 1.

In our experiments, we remove the rare tags, which has been described in Sect. 3.2. For the two medium-scale and three small-scale sites, we remove the software object if all of its tags appear less than 50 times and for a large-scale site if all its tags appear less than 10000 times. Table 1 presents the number of *Software Objects* and *Tags* after removing the rare tags.

4.2   Evaluation Metrics

We employ three widely used evaluation metrics [3–5]: top-k recommendation recall ($Recall@k$), top-k recommendation precision ($Precision@k$) and top-k recommendation F1-score ($F1 - score@k$). Given a validation set V composed of n software objects $o_i\{1 \leq i \leq n\}$, we can eventually get the top-k recommended tags $TR_i^{predict}$ and the actual tags TR_i^{actual} of each software object o_i.

Recall@k: $Recall@k$ indicates the percentage of tags actually used by the software object coming from the recommended lists $TR_i^{predict}$. For a software object o_i in the validation set V, $Recall@k_i$ of it is computed by Eq. (9), and $Recall@k$, the mean prediction recall of the validation set V is defined by Eq. (10).

$$Recall@k_i = \begin{cases} \frac{|TR_i^{predict} \cap TR_i^{actual}|}{|k|}, & |TR_i^{actual}| > |k|; \\ \frac{|TR_i^{predict} \cap TR_i^{actual}|}{|TR_i^{actual}|}, & |TR_i^{actual}| < |k|. \end{cases} \tag{9}$$

$$Recall@k = \frac{\sum_{i=1}^{|n|} Recall@k_i}{|n|} \tag{10}$$

Precision@k: $Precision@k$ denotes the percentage of the truth tags of a software object in the recommended lists $TR_i^{predict}$. For a software object o_i in the validation set V, $Precision@k_i$ of it is computed by Eq. (11), and $Precision@k$, the mean prediction precision of the validation set V is defined by Eq. (12).

$$Precision@k_i = \begin{cases} \frac{|TR_i^{predict} \cup TR_i^{actual}|}{|k|}, & |TR_i^{actual}| > |k|; \\ \frac{|TR_i^{predict} \cup TR_i^{actual}|}{|TR_i^{actual}|}, & |TR_i^{actual}| < |k|. \end{cases} \tag{11}$$

$$Precision@k = \frac{\sum_{i=1}^{|n|} Precision@k_i}{|n|} \tag{12}$$

F1-score@k: This metric is the combination of $Precision@k$ and $Recall@k$. For a software object o_i in the validation set V, $F1 - score@k_i$ of it is computed by Eq. (13), and $F1 - score@k$, the mean prediction f1-score of the validation set V is defined by Eq. (14).

$$F1 - score@k_i = 2 * \frac{Precision@k_i - Recall@k_i}{Precision@k_i + Recall@k_i} \tag{13}$$

$$F1 - score@k = \frac{\sum_{i=1}^{|n|} F1 - score@k_i}{|n|} \tag{14}$$

4.3   Experiments Results

Table 2. TagDeepRec vs. FastTagRec & TagMulRec using metrics Recall@k, Precision@k, and F1-score@k

Sites	Recall@5			Precision@5			F1-score@5		
	TagDeep Rec	TagMul Rec	FastTag Rec	TagDeep Rec	TagMul Rec	FastTag Rec	TagDeep Rec	TagMul Rec	FastTag Rec
StackOverflow@small@	**0.817**	0.680	0.805	0.344	0.284	**0.346**	0.463	0.454	**0.482**
AskDifferent	**0.780**	0.708	0.689	**0.405**	0.372	0.357	**0.511**	0.488	0.471
Freecode	0.640	**0.659**	0.588	**0.392**	0.383	0.343	0.449	**0.485**	0.434
Askubuntu	**0.728**	0.603	0.684	**0.361**	0.271	0.346	**0.458**	0.374	0.437
Unix	**0.706**	0.604	0.621	**0.348**	0.294	0.309	**0.447**	0.395	0.397
StackOverFlow@large	**0.885**	0.809	0.870	**0.357**	0.310	0.349	**0.487**	0.449	0.476
Average	**0.760**	0.677	0.709	**0.368**	0.319	0.342	**0.469**	0.441	0.450
Sites	Recall@10			Precision@10			F1-score@10		
	TagDeep Rec	TagMul Rec	FastTag Rec	TagDeep Rec	TagMul Rec	FastTag Rec	TagDeep Rec	TagMul Rec	FastTag Rec
StackOverflow@small	**0.900**	0.777	0.887	**0.194**	0.165	0.187	**0.309**	0.293	0.303
AskDifferent	**0.889**	0.827	0.815	**0.236**	0.222	0.216	**0.361**	0.350	0.342
Freecode	**0.775**	0.758	0.692	0.244	**0.245**	0.219	0.347	**0.364**	0.332
Askubuntu	**0.850**	0.721	0.770	**0.215**	0.166	0.198	**0.331**	0.270	0.303
Unix	**0.835**	0.682	0.722	**0.211**	0.169	0.182	**0.327**	0.271	0.282
StackOverFlow@large	**0.949**	0.892	0.919	**0.195**	0.176	0.187	**0.314**	0.294	0.301
Average	**0.867**	0.776	0.801	**0.216**	0.191	0.198	**0.332**	0.307	0.311

Table 3. Recall@k, Precision@k, and F1-score@k of different TagDeepRec model

	Recall@5	Precision@5	F1-score@5	Recall@10	Precision@10	F1-score@10
Bi-LSTM	0.803	0.336	0.453	0.882	0.187	0.304
Bi-LSTM+Attention	0.812	0.341	0.461	0.892	0.191	0.306
Bi-LSTM+New Loss Function	0.811	0.341	0.460	0.890	0.191	0.305
TagDeepRec	0.817	0.344	0.463	0.900	0.194	0.309

RQ1. Compared with the state-of-the-art approaches, how effective is our TagDeepRec? In order to answer RQ1, we compare TagDeepRec with another two state-of-the-art approaches: TagMulRec [4] and FastTagRec [5] on six software information sites (see Table 1). TagMulRec is an information retrieval tool based on semantics similarity and FastTagRec is a classification technique based on neural network. We evaluate their performances through *Recall@k*, *Precision@k* and $F1 - score@k$ with different k values: 5 and 10. A ten-fold cross validation [24] is performed for evaluation. We randomly split it into ten subsamples. Nine of them are used as training data and one subsample is used for testing. We repeat the process ten times and compute the mean to get more credible results.

The results of these methods are presented in Table 2 and the best values of each site are highlighted in bold. The results show that TagDeepRec achieves a better performance than another two methods except on the Freecode site. Compared to FastTagRec, the average improvement of all sites in $Recall@5$, $Precision@5$, $F1 - score@5$, $Recall@10$, $Precision@10$ and $F1 - score@10$ is 5.1%, 2.6%, 1.9%, 6.6%, 1.8% and 2.1%, and compared to TagMulRec, the average improvement of all sites in $Recall@5$, $Precision@5$, $F1 - score@5$, $Recall@10$, $Precision@10$ and $F1 - score@10$ is 8.3%, 9.0%, 8.4%, 9.1%, 2.5% and 2.5%, respectively. Experimental results also show that the larger the scale of software information site, the better the effectiveness of our approach TagDeepRec.

In addition, in order to verify whether TagDeepRec has a statistically significant difference compared with other approaches, we adopt Wilcoxon signed-rank test [17] at 95% significance level on 36 paired value corresponding to the evaluation metrics. Across the six datasets, the corresponding $p - value$ is very small ($p < 0.01$), which confirms that our approach is statistically effective for tag recommendation.

RQ2. Do the attention mechanism and new loss function improve the performance of TagDeepRec? To evaluate the effectiveness of the attention mechanism and new loss function, we designed four different experiments, including the original Bi-LSTM model, attention-based Bi-LSTM model, "Bi-LSTM+new loss function" model and TagDeepRec combined with the attention-based Bi-LSTM model and new loss function. All four experiments are conducted on the StackOverflow@small which is the most commonly used dataset in the field of tag recommendation. And the experimental results are represented in Table 3.

As shown in Table 3, the attention-based Bi-LSTM model outperforms the original Bi-LSTM. The improvement in terms of $Recall@5$, $Precision@5$, $F1 - score@5$, $Recall@10$, $Precision@10$ and $F1 - score@10$ is 0.9%, 0.5%, 0.8%, 1.0%, 0.4% and 0.2% respectively. The result confirms the effectiveness of the attention-based Bi-LSTM model used in our approach. Table 3 also indicates that the enhanced Bi-LSTM model with the new cost function leads to better results as compared to the original Bi-LSTM model. The improvement in terms of $Recall@5$, $Precision@5$, $F1 - score@5$, $Recall@10$, $Precision@10$ and $F1 - score@10$ is 0.8%, 0.5%, 0.7%, 0.8%, 0.4% and 0.1% respectively. The results confirm the usefulness of the new loss function. Additionally, TagDeepRec, which combines the two techniques achieves better performance than another three models.

RQ3. How does the number of hidden states in LSTM affect the performance of TagDeepRec? For RQ3, we choose three small-scale sites including StackOverflow@small, AskDifferent and Freecode to better capture the change of experimental results. We gradually change the values of LSTM hidden states from 50 to 1000 and observe the trend of experimental results. For these three small-scale datasets, Fig. 3(a)–(f) respectively depict the changes of $Recall@5$, $Precision@5$, $F1-score@5$, $Recall@10$, $Precision@10$ and $F1-score@10$ along with the number of hidden states.

The results show that the number of LSTM hidden states affects all the evaluation metrics. For each evaluate metric, there is an optimum range of hidden states. With the number of LSTM hidden states increases, the values of these evaluation metrics rise steadily first, and then gradually decline. Therefore, for small-scale datasets, more hidden states do not always correspond to better performance.

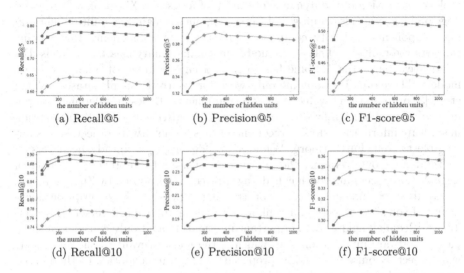

(a) Recall@5   (b) Precision@5   (c) F1-score@5

(d) Recall@10   (e) Precision@10   (f) F1-score@10

Fig. 3. The effect of the number of hidden states in LSTM: StackOverflow@small (blue), AskDifferent (green), Freecode (orange) (Color figure online)

5 Threats to Validity

Internal Validity. Threats to internal validity are the reliability of our experimental data. Because the tags of the software object are chosen freely by developers, errors are inevitable. We assume that the tags of software objects are correct by following prior studies. In order to mitigate this issue, we have taken some measures including selecting common software information sites, selecting the older data in a software information site and filtering out objects with low-frequency and incorrect tags.

External Validity. Threats to external validity are the generalizability of our approach. We have evaluated TagDeepRec on six software information sites and approximately 11 million software objects. In the future, we will further evaluate TagDeepRec from more software information sites to generalize our findings.

Construct validity. Threats to construct validity are the suitability of our evaluation metrics. We use $Recall@k$, $Precision@k$, and $F1-score@k$ to evaluate the proposed TagDeepRec. The metrics used in our study have been widely used in previous studies [3–5]. Thus, we believe we have little threats to construct validity.

6   Related Work

Many approaches have been proposed for automatic tag recommendation recently. TagRec, proposed by Al-Kofahi et al. [1], automatically recommends tags for work items in IBM Jazz. TagRec was based on the fuzzy set theory and took consideration of the dynamic evolution of a system. Xia et al. [2] proposed TagCombine, which is composed of three components including multi-label ranking component, similarity component and tag-term component. TagCombine converts the multi-label classifier model into many binary classifier models. For a large-scale site, TagCombine has to train a large number of binary classifier models. Therefore, TagCombine only work for relatively small datasets. Wang et al. [3] proposed EnTagRec with two components: Bayesian inference component and Frequentist inference component. EnTagRec relies on all information in software information sites to recommend tags for a software object, so it's not scalable as well. Furthermore, Wang et al. [25] proposed an advanced version EnTagRec++ by leveraging the information of users to improve the quality of tags. A more recent approach called TagMulRec was proposed by Zhou et al. [4]. TagMulRec recommends tags by constructing indices for the description documents of software objects and ranking all tags in the candidate set. However, TagMulRec may ignore some important information as it only considers a small part of software information sites which is the most relevant to the given software object. Beomseok et al. [21] proposed a tag recommendation method based on topic modeling approaches, which recommends tags by calculating tag scores based on the document similarity and the historical tag occurrence. Lately, A novel approach called FastTagRec based on neural networks was proposed by Liu et al. [5], which is the prior state-of-the-art work. FastTagRec is not only accurate and scalable, but also faster than existing methods. It recommend tags by learning the relationship between existing postings and their tags.

In the field of software engineering, tags studies have become a hot research problem. Treude et al. [19] implemented an empirical study of a large project on how tagging had been adopted and adapted in the last two years, and showed that tagging mechanism made a contribution to bridging the gap between technical and social aspects of managing work items. Thung et al. [20] concluded that collaborative tagging was useful for detecting similar software applications as a promising information source by performing a user study related to several participants. Wang et al. [21] described the relationships among tags on Freecode and defined them as tag synonyms. Beyer et al. [22] designed TSST, a tag synonym suggestion tool to address the problems of tag synonyms on StackOverflow. And Beyer et al. [23] continued their previous studies and presented an approach to alleviate the issue of tag synonyms by grouping tag synonyms to meaningful topics.

7   Conclusion and Future Work

In this paper, we proposed TagDeepRec, a new tag recommendation approach for software information sites using attention-based Bi-LSTM. We evaluated the performance of TagDeepRec on six software information sites with approximately 11 million software objects. The experimental results show that TagDeepRec is scalable enough to handle both small and large software information sites and has achieved better performance compared with the state-of-the-art approaches (i.e., TagMulRec and FastTagRec). In summary, TagDeepRec can achieve promising performance for the following three reasons: (1) Bi-LSTM model can accurately express the potential semantics of the software objects from both the forward and backward directions. (2) Attention mechanism can capture the key information of the posted questions by attaching different weights to each time step of Bi-LSTM hidden layers. (3) Weighted binary cross entropy loss function can solve the unbalance distribution problems of tags between positive samples and negative samples.

Our current work is based on the question descriptions only. In the future, we plan to consider more features such as code snippets and screenshots to improve effectiveness of tag recommendation. We also intend to explore the tag relationships between the new software object and the historical terms.

References

1. Al-Kofahi, JM., Tamrawi, A., Nguyen, T.T., et al.: Fuzzy set approach for automatic tagging in evolving software. In: 2010 IEEE International Conference on Software Maintenance, pp. 1–10. IEEE (2010)
2. Xia, X., Lo, D., Wang, X., et al.: Tag recommendation in software information sites. In: 2013 10th Working Conference on Mining Software Repositories (MSR), pp. 287–296. IEEE (2013)
3. Wang, S., Lo, D., Vasilescu, B., et al.: EnTagRec: an enhanced tag recommendation system for software information sites. In: 2014 IEEE International Conference on Software Maintenance and Evolution, pp. 291–300. IEEE (2014)
4. Zhou, P., Liu, J., Yang, Z., et al.: Scalable tag recommendation for software information sites. In: 2017 IEEE 24th International Conference on Software Analysis, Evolution and Reengineering (SANER), pp. 272–282. IEEE (2017)
5. Liu, J., Zhou, P., Yang, Z., et al.: FastTagRec: fast tag recommendation for software information sites. Autom. Softw. Eng. $25(4)$, 675–701 (2018)
6. Joorabchi, A., English, M., Mahdi, A.E.: Automatic mapping of user tags to Wikipedia concepts: the case of a Q&A website-StackOverflow. J. Inf. Sci. $41(5)$, 570–583 (2015)
7. Barua, A., Thomas, S.W., Hassan, A.E.: What are developers talking about? An analysis of topics and trends in stack overflow. Empir. Softw. Eng. $19(3)$, 619–654 (2014)
8. Deshmukh, J., Podder, S., Sengupta, S., et al.: Towards accurate duplicate bug retrieval using deep learning techniques. In: 2017 IEEE International Conference on Software Maintenance and Evolution (ICSME), pp. 115–124. IEEE (2017)
9. Li, L., Feng, H., Zhuang, W., et al.: Cclearner: a deep learning-based clone detection approach. In: 2017 IEEE International Conference on Software Maintenance and Evolution (ICSME), pp. 249–260 IEEE (2017)
10. Cho, K., Van Merriënboer, B., Bahdanau, D., et al.: On the properties of neural machine translation: encoder-decoder approaches. arXiv preprint arXiv:1409.1259 (2014)

11. Zhou, P., Shi, W., Tian, J., et al.: Attention-based bidirectional long short-term memory networks for relation classification. In: Proceedings of the 54th Annual Meeting of the Association for Computational Linguistics (Volume 2: Short Papers), vol. 2, pp. 207–212 (2016)

12. Huang, Z., Xu, W., Yu, K.: Bidirectional LSTM-CRF models for sequence tagging. arXiv preprint arXiv:1508.01991 (2015)

13. Vaswani, A., Shazeer, N., Parmar, N., et al.: Attention is all you need. In: Advances in Neural Information Processing Systems, pp. 5998–6008 (2017)

14. Bird, S., Klein, E., Loper, E.: Natural Language Processing with Python: Analyzing Text With the Natural Language Toolkit. O'Reilly Media Inc., Sebastopol (2009)

15. Mikolov, T., Chen, K., Corrado, G., et al.: Efficient estimation of word representations in vector space. arXiv preprint arXiv:1301.3781 (2013)

16. Xie, S., Tu, Z.: Holistically-nested edge detection. In: Proceedings of the IEEE International Conference on Computer Vision, pp. 1395–1403 (2015)

17. Wilcoxon, F.: Individual comparisons by ranking methods. Biom. Bull. **1**(6), 80–83 (1945)

18. Hong, B., Kim, Y., Lee, S.H.: An efficient tag recommendation method using topic modeling approaches. In: Proceedings of the International Conference on Research in Adaptive and Convergent Systems, pp. 56–61. ACM (2017)

19. Treude, C., Storey, M.A.: How tagging helps bridge the gap between social and technical aspects in software development. In: Proceedings of the 31st International Conference on Software Engineering, pp. 12–22. IEEE Computer Society (2009)

20. Thung, F., Lo, D., Jiang, L.: Detecting similar applications with collaborative tagging. In: 2012 28th IEEE International Conference on Software Maintenance (ICSM), pp. 600–603. IEEE (2012)

21. Wang, S., Lo, D., Jiang, L.: Inferring semantically related software terms and their taxonomy by leveraging collaborative tagging. In: 2012 28th IEEE International Conference on Software Maintenance (ICSM), pp. 604–607. IEEE (2012)

22. Beyer, S., Pinzger, M.: Synonym suggestion for tags on stack overflow. In: Proceedings of the 2015 IEEE 23rd International Conference on Program Comprehension, pp. 94–103. IEEE Press (2015)

23. Beyer, S., Pinzger, M.: Grouping android tag synonyms on stack overflow. In: Proceedings of the 13th International Conference on Mining Software Repositories, pp. 430–440. ACM (2016)

24. Kohavi, R.: A study of cross-validation and bootstrap for accuracy estimation and model selection. IJCAI **14**(2), 1137–1145 (1995)

25. Wang, S., Lo, D., Vasilescu, B., et al.: EnTagRec++: an enhanced tag recommendation system for software information sites. Empir. Softw. Eng. **23**(2), 800–832 (2018)

Application of Probabilistic Process Model for Smart Factory Systems

Junsup Song, Yeongbok Choe, and Moonkun Lee$^{(\boxtimes)}$

Chonbuk National University, 567 Baekje-daero, Deokjin-gu,
Jeonju-si, Jeonbuk 54896, Republic of Korea
moonkun@jbnu.ac.kr

Abstract. Process algebra is one of the best suitable formal methods to model smart systems based on IoT, especially Smart Factory. However, because of some uncertainty, it is necessary to model predictability of the systems, based on the uncertainty. There have been several process algebras with probability, such as, PAROMA, PACSR, etc. However they are not well suitable for the smart systems, since they are based only on discrete model or exponential model. Consequently, only simple or targeted probability can be specified and analyzed. In order to handle such limitations, the paper presents a new formal method, called dTP-Calculus, extended from the existing dT-Calculus with discrete, normal, exponential, and uniform probability models. It provides all the possible probability features for Smart Factory with complex uncertainty. The specification of the modeling will be simulated statistically for Smart Factory, and further the simulation results will be analyzed for probabilistic properties of the systems. For implementation, a tool set for the calculus has been developed in the SAVE tool suite on the ADOxx Meta-Modeling Platform, including Specifier, Analyzer and Verifier. A Smart Factory example from Audi Cell Production System has been selected as an example to demonstrate the feasibility of the approach.

Keywords: dTP-Calculus · Formal method · Probability · Smart Factory · SAVE · ADOxx Meta-Modeling Platform

1 Introduction

Smart Factory is one of the main themes in the Industry 4.0 to improve productivity of factories effectively. Smart factory implies intelligent factory controlled by Big Data and AI in IoT system environments [1]. Since all the infrastructure and systems are connected by wireless communication, manufacturing processes are proceeded more effectively and efficiently. Smart Factory Systems must not only be verified for their operational safety and correctness for sound industrial activities by workers, but also the system behaviors must be predictable formally in order to prevent unexpected system errors or failures from occurring. Further the systems must guarantee their productivity and reliability through probabilistic analysis of the system behaviors. In order to satisfy system characteristics and safety requirements of Smart Factory Systems, it is necessary to apply formal methods and tools to model the systems, since formal methods are used

© Springer Nature Switzerland AG 2019
C. Douligeris et al. (Eds.): KSEM 2019, LNAI 11776, pp. 25–36, 2019.
https://doi.org/10.1007/978-3-030-29563-9_3

to specify and verify such system behaviors with the properties of distributivity, mobility and communicativity in real-time.

Generally, it is very difficult to predict system behaviors with process algebra because of nondeterministic choice operations. In order to overcome the limitation, a new type of process algebras, such as, PAROMA [2] and PACSR [3], were defined based on the notion of probability. However, these process algebras have limitations to specify and analyze very complex systems like smart systems with IoT or IIoT, especially Smart Factory, since PACSR is capable of specifying probabilistic choice operations only in one form of probability model, that is, discrete model and PAROMA is only based on exponential distribution model. In the smart systems based on IoT systems, especially, Smart Factory, various behaviors cannot be predicted from the explicitly fixed or exponentially distributed probabilistic branches of choice operations, since the systems behave differently according to different specification and requirements. Therefore, it is necessary to apply various probabilistic models based on normal, exponential, and other distributions in order to predict various behaviors, instead of being on the fixed or exponential models.

In order to handle the limitations, this paper presents dTP-Calculus [4], a probabilistic process algebra extended from dT-Calculus [5] with a set of probability models. Further the paper presents a dedicated tool to specify, analyze and verify such systems with dTP-Calculus, namely SAVE [6], developed on ADOxx Meta-Modeling Platform [7]. The paper also presents the application steps how the calculus and the tool are used to predict system behaviors at the time of modeling smart systems to prevent unexpected system behaviors.

dTP-Calculus allows to specify formally the components of Smart Factory Systems, as well as their communication and mobility with probability properties. SAVE consists of Specifier, Analyzer and Verifier. Specifier allows visual specification of the system with dTP-Calculus. Analyzer performs simulation of the system based on their specification in dTP-Calculus. As results of the simulation, it generates Geo-Temporal Space (GTS) data, representing all the spatial and temporal events among the components of the system, including probabilistic properties. Further, it allows to predict probabilistic behaviors of the system, such as productivity, reliability, etc., based on probabilistic analysis on the GTS data from the simulation. In order to demonstrate the feasibility of the approach with dTP-Calculus and SAVE, a smart factory example from the Audi Cell Production System has been selected and implemented in SAVE with dTP-Calculus.

The paper consists of the following sections. In Sect. 2, dTP-Calculus is described. In Sect. 3, a smart factory example is specified and analyzed using dTP-Calculus and SAVE. In Sect. 4, the SAVE tool is described. In Sect. 5, the approach in the paper is compared with other approaches for its advantages. In Sect. 6, conclusions and future research are made.

2   dTP-Calculus

2.1   Syntax

dTP-Calculus is a process algebra extended from existing dT-Calculus in order to define probabilistic behavioral properties of processes on the choice operation. Note that dT-Calculus is the process algebra originally designed by the authors of the paper in order to specify and analyze various timed movements of processes on the virtual geo-graphical space. The syntax of dTP-calculus is shown in Fig. 1.

$P ::= A$	Action .... (1)	$A ::= \emptyset$	Empty .... (12)
$\mid A^{p,n}_{[r,to,e,d]}$	Timed action .... (2)	$\mid r(\overline{msg})$	Send .... (13)
$\mid P^{p,n}_{[r,to,e,d]}$	Timed process .... (3)	$\mid r(msg)$	Receive .... (13)
$\mid P_{(n)}$	Priority .... (4)	$\mid M$	Movement action
$\mid P[Q]$	Nesting .... (5)	$\mid C$	Control action
$\mid P(r)$	Channel .... (6)	$M ::= m^p(k)\, P$	Movement request ..... (14)
$\mid P + Q$	Choice .... (7)	$\mid P\, m(k)$	Movement permission (15)
$\mid P\{c\} +_F Q\{c\}$	Probabilistic choice .... (8)	$m ::= in$	In movement
$\mid P \parallel Q$	Parallel .... (9)	$\mid out$	Out movement
$\mid P\backslash E$	Exception .... (10)	$\mid get$	Get movement
$\mid A \cdot P$	Sequence .... (11)	$\mid put$	Put movement
$F ::= D$	Discrete distribution	$C ::= new\, P$	Create process .... (16)
$\mid N(\mu,\sigma)$	Normal distribution	$\mid kill\, P$	Kill process .... (17)
$\mid E(\lambda)$	Exponential distribution	$\mid exit$	Exit process .... (18)
$\mid U(l,u)$	Uniform distribution		

Fig. 1.   Syntax of dTP-Calculus

Each part of the syntax is defined as follows:

(1)   *Action*: Actions performed by a process.

(2)   *Timed action*: The execution of an action with temporal restrictions. The temporal properties of [r, to, e, d] represent *ready time, timeout, execution time,* and *deadline*, respectively. p and n are properties for periodic action or processes: p for period and n for the number of repetition.

(3)   *Timed process*: Process with temporal properties.

(4)   *Priority*: The priority of the process P represented by a natural number. The higher number represents the higher priority. Exceptionally, 0 represents the highest priority.

(5)   *Nesting*: P contains Q. The internal process is controlled by its external process. If the internal process has a higher priority than that of its external, it can move out of its external without the permission of the external.

(6)   *Channel*: A channel r of P to communicate with other processes.

(7)   *Choice*: Only one of P and Q will be selected nondeterministically for execution.

(8)   *Probabilistic choice*: Only one of P and Q will be selected probabilistically. Selection will be made based on a probabilistic model specified with F, and the condition for each selection will be defined with c.

(9)   *Parallel*: Both P and Q are running concurrently.

(10)   *Exception*: P will be executed. But E will be executed in case that P is out of timeout or deadline.

(11) *Sequence*: *P* follows after action *A*.
(12) *Empty*: No action.
(13) *Send/Receive*: Communication between processes, exchanging a message by a channel *r*.
(14) *Movement request*: Requests for movement. *p* and *k* represent priority and key, respectively.
(15) *Movement permission*: Permissions for movement.
(16) *Create process*: Creation of a new internal process. The new process cannot have a higher priority than its creator.
(17) *Kill process*: Termination of other processes. The terminator should have the higher priority than that of the terminatee.
(18) *Exit process*: Termination of its own process. All internal processes will be terminated at the same time.

2.2 Probability

There are 4 types of probabilistic models to specify probabilistic choice as follows. Each model may require variables to be used to define probability:

(1) Discrete distribution: It is a probabilistic model without variable. It simply defines specific value of probability for each branch of the choice operation. There are some restrictions. For example, the summation of the probability branches cannot be over 100%.
(2) Normal distribution: It is a probabilistic model based on the normal distribution with the mean value of μ and the standard deviation of σ, whose density function is defined by $f(x|\mu, \sigma^2) = \frac{1}{\sigma\sqrt{2\pi}} \exp\left(-\frac{(x-\mu)^2}{2\sigma^2}\right)$.
(3) Exponential distribution: This is a probabilistic model based on the exponential distribution with frequency of λ, whose density function is defined by $f(x; \lambda) = \lambda e^{-\lambda x} (x \geq 0)$.
(4) Uniform distribution: This is a probabilistic model based on the uniform distribution with the lower bound l and the upper bound u, whose density function is defined by $f(x) = \begin{cases} 0 & (x < a \lor x > b) \\ \frac{1}{u-l} & (l \leq x \leq u) \end{cases}$.

Once a model is defined, the conditions for the selection of the branches should be specified. There are differences in the specifications for the conditions in the models. In the discrete distribution, the values of the probabilities are specified directly in the condition as shown in Expression (1).

$$P\{0.7\} +_D Q\{0.3\} \tag{1}$$

In other cases, that is, other distribution models, such as, normal, exponential and uniform, a set of specific ranges is to be specified in the conditions. The following Expressions (2), (3) and (4) are the examples for normal distribution, exponential distribution and uniform distribution, respectively.

$$P(v > 52) + {}_{N(50,5)}Q(v \leq 52) \tag{2}$$

$$P(v > 2.5) + {}_{E(0.33)}Q(v \leq 2.5) \tag{3}$$

$$P(v > 5) + {}_{U(3,7)}Q(v \leq 5) \tag{4}$$

During the specification, it is very important to check that the summation of the probabilities in the conditions on the branches should be less than or equal to 1. In the discrete distribution, the summation should be 1, since the values are specified directly. However, in other case, such as, normal, exponential and uniform distributions, the conjunction of all the ranges in the conditions on the branches should be the set of the real numbers, since the ranges are specified in the conditions. Note that the restriction on is based on the facts that, if the summation is less than 1, it is possible for no branch to be selected, and, if it is greater than 1, it is possible for some branches to be selected at the same time, violating the notion of selection on the choice.

3   Application: Audi Smart Factory System

Audi Smart Factory System (ASFS) [8] is based on Production Cell Method (PCM), where AGVs (*Automated Guided Vehicle*) are moving through the cells, in which each production processes are performed smartly as planned for production.

This section presents the probabilistic specification and analysis for a smart factory system based on the basic concept of ASFS, using dTP-Calculus and SAVE.

3.1   Specification

Smart Factory System (SFS) is assumed to consist of the following components:

(1) AGV: It represents an ambient, that is, a mobile entity with carrier capability.
(2) Cell: It represents space where each manufacturing processes of SFS are performed. Each Cell has its own fault rate during its process as follows

- Cell A: 4%
- Cell B: 3%
- Cell C: 5%
- Cell D: 3%

SFS operates as follows:

(1) AGV is processed to be a product through the manufacturing process of each Cell.
(2) Each Cell performs its manufacturing process through communication with AGV. Each Cell requires the following production time.

- Cell A: 2 (Time Unit)
- Cell B: 3
- Cell C: 1
- Cell D: 5

Figure 2 shows the specification of the manufacturing process of SFS, using dTP-Calculus, and Fig. 3 shows the visual representation of the specification on SAVE.

$$
\begin{aligned}
&\textit{Cell Production} ::= AGV \parallel \textit{Cell A} \parallel \textit{Cell B} \parallel \textit{Cell C} \parallel \textit{Cell D};\\
&\textit{Cell A} ::= \emptyset_{[0,-,1,-]} \cdot \left(\emptyset\{0.04\} +_D \left(SA(ReadyA) \cdot AGV\ in \cdot \emptyset_{[0,-,2,-]} \cdot SA(\overline{DoneA}) \cdot AGV\ out\right)\{0.96\}\right);\\
&\textit{Cell B} ::= \emptyset_{[0,-,2,-]} \cdot \left(\emptyset\{0.03\} +_D \left(SB(ReadyB) \cdot AGV\ in \cdot \emptyset_{[0,-,3,-]} \cdot SB(\overline{DoneB}) \cdot AGV\ out\right)\{0.97\}\right);\\
&\textit{Cell C} ::= \emptyset_{[0,-,3,-]} \cdot \left(\emptyset\{0.05\} +_D \left(SC(ReadyC) \cdot AGV\ in \cdot \emptyset_{[0,-,1,-]} \cdot SC(\overline{DoneC}) \cdot AGV\ out\right)\{0.95\}\right);\\
&\textit{Cell D} ::= \emptyset_{[0,-,4,-]} \cdot \left(\emptyset\{0.03\} +_D \left(SD(ReadyD) \cdot AGV\ in \cdot \emptyset_{[0,-,5,-]} \cdot SD(\overline{DoneD}) \cdot AGV\ out\right)\{0.97\}\right);\\
&AGV ::= \left(SA(\overline{ReadyA}) \cdot in\ Cell\ A \cdot \emptyset_{[0,-,2,-]} \cdot SA(DoneA) \cdot out\ Cell\ A\right)_{[0,3,-,-]} \backslash \emptyset_{[0,-,9,-]}\\
&\qquad \cdot \left(SB(\overline{ReadyB}) \cdot in\ Cell\ B \cdot \emptyset_{[0,-,3,-]} \cdot SB(DoneB) \cdot out\ Cell\ B\right)_{[0,3,-,-]} \backslash \emptyset_{[0,-,5,-]}\\
&\qquad \cdot \left(SC(\overline{ReadyC}) \cdot in\ Cell\ C \cdot \emptyset_{[0,-,1,-]} \cdot SC(DoneC) \cdot out\ Cell\ C\right)_{[0,3,-,-]} \backslash \emptyset_{[0,-,4,-]}\\
&\qquad \cdot \left(SD(\overline{ReadyD}) \cdot in\ Cell\ D \cdot \emptyset_{[0,-,5,-]} \cdot SD(DoneD) \cdot out\ Cell\ D\right)_{[0,3,-,-]} \backslash \emptyset_{[0,-,7,-]};
\end{aligned}
$$

Fig. 2. dTP-Calculus: a specification of product specification for Audi SFS

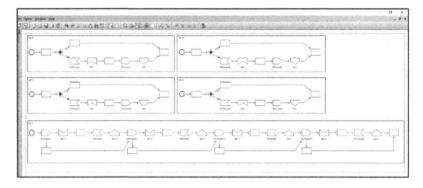

Fig. 3. SAVE: visual representation of the specification in Fig. 2

The specification describes that AGV of SFS moves through the cells in order to perform manufacturing, and that there are 4%, 3%, 5% and 3% fault rates for Cells A, B, C and D, respectively. If some fault occurs in a cell, AGV moves to another cell in order to complete the specified manufacturing task. In Cell Production of SFS, Cells A, B, C and D are operating concurrently, and the failure and success rates of each cells are specified with probabilistic choice formulas, as shown in the following Expressions (5), (6), (7) and (8). Note that these Expressions are based on Expression (1), that is, Discrete Distribution.

$$
\emptyset\{0.04\} +_D \left(SA(ReadyA) \cdot AGV\ in \cdot \emptyset_{[0,-,2,-]} \cdot SA(\overline{DoneA}) \cdot AGV\ out\right)\{0.96\} \tag{5}
$$

$$
\emptyset\{0.03\} +_D \left(SB(ReadyB) \cdot AGV\ in \cdot \emptyset_{[0,-,3,-]} \cdot SB(\overline{DoneB}) \cdot AGV\ out\right)\{0.97\} \tag{6}
$$

$$
\emptyset\{0.05\} +_D \left(SC(ReadyC) \cdot AGV\ in \cdot \emptyset_{[0,-,1,-]} \cdot SC(\overline{DoneC}) \cdot AGV\ out\right)\{0.95\} \tag{7}
$$

$$
\emptyset\{0.03\} +_D \left(SD(ReadyD) \cdot AGV\ in \cdot \emptyset_{[0,-,5,-]} \cdot SD(\overline{DoneD}) \cdot AGV\ out\right)\{0.97\} \tag{8}
$$

Expression (5) shows that Cell A cannot perform its manufacturing task with the 4% probability and can complete its task with the 96% probability. SA implies a channel between Cell A and AGV, and the 2 time units of Cell A is specified as $\emptyset_{[0,-,2,-]}$. Cells B, C and D are specified in the same manner.

3.2 Analysis

This section shows how the system from Sect. 3.1 can be analyzed to predict its behavior based on probabilistic specification, represented as safety requirements.

The basic requirements for SFS are as follows:

(R1) The error cannot be occurred 3 times in the 1st product manufacturing process.
(R2) The 1st process will take in 38 time units.
(R3) The types can be classified as follows, according to satisfaction of the requirements in the 1st process:

- Type A: All requirements are satisfied.
- Type B: R1 is satisfied, but R2 is not.
- Type C: R1 is not satisfied.

It can be interpreted as that the C of R3 can be of the products without any problem, but that the B of R3 can be of the products with some improvement because of not satisfying R1, that is, of 3 errors, and that the C of R3 can be of the products irreplaceable in other Cells due to overdue errors.

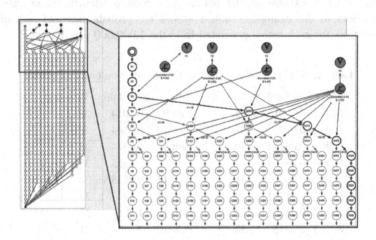

Fig. 4. The overall system behaviors of SFS

Figure 4 shows overall system behaviors of SFS. There are total 16 system behaviors extracted from the specification using SAVE:

- Path 1: It is of Type C, since there were errors in all the Cells.
- Path 2: It is of Type C, since there were errors in Cells A, B and C.
- Path 3: It is of Type C, since there were errors in Cells A, B and D.

- Path 4: It is of Type A, since there were errors in Cells A and B, and R2 is satisfied.
- Path 5: It is of Type C, since there were errors in Cells A, C and D.
- Path 6: It is of Type B, since there were errors in Cells A and C, and R2 is not satisfied.
- Path 7: It is of Type A, since there were errors in Cells A and D, and R2 is satisfied.
- Path 8: It is of Type A, since there was an error in Cell A, and R2 is satisfied.
- Path 9: It is of Type C, since there were errors in Cells B, C and D.
- Path 10: It is of Type A, since there were errors in Cells B and C, and R2 is satisfied.
- Path 11: It is of Type A, since there were errors in Cells B and D, and R2 is satisfied.
- Path 12: It is of Type A, since there was an error in Cell B, and R2 is satisfied.
- Path 13: It is of Type A, since there were errors in Cells C and D, and R2 is satisfied.
- Path 14: It is of Type A, since there was an error in Cell C, and R2 is satisfied.
- Path 15: It is of Type A, since there was an error in Cell D, and R2 is satisfied.
- Path 16: It is of Type A, since there was no error, and R2 is satisfied.

It is possible in SAVE to calculate real occurrence probability of system behaviors form the probabilistic specification using dTP-Calculus, that is, the execution paths from the numerous simulations. The calculation of probability thorough numerous simulations in SAVE are performed by Path Analysis Tool of ADOxx Meta-Modeling Platform.

For the paper, 1,000,000 simulations are performed to calculate the probability of each behaviors in the example. Table 1 shows the probabilities and execution or production time for each paths, generated from the 1,000,000 simulations.

Table 1. The probabilities and execution/production times for paths

Path	Probability	Time unit	Path	Probability	Time unit
Path 1	0.0001	43	Path 9	0.0014	38
Path 2	0.0023	41	Path 10	0.0744	36
Path 3	0.0011	40	Path 11	0.0374	35
Path 4	0.0540	38	Path 12	1.8353	33
Path 5	0.0022	41	Path 13	0.0828	36
Path 6	0.1131	39	Path 14	3.6973	34
Path 7	0.0585	38	Path 15	1.8214	33
Path 8	2.7893	36	Path 16	89.4294	31
Sum of probabilities for all paths			100%		

Table 2 shows a general analysis table for the requirements. As a result of the analysis, it can be seen that the probability of being Types B and C is 0.1202%, and there are 1202 occurrences from the 1,000,000 simulations. Since, in general, the level of product quality by 6-sigma is of 3.4 occurrences from the 1,000,000 simulations, it can be considered that the system needs to be improved.

If it is necessary to prepare for another additional Cell, the above analysis data can be utilized to determine for which Cell it can be prepared to improve the system performance. The number of errors occurred at Cells with respect to Types B and C can be summarized in analysis as follows:

- Cell A: 5 times
- Cell B: 4 times
- Cell C: 5 times
- Cell D: 4 times

Regarding error occurrences for Types B and C, it is necessary to prepare an additional cell for Cells A or C, which have the highest frequency of the occurrences. The additional work time for Cell A is 5 time units and the additional work time for Cell C is 4 time units. That is, if an error occurs, it means that Cell A has higher risk than Cell C. Therefore, it can be considered that there will be high probability of satisfying R2 by preparing an additional cell for Cell A.

Table 2. The analysis table for the requirements

Type	Path	Time unit	Probability	Sum 1	Sum 2
A	Path 4	38	0.0540	99.8798	99.8798
	Path 7	38	0.0585		
	Path 8	36	2.7893		
	Path 10	36	0.0744		
	Path 11	35	0.0374		
	Path 12	33	1.8353		
	Path 13	36	0.0828		
	Path 14	34	3.6973		
	Path 15	33	1.8214		
	Path 16	31	89.4294		
B	Path 6	39	0.1131	0.1131	0.1202
C	Path 1	43	0.0001	0.0071	
	Path 2	41	0.0023		
	Path 3	40	0.0011		
	Path 5	41	0.0022		
	Path 9	38	0.0014		
Sum of probabilities for all paths			100%		

4 SAVE

SAVE is a suite of tools to specify and analyze the IoT systems with dTP-Calculus. It is developed on the ADOxx Meta-Modeling Platform. Figure 5 shows the basic tools and system architecture of SAVE on ADOxx.

SAVE consists of the basic three components: Specifier, Analyzer and Verifier. Specifier, as shown in Fig. 6, is a tool to specify the IoT systems with dTP-Calculus, visually in the diagrammatic representations [9]. The left side of Fig. 6 is the In-the-Large (ITL) model, or system view, representing both inclusion relations among components of the system and communication channels among them. The right side of the Fig. 6 is In-the-Small (ITS) models, or process view, representing a sequence of the detailed actions, interactions and movements performed by a process.

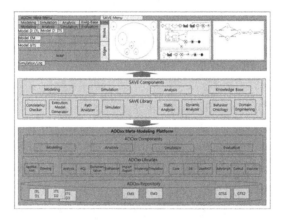

Fig. 5. SAVE architecture

Analyzer is a tool to generate the execution model from the specification in order to explore all the possible execution paths or cases, as the left side of Fig. 7 shows in the form of a tree, and to perform trial-based simulation of each execution from the execution model in order to analyze probabilistic behaviors of the specified system.

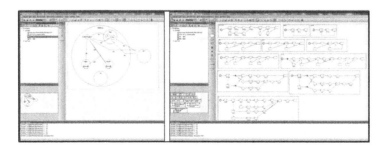

Fig. 6. Specification tool of SAVE

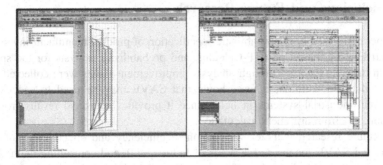

Fig. 7. Analysis and verification tool of SAVE

Verifier is a tool to verify a set of system requirements on the geo-temporal space generated, as output, from each simulation for all the execution paths or cases in the execution model, as the right side of Fig. 7 shows. This model allows both confirming the behavior and movements of the system and comprehending the security of the system by visualizing systems requirements and their verification results.

5   Comparative Study

The representative process algebras to specify probability properties of systems can be PAROMA and PACSR. These process algebras allow specifying various probability properties, but they have some limitations to the properties required by the IoT systems. PAROMA allows specifying exponential distribution probability model by using the λ parameter, at the time of defining location information of each agent. Further it is suitable to analyze systems consisting of geographically distributed agents by applying M2MAM (Multi-class, Multi-message Markovian Agent Models) [10]. However, the location information is simply a parameter used for communication, but mobility of the location cannot be expressed properly. PACSR is the process algebra to express resources and probability. It allows specifying three properties of resources, time and probability, as well as exceptional handling using time property, but only a simple form of probability using discrete distribution is allowed.

However dTP-Calculus allows specifying various properties of geographical space, time and probabilities, suitable for Smart Factory. Geographical mobility, not just simple geographical information, can be expressed, and various types of time properties can be specified, too. More importantly, various probability properties can be specified with 4 kinds of probability models, and change of probability from the Smart Factory environment can be more easily specified with probability density function, not with specific predefined probability. In addition, complex probability computation and simulation are automatically performed using the SAVE tool. Since the probability calculation performed by SAVE is not of arithmetic calculation but of statistical results from the simulation, it can support to obtain statistical data more easily than real industrial environments. Such statistical data can be used to discover improvement issues of Smart Factory Systems and increase reliability of their system behaviors.

6   Conclusions and Future Research

This paper performed both probabilistic specification of product manufacturing system for Smart Factory, based on dTP-Calculus, and probabilistic analysis for the specification on the SAVE tool. Through analysis, improvement issues were collected from statistical data. In addition, it was shown that SAVE may be used to specify and analyze real industrial systems in field, since it provides statistical results from the simulation, not from arithmetic calculation.

The future research includes verification of efficiency and effectiveness of dTP-Calculus and SAVE for the real systems of Industry 4.0, and controlling methods for nondeterministic system behaviors of the systems, with high reliability, using probability.

Acknowledgment. This work was supported by Basic Science Research Programs through the National Research Foundation of Korea (NRF) funded by the Ministry of Education (2010-0023787), Space Core Technology Development Program through the National Research Foundation of Korea (NRF) funded by the Ministry of Science, ICT and Future Planning (NRF-2014M1A3A3A02034792), Basic Science Research Program through the National Research Foundation of Korea (NRF) funded by the Ministry of Education (NRF-2015R1D1A3A01019282), and Hyundai NGV, Korea.

References

1. IEC. White Paper: Factory of the future (2017)
2. Feng, C., Hillston, J.: PALOMA: a process algebra for located Markovian agents. In: Norman, G., Sanders, W. (eds.) QEST 2014. LNCS, vol. 8657, pp. 265–280. Springer, Cham (2014). https://doi.org/10.1007/978-3-319-10696-0_22
3. Lee, I., Philippou, A., Sokolsky, O.: Resources in process algebra. J. Logic Algebraic Program. **72**(1), 98–122 (2007)
4. Choe, Y., Lee, M.: Process model to predict nondeterministic behavior of IoT systems. In: Proceedings of the 2nd International Workshop on Practicing Open Enterprise Modelling Within OMiLAB (PrOse) (2018)
5. Choe, Y., Lee, S., Lee, M.: dT-Calculus: a process algebra to model timed movements of processes. Int. J. Comput. **2**, 53–62 (2017)
6. Choe, Y., Lee, S., Lee, M.: SAVE: an environment for visual specification and verification of IoT. In: 2016 IEEE 20th International Enterprise Distributed Object Computing Workshop (EDOCW), pp. 1–8. IEEE (2016)
7. Fill, H.G., Karagiannis, D.: On the conceptualisation of modeling methods using the ADOxx meta modeling platform. Proc. Enterp. Model. Inf. Syst. Architect. (EMISAJ) **8**(1), 4–25 (2013)
8. Audi Homepage. https://www.audi-mediacenter.com/en/overview-of-audi/5702/digitalized-production-of-the-future-5708. Accessed 01 May 2019
9. Choe, Y., Lee, M.: Algebraic method to model secure IoT. In: Karagiannis, D., Mayr, H., Mylopoulos, J. (eds.) Domain-Specific Conceptual Modeling, pp. 335–355. Springer, Cham (2016). https://doi.org/10.1007/978-3-319-39417-6_15
10. Cerotti, D., Gribaudo, M., Bobbio, A., Calafate, Carlos T., Manzoni, P.: A Markovian agent model for fire propagation in outdoor environments. In: Aldini, A., Bernardo, M., Bononi, L., Cortellessa, V. (eds.) EPEW 2010. LNCS, vol. 6342, pp. 131–146. Springer, Heidelberg (2010). https://doi.org/10.1007/978-3-642-15784-4_9

A Distributed Topic Model for Large-Scale Streaming Text

Yicong Li[1,2] ⓘ, Dawei Feng[1,2(✉)], Menglong Lu[1,2],
and Dongsheng Li[1,2]

[1] College of Computer Science and Technology,
National University of Defense Technology, Changsha 410073, China
{liyicong17, dsli}@nudt.edu.cn, davyfeng.c@gmail.com,
lumenglong2018@163.com
[2] National Key Laboratory of Parallel and Distributed Processing,
National University of Defense Technology, Changsha 410073, China

Abstract. Learning topic information from large-scale unstructured text has attracted extensive attention from both the academia and industry. Topic models, such as LDA and its variants, are a popular machine learning technique to discover such latent structure. Among them, online variational hierarchical Dirichlet process (onlineHDP) is a promising candidate for dynamically processing streaming text. Instead of a static assignment in advance, the number of topics in onlineHDP is inferred from the corpus as the training process proceeds. However, when dealing with large scale streaming data it still suffers from the limited model capacity problem. To this end, we proposed a distributed version of the onlineHDP algorithm (named as DistHDP) in this paper, the training task is split into many sub-batch tasks and distributed across multiple worker nodes, such that the whole training process is accelerated. The model convergence is guaranteed through a distributed variation inference algorithm. Extensive experiments conducted on several real-world datasets demonstrate the usability and scalability of the proposed algorithm.

Keywords: Distributed topic model · Hierarchical Dirichlet process · Variational inference

1 Introduction

In recent years, unstructured and unlabeled data in the network such as news and literature have become more and more extensive [15]. These data generally share the following characteristics. Firstly, the data size is huge. For example, there are around 500 million tweets posted on Twitter per day [16]. If one wants to monitor the trend of Twitter's public opinion, then he needs to process an extremely massive amount of data. Secondly, most of the data arrive in a streaming manner, which consequently leads to the data volume increasing over time and the content topics drifting dynamically [4].

Obtaining latent topic information from such texts is becoming an issue of concern both to the academia and the industry [19]. Among many of the potential techniques,

---

The original version of this chapter was revised: References and equation citations were modified. The correction to this chapter is available at https://doi.org/10.1007/978-3-030-29563-9_37

© Springer Nature Switzerland AG 2019
C. Douligeris et al. (Eds.): KSEM 2019, LNAI 11776, pp. 37–48, 2019.
https://doi.org/10.1007/978-3-030-29563-9_4

topic models are a popular machine learning method to find useful latent structure in such otherwise unstructured text collection, which can identify interpretable low dimensional components in very high dimensional text data. Therefore, topic models serve as the foundation of a wide range of applications: recommendation systems [2], information retrieval [3], advertising, network analysis, genetics and so on.

Although traditional methods can effectively infer the topics, it is difficult to process large-scale text in a short time. Because of the limitation in a single machine's storage capacity and computing capability, it is always insufficient to store and calculate the whole parameter set of a large topic model [5]. For instance, there are one trillion parameters when training the topic model of billions of documents, with the setting of one million topic number and one million vocabulary size. Many researchers have conducted extensive research on large-scale topic model algorithms for this problem. Among them, the method of optimizing sampling accounts for the majority [4, 12, 13], which aims to optimize the time complexity of the algorithms. There are also some distributed algorithms based on decoupling sampling [5, 11], which are focused on reducing the training time and maintaining high scalability.

All aforementioned algorithms show improved performance. However, due to the assumption of the LDA generation model, it is necessary to specify the number of topics (clusters) before the model training, which does not apply to streaming text that increases over time. In this respect, the non-parametric Bayesian model has its advantages. Hierarchical Dirichlet process (HDP) [8] is one of the most popular non-parametric Bayesian models, where the number of topics is determined during the training of an HDP model. The topic number does not need to be specified in advance, while the model evolves as the data changes, which makes it suitable for processing streaming data. However, one of the limitations in HDP is that it always requires to pass through the whole data set multiple times, and consumes considerably long time, makes it intractable for large-scale corpus. To alleviate this problem, Wang et al. proposed an online variational inference method [10], which fetches a random set of text iteratively and updates the variational objective parameters. But it is still intractable for very large corpus.

In this paper, we propose a distributed online HDP (DistHDP) based on the distributed online variational inference method. DistHDP not only supports the online model updating, but also does not acquire to specify the number of topics in advance. Besides, as a distributed algorithm, it demonstrates good scalability through experiments.

In summary, the main contributions of this paper include:

- To process massive text data effectively, we utilize a distributed online variational inference (DistVI) to implement the distributed online variational HDP based on message passing interface (MPI), the proposed method is able to learn topic models dynamically on streaming data in a distributed manner;
- Extensive experiments are conducted to demonstrate the applicability and efficiency of the proposed method with comparison to the classical LDA and onlineHDP model.

The following paper is structured as follows. In the second section, we introduce the related work and discuss their advantages and disadvantages. The proposed method and experiment results are given in Sects. 3 and 4, respectively. We summarize our work and future direction in the last section.

2 Related Work

Topic model can date back to LDA proposed by Blei et al. [6] in 2003, which is proposed to discover the coherent topics and the topic proportions from text corpus. LDA is a probabilistic topic generation model that each document is associated with a mixture of latent topics and each topic is based on the distribution of words.

Many efforts have been put into scaling LDA to ever-larger data and model capacity in recent years, such as LightLDA [5], WrapLDA [11], LDA^* [7] and so on. LightLDA utilizes a new proposal scheme and a highly efficient architecture to improve the sample throughput and convergence rate. WrapLDA is built on an MCEM algorithm which reduces the latency of random accesses of parameters during training. LDA^* is based on a hybrid sampler and an asymmetric architecture, which has been running to provide services for industry.

LDA requires to specify the number of clusters (topics) in advance, which can be determined by experimental methods, such as cross-validation, held-out likelihood and so on. However, the above methods are impractical to process the streaming data. In 2006, Teh et al. [8] proposed the hierarchical Dirichlet process (HDP), which is a nonparametric Bayesian model. It adds the Dirichlet process to the model and considers the sharing of clusters across multiple, nested groupings of data [9, 17]. Specifically, in HDP the whole dataset shares the topics, and the topic distribution of each document comes from a base distribution. In addition, HDP considers the number of topics to be an unknown parameter and infer it during the training process. As a result, there is no need to specify the number of topics in advance.

However, HDP is still not suitable to deal with large datasets, because of the limitation of a single machine's storage and computing capacity. In addition, the algorithm is not convenient for incremental model updates because when the data is updated, the common way to update the model is to resample the whole dataset and get a new topic distribution. Besides, HDP requires multiple passes through the whole dataset, which is always impractical for large scale corpus.

In 2011, Wang et al. [10] proposed online variational inference algorithms for the HDP (onlineHDP), which utilizes Sethuraman's stick-breaking construction [20] in the online variational inference method to make an incremental model updating possible. However, due to its non-distributed implementation, it is not suitable for processing large scale dataset.

3 DistHDP Methodology

Inspired by the work of onlineHDP, we implement the DistHDP. For the sake of concise expression, the formulas presented in this paper are consistent with those in [10].

3.1 HDP Generation Model

HDP is a non-parametric topic model which has the ability to find low-dimensional latent structures in document collections. We describe the graphical model of HDP in

Fig. 1. As shown, H is a base distribution, from which the discrete corpus-level topic distribution G_0 is obtained. For each document m, the discrete document-level distribution G_m is drawn from G_0. θ_{mn} is the posterior topic distribution from G_m, where each word w_{mn} is generated from.

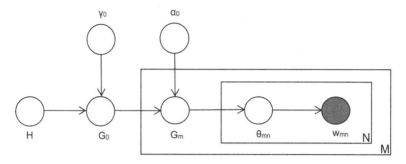

Fig. 1. The graphical model of HDP

In detail, to generate a document according to the HDP model, it firstly samples the discrete topic mixture distribution from H (continuously base distribution) with the hyperparameter γ_0. G_0 is also a base distribution, from which HDP samples all document-level topic distributions with the hyperparameter α_0. Formally,

$$G_0 | \gamma_0, H \sim DP(\gamma_0, H), \tag{1}$$

$$G_m | \alpha_0, G_0 \sim DP(\alpha_0, G_0), \tag{2}$$

where DP is a Dirichlet Process. Hyperparameter α_0 determines the number of clusters (topics). Hyperparameter γ_0 and α_0 jointly determine the atomic correlation among each G_m distribution.

For each document m, each topic distribution θ_{mn} is drawn from G_m. Finally, each word w_{mn} is sampled from the topic distribution θ_{mn}. Mathematically,

$$\theta_{mn} | G_m \sim G_m, \tag{3}$$

$$w_{mn} | \theta_{mn} \sim Mult(\theta_{mn}), \tag{4}$$

where *Mult(.)* is the multinomial sampling. According to the above process, a document corresponding to the topic distribution can be generated.

3.2   Dirichlet Process Construction for the HDP

OnlineHDP utilizes the Sethuraman's Stick Breaking to construct HDP, it follows a two-layer stick breaking process [17]. It addresses the coupling problem in the traditional variational inference method, and makes the variation update more convenient.

The first layer of the stick breaking is to learn the corpus-level discrete topic distribution parameters, and the base distribution G_0 can be represented by Eq. (5).

$$G_0 = \sum_{k=1}^{\infty} \beta_k \delta_{\phi_k}, \tag{5}$$

where β_k is the topic weight of each topic ϕ_k. δ_{ϕ_k} is the probability measure of the topic. And all topics with its weights make up the discrete base distribution G_0. Each topic is sampled from H, mathematically,

$$\phi_k \sim H, \tag{6}$$

where H is the continuously base distribution in Eq. (1). At the same time, β_k is obtained by the following formula,

$$\beta_k' | \gamma \sim \text{Beta}(1, \gamma), \tag{7}$$

$$\beta_k = \beta_k' \prod_{t=1}^{k-1} (1 - \beta_t'), \tag{8}$$

where γ is the parameter of the Beta distribution, from which the weights of corpus-level topics are drawn. It is important to note that the sequence $\beta = (\beta_k)_{k=1}^{\infty}$ constructed by Eqs. (5)–(8) satisfies $\sum_{k=1}^{\infty} \beta_k = 1$. [8] The second layer is also a stick breaking step, which gets the document-level topic distribution. For each document m, G_m can be represented by Eq. (9).

$$G_m = \sum_{t=1}^{\infty} \pi_{mt} \delta_{\psi_{mt}}, \tag{9}$$

where π_{mt} is the topic weight of each topic ψ_{mt}. Each of the parameters follows Eqs. (10)–(12)

$$\psi_{mt} \sim G_0, \tag{10}$$

$$\pi_{mt}' \sim \text{Beta}(1, \alpha_0), \tag{11}$$

$$\pi_{mt} = \pi_{mt}' \prod_{l=1}^{t-1} (1 - \pi_{mt}'), \tag{12}$$

where α_0 is the parameter of the second level (document-level) Beta distribution.

Based on the stick breaking construction above, onlineHDP uses the online variational inference [17] method to train the HDP model. It is based on the assumption that the implicit variables are independent with each other, and uses the coordinate ascent variation [1] to maximize the log-likelihood.

3.3   Distributed Online Variational Inference for the HDP

We utilize a distributed online variational inference method (DistVI) to construct the implementation of DistHDP, and accelerate the processing speed without substantially reducing the clustering performance.

The process of our proposed algorithm is as follows. Firstly, each worker fetches a batch of documents B_m and updates the second level (document-level) stick breaking beta distribution parameters described in Eqs. (13) and (14). Because the document-level parameters are independent among each batch, the calculation of these parameters only depends on local parameters associated with each batch. When updating the document-level Beta distribution parameters, each worker calculates as follows.

$$a_{mt} = \sum\nolimits_{n} \zeta_{mnt} + 1, \text{ for each } B_m, \tag{13}$$

$$b_{mt} = \sum\nolimits_{n} \sum\nolimits_{s=t+1}^{T} \zeta_{mns} + \alpha_0, \text{ for each } B_m, \tag{14}$$

where (a_{mt}, b_{mt}) is the second-level stick breaking Beta distribution parameters. The constant 1 and the parameter α_0 in Eqs. (13) and (14), respectively, represent the initial Beta distribution parameters in Eq. (11). t is the document-level topic truncation. ζ means document topic indicators.

According to the observations, the per word topic indicators and the parameters to the per document topic indicators are computed as follows,

$$\varphi_{mtk} \propto \exp \left(\sum\nolimits_{n} \zeta_{mnt} E_q[\log p(w_{mn}|\varphi_k)] + E_q[\log \beta_k] \right), \text{ for each } B_m, \tag{15}$$

$$\zeta_{mnt} \propto \exp \left(\sum\nolimits_{n} \varphi_{mnt} E_q[\log p(w_{mn}|\varphi_k)] + E_q[\log \pi_{mt}] \right), \text{ for each } B_m, \tag{16}$$

where β_k and π_{mt} are the first-level topic weights and the second-level topic weights of the topic atoms, respectively. w_{mn} is the n-th word in the m-th document φ_k is the k-th first-level topic atom.

Then, the server gathers all document-level parameters from workers. By computing the natural gradient, corpus-level parameters are updated according to Eqs. (17)–(19). This process is repeated until all documents are iteratively processed.

$$\lambda = \lambda + \rho(-\lambda + \eta + D \sum\nolimits_{s=1}^{S} \sum\nolimits_{t=1}^{T} \varphi_{mtks} (\sum\nolimits_{n} \zeta_{mnt} I[w_{mn} = w])), \tag{17}$$

$$u = u + \rho(-u + 1 + D \sum\nolimits_{S=1}^{S} \sum\nolimits_{t=1}^{T} \varphi_{mtks}), \tag{18}$$

$$v = v + \rho(-v + \gamma + D \sum\nolimits_{s=1}^{S} \sum\nolimits_{t=1}^{T} \sum\nolimits_{l=k+1}^{k} \varphi_{mtls}), \tag{19}$$

where (u, v) is the first-level stick breaking beta distribution parameters, and k is the corpus-level topic truncation. ρ is the learning rate. $I[.]$ is an indicator function to represent if there is word w. S means the number of workers. The pseudo code of the algorithm is shown in Table 1.

Table 1. Pseudo code of DistHDP

Algorithm 1. DistHDP
1: **Input:**
2: B_m: a batch of documents
3: D: the document set
4: V: vocabulary
5: η: topic word Dirichlet prior hyperparameter
6: α: document-level stick breaking hyperparameter
7: γ: corpus-level stick breaking hyperparameter
8: **Output:**
9: λ: corpus-level topics parameter
10: **procedure** DistHDP trained on **workers**
11:   **begin**
12:       initialize global corpus-level stick parameters u_D, v_D, and the topics λ_D
13:       **while** not finish **do**
14:           fetch random B_m from D
15:           compute document-level stick parameters a_m, b_m
16:           compute word topic indicators φ_m and document topic indicators ζ_m
17:           push document-level parameters (φ_m, ζ_m) to server
18:           receive push response and update corpus-level parameters (u_D, v_D, λ_D)
19:       **end while**
20:   **end begin**
21: **end procedure**
22: **procedure** DistHDP trained on **masters**
23:   **begin**
24:       **while** receiving pushing request **do**
25:           compute natural gradients ∂u_D, ∂v_D, $\partial \lambda_D$
26:           update corpus-level parameters u_D, $v_{D,}$ λ_D
27:           push back corpus-level parameters (u_D, v_D, λ_D)
28:       **end while**
29:   **end begin**
30: **end procedure**

As shown in Fig. 2, DistHDP implementation is made up of two parts, workers and master. The workers are focused on calculating document-level (local) parameters. After calculating the local parameters, the workers push document-level parameters to the master side to attend the calculation of the corpus-level parameters. On the master node, corpus-level (global) parameters are updated according to the received local parameters. Once finishing updating, the global parameters will be broadcasted to all workers to start a new iteration.

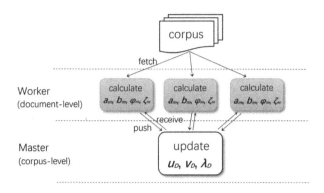

Fig. 2. Working process between worker and master in DistHDP

4 Experiments

In this section, we present empirical studies of DistHDP by comparing with onlineHDP and variational EM for LDA. OnlineHDP is the single-machine version of DistHDP, and variational EM for LDA is a classical topic model. We compare them in terms of time efficiency and model performance. In addition, the scalability experiment for DistHDP is conducted in the end.

4.1 Datasets

The datasets used in our experiments are described in Table 2. Among them, two are in English and the others are in Chinese. In Table 2 V represents the vocabulary size, D is the number of documents, T is the number of tokens, and T/D represents the average length of each document. Webhose.io[1] is a news dataset containing 87,201 documents, with a vocabulary size of 87,201. PubMed[2] [18] is with regard to medicine papers containing 21,148,298 documents, and a vocabulary size of 196,425. Wanfang[3] and cnki[4] are academic datasets containing 720,000 and 1,307,312 documents, respectively.

Table 2. Datasets information

Language	Dataset	V	D	T	T/D
English	webhose.io	37,886	87,201	19,641,405	225
	PubMed	196,425	21,148,298	1,283,644,290	61
Chinese	wanfang	67,580	720,000	41,604,342	58
	cnki	73,375	1,307,312	59,953,531	46

---

[1] https://webhose.io/.

[2] https://www.ncbi.nlm.nih.gov/pubmed/.

[3] http://www.wanfangdata.com.cn/index.html.

[4] https://www.cnki.net/.

4.2   Evaluation Methods

In our experiments, the perplexity (PPL) and the normalized pointwise mutual information (NPMI) [14] are employed to measure the performance of the proposed algorithm.

PPL is one of the most popular measurements in the natural language processing field, which is defined as the reciprocal of the geometric mean of each word likelihood on a given test set. The perplexity of a held-out abstract consisting of words $w_1, \ldots, w_N$ is defined to be:

$$\exp(-\frac{1}{N}\log p(W_1, \ldots, W_N|M)), \tag{20}$$

where M is the trained model and $p(.)$ is the probability mass function for a given model.

NPMI is a word intrusion task by calculating the coherence of the words. It is widely used to estimate topic interpretability and is claimed to be very close to human judgment. Mathematically,

$$\text{NPMI(t)} = \sum_{j=2}^{N} \sum_{i=1}^{j-1} \frac{\log \frac{P(w_j, w_i)}{P(w_i)P(w_j)}}{-\log P(w_i, w_j)}, \tag{21}$$

where t is the t-th topic and N is the number of topic words displayed to the human users according to the existed topic word model.

4.3   Results

Time. To illustrate the running time of our algorithm, we use the onlineHDP as a baseline. In the experiment, we set the number of DistHDP processors to 30, and the corpus-level topic number to 100, document level topic number to 10. All other hyperparameters are the same. The batch size of onlineHDP is 30 times larger than that in DistHDP as we need to keep the global batch size be the same. Table 3 illustrates the run time comparison of each dataset.

Table 3. Run time comparison between onlineHDP and DistHDP (in minutes)

Algorithm	webhose.io	PubMed	wanfang	cnki
onlineHDP	5.32	2338.18	21.54	37.99
DistHDP	0.29	30.59	0.99	1.40

As shown in Table 3, it can be observed that DistHDP is constantly faster than onlineHDP, especially on large-scale datasets. Specifically, in the PubMed dataset the time consumed by onlineHDP is more than one day while that of DistHDP is only about half an hour.

Performance. To measure the validity and the interpretability of topics (clusters), we utilize PPL and NPMI to compare DistHDP with the variational EM for LDA[5] [6] and onlineHDP. The number of iterations is set to 500 for all three algorithms. Results are shown in Table 4. For the NPMI results (row 4–6), the left value is the average NPMI of all topics and the right one is their median.

As we can see from Table 4, for the NPMI DistHDP is almost the same as that of onlineHDP. In other words, the clustering performance of DistHDP is roughly equivalent to onlineHDP. Variational EM for LDA takes a long time to converge and get the worst NPMI among the three algorithms. For the PPL, we randomly selected 100 documents from the webhose.io and wanfang dataset as test dataset, the result exhibits DistHDP has obtained a better performance.

Table 4. PPL and NPMI comparison among onlineHDP, variational EM for LDA and DistHDP

Evaluation	Algorithm	webhose.io	PubMed	wanfang	cnki
PPL	OnlineHDP	1.555e+301	–	5.105e+73	–
	DistHDP	4.768e+95	–	4.425e+12	–
NPMI	LDA	0.004/0.003	–	0.001/0.001	–
	OnlineHDP	0.051/0.03	0.035/0.035	0.042/0.039	0.045/0.039
	DistHDP	0.048/0.032	0.035/0.034	0.042/0.037	0.013/0.013

Scalability. We evaluate the scalability of DistHDP by scaling it to different number of processors. Figure 3 illustrates the result, where the *x-axis* represents the number of processors and the *y-axis* shows the parallel efficiency. The parallel efficiency is computed as follows,

$$E(n) = DT_1/DT_n/n, \tag{22}$$

where n is the number of processors and DT_1 represents the time when running DistHDP on one processor. DT_n means the time when running DistHDP on n processors.

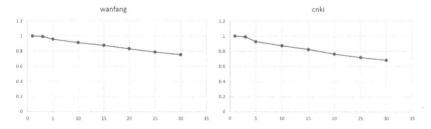

Fig. 3. Scalability of DistHDP

[5] https://github.com/blei-lab/lda-c.

As shown in the figure, a fairly good acceleration efficiency is obtained on both datasets. Specifically, even when the number of processors scales to 30, the parallel efficiency on both the wanfang and cnki datasets is still greater than 70%.

5   Conclusion

Learning informative topic information from streaming text corpus has been a widely concerned research interest. Traditional topic models such as onlineHDP suffer from the limited model capacity problem. To this end, we implemented a distributed online variational inference based HDP (DistHDP) to accelerate the topic learning process. Experimental results on several real-world datasets demonstrate that DistHDP is capable of processing large scale streaming data while maintaining improved performance compared to baseline methods. Nevertheless, there are still some limitations in our work. The currently distributed implementation applies synchronous parallelism, in which when updating the global model parameters those faster worker nodes have to wait for other delayed nodes (stragglers) to accomplish their computation (reaching the synchronized barrier) in each iteration. This problem might be alleviated by implementing the algorithm in an asynchronous updating manner. Therefore, in the future we will explore an asynchronous DistHDP to further improve the computation efficiency and the system scalability.

Acknowledgments. This work is sponsored by the National Key R&D Program of China [grant number 2018YFB0204300].

References

1. Sato, M.: Online model selection based on the variational Bayes. Neural Comput. **13**(7), 1649–1681 (2005)
2. She, J., Chen, L.: Tomoha: topic model-based hashtag recommendation on twitter. In: Proceedings of the 23rd International Conference on World Wide Web, pp. 371–372 (2014)
3. Wei, X., Croft, W.B.: LDA-based document models for ad-hoc retrieval. In: Proceedings of the 29th Annual International ACM SIGIR Conference on Research and Development in Information Retrieval, pp. 178–185 (2016)
4. Yao, L., Mimno, D., McCallum, A.: Efficient methods for topic model inference on streaming document collections. In: SIGKDD, pp. 937–946 (2009)
5. Yuan, J., et al.: LightLDA: big topic models on modest compute clusters. In: The International World Wide Web Conference, pp. 1351–1361 (2015)
6. Blei, D.M., Ng, A.Y., Jordan, M.I.: Latent Dirichlet allocation. J. Mach. Learn. Res. **3**(4–5), 993–1022 (2003)
7. Lele, Yu., Zhang, C., Shao, Y., Cui, B.: LDA*: a robust and large-scale topic modeling system. Proc. VLDB Endow. **10**(11), 1406–1417 (2017)
8. Teh, Y.W., Jordan, M.I., Beal, M.J., Blei, D.M.: Hierarchical Dirichlet processes. J. Am. Stat. Assoc. **101**(476), 1566–1581 (2006)
9. Tang, Y.-K., Mao, X.-L., Huang, H., Shi, X., Wen, G.: Conceptualization topic modeling. Multimedi Tools Appl. **3**(77), 3455–3471 (2018)

10. Wang, C., Paisley, J., Blei, D.M.: Online variational inference for the hierarchical Dirichlet process. In: 14th International Conference on Artificial Intelligence and Statistics, pp. 752–760 (2011)
11. Chen, J., Li, K., Zhu, J., Chen, W.: WrapLDA: a cache efficient O(1) algorithm for Latent Dirichlet allocation. Proc. VLDB Endow. **9**(10), 744–755 (2016)
12. Li, A.Q., Ahmed, A., Ravi, S., Smola, A.J.: Reducing the sampling complexity of topic models. In: SIGKDD, pp. 891–900 (2014)
13. Yu, H.-F., Hsieh, C.-J., Yun, H., Vishwanathan, S., Dhillon, I.S.: A scalable asynchronous distributed algorithm for topic modeling. In: The International World Wide Web Conference, pp. 1340–1350 (2015)
14. Lau, J.H., Newman, D., Baldwin, T.: Machine reading tea leaves: automatically evaluating topic coherence and topic model quality. In: 14th Conference of the European Chapter of the Association for Computational Linguistics, pp. 530–539 (2014)
15. Fu, X., et al.: Dynamic Online HDP model for discovering evolutionary topics from Chinese social texts. Neurocomputing **171**, 412–424 (2016)
16. Internet Live Stats, Twitter Usage Statistics page. https://www.internetlivestats.com/twitter-statistics. Accessed 01 June 2019
17. Sethuraman, J.: A constructive definition of Dirichlet priors. Statistica Sinica **4**, 639–650 (1994)
18. U.S. National Library of Medicine, Download PubMed Data. https://www.nlm.nih.gov/databases/download/pubmed_medline.html. Accessed 05 June 2019
19. Canini, K., Shi, L., Griffiths, T.: Online inference of topics with latent Dirichlet allocation. In: Artificial Intelligence and Statistics, pp. 65–72 (2009)
20. Fox, E., Sudderth, E., Jordan, M., et al.: An HDP-HMM for systems with state persistence. In: 25th International Conference on Machine Learning, pp. 312–319 (2008)

$AutoSimP$: An Approach for Predicting Proteins' Structural Similarities Using an Ensemble of Deep Autoencoders

Mihai Teletin[ID], Gabriela Czibula[✉][ID], and Carmina Codre[ID]

Department of Computer Science, Babeş-Bolyai University,
1, M. Kogalniceanu Street, 400084 Cluj-Napoca, Romania
{mihai.teletin,gabis}@cs.ubbcluj.ro, ccic1510@scs.ubbcluj.ro

Abstract. This paper investigates the problem of supervisedly classifying proteins according to their structural similarity, based on the information enclosed within their conformational transitions. We are proposing $AutoSimP$ approach consisting of an ensemble of *autoencoders* for predicting the similarity class of a certain protein, considering the similarity predicted for its conformational transitions. Experiments performed on real protein data reveal the effectiveness of our proposal compared with similar existing approaches.

Keywords: Proteins · Deep learning · Autoencoders

1 Introduction

Proteins have a vital role for the well-functioning of all living organisms [11], contributing in the chemical processes essential for life. They are sequences of smaller molecules, amino acids, that form the primary structure of a protein [3]. As a result of the interaction between the amino acids due to their chemical composition, as well as their interaction with the external environment, the protein folds in a three dimensional shape known as its native state. A protein suffers multiple changes until it reaches its stable final form and undergoes through the so called *conformations*. *Structural alphabets* (SAs) [14] offer means for encoding the three dimensional representation of a conformation into a one dimensional representation, in which a conformation may be visualized as a string. The representation of a protein composed by a sequence n amino acids in its primary structure is a sequence of length $n - 3$ of SA letters. Families [15] are groups of proteins which have high sequence identity and also similar structure and functions. Furthermore, superfamilies are formed of families which have lower sequence identities, but whose structural and functional properties are alike. Thus, studying the similarity among proteins at the superfamily level could bring insights into their features, but it also imposes a challenge since this level sequences are more diverse and their similarity is harder to predict.

Autoencoders [7] are powerful self-supervised learning models used for learning how to reconstruct the input by approximating the identity function. Their applicability

C. Douligeris et al. (Eds.): KSEM 2019, LNAI 11776, pp. 49–54, 2019.
https://doi.org/10.1007/978-3-030-29563-9_5

spans multiple areas from image analysis to speech processing. We are further introducing a supervised classifier $AutoSimP$ based on an ensemble of *autoencoders* for predicting the superfamily to which a protein belongs, based on the similarity between its conformations and the conformations of the proteins from each superfamily. We are focusing towards answering the following research questions: (1) *How to use an ensemble of autoencoders to supervisedly classify proteins in superfamilies, considering the structural information encoded for each superfamily?*; and (2) *To what extent the proposed approach can be applied at the conformational level, for detecting protein conformations that are likely to be anomalous in relation to the protein's superfamily (i.e. conformations whose structure does not resemble to their encoded information)?*

The rest of the paper is organized as follows. Section 2 introduces our supervised classifier $AutoSimP$ for predicting the superfamily of a certain protein using an ensemble of autoencoders. The experimental results and their analysis, as well as a comparison to existing similar work are given in Sect. 3. The conclusions of the paper and directions for future research and improvements are outlined in Sect. 4.

2   Methodology

$AutoSimP$ consists of on an ensemble of autoencoders for predicting the superfamily to which a protein belongs, based on how similar are its conformational transitions with those of the proteins from that superfamily (encoded into an *autoencoder*). For each superfamily, an autoencoder is used for capturing biologically relevant structural patterns from that superfamily. The autoencoders are used (through their hidden state representation) in order to unsupervisedly learn features that are specific to a particular superfamily. These feature will be further used for classification.

$AutoSimP$ involves four steps: *data representation and preprocessing*, *training* and *testing* (*evaluation*). The main steps of $AutoSimP$ will be further detailed. The ensemble of models represents a set of fully convolutional neural networks that take as input an integer real numbered vector representing a conformation. Let us consider that $\mathcal{F} = \{F_1 \ldots F_{nf}\}$ are protein superfamilies. A superfamily F_i consists of n_i proteins. For each protein, a number m of different conformations obtained by molecular dynamics simulations are given. As a first preprocessing step, the proteins' conformations are transformed into numerical vectors, by replacing each SA letter with its rank within the alphabet. Then, depending on each protein, a zero padding approach will be used, if needed. For each superfamily F_i ($1 \leq i \leq nf$), a data set D_i (consisting of $m \cdot n_i$ conformations) is built using all conformations for all the proteins from that superfamily. An ensemble of nf autoencoders will be trained, one autoencoder A_i for each superfamily F_i. For training each autoencoder A_i ($\forall 1 \leq i \leq nf$) we will use 60% of D_i (i.e. 60% conformations for each protein from the i-th superfamily). 16% of D_i are used for the model validation and the remaining of 24% will be further used for testing.

In the current study we use fully convolutional undercomplete autoencoders to learn meaningful, lower-dimensional representations for proteins' structures from their conformational transitions. The classical *mean squared error* is employed as the *loss function* of the autoencoder. The first operation of the autoencoder is the embedding. The vector of n SA letters representing a protein conformation is mapped into a $64 \cdot n$ - dimensional space using an embedding layer [6]. Such a representation is a dense one and is similar to the word embedding technique. This high dimensional vector is going to be encoded using 1D convolutional layers (filters sizes are 32, 12 and 7) into a $3 \cdot \frac{n}{8}$-dimensional space. Afterwards, the decoder upsamples from this representations using the same number of filters as the encoder. The encoder uses 1D convolutional layers with kernel size equal to 3 and strides of 2. On the other hand, the decoder uses the same type of convolutional layers with stride of 2 and 1D Upsampling layers. The network uses ELU [4] activation function and Batch Normalization layers [7]. As a regularization strategy, we use the $l1 - l2$ technique [7] with a value of 10^{-2} for the regularization parameter λ. Optimization of the autoencoder is achieved via stochastic gradient descent enhanced with the *RMSprop* optimizer [7]. We employ the algorithm in a minibatch perspective by using a batch size of 32. The data set is shuffled and 16% is retained for validation. We keep the best performing model on the validation phase by measuring the validation loss. The hyperparameters of the autoencoders were selected using a grid search approach.

After training, $AutoSimP$ is evaluated on 24% from each data set D_i ($\forall 1 \leq i \leq nf$), i.e. 24% conformations for each protein from each superfamily F_j which were unseen during training. The loss value computed for conformation c by the autoencoder A_j which measures how close the output $\widehat{c}$ of the model is to its input c is further denoted by $L_j(\widehat{c}, c)$. When testing is performed at the conformation level, a conformation c is classified by $AutoSimP$ as belonging to the superfamily F_i such that $i = \mathrm{argmin}_{j=1,nf} L_j(\widehat{c}, c)$. When testing is performed at the protein level, a protein p represented in the testing set as a sequence $(c_1, c_2, \ldots, c_t)$ of conformations ($t = \frac{24 \cdot m}{100}$ as previously mentioned) will be classified as belonging to the superfamily F_i whose autoencoder A_i minimizes the average loss of its t conformations.

For measuring the performance of $AutoSimP$ after testing, the F-*measure* (Fm_i) for each superfamily F_i is computed as the harmonic mean between the *Precision* and *Recall* values [8]. Due to the imbalanced nature of the data sets D_i, an aggregated F-*measure* is computed as the weighted average of the Fm_i values.

3 Results and Discussion

Experiments on 57 proteins belonging to 9 superfamilies will be conducted, using the methodology introduced in Sect. 2. The data set was obtained from the MoDEL database available at [13]. For each protein we consider the structural alphabet representation. Each protein from the data set is characterized by a sequence of 10000 experimentally determined conformations (i.e. $m = 10000$). The proteins have different lengths, varying from 99 to 668 SA letters.

As shown in Sect. 2, for each superfamily F_i a data set D_i is formed by all conformations for all the proteins for the superfamily. 6000 conformations from D_i are used for training, 1600 for validation and the remaining 2400 for testing. Experiments were performed both at the *protein* level and at a *conformation* level (for predicting the superfamily for a certain protein conformation). The results from Table 1 reveal high $F\text{-}measure$ values for all superfamilies, excepting F_5 and F_8. The lower performance on these superfamilies may be due to the fact that the conformations for their proteins are highly similar to conformations from proteins belonging to other superfamilies. Thus, these conformations are hardly distinguishable by the autoencoders. Further investigations will be performed in this direction.

Table 1. Experimental results.

Level	Measure	F_1	F_2	F_3	F_4	F_5	F_6	F_7	F_8	F_9
	Precision	1	1	1	0.857	0.6	1	0.857	0.444	1
Protein	*Recall*	1	1	0.8	1	0.5	1	0.666	0.666	1
	F-measure	1	1	0.888	0.923	0.545	1	0.75	0.533	1
	Precision	0.997	0.969	0.994	0.809	0.695	0.983	0.858	0.433	0.996
Conformation	*Recall*	0.963	1	0.803	0.955	0.508	0.999	0.638	0.696	1
	F-measure	0.980	0.984	0.888	0.876	0.587	0.991	0.732	0.534	0.998

The supervised classifier $AutoSimP$ proposed in this paper for predicting the superfamily of a protein using an ensemble of autoencoders is new. There are approaches in the literature using *autoencoders* for protein structure analysis, but from perspectives which differ from ours. Wei and Zhou [15] compare multiple supervised methods for protein classification, the study being conducted at fold level on 27 classes. A fuzzy approach for protein superfamily classification was introduced by Mansoori et al. [12]. The data set is formed by selecting the five unambiguous proteins from UniProt [1]. Different from our approach, they used exchange grams [5] to represent similarities among amino acids. Taeho et al. [10] proposed a method which uses a feed forward neural network for classifying if a pair of proteins belongs to the same group. The data set was selected from SCOP 1.75 [9] and for the superfamily level they reached 61.5% recognition rate.

The previously described related work use different approaches from the one used in this study starting from the data set, how features are selected or even engineered and the models used. Although an exact comparison is not attainable, the scores obtained by our experiments demonstrate that the methodology described in this paper is capable of modelling the characteristics of proteins superfamilies and when it comes to their distinction it outperforms other techniques. The approach which is the most similar to $AutoSimP$ is the one introduced by Albert et al. [2] for detecting inter-protein similarity using *self-organizing maps* (SOM) and *fuzzy self-organizing maps* (FSOM). The approach from [2] is evaluated on the same data set as in our experiments. Table 2 summarizes the results of the comparison and highlight that $AutoSimP$ approach proposed in this paper outperforms the related approach [2].

Table 2. Comparison to previous work

Model	Precision	Recall	F-measure
Our AutoSimP (protein level)	0.861	0.842	0.845
Our AutoSimP (conformation level)	0.858	0.833	0.837
SOM [2]	0.667	0.675	0.671
FSOM 9x1 [2]	0.662	0.647	0.654
FSOM 5x2 [2]	0.696	0.741	0.718

4 Conclusions and Future Work

We have introduced a supervised learning approach $AutoSimP$ consisting of an ensemble of *deep autoencoders* for classifying proteins in superfamilies based on the information enclosed within their conformational transitions. The main reason we opted for autoencoders instead of a neural network classifier is that an autoencoder trained on a certain superfamily will subsequently reject any other superfamily, while a shallow or a convolutional network will recognize only the superfamilies seen during the training. Experiments conducted on 57 proteins belonging to 9 superfamilies highlighted the effectiveness of autoencoders and their ability to uncover the structure of proteins and their structural similarity. The experiments have been conducted both at the protein level, as well as at the conformation level, emphasizing this way the generality of our proposal.

We plan to extend our work by applying *variational* and *contractive* autoencoders. We also aim to further study the applicability of autoencoders for detecting protein conformations that are likely to be anomalous in relation to the protein's superfamily, i.e. conformations whose structure does not resemble to their encoded information.

Acknowledgments. The authors thank lecturer Alessandro Pandini from Brunel University, London for providing the protein data sets used in the experiments.

References

1. The UniProt Consortium: The universal protein resource (UniProt). Nucleic Acids Res. **35**(Database-Issue), 193–197 (2007). https://doi.org/10.1093/nar/gkl929
2. Albert, S., Teletin, M., Czibula, G.: Analysing protein data using unsupervised learning techniques. Int. J. Innov. Comput. Inf. Control **14**, 861–880 (2018)
3. Ambrogelly, A., Palioura, S., Soll, D.: Natural expansion of the genetic code. Nat. Chem. Biol. **3**, 29–35 (2007)
4. Clevert, D.A., Unterthiner, T., Hochreiter, S.: Fast and accurate deep network learning by exponential linear units (elus). arXiv preprint arXiv:1511.07289 (2015)
5. Dayhoff, M.O., Schwartz, R.M.: A model of evolutionary change in proteins (Chap. 22). In: Atlas of Protein Sequence and Structure (1978)
6. Gal, Y., Ghahramani, Z.: A theoretically grounded application of dropout in recurrent neural networks. In: Advances in Neural Information Processing Systems, pp. 1019–1027 (2016)
7. Goodfellow, I., Bengio, Y., Courville, A.: Deep Learning. MIT Press, Cambridge (2016)

8. Gu, Q., Zhu, L., Cai, Z.: Evaluation measures of the classification performance of imbalanced data sets. In: Cai, Z., Li, Z., Kang, Z., Liu, Y. (eds.) ISICA 2009. CCIS, vol. 51, pp. 461–471. Springer, Heidelberg (2009). https://doi.org/10.1007/978-3-642-04962-0_53

9. Hubbard, T.J.P., Ailey, B., Brenner, S.E., Murzin, A.G., Chothia, C.: SCOP: a structural classification of proteins database. Nucleic Acids Res. **27**(1), 254–256 (1999)

10. Jo, T., Hou, J., Eickholt, J., Cheng, J.: Improving protein fold recognition by deep learning networks. Sci. Rep. **5**, 17573 (2015)

11. Lesk, A.: Introduction to Protein Science. Oxford University Press, Oxford (2004)

12. Mansoori, E.G., Zolghadri, M.J., Katebi, S.D.: Protein superfamily classification using fuzzy rule-based classifier. IEEE Trans. NanoBiosci. **8**(1), 92–99 (2009)

13. Meyer, T., et al.: MoDEL: a database of atomistic molecular dynamics trajectories. Structure **18**(11), 1399–1409 (2010)

14. Pandini, A., Fornili, A., Kleinjung, J.: Structural alphabets derived from attractors in conformational space. BMC Bioinform. **11**(97), 1–18 (2010)

15. Wei, L., Zou, Q.: Recent progress in machine learning-based methods for protein fold recognition. Int. J. Mol. Sci. **17**(12), 2118 (2016). PMID: 27999256

Overview of Generation Methods for Business Process Models

Piotr Wiśniewski, Krzysztof Kluza[✉], Krystian Jobczyk,
Bernadetta Stachura-Terlecka, and Antoni Ligęza

AGH University of Science and Technology,
al. A. Mickiewicza 30, 30-059 Krakow, Poland
{wpiotr,kluza,jobczyk,bstachur,ligeza}@agh.edu.pl

Abstract. Business process models are a way of knowledge representation which is widely exploited in various areas of economy and industry. They illustrate workflows executed manually by people, as well as automated sequences of tasks processed by computer software. Manual creation of a workflow model is a complex activity which requires a significant workload. This is caused by the necessity to collect and transform input data from different sources. As a solution to this problem, several techniques have been elaborated to extract knowledge from different representations in order to generate a correct business process model. In this paper, an overview and classification of such techniques which include generating process models from representations such as: natural language text, various notations, other models or logs obtained from an information system is put forward.

1   Introduction

Manual designing of process models or extraction of such models from e.g. a technical documentation is a time-consuming task. Moreover, process models in companies are frequently updated to improve the quality or extend the services. Manually designed models can differ depending on the designer modeling the process which can negatively impact the standardization of created models. Automatic business process models generation constitute a convenient support in dealing with such problems. Thus, a number of approaches for automatic business process models generation have been proposed in recent years. In the following section, an overview of methods for generating business process models based on various input and using sundry techniques is presented.

2   Automated Generation of Process Models

This paper is aimed at the giving an overview of the methods that generates a process model. We distinguished five main categories of such methods. Figure 1

The paper is supported by the AGH UST research grant.

C. Douligeris et al. (Eds.): KSEM 2019, LNAI 11776, pp. 55–60, 2019.
https://doi.org/10.1007/978-3-030-29563-9_6

presents this categorization of different methods which may be used to generate a Business Process Model and Notation (BPMN) diagram depending on the provided source data. These five classes have been described in details in the following subsections.

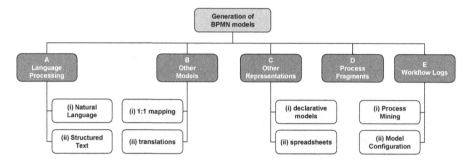

Fig. 1. Automated generation of business process model methods classification.

2.1   Generating Models from Language Description (A)

According to the current state-of-the-art analysis in the area of mining process models from natural language description [1], there is a variety of solutions. A part of them work with a form of structured text (use cases, group stories), and some of them – with natural language description.

An important approach in this area was developed by Friedrich et al. [2]. As a result of such a rich text analysis, the output constitutes a sound and complete model, often with supplementary elements like lanes or data sources.

As stated in the survey [3], even experienced process designers find creating a process model easier when a rule-mapped text is used as a specification, than based only on natural language descriptions. Thus, in many cases, a description can be structured in some way. Using Semantics of Business Vocabulary and Business Rules (SBVR) may be indicated as an illustrative example of structured English description.

A more advanced method – taking into account obtaining structured information – is a semantic information extraction [4]. Such information can be also useful for semantization of the process model [5], e.g. using a domain ontology [6].

2.2   Generating Models from Other Models (B)

In such a class of approaches, process models can be acquired using mapping or translation from other representations. Such representations usually take form of diagrams in other notations, such as: Unified Modeling Language (UML), Decision Model and Notation (DMN) or Case Management Model and Notation (CMMN).

In the case of UML diagrams, some integration approaches, which can be often considered as a basis for a mapping or translation, concerns use case diagrams [7], activity diagrams [8], sequence diagrams [9] or several different UML diagrams integrated with the process [10]. Much less research concerns DMN models (e.g. [11]) or CMMN models (e.g. [12]). Unfortunately, a mapping translation from other notations requires the other models designed. However, such models do not provide enough information and – often – even do not exist.

2.3 Generating Process Models from Other Representations (C)

An imperative approach to modeling processes focuses on explicit specification of the workflow within the process. Obviously, these approaches should restrict or constrain the potential ways of process goal achievement [13]. Although imperative and declarative models are not so distant [14], practitioners usually expect some kind of hybrid solutions [15]. Thus, there are many solutions, which present imperative process model generation based on declarative ones [14,16]. Such structured process information can be an unordered list of tasks which include also the initial state and outcomes of the process [17]. Sometimes, intermediate representation such as spreadsheets can be used for managing the creation of the process model [18].

Finally, a similar group of approaches which relies on translations from data models must be also indicated. They use various representations, such as Bill Of Materials [19], Product Based Workflow Design [20], Product Structure Tree [21], Decision Dependency Design [22], Attribute Relationship Diagrams [23].

2.4 Generating Models from Process Fragments (D)

In many organizations, there is a repository of process models which can be reused. However, it is also possible to obtain from such a repository reusable process fragments, like sub-diagrams, domain patterns [24] or services [25]. Using such patterns, it is possible to improve the process of creating high-quality business process models [26].

A similar approach is creating or composing a business process model based on a collection of the existing diagrams representing different execution variants. One of the implementations of such an approach is called Decomposition Driven Consolidation [27] and supports process modeling by reducing redundancies as well as possible inconsistencies that may occur in manually created models.

2.5 Modeling Processes Based on Logs (E)

A classic group of methods exploits event logs for generating process model. Among these methods, process discovery is one of the most spread process mining solution [28]. Thanks to variety of process mining algorithms, it is a flexible technique that allows a user to discover the process models that is needed. There are techniques to mine process models represented directly in BPMN [29].

Some pieces of information about a process may be also retrieved by exploration of the workflow log. A set of execution sequences may be analyzed to determine temporal relationships between activities [30].

3   Conclusion and Future Works

In this paper, we have presented and classified different methods for automated generation of business process models. The set of implementable techniques was divided into five main groups in terms of the format of source data.

References

1. Riefer, M., Ternis, S.F., Thaler, T.: Mining process models from natural language text: a state-of-the-art analysis. In: Multikonferenz Wirtschaftsinformatik (MKWI-16), 9–11 March (2016)
2. Friedrich, F., Mendling, J., Puhlmann, F.: Process model generation from natural language text. In: Mouratidis, H., Rolland, C. (eds.) CAiSE 2011. LNCS, vol. 6741, pp. 482–496. Springer, Heidelberg (2011). https://doi.org/10.1007/978-3-642-21640-4_36
3. Mayr, H.C., Guizzardi, G., Ma, H., Pastor, O. (eds.): ER 2017. LNCS, vol. 10650. Springer, Cham (2017). https://doi.org/10.1007/978-3-319-69904-2
4. Adrian, W.T., Leone, N., Manna, M.: Semantic views of homogeneous unstructured data. In: ten Cate, B., Mileo, A. (eds.) RR 2015. LNCS, vol. 9209, pp. 19–29. Springer, Cham (2015). https://doi.org/10.1007/978-3-319-22002-4_3
5. Kluza, K., et al.: Overview of selected business process semantization techniques. In: Pełech-Pilichowski, T., Mach-Król, M., Olszak, C.M. (eds.) Advances in Business ICT: New Ideas from Ongoing Research. SCI, vol. 658, pp. 45–64. Springer, Cham (2017). https://doi.org/10.1007/978-3-319-47208-9_4
6. Nalepa, G., Slazynski, M., Kutt, K., Kucharska, E., Luszpaj, A.: Unifying business concepts for SMEs with prosecco ontology. In: FedCSIS 2015, pp. 1321–1326 (2015)
7. Zafar, U., Bhuiyan, M., Prasad, P., Haque, F.: Integration of use case models and BPMN using goal-oriented requirements engineering. J. Comput. **13**(2), 212–222 (2018)
8. Salma, K., Khalid, B., et al.: Product design methodology for modeling multi business products: comparative study between UML and BPMN modeling for business processes. J. Theor. Appl. Inf. Technol. **79**(2), 279 (2015)
9. Suchenia (Mroczek), A., Kluza, K., Jobczyk, K., Wiśniewski, P., Wypych, M., Ligęza, A.: Supporting BPMN process models with UML sequence diagrams for representing time issues and testing models. In: Rutkowski, L., Korytkowski, M., Scherer, R., Tadeusiewicz, R., Zadeh, L.A., Zurada, J.M. (eds.) ICAISC 2017. LNCS (LNAI), vol. 10246, pp. 589–598. Springer, Cham (2017). https://doi.org/10.1007/978-3-319-59060-8_53
10. Aversano, L., Grasso, C., Tortorella, M.: Managing the alignment between business processes and software systems. Inf. Softw. Technol. **72**, 171–188 (2016)
11. Hasić, F., De Smedt, J., Vanthienen, J.: Towards assessing the theoretical complexity of the decision model and notation (DMN). In: 8th International Workshop on Enterprise Modeling and Information Systems Architectures (EMISA), pp. 64–71 (2017)

12. Nešković, S., Kirchner, K.: Using context information and CMMN to model knowledge-intensive business processes. In: 6th International Conference on Information Society and Technology ICIST 2016, pp. 17–21 (2016)
13. Goedertier, S., Vanthienen, J., Caron, F.: Declarative business process modelling: principles and modelling languages. Enterp. Inf. Syst. **9**(2), 161–185 (2015)
14. De Giacomo, G., Dumas, M., Maggi, F.M., Montali, M.: Declarative process modeling in BPMN. In: Zdravkovic, J., Kirikova, M., Johannesson, P. (eds.) CAiSE 2015. LNCS, vol. 9097, pp. 84–100. Springer, Cham (2015). https://doi.org/10. 1007/978-3-319-19069-3_6
15. Reijers, H.A., Slaats, T., Stahl, C.: Declarative modeling–an academic dream or the future for BPM? In: Daniel, F., Wang, J., Weber, B. (eds.) BPM 2013. LNCS, vol. 8094, pp. 307–322. Springer, Heidelberg (2013). https://doi.org/10.1007/978-3-642-40176-3_26
16. Mrasek, R., Mülle, J., Böhm, K.: Automatic generation of optimized process models from declarative specifications. In: Zdravkovic, J., Kirikova, M., Johannesson, P. (eds.) CAiSE 2015. LNCS, vol. 9097, pp. 382–397. Springer, Cham (2015). https://doi.org/10.1007/978-3-319-19069-3_24
17. Wiśniewski, P., Kluza, K., Ligęza, A.: An approach to participatory business process modeling: BPMN model generation using constraint programming and graph composition. Appl. Sci. **8**(9), 1428 (2018)
18. Honkisz, K., Kluza, K., Wiśniewski, P.: A concept for generating business process models from natural language description. In: Liu, W., Giunchiglia, F., Yang, B. (eds.) KSEM 2018. LNCS (LNAI), vol. 11061, pp. 91–103. Springer, Cham (2018). https://doi.org/10.1007/978-3-319-99365-2_8
19. van der Aalst, W.: On the automatic generation of workflow processes based on product structures. Comput. Ind. **39**(2), 97–111 (1999)
20. Vanderfeesten, I., Reijers, H.A., van der Aalst, W.M.P.: Product-based workflow support. Inf. Syst. **36**(2), 517–535 (2011)
21. Li, S., Shao, X., Zhang, Z., Chang, J.: Dynamic workflow modeling based on product structure tree. Appl. Math. **6**(3), 751–757 (2012)
22. Wu, F., Priscilla, L., Gao, M., Caron, F., De Roover, W., Vanthienen, J.: Modeling decision structures and dependencies. In: Herrero, P., Panetto, H., Meersman, R., Dillon, T. (eds.) OTM 2012. LNCS, vol. 7567, pp. 525–533. Springer, Heidelberg (2012). https://doi.org/10.1007/978-3-642-33618-8_69
23. Kluza, K., Nalepa, G.J.: Towards rule-oriented business process model generation. In: Ganzha, M., Maciaszek, L.A., Paprzycki, M. (eds.) Proceedings of the Federated Conference on Computer Science and Information Systems - FedCSIS 2013, Krakow, Poland, 8–11 September 2013, pp. 959–966. IEEE (2013)
24. Fellmann, M., Delfmann, P., Koschmider, A., Laue, R., Leopold, H., Schoknecht, A.: Semantic technology in business process modeling and analysis. part 1: matching, modeling support, correctness and compliance. In: EMISA Forum, vol. 35, pp. 15–31 (2015)
25. Klimek, R.: Towards formal and deduction-based analysis of business models for soa processes. In: ICAART, vol. 2, pp. 325–330 (2012)
26. Koschmider, A., Reijers, H.A.: Improving the process of process modelling by the use of domain process patterns. Enterp. Inf. Syst. **9**(1), 29–57 (2015)
27. Milani, F., Dumas, M., Matulevičius, R.: Decomposition driven consolidation of process models. In: Salinesi, C., Norrie, M.C., Pastor, Ó. (eds.) CAiSE 2013. LNCS, vol. 7908, pp. 193–207. Springer, Heidelberg (2013). https://doi.org/10.1007/978-3-642-38709-8_13

28. van der Aalst, W.M.P.: Process Mining: Discovery, Conformance and Enhancement of Business Processes, 1st edn. Springer, Heidelberg (2011). https://doi.org/10.1007/978-3-642-19345-3

29. Kalenkova, A.A., de Leoni, M., van der Aalst, W.M.: Discovering, analyzing and enhancing BPMN models using ProM? In: Business Process Management-12th International Conference, BPM, pp. 7–11 (2014)

30. Tang, Y., Mackey, I., Su, J.: Querying workflow logs. Information **9**(2), 25 (2018)

Text Mining and Document Analysis

Dynamic Task-Specific Factors
for Meta-Embedding

Yuqiang Xie[1,2], Yue Hu[1,2(✉)], Luxi Xing[1,2], and Xiangpeng Wei[1,2]

[1] Institute of Information Engineering, Chinese Academy of Sciences, Beijing, China
[2] School of Cyber Security, University of Chinese Academy of Sciences,
Beijing, China
{xieyuqiang,huyue,xingluxi,weixiangpeng}@iie.ac.cn

Abstract. Meta-embedding is a technology to create a new embedding by combining different existing embeddings, which captures complementary aspects of
lexical semantics. The supervised learning of task-specific meta-embedding is a
convenient way to make use of accessible pre-trained word embeddings. However, the weights for different word embeddings are hard to calculate. We introduce the dynamic task-specific factors into meta-embedding (DTFME), which
are utilized to calculate appropriate weights of different embedding sets without
increasing complexity. Then, we evaluate the performance of DTFME on sentence representation tasks. Experiments show that our method outperforms prior
works in several benchmark datasets.

Keywords: Meta-embedding · Task-specific factors ·
Sentence representation

1 Introduction

Word embeddings have revolutionized natural language processing (NLP). Early, a simplified approach to represent the meaning of a word is to embed it in fixed-dimensional
vector space. In contrast to sparse and high-dimensional counting-based word representation methods that use co-occurring contexts of a word as its representation, dense
and low-dimensional prediction-based distributed word representations [17,19] have
obtained impressive performances in numerous NLP tasks.

It is well known that the performances of different word embeddings vary significantly over different tasks. A great deal of literature has emerged as to which types of
embedding are most useful for which tasks. For example, [11] try to understand what
word embeddings learn. Also, [24] evaluate word embeddings systematically.

Recent works in so-called "meta-embedding", which try to combine the strengths
of different word embeddings, have been gaining attention [18,29]. In other words,
meta-embedding is utilized to create a new embedding by combining different existing
embeddings, which captures complementary aspects of lexical semantics. [1] also show
that an ensemble of different word representations improves the accuracy of dependency
parsing, implying the complementarity of the different word embeddings.

© Springer Nature Switzerland AG 2019
C. Douligeris et al. (Eds.): KSEM 2019, LNAI 11776, pp. 63–74, 2019.
https://doi.org/10.1007/978-3-030-29563-9_7

However, there are two issues in meta-embedding researches: **First**, meta-embedding is usually created in a separate pre-processing step, rather than in a process that is adapted to the task dynamically; **Second**, it is difficult to obtain appropriate weights for different embeddings. Recently, dynamic meta-embeddings [8] implements the supervised learning of task-specific meta-embeddings, which proposes a basic framework to solve the first problem. Nonetheless, dynamic meta-embeddings uses sentence-level self-attention [13] to determine the weights of different embedding sets, where the self-attention method focuses on the linear regression for elements in one word embedding independently and lack of the pairwise element interactions. Besides, it is difficult to select a proper gate function. The second question still exists which is full of challenges.

To resolve the problem of obtaining appropriate weight, we propose to introduce dynamic task-specific factors into meta-embedding (DTFME) with factorization operation and pooling mechanisms. Different from dynamic meta-embeddings, task-specific factors will calculate the element pairwise interaction of each embedding, not just a simple linear regression. Particularly, the parameters in every factor are learned with training the whole model. In addition, dynamic task-specific factors can be computed efficiently in linear time which would bring no complexity into meta-embedding. Then, we evaluate the performance of DTFME on sentence representation tasks.

The contributions of our work are summarized as follows:

- We introduce the dynamic task-specific factors into meta-embedding (DTFME), which are utilized to calculate appropriate weights of different embedding sets.
- We utilize factorization operation and pooling mechanism which can be efficiently computed in linear time without increasing complexity of meta-embedding.
- We evaluate the performance of DTFME on sentence representation tasks. Experiments show that our method outperforms prior works in several benchmark datasets. Compared to the baseline, we get about 0.5% to 0.7% improvements on NLI benchmark datasets. For Quora, we obtain nearly 0.4% growth. And on SST2, our methods can acquire around 0.8% improvements.

2 Related Work

Word embeddings are popularly used in the NLP field. There have been too many researches about learning and applying word embeddings, so we focus on previous works that combine multiple embeddings for downstream tasks.

[28] learn to combine word-level and character-level embeddings. Context representations have also been used for neural machine translation, for example, to learn context word vectors and apply them to other tasks [15] or to learn context-dependent representations to address disambiguation issues in machine translation [5].

Neural tensor skip-gram models learn to combine word, topic and context embeddings [14]. Context2vec [16] learns a more complex context representation separately from target embeddings. [12] learn word representations with distributed word representation with multi-contextual mixed embedding.

There are also a number of works on learning multiple embeddings per word [4], including many works in sense embeddings where the senses of a word have their own individual embeddings [22], as well as on how to apply such sense embeddings in downstream NLP tasks [21].

The usefulness of different embeddings as initialization has been explored [10], and different architectures and hyper-parameters have been extensively examined [11]. Besides, various alternatives for evaluating word embeddings in downstream tasks have been proposed [26].

Recent works in "meta-embedding", which ensembles embedding sets, have been gaining attention [29]. However, these works obtain meta-embedding as a preprocessing step. Recently, [8] apply meta-embedding idea to sentence representation, which learns attention weights for different embedding sets dynamically. Additionally, this work gives the basic framework for calculating weights and proposes a contextualized method to enhance projection embeddings. Nonetheless, dynamic meta-embeddings uses sentence-level self-attention [13] to determine the weights of different embedding sets, where the self-attention method focuses on the linear regression for elements independently and lack of the pairwise element interactions.

Our work can be seen as an improvement of dynamic meta-embeddings. Here, appropriate weights for different word embeddings are expected. We propose DTFME, which utilizes factorization operation [23] and pooling mechanisms for computing more suitable task-specific weights. Factorization operation is a good mechanism for extracting useful pairwise interaction of the elements in one vector. Furthermore, our method can be efficiently computed in linear time without increasing the complexity of meta-embedding. By applying DTFME to sentence representations, we can more easily use our work in a wide variety of NLP tasks that require sentence-level semantic information.

3   Dynamic Task-Specific Factors for Meta-Embedding (DTFME)

For dynamic meta-embeddings, weights for different embedding types are the most important components. We propose DTFME, which are utilized to calculate appropriate weights of different embedding sets. In this section, we first introduce the basic framework of dynamic meta-embeddings and the contextualized method. Then, we give the details of our method DTFME that modifies the function used for calculating weights. Lastly, we describe the sentence encoder and the matching layer.

Consider a sentence represented as S, composed of s tokens $\{t_j\}_{j=1}^s$. We have n word embedding types, leading to sequences $\{w_{i,j}\}_{j=1}^s \in \mathbb{R}^{d_i} (i = 1, 2, ..., n)$. We use a setting which centers each type of word embedding to zero mean.

3.1   Basic Framework

We utilize the basic framework which proposed by dynamic meta-embeddings [8]. It projects the embeddings into a d'-dimensional space by learned linear functions:

$$w'_{i,j} = P_i w_{i,j} + b_i (i = 1, 2, ..., n) \qquad (1)$$

where $P_i \in \mathbb{R}^{d' \times d}$ and $b_i \in \mathbb{R}^{d'}$. Then, dynamic meta-embeddings combines the projected embeddings by taking the weighted sum:

$$w_{i,j} = \sum \alpha_{i,j} w'_{i,j} \qquad (2)$$

where $\alpha_{i,j} = g(\{w'_{i,j}\}_{j=1}^s)$ are scalar weights from a linear projection and a gate function:

$$\alpha_{i,j} = g(w'_{i,j}) = \phi(a \cdot w'_{i,j} + b) \tag{3}$$

where $a \in \mathbb{R}^{d'}$ and $b \in \mathbb{R}$ are learned parameters and ϕ is a softmax (or could be a sigmoid or tanh, for gating). The calculation between elements is independent of each other. Also, gate functions are useful for dynamic meta-embeddings but have unpredictable effects.

Besides, [8] give a contextualized dynamic meta-embeddings to enhance projection embeddings:

$$\alpha_{i,j} = g(\{w'_{i,j}\}_{j=1}^s) = \phi(a \cdot h_j + b) \tag{4}$$

where $h_j \in \mathbb{R}^{2m}$ is the jth hidden state of a Bi-LSTM taking $\{w'_{i,j}\}_{j=1}^s$ as input, $a \in \mathbb{R}^{2m}$ and $b \in \mathbb{R}$.

Our work bases on the basic framework and its contextualized method. Then, we modify the g function for more suitable weights.

3.2   DTFME

Our method includes two key components: factorization operation and pooling mechanisms. We utilize factorization operation to extract task-specific factors which used for computing appropriate weights. The parameters in every factor are learned with training the whole model. Then we try different pooling operations for receiving more critical information on all task-specific factors. In all, we give six strategies for DTFME.

Factorization Operation: Given an input vector $x \in \mathbb{R}^D$ with the dimension D, the factorization operation [23] is defined as:

$$f_{Linear}(x) = w_0 + \sum_{p=1}^{D} w_p x_p \tag{5}$$

$$f_{Factors}(x) = \sum_{p=1}^{D} \sum_{q=p+1}^{D} \langle v_p, v_q \rangle x_p x_q \tag{6}$$

$$f_{FM}(\cdot) = f_{Linear}(x) + f_{Factors}(x) \tag{7}$$

where the output of $f_{FM}(\cdot)$ is a scalar value, $\langle v_p, v_q \rangle$ is the dot product between two vectors, and w_0 is the global bias. Parameters of the factorization operation are $w_0 \in \mathbb{R}$, $w \in \mathbb{R}^D$ and $v \in \mathbb{R}^{D \times K}$, K is a hyper-parameter which stand for the number of factors. v is learned with training the whole model for downstream tasks. In all, $f_{FM}(\cdot)$ gives K task-specific factors for an input vector.

As shown in Eq. 7, factorization operation is divided into two parts, one is $f_{Linear}(x)$ which represents a linear regression. The calculation between elements is independent of each other. The second part, $f_{Factors}(x)$, a key point, learns pairwise interaction of each element in a vector which is used for calculating task-specific factors.

It is worth pointing out that the second part of factorization operation can be computed in linear time efficiently:

$$f_{Factors}(x) = \frac{1}{2} \sum_{f=1}^{K} ((\sum_{p=1}^{D} v_{p,f} x_p)^2 - \sum_{p=1}^{D} v_{p,f}^2 x_p^2) \tag{8}$$

For DTFME, we use K task-specific factors to exact more useful information from word embeddings. The first projection layer is the same as dynamic meta-embeddings. We project word embeddings of different dimensions to the same and lower dimension by using a linear function. Then, with the new representation $\{w'_{i,j}\}_{j=1}^{s} \in \mathbb{R}^{d'_i} (i = 1, 2, ..., n)$ which used for factorization operation. We define the vector:

$$w'_{i,j} = [x_1, x_2, ..., x_{d'}] \tag{9}$$

where x_i stands for elements in the ith new word representation. We combine the different word embeddings by taking the weighted sum:

$$w_j^{DTFME} = \sum \alpha_{i,j} w'_{i,j} \tag{10}$$

where $\alpha_{i,j} = g(\{w'_{i,j}\}_{j=1}^{s})$ are scalar weights from g operation (factorization operation and a sigmoid function):

$$\alpha_{i,j} = g(w'_{i,j}) = \sigma(f_{FM}(w'_{i,j})) \tag{11}$$

Then, we give three strategies for combining task-specific factors from factorization operation with associated pooling mechanisms.

DTFME-Sum: For this strategy, we keep the dot product in $f_{Factors}(x)$ unchanged which is the same as described in Eq. 8:

$$f_{Factors}(x) = \frac{1}{2} \sum_{f=1}^{K} ((\sum_{p=1}^{d'} v_{p,f} x_p)^2 - \sum_{p=1}^{d'} v_{p,f}^2 x_p^2) \tag{12}$$

DTFME-Max: The most important part is computing pairwise element interactions of each word embedding. Max-pooling is an easy and effective method to get the most important features. We apply it to dynamic task-specific factors. Finally, we can combine all factors into one vector. Here, we define the max-pooling function: $\hat{v}_{max} = Maxpooling(v_1, v_2, ...v_K)$, and the pairwise interaction part of factorization operation:

$$f_{Factors}(x) = \frac{1}{2} ((\sum_{p=1}^{d'} \hat{v}_{max,p} x_p)^2 - \sum_{p=1}^{d'} \hat{v}_{max,p}^2 x_p^2) \tag{13}$$

where $\hat{v}$ stands for the most task-specific factor which could contain key features of corresponding word representation.

DTFME-Aver: Average pooling is also a method that has effects on some tasks. Empirically, it can be seen as a structured regular for all factors which leads to a stable performance for DTFME. Here, we define the max-pooling function: $\hat{v}_{aver} = Averpooling(v_1, v_2, ...v_K)$, and the pairwise interaction part of factorization operation:

$$f_{Factors}(x) = \frac{1}{2}((\sum_{p=1}^{d'} \hat{v}_{aver,p}x_p)^2 - \sum_{p=1}^{d'} \hat{v}_{aver,p}^2 x_p^2) \tag{14}$$

The results in experiments (see Sect. 4) prove that these three strategies have their own advantages. DTFME-Aver has the best performance mostly.

In addition, we implement contextualized DTFME (CDTFME) according to the basic contextualized method (see Eq. 4):

$$\alpha_{i,j} = g(\{w'_{i,j}\}_{j=1}^{s}) = \sigma(f_{FM}(h_j)) \tag{15}$$

Then, same as DTFME, we improve CDTFME by sum, max-pooling and aver-pooling. We define the pairwise interaction part of factorization operation in **CDTFME-Sum**:

$$f_{Factors}(x) = \frac{1}{2}\sum_{f=1}^{K}((\sum_{z=1}^{d'} v_{z,f}x_z)^2 - \sum_{z=1}^{d'} v_{z,f}^2 x_z^2) \tag{16}$$

where x_z stands for an element in h_j. The process of task-specific factors in **CDTFME-Max** and **CDTFME-Aver** is the same as DTFME.

3.3 Sentence Encoder

We apply DTFME into a BiLSTM-Max sentence encoder [6] for sentence representation. It computes two sets of s hidden states, one of each direction:

$$\overrightarrow{h_j} = \overrightarrow{LSTM_j}(w_1, w_2, ..., w_j) \tag{17}$$

The opposite direction is the same:

$$\overleftarrow{h_j} = \overleftarrow{LSTM_j}(w_j, w_{j+1}, ..., w_s) \tag{18}$$

We use max-pooling operation after the concatenation these two hidden states each time step. Then, the final sentence representation:

$$h = Maxpooling([\overrightarrow{h_j}, \overleftarrow{h_j}]_{j=1,2,...,s}) \tag{19}$$

3.4 Matching Layer

Our work focuses on sentence representation-based architecture, and so we do not compute any other interaction between the two sentence representations. For comparison with dynamic meta-embeddings, we use the standard combination operation between two sentence representations: $m = [u, v, u * v, |u - v|]$, where u and v are the representations of two sentences. Then, we use ReLU for better-combined representation. On top of our model is a two-layer MLP classifier.

4 Experiments and Results

4.1 Datasets

We evaluate our method on three popular and well-studied NLP tasks: (i) natural language inference (**SNLI, MultiNLI and AllNLI**); (ii) paraphrase identification (**Quora**); (iii) sentiment classification (**SST2**).

Natural language inference (NLI), also known as recognizing textual entailment (RTE), is the task of classifying pairs of sentences according to whether they are neutral, entailing or contradictive. Inference about entailment and contradiction is fundamental to understanding natural language, and there are two established datasets to evaluate semantic representations in that setting. **SNLI** contains 570k hypotheses written by crowdsourcing workers given the premises. The data splits are provided in [3]. **MultiNLI**, also known as Multi-Genre NLI, has 433k sentence pairs whose size and mode of the collection are modeled closely like SNLI. We also evaluate our method on both SNLI and MultiNLI (**AllNLI**) [6].

Paraphrase identification (PI) identifies whether two sentences express the same meaning. **Quora** contains 400k question pairs collected from the Quora website. This dataset has balanced positive and negative labels which indicate whether the questions are duplicated or not. The training-dev-test splits for this dataset are provided in [27].

Sentiment classification (SC) classifies a single sentence to correct sentiment label. The binary SST task (**SST2**), consisting of 70k sentences with a corresponding binary (positive or negative) sentiment label. The training-dev-test splits for this dataset are provided in [25].

4.2 Settings

Word embeddings are pre-loaded with 840B-300d GloVe [19] and 300d FastText [2]. Why not use ELMo [20] or BERT [7]? The representation for each word from these two large language models depends on the entire context in which it is used, which is quite different with GloVe and so on. Besides, to compare with the baseline, we select the same two common word embeddings for experiments. We implement our model based on codes provided by dynamic meta-embeddings[1]. The batch size is 64. The dimension of hidden state for CDTFME is set to 2. K is a hyperparameter standing for the number of latent task-specific factors. We set K to 5 for DTFME and 2 for CDTFME based on the analysis (see Sect. 5.1). Parameters of the model are initialized with Xavier initialization except that parameters in factorization operation are initialized with uniform initialization. The initial learning rate is set to 0.0004 and dropped by a factor of 0.2 when dev accuracy stops improving and we use Adam for optimization [9]. To avoid overfitting, we use the early-stopping method. The loss function for all tasks is standard cross-entropy.

4.3 Results on NLI

Table 1 shows the results of natural language inference tasks. Our baseline includes dynamic meta-embeddings (DME) and contextualized dynamic meta-embeddings

---

[1] Based on facebookresearch/DME: https://github.com/facebookresearch/DME.

Table 1. Accuracy scores on NLI tasks, including dev and test sets of SNLI, MNLI(MultiNLI mismatched and matched sets) and AllNLI test set. Our methods include DTFME-Aver and CDTFME-Aver which were selected by analysis on the dev set of SNLI (see Sect. 5.3). Concat* stands for the BiLSTM-Max sentence encoder which combines pre-trained word embeddings by naïvely concatenation.

Model	Params	SNLI Dev	SNLI test	MNLI mismatched	MNLI matched	AllNLI
InferSent	40.0M	-	84.5	-	-	-
Concat*	9.8M	86.2	85.6	72.1	72.1	79.6
Baseline						
DME	8.6M	86.7	86.2	74.3	73.5	80.3
CDME	8.6M	87.1	86.4	74.3	74.2	80.5
Our methods						
DTFME-Aver	8.6M	87.2	**86.7**	**74.7**	74.2	**81.0**
CDTFME-Aver	8.6M	87.4	**87.1**	74.4	**74.7**	**80.8**

(CDME) [8]. We focus on the model which encodes sentence individually and does not proceed interaction between the two sentences[2]. We include InferSent [6], which also makes use of a BiLSTM-Max sentence encoder. Besides, we compare our approach against the Concat* which naïvely concatenates pre-trained word embeddings.

We observe that DTFME with aver-pooling outperforms the baseline DME. Also, CDTFME is the same. Compared to DME, we obtain around 0.5% improvement on average by introducing task-specific factors into the basic framework. Besides, CDTFME-Aver outperforms CDME with 0.6% improvement, which indicates the effect of task-specific factors is also applicable to the contextual representation of original projection embedding. From the results on MultiNLI and AllNLI, our methods perform higher than the baseline. Furthermore, we can conclude that aver-pooling works on task-specific factors.

Finally, we do note that we found the highest maximum performance for the DTFME-Aver and CDTFME-Aver. It is important to note that pooling provides additional interpretability without sacrificing performance. These results further strengthen the point that dynamic task-specific factors help in interpretable ways and that we can learn to combine different embeddings efficiently with more suitable weights.

4.4   Results on Quora

From the results in Table 2, we can see a similar pattern as we observed with NLI tasks: DTFME and CDTFME with three strategies outperform the baseline (DME and CDME), with aver-pooling strategy appearing to work best. Especially, DTFME-Aver and CDTFME-Aver show the best performance of all with 0.4% improvement. Compared to the baseline, we get nearly 0.3% improvements on average.

These results indicate that dynamic task-specific factors can learn to combine different embedding sets with appropriate weights. With the help of aver-pooling, dynamic task-specific factors can improve the ability of generalization.

---

[2] This is a common distinction, see e.g., the SNLI leaderboard at https://nlp.stanford.edu/projects/snli/.

Table 2. Accuracy on Quora and SST2 test set.

Model	Quora test	SST2 test
Baseline		
DME	87.7	88.7
CDME	87.6	89.2
DTFME		
DTFME-Sum	87.7	88.7
DTFME-Max	87.9	89.2
DTFME-Aver	**88.1**	**89.5**
CDTFME		
CDTFME-Sum	87.5	89.3
CDTFME-Max	87.6	89.4
CDTFME-Aver	**88.0**	89.3

Table 3. Ablation study on SNLI dev set with the model DTFME-Aver. (1–2) remove the components of g function in DTFME. (3–4) replace aver-pooling operation with sum or max-pooling. (5–7) is the contextualized method for DTFME.

DTFME-Aver		SNLI Dev
Full Model		87.22
(1) w/o Linear		86.89
(2) w/o Factors		86.75
(3) replace Aver w/ Sum		86.99
(4) replace Aver w/ Max		86.97
contextualized	(5) w/ Aver	**87.41**
	(6) w/ Sum	87.12
	(7) w/ Max	87.14

4.5   Results on SST2

To analyze the results in Table 2, we can see some differences from NLI and PI: DTFME with three strategies outperform the baseline DME and performs similarly to CDME. For the strategies on DTFME, aver-pooling also performs best of all. However, for CDTFME, max-pooling is the best performance this time. We can not get the explanation for this phenomenon, which could be affected by the random seed or other parameters. Besides, we infer that sum operation contains all information of task-specific factors; max-pooling extracts the most important features of all factors; aver-pooling can be seen as a structured regular for all factors which leads to a stable performance for DTFME.

Furthermore, DTFME-Aver outperforms the comparable models listed in the above table. Compared to the baseline, we get nearly 0.3 improvements on average. Lastly, the results from Table 2 reveal that aver-pooling may be the most appropriate strategy for dynamic task-specific factors.

5   Discussion and Analysis

5.1   The Effect of K

We perform a fine-grained analysis about the effect of K for DTFME and CDTFME on the test set of SNLI. K stands for the number of latent task-specific factors. Commonly, the hyper-parameters have great relationships with the model structure. So, we inference that the number of task-specific factors is important for different model structures. Then, we perform experiments with different K amongst $\{1, 50\}$ on the test set of SNLI with DTFME-Sum and CDTFME-Sum.

From $K = 1$ to $K = 5$, the step size is one. From $K = 10$ to $K = 50$, the step size is ten. Figure 1 shows the best K are 5 and 2 for DTFME and CDTFME respectively.

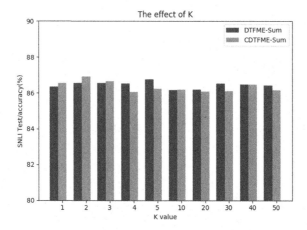

Fig. 1. This is an analysis for the effect of K on SNLI with DTFME-Sum and CDTFME-Sum. Horizontal axis stands for K and vertical axis stands for the accuracy on test set.

For DTFME-Sum, accuracy on SNLI increases beyond $K = 5$ and the performance is gradually stable from $K = 10$ to $K = 50$. For CDTFME-Sum, two factors are best. To analyze the law between data in the histogram, we can note that K has great robustness no matter which method we evaluate. After undergoing a decay, the accuracy keeps smooth which is not affected by the increase in K.

5.2 Ablation Study

Table 3 reports ablation studies on the SNLI dev set with DTFME-Aver. We hold other parameters and initialization fixed. Besides, we set the maximal number of epochs to the same.

First of all, the accuracy of the full model is 87.22. Then, we drop linear regression (1), and we notice a slight decline in performance. Without linear regression, task-specific factors can also perform well. Ablation (2) explores the importance of task-specific factors in DTFME, which impacts the model performance significantly. We can conclude that the status of task-specific factors is more important than linear regression in this structure. Then, (3–4) replaces aver-pooling with sum operation and max-pooling respectively for task-specific factors, which influences on the model with a nearly 0.5 decline. Next, (5–7) adds Bi-LSTM to projection layer (see Sect. 3.2). (5) explores the effectiveness of aver-pooling with contextualized DTFME with a nearly 0.2 improvement. We can also conclude that aver-pooling is the best strategy for both DTFME and CDTFME. Finally, (6–7) replaces aver-pooling with sum operation and max-pooling respectively with a nearly 0.3 decline.

Above all, we observe that task-specific factors, aver-pooling and contextualized operation are more important than linear regression, sum and max-pooling. We infer that the former three components can be more focused on pairwise interaction of the elements in each embedding which help calculate more suitable weights.

Table 4. Case analysis on two examples from SNLI dev set. The ground truth of these two examples is all entailment. N stands for neutral, and E stands for entailment. The number in the brackets is the probability of prediction result.

Premises and Hypotheses (Entailment)	DME	CDME	DTFME-Aver	CDTFME-Aver
Premise: A crowd of people are packed into a subway car Hypothesis: A crowd of people are together	N(0.55)	N(0.55)	E(0.78)✓	E(0.84)✓
Premise: Man chopping wood with an axe Hypothesis: The man is outside	N(0.67)	N(0.78)	E(0.92)✓	E(0.94)✓

5.3 Case Analysis

In Table 4, we perform a case analysis on two sentence pairs from the SNLI dev set. From the example, DME and CDME fail to give the correct answer. Instead, our method can estimate a related high probability of the ground truth label and CDTFME performs better. In all, we infer that baselines tend to give a neutral answer for some hard NLI questions. To some degree, dynamic task-specific factors lead to taking advantage of the semantic features in the word embedding itself. Besides, the averpooling is helpful for the generalization which can be seen as a structured regular for all factors.

6 Conclusion and Future Work

While learning meta-embedding dynamically, the weights of different embedding sets are important and difficult to calculate. We argue that dynamic task-specific factors help a lot, which are utilized to obtain appropriate weights. We also explore the best K for different model structures on the same dataset, give an interesting case analysis, and perform ablation studies for DTFME-Aver.

In future work, it would be interesting to apply this idea to different tasks. Also, it is worth considering the effects of dynamic task-specific factors for combining word representation from large pre-trained language models, such as ELMo and BERT. Besides, it would be meaningful to further examine the relationship between parameters and initialization, e.g., introducing a normalization factor for loss function might improve results or interpretability further.

References

1. Bansal, M., Gimpel, K., Livescu, K.: Tailoring continuous word representations for dependency parsing. In: ACL, pp. 809–815 (2014)
2. Bojanowski, P., Grave, E., Joulin, A., Mikolov, T.: Enriching word vectors with subword information. In: TACL, pp. 135–146 (2017)
3. Bowman, S.R., Angeli, G., Potts, C., Manning, C.D.: A large annotated corpus for learning natural language inference. arXiv preprint arXiv:1508.05326 (2015)

4. Chen, X., Liu, Z., Sun, M.: A unified model for word sense representation and disambiguation. In: EMNLP, pp. 1025–1035 (2014)
5. Choi, H., Cho, K., Bengio, Y.: Context-dependent word representation for neural machine translation. Comput. Speech Lang. **45**, 149–160 (2017)
6. Conneau, A., Kiela, D., Schwenk, H., Barrault, L., Bordes, A.: Supervised learning of universal sentence representations from natural language inference data. arXiv (2017)
7. Devlin, J., Chang, M.W., Lee, K., Toutanova, K.: Bert: pre-training of deep bidirectional transformers for language understanding. arXiv (2018)
8. Kiela, D., Wang, C., Cho, K.: Dynamic meta-embeddings for improved sentence representations. In: EMNLP (2018)
9. Kingma, D.P., Ba, J.: Adam: a method for stochastic optimization. arXiv (2014)
10. Kocmi, T., Bojar, O.: An exploration of word embedding initialization in deep-learning tasks. arXiv preprint arXiv:1711.09160 (2017)
11. Levy, O., Goldberg, Y., Dagan, I.: Improving distributional similarity with lessons learned from word embeddings. In: TACL (2015)
12. Li, J., Li, J., Fu, X., Masud, M.A., Huang, J.Z.: Learning distributed word representation with multi-contextual mixed embedding. Knowl. Based Syst. **106**, 220–230 (2016)
13. Lin, Z., et al.: A structured self-attentive sentence embedding. arXiv (2017)
14. Liu, P., Qiu, X., Huang, X.: Learning context-sensitive word embeddings with neural tensor skip-gram model. In: IJCAI, pp. 1284–1290 (2015)
15. McCann, B., Bradbury, J., Xiong, C., Socher, R.: Learned in translation: contextualized word vectors. In: Advances in Neural Information Processing Systems, pp. 6294–6305 (2017)
16. Melamud, O., Goldberger, J., Dagan, I.: context2vec: Learning generic context embedding with bidirectional LSTM. In: Proceedings of The 20th SIGNLL Conference on Computational Natural Language Learning, pp. 51–61 (2016)
17. Mikolov, T., Chen, K., Corrado, G., Dean, J.: Efficient estimation of word representations in vector space. arXiv preprint arXiv:1301.3781 (2013)
18. Muromägi, A., Sirts, K., Laur, S.: Linear ensembles of word embedding models. arXiv preprint arXiv:1704.01419 (2017)
19. Pennington, J., Socher, R., Manning, C.: Glove: global vectors for word representation. In: EMNLP, pp. 1532–1543 (2014)
20. Peters, M.E., et al.: Deep contextualized word representations. arXiv (2018)
21. Pilehvar, M.T., Camacho-Collados, J., Navigli, R., Collier, N.: Towards a seamless integration of word senses into downstream NLP applications. arXiv (2017)
22. Qiu, L., Tu, K., Yu, Y.: Context-dependent sense embedding. In: EMNLP (2016)
23. Rendle, S.: Factorization machines. In: ICDM, pp. 995–1000 (2010)
24. Schnabel, T., Labutov, I., Mimno, D., Joachims, T.: Evaluation methods for unsupervised word embeddings. In: EMNLP (2015)
25. Socher, R., et al.: Recursive deep models for semantic compositionality over a sentiment treebank. In: EMNLP (2013)
26. Tsvetkov, Y., Faruqui, M., Ling, W., Lample, G., Dyer, C.: Evaluation of word vector representations by subspace alignment. In: EMNLP (2015)
27. Wang, Z., Hamza, W., Florian, R.: Bilateral multi-perspective matching for natural language sentences. In: IJCAI (2017)
28. Yang, Z., Dhingra, B., Yuan, Y., Hu, J., Cohen, W.W., Salakhutdinov, R.: Words or characters? fine-grained gating for reading comprehension. arXiv (2016)
29. Yin, W., Schütze, H.: Learning meta-embeddings by using ensembles of embedding sets. arXiv preprint arXiv:1508.04257 (2015)

Automated Mining and Checking of Formal Properties in Natural Language Requirements

Xingxing Pi[1], Jianqi Shi[1,2](✉) ⓘ, Yanhong Huang[1,3], and Hansheng Wei[1]

[1] National Trusted Embedded Software Engineering Technology Research Center,
East China Normal University, Shanghai, China
{xingxing.pi,hansheng.wei}@ntesec.ecnu.edu.cn
[2] Hardware/Software Co-Design Technology and Application Engineering,
Research Center, Shanghai, China
[3] Shanghai Key Laboratory of Trustworthy Computing, Shanghai, China
{jqshi,yhhuang}@sei.ecnu.edu.cn

Abstract. Bridging the gap between natural language requirements (NLR) and precise formal specifications is a crucial task of knowledge engineering. Software system development has become more complex in recent years, and it includes many requirements in different domains that users need to understand. Many of these requirements are expressed in natural language, which may be incomplete and ambiguous. However, the formal language with its rigorous semantics may accurately represent certain temporal logic properties and allow for automatic validation analysis. It is difficult for software engineers to understand the formal temporal logic from numerous requirements. In this paper, we propose a novel method to automatically mine the linear temporal logic (LTL) from the natural language requirements and check the consistency among different formal properties. We use natural language processing (NLP) to parse requirement sentences and map syntactic dependencies to LTL formulas by using our extraction rules. Also, we apply the automata-based model checking to assess the correctness and consistency of the extracted properties. Through implementation and case studies, we demonstrate that our approach is well suited to deal with the temporal logic requirements upon which the natural language is based.

1 Introduction

Requirements denote the essential properties knowledge of software systems and assist in software development. In practice, software requirements written in natural language are subject to considerable ambiguity. Most errors in software development are introduced in the early stages of the requirements design and writing phases. Correctly understanding and analyzing NLR is difficult for engineers; considerable time and professional knowledge are required to evaluate the accuracy and consistency of these requirements. Using formal language instead of natural language can accurately describe the temporal and logical properties

ⓒ Springer Nature Switzerland AG 2019
C. Douligeris et al. (Eds.): KSEM 2019, LNAI 11776, pp. 75–87, 2019.
https://doi.org/10.1007/978-3-030-29563-9_8

in NLR, eliminating syntactic errors and semantic ambiguities, and provide the basis for performing advanced verification techniques such as model checking. Formal language, like LTL expressions, has rigorous semantics and a high learning cost. Given the advancements in the scale and complexity of modern software requirements, it is difficult to translate NLR to formal language manually.

Much previous research has been dedicated to translating NLR into a specific formal expression. In [5], a controlled subset of English has translated into target temporal formalism by using an aspectual DCG parser. However, the author did not give the actual experimental data, and we do not know whether the practical application of these methods is satisfactory. An approach of ontology population focused on instance property identification from NLR and represented in a formal manner [12]. This approach failed to cope with temporal properties of NLR. The author of [10] dealt with the translation of the natural language to temporal logic through discourse representation structure. The translation work was done with high-quality, but there was no in-depth study of the requirements analysis. Similar research in [15] turned NLR into LTL and detected the realizability of specifications. But our methods are essentially different and have achieved good results in practical applications.

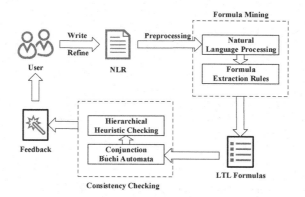

Fig. 1. The workflow of mining and checking framework

In this paper, we use the idea of tree-to-tree to mine LTL from NLR, and then check the consistency of multiple properties formalized in LTL formulas. Our framework has a well-established closed-loop workflow (shown in Fig. 1). The two main parts are formula mining and consistency checking. At the beginning, the untrained users (the people who lack knowledge of NLP and FM) write the NLR. Through the preprocessing, we use natural language processing technology to parse the requirements sentences to obtain syntactic dependencies and map them to LTL by applying formula extraction rules. Then, we use the automata-based model checking to analyze the consistency of the extracted LTL formulas. The hierarchical heuristic checking makes our consistency checking method more efficient. Finally, we rely on feedback to enable users to refine the initial requirements. We continue this same procedure until there is no abnormal feedback. To demonstrate the effectiveness of automatic mining and checking in complex situations, we conduct experiments on different application requirements with positive results. Our approach can reduce the burden of requirements engineers and formal modelers, and improve the efficiency and accuracy of software development.

2 Preliminary

2.1 Nature Language Processing

Natural Language Processing (NLP) is a branch of artificial intelligence that helps computers understand, interpret and manipulate human language in a cogent and useful way. Based on machine learning and deep learning, NLP takes a natural language sentence as the input and works out the grammatical information of the sentence. It has a variety of contributions such as automatic text summarization, named entity recognition, part-of-speech tagging, information extraction, and knowledge acquisition. To bridge the gap between natural language and formal language, we use NLP for parsing and semantic reasoning to get the final formal expression.

The Stanford Parser[1] is a Java implementation of probabilistic natural language parser created by researchers from the Stanford Natural Language Processing Group [9]. With input text in natural language, including English, Chinese, German, etc., the Stanford Parser can quickly and correctly work out the syntactic dependency relationship of sentences that can easily be understood and effectively applied by users. Our mining methods use parsing results to help us extract formal properties from NLR.

2.2 Linear Temporal Logic

Linear Temporal Logic (LTL) is a temporal logic formalism that extends propositional or predicate logic and provides intuitive and mathematically precise notations for expressing linear-time properties [3]. LTL formulas over the set AP of the atomic proposition are formed according to the following grammar:

$$\varphi ::= true \mid a \mid \varphi_1 \wedge \varphi_2 \mid \neg\varphi \mid \bigcirc\varphi \mid \varphi_1 \cup \varphi_2$$

Where $a \in$ AP is a propositional variable, $\wedge$ is conjunction, $\neg$ is negation, $\bigcirc$ is the temporal operator next and $\cup$ is the temporal operator until. The formula $\bigcirc\varphi$ expresses that φ is true in the next state. $\varphi_1 \cup \varphi_2$ indicates that φ_2 is true in a certain state, and φ_1 is always true before this state. Disjunction $\vee$, implication $\rightarrow$, eventually $\Diamond$ and always $\Box$ can be derived from the above four operators. For more formal definition of LTL syntax and semantics, see [4].

---

[1] http://nlp.stanford.edu:8080/parser/index.jsp.

A parse tree of an LTL formula is a nested list, where each branch is either a single atomic proposition or a formula. The LTL parse tree is a structure which is designed to be eventually transformed to LTL formula. They are in different forms, but their essence is to reflect temporal and logical properties. So, we can build a LTL parse tree to get to the LTL formula.

LTL is a dominant language of model checking in formal methods. Classical LTL model checking translates the negation of LTL formulas into a Büchi automata, and checks the emptiness of its intersection with the Büchi automata of the current model [13]. A Büchi automata is a five-tuple $(Q, \sum, \triangle, Q_0, F)$ where Q is a finite set of states, $\sum$ is a finite alphabet, $Q_0 \subseteq Q$ is a set of initial states, $\triangle: Q \times \sum \to 2^Q$ is the transition function, and $F \subseteq Q$ is a set of acceptance states. Given an LTL formula φ, we can construct a finite-state automata A_φ according to infinite words that accept all computations that satisfy φ. In Sect. 4, we use this approach to check the consistency of the multiple properties extracted in LTL.

3   Mining Methodology

In this section, we will elaborate on our mining method, which focuses on the automatic extraction of formal temporal and logical properties from the NLR, including Preprocessing, Natural Language Processing, Formula Extraction Rules. Finally, we introduce our mining algorithm in Formula Synthesis.

3.1   Preprocessing

When given a natural language requirement document, we use preprocessing to properly handle it instead of using NLP and formula extraction immediately. We decompose the stream of natural language text into individual sentences to isolate the independent temporal and logical properties. This preprocessing does not require that engineers know NLP or FM knowledge but some domain knowledge. Domain knowledge can help us identify entity phrases. We convert domain-specific nominal phrases into a single term, such as Cancel_Button, Temperature_Sensor or Electronics_Display; these are professional phrases that appear in the different domain. In addition, we replace special symbols and arithmetic expressions with their intuitive meaning, such as $\rightleftharpoons$, which converts to a term like leftright_harpoons. Similarly, we replace the arithmetic expression $x \pm 1$ with x_pm_1. The NLP parser treat this three symbols as a single term. The purpose of the preprocessing is to facilitate the later NLP and make it parse the sentences correctly.

3.2   Natural Language Processing

In the natural language processing stage, we use the Stanford Parser, which takes the NLR as input and works out the potential information of the sentences. We use this information to help us mine out the formal properties implied in the sentences. The Stanford Parser can identify which words act as nouns, verbs, adverbs, etc., and determine the grammatical relationships of sentences, such as which words are the subject or object of a verb.

For example, the following requirement REQ is parsed by the Stanford Parser and delivers a set of syntactic dependencies. We can intuitively depict the dependencies of REQ and present the information in a human-friendly form. See the following syntactic dependency tree (Fig. 2(a)). We represent a single syntactic dependency with a triplet: *type*(*gov*, *dep*). Note that "*gov*" and "*dep*" are words that occur in natural language sentences, whereas the relation type name "*type*" is automatically generated by the parser. The dependency triplet indicates the grammatical relationship between two words in a sentence: the word "*gov*" is related to the word "*dep*" via the dependency relation "*type*".

REQ: If the current_speed equals 60 km/h, the indicator_light will be set to On eventually.

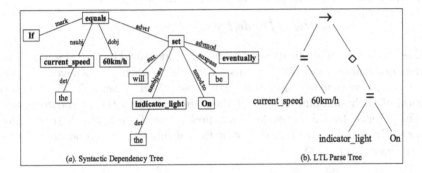

Fig. 2. Syntactic dependency tree and LTL parse tree of the REQ

The structure of the dependency tree in the figure above is similar to the LTL parse tree. However, the gap between the two tree is large so we need to address that. Transforming from a syntactic dependency tree to an LTL parse tree is novel, and this presents an idea to solve the problem of formal properties mining. Next, we define a series of extraction rules to map the dependencies tree to the LTL parse tree.

3.3   Formula Extraction Rules

Before introducing our formula extraction rules, we define an expression for the LTL parse tree, which we call the **LTL parse expression**. The LTL parse expression is a prefix expression designed to be transformed into an LTL formula. LTL parse expressions are composed of unary operators ($\square$, $\bigcirc$, $\lozenge$, $\neg$) and binary operators ($\rightarrow$, $\cup$, $\vee$, $\wedge$, $=$, $<$, $>$). The binary operator indicates that there are two children in the parse tree and the unary operator has only one child. For example, a parse tree represented by an LTL parse expression $\rightarrow (A, \bigcirc(B))$ can be transformed into an LTL formula $(A \to \bigcirc B)$. Therefore, in order to get the LTL formula, we can extract the LTL parse expression from NLR first.

Formula extraction rules aim to identify temporal and logical properties in terms of syntactic dependencies. We need to map the syntactic dependencies to the LTL parse expression. Extraction rules are a bridge between informal language and formal language. Based on the semantic analysis of dependencies and the syntactic analysis of LTL languages, we propose a set of extraction rules.

The formula extraction rules are shown in the following form:

$$< preconditions > \Longrightarrow < mapped\ expressions >$$

The preconditions of the rules are composed of dependencies triplets. The extraction results of the rules are mapped expressions, which can be combined into LTL parse expressions. A concrete example is the following rules that maps two dependencies $mark(\omega_1, If)$ and $advcl(\omega_2, \omega_1)$ for any two single entities word ω_1 and ω_2 to the mapped expressions $\to (\omega_1, \omega_2)$.

$$mark(\omega_1, If); advcl(\omega_2, \omega_1) \Longrightarrow \to (\omega_1, \omega_2)$$

The extraction of implication relationships is identified by the presence of particular conditional words as: "if", "once", "while", "when", "whenever", "after". There is also particular consequence words as: "until", "before". The semantic relation of their mapping is $\cup$, and they are related to the predicate word ω of the sentence by the dependencies: $mark(\omega, until)$, $mark(\omega, before)$. More importantly, we will introduce the extraction of three unary temporal properties in LTL, namely $\square$, $\bigcirc$, $\diamond$.

- $\square$ Natural language expresses global temporal property by some specific adverbs, such as "globally", "always", "forever", "from now on", etc. By examining dependencies of a sentence with those adverbs, we can have the rules for the extraction of temporal properties. Dependencies include $advmod(\omega, globally)$, $advmod(\omega, always)$, $advmod(\omega, forever)$ and $case(now, from); nmod(\omega, now); case(now, on)$.
- $\bigcirc$ If some phrases or clauses in a sentence contain "in the next state", "in X second", "X cycles later", etc. We mark the unit time with a $\bigcirc$. Dependencies include $nmod : in(\omega, state); amod(state, next)$ and $nmod : in(\omega, second); nummod(second, X)$
- $\diamond$ By using specific phrases to express temporal property at some point in the future, such as "eventually", "in the future", "sometimes", etc. We mark them with corresponding temporal operator $\diamond$. Dependencies include $advmod(\omega, eventually)$, $advmod(\omega, sometimes)$ and $nmod : in(\omega, future)$.

Finally, we show some other common extraction rules as follows.

$$neg(\omega, not) \Longrightarrow \omega := \neg(\omega)$$
$$conj : and(\omega_1, \omega_2) \Longrightarrow \omega_1 := \wedge(\omega_1, \omega_2)$$
$$conj : or(\omega_1, \omega_2) \Longrightarrow \omega_1 := \vee(\omega_1, \omega_2)$$
$$nsubj(equals, \omega_1); dobj(equals, \omega_2) \Longrightarrow equals := = (\omega_1, \omega_2)$$
$$nsubjpass(set, \omega_1); nmod : to(set, \omega_2) \Longrightarrow set := = (\omega_1, \omega_2)$$
$$nsubj(less, \omega_1); nmod : than(less, \omega_2) \Longrightarrow less := < (\omega_1, \omega_2)$$
$$nsubj(greater, \omega_1); nmod : than(greater, \omega_2) \Longrightarrow greater := > (\omega_1, \omega_2)$$

We define that the left-hand parts of the symbol ":=" can be replaced by the right-hand parts. It is noteworthy that all replacements follow a principle that we refer to as a **combined strategy**. The principle of the combined strategy is to get the LTL parse expression in a correct combination order. When multiple mapped expressions exist, they are iteratively combined in the following order:

$$(\rightarrow \| \cup), (\vee \| \wedge), (\bigcirc \| \square \| \Diamond), (\neg), (= \| < \| >)$$

The symbol "‖" indicates that the front and rear operators have the same binding priority. The mapped expressions cannot be combined by themselves, and the combined expression is the final LTL parse expression when no other mapped expressions can be combined. Therefore, for the mapped expression of REQ above, we can get the following LTL parse expression based on combined strategy, and the corresponding LTL parse tree is shown in Fig. 2(b).

$$\rightarrow (= (current\_speed, 60\,km/h), \Diamond(= (indicator\_light, On)))$$

To handle complex grammatical structure of the requirement sentences, our rules can add more constraints or preconditions. The words "equals" and "set" can be replaced by other predicates. Moreover, we have created 110 extraction rules or even more to ensure that most of the different forms of NLR can be extracted correctly.

3.4   Formula Synthesis

Our extraction rules successfully get the LTL parse expression in an innovative way. The goal of automation is to quickly mine LTL formulas from a large number of requirements. For the formula extraction of multiple requirements, we will introduce our mining algorithm. The details on the mining process are depicted in Algorithm 1, where the input is the original large amount of NLR, and output LTL formula set.

In the beginning, some set variables need to be initialized. In the preprocessing stage, we identify domain-specific terms and rewrite some complex expression. Then, the Stanford Parser is applied to produce a set of dependencies D for each sentence s in NLR. If the subset of dependencies satisfies the precondition

Algorithm 1. Formula Mining Algorithm

Input: Natural Language Requirements NLR
Output: LTL Formula Set Φ
$R \leftarrow$ *Formula Extraction Rules Set*;
$D = \varnothing$;   //Syntactic Dependencies Set
$E = \varnothing$;   //Mapped Expression Set
$\xi = null$;   //LTL Parse Expression
$NLR \leftarrow preProcessing(NLR)$;
for $\forall s \in NLR$ **do**
  $D \leftarrow nlpParse(s)$;
  for $\forall d \subseteq D$ **do**
    if $satPrecond(R, d)$ **then**
      $E \leftarrow mapExp(R, d)$;
    end
  end
  for $\forall e \in E$ **do**
    if $higherPri(e)$ **then**
      $\xi \leftarrow combine(\xi, e)$;
    end
  end
  $\varphi = preToMid(\xi)$;
  $\Phi = \Phi \cup \{\varphi\}$;
  $D = \varnothing; E = \varnothing; \xi = null$;
end
return Φ

($satPrecond$), the corresponding mapped expression is generated according to the extraction rules ($mapExp$). $satPrecond()$ require that $type.gov$ and $type.dep$ meet the preconditions simultaneously. The mapped expressions are combined in order of high priority to low priority. Since LTL parse expression is the prefix expression of the LTL formula, we use a recursive function $preToMid()$ to get the final LTL formula. If the outermost operator of the expression is a binary operator, this operator is placed in the middle of its two parameters. If the outermost operator is a unary operator, we put this unary operator in front of its parameter. If the parameter is a word, we output it to our formula. By recursively applying for all parameter, we correctly print out the LTL formula and add it to Φ. The following is the LTL result of the requirement REQ.

$$(current\_speed = 60 \, \text{km/h}) \rightarrow \Diamond(indicator\_light = On))$$

Once we successfully mine a set of formulas from NLR, it is desirable to distinguish the atomic propositions in an LTL formula. The same atomic proposition in a system requirement's extracted formulas uses the same variable instead. Generally speaking, "$=$", "$<$" or "$>$" and the parameters on both sides of it form an atomic proposition. Of course, our rules are far from covering the whole range of linguistic phenomena. We judge the correctness of the formula itself by LTL satisfiability checking, which can be reduced to automata-based non-emptiness checking. Requirements corresponding to incorrect formulas also needs asks the user for the assistance. The performance of the mining work directly affects the subsequent consistency checking. Through a lot of experiments show that our extraction rules are sufficient for many applications.

4   Consistency Checking

Natural language requirements are not supported any consistency checks among the multiple system properties. Whereas formal languages like LTL, by their nature, are very suitable for formal analysis and consistency checking. The inconsistency between different LTL formulas means that there are some contradictions in the requirements, which increases the difficulty of system development.

In this work, the automata-based model checking is used to analyse the consistency of formal properties. The consistency of a set of extracted LTL formulas can be reduced to checking the emptiness of the Büchi automata, which is the conjunction of the multiple LTL formulas. If the conjunction Büchi automata is non-empty, these formulas are considered to be consistent. Checking for non-emptiness of a Büchi automata is equivalent to finding a strongly connected component that is reachable from an initial state and contains an accepting state, which is visited infinitely often [4]. If we can find a reachable acceptance state that falls within a cycle, the LTL formulas are deemed consistent.

Specifically, we use the principle of **hierarchical heuristic checking** to detect inconsistencies in multiple LTL formulas. It is inefficient to check consistency by traversing all the combinations of every formula. Our approach is to find out the minimal inconsistent subsets through heuristic checking, which means that we exclude the subsets with known consistent supersets, and only check the subset of the inconsistent supersets downwards until there is no inconsistent subset at a certain level.

For a practical example, we collected requirements from the power window controller (PWC) system [1] to demonstrate our checking method. The power window control system is adopted by many modern cars, which is convenient for drivers and passengers to operate the windows. We selected the following requirements sentences and extracted formulas according to the mining method. ("Driver_Up_Switch = OFF", "Power_Window = CLOSED" are represented by atomic proposition p and q respectively)

S_1: The Power Window will be set to CLOSED in the future. ($\varphi_1 : \Box(\Diamond q)$)
S_2: If the Driver Up Switch not equals OFF, the Power Window will be set to CLOSED eventually. ($\varphi_2 : \Box(\neg p \rightarrow \Diamond q)$)
S_3: The Power Window is set to CLOSED until the Driver Up Switch is turned to OFF. ($\varphi_3 : \Box(q \cup p)$)
S_4: If the Driver Up Switch equals OFF, the Power Window will never be set to CLOSED. ($\varphi_4 : \Box(p \rightarrow \Box \neg q)$)

The process of hierarchical heuristic checking of the LTL set $\{\varphi_1, \varphi_2, \varphi_3, \varphi_4\}$ is illustrated in Fig. 3. The sets with dashed outline are the inconsistent sets, and the arrows with the solid line are the process we need to check. For example, we check the emptiness of the conjunction Büchi automata ($\varphi_1 \wedge \varphi_2 \wedge \varphi_3$). It contains an accepting state, which is visited infinitely often, means that these three LTL formulas are consistent. Finally, there is no inconsistent subset at the last level, and $\{\varphi_1, \varphi_3, \varphi_4\}$ is the minimal inconsistent subset. In this way, users can narrow their error detection scope and reduce their workload.

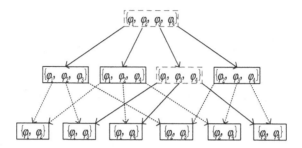

Fig. 3. Hierarchical heuristic checking

Through consistency checking, we can provide feedback on errors or contradictions in the NLR to users. Inconsistency does not mean that the formula is wrong, but consistency means the formula is satisfiable. For the minimal inconsistent subsets, we assume that some of the requirements are consistent, and the remaining requirements are compared by the state path. Users can properly handle the failed requirements based on the correct prompt information. Assumption method provide users with traceable feedback on the corresponding requirements so that the users can correct the initial requirements at an early stage. Providing users with feedback about inconsistent requirements specification is valuable. By filtering out inconsistent formulas or modifying inconsistent requirements, our work can be cycled until there is no contradiction.

5   Experiments and Evaluations

To evaluate the methods discussed in this paper, we implemented a research prototype of our framework for more practical and complex case studies. For the formulas extraction, we implemented the mining system utilized by JAVA 8 (JDK1.8) and an integrated version 3.8.0 of the Stanford Parser Package[2]. Besides, we loaded the language model "englishPCFG" for English text requirements. In the aspect of the consistency checking, our prototype tool interfaced with LTL2BA [6], and checked the consistency by intersecting Büchi Automata and monitoring state cycles. If we link all reachable states and figure out an acceptable cycle, the input formulas will be declared consistent. This framework integrated mining system and consistency checking to achieve a united platform.

---

[2] https://nlp.stanford.edu/software/lex-parser.shtml.

We collected requirements from six different application areas to demonstrate the ability of our tool to handling complex NLR sentences and measuring the robustness relative to noise.

- CCS: The Cruise Control System (CCS) main function is to automatically control the speed of the car. The requirements document is provided by SCADE [7]. We used existing requirements statements as our test NLR.
- PWC: We focused on the window switches control system requirements in the PWC [1]. The up and down motion of the window switches were treated as separate inputs to the control system, and the window states were treated as outputs. Moreover, the driver's inputs took precedence over the passenger's.
- AVC: The Autonomous Vehicles Controller (AVC) system is a hierarchical embedded control architecture [14] that can solve communications problems and urban navigation. We experimented with the requirements of two software modules, namely "Path Follower" and "Gcdrive".
- ITS: The Isolette Thermostat System (ITS) is designed to maintain the air temperature of an Isolette within the desired range [8]. The functional requirements of thermostat have been expressed in itemized natural language sentences. Different submodules were considered, including "Regulate Temperature", "Monitor Temperature".
- SOS: The Satellite Operations Software (SOS) is a software component of the space vehicle [11]. Each requirement was numbered for tracing purposes, and we chose suitable samples from them.
- CARA: The Computer Assisted Resuscitation Algorithm (CARA) can determine the rate at which the infusion pump should infuse fluid into a patient based on the blood pressure [2]. We collected 70 requirements of Blood Pressure Monitor components for our work.

Table 1. The results of mining and checking

Corpus name	Total requirements	Correct mining	Incorrect mining	Mining accuracy	Consistent formulas	Checking time (s)
CCS	20	19	1	95%	19	8.6
PWC	25	23	2	92%	22	12.7
AVC	36	31	5	86%	29	125.6
ITS	42	38	4	90%	36	692.5
SOS	53	44	9	83%	39	1453.4
CARA	70	58	12	83%	53	8516.0

The results of six cases are summarized in Table 1. From the results data, we can see that the mining accuracy exceeds 80%. With the increasing scale and complexity of the system, the effectiveness of mining decreases generally and the checking times increase exponentially. The change of checking time is mainly related to the automaton generation: the longer the length of conjunction formula, the more time it takes to generate the automaton. We also measured the mining accuracy of different operators, where the mining accuracy of the temporal operators (about 80%) is less than that of the logical operator (about 92%). Because the temporal properties are more diverse and obscure in expression than logical properties. Therefore, the above problems are exactly what we need to improve in the future. Most of the NLR can be correctly converted to LTL formulas, and the number of consistent formulas can be checked based on correct mining. Accurate consistency checking reduces design errors in the early stage. Moreover, the speed of formulas mining and consistency checking is thousands of times faster than manual processing, which saves time and energy.

6   Conclusion and Future Work

In this paper, we propose a novel method to automatically extract formal language LTL from NLR, and we demonstrate a formal analysis for the consistency between extracted LTL formulas. Based on our proposed approach, we use natural language processing and formula extraction rules to extract LTL formulas. This eliminates the ambiguity of the NLR. To ensure the consistency between requirements at early stages of analysis, we use automata-based model checking to discover the inconsistencies among multiple LTL formulas. The hierarchical heuristic checking is used to optimize the checking method and the feedback information assist users in refining the original requirements. Our approach is evaluated by different domain requirements with positive results. In the future, we will focus on making our mining system more robust and then extracting other formal languages other than LTL, like CTL. In addition, we would like to enhance the ability of formal analysis and complete the whole sanity checking of the requirements.

Acknowledgements. This work is partially supported by the National Natural Science Foundation of China (No. 61602178), Shanghai Science and Technology Committee Rising-Star Program (No. 18QB1402000).

References

1. Akhtar, Z.: Model based automotive system design: a power window controller case study. Master's thesis, University of Waterloo (2015)
2. Alur, R., et al.: Formal specifications and analysis of the computer-assisted resuscitation algorithm (CARA) infusion pump control system. Int. J. Softw. Tools Technol. Transfer **5**(4), 308–319 (2004)
3. Baier, C., Katoen, J.P.: Principles of Model Checking. MIT Press, Cambridge (2008)
4. Clarke Jr., E.M., Grumberg, O., Peled, D.A.: Model Checking. MIT Press, Cambridge (1999)
5. Fazaeli, R.: Translating from a natural language to a target temporal formalism. Final Year Project (2002)

6. Gastin, P., Oddoux, D.: Fast LTL to Büchi automata translation. In: Berry, G., Comon, H., Finkel, A. (eds.) CAV 2001. LNCS, vol. 2102, pp. 53–65. Springer, Heidelberg (2001). https://doi.org/10.1007/3-540-44585-4_6

7. Heim, S., Dumas, X., Bonnafous, E., Dhaussy, P., Teodorov, C., Leroux, L.: Model checking of SCADE designed systems. In: 8th European Congress on Embedded Real Time Software and Systems (ERTS 2016) (2016)

8. Lempia, D.L., Miller, S.P.: Requirements Engineering Management Handbook. National Technical Information Service (NTIS), vol. 1 (2009)

9. Marneffe, M.C.D., Maccartney, B., Manning, C.D.: Generating typed dependency parses from phrase structure parses. In: LREC, pp. 449–454 (2006)

10. Nelken, R., Francez, N.: Automatic translation of natural language system specifications into temporal logic. In: Alur, R., Henzinger, T.A. (eds.) CAV 1996. LNCS, vol. 1102, pp. 360–371. Springer, Heidelberg (1996). https://doi.org/10.1007/3-540-61474-5_83

11. Prowell, S.J., Trammell, C.J., Linger, R.C., Poore, J.H.: Cleanroom Software Engineering: Technology and Process. Pearson Education, London (1999)

12. Sadoun, D., Dubois, C., Ghamri-Doudane, Y., Grau, B.: From natural language requirements to formal specification using an ontology. In: IEEE International Conference on TOOLS with Artificial Intelligence, pp. 755–760 (2013)

13. Vardi, M.Y.: An automata-theoretic approach to linear temporal logic. In: Moller, F., Birtwistle, G. (eds.) Logics for Concurrency. LNCS, vol. 1043, pp. 238–266. Springer, Heidelberg (1996). https://doi.org/10.1007/3-540-60915-6_6

14. Wongpiromsarn, T.: Formal methods for design and verification of embedded control systems: application to an autonomous vehicle. Ph.D. thesis, California Institute of Technology (2010)

15. Yan, R., Cheng, C.H., Chai, Y.: Formal consistency checking over specifications in natural languages. In: Proceedings of the 2015 Design, Automation & Test in Europe Conference & Exhibition, pp. 1677–1682. EDA Consortium (2015)

A Shallow Semantic Parsing Framework for Event Argument Extraction

Zhunchen Luo[1], Guobin Sui[2], He Zhao[3], and Xiaosong Li[1(✉)]

[1] Information Research Center of Military Science,
PLA Academy of Military Science, Beijing, China
zhunchenluo@gmail.com, 164832732@qq.com
[2] School of Computer Science and Engineering, Beihang University , Beijing, China
suigb@buaa.edu.cn
[3] School of Computer Science, Beijing Institute of Technology, Beijing, China
zhaohe1995@outlook.com

Abstract. Currently, many state-of-the-art event argument extraction systems are still based on an unrealistic assumption that gold-standard entity mentions are provided in advance. One popular solution of jointly extracting entities and events is to detect the entity mentions using sequence labeling approaches. However, this methods may ignore the syntactic relationship among triggers and arguments. We find that the constituents in the parse tree structure may help capture the internal relationship between words in an event argument. Besides, the predicate and the corresponding predicate arguments, which are mostly ignored in existing approaches, may provide more potential to represent the close relationship. In this paper, we address the event argument extraction problem in a more actual scene where the entity information is unavailable. Moreover, instead of using word-level sequence labeling approaches, we propose a shallow semantic parsing framework to extract event arguments with the event trigger as the predicate and the event arguments as the predicate arguments. In specific, we design and compare different features for the proposed model. The experimental results show that our approach advances state-of-the-arts with remarkable gains and achieves the best F1 score on the ACE 2005 dataset.

Keywords: Event argument extraction · Entity ·
Shallow semantic parsing

1 Introduction

In recent years, event extraction, which aims to discover event triggers with specific types and their arguments, has attracted increasing interests in the research communities. In the Automatic Context Extraction (ACE) event extraction program[1], an event is represented as a structure, comprising an event trigger and a set of arguments. This work tackles the event argument extraction (EAE) task, which is a crucial part of event extraction (EE) and focuses on identifying event arguments and categorizing them into

---

[1] https://www.ldc.upenn.edu/collaborations/past-projects/ace.

© Springer Nature Switzerland AG 2019
C. Douligeris et al. (Eds.): KSEM 2019, LNAI 11776, pp. 88–96, 2019.
https://doi.org/10.1007/978-3-030-29563-9_9

roles in the events triggered by the given triggers. The following is an example to illustrate the EAE task.

E1: *Controversial PLO leader Yasser Arafat **died** in a Paris hospital on Sunday.*
In this example, given the sentence **E1** and the trigger word *"died"* which triggered a *Die* event, an EAE system is expected to detect *"Controversial PLO leader Yasser Arafat"* as a *Victim* argument, *"a Paris hospital"* as a *Place* argument, and *"Sunday"* as a *Time* argument.

Current state-of-the-art methods [1–7] often model the EAE task as an entity-level classification problem with an unrealistic assumption that the gold-standard entity annotations are provided in advance. However, in real-life applications, the entity-level classification approach can hardly be directly applied to EAE, because the gold-standard entity annotations are not always available. Therefore, how to recognize the entity mentions remains a challenging issue. Besides, previous research on joint entity and event extraction models the entity mention recognization problem as a word-level sequence labeling problem by classifying the words using the BIO schema and then feed the sequence labeling results into the later EAE models [8]. However, in those entity-event pipeline frameworks, the errors in entity mention recognition will propagate and affect the final extraction result. What's more, there are some shortages of the current sequence labeling approaches to EAE. First, the words in an argument are assumed to be independent to each other. So that the internal mutual relationship between words are ignored for extracting a complete event argument. For example, in **E1**, the *Victim* argument is *"Controversial PLO leader Yasser Arafat"*, and it contains several words. If ignoring the relationship among words, the modified parts *"Controversial PLO"* might be ignored, hence an incomplete argument *"leader Yasser Arafat"* will be extracted.

E2: *Melony Marshall was **married** just a month before she **left** for Iraq.*
Second, the sequence labeling approaches often use the contextual information of the arguments but ignore the relationship among the arguments and the event triggers. For example, in **E2**, there are two events which are triggered by *"married"* and *"left"*, respectively. It is essential to know the relationship between the phrase *"just a month before"* and each trigger to determine which event trigger it belongs to. Therefore, it remains immature to model the close relationship between an event trigger and its arguments in current approaches.

In this paper, we propose a novel approach which simultaneously extracts event arguments and classifies them into the roles in the events to solve the above two main critical issues. We model this task from a parse tree structure perspective and adopt a shallow semantic parsing and classifying framework. More specifically, first we use the abundant constituents provided by the pars tree structure to capture the internal relationship between words in an event argument. Second, we use a rule-based argument merger to find the appropriate constituents which indicates the event argument candidates in the given parse tree. And then, we introduce an argument pruning procedure to filter the candidates which are most likely non-arguments of a predicate. Finally, we use the well-designed parse tree structure features to infer whether the argument is related to the event and the corresponding role. In experiments, we systematically conduct comparisons on a widely used benchmark dataset, ACE2005[2].

---

[2] https://catalog.ldc.upenn.edu/LDC2006T06.

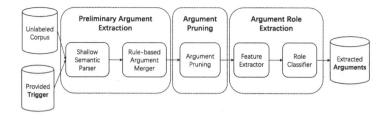

Fig. 1. An overview of the shallow semantic parsing and classifying framework.

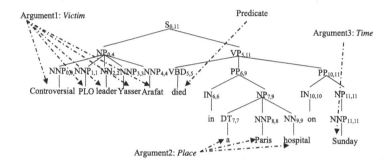

Fig. 2. Illustration of an event trigger (predicate) and its corresponding event arguments in a parse tree of the sentence **E1** (*Controversial PLO leader Yasser Arafat **died** in a Paris hospital on Sunday*).

The experimental results demonstrate that our proposed approach is effective for the EAE task, and it outperforms state-of-the-art approaches with remarkable gains.

2 Approach

We formulate the EAE task as a shallow semantic parsing problem and solve it in a simplified shallow semantic parsing and classifying framework. As shown in Fig. 1, our proposed framework can be divided into three subsections: Preliminary Argument Extraction, Argument Pruning, and Argument Role Extraction, which will be introduced respectively.

Preliminary Argument Extraction

To capture the internal and mutual syntactic relationship among triggers and arguments, we convert the original word sequences to semantic parse trees given the event triggers as predicates. Preliminary event arguments are recast as the predicate arguments in parse trees. The task of shallow semantic parsing is to map all the constituents in the sentence into their corresponding semantic arguments (roles) of the predicate given the sentence's parse tree and a predicate in it. For EAE, the event trigger is considered as the predicate, while the event arguments are mapped into the predicate's arguments. Figure 2 shows the parsing tree structure of the sentence in **E1**, together with the event trigger and its corresponding event arguments. To find the proper constituents in parse trees containing those separated tokens respectively, given the trigger and the sentence

Table 1. Basic Features with Regard to Fig. 2. And the contents between the parentheses are corresponding extracted basic features with regard to the sentence **E1**.

Category	Features	Description
B-Pre	**B-Pre1**	The predicate and, its POS and type. (died, VBD, Life/Die)
B-Arg	**B-Arg1**	The argument candidate and its POS. (controversial plo leader Yasser Arafat, NNP_NNP_NN_NNP_NNP)
	B-Arg2	The headword of the argument candidate and its POS. (controversial, NNP)
	B-Arg3	The last word of the argument candidate and its POS. (Arafat, NNP)
	B-Arg4	The left word of the argument candidate and its POS. (null, null)
	B-Arg5	The right word of the argument candidate and its POS. (died, VBD)
	B-Arg6	Whether the argument candidate includes a time word. (no)
B-Arg-Pre	**B-Arg-Pre1**	The predicate and the positional relationship of the argument candidate with the predicate ("left" or "right"). (died_left)
	B-Arg-Pre2	The distance from the headword of the argument candidate to the predicate. (5)

which contains m words: $word_1$, ..., $word_m$, we propose a rule-based argument merger consisting of the following three heuristic rules to merge the separated tokens to the appropriate constituents indicating event arguments in the given parse tree.

PAE-Rule(1): The trigger itself and all of its ancestral components are non-arguments.

PAE-Rule(2): If all child constituents of constituent X are recognized as arguments, X is labeled as an argument, and all its child constituents are re-labeled as non-arguments.

PAE-Rule(3): If not all of the child constituents of constituent X are recognized as arguments, X is labeled as a non-argument.

After applying the rule-based argument merger, we can obtain event argument candidates given a particular event trigger.

Argument Pruning

However, the previous preliminary argument extraction step may bring in extra noises of event argument candidates which are most likely non-arguments of a predicate. To filter the noises, we introduce an argument pruning procedure based on three heuristic rules to obtain the extracted event argument candidates. The heuristics in the argument pruning are executed sequentially in the given order:

AP-Rule(1): The constituents which contain more than five words are filtered out as non-arguments and instead, their child constituents are considered as argument candidates.

AP-Rule(2): The predicate constituent itself and its ancestral constituents in the parse tree are filtered out as non-arguments.

AP-Rule(3): The constituents which have no brother constituents are filtered out as non-arguments.

Table 2. Syntactic Features with Regard to Fig. 2. And the contents between the parentheses are corresponding extracted syntactic features with regard to the sentence **E1**.

Category	Features	Description
S-Arg	**S-Arg1**	The node name of the argument candidate. (NP)
	S-Arg2	Whether the node of the argument candidate is the largest NP node including a time word. (no)
S-Arg-Pre	**S-Arg-Pre1**	The path from the headword of the argument candidate to the predicate. (NP<S>VP>VBD)
	S-Arg-Pre2	The number of the nodes in S-Arg-Pre1. (4)
	S-Arg-Pre3	The partial syntactic path from the argument candidate node to the least governing node of both the argument candidate and the predicate. (NP<S)
	S-Arg-Pre4	The partial syntactic path from the predicate to the least governing node of both the argument candidate and the predicate. (VBD<VP<S)
	S-Arg-Pre5	Whether there is a clause tag (S) between the predicate and the argument candidate nodes. (yes)
	S-Arg-Pre6	Whether there are more than 3 clause tags (S) between the predicate and the argument candidate nodes. (no)

Argument Role Extraction

Event argument extraction (EAE) involves typically two sub-tasks, namely argument identification, and argument classification. The former is to identify whether an event argument has been playing a particular role in the event triggered by a given trigger. The latter, however, is to categorize an event argument to the role played in that event. In our approach, we deal with these two sub-tasks together by considering the non-argument (the event argument has not played a specific role in that event) as an extra and particular category of event argument roles. Thus, the whole argument extraction is formulated as an argument-level multi-category classification problem.

To address the multi-category classification problem, we use the conditional random fields (CRFs) and exploit two groups of features: **basic features** and **syntactic features**, as shown in Table 1. The features are categorized into three groups: the predicate-related features, B-Pre; the argument-related features, B-Arg; the features related to both the argument and predicate, B-Arg-Pre. Besides the basic features, various kinds of syntactic features in Table 2 are explored to capture more details regarding the argument candidate and the predicate. In the same spirit, we categorize the syntactic features into two groups, namely S-Arg and S-Arg-Pre. The first group contains the argument-related features and the second group contains the argument and predicate related features.

3 Experiments

In our approach, argument pruning is an important strategy to reduce the amount of argument candidates. Table 3 shows the numbers of argument candidates when the pruning rules as discussed in Sect. 3.2 are used. From this table, we can see that the first

Table 3. The effectiveness of the argument pruning rules

Action	#Argument candidates (Percentage)
Without Pruning	20920 (100%)
After **AP-Rule(1)**	16719 (79.9%)
After **AP-Rule(1)+(2)**	15841 (75.7%)
After **AP-Rule(1)+(2)+(3)**	14192 (67.8%)

Table 4. Performance comparison between word-sequence and parsing level approaches to argument extraction

Features	Argument identification			Argument classification		
	P(%)	R(%)	F1(%)	P(%)	R(%)	F1(%)
Word-sequence level (Basic)	63.36	38.52	47.91	60.14	**36.55**	45.47
Parsing level (Basic)	66.82	40.06	50.09	**82.17**	32.91	47.00
Parsing level (Basic + Syntactic)	**67.48**	**42.44**	**52.11**	81.52	34.59	**48.57**

rule **AP-Rule(1)** (filtering the constituent with more than five words) is most effective, which filters about 20% candidates. When all rules are used, 32.2% argument candidates are filtered.

Experimental Settings

For dataset, we use the English corpus for event extraction in ACE2005, which involves 8 types and 33 subtypes of events. Among all the 599 documents, we use 559 of them for training and the rest 40 for test. Different from previous studies [1–7], the gold-standard entity information is not available in our experiment.

We use the Stanford Parser[3] to get the POS tags and shallow semantic parse trees of the sentences. And for the multi-category classification problem, we use the conditional random fields (CRFs), which is implemented with a public tool CRF++[4].

For evaluation, we use the following criteria to determine the correctness of an predicted event mention: (1) An argument is correctly identified if its event subtype and offsets match any of the reference argument mentions. (2) An argument is correctly identified and classified if its event subtype, offsets and argument role match any of the reference argument mentions. Finally we use Precision (P), Recall (R) and F_1-measure (F_1) to evaluate the performance of event argument extraction.

Experimental Results

Table 4 shows the comparison between word-sequence and parsing level approaches to argument extraction. We can see that even using the basic features only, our parsing level approach is apparently superior to the word-sequence level approach in both argument identification, 47.91% vs. 50.09% and argument classification, 45.47% vs. 47.00%. Significance test with t-test shows that the improvement of our parsing level

---

[3] https://nlp.stanford.edu/software/lex-parser.html#Citing.
[4] https://code.google.com/p/crfpp/.

Table 5. Contribution of syntactic features in argument identification

Feature	P(%)	R(%)	F1(%)	Feature	P(%)	R(%)	F1(%)
Basic	66.82	40.06	50.09	Basic	66.82	40.06	50.09
+S-Arg1	66.36	40.34	50.17	+S-Arg1	66.36	40.34	50.17
+S-Arg2	66.51	39.22	49.34	+S-Arg2	66.51	39.22	49.34
+S-Arg-Pre1	**68.35**	39.92	50.40	+S-Arg-Pre1	**68.35**	39.92	50.40
+S-Arg-Pre2	65.32	40.62	50.09	+S-Arg-Pre2	65.32	40.62	50.09
+S-Arg-Pre3	67.12	41.74	51.47	+S-Arg-Pre3	67.12	41.74	51.47
+S-Arg-Pre4	67.50	41.60	51.47	+S-Arg-Pre4	67.50	41.60	51.47
+S-Arg-Pre5	66.67	39.78	49.82	+S-Arg-Pre4	67.50	41.60	51.47
+S-Arg-Pre6	67.61	40.34	50.53	+S-Arg-Pre6	67.61	40.34	50.53
All	67.48	**42.44**	**52.11**	All	67.48	**42.44**	**52.11**

Table 6. Comparison to the state-of-the-art

Approach	Performance on argument classification
Li et al. [5] with gold-standard entity information	52.7%
Li et al. [5] with entity extraction system	41.8%
Nguyen et al. [7] with gold-standard entity information	55.4%
Nguyen et al. [7] with entity extraction system	45.3%
Yang et al. [8]	48.4%
Our Approach	**48.6%**

approach (Basic+Syntatic) over the word-level approach is significant (p-value¡0.05). Especially, in argument classification, our parsing level approach outperforms word-sequence level approach in precision with a very large margin, i.e., 22.03%. Once the syntactic features are leveraged, the performance of our approach could be further improved.

Table 5 (left) shows the contribution of syntactic features in argument identification. The syntactic path features of S-Arg-Pre3, S-Arg-Pre4, and S-Arg-Pre6 are very effective for argument identification. Compared to using basic features only, using all these syntactic features yields a better performance in both precision and recall. And Table 5 (right) shows the contribution of syntactic features in argument classification. We can see that using all syntactic features is superior in terms of recall but a bit inferior in terms of precision. Overall, using syntactic features improves the performance in F-measure.

Table 6 shows the result comparison to the results provided by the state-of-the-art work of Li et al. [5], Nguyen et al. [7], and Yang et al. [8]. Our approach performs 3%-6% better than using an automatic system for extracting entities. Besides, our approach also outperforms the method of jointly extracting entities, event triggers, and event arguments. It can be seen the internal and mutual syntactic relationship among triggers and arguments is essential. Although our approach performs worse than their approach when gold-standard entity information is used, our approach does not employ the global features as their approach applies.

4 Conclusion

In this paper, we focus on a more realistic scenario in event extraction when the gold-standard entity annotations are not available in the test phase. We present a novel approach to event argument extraction by formulating it as a shallow semantic parsing problem. And various kinds of basic and syntactic features are employed to extract event arguments. Empirical studies demonstrate that our approach considerably outperforms traditional sequence labeling approaches. In the future work, we will improve our approach by leveraging a stronger parser or introducing some operations to recall more event arguments. And we will exploit higher-level knowledge, such as the cross-event and the cross-entity information.

Acknowledgements. This work was supported by the National Natural Science Foundation of China (No. 61602490).

References

1. Chen, Y., Xu, L., Liu, K., Zeng, D., Zhao, J.: Event extraction via dynamic multi-pooling convolutional neural networks. In: Proceedings of the 53rd Annual Meeting of the Association for Computational Linguistics and the 7th International Joint Conference on Natural Language Processing of the Asian Federation of Natural Language Processing, ACL 2015, Volume 1: Long Papers, Beijing, China, 26–31 July 2015, pp. 167–176 (2015). http://aclweb.org/anthology/P/P15/P15-1017.pdf
2. Hong, Y., Zhang, J., Ma, B., Yao, J., Zhou, G., Zhu, Q.: Using cross-entity inference to improve event extraction. In: The 49th Annual Meeting of the Association for Computational Linguistics: Human Language Technologies, Proceedings of the Conference, Portland, Oregon, USA, 19–24 June 2011, pp. 1127–1136 (2011). http://www.aclweb.org/anthology/P11-1113
3. Ji, H., Grishman, R.: Refining event extraction through cross-document inference. In: ACL 2008, Proceedings of the 46th Annual Meeting of the Association for Computational Linguistics, Columbus, Ohio, USA, 15–20 June 2008, pp. 254–262 (2008). http://www.aclweb.org/anthology/P08-1030
4. Li, Q., Ji, H., Hong, Y., Li, S.: Constructing information networks using one single model. In: Proceedings of the 2014 Conference on Empirical Methods in Natural Language Processing, EMNLP 2014, Doha, Qatar, A meeting of SIGDAT, a Special Interest Group of the ACL, 25–29 October 2014, pp. 1846–1851 (2014). http://aclweb.org/anthology/D/D14/D14-1198.pdf
5. Li, Q., Ji, H., Huang, L.: Joint event extraction via structured prediction with global features. In: Proceedings of the 51st Annual Meeting of the Association for Computational Linguistics, ACL 2013, Volume 1: Long Papers, Sofia, Bulgaria, 4–9 August 2013, pp. 73–82 (2013). http://aclweb.org/anthology/P/P13/P13-1008.pdf

6. Liao, S., Grishman, R.: Using document level cross-event inference to improve event extraction. In: ACL 2010, Proceedings of the 48th Annual Meeting of the Association for Computational Linguistics, Uppsala, Sweden, 11–16 July 2010, pp. 789–797 (2010). http://www.aclweb.org/anthology/P10-1081

7. Nguyen, T.H., Cho, K., Grishman, R.: Joint event extraction via recurrent neural networks. In: NAACL HLT 2016, The 2016 Conference of the North American Chapter of the Association for Computational Linguistics: Human Language Technologies, San Diego California, USA, 12–17 June 2016, pp. 300–309 (2016). http://aclweb.org/anthology/N/N16/N16-1034.pdf

8. Yang, B., Mitchell, T.M.: Joint extraction of events and entities within a document context. In: NAACL HLT 2016, The 2016 Conference of the North American Chapter of the Association for Computational Linguistics: Human Language Technologies, San Diego California, USA, 12–17 June 2016, pp. 289–299 (2016). http://aclweb.org/anthology/N/N16/N16-1033.pdf

Training-Less Multi-label Text Classification Using Knowledge Bases and Word Embeddings

Wael Alkhatib[(✉)], Steffen Schnitzer, and Christoph Rensing

Communication Multimedia Lab, TU Darmstadt,
Rundeturmstr. 10, 64283 Darmstadt, Germany
{wael.alkhatib,steffen.schnitzer,christoph.rensing}@kom.tu-darmstadt.de

Abstract. Traditional multi-label text classifiers suffer from the high dimensionality of feature space, label imbalance, and training overhead. In this work, we depart from traditional approaches with intensive feature engineering and linguistic analysis by introducing a novel ontology-based training-less multi-label text classifier. We transform the classification task into a graph matching problem to have a training-less classifier. The experiment results, using the EUR-Lex dataset, proved that our method offers competitive performance with respect to the above-mentioned approaches in terms of $F1_{macro}$ giving fair performance over the different labels despite of the training-less configurations.

Keywords: Semantics · Knowledge base · Ontology · Text classification

1 Introduction

Multi-label text classification is a predictive data mining task which focuses on organizing text documents into several not mutually exclusive categories. Multi-label classification can be accomplished through different strategies namely, method adaptation, data transformation, and the use of ensembles of classifiers. For all methods, text representation is a crucial step in the preprocessing pipeline. Documents have to be transformed into a reduced feature space by building a vector of words as features. Selecting the most representative features of documents largely affects the predictive performance of the classifier. However, there are no rules for deciding what is the best feature selection technique or how many features to be used. Instead, expert knowledge is necessary. In addition, traditional classifiers tend to perform better for more frequent labels. Moreover, multi-label datasets with millions of instances are increasingly common, which makes building and updating the classifiers an extremely tedious and time-consuming process.

In this work, we address these challenges and improve previous research by proposing a novel training-less multi-label text classifier. We shift the classification problem to graph matching problem: the ontology effectively becomes the

© Springer Nature Switzerland AG 2019
C. Douligeris et al. (Eds.): KSEM 2019, LNAI 11776, pp. 97–104, 2019.
https://doi.org/10.1007/978-3-030-29563-9_10

classifier. Thus, we eliminate the need for a pre-trained classifier. The classification process is based on measuring the similarity between ontologies representing the labels and the topics covered in a document. The overall performance of our method is better compared to the baseline in term of $F1_{macro}$ and shows less sensitivity to imbalanced datasets.

2 Proposed Methodology

Some approaches in related work try to use ontologies as classifiers in order to partially address these challenges of feature selection and extraction, label imbalance and training overhead in specific domains [2, 5, 10]. In related work, authors rely on manually built ontologies by domain experts, structured text and predefined categories hierarchy. These assumptions significantly limit the applicability of these methods across other domains where such an ontology or domain experts are not available. In this work, we transform the classification problem into graph matching by relying on a set of automatically generated ontologies.

The main components of an ontology are concepts, the relationships between them, instances and axioms [9]. The proposed approach constitutes of four main parts: The *Domain Ontology*, which is built using the document corpus and a set of existing external knowledge bases. A *Label Ontology* represents the concepts related to a specific label. The *Document Representation Module* converts a text document to a set of topics. Finally, the *Matching Module* converts the classification task into a matching between the topics representing a document and all the label ontologies.

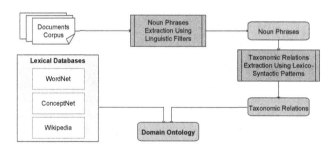

Fig. 1. Workflow of developing the domain ontology in the proposed approach

2.1 Domain Ontology Construction

Figure 1 presents the workflow of developing the domain ontology. The domain ontology consists of concepts describing the domain and different relations between the concepts. In order to build a comprehensive ontology we combine different existing lexical databases, namely *WordNet* [7], *YAGO* [6] and *Concept-Net* [8] to build a basic ontology. The extracted semantic relations from *Wordnet* are namely, *Part-meronym*, *Substance-meronym*, *Synonyms* and *Hyponyms*.

While, the extracted semantic relations from *ConceptNet* and *Yago* are namely, *Hyponyms, Derived-from, Form-of, Has-a, Part-of, Manner-of* and *Synonyms*.

We expand this first ontology by extracting additional taxonomic relations from the document corpus using the six Hearst lexico-syntactic patterns [4]. We crawl new semantic relations from *Wikipedia* and keep relations occurring at least 3 times to guarantee a higher precision of the extracted relations.

2.2   Label Ontology Construction

A label ontology consists of concepts which are related to a single label and relations between these concepts are obtained from the domain ontology. We distinguish between two types of labels, namely *non-concrete labels* and *concrete labels*. *Non-concrete labels* are the labels which are not found in the domain ontology. In order to find representative features for non-concrete labels, statistical-based feature selection methods should be used. We extract noun phrases from the document corpus as the first step. A statistical-based filter is applied after that, in order to select the noun phrases/features which are representative for each of the given labels. There are different approaches to analyze the dependencies between the noun phrases and the labels, namely information gain, information gain ratio, chi-squared statistic, and correlation.

Labels which are found in the domain ontology are called *concrete labels*. The label ontology is a subgraph/sub-ontology of the domain ontology. It is built by adding the relations between the concepts with direct semantic relation to the label in the domain ontology.

Concrete label ontologies and non-concrete label ontologies can be extended by attaching semantically similar concepts using *Word Embeddings*. Word embeddings are numerical vectors that can capture the word semantic and context. This means semantically-related words are close in the vector space. Based on that, the generated word embeddings vectors are used to enrich the ontologies with semantically-similar words. Using Wikipedia, *FastText* [3] model is trained and the generated word vectors are used. We add any concept with high cosine similarity to a concept already in the ontology. We set a hard threshold of 0.9 which reflects words with similar context or meaning.

2.3   Document Representation and Matching Modules

The domain and the label ontologies are created once and used for subsequent classification tasks. The multi-label classification is conducted in two steps: document representation and matching.

A document to which labels are to be assigned might cover one or more topics. Therefore in the document representation step, we select the main topics. Firstly, we extract the noun phrases of a text document using a linguistic filter: $(Adj| Noun) + Noun$.

After that, a weighting technique is triggered to weight each noun phrase. Weighting techniques always aim to give quantitative importance for terms.

Both *Tf-Idf* and Term Frequency *(Tf)* are calculated. The noun phrases are then converted to word vectors using trained *FastText* model. Having the representing vectors, a naive clustering procedure could is applied. The vectors which are similar to each other are clustered together into one set. At this point, each set is considered to be representing one topic of the document.

Then, topic selection methods are applied to rank the topics based on their importance to the document. Topics that are composed of one noun phrase, topics which are not in English and topics including groups of numbers are filtered out. Then, we weight the noun phrases using *Tf-Idf* and *Tf*. To rank the topics we perform the following procedure:

1. The average *Tf-Idf* weight is calculated for all noun phrases of the document.
2. The topics which do not have at least one noun phrase with a weight above the average is removed.
3. The total sum of *Tf-Idf* is calculated for each topic according to the following formula:

$$Imp(Topic) = \sum_{i=1}^{n} Tf - Idf(np_i) \quad where \quad np \in Topic \qquad (1)$$

4. The topics are ranked based on the calculated *Tf-Idf* scores.

Finally, a direct matching process is triggered to match the main topics (set of noun phrases) of the document to each label ontology (concrete or non-concrete). If there are terms which are included in the set of topics and a label ontology, then the label is considered to be a label for the document. How many co-occurrences are necessary is subject of the evaluation.

3   Dataset and Evaluation Settings

We conduct our evaluation on the imbalanced-dataset EUR-Lex [1]. EUR-Lex contains around 19348 documents covering European Union laws, treaties and other public documents. The *Subject-matters* labelling scheme was used here. This scheme includes 201 *labels* with *Label Cardinality* of 2.21 and *Label Density* of 1.10. Figure 2 represents the imbalanced label distribution of the EUR-Lex.

4   Evaluation Results

We conduct several experiments to optimize different configurable parameters of our approach. In addition, we compare the performance against the best performance achieved on this dataset in a previous work using Multi-label K-Nearest-Neighbors (ML-KNN) with semantic-based feature selection [1]. ML-KNN results from the modification of the k Nearest Neighbors (KNN) lazy learning algorithm using a Bayesian approach in order to deal with multi-label classification problems. We further compare the performance with four statistical feature selection techniques using ML-KNN as a classifier. All the experiments have been performed on the full dataset since no training phase is needed.

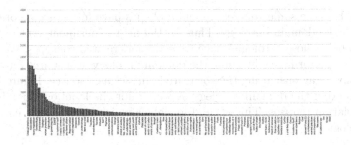

Fig. 2. Distribution of th labelset sizes for the EUR-Lex dataset.

4.1 Correlation Threshold for Non-concrete Labels

Creating ontologies for non-concrete labels requires a statistical measure for feature selection. We have considered four widely used techniques, namely correlation, information gain, chi-squared statistic, and information gain ratio. On one hand, the number of label features based on chi-squared, information gain ratio, information gain is proportional to the label frequency which makes them less favorable for building the ontology of non-concrete labels. Using terms with correlation coefficient of 0.15 or more, we notice that the average number of features representing less-frequent labels compared to the most common labels are similar with a maximum of 63 features per label. For that, the statistical measure used in the following experiments is *Pearson's correlation coefficient*.

4.2 Feature Enrichment for Concrete Label Ontologies

We compare five different combinations of sources for building the ontologies of concrete labels using the *Domain Ontology*, the correlated noun phrases, and the correlated terms. The same settings are applied here. Figure 3 illustrates the performance of the model for different combinations. It shows that using a statistical measure to extract features from the dataset is better than depending on domain ontology, which is contradictory to our assumptions.

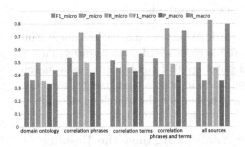

Fig. 3. Using the different combinations of sources for concrete label ontologies.

This is because some concrete label ontologies have few concepts or even no concepts in the domain ontology. Thus, in the next experiment, we consider 13 concrete labels whose ontologies have more than 45 related concepts. We analyze the classifier performance by using the domain ontology as a source for concrete label ontologies against using the correlated phrases as a source. Figure 4 proves that considering the domain ontology as source for the label ontology is better than correlation phrases. This is valid for labels which have enough concepts in their ontologies.

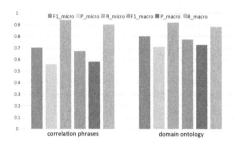

Fig. 4. Using correlation phrases vs domain ontology for features enrichment for concrete label ontologies.

4.3   Number of Topics per Document

After topics extraction, a subset of representative topics should be selected. Using *Tf-Idf* for topics selection, we investigate the performance based on the number of selected topics. The threshold to be defined is the minimal number of topics required to represent a document. Figure 5 illustrates the model performance with regard to the number of selected topics. It is clear that the performance is decreasing by increasing the number of topics representing a document. The best performance reached by using the top 2 topics representing a document which conforms to the *label cardinality* of the dataset.

4.4   Matching Process Analysis

The matching process is done between a topic in a document and a label ontology. We analyse the required percentage of noun phrases in a topic set that should be covered by the label ontology to be considered as a match. Figure 6 illustrates the experimental results. It indicates that using a matching threshold of 5% of the topic set is the best option for the matching decision.

4.5   Comparative Analysis Against the Baseline

Finally, we compare our best approach against ML-KNN with semantic-based approach for feature selection [1] and four statistical feature selection methods,

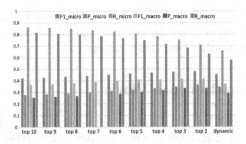

Fig. 5. The performance based on the number of topics representing a document.

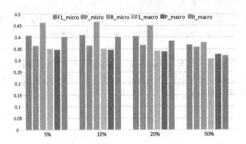

Fig. 6. The performance based on the proportion of noun phrases in a topic set covered by the label ontology.

namely, *information gain, information gain ratio, chi-squared statistic,* and *correlation.* The methods are applied to the documents after stemming and removing the stop words. Also, for ML-KNN, the number of nearest neighbours K=10 is used and the number of features is fixed to 5000 features to align with the baseline.

Table 1. Evaluating our model against the baseline

Model	Features	$F1_{micro}$	$F1_{macro}$
ML-KNN	C-DF [1]	**0.6642**	0.3162
ML-KNN	Info Gain	0.6059	0.3781
ML-KNN	Gain Ratio	0.5993	0.3556
ML-KNN	$Chi-2$	0.6175	0.3845
ML-KNN	Correlation	0.6179	0.3838
Our Classifier	Ontologies	0.5003	**0.4581**

Table 1 summarizes the results. The baseline performs better in terms of $F1_{micro}$ and lower in terms of $F1_{macro}$. This conforms with the fact that traditional classifiers tend to perform better for high frequent labels. Our training-less classifier has a fair performance across all labels with close scores for both metrics. It outperforms the best performance on the EUR-Lex dataset in terms of $F1_{macro}$ despite the training-less configurations.

5   Conclusion and Future Work

Ontology-based training-less text classifiers can overcome the challenges of label imbalance in traditional methods. Our approach solely relies on developing a domain ontology to be used as a training-less classifier without a pre-classified set of training documents. Our intensive experiments proved that our method significantly outperforms the baseline in terms of $F1_{macro}$. More work can be done in the area of building the domain ontology by integrating more lexical resources to improve the ontology coverage with regard to the labels set.

Acknowledgment. This work has been co-funded by the German Federal Ministry of Education and Research (BMBF) within in the framework of the Software Campus project "PIOBRec" [01IS17050].

References

1. Alkhatib, W., Rensing, C., Silberbauer, J.: Multi-label text classification using semantic features and dimensionality reduction with autoencoders. In: Gracia, J., Bond, F., McCrae, J.P., Buitelaar, P., Chiarcos, C., Hellmann, S. (eds.) LDK 2017. LNCS (LNAI), vol. 10318, pp. 380–394. Springer, Cham (2017). https://doi.org/10.1007/978-3-319-59888-8_32
2. Alkhatib, W., Sabrin, S., Neitzel, S., Rensing, C.: Towards ontology-based training-less multi-label text classification. In: Silberztein, M., Atigui, F., Kornyshova, E., Métais, E., Meziane, F. (eds.) NLDB 2018. LNCS, vol. 10859, pp. 389–396. Springer, Cham (2018). https://doi.org/10.1007/978-3-319-91947-8_40
3. Bojanowski, P., Grave, E., Joulin, A., Mikolov, T.: Enriching word vectors with subword information. arXiv preprint arXiv:1607.04606 (2016)
4. Hearst, M.A.: Automatic acquisition of hyponyms from large text corpora. In: Proceedings of the 14th conference on Computational linguistics-Volume 2, pp. 539–545. Association for Computational Linguistics (1992)
5. Janik, M.G.: Training-less ontology-based text categorization. Ph.D. thesis, UGA (2008)
6. Mahdisoltani, F., Biega, J., Suchanek, F.: Yago3: a knowledge base from multilingual wikipedias. In: 7th Biennial Conference on Innovative Data Systems Research, CIDR Conference (2014)
7. Miller, G.A.: WordNet: a lexical database for english. Commun. ACM **38**(11), 39–41 (1995)
8. Speer, R., Havasi, C.: Representing general relational knowledge in ConceptNet 5. In: LREC, pp. 3679–3686 (2012)
9. Uschold, M., King, M., Moralee, S., Zorgios, Y.: The enterprise ontology. Knowl. Eng. Rev. **13**(1), 31–89 (1998)
10. Zhou, P., El-Gohary, N.: Ontology-based multilabel text classification of construction regulatory documents. J. Comput. Civil Eng. **30**(4), 04015058 (2015)

Text-Based Fusion Neural Network for Rumor Detection

Yixuan Chen, Liang Hu, and Jie Sui$^{(\boxtimes)}$

University of Chinese Academy of Sciences, Beijing, China
suijie@ucas.ac.cn

Abstract. Rumor detection is a very challenging and urgent issue. Text is the most fundamental and significant owing to its high usability and accessibility. In this paper, we propose a fusion neural network based on the text for rumor detection, which is called Text-based Fusion Neural Network (T-FNN). For accurately extracting contextual features, we present a new data processing algorithm, and construct a fusion neural network including bi-directional gated recurrent unit, convolutional model, and attention mechanism. Experimental results on two real-life datasets show that our proposed T-FNN has much better performance than other text-based state-of-art models on rumor detection.

Keywords: Rumor detection · Textual feature ·
Convolution neural network · Recurrent neural network

1 Introduction

In order to minimize the rumor's negative influence, it is important to detect rumors accurately. Compared to an individual microblog, a collection composed of multiple conflicting microblogs contains more information. Thus, we focus on the event-level rumor detection problem, where microblogs are seen as time series. For rumor detection, some study focused on text-based neural network to produce detection results [1–3]. But their rumor detection accuracies are limited by the use of content properties. Some works contributed to integrate multiple features to improve accuracy of rumor detection task. Guo et al. [4] proposed a hierarchical social attention network, combining social signals via attention mechanism. However, multiple features can not be easily obtained.

In this paper, we propose a model based on text to verify debunking rumors. First, we present a new data processing algorithm, which computes content vector by using unweighted averaging operation, and evenly distributes all posts of an event over multiple time intervals. Second, we propose a fusion neural network model. In detail, we apply CNN based on processed data to calculate local correlation of several posts in an event. Then, we pose a BiGRU layer to learn temporal and structure informations in order to obtain global features. Based on the global feature, we apply an attention layer to selectively learn important feature.

© Springer Nature Switzerland AG 2019
C. Douligeris et al. (Eds.): KSEM 2019, LNAI 11776, pp. 105–109, 2019.
https://doi.org/10.1007/978-3-030-29563-9_11

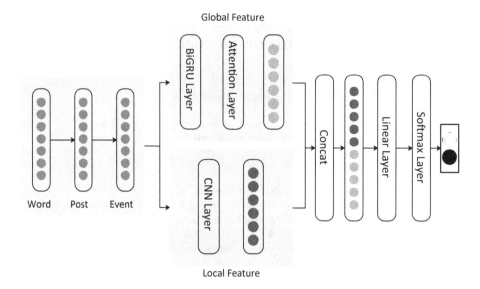

Fig. 1. The overall architecture of proposed framework

The contributions of this paper can be summarized as follows:

1. We propose a text-based fusion neural network to rumor detection by deeply exploiting use of global and local textual features. Besides, the data processing part is especially efficient.
2. Experiment evaluations on two real world datasets Weibo and Twitter demonstrate T-FNN has a good performance on rumor detection.

2 Methodology

The overall architecture of T-FNN is shown in Fig. 1. We define the event set is $E = \{E_i\}$, where $E_i = \{p_{i,j}\}$ is a specific event composed of all related posts $p_{i,j}$. And each post $p_{i,j}$ contains variable count of m word $p_{i,j} = \{w_{i,j}^m\}$. We build a classification model to learn a projection $F(E) \to (1, 0)$, where 1 and 0 denote rumor class label and non-rumor class label, respectively.

2.1 Data Processing

First, we define that the number of time intervals N is fixed, which is input sequence length of our model. Next we distribute an event's cleaned posts evenly over all time intervals. Then, we apply pre-trained word embedding vector with dimension D to represent word. To compute posts sentence, we operate unweighted average on word, which presented by pre-trained word embeddings.

2.2 Convolutional Model

In the convolution model, input matrix is subjected to a filter $f \in \mathbb{R}^{Y \times D}$ with a window size of Y to capture local correlation. The stride of a filter is set to 1 by default. For instance, a new feature $FM \in \mathbb{R}^{C \times N-Y+1}$ extracted by a filter f follows can be computed as $FM = ReLU\left(f[iv_1, iv_2, \ldots, iv_N] + b\right)$. Where $FM \in \mathbb{R}^{C \times N-Y+1}$ is the local feature matrix extracted by the filter f, C is the number of channels in f. Next we perform maxpooling operation on the FM sequence to preserve the most important features $\widehat{FM} \in \mathbb{R}^C = max\left(FM\right)$, while reducing the dimension of the parameters.

In order to obtain a variety of features, we select multiple filters with different window size. Finally, the convolution model output matrix $MultiFM$ of all local correlations computed by concatenating all individual features: $MultiFM = concat\left(\widehat{FM}_1, \widehat{FM}_2, \cdots, \widehat{FM}_m\right)$. Here m is the number of filters. The details of convolutional model is shown in Fig. 2(a).

2.3 BiGRU

BiGRU is capable to capture the trend changes in the process of event development, and learn the complex interaction between posts. Bidirectional GRU(BiGRU) takes advantage in possessing data by combining forward hidden state and backward hidden state to capture more efficient context representations.

2.4 Attention Mechanism

In order to alleviate negligible noisy and select significant posts, we apply attention mechanism to give a large weight to relatively important information. As shown in Fig. 2(b), we adapt attention operation over a set of queries Q, simultaneously the input includes keys and values, which are packed into matrix K and V, respectively. The attention layer output will be computed as: $Attention\left(Q, K, V\right) = softmax\left(\frac{QK^T}{\sqrt{d_k}}\right)V$.

2.5 Pipeline

First, we propose CNN to capture local correlations between each interval based on initial data. Second, we build BiGRU combined with attention model to selectively preserve global properties. The two output feature matrix are then concatenate as the final context representation matrix. The classifier contains a full connected layer and a softmax layer to detect whether an event is a rumor or not.

3 Experiments

3.1 Dataset

In order to validate performance of our model, we possess public datasets [1] that have been used in previous work, including Weibo and Twitter. In experiments, each dataset is randomly assigned in a 4 : 1 ratio for training and testing.

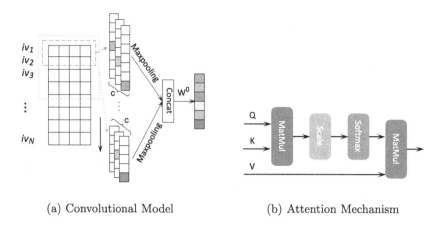

(a) Convolutional Model   (b) Attention Mechanism

Fig. 2. Architecture of convolutional model and attention mechanism

Table 1. Performance comparison on two datasets: Weibo (top) and Twitter (bottom).

Dataset	Method	Accuracy	Rumor			Non rumor		
			Precision	Recall	F-1	Precision	Recall	F-1
Weibo	ML-GRU	0.862	0.858	0.864	0.861	0.865	0.860	0.863
	CallAtRumor	0.887	0.918	0.847	0.881	0.860	0.926	0.892
	HSA	0.943	0.946	0.940	0.943	0.941	**0.947**	0.944
	T-FNN	**0.949**	**0.956**	0.940	**0.948**	0.958	0.943	**0.951**
Twitter	ML-GRU	0.784	0.870	0.670	0.757	0.730	0.899	0.805
	CallAtRumor	0.804	0.821	0.780	0.800	0.789	0.828	0.808
	HSA	0.844	**0.948**	0.730	0.825	0.779	**0.960**	**0.863**
	T-FNN	**0.870**	0.847	**0.926**	**0.885**	**0.902**	0.804	0.851

3.2 Models for Comparison

The models used in comparison experiments are as follows:

- ML-GRU [1] uses GRU to learn text representation for rumor detection.
- CallAtRumor [2] combines BiLSTM with attention model.
- HSA [4] proposes a hierarchical LSTM network combining text features with social information.
- T-FNN is the proposed text-based fusion neural network.

3.3 Performance Comparison

Table 1 shows the performance of all comparison methods with details. We observe that T-FNN outperforms all other methods on two different datasets. The rumor detection accuracy on Weibo and Twitter datasets reach 94.9% and

87.0%, respectively. It is proved that the model we propose has a good applicability to different types of online social network dataset via the modeling of strengthening textual feature representations.

Compared to two text-based methods ML-GRU and CallAtRumor, T-FNN outperforms by a large margin, demonstrating that T-FNN can learn powerful representation of textual features. HSA outperforms other baselines, the phenomena demonstrates multi-modal fusion features can improve accuracy. Compared to the complex model, T-FNN also shows good performance on two datasets. This result proves a good applicability to different datasets and the competitiveness in rumor detection task.

4   Conclusions

In this article, we proposed a fusion neural network based on text for rumor detection. Unlike many other multimodal features fusion model, we adapted multiple layers to exploit the use of discourse properties. Experiments on two datasets prove that proposed model (T-FNN) is significantly superior to other text-based models, and competitive to complex models combining with fusion features.

Acknowledgment. This work is supported by The National Key Research and Development Program of China (Grant No. 2017YFB0803001) and The National Natural Science Foundation of China (Grant No. 61572459).

References

1. Ma, J., et al.: Detecting rumors from microblogs with recurrent neural networks. In: IJCAI, pp. 3818–3824 (2016)
2. Chen, T., Li, X., Yin, H., Zhang, J.: Call attention to rumors: deep attention based recurrent neural networks for early rumor detection. In: Ganji, M., Rashidi, L., Fung, B.C.M., Wang, C. (eds.) PAKDD 2018. LNCS (LNAI), vol. 11154, pp. 40–52. Springer, Cham (2018). https://doi.org/10.1007/978-3-030-04503-6_4
3. Liu, Q., Yu, F., Wu, S., Wang, L.: Mining significant microblogs for misinformation identification: an attention-based approach. ACM Trans. Intell. Syst. Technol. (TIST) **9**(5), 50 (2018)
4. Guo, H., Cao, J., Zhang, Y., Guo, J., Li, J.: Rumor detection with hierarchical social attention network. In: Proceedings of the 27th ACM International Conference on Information and Knowledge Management, pp. 943–951. ACM (2018)

Text to Image Synthesis Using Two-Stage Generation and Two-Stage Discrimination

Zhiqiang Zhang[1], Yunye Zhang[1], Wenxin Yu[1(✉)], Gang He[1], Ning Jiang[1], Gang He[2], Yibo Fan[3], and Zhuo Yang[4]

[1] Southwest University of Science and Technology, Mianyang, China
zzq.zhangzhiqiang2018@gmail.com, yuwenxin@swust.edu.cn,
star_yuwenxin27@163.com
[2] Xidian University, Xi'an, China
[3] State Key Laboratory of ASIC and System, Fudan University, Shanghai, China
[4] Guangdong University of Technology, Guangzhou, China

Abstract. In this paper, the method of two-stage generation and two-stage discrimination (2G2D) is proposed to generate high-resolution and more realistic images. It is a simple but effective way to synthesize images based on text descriptions. Our method generates the refined foreground image in the first stage, and then combines the text description to generate the final high-resolution image in second stage. We demonstrate the performance of the proposed method on the Caltech-UCSD Birds (CUB) dataset. Through the experimental results, our model can improve the resolution and the authenticity of content of the synthetic image better than the existing state-of-the-art methods.

Keywords: Deep learning · Generative Adversarial Networks · Computer vision · Image synthesis

1 Introduction

In computer vision, the field of text-to-image synthesis has received more and more attention and has enormous potential applications, such as computer-aided design and image editing.

Using text descriptions to generate images is more flexible than using image attributes such as category labels, and is more conform with people's usage habits. Recently, Reed et al. [1] successfully implemented the synthesis from text description to image using Generative Adversarial Networks (GAN) [2]. The results are highly consistent with the text description. However, the corresponding resolution of the result is not high. In order to improve the resolution, [3] and [4] proposed StackGAN and AttnGAN respectively to generate high-resolution results. Their results have been greatly improved in resolution, but there is still a certain gap compared with real images.

In order to further approximate the real image, the method of two-stage generation and two-stage discrimination (2G2D) is proposed. The refined foreground image is generated in the first stage and the final image is generated

© Springer Nature Switzerland AG 2019
C. Douligeris et al. (Eds.): KSEM 2019, LNAI 11776, pp. 110–114, 2019.
https://doi.org/10.1007/978-3-030-29563-9_12

in the second stage. Since the first stage does not need to generate background information, it can focus more on generating foreground information, so that the refined foreground image is obtained. Then the refined foreground image is combined with the corresponding text description to generate final result. The task of second stage is simple, it only needs to add background information and further modify the defects in the first stage. Through the adjustment of the second stage, the high-resolution and more realistic image can be finally obtained.

The rest of this paper is arranged as follows. The preliminary work and the detail content of our method are presented in Sect. 2. The experimental results are shown in Sect. 3. Section 4 concludes our work.

2   Our Method

2.1   First Stage

In the first stage, it can generate refined foreground image by using foreground images in the discriminator. For the acquisition of foreground images, we first download binary images from the official website. By comparing the binary image with the original image, the area of original image corresponding to the background area of binary image are converted to white. In this way, the refined foreground images are obtained. The structure of the first stage is shown in Fig. 1. This structure trains G and D primarily by minimizing G_{loss1} and D_{loss1}.

$$G_{loss1} = \sum_{z \sim P_{Z(z)}} [\log(1 - D_1(G_1(z, \phi(t))))] \tag{1}$$

$$D_{loss1} = \sum_{z \sim P_{sample(x)}} \log[D_1(x, \varphi(t))] + \sum_{z \sim P_{Z(z)}} [\log(1 - D_1(G_1(z, \varphi(t))))] \tag{2}$$

where $\varphi(t)$ denotes the encoded text vector, G_1 and D_1 denotes the generator and discriminator in the first stage, respectively.

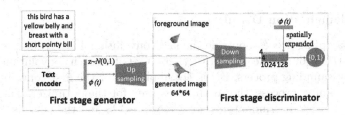

Fig. 1. The generator and discriminator structure of the first stage.

In the generator, the text description is first encoded into a text vector, and then combined with the noise vector to generate the fake image by up-sampling. The operation of up-sampling is mainly performed by de-convolution [5]. In the discriminator, the received images are primarily down-sampling and then combined with the spatially expanded text vector to produce the decision score through a convolution layer and a full connected layer.

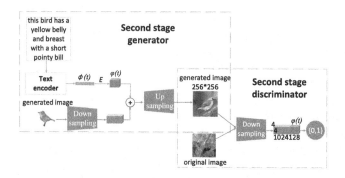

Fig. 2. The generator and discriminator structure of the second stage.

2.2   Second Stage

The structure of the second stage is shown in Fig. 2. This structure trains G and D primarily by minimizing G_{loss2} and D_{loss2}.

$$G_{loss2} = \sum_{f \sim P_{G_1}} [\log(1 - D_2(G_2(f, \varphi(t))))] \tag{3}$$

$$D_{loss2} = \sum_{x \sim P_{sample(x)}} [\log D_2(x, \varphi(t))] + \sum_{f \sim P_{G_1}} [\log(1 - D_2(G_2(f, \varphi(t))))] \tag{4}$$

where f denotes the fake image generated in the first stage, G_2 and D_2 denotes the generator and discriminator in the second stage, respectively.

In the generator, while the text is encoded, the result of the first stage corresponding to the input text is down-sampled. Then the down-sampling result is combined with the spatially expanded text vector to generate the fake image of the second stage by up-sampling. The discriminator operation of the second stage is identical to the first stage.

2.3   Implementation Details

In the up-sampling process, outside the last convolutional layer, the Batch Normalization (BN) [6] and Leaky-ReLU [7] are used after each convolutional layer. In the down-sampling process, BN is not applied after the first convolution.

In the training process, the Adam [8] is used for the optimizer. The dimensions of generator, discriminator, text vector are 128 and the noise is 100. The value of Batch Size is 64 and the initial learning rate is 0.0002. In this work, 600 epochs are required at each stage.

3   Experiments

We validate the effectiveness of our method on the CUB dataset [9]. The CUB dataset contains 11,788 bird images and 200 categories. Each image has 10 corresponding text descriptions. In the experiment, the CUB dataset is split to 150 train classes and 50 test classes.

Fig. 3. The results of compared with the GAN-CLS-INT, AttnGAN and StackGAN.

3.1 Comparison Results and Generalization Results

Our method is compared with GAN-CLS-INT [1], StackGAN [3] and AttnGAN [4], which are the previous state-of-the-art text-to-image synthesis methods. The compared results are shown in Fig. 3. The resolution of the results of GAN-CLS-INT is look bad. In contrast, the resolution of the results of AttnGAN has been improved a lot. But there are many deficiencies in the content, which make the results unreal. The results of StackGAN are good in resolution and content, but there is still some certain distance from the real image. Compared with them, our results are significantly better than GAN-CLS-INT, are better than AttnGAN in terms of content, and are closer to real images than StackGAN. It performs best in detail and content.

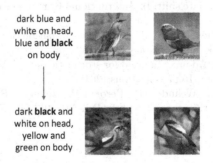

Fig. 4. The demonstration of generalization results (Change the color words).

The results of generalization are shown in Fig. 4. Figure 4 shows the comparison after changing some words (such as color). These results show the universality of the model.

4   Conclusion

In this paper, a novel text-to-image synthesis (2G2D) method is proposed, which promotes the generation of high-resolution and more authentic images in the second stage by generating the refined foreground in the first stage. The experiment results show that the effective and generalization of our method in details and content. Our results are closest to the real image and almost as same as the real.

Acknowledgement. This research was supported by 2018GZ0517, 2019YFS0146, 2019YFS0155 which supported by Sichuan Provincial Science and Technology Department, 2018KF003 Supported by State Key Laboratory of ASIC & System, Science and Technology Planning Project of Guangdong Province 2017B010110007.

References

1. Reed, S., Akata, Z., Yan, X., Logeswaran, L., Schiels, B., Lee, H.: Generative adversarial text-to-image synthesis. In: International Conference on Machine Learning, pp. 1060–1069 (2016)
2. Goodfellow, I.J., et al.: Generative adversarial nets. In: Advances in Neural Information Processing Systems, pp. 2672–2680 (2014)
3. Zhang, H., et al.: StackGAN: text to photo-realistic image synthesis with stacked generative adversarial networks. In: International Conference on Computer Vision, pp. 5908–5916 (2017)
4. Xu, T., et al.: AttnGAN: fine-grained text to image generation with attention generative adversarial networks. In: Computer Vision and Pattern Recognition, pp. 1316–1324 (2018)
5. Zeiler, M.D., Fergus, R.: Visualizing and understanding convolutional networks. In: Fleet, D., Pajdla, T., Schiele, B., Tuytelaars, T. (eds.) ECCV 2014. LNCS, vol. 8689, pp. 818–833. Springer, Cham (2014). https://doi.org/10.1007/978-3-319-10590-1_53
6. Ioffe, S., Szegedy, C.: Batch normalization: accelerating deep network training by reducing internal covariate shift. In: International Conference on Machine Learning, pp. 448–456 (2015)
7. Xu, B., Wang, N., Chen, T., Li, M.: Empirical evaluation of rectified activations in convolutional network. abs/1505.00853 (2015)
8. Kingma, D.P., Ba, J.: Adam: a method for stochastic optimization. In: International Conference on Learning Representations (2015)
9. Wah, C., Branson, S., Welinder, P., Perona, P., Belongie, S.: The caltech-UCSD birds-200-2011 dataset. Technical report CNS-TR-2011-001, California Institute of Technology (2011)

Word Embeddings for Unsupervised Named Entity Linking

Debora Nozza[(✉)] ⓘ, Cezar Sas ⓘ, Elisabetta Fersini ⓘ, and Enza Messina ⓘ

University of Milano - Bicocca, Milan, Italy
{debora.nozza,elisabetta.fersini,enza.messina}@unimib.it,
c.sas@campus.unimib.it

Abstract. The huge amount of textual user-generated content on the Web has incredibly grown in the last decade, creating new relevant opportunities for different real-world applications and domains. In particular, microblogging platforms enables the collection of continuously and instantly updated information. The organization and extraction of valuable knowledge from these contents are fundamental for ensuring profitability and efficiency to companies and institutions. This paper presents an unsupervised model for the task of Named Entity Linking in microblogging environments. The aim is to link the named entity mentions in a text with their corresponding knowledge-base entries exploiting a novel heterogeneous representation space characterized by more meaningful similarity measures between words and named entities, obtained by Word Embeddings. The proposed model has been evaluated on different benchmark datasets proposed for Named Entity Linking challenges for English and Italian language. It obtains very promising performance given the highly challenging environment of user-generated content over microblogging platforms.

Keywords: Word Embeddings · Named Entity Linking · Social media

1 Introduction

With the continuous and fast evolution of the Internet and the advent of Social-Web, or Web 2.0, the amount of unstructured textual data produced by the social interactions between people has become an immense hidden treasure of knowledge [26]. Organizing and extracting valuable information from these data has become an important issue both for companies and institutions to ensure maximum profits and efficiency. In this context, the task of Information Extraction, and in particular Named Entity Linking, can provide a crucial advantage on automatically derive structured meaningful information from large collection of textual data.

Named-Entity Linking (NEL) is the task of determining the identity of entities mentioned in a textual document, that are usually extracted in the Named Entity Recognition (NER) task phase. NEL can be of great importance

© Springer Nature Switzerland AG 2019
C. Douligeris et al. (Eds.): KSEM 2019, LNAI 11776, pp. 115–132, 2019.
https://doi.org/10.1007/978-3-030-29563-9_13

in many fields: it can be used by search engines for disambiguating multiple-meanings entities in indexed documents or for improving queries precision, as named entities are averagely present in 70% of cases [29]. NEL systems can also be used in combination with other Natural Language Processing systems, such as Sentiment Analysis, for the generation of additional knowledge to describe users preferences towards companies, politicians, and so on.

The common NEL process typically requires annotating a potentially ambiguous entity mention with a link to global identifiers with unambiguous denotation, such as Uniform Resource Identifier (URI) in Knowledge Bases (KBs), describing the entity. A popular choice for the KB is Wikipedia, in which each page is considered as a named entity, or DBpedia, which is used as structured background knowledge in many NEL systems [2,8,10,16–18,21,25,43,44]. An example of a sentence processed for the Named Entity Linking task is shown in Fig. 1. In this example, it is possible to notice that the mention *@EmmaWatson* is correctly linked to the actress. A more difficult case regards the word *hermione*, since it can assume very different meanings, e.g. the name of an autobiographical novel, a common given name or the character of the movie Harry Potter.

Traditionally, Information Extraction studies has been successfully investigated on well-formed text, such as news or scientific publications [13,19,30,31]. Recently, a large number of studies focused on user-generated content as source data, in particular messages originated from users in micro-blogging platforms such as Twitter [2,5,12,22,33]. Due to its dynamic and informal nature, Twitter provides its users an easy way to express themselves and communicate thoughts and opinions in a highly colloquial way. This, in addition to the limitation of characters, induces the users to use abbreviations, slangs, and made-up words increasing the difficulty in recognizing and disambiguating the involved named entities. The achievement of obtaining results for social media content equally accurate to the ones on well-written text is still a long way off [9].

Fig. 1. Example of a sentence processed by Named Entity Linking.

In order to address the issues on dealing with a micro-blogging environment, we propose a model for the exploitation of Named Entity Linking task in unsupervised settings for noisy social media texts, called *UNIMIB-WE*. The proposed model first investigates the contribution of ad-hoc preprocessing techniques for noisy text from social media, then it makes use of Word Embeddings to better deal with new emerging named entities and commonly used slangs and abbreviations. Moreover, it is expected that the use of Word Embeddings will improve the semantic similarity of the words comprising the named entities and the corresponding entries in the KB. By using the joint representation obtained with Word Embeddings models, the similarity measure will gain on semantic expressiveness resulting in a more accurate discrimination of the entities and coverage as it has been preliminary shown in [6].

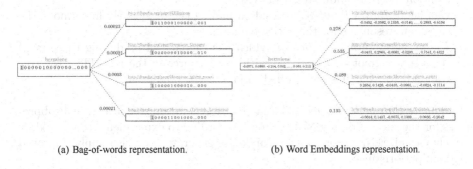

(a) Bag-of-words representation.   (b) Word Embeddings representation.

Fig. 2. Example of Named Entity Linking similarity computation.

In order to demonstrate the advantage of employing Word Embeddings as word representation models, let us consider the tweet "@EmmaWatson no1 can play hermione better than u" and in particular the case of linking the entity mention "hermione". This ambiguous named entity must be disambiguated and consequently associated with several possible unambiguous entity candidates (e.g. with respect to DBpedia), comprising the correct one, i.e. the character of Hermione Granger. Figure 2 reports two possible scheme representations, one using the popular bag-of-words textual representation and the other using the more meaningful textual distributional representation of Word Embeddings. The numbers in the boxes represent the numerical vector representation associated with the text, i.e. the tweet text on the left and the textual description of the candidate KB resources on the right. The use of bag-of-words representation has been reported in Fig. 2(a), highlighting in light blue the presence (1) of the word "hermione" in each box. It is possible to note that the bag-of-words representation is very sparse, resulting in a low representative similarity measure which corresponds to 0.00021 with respect to the correct KB resource. Otherwise, the representation derived from Word Embeddings (Fig. 2(b)) permits to correctly rank as first the correct KB resource (*Hermione Granger*) with a similarity score of 0.535, as it provides a metric that better expresses the semantic properties for words and entities and consequently the similarity between them.

Following, Sect. 2 provides an overview of the state of the art approaches. Then, the proposed model for the exploitation of Word Embeddings representation is described in Sect. 3. Section 4 describes the developed framework, giving an overview of all the module components. The evaluation results on three benchmark datasets on different languages are reported in Sect. 5.

2   Related Works

The state of the art approaches in NEL can be mainly distinguished considering the specific task that they are addressing [36]:

- *Candidate Entity Generation*, which is aimed at extracting for each entity mention a set of candidates resources;
- *Candidate Entity Ranking*, focused on finding the most likely link among the candidate resources for the entity mention.
- *Unlinkable Mention Prediction*, which has the goal of predicting those mentions that cannot be associated with any resource in the KB. This step corresponds to what has been called so far as NIL prediction.

Candidate Entity Generation. The candidate generation step is a critical subprocess for the success of any NEL system. According to experiments conducted by Hachey et al. [17], a more precise candidate generator can also imply improved linking performance.

In the literature, candidate generation techniques can be mainly distinguished in Name Dictionary and Search Engine based methods. The former consists in constructing a dictionary-based structure where one or more KB resources are associated with a given named entity (dictionary key) based on some useful features available in the KB, such as redirect pages, disambiguation pages, bold phrases, etc. [10,43,44]. Given an entity mention extracted from text, the set of its candidate entities is obtained by using exact matching or partial matching with the corresponding dictionary keys [40]. An alternative solution for Candidate Entity Generation is represented by Search Engine based techniques, which make use of Web search engines for retrieving the list of candidate resources associated with an entity mention [18,21,25].

Candidate Entity Ranking. After the candidates' extraction, the list of candidates should be ranked in order to extract the most probable one. Most of the approaches are mainly based on Machine Learning algorithms for learning how to rank the candidate entities [2,8,16,19]. These approaches usually consider several features related to the named entity or the KB entry, such as *entity popularity*, the *ontology type* extracted by NER systems and vector-based representation of the context surrounding the named entity. Beyond Machine Learning models, it has also been proved that the combination of multiple features can be useful for ranking the mention candidates [5].

Unlinkable Mention Prediction. An entity mention does not always have a corresponding entity in the KB, therefore systems have to deal with the problem of predicting NIL entities (unlinkable mentions). Some approaches [8] use a simple heuristic to predict unlinkable entity mentions: if it is not possible to retrieve any candidate for an entity mention, then the entity mention is unlinkable. Many NEL systems are based on a threshold method to predict the unlinkable entity mention [4,11,14,28,37,38]. In these systems, each ranked candidate is associated to a confidence score and if the score is lower than a given threshold, then the entity mention is considered a NIL. The NIL prediction can be also accomplished using approaches based on supervised Machine Learning, such as binary classification techniques [32,44].

As stated above, the candidate generation is a crucial part for any NEL task. The process of generating the candidate resource set for a given entity mention is usually obtained by exact or partial matching between the entity mention and the labels of all the resources in the KB. However, these approaches can be error-prone, especially when dealing with microblog posts that are rich in misspellings, abbreviations, nicknames and other noisy forms of text. In order to deal with these issues, the proposed NEL approach has been defined for taking into account specific preprocessing techniques for this data and subsequently exploit a similarity measure between the high-level representation of entity mentions and KB resources. These meaningful and dense representation of entity mentions and KB resources has been obtained by taking advantage of one of the most widely used neural network language models, i.e. Word Embeddings [23].

3   Representation and Linking Model

The task of Named Entity Linking (NEL) is defined as associating an entity mention $t_i \in T$, with an appropriate KB candidate resource $k_j \in K \subset \Omega$, where $K = \{k_1, k_2, \cdots, k_{n_k}\}$ is a set of candidate resources selected from the complete set of KB resources Ω.

The main contribution consists in creating a Word Embeddings model that is able to learn a heterogeneous representation space where similarities between KB resources and named entities can be compared. In particular, given a Word Embeddings training set composed of a large but finite set of words denoting a vocabulary V and the set Ω of KB resources, the Word Embeddings model can be expressed as a mapping (or embedding) function $C : \Gamma \to \mathbb{R}^m$ with $\Gamma = V \cup \Omega$. Therefore, the embedding function is trained on a heterogeneous space of KB resources and words, ensuring that the embedded representation will be inferred from the same Word Embeddings model. More details about the training process of this heterogeneous space Word Embeddings are given in Sect. 5.

Given an entity mention t_i and a KB resource k_j, the similarity function s_C can be written as:

$$s_C(t_i, k_j) = sim(C(t_i), C(k_j)), \tag{1}$$

where sim is a similarity function, e.g. cosine similarity. The candidate resource set K for t_i is then obtained by taking the top-n_k KB resources ranked by the similarity score $s_C(t_i, k_j)$. The predicted KB resource k^* is then the k_j with the highest similarity score. If K is an empty set, t_i is considered as a NIL entity.

This can be generalized in the case of a multi-word entity, i.e. entities composed by two or more words in a vocabulary $w \in V$, defined as $t_i = \{w_1^i, \ldots, w_n^i\}$. Since words can be considered as point in an m-dimensional feature space, the top-n_k similar KB resources will be the set K that maximizes the sum of the similarities between k_j and all the entity mention words.

4   Experimental Settings

For performing the experiments, the *UNIMIB-WE* system proposed in Fig. 3 has been implemented, starting from the input named entities (extracted by a NER system from user-generated content) to the output (KB resources). Following, each module of the pipeline is described for a broader understanding.

4.1   Model Training

In order to obtain a Word Embeddings model able to map both words and KB resources in the same representation space, its training process has been performed over a corpus that comprises both of them. For this reason, a dump of Wikipedia has been considered as the training set. The structure of a Wikipedia article fits well the model's needs since a named entity can be directly associated with the corresponding Wikipedia article title. The following snippet reports a sentence from the Wikipedia page of Harry Potter and the Philosopher's Stone related to the character of Hermione Granger.

"... he quickly befriends fellow first-year Ronald Weasley and Hermione Granger ..."

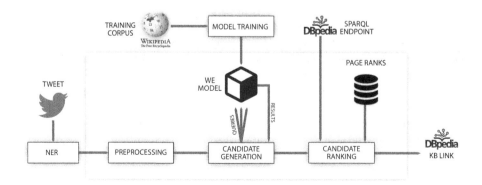

Fig. 3. Pipeline of the proposed *UNIMIB-WE* Named Entity Linking framework.

In this sentence it is possible to identify two named entities (Ronald Weasley and Hermione Granger) that, thanks to the favorable article structure, are represented as a link to their Wikipedia articles which corresponds to https://en.wikipedia.org/wiki/Ron_Weasley and https://en.wikipedia.org/wiki/ Hermione_Granger respectively. The training corpus is then obtained by merging and processing all the Wikipedia articles by specifically identifying each KB resources with the tag "KB_ID/" that corresponds to the article links (e.g. "KB_ID/Hermione_Granger"). After this process, the previous sentence will result as:

"... he quickly befriends fellow first-year *KB_ID/Ron_Weasley* and
KB_ID/Hermione_Granger ..."

Then, the Skip-Gram model [23] has been used as effective Word Embeddings model for learning the function $C : \Gamma \rightarrow \mathbb{R}^m$.

Given a sequence $s_1, \ldots, s_{n_T}$ such that $s_i \in \Gamma$, containing words and KB resources, the objective function of the Skip-gram model is defined as:

$$\mathcal{L}_{Skip-gram} = \frac{1}{n_T} \sum_{i=1}^{n_T} \sum_{-k \leq j \leq k, j \neq 0} \log P(s_{i+j} \mid s_i) \tag{2}$$

where $s_i \in \{s_1, \ldots, s_{n_T}\}$ and n_T is the sequence length.

Given the large amount of data comprised in the Wikipedia dump, the processing and the learning process of the Skip-Gram model have been performed using the efficient Wiki2Vec tool [41], a software developed using Scala, Hadoop, and Spark that processes a large amount of text and makes it usable for our requirements. It is important to mention that, given the large amount of publicly available information particularly suitable for the proposed model, Wikipedia has been used for training the Word Embeddings model. Analogously to what has been done in numerous studies and organized challenges in the state of the art [34, 35], DBpedia has been used as structured background knowledge for the the Named Entity Linking process. Nevertheless, since DBpedia is a a large-scale Knowledge Base built by extracting structured data from Wikipedia [20], there is a correspondence between the entities included in these two KBs.

4.2   Preprocessing

Since the input entity mention is originated from a microblog post, it is expected to increase the number of correctly linked named entities by performing textual preprocessing because of its noisy nature. Common preprocessing involves capitalization solving and typographical error correction, such as missing spaces or wrong word separators. Moreover, for improving the retrieval performance, some query expansion techniques have been adopted, i.e. appending the "KB_ID/" token before the named entity.

4.3 Candidates Generation, Ranking and NIL Prediction

As presented in Sect. 3, the candidate generation process is performed by computing a similarity measure between the entity mention t_i and all the words or resources present in the Word Embeddings training set. As for any NNLM, the fundamental property is that semantically similar words have a similar vector representation. Given an entity mention t_i, the model returns the candidate resource set K composed of the top-n_k similar KB resources or words ranked by the similarity measure s_C, from which only the KB resources k_j are extracted. The candidate resource set can be further reduced by considering the ontology type initially inferred by a given NER model. In particular, this reduction has been performed by considering only the KB resources k_j that have the same ontology type of the named entity t_i. While the ontology type of k_j can be obtained by querying the Knowledge Base, the one of t_i can be inferred with a given NER model[1]. Finally, the candidate k^* that has the highest similarity score compared to the entity t_i is selected as the predicted KB resource.

In the proposed system, an entity mention t_i has been considered as a NIL entity, if either the similarity between t_i and the predicted resource k^* is lower than a threshold or t_i is not present in the Word Embeddings training set.

5 Experimental Results

This section discusses the datasets and the performance measures involved in the evaluation of the proposed NEL system.

5.1 Datasets

The datasets adopted for the system evaluation are three benchmark datasets of microblog posts that have been made available for different Named Entity Recognition and Linking Challenges. The #Microposts2015 and #Microposts2016 datasets have been divulgated by the Making Sense of Microposts challenge [34,35]. Moreover, a dataset of Twitter posts in the Italian language, as promoted by the NEEL-IT challenge organized by EVALITA [1,3], has been considered. In this study, all the datasets provided by the challenges (i.e. Training, Test, Dev) have been used to perform the evaluation.

In Table 1, several statistics for both English and Italian micropost challenge datasets are reported. The tables contain the total number of entities, the number of linkable entities, and the number of NIL entities.

---

[1] In the experimental investigation, the considered NER model is the one proposed by Ritter et al. [33], which has been specifically designed for dealing with user-generated content.

Table 1. Datasets statistics.

	#Micropost2015			#Micropost2016		
	# Entities	# Linkable Entities	# NIL Entities	# Entities	# Linkable Entities	# NIL Entities
Training	4016	3565	451	8665	6374	2291
Dev	790	428	362	338	253	85
Test	3860	2382	1478	1022	738	284

	EVALITA NEEL-IT 2016		
	# Entities	# Linkable Entities	# NIL Entities
Training	787	520	267
Test	357	226	131

5.2 Performance Measures

NEL systems are commonly evaluated using Strong Link Match (SLM) [34,35]. Given the ground truth (GT), a pair $<t_i, k_j>$ can be considered as:

- True Positive (TP): if the system correctly recognizes the link of the entity.
- False Positive (FP): if the link recognized by the system is different by the one in the GT.
- True Negative (TN): if the link is not recognized by the system and in the GT. In this case the link is NIL.
- False Negative (FN): if the system recognizes the entity, but the entity is not recognized by the GT. In other words, the system returns NIL but the GT has a link.

Using these definitions, the traditional performance measure for the SLM score, i.e. *Precision*, *Recall* and *F-measure*, can be computed. In addition, NEL systems usually measure the *NIL Score*, as the equivalent to the Recall for the NIL labeled entities.

6 Experimental Evaluation

In this section, the results achieved by the proposed approach are introduced, analyzed and presented, showing the impact of the different pipeline components on the performance measures. In particular, the system has been investigated by considering three different configurations: without preprocessing, with preprocessing and by including the ontology type into the candidate generation process. Finally, a comparison with the available state of the art approaches is discussed.

In Tables 2, 3, and 4, the results of the proposed approach without preprocessing for both English and Italian challenges are shown. As it is possible to notice, the results are promising, achieving an overall *F-measure* of 40%.

Table 2. Results for #Micropost2015 without preprocessing.

	SLM scores for #Micropost2015			
	Precision	Recall	F-measure	NIL Score
Training	0.4604	0.5186	0.4877	0.7472
Dev	0.2265	0.4182	0.2939	0.8895
Test	0.3370	0.5417	0.4168	0.8748

Table 3. Results for #Micropost2016 without preprocessing.

	SLM scores for #Micropost2016			
	Precision	Recall	F-measure	NIL Score
Training	0.3840	0.5221	0.4425	0.8520
Dev	0.3461	0.4624	0.3959	0.8235
Test	0.2563	0.3550	0.2977	0.8380

Table 4. Results for EVALITA NEEL-IT 2016 without preprocessing.

	SLM scores for EVALITA NEEL-IT 2016			
	Precision	Recall	F-measure	NIL Score
Training	0.2477	0.3750	0.2983	0.6779
Test	0.2380	0.3761	0.2915	0.5954

In order to deal with the variety of problems related to the language register of Web 2.0, the **preprocessing** step has been performed. The results are reported in Tables 5 and 6. As expected, all the performance measures have been increased of 10%–15% with respect to previous experimental settings.

An example of correctly linked entity mention after preprocessing is *"f1"*: in the baseline experiment it has been labeled with the wrong link *"dbpedia.org/resource/Family_1"*, while, if properly capitalized in *"F1"*, the result is the correct link *"dbpedia.org/resource/Formula_One"*. Another example for the Italian dataset (Table 7) regards the entity *"FEDEZ"*, an Italian singer, that has been linked to a NIL entity in the baseline. By performing the capitalization resolution, the model is able to correctly link the entity to *"dbpedia.org/resource/Fedez"*.

In spite of the overall performance improvements, for some entities, the preprocessing module associates erroneous links that were correctly given by the baseline method. An example is the entity *"repubblicait"*, from Italian tweets, which is the account of an Italian newspaper called "La Repubblica", that after the preprocessing step is determined as NIL.

Table 5. Results for #Micropost2015 with preprocessing.

	SLM scores for #Micropost2015			
	Precision	Recall	F-measure	NIL Score
Training	0.53	0.60	0.56	0.72
Dev	0.28	0.53	0.37	0.87
Test	0.40	0.65	0.50	0.86

Table 6. Results for #Micropost2016 with preprocessing.

	SLM scores for #Micropost2016			
	Precision	Recall	F-measure	NIL Score
Training	0.45	0.61	0.52	0.84
Dev	0.53	0.71	0.61	0.78
Test	0.43	0.59	0.50	0.82

Table 7. Results for EVALITA NEEL-IT 2016 with preprocessing.

	SLM scores for EVALITA NEEL-IT 2016			
	Precision	Recall	F-measure	NIL Score
Training	0.3100	0.4692	0.3733	0.6479
Test	0.2689	0.4247	0.3293	0.6183

Another investigated experimental setting consists of considering the **ontology type** of the entity mention in the candidate generation process, taking advantage of the preprocessing step. The ontology type can be obtained by performing a type classification with a Named Entity Recognition and Classification method. It is expected that considering the ontology type of entity will help the linking process. For instance, given the entity mention *"Paris"*, the corresponding inferred type *Person* will contribute to link *"Paris"* to the celebrity Paris Hilton, instead of the France capital. The achieved results are shown in Tables 8, 9, and 10.

Differently from the expectations, with the introduction of the entity types, the performance have barely improved with respect to the configuration with only preprocessing (Tables 5, 6 and 7). This behavior can be justified by the fact that the candidate resources k_j of an entity mention t_i are already mostly related to the same ontology class. Thus, do not providing any additional discriminative information, e.g. the most similar entities to a birth name will very likely be of type *Person*.

Table 8. Results for #Micropost2015 with preprocessing and considering entity types.

	SLM scores for #Micropost2015			
	Precision	Recall	F-measure	NIL Score
Training	0.5333	0.6008	0.5650	0.7184
Dev	0.2860	0.5280	0.3711	0.8729
Test	0.4015	0.6507	0.4966	0.8626

Table 9. Results for #Micropost2016 with preprocessing and considering entity types.

	SLM scores for #Micropost2016			
	Precision	Recall	F-measure	NIL Score
Training	0.4520	0.6145	0.5209	0.8358
Dev	0.5355	0.7154	0.6125	0.7764
Test	0.4015	0.6507	0.4966	0.8626

Table 10. Results for EVALITA NEEL-IT 2016 with preprocessing and considering entity types.

	SLM scores for EVALITA NEEL-IT 2016			
	Precision	Recall	F-measure	NIL Score
Training	0.3672	0.5557	0.4422	0.6479
Test	0.3165	0.5000	0.3876	0.6183

A small improvement in terms of F-measure can be observed when the candidate list is composed of resources with different ontology types. An example is the entity mention "*Interstellar*": the first match of the system based only on the preprocessing step is "*dbpedia.org/resource/Interstellar_travel*", while including the entity type *Product* gives the correct resource "*dbpedia.org/resource/Interstellar_(film)*".

6.1 State of the Art Comparison

This section presents a comparison between the proposed NEL system and the current state of the art solutions. Tables 11 and 12 report a comparison of the proposed approach with the state of the art (only those approaches providing individual results for the specific NEL task have been considered). From the results, it is possible to notice that the proposed system (**UNIMIB-WE**) has comparable performance to the top performant systems proposed at #Micropost challenges. In the #Micropost2015 challenge UNIMIB-WE places in the third position, close to the solution proposed by *Acubelab* [27] in second place. In the 2016 edition, UNIMIB-WE achieves the second place, with 60% of F-measure. The main reason why the proposed system is overcome by *KEA* [40] regards the specific optimization that this model has performed on the challenge dataset, in fact this domain-specific optimization process induced an increase of 40% in terms of F-measure compared to the not optimized version. Similarly, the *Ousia* model [42] is a supervised learning approach which exploits an ad-hoc acronym expansion dictionary.

In spite of the better-achieved results, these models have the main problem of limited generalization abilities and the need of a manually label dataset, which is very expensive in terms of human effort. Differently, the proposed NEL system does not need any supervision or labeled dataset and, given the wider range of named entities that can cover, it provides good generalization abilities to other domains.

Table 13 reports the results related to the participants of the EVALITA NEEL-IT challenge that provided the specific NEL performance. Regarding the comparison with the model proposed in [24], UNIMIB-WE obtains similar performance in terms of F-measure, but different in terms of Precision and Recall. UNIMIB-WE is less precise, but it has a higher Recall. The same performance gap occurs when comparing with the *sisinflab*'s solution [7], in this case, the higher Precision is due to the combined specific three different approaches that they used in the NEL system. They make use of DBpedia Spotlight for span and URI detection, DBpedia lookup for URI generation given a keyword, and a Word Embeddings model trained over tweets with a URI generator. Both of these solutions use an ensemble of state of the art techniques, that gives them the ability to overcome the problems of individual methods and achieve better overall performance.

Table 11. Comparison for #Micropost2015 sorted by F-measure.

#Micropost2015 Test set		
Team Name	Reference	F-measure
Ousia	[42]	0.7620
Acubelab	[27]	0.5230
UNIMIB-WE	[6]	0.5059
UNIBA	[2]	0.4640

Table 12. Comparison for #Micropost2016 sorted by F-measure.

#Micropost2016 Dev set				
Team Name	Reference	Precision	Recall	F-measure
KEA	[40]	0.6670	0.8620	0.7520
UNIMIB-WE	[6]	0.5295	0.7075	0.6057
MIT Lincoln Lab	[15]	0.7990	0.4180	0.5490
Kanopy4Tweets	[39]	0.4910	0.3240	0.3900

Table 13. Comparison for EVALITA NEEL-IT 2016.

EVALITA NEEL-IT 2016				
Team Name	Reference	Precision	Recall	F-measure
FBK-NLP (train)	[24]	0.5980	0.4540	0.5160
UNIMIB-WE (train)	[6]	0.4231	0.6403	0.5095
UNIMIB-WE (test)	[6]	0.3529	0.5575	0.4322
sisinflab (test)	[7]	0.5770	0.2800	0.3800

As a conclusion, it is possible to state that the results obtained by the proposed model are very promising, given the highly challenging environment of user-generated content over microblogging platforms. This supports the evidence of Word Embeddings as providers of semantically meaningful word representation. The model would certainly gain with the addition of a supervision procedure able to learn which module should be used with respect to the similarity score. For instance, if the similarity score between "*dbpedia.org/resource/La_Repubblica_(quotidiano)*" and "*repubblicait*" is higher than the one to "*RepubblicaIT*", the capitalization module would not be activated.

7   Conclusion

This paper introduces a Named Entity Linking system based on Word Embeddings in unsupervised settings. We addressed different issues of noisy microblogging data with an ad-hoc preprocessing that experimentally demonstrates to be an important step for this task. The introduction of Word Embeddings permits to improve the semantic similarity of the words comprising the named entities and the corresponding entries in the KB and also to better capture new emerging named entities and commonly used slangs and abbreviations. Considering the difficulties of the investigated environment, the obtained results are very promising, proving the potential of the Word Embedding model as a high-level word representation.

One of the main problems in standard Word Embeddings representation is that each word must encode all of its possible meaning into a single vector. This causes some word representation to be placed into a position that is the average of all the possible meaning of that word. Future studies could explore this issue by conveying the representation of each word occurrence considering its specific meaning.

Acknowledgements. This work has been partially supported by PON I&R 2014-20, with the grant for research project "SmartCal", CUP B48I15000180008.

References

1. Basile, P., Caputo, A., Gentile, A.L., Rizzo, G.: Overview of the EVALITA 2016 Named Entity rEcognition and Linking in Italian Tweets (NEEL-IT) Task. In: Proceedings of 3rd Italian Conference on Computational Linguistics & 5th Evaluation Campaign of Natural Language Processing and Speech Tools for Italian, vol. 1749 (2016)
2. Basile, P., Caputo, A., Semeraro, G., Narducci, F.: UNIBA: exploiting a distributional semantic model for disambiguating and linking entities in tweets. In: Proceedings of the 5th Workshop on Making Sense of Microposts Co-located with the 24th International World Wide Web Conference, vol. 1395, p. 62 (2015)
3. Basile, P., et al. (eds.): Proceedings of 3rd Italian Conference on Computational Linguistics & 5th Evaluation Campaign of Natural Language Processing and Speech Tools for Italian, vol. 1749 (2016)
4. Bunescu, R.C., Pasca, M.: Using encyclopedic knowledge for named entity disambiguation. In: Proceedings of the 11th Conference of the European Chapter of the Association for Computational Linguistics (2006)
5. Caliano, D., Fersini, E., Manchanda, P., Palmonari, M., Messina, E.: UniMiB: entity linking in tweets using Jaro-Winkler distance, popularity and coherence. In: Proceedings of the 6th Workshop on Making Sense of Microposts Co-located with the 25th International World Wide Web Conference, vol. 1691, pp. 70–72 (2016)
6. Cecchini, F.M., et al.: UNIMIB@NEEL-IT: named entity recognition and linking of italian tweets. In: Proceedings of 3rd Italian Conference on Computational Linguistics & 5th Evaluation Campaign of Natural Language Processing and Speech Tools for Italian, vol. 1749 (2016)
7. Cozza, V., Bruna, W.L., Noia, T.D.: sisinflab: an ensemble of supervised and unsupervised strategies for the NEEL-IT challenge at Evalita 2016. In: Proceedings of 3rd Italian Conference on Computational Linguistics & 5th Evaluation Campaign of Natural Language Processing and Speech Tools for Italian, vol. 1749 (2016)
8. Cucerzan, S.: Large-scale named entity disambiguation based on wikipedia data. In: Proceedings of the 2007 Joint Conference on Empirical Methods in Natural Language Processing and Computational Natural Language Learning, pp. 708–716 (2007)
9. Derczynski, L., Maynard, D., Aswani, N., Bontcheva, K.: Microblog-genre noise and impact on semantic annotation accuracy. In: Proceedimgs of the 24th ACM Conference on Hypertext and Social Media, pp. 21–30 (2013)
10. Dredze, M., McNamee, P., Rao, D., Gerber, A., Finin, T.: Entity disambiguation for knowledge base population. In: Proceedings of the 23rd International Conference on Computational Linguistics, pp. 277–285 (2010)

11. Ferragina, P., Scaiella, U.: TAGME: on-the-fly annotation of short text fragments (by Wikipedia entities). In: Proceedings of the 19th ACM Conference on Information and Knowledge Management, pp. 1625–1628 (2010)

12. Fersini, E., Manchanda, P., Messina, E., Nozza, D., Palmonari, M.: Adapting named entity types to new ontologies in a microblogging environment. In: Mouhoub, M., Sadaoui, S., Ait Mohamed, O., Ali, M. (eds.) IEA/AIE 2018. LNCS (LNAI), vol. 10868, pp. 783–795. Springer, Cham (2018). https://doi.org/10.1007/978-3-319-92058-0_76

13. Fersini, E., Messina, E., Felici, G., Roth, D.: Soft-constrained inference for Named Entity Recognition. Inf. Process. Manag. **50**(5), 807–819 (2014)

14. Gottipati, S., Jiang, J.: Linking entities to a knowledge base with query expansion. In: Proceedings of the 2011 Conference on Empirical Methods in Natural Language Processing, pp. 804–813 (2011)

15. Greenfield, K., et al.: A reverse approach to named entity extraction and linking in microposts. In: Proceedings of the 6th Workshop on Making Sense of Microposts Co-located with the 25th International World Wide Web Conference, vol. 1691, pp. 67–69 (2016)

16. Guo, S., Chang, M., Kiciman, E.: To link or not to link? A study on end-to-end tweet entity linking. In: Proceedings of the 2013 Conference of the North American Chapter of the Association of Computational Linguistics: Human Language Technologies, pp. 1020–1030 (2013)

17. Hachey, B., Radford, W., Nothman, J., Honnibal, M., Curran, J.R.: Evaluating Entity Linking with Wikipedia. Artif. Intell. **194**, 130–150 (2013)

18. Han, X., Zhao, J.: NLPR_KBP in TAC 2009 KBP track: a two-stage method to entity linking. In: Proceedings of the 2nd Text Analysis Conference (2009)

19. Hoffart, J., et al.: Robust disambiguation of named entities in text. In: Proceedings of the 2011 Conference on Empirical Methods in Natural Language Processing, pp. 782–792 (2011)

20. Lehmann, J., et al.: DBpedia - a large-scale, multilingual knowledge base extracted from Wikipedia. Semant. Web **6**(2), 167–195 (2015)

21. Lehmann, J., Monahan, S., Nezda, L., Jung, A., Shi, Y.: LCC approaches to knowledge base population at TAC 2010. In: Proceedings of the 3rd Text Analysis Conference (2010)

22. Manchanda, P., Fersini, E., Palmonari, M., Nozza, D., Messina, E.: Towards adaptation of named entity classification. In: Proceedings of the Symposium on Applied Computing, pp. 155–157 (2017)

23. Mikolov, T., Chen, K., Corrado, G., Dean, J.: Efficient estimation of word representations in vector space. In: Proceedings of the 1st International Conference on Learning Representations (2013)

24. Minard, A., Qwaider, M.R.H., Magnini, B.: FBK-NLP at NEEL-IT: active learning for domain adaptation. In: Proceedings of 3rd Italian Conference on Computational Linguistics & 5th Evaluation Campaign of Natural Language Processing and Speech Tools for Italian, vol. 1749 (2016)

25. Monahan, S., Lehmann, J., Nyberg, T., Plymale, J., Jung, A.: Cross-lingual cross-document coreference with entity linking. In: Proceedings of the Fourth Text Analysis Conference (2011)

26. Nozza, D., Ristagno, F., Palmonari, M., Fersini, E., Manchanda, P., Messina, E.: TWINE: a real-time system for TWeet analysis via INformation Extraction. In: Proceedings of the 15th Conference of the European Chapter of the Association for Computational Linguistics, pp. 25–28 (2017)

27. Piccinno, F., Ferragina, P.: From TagME to WAT: a new Entity Annotator. In: Proceedings of the 1st ACM International Workshop on Entity Recognition & Disambiguation, pp. 55–62 (2014)
28. Pilz, A., Paaß, G.: From names to entities using thematic context distance. In: Proceedings of the 20th ACM Conference on Information and Knowledge Management, pp. 857–866 (2011)
29. Pound, J., Mika, P., Zaragoza, H.: Ad-hoc object retrieval in the web of data. In: Proceedings of the 19th International Conference on World Wide Web, pp. 771–780 (2010)
30. Rao, D., McNamee, P., Dredze, M.: Entity linking: finding extracted entities in a knowledge base. In: Poibeau, T., Saggion, H., Piskorski, J., Yangarber, R. (eds.) Multi-source, Multilingual Information Extraction and Summarization. Theory and Applications of Natural Language Processing, pp. 93–115. Springer, Heidelberg (2013). https://doi.org/10.1007/978-3-642-28569-1_5
31. Ratinov, L., Roth, D.: Design challenges and misconceptions in named entity recognition. In: Proceedings of the 13th Conference on Computational Natural Language Learning, pp. 147–155 (2009)
32. Ratinov, L., Roth, D., Downey, D., Anderson, M.: Local and global algorithms for disambiguation to wikipedia. In: Proceedings of the 49th Annual Meeting of the Association for Computational Linguistics: Human Language Technologies, pp. 1375–1384 (2011)
33. Ritter, A., Clark, S., Mausam, Etzioni, O.: Named entity recognition in tweets: an experimental study. In: Proceedings of the 2011 Conference on Empirical Methods in Natural Language Processing, pp. 1524–1534 (2011)
34. Rizzo, G., Basave, A.E.C., Pereira, B., Varga, A.: Making sense of microposts (#Microposts2015) Named Entity rEcognition and Linking (NEEL) challenge. In: Proceedings of the the 5th Workshop on Making Sense of Microposts Co-located with the 24th International World Wide Web Conference, vol. 1395, pp. 44–53 (2015)
35. Rizzo, G., van Erp, M., Plu, J., Troncy, R.: Making sense of microposts (#Microposts2016) Named Entity rEcognition and Linking (NEEL) challenge. In: Proceedings of the 6th Workshop on 'Making Sense of Microposts' Co-located with the 25th International World Wide Web Conference, vol. 1691, pp. 50–59 (2016)
36. Shen, W., Wang, J., Han, J.: Entity linking with a knowledge base: issues, techniques, and solutions. IEEE Trans. Knowl. Data Eng. 27(2), 443–460 (2015)
37. Shen, W., Wang, J., Luo, P., Wang, M.: LINDEN: linking named entities with knowledge base via semantic knowledge. In: Proceedings of the 21st World Wide Web Conference 2012, pp. 449–458 (2012)
38. Shen, W., Wang, J., Luo, P., Wang, M.: Linking named entities in tweets with knowledge base via user interest modeling. In: Proceedings of the 19th ACM SIGKDD International Conference on Knowledge Discovery and Data Mining, pp. 68–76 (2013)
39. Torres-Tramón, P., Hromic, H., Walsh, B., Heravi, B.R., Hayes, C.: Kanopy4Tweets: entity extraction and linking for Twitter. In: Proceedings of the 6th Workshop on 'Making Sense of Microposts' Co-located with the 25th International World Wide Web Conference, vol. 1691, pp. 64–66 (2016)
40. Waitelonis, J., Sack, H.: Named Entity Linking in #Tweets with KEA. In: Proceedings of the 6th Workshop on 'Making Sense of Microposts' Co-located with the 25th International World Wide Web Conference, vol. 1691, pp. 61–63 (2016)

41. Yamada, I., Asai, A., Shindo, H., Takeda, H., Takefuji, Y.: Wikipedia2Vec: an optimized tool for learning embeddings of words and entities from Wikipedia. CoRR abs/1812.06280 (2018)
42. Yamada, I., Takeda, H., Takefuji, Y.: An end-to-end entity linking approach for tweets. In: Proceedings of the 5th Workshop on Making Sense of Microposts Co-located with the 24th International World Wide Web Conference, vol. 1395, pp. 55–56 (2015)
43. Zhang, W., Su, J., Tan, C.L., Wang, W.: Entity linking leveraging automatically generated annotation. In: Proceedings of the 23rd International Conference on Computational Linguistics, pp. 1290–1298 (2010)
44. Zheng, Z., Li, F., Huang, M., Zhu, X.: Learning to link entities with knowledge base. In: Proceedings of the 2010 Conference of the North American Chapter of the Association for Computational Linguistics: Human Language Technologies, pp. 483–491 (2010)

Effectively Classify Short Texts with Sparse Representation Using Entropy Weighted Constraint

Ting Tuo[1], Huifang Ma[1,2,3(✉)], Zhixin Li[3], and Xianghong Lin[1]

[1] College of Computer Science and Engineering, Northwest Normal University, Lanzhou 730070, Gansu, China
mahuifang@yeah.net
[2] Guangxi Key Laboratory of Trusted Software, Guilin University of Electronic Technology, Guilin 541004, China
[3] Guangxi Key Lab of Multi-source Information Mining and Security, Guangxi Normal University, Guilin 541004, Guangxi, China

Abstract. Short texts have become a kind of prevalent source of information, and the classification of these short texts in various forms is valuable to many applications. However, most existing short text classification approaches circumvent the sparsity problem by extending short texts (or their feature representations) or exploiting additional information to adapt short texts to traditional text classification approaches. In this paper, we try to solve the sparsity problem of short text classification in a different direction: adapting the classifier to short texts. We propose a sparse representation short text classification method based on entropy weighted constraint. The main idea behind this study is to consider that the short texts are similar in potentially specific subspace. Specifically, we first introduce word embedding to represent the initial sparse representation dictionary, and then a fast feature subset selection algorithm is used to filter the dictionary. Again, we design an objective function based on sparse representation of entropy weight constraint. The optimal value of the objective function is obtained by Lagrange multiplier method. Finally, the distance between the short text to be classified and the short text in each class is calculated under the subspace, and the short text is classified according to three classification rules. Experiments over five datasets show that the proposed approach can effectively alleviate the problem of sparse feature of short text and is more efficient and effective than the existing short text classification method.

Keywords: Word embedding · Entropy · Sparse representation · Short text classification

1 Introduction

Short texts have become a fashionable form of information on the Internet. Examples include web page snippets, text advertisements, and question/answer pairs. Given the large volume of short texts available, effective and efficient classification short texts become fundamental to many applications that require semantic understanding of

C. Douligeris et al. (Eds.): KSEM 2019, LNAI 11776, pp. 133–145, 2019.
https://doi.org/10.1007/978-3-030-29563-9_14

textual content, such as social website-based short text classification, topic detection [1] and emotions categorization. However, traditional text classification approaches do not work well with short texts if being applied straightforwardly, due to feature sparsity.

Several ingenious strategies have been proposed to deal with the data sparsity problem in short texts. One strategy is to aggregate a subset of short texts to form a longer pseudo-document, after text expansion, a traditional text classification approach (e.g. Support Vector Machine, SVM) is then used to classify the extended short texts. Nevertheless, the limitations of these researches are that they are difficult to obtain guarantee additional metadata effectively [2]. The other solution is to exploit additional information. Typical work includes web-based search method and classification/topic-based method. Previous studies have shown that web-based search method can significantly improve classification performance [3, 4]. Nevertheless, the search engine used greatly affects the performance of the method. In contrast, the categorization/topic-based approach uses explicit classification or implicit topic. For example, in [5], the authors used link information of tweets to construct a graph, and then they employed the collective classification method to do tweets classification. Recently, Mikolov et al. [6] put forward the concept of word embedding, which provides a new idea for short text categorization. And then Boom et al. [7] proposed a method based on semantic word embedding and frequency information for low-dimensional representation of short text. Essentially, these approaches circumvent the sparsity problem by extending short texts or exploiting additional information to adapt short texts to traditional text classification approaches.

Different from the above views, Gao et al. [8] proposed a structured sparse representation classifier to classify short text effectively, thus trying to solve the sparse problem of short text classification from different directions. But this method ignores the fact that in short text classification tasks, the text is similar in a specific potential subspace rather than in the whole space.

In this paper, we propose an effectively classify short texts with sparse representation using entropy weighted constraint (i.e., EWC-SR). The difference between this and previous methods is that we will make use of the sparsity of short text in the classification. Firstly, the word in the dictionary is represented as word embedding form via using Word2vec tool, and then the original dictionary is reduced according to the average weighted vectors. Secondly, a fast feature subset selection algorithm is introduced to filter the dictionary. Thirdly, by introducing the concept of subspace, we design an objective function based on sparse representation of entropy weight constraint. The optimal value of the objective function is obtained by Lagrange multiplier method. Finally, the distance between the short text to be classified and the short text in each class is calculated under the subspace, and the short text is classified according to three classification rules. Experiments over five datasets show that the proposed approach can effectively alleviate the problem of sparse feature of short text and is better than the existing methods of short text classification.

The basic outline of this paper is as follows: the learning of sparse representation dictionary is given in Sect. 2 and the short text sparse representation classifier via entropy weighted constraint is given in Sect. 3. In Sect. 4, experiments are applied to short text with five classical short text dataset for classification. And the concluding remarks in Sect. 5.

2   The Sparse Representation Dictionary Learning

Sparse representation dictionary learning is a representation learning method which aims at finding a sparse representation of the input data. Although, sparse representation provides more information that helps us determine the class label of the short texts, sparse representation can be seriously impacted by data correlation in the dictionary, especially when the dictionary is very large. In order to address this problem, there are two key steps. One is to reduce the dimension of the original dictionary by using word embedding. The other is to filter the original dictionary by using a fast feature subset selection method to reduce data correlation and redundancy.

2.1   Short Text Vector Representation

In a broad sense, word embedding is the collective name for a set of language modeling and feature learning techniques in natural language processing (NLP) where words or phrases from the vocabulary are mapped to vectors of real numbers.

With the rapid development of neural networks, there has been a corresponding word and phrase embedding, which helps to boost the performance in NLP tasks such as syntactic parsing [9] and sentiment analysis. Therefore, in our work, a short text low dimensional representation method based on semantic word embedding is introduced to learn sparse representation dictionary.

Let $D = \{d_1, d_2, ..., d_n\}$ is the set of n short texts in a document set D, and $T = \{t_1, t_2, ..., t_m\}$ is the set of m terms in a vocabulary set T. $C = \{C_1, C_2, ..., C_l...C_c\}$ is the collection of all classes. Assume n short text as training samples that constitute the original dictionary $A^{m \times n}$, they are transformed into feature vectors of m-dimension, formally $v_i \in R^m (i \in [1, n])$, using the raw term frequency (TF), and no other preprocessing procedure is performed for the reason that stemming and stop-word removal are harmful for short text classification [10]. Formally, the word embedding of t_i is represented as $\textbf{\textit{Word2vec}}(t_i)$, where the dimension of $\textbf{\textit{Word2vec}}(t_i)$ is k, and its 300-dimensional vector representation was listed. In this paper, we make use of the Word2vector tool to calculate word embedding. Mainstream word embedding training tools have continuous bag-of-words (CBOW) and continuous skip-gram. The CBOW model is used in our work. After that, every embedding vector for each term in the short text is multiplied with a weight that its IDF value. Finally, the weighted vectors are averaged to arrive at a single short text representation $\textbf{\textit{V}}(\textbf{\textit{d}}_i)$. To encode short text d_i, the vector representation of d_i is formalized as:

$$V(d_i) = \frac{1}{|d_i|} \sum\nolimits_{j=1}^{|d_i|} w_j \times Word2vec(t_j) \tag{1}$$

In which, $\textbf{\textit{V}}(\textbf{\textit{d}}_i)$ is the vector representation of the short text d_i, $|d_i|$ is the number of terms in the d_i of the short text, w_j is the idf weight of term j in d_i, $\textbf{\textit{Word2vec}}(t_j)$ is the word embedding of the term j in d_i.

Each short text d_i in $\textbf{\textit{A}}$ are represented as a $1 \times k$ dimensional vector through (1), that is, the low-dimension dictionary $A' = [V_{d_1}, V_{d_2}, ..., V_{d_i}..., V_{d_n}]^T \in R^{k \times n}$.

2.2 Dictionary Filtering

One of the key principles of sparse representation learning is that the dictionary has to be inferred from the input data. However, there is a great correlation and redundancy between the same training samples in dictionaries. Thus, it is crucial to select a good subset of discriminative to filter the dictionary. In our method, we use a fast feature subset selection algorithm to filter the sparse representation dictionary.

Let n_l be the number of the short text documents of l-th class, first at all, the Word2evc model is capable of representing each class feature vectors, that is **Word2vec(l)**, using a fixed-length k vector. And then, as for l-th class, the similarity between each short text d_i and class feature vector is computed as:

$$S(d_i, l) = \exp(-||V(d_i), word2vec(l)||_2), d_i \notin l \tag{2}$$

If $S(d_i, l)$ is less than a predetermined threshold θ, we say that d_i is an irrelevant short text to class l, pruning these short text, ultimately, the relevant short text for class l is denoted as $l' = \{d_1, d_2, \ldots, d_{n'_l}\}$.

The next step is to eliminate the redundant short text in each class, which involves three steps: (1) constructing complete G from relative ones. For l' class, an undirected complete graph $G = (V, E)$ is constructed with all relevant short text construct. Where, $V = \{d_i | d_i \in l' \wedge i \in [1, n'_l]\}$, the similarity value of the related short texts as the weight of the edges. $E = \{(d_i, d_j) | d_i, d_j \in l' \wedge i, j \in [1, n'_l] \wedge i \neq j\}$, the similarity between the related short texts as the weight of the edge. (2) Generating the minimal spanning tree MST based on G, in our work we build an MST using the well-known Prim algorithm [11]. (3) Partitioning the MST and selecting representative features. After building the MST, we first remove the edges whose weights are smaller than both of the similarity value between the vertices and their classes from the MST. Afterwards removing all the unnecessary edges, a forest is obtained, each tree in the forest represents a cluster. As illustrated above, the short texts in each cluster are redundant, so for each cluster we choose a representative short text as the final subset whose similarity with class vectors is the greatest. At the end, redundant dictionary is represented as $A^* \subset A'$.

3 Entropy Weighted Constraint for Short Text Sparse Representation Classifier

In this section, we first introduce the whole idea of the proposed method and give our objective function, and then, the solving process of the objective function is given. Finally, we present the classification rules for our sparse representation classifier.

3.1 Subspace Learning Based on Entropy Weighted Constraints

The sparse representation method represents an unmarked test text as a linear combination of a set of known class markers training short text, where the coefficient vector is sparse [12]. In more detail, given n short texts as training samples that constitute the dictionary $A^{k \times n}$, we try to reconstruct y from A by solving the equation $y = A = \beta_1 A_1 + \beta_2 A_2 + \ldots + \beta_n A_n$, where $\beta = [\beta_1, \beta_2, \ldots, \beta_n]^T \in R^n$ is the coefficient vector.

Intuitively, an interesting phenomenon in short text categorization is that short texts of the same class are usually similar in a potential subspace rather than in the whole space. In this work we define a novel sparse representation subspace learning objective function using entropy weight constraints to learn subspaces of each class. Simultaneously, we do not have the method of iterative computation of subspace, the reason is the short text in each class we are known beforehand. Next, we take the l-th class as an example to show the objective functions of subspace learning:

$$F(\beta_l) = \sum_{i=1}^{n_l} \sum_{j=i+1}^{n_l} \sum_{t=1}^{k} \beta_{lt}(x_{it} - x_{jt})^2 + \gamma \sum_{t=1}^{k} \beta_{lt} \log_2 \beta_{lt}, \sum_{t=1}^{k} \beta_{lt} = 1 \qquad (3)$$

Here, $\beta_l = [\beta_{l1}, \beta_{l2}, \ldots, \beta_{lk}]^T \in R^n$ is the coefficient vector, $n_{l'}$ the number of the short text assigned to the l-th class, x_{it} is value of the i-th short text of the t-th dimension, k is the dimension of short text vectors, and γ is a positive parameter to control the intensity of excitation in subspace.

The first term in (3) is the sum of the within class distance, and the second term the negative weight entropy. The positive parameter γ controls the strength of the incentive for on more dimensions. Minimization of F in (3) means minimizing both intra class distance and negative entropy weights. It is more specifically, intra class distance means to make the class in short text similar to each other; minimizing the negative entropy weight implies the need to stimulate more dimensions. In this way, we can avoid the problem of identifying short text by few dimensions in sparse data.

F is minimized if:

$$\beta_{lt} = \frac{\exp(\frac{-D_{lt}}{\gamma})}{\sum_{t=1}^{k} \exp(\frac{-D_{lt}}{\gamma})} \qquad (4)$$

Where $D_{lt} = \sum_{i=1}^{n_l} \sum_{j=i+1}^{n_l} (x_{it} - x_{jt})^2$

Proof. We use the Lagrange multiplier technique to obtain the following unconstrained minimization problem:

$$\min F_1(\beta_l, \delta_l) = \sum_{i=1}^{n_l} \sum_{j=i+1}^{n_l} \sum_{t=1}^{k} \beta_{lt}(x_{it} - x_{jt})^2 + \gamma \sum_{t=1}^{k} \beta_{lt} \log_2 \beta_{lt} - \delta_l(\sum_{t=1}^{k} \beta_{lt} - 1) \quad (5)$$

By setting the gradient of $F_1(\beta_l, \delta_l)$ with respect to β_{lt} and δ_l to zero, we obtain:

$$\frac{\partial F_1}{\partial \delta_l} = (\sum_{t=1}^{k} \beta_{lt} - 1) = 0 \qquad (6)$$

$$\frac{\partial F_1}{\partial \beta_{lt}} = \sum_{i=1}^{n_l} \sum_{j=i+1}^{n_l} (x_{it} - x_{jt})^2 + \gamma(1 + \log_2 \beta_{lt}) - \delta_l = 0 \qquad (7)$$

Let $D_{lt} = \sum_{i=1}^{n_l} \sum_{j=i+1}^{n_l} (x_{it} - x_{jt})^2$, from (7), we obtain:

$$\beta_{lt} = \exp(\frac{-D_{lt} - \gamma + \delta_l}{\gamma}) = \exp(\frac{\delta_l - \gamma}{\gamma}) \cdot \exp(\frac{-D_{lt}}{\gamma}) \tag{8}$$

Substituting (8) into (6), we have:

$$\sum_{t=1}^{k} \beta_{lt} = \sum_{t=1}^{k} \exp(\frac{\delta_l - \gamma}{\gamma}) \cdot \exp(\frac{-D_{lt}}{\gamma}) = \exp(\frac{\delta_l - \gamma}{\gamma}) \cdot \sum_{t=1}^{k} \exp(\frac{-D_{lt}}{\gamma}) = 1 \tag{9}$$

It follows that:

$$\exp(\frac{\delta_l - \gamma}{\gamma}) = \frac{1}{\sum_{t=1}^{k} \exp(\frac{-D_{lt}}{\gamma})}$$

Substituting this expression back to (8), we obtain:

$$\beta_{lt} = \frac{\exp(\frac{-D_{lt}}{\gamma})}{\sum_{t=1}^{k} \exp(\frac{-D_{lt}}{\gamma})}$$

3.2   Classification Rules

In this subsection, we will calculate the distance between the text to be classified and each class based on subspace, meanwhile, three classification rules are defined to classify short texts.

Rule 1 (*Minimum Distance*) given short text Y, the short text Y label based on the minimum distance is defined as follows:

$$label(Y) = \min_l \{l| \sum_{i=1}^{n_l} \sum_{t=1}^{k} \beta_{lt}(x_{it} - y_t)^2, l = 1, 2, \ldots, c\} \tag{10}$$

Rule 2 (*Average Distance*) given short text Y, the label of text Y based on the average distance is defined as follows:

$$label(Y) = \min_l \{l| \frac{1}{n_l} \times \sum_{i=1}^{n_l} \sum_{t=1}^{k} \beta_{lt}(x_{it} - y_t)^2, l = 1, 2, \ldots, c\} \tag{11}$$

Rule 3 (*Center Distance*) We first calculate the class center of each class, assume that Z_l is the class center vector of class l, where $Z_l = [z_{l1}, z_{l2}, \ldots, z_{lt}, \ldots, z_{lk}]$, z_{lt} is defined as follows:

$$z_{lt} = \frac{1}{n_{l'}} \times \sum_{i=1}^{n_{l'}} x_{it} \tag{12}$$

Therefore, the text Y label based on the center distance is defined as follows:

$$label(Y) = \min_{l} \{l| \sum_{t=1}^{k} \beta_{lt}(Z_{lt} - y_t)^2, l = 1, 2, \ldots, c\} \tag{13}$$

As stated before, the calculation of subspace is the emphasis of this paper. According to (1), the complexity of dictionary construction is $O(mn)$. In the stage of dictionary filtering, its complexity has been proved to be much less than $O((n_l)^2)$. There are c classes that need to be traversed in our work, obviously, the time complexity is less than $O(c \times (n_l)^2)$. Observe the (3) shows that the subspace computing complexity is $O(c \times k \times n_{l'}^2)$. At the end of, according to the classification rules, the complexity is $O(c \times k \times n_{l'})$. Overall, the complexity of our algorithm is $O(mn + c \times (n_l)^2 + (c \times k \times n_{l'}^2) + O(c \times k \times n_{l'}))$. Since the values of prior c and k are very small, our method is effective.

The details of the EWC-SR algorithm are shown in Algorithm 1.

Algorithm 1: Effectively Classify Short Texts with Sparse Representation using Entropy Weighted constraint (EWC-SR)

Input: A set of short texts D= $\{d_1,d_2,\ldots,d_n\}$, a set of short text class :C=$\{1,2,\ldots,l,\ldots,c\}$, a set of terms T=$\{t_1,t_2,\ldots,t_m\}$, an unclassified short text Y;

output: label(Y); #The class label of Y;

1: for i=1 to m

    Word2vec(t_i)= word2vec(t_i); #Represent each term t_i using Word2vec;

2: end for;

3: A'= $[\ ]_{k \times n}$; # Initialize the text matrix

4: for i=1 to n

5:    According to (1), the short text d_j as vectors $V(d_j)$;

6:    $A'[:i]$= $V(d_j)$;

7: end for;

8: According to (1), the unclassified short text Y as vectors $V(Y)$;

9: A^*=FAST(A'); #Using the FAST[13] algorithm to get the final de-redundant dictionary A^*;

10: $\beta[\ ]_{k \times c}$; # Initialize subspace matrix

11: for l=1, 2, ..., c

    $\beta[:l]$= β_l ; #According to (3), the corresponding subspaces are calculated in class l that after eliminating redundant features.

12: end for;

13: Evaluate label(Y) according to classification rule 1/2/3;

14: return label(Y).

---

4   Experiments and Results

We implemented our experiments under five real world datasets. At the beginning, the used datasets are briefly described. Then, we analyze the parameters involved in the experiment. In the end, we present our experimental results.

4.1   Dataset Description

Five datasets are used to evaluate the proposed method. The first dataset is the 20 newsgroups corpus[1], this dataset contains 20 classes, each of which has 1000 texts of news stories. In the experiment, we use only the titles. The second dataset is a ChineseNews dataset[2] consists of 2814 news stories and commentaries from People's Daily. Similarly, only titles are used in the experiment. The third dataset is from the Twitter Emotional Analysis Corpus[3] of the University of Michigan Emotional Analysis Competition. This dataset contains 157862 classified tweets. Each row is marked with 1 for positive emotions and 0 for negative emotions. The fourth dataset is a JSC corpus[4] consisting of 1002 legitimate emails and 322 spam emails extracted from GrumbleText. Positive and negative comments account for half. The fifth is the dataset is an IMDB movie review dataset[5], which consists of collection from the website of imdb.com movie reviews. The dataset is used as a binary emotion classification dataset contains a total of 50000 movie reviews, it contains 50000 movie reviews, of which positive and negative reviews account for half.

In experiment, the 5-fold cross validation method was conducted for each dataset to acquire the training samples and test samples. The experimental performance was measured with Accuracy and F1 [14]. Table 1 presents the statistics of the five datasets. Note that the last row of Table 1 is the average number of keywords per document, which are 5.40, 10, 19.5, 7.56 and 17.35 for the five datasets respectively. Hence, they are really short texts.

Table 1. The statistics of five datasets

Datasets	20 news group	Chinese news	Twitter	JSC	IMDB
Classes	20	10	2	2	2
Doc	20000	2814	157862	1324	50000
Keywords	8866	7437	20135	6375	11035
keywords/doc	5.4	10	19.5	7.56	17.35

---

[1] http://kdd.ics.uci.edu/databases/20newsgroups/20newsgroups.html.

[2] http://www.people.com.cn/.

[3] http://thinknook.com/twitter-sentiment-analysis-training-corpus-dataset-2012-09-22/.

[4] http://www.esp.uem.es/jmgomez/smsspamcorpus/.

[5] http://ai.stanford.edu/∼amaas/data/sentiment/aclImdb_v1.tar.gz.

4.2   Experimental Results

In order to verify the effectiveness of our algorithm, we design two experiments. (1) We test the most suitable parameter γ via experiments. (2) We make a deep analysis of our algorithm with the five baselines.

Parameter Analysis. As mentioned early in this article, our approach is based on the fact that in short text classification tasks, the text is similar in a specific potential subspace rather than in the whole space. Therefore, to investigate how the parameter γ affects the subspace learning, we start to use all datasets for EWC-SR algorithm to get the most appropriate number of parameters with the increase of parameter γ from 0.1 to 7. Results are reported below.

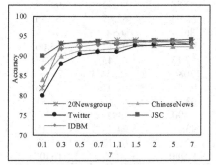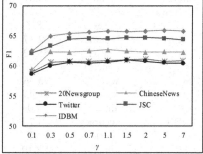

Fig. 1. The accuracy and F1-score of subspace clustering on different datasets

Figure 1 show the results of subspace learning on five types of datasets respectively. We can see that high accuracy was obtained in a large range of γ values [0.3, 7] on all datasets. These results indicate that the clustering results were not sensitive to the change of γ values, which is a good property of the algorithm. Therefore, in the next experiment, we set the parameter γ is 0.5.

Result Analysis. First of all, we compare our method with the SSR-DF method, the main reasons are as follows: (1) our method and the SSR-DF method use the sparsely of short text to classify them, so our method and SSR-DF method in this paper is compared is reasonable. (2) Our proposed method and SSR-DF method both improve the dictionary of sparse representation, and the design of the different classification rules, so similar with SSR-DF method. Nevertheless, in detail, we adopt the entropy weight constraint to improve the objective function to avoid the shortcoming of using sparse data to identify short text through several dimensions. The experimental results are shown in Table 2.

Tables 2 presents the classification results and run time for our EWC-SR method and the SSR-DF on the five datasets. As a whole, we can see that after dictionary filtering, classification performance is improved on the five datasets, and our approach gets the best performance. On ChineseNews, our approach obtains the best F1-measure, while its accuracy is a little lower than that of the case without filtering (concretely, 94.53 vs. 94.68). The reason may be that there are not enough training texts after decorrelation. On the other hand, our method of running time is far less than the SSR-DF method, in the best case, even more than SSR-DF running time increased four times.

Table 2. The effect of dictionary filtering on algorithm

		SSR-DF		EWC-SR	
		filtered	unfiltered	filtered	unfiltered
20news	Accuracy	94.24	93.64	**95.03**	94.87
group	F1	54.76	51.32	**58.68**	56.39
	time(s)	22409	67628	**5742**	11064
Chinese	Accuracy	93.87	92.88	94.53	94.68
News	F1	61.77	58.94	**62.87**	62.56
	time(s)	1826	8623	**658**	1013
Twitter	Accuracy	92.37	92.04	**93.14**	93.06
	F1	55.32	52.13	**56.43**	55.47
	time(s)	57716	120864	**16304**	29863
JSC	Accuracy	**93.56**	93.17	93.42	93.26
	F1	**65.93**	63.07	65.51	63.31
	time(s)	769	3890	**392**	937
IMDB	Accuracy	93.76	93.16	**94.43**	94.18
	F1	68.33	62.59	**62.17**	61.53
	time(s)	40619	17980	**8176**	16407

As for sparse representation, a lower dimensional dictionary may lead to more iterations of computation, thus incurs more time cost. Interestingly, our method not only considers the subspace, but also avoids the iterative computation of the subspace when classifying short text, which greatly saves time.

Table 3. The effect of classification rule

Datasets		Rule 1	Rule 2	Rule 3
20 news	Accuracy	**95.03**	94.31	94.96
group	F1	**60.68**	59.61	60.47
Chinese	Accuracy	94.53	94.62	**94.67**
News	F1	65.13	63.83	**65.87**
Twitter	Accuracy	94.14	**94.28**	94.13
	F1	66.35	**66.39**	66.34
JSC	Accuracy	94.01	94.17	**94.42**
	F1	**67.87**	64.87	67.51
IMDB	Accuracy	**94.47**	94.38	94.12
	F1	**72.17**	69.71	70.97

As can be seen from Table 3, Rule 1 and Rule 3 are superior to Rule 1 on all datasets. Between Rule 1 and Rule 3, Rule 1 performs better than Rule 3 on 20Newsgroups and IMDB, while Rule 3 outperforms Rule 1 on ChineseNews and JSC. These two rules achieve nearly similar performance on Twitter dataset. Overall, the performance differences between Rule 1 and Rule 3 are not apparent in the five datasets. So, in the rest experiments, we use only Rule 1.

In addition, in order to make our method more convincing, we plan to compare our method with several existing advanced short text classification methods. Namely, two classical short text classification methods SVM and KNN to use them as a baseline for the analysis, three sparse representation-based classification methods SRC [15] and SR-SVM [16] and SSR-DF. We use the package libSVM to implement SVM. In KNN, the sklearn package in python is used to solve the parameter setting problem. As to SRC and SR-SVM, we use weighted decomposition principal component analysis (WDPCA) to discriminate the similar classes. In SR-SVM, we seed the dictionary using principal components of TF vector representation corresponding to training text documents. In the next experiment, 20 newsgroups and Chinese news datasets are selected to compare the results.

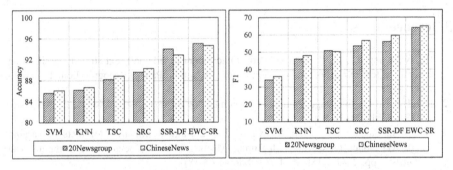

Fig. 2. Comparison of accuracy and F1 values of four methods on two datasets

The same setup of experimental data, the comparisons of our method against the 5 baselines are demonstrated in Fig. 2. As a whole, our proposed method EWC-SR achieves the best performance. From the Fig. 2, we can see that our approach EWC-SR outperforms the other five methods in both accuracy and F1-measure. Even though the accuracy value of all the methods on the two datasets differs slightly, in the case of F1 value can be seen in the SVM and KNN methods F1 values were less than 50%. Among them, the performance of SVM method is not satisfactory. The main reason is that in sparse dimension space, distance measure cannot distinguish vectors with different non-overlapping non-zero dimensions, which makes SVM unable to select support vectors perfectly. On the other hand, notwithstanding, SRC and SRC-SVM use sparse representation theory, they still use the original word frequency. The classification performance of SSR-DF method has been greatly improved, but still less than 60%. The reason is that these two methods neglect the potential subspace.

The F1 values of our method are all over 60%, and there is no iteration when calculating subspace. The running time of our method is much lower than that of SSR-DF method. Hence, our method can classify short text better.

5   Conclusions and Future Work

In this paper, we propose a sparse representation classifier for short text based on entropy weight constraint, which is different from the classification method which can avoid the sparse problem of short text by extending short text or using additional information. Our extensive experiments demonstrate the effectiveness of our approach. In the future, we will try to find more efficient classification rules to better classify short texts.

Acknowledgment. The work is supported by the National Natural Science Foundation of China (No. 61762078, 61363058, 61663004) Guangxi Key Laboratory of Trusted Software (No. kx201910) and Research Fund of Guangxi Key Lab of Multi-source Information Mining & Security (MIMS18-08).

References

1. Hu, X., Wang, H., Li, P.: Online biterm topic model based short text stream classification using short text expansion and concept drifting detection. Pattern Recognit. Lett. **116**, 187–194 (2018)
2. Uysal, A.K.: On two-stage feature selection methods for text classification. IEEE Access **6**, 43233–43251 (2018)
3. Gong, H., Sakakini, T., Bhat, S., Xiong, J.J.: Document similarity for texts of varying lengths via hidden topics. In: 56th Annual Meeting of the Association for Computational Linguistics, pp. 2341–2351. ACL, Melbourne (2018)
4. Wang, J., Shen, J., Li, P.: Provable variable selection for streaming features. In: International Conference on Machine Learning, pp. 5158–5166. ICML, Stockholm (2018)
5. Srishti, G., Abhinav, K., Gogia, A., Kumaraguru, P.T., Chakraborty, T.: Collective classification of spam campaigners on twitter: a hierarchical meta-path based approach. In: The International World Wide Web Conference WWW 2018, pp. 529–538. WWW, Lyon (2018)
6. Mikolov, T., Sutskever, I., Chen, K., Corrado, G.S., Dean, J.: Distributed representations of words and phrases and their compositionality. In: NIPS, pp. 3111–3119 (2013)
7. Boom, C.D., Canneyt, S.V., Demeester, T., Dhoedt, B.: Representation learning for very short texts using weighted word embedding aggregation. v **80**, 150–156 (2016)
8. Gao, L., Zhou, S., Guan, J.: Effectively classifying short texts by structured sparse representation with dictionary filtering. Inf. Sci. **323**, 130–142 (2015)
9. Zhang, W., Du, Y.H., Yoshida, T., Yang, Y.: DeepRec: a deep neural network approach to recommendation with item embedding and weighted loss function. Inf. Sci. **470**, 121–140 (2019)
10. Wang, J., Wang, Z.Y., Zhang, D.W., Yan, J.: Combining knowledge with deep convolutional neural networks for short text classification. In: the 26th International Joint Conference on Artificial Intelligence, pp. 2915–2921. IJCAI, Melbourne (2017)

11. Li, W.M., Zhu, H., Liu, W., Chen, D.H., Jiang, J.L.: An anti-noise process mining algorithm based on minimum spanning tree clustering. IEEE, pp. 48756–48764 (2018)
12. Sun, J.Y., Wang, X.Z., Xiong, N.X., Shao, J.: Learning sparse representation with variational auto-encoder for anomaly detection. IEEE Access **6**, 33353–33361 (2018)
13. Song, Q., Ni, J., Wang, G.: A fast clustering-based feature subset selection algorithm for high-dimensional data. TKDE **25**(1), 1–14 (2013)
14. Kiela, D., Grave, E., Joulin, A., Mikolov, T.: Efficient large-scale multi-modal classification. In: The 32th AAAI Conference on Artificial Intelligence, pp. 5198–5204. AAAI, New Orleans (2018)
15. Stein, R.A., Jaques, P.A., Valiati, J.F.: An analysis of hierarchical text classification using word embeddings. Inf. Sci. **471**, 216–232 (2019)
16. Li, X.R., Zhu, D.X., Dong, M.: Multinomial classification with class-conditional overlapping sparse feature groups. Pattern Recognit. Lett. **101**, 37–43 (2018)

A New Method for Complex Triplet Extraction of Biomedical Texts

Xiao Wang[1] , Qing Li[1] , Xuehai Ding[1(✉)] , Guoqing Zhang[2] ,
Linhong Weng[1] , and Minjie Ding[1]

[1] School of Computer Engineering and Science, Shanghai University,
Shanghai, China
{wangxiao2017,qli,dinghai,wenglinhong,
hhhhw}@shu.edu.cn
[2] Bio-Med Big Data Center, CAS-Key Laboratory of Computational Biology,
CAS-MPG Partner Institute for Computational Biology,
Shanghai Institute of Nutrition and Health,
Shanghai Institutes for Biological Sciences,
University of Chinese Academy of Sciences,
Chinese Academy of Sciences, Shanghai, China
gqzhang@picb.ac.cn

Abstract. Extracting biomedical triplet is one of the most important tasks in medical knowledge graph construction. Relations in complex biomedical text are overlap heavily. Although existing biomedical relation extraction methods have higher accuracy, they still have two problems. First, most of those methods hardly consider relations overlap problem. A lot of precious biomedical information is neglected. In addition, the entities in biomedical text are intensive, and the contextual information association also affects the understanding of the meaning of biomedical texts. Methods often used to encode sentence, like canonical bidirectional recurrent neural networks (BiRNN) or convolutional neural networks (CNN), are difficult to capture enough information from biomedical text. In this paper, we propose a new end-to-end triplet extraction method to address the complex triplet extraction problem in biomedical text. In our model, sentences are encoded by Recurrent Convolutional Neural Network (RCNN), which combines the advantages of BiRNN and CNN flexibly, containing more information of sentence. Experimental results on biomedical dataset and general field dataset show that our method is effective.

Keywords: Triplet extraction · Biomedical text · Neural network ·
Relation overlap · Semantic vector

1 Introduction

With the reality that medical resources are very limited as well as the introduction of precision medicine and intelligent medical, the application of medical knowledge maps has attracted more attention. The main job of constructing medical knowledge maps is to extract entities, relations and attributes from massive unstructured biomedical data. The cost of manual information extraction from these data is very expensive.

© Springer Nature Switzerland AG 2019
C. Douligeris et al. (Eds.): KSEM 2019, LNAI 11776, pp. 146–158, 2019.
https://doi.org/10.1007/978-3-030-29563-9_15

Therefore, how to extract valid information automatically from these texts becomes very important. Triplet extraction is an essential process of information extraction, where triplet is in the form of "entity1-relation-entity2", which indicates the relation of two entities.

Biomedical text triplet extraction task refers to extracting relations and named entities in biomedical text. Existing methods committed to classifying the relation of entity pair [1–3]. In i2b2/VA challenge dataset [4], the F1 score in some classes of classification results has reached 82% [2]. But most of them ignore entity extraction. While few methods can extract triplet [5], none of these models completely addresses the problem of entities overlap in complex relations.

In biomedical text, the relations between entities are very complicated. In a sentence, it is often the case that a entity is involved in different triplets at same time (Single entity overlap [6]), or that there are multiple relations in a entity pair (Entity pair overlap [6]).

For example, as shown in Fig. 1, relational triplets (Pprom, Bleeding, PIP) and (Pprom, Transverse lie, PIP) exist in the sentence "Pprom with bleeding and transverse lie prompted cesarean section.", where the entity "Pprom" is involved in both triplets. And for another example, relational triplets (Gallbladder cavity, Dense shadow, produce) and (Gallbladder cavity, Dense shadow, contains) exist in the sentence "Multiple gallbladder-like dense shadows can be seen in the gallbladder cavity.", where there are two kinds of relations between "Gallbladder cavity" and "Dense shadow".

Fig. 1. The example of single entity overlap (left) and entity pair overlap (right).

But in most of existing methods, a word corresponds to a label, or one entity pair corresponds to one relation. When there are multiple relations in an entity pair, these methods only retain the one with the highest probability. Therefore, it is difficult to use these methods to analyze the entities and relations in complex biomedical sentence.

Recently, a method (CopyRE) [6] can deal with this situation by predicting relation first. This method also has some limitations: they only aimed at the general field and the sentence representation is obtain through Bidirectional Long short-term Memory (BiLSTM). Biomedical text is rigorous and concise. Entities in biomedical text are intensive. For example, entities "cesarean section", "pprom", "bleeding" and "transverse lie" exist in the sentence "Pprom with bleeding and transverse lie prompted cesarean section.". These entities can be arranged into multiple entity pairs. BiLSTM is not good enough to get sentence representation.

To solve this problem, we propose a new method. Our method use RCNN to improve the encoder of CopyRE and is applied to the biomedical field. The neural network triplet extraction models often take sentences into the Recurrent Neural

Network (RNN) or CNN to obtain a sentence representation. RNN can capture the contextual information, but it is a biased model [7]. The information is passed backwards in RNN, the latter words become more important, but the reality is that each word may be an important word. CNN is an unbiased model compared to RNN. It can get the most important features through a max-pooling layer [7]. Unbiasedness also makes CNN capturing more semantic information. However, CNN also has a limitation: it needs to set the convolution kernel in advance when the training situation is unknown. Early methods try to solve this problem by setting the convolution kernel to multiple sizes [8]. The bidirectional recurrent structure (BiRNN), is less noisy than traditional window-based neural networks and can maximize context information. The RCNN [7] flexibly combines BiRNN with CNN to construct a new structure, taking advantage of these two models. Sentence representation output by the RCNN will perform better. Our model use the idea of RCNN to encode sentence. Sentences are first fed into BiLSTM. The output of BiLSTM and the words embedding are regrouped in the same way as RCNN. Our method uses only word-embedding features without manual feature engineering. And then, the decoder use the sentence representation to predict relations and copy entities.

The main contributions of our work are as follows:

(1) We used the idea of RCNN instead of BiLSTM as an encoder to improve the CopyRE model, and extracted the triplets in the complex sentences in a joint learning manner.
(2) We apply the improved method to medical field. In the case of using randomly initialized word vectors and using pretrained word embedding vectors, our method is outperform than the original method.

2   Related Work

The two parts in "entity1-relation-entity2", relation and entities, can be extracted one by one. This method is called Pipelined Method. Most methods use BiLSTM to extract entities [9] and use CNN containing attention vector to extract relations [10]. The two parts can also be extracted in triplet form (entity 1, entity 2, relation) [11–13], known as Joint Learning. The pipeline method ignores the relation between the two subtasks and the joint extraction method avoids the accumulation of errors in the pipeline method. Some early studies noted the sub-task association [14–16], but these methods cost much in feature engineering. Within the scope of the method with neural network, there are two ways to achieve the combination of two subtasks: one is Parameter Sharing [1, 12], and the other is Tagging Scheme, such as The Novel tagging model [17].

Despite their success, none of these models completely addresses the problem of complex relations mentioned in the first section. In these models, one word corresponds to one label, or one entity pair corresponds to only one relation. They have great limitation on knowledge extraction.

CopyRE solves the problem of complex relation and entity overlap in a clever way which extracts the relation first and then copies the entities involved in the relation. CopyRE is an improvement on The novel tagging model [3]. The limitations of

CopyRE are that they only aimed at the general field and the sentence representation is only obtained through BiLSTM, which may lost information when the sentence is too long.

In the medical field, most models are used to extract the relations in the case that the entities have already been known [1, 2]. Some of these methods use segmented convolutional neural networks (seg-CNN) [1] or segmented Recurrent neural networks (seg-RNN) [2] to classify the relation of entity pair. Few biomedical models consider the connection of two subtasks [5]. In fact, it is not a real joint learning because relations and entities is not extracted in one model. Besides, these biomedical triplets extraction methods do not consider the problem of relation overlap in complex sentences.

Our work is based on CopyRE model, the sentence representation is optimized by the idea of RCNN. Then we applied this improved model to the medical field.

3 Our Model

In this section, we will introduce our triplet extraction model in details. Our model is a sequence to sequence model which is shown in Fig. 2 (left), and it contains two parts: encoder and decoder. Encoder is our main work. In the part of encoder, we use the thought of RCNN to get the representation of the sentence. In the part of decoder, we use multi-decoder which can decode several triplets in one time.

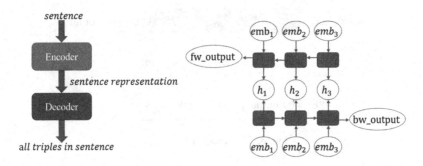

Fig. 2. Model overview (left) and the input and Output of BiLSTM (right).

3.1 Encoder

Embedding. The input of the model is a complete sentence consisting of n words, $s = $ "$w_1\ w_2\ w_3\ \cdots\ w_n$". Firstly, we use the word segmentation algorithm to segment the sentence, and then after the word segmentation, we get a new sentence representation of length n: $S = ($"w_1", "w_2", "w_3", $\cdots$,"w_n"$)$. Secondly, Each word w_i in a sentence produces a word vector emb_i through the word embedding layer. Then the sentence form output by the word embedding layer is $S_{emb} = ($"emb_1", "emb_2", "emb_3", $\cdots$, "emb_n"$)$.

Bi-LSTM. The word vectors in S_{emb} will pass through a bidirectional RNN [18]. As we all know LSTM [19] will produce an output and a hidden state in every time step. That means that the Bi-LSTM will output a forward_output$_i$, a backwards_output$_i$ and a hidden state h_i in every time step i as Fig. 2 (right) shows.

Regroup. Then we use the thought of RCNN to encode the sentence. We merge three parts: the last output of forward-LSTM (fw_output$_i$), the embedding of current word ($emb(w_i)$) and the last output of backwards-LSTM (bw_output$_i$). A new form of sentence representation was produced as Eq. (1) shows. We do not do max-pooling, because we will extract triplets in a sentence and we want to retain more information as much as possible.

$$output_i^{en} = [\text{fw\_output}_i; emb(w_i); \text{bw\_output}_i] \tag{1}$$

The superscript "en" in the equations means that it is the output of encoder. Finally, the word representations of words are connected together as a new sentence representation, as shown in Eq. (2). The new sentence representation covers more information of the sentence. The encoder also outputs all states like Eq. (3) (Fig. 3).

$$output^{en} = \left[output_1^{en}, output_2^{en}, \cdots, output_n^{en}\right] \tag{2}$$

$$state^{en} = \left[h_1^{en}, h_2^{en}, \cdots, h_n^{en}\right] \tag{3}$$

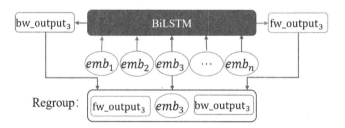

Fig. 3. The encoder of $word_3$.

3.2   Decoder

The general structure of decoder part is a recurrent structure. In decoder part, we will predict a relation first, then copy two entities. In case of using multi-decoder, we can predict several triplets at same time.

Equation (4) shows the frame of decoder. $f^{de_i}(\cdot)$ is decoder function. The condition $t \bmod 3 = 2,0$ represents the second and third element (the first entity and the second entity) in the predicted triplet and The condition $t \bmod 3 = 1$ represents the first elements (the relation) in the predicted triplet. $h_t^{de_i}$ is hidden state of decoder in time step t − 1. When we predict a relation, we input $\hat{h}_{t-1}^{de_i}$. When we copy entities, we input $h_{t-1}^{de_i}$. Because we need both sentence representation $output_i^{en}$ and the last hidden state $h_{t-1}^{D_{i-1}}$ to predict relation. When it is first relation that predicted in a sentence, we only input the output of encoder ($output_i^{en}$). The specific algorithm is shown in Eq. (5). u_t is a vector that calculate by h_{t-1}^{de} and $output_i^{en}$, we will introduce it in detail in Eq. (9) (Fig. 4).

$$output_t^{de}, h_t^{de} = \begin{cases} f^{de_i}\left(u_t, \hat{h}_{t-1}^{de_i}\right), t\%3 = 1 \\ f^{de_i}\left(u_t, h_{t-1}^{de_i}\right), t\%3 = 2, 0 \end{cases} \tag{4}$$

$$\hat{h}_{t-1}^{D_i} = \begin{cases} output_i^{en}, i = 1 \\ \frac{1}{2}\left(output_i^{en} + h_{t-1}^{D_{i-1}}\right), i > 1 \end{cases} \tag{5}$$

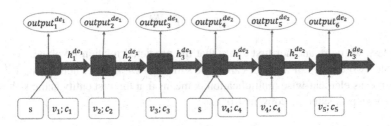

Fig. 4. The decoder frame.

$output_i^{en}$ is the output of encoder, $\alpha = [\alpha_1, \alpha_2, \cdots, \alpha_n]$ and $\beta = [\beta_1, \beta_2, \cdots, \beta_n]$ are vectors. Every w means a weight vector and the superscript is use to distinguish them. For example, w^c is a weight vector of c_t. Activation function is selu($\cdot$) [20]. v_t is word embedding of the last prediction. In other words, it is word embedding of an entity or a relation.

$$\beta_i = selu\left(\left[h_{t-1}^{de}; output_i^{en}\right] \cdot w^c\right) \tag{6}$$

$$\alpha = softmax(\beta) \tag{7}$$

$$c_t = \sum_{i=1}^{n} \alpha_i \times output_i^{en} \tag{8}$$

Finally, we can get the output of decoder: $output_i^{de}$ and h_t^{de}. The u_t is calculated in Eq. (9)

$$u_t = [v_t; c_t] \cdot W^u \tag{9}$$

$$output_i^{de}, h_t^{de} = f(u_t, h_{t-1}^{de}) \tag{10}$$

Prediction. There are m relations, the score of each relation $q^r = [q_1^r, \cdots, q_m^r]$. The superscript "r" means relation, and the superscript "NA" means that we have predicted all triplets in this sentence already. We can calculate the probability in this way:

$$q^r = selu(output_i^{de} \cdot w^r + b^r) \tag{11}$$

$$q^{NA} = selu(output_i^{de} \cdot w^{NA} + b^{NA}) \tag{12}$$

$$p^r = softmax([q^r; q^{NA}]) \tag{13}$$

Copy. Then we copy the first entity that the predicted relation involved. The superscript "e" means entity.

$$q_i^e = selu([output_i^{de} \cdot output^{en}] \cdot w^e) \tag{14}$$

$$p^e = softmax([q^e; q^{NA}]) \tag{15}$$

At last, we copy another first entity that the predicted relation involved. As we all know, the two entities of a triplet cannot be same. So we set a switch vector V^M. The note ⊛ means element-wise multiplication. k means that the first entity is the k-th word. The copy step is same as copy first one.

$$V_i^M = \begin{cases} 1, & i \neq k \\ 0, & i = k \end{cases} \tag{16}$$

$$p^e = softmax([V^M \circledast q^e; q^{NA}]) \tag{17}$$

3.3   Training

We set loss function in Eq. (18). We train all the data in the train corpus into the model for training, and there are b data in one batch. That means the input is $S_b = \{s_1, \ldots, s_b\}$, and the prediction output is $Y = \{y_1, \ldots, y_b\}$, where y_i contains all prediction of sentence s_i. For example, we will predict x triplets in a sentence, the $y_i = [y_i^1, y_i^2, y_i^3, \cdots, y_i^{3x}]$, and we use T representation 3x.

$$L = \frac{1}{b \times T} \sum_{i=1}^{b} \sum_{t=1}^{T} -\log(p(y_i^t | y_i^{<t}, s_i, \theta)) \tag{18}$$

4   Experiments

4.1   Dataset

The New York Times Annotated Corpus. It contains more than 1.8 million news articles written and published by the New York Times for about twenty years from January 1, 1987 to June 19, 2007. There are 24 relations in the relation library. The data set is treated the same as CopyRE: Filters the entire data set, leaving only sentences with a sentence length of 100 and a triplet.

WebNLG Dataset. There are 246 relations in the relational library of this data set. The preprocessing method for this data set is the same as CopyRE.

2010 i2b2/VA Relation Corpus. We did not get the full data when downloading the data. There are eight relation types among them: treatment caused medical problems (TrCP), treatment administered medical problem (TrAP), treatment worsen medical problem (TrWP), treatment improve or cure medical problem (TrIP), treatment was not administered because of medical problem (TrNAP), test reveal medical problem (TeRP), test conducted to investigate medical problem (TeCP), medical problem indicates medical problems (PIP) [4]. Our data preprocess follows a past research [21].

Table 1. The number of instance in 2010 i2b2/VA relation corpus.

	TeCP	TeRP	TrAP	PIP	TrCP
Train	182	1153	875	810	211
Test	52	338	311	305	63

4.2 Preprocessing and Evaluation

We use the NLTK toolkit [22] to tokenize the sentence. We use standard precision, recall and F1 scores to evaluate the results which are commonly used evaluation criteria in neural network models. Only if the relation and entities of the triplet are all correct, the triplet is considered correct. When the number of extracted triples reaches a preset amount, the extraction is ended.

4.3 Settings

We use LSTM [19] as the basic unit; The number of the cell unit is set to 1000. We set embedding dimension to 100 for dataset NYT and WebNLG. The batch size, $b = 100$, and the learning rate is 0.001. Parameter optimizer is Adam [23].

Operating environment: All the experiments are tested with the computer with configuration described as follows: OS system: Ubuntu 14.04 LTS; GPU Memory: 16 GB; Python: 3.5.2; Tensorflow: 1.7.0.

4.4 Result

Comparison with the Baselines. We first let all the settings same as CopyRE. Learning rate is set to 0.001. We set that five triplets is predicted in a sentence. The performance results are displayed in Table 1. In WebNLG dataset, the recall and F1 score of our method are better than baseline. But for NYT dataset, our model performs not very good. This might because the settings of CopyRE are not suitable for our model. If we reduce learning rate or reduce the cell unit number of LSTM, our method perform better than CopyRE in NYT dataset. And when the learning rate reduce to 0.0005, our method perform performs better than the best result of CopyRE in NYT dataset, which is shown in the last line of Table 3. The precision is lower than the Novel tagging model and the reason is that the Novel tagging model do not consider entity overlap and predicted fewer triplets. But recall and F1 score have been improved significantly.

Table 2. Results of different models in WebNLG dataset and NYT dataset.

Dataset	WebNLG			NYT		
	Precision	Recall	F1	Precision	Recall	F1
Novel tagging	0.525	0.193	0.283	0.624	0.317	0.420
CopyRE	0.377	0.364	0.371	**0.610**	**0.566**	**0.587**
Our model	**0.385**	**0.376**	**0.380**	0.607	0.562	0.583

Table 3. Results of different settings in NYT dataset.

	Learning rate	Unit number	Precision	Recall	F1
CopyRE	0.01	1000	0.406	0.327	0.362
Our model			**0.468**	**0.432**	**0.449**
CopyRE	0.001	300	0.568	0.507	0.536
Our model			**0.593**	**0.538**	**0.564**
Our model	0.0005	1000	**0.622**	**0.568**	**0.594**

Biomedical Text Application. Then we test our model in biomedical text, 2010 i2b2/VA relation corpus. The entities in this dataset are overlap. The example of entity overlap in Fig. 1 is from this dataset.

We set that predict 5 triplets in a sentence. Learning rate is set to 0.001 and the cell unit number is set to 1000. It is the best settings for CopyRE. The comparison results between CopyRE and our model is shown in Tables 2 and 3. Our model do not depend on any external features while CopyRE add part-of-speech (POS) to their model. And both our model and CopyRE, not add word position embeddings.

Model performance is evaluated under two word embedding initializations:

Randomly initialized: We set the embedding dimension to 100 and predict 5 triplets in a sentence. Our model performs better than CopyRE which is shown in Table 4.

Table 4. Results of different models when word embedding randomly initialized.

Model	Precision	Recall	F1
CopyRE	0.208	0.190	0.199
Our model	**0.238**	**0.212**	**0.224**

Pre-trained: word embedding are initialized by pre-trained word embeddings: PubMed-w2v.bin [24]. We set the embedding dimension to 200 and predict 5 triplets in a sentence. The learning rate and unit number are set follow CopyRE. The comparison results between CopyRE and our model are shown in Table 5. Our model still performs better than CopyRE.

Table 5. Results of different methods when word embedding are initialized by pretrained word embedding.

Model	Precision	Recall	F1
CopyRE	0.280	0.250	0.264
Our model	**0.288**	**0.256**	**0.271**

In both two word embedding initializations, our model is better than the CopyRE. When add pre-trained word embeddings, the implement of our model does not as obvious as CopyRE. From the results we suppose that CopyRE is more sensitive to external knowledge, and our model is more suitable when there is no enough knowledge to supplement it.

Finally, we test the effect of our model in predicting different numbers of triplets and compare it with CopyRE. The learning rate and cell unit number are set follow CopyRE. The result is shown in Fig. 5.

As shows in the Fig. 5, for 2010 i2b2/VA relation corpus, in most cases, our method behaves better than CopyRE. That means that when entity in sentence is overlap heavily, our method can capture more information than CopyRE. The training set is not complete, but our model is still better than the original model in comparison to the improved model. These observations verify the effectiveness of RCNN in biomedical triplets extraction.

But the F1 score of methods are still too low which might because of Incomplete data set. The limitation of both CopyRE and Our model is that the models only keep the last word of the entity to represent the entity, which might affect the precision of result.

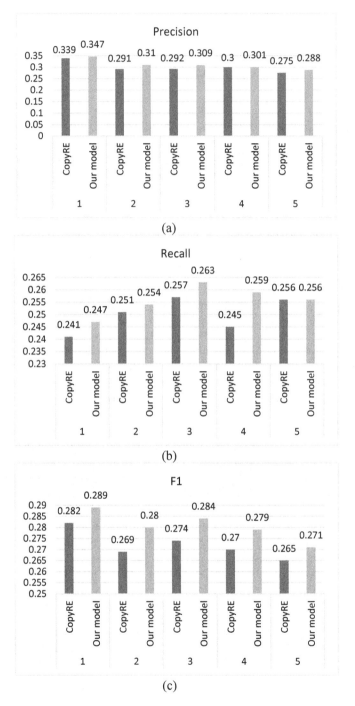

Fig. 5. The results of extracting different number triplets from one sentence. (a)The precision of result. (b) The recall of result. (c)F1 score of result. The number in the bottom means triplets number of a sentence.

5   Conclusion and Future Work

Relations in complex biomedical text are overlap heavily. Most of existing triplet extraction methods do not consider this problem. To address this problem, we propose a new end-to-end triplet extraction method which use RCNN to get sentence representation. We first test our method on public general field datasets, and it achieves the baseline. Then we test our method on complex biomedical text to extract triplets with entity overlap problem, and it outperform than baseline. The results show that our method is effective when it is used to extract complex triplet in biomedical text.

But the F1 scores of methods are still too low to meet the standards that can be used by doctors. To solve complex biomedical text triplets extraction problem completely, there still a long way to go. This work is just a beginning. In the future, we will keep trying to improve this model.

Acknowledgments. This work was supported by the National key research and development program of China (No. 2017YFE0117500), National Key R&D Program of China, Grant (NO. 2016YFC0901904, 2016YFC0901604) and Science and Technology Committee of Shanghai Municipality (No. 16010500400).

References

1. Luo, Y., et al.: Segment convolutional neural networks (Seg-CNNs) for classifying relations in clinical notes. J. Am. Med. Inform. Assoc. **25**(1), 93–98 (2018)
2. Luo, Y.: Recurrent neural networks for classifying relations in clinical notes. J. Biomed. Inform. **72**, 85–95 (2017)
3. He, B., Guan, Y., Dai, R.: Classifying medical relations in clinical text via convolutional neural networks. Artif. Intell. Med. **93**, 43–49 (2019)
4. Uzuner, Ö., South, B.R., Shen, S., et al.: 2010 i2b2/VA challenge on concepts, assertions, and relations in clinical text. J. Am. Med. Inform. Assoc. **18**(5), 552–556 (2011)
5. Li, F., Zhang, M., Fu, G., et al.: A neural joint model for entity and relation extraction from biomedical text. BMC Bioinform. **18**(1), 198 (2017)
6. Zeng, X., et al.: Extracting relational facts by an end-to-end neural model with copy mechanism. In: Proceedings of the 56th Annual Meeting of the Association for Computational Linguistics. Long Papers, vol. 1 (2018)
7. Lai, S., Xu, L., Liu, K., Zhao, J.: Recurrent convolutional neural networks for text classification. In: Twenty-Ninth AAAI Conference on Artificial Intelligence (2015)
8. Nguyen, T.H., Grishman, R.: Relation extraction: perspective from convolutional neural networks. In: Proceedings of the 1st Workshop on Vector Space Modeling for Natural Language Processing, pp. 39–48 (2015)
9. Xu, K., Zhou, Z., Hao, T., Liu, W.: A bidirectional LSTM and conditional random fields approach to medical named entity recognition. In: Hassanien, A.E., Shaalan, K., Gaber, T., Tolba, Mohamed F. (eds.) AISI 2017. AISC, vol. 639, pp. 355–365. Springer, Cham (2018). https://doi.org/10.1007/978-3-319-64861-3_33
10. Zhu, Ji., et al.: Relation classification via target-concentrated attention CNNs (2017)
11. Miwa, M., Bansal, M.: End-to-end relation extraction using LSTMs on sequences and tree structures. In: Proceedings of ACL, pp. 1105–1116 (2016)

12. Zheng, S., et al.: Joint entity and relation extraction based on a hybrid neural network. Neurocomputing **257**, 59–66 (2017)
13. Gupta, P., Schtze, H., Andrassy, B.: Table filling multi-task recurrent neural network for joint entity and relation extraction. In: Proceedings of COLING, pp. 2537–2547 (2016)
14. Li, Q., Ji, H.: Incremental joint extraction of entity mentions and relations. In: Proceedings of ACL, pp. 402–412 (2014)
15. Miwa, M., Sasaki, Y.: Modeling joint entity and relation extraction with table representation. In: Proceedings of EMNLP, pp. 1858–1869 (2014)
16. Yu, X., Lam, W.: Jointly identifying entities and extracting relations in encyclopedia text via a graphical model approach. In: Proceedings of COLING, pp. 1399–1407 (2010)
17. Zheng, S., et al.: Joint extraction of entities and relations based on a novel tagging scheme (2017)
18. Chung, J., Gulcehre, C., Cho, K., Bengio, Y.: Empirical evaluation of gated recurrent neural networks on sequence modeling (2014). arXiv preprint: arXiv:1412.3555
19. Hochreiter, S., Schmidhuber, J.: Long short-term memory. Neural Comput. **9**(8), 1735–1780 (1997)
20. Klambauer, G., Unterthiner, T., Mayr, A., Hochreiter, S.: Self-normalizing neural networks. In: Advances in NIPS, pp. 971–980 (2017)
21. Sahu, S.K., Anand, A., Oruganty, K., Gattu, M.: Relation extraction from clinical texts using domain invariant convolutional neural network (2016). arXiv preprint: arXiv:1606.09370
22. Nltk toolkit. https://www.nltk.org/_modules/nltk/tokenize.html
23. Kingma, D.P., Ba, J.L.: Adam: a method for stochastic optimization. In: Proceedings of ICLR, pp. 1–15 (2015)
24. PubMed-w2v.bin word vector. http://evexdb.org/pmresources/vec-space-models/

Assessing Semantic Similarity Between Concepts Using Wikipedia Based on Nonlinear Fitting

Guangjian Huang[1], Yuncheng Jiang[1(✉)], Wenjun Ma[1], and Weiru Liu[2]

[1] School of Computer Science, South China Normal University, Guangzhou, China
ycjiang@scnu.edu.cn
[2] School of Computer Science, Electrical and Electronic Engineering,
and Engineering Maths, University of Bristol, Bristol, UK

Abstract. Feature-based methods of semantic similarity with Wikipedia achieve fruitful performances on measuring the "likeness" between objects in many research fields. However, since Wikipedia is created and edited by volunteers around the world, the preciseness of these methods more or less are influenced by the incompleteness, invalidity and inconsistency of the knowledge in Wikipedia. Unfortunately, this problem has not got enough attention in the existing work. To address this issue, this paper proposes a novel feature-based method for semantic similarity, which has three parts: low frequency features removal, the similarities of generalized synonyms computing, and weighted feature-based methods based on nonlinear fitting. Moreover, we show that our new method can always get a better Pearson correlation coefficient on one or more benchmarks through a set of experimental evaluations.

Keywords: Semantic similarity · Wikipedia · Nonlinear fitting

1 Introduction

Semantic similarity computation can estimate the "likeness" (similar) between objects (words, concepts or sentences) based on background knowledge and contextual awareness. Thus, it plays an essential role in many research fields, such as information retrieval [3] and natural language processing [11]. Despite its usefulness, robust measurement of semantic similarity for large scale natural language processing application remains a challenging task. Many works have been developed in the last few years, especially with the increase in feature-based methods with Wikipedia [2,5,6,11,14]. For these methods, Wikipedia serves as a huge size knowledge resource with significant coverage and feature-based measures can exploit more semantic knowledge than edge-counting approaches with the evaluations about the commonalities and differences of compared concepts. Thus, such methods have the potential to solve the task.

However, since Wikipedia is a free encyclopedia that anyone can edit, it is too hard to be sure about the quality of the knowledge in Wikipedia. As a

© Springer Nature Switzerland AG 2019
C. Douligeris et al. (Eds.): KSEM 2019, LNAI 11776, pp. 159–171, 2019.
https://doi.org/10.1007/978-3-030-29563-9_16

result, by relying on the features extracted from Wikipedia, this kind of methods suffer from a critical drawback: the precision of the semantic similarity results is deeply influenced by the incompleteness, invalidity and inconsistency of the knowledge in Wikipedia. Unfortunately, in the existing researches, this issue has been ignored. Another problem of feature-based approaches is their dependency on the weighting parameters that balance the contribution of each feature: (a) in the methods that without weights [6], features are treated equally. Thus, the important underlying statistics of knowledge resource is ignored. (b) In the weighted methods, it is a complex task to assign weights for each feature with Wikipedia. In the literature [5, 6, 11], researches usually use some small subsets of whole Wikipedia (*i.e.*, Wikipedia category graph) for feature weights assignment. But such subsets do not offer as much coverage as Wikipedia.

To address the above issues, in this paper, based on [6], we propose some new weighted feature-based methods by the nonlinear fitting. So we can make sure different features make different contributions to semantic similarity computation. Specifically, we first remove low-frequency features to reduce noise. Then we provide a new way to compute the similarities of generalized synonyms, based on the number of their categories. After that, we use nonlinear fitting to construct some weighted feature-based methods for semantic similarity. Finally, we show that our new methods can always get a better Pearson correlation coefficient on some benchmarks through a set of experimental evaluations. We will test our methods in the following benchmarks, RG65 [13], MC30 [9], 353tc [1], Sim666 [4], Jiang30 [6].

This paper advances the state-of-the-art on the topic of semantic similarity computation in the following aspects: (i) we propose a set of methods based on nonlinear fitting to increase the precision of semantic similarity results based on Wikipedia. (ii) Our new methods can reduce the influence of the incompleteness, invalidity and inconsistency of the knowledge in Wikipedia on the semantic similarity computation results. (iii) We give a new features weights assignment method for semantic similarity by the nonlinear fitting. (iv) Several widely used benchmarks have been considered to enable an objective comparison.

The rest of the paper is organized as follows. Section 2 discusses some background knowledge and related work. Section 3 analyzes some limitations of previous researches and talks about how to improve those limitations step by step. Then we evaluate our methods on benchmarks in the next section. Finally, Sect. 5 concludes the paper with future work.

2   Background and Related Work

This section provides a brief introduction about Wikipedia and discusses related work about feature-based methods of semantic similarity between concepts.

Wikipedia is a free, multilingual, largest, most widely used and up to date encyclopedia in existence. English version of Wikipedia contains over 5 million articles. A Wikipedia article offers a great deal of textual information and features (such as redirects, glosses, hyperlinks, disambiguation pages and categories). An article is the basic unit of Wikipedia, which contains text about a specific concept. Each article is assigned a *title* which is also referred as a *concept*. The opening paragraph of an article provides its summary, referred as *gloss*. An article has a set of anchors, which are internal hyperlinks to other related Wikipedia articles and categories are used to group related articles. Some synonyms share the same article and polysemic words refer to many articles. Our experiments are based on the Wikipedia dump of 05 January 2019.

The basic idea of feature-based methods based on Wikipedia is that concepts with more shared features are more similar than the concepts with less shared features [7]. Thus, the similarity of compared concepts can be obtained by their features comparison. To this end, in [5,6,11], they propose a series of feature-based methods that concepts are defined by four features (*i.e.*, anchor, category, gloss, and synonym) extracted from the concepts' articles in Wikipedia. In their definitions, a concept is denoted as Con, and $Con = (Anchor(A), Category(C),$ $Gloss(G), Synonym(S))$, where $A = \{a_1, \cdots a_n\}$ is the set of all the internal hyperlinks to other Wikipedia concepts in the Wikipedia article of Con and $C = \{c_1, \cdots c_k\}$ is set of categories that Con belongs to, $G = \{t_1, \cdots t_i\}$ is the set of all the terms that extracted from the first paragraph of the article of Con and $S = \{s_1, \cdots s_m\}$ is a set of alternative aliases (Redirects) or synonyms of Con. Thus, the similarity between two concepts Con_1 and Con_2 is defined as:

$$Sim(Con_1, Con_2) = S_{con}(\Im(A), \Im(C), \Im(G), \Im(S)) \qquad (1)$$

where $\Im(K)$, $K \in \{A, C, G, S\}$ represents the similarity of four feature sets of anchors, categories, glosses, and synonyms respectively. $K \in \{A, C, G, S\}$ is a pair of feature sets for the compared concepts. For example, $\Im(A) = \Im(A_1, A_2)$ and A_1 (or A_2) represents the sets of anchors of $Con1$ (or $Con2$) respectively. Hence, function $\Im(K) = \Im(x, y)$ is the similarity of set x and set y. Specifically, $\Im(x, y)$ can be defined based on X-similarity [10] or RE-approach [12], i.e.,

$$\Im_X(x, y) = \frac{|x \cap y|}{|x \cup y|}, \qquad (2)$$

$$\Im_{RE}(x, y) = \frac{|x \cap y|}{|x \cap y| + \alpha|x \setminus y| + (1 - \alpha)|y \setminus x|}. \qquad (3)$$

Finally, function S_{con} can be considered as an aggregation operator to combine the similarity of four feature sets of anchors, glosses, categories and synonyms. Thus, it can be mean function or max function, and so on.

Based on Eq. (1), Jiang *et al.* have chosen different forms for function S_{con} and $\Im_X$ (or $\Im_{RE}$) in Eqs. (2) and (3) to get different methods of semantic similarity in [6]. After comparing the experimental results of twelve different methods, it is concluded that the following four methods will get a better results in different benchmarks than other methods:

$$SimFir(Con_1, Con_2) = (\Im_X(A) + \Im_X(C) + \Im_X(G) + \Im_X(S)) \times 0.25, \qquad (4)$$

$$SimSec(Con_1, Con_2) = (\Im_{RE}(A) + \Im_{RE}(C) + \Im_{RE}(G) + \Im_{RE}(S)) \times 0.25, \qquad (5)$$

$$SimThi(Con_1, Con_2) = \max(\Im_X(A), \Im_X(C), \Im_X(G), \Im_X(S)), \qquad (6)$$

$$SimFou(Con_1, Con_2) = \max(\Im_{RE}(A), \Im_{RE}(C), \Im_{RE}(G), \Im_{RE}(S)), \qquad (7)$$

where function $\Im_X(x, y)$ is defined as Eq. (2) and $\Im_{RE}(x, y)$ is defined as Eq. (3). In $\Im_{RE}(x, y)$, α is defined as 0.5 in default in [6]. In this paper, we will show how to improve the above four methods step by step.

3   Weighted Feature-Based Methods with Nonlinear Fitting

Since Wikipedia is a free encyclopedia that anyone can edit, the contents of an article are influenced by the knowledge and culture of the people who edit this article. It will lead to the following issues. Firstly, incompleteness, some features of a concept are not included in the contents. Secondly, inconsistency, a feature is supposed to be a common feature between two concepts, but in fact, it belongs to only one concept. Finally, invalidity: a feature is not the right or appropriate feature for a concept. For instance, both "Potato" and "Tomato" are not in the category "Vegetables", but "Pomato" is. There are many terms extracted from glosses just appeared in only one article, such as "medula", "mmeli", "treatmentknown", "treatmentth" and "absolutein".

To reduce the influence of such issues for the semantic similarity computation result, in this section, based on the four methods in Eqs. (4)–(7), we propose our new weighted feature-based method with nonlinear fitting. These methods include two stages: first, we remove the low-frequency features to reduce noise (i.e., reduce the influence of invalidity) and the similarities computation of generalized synonyms (i.e., reduce the influence of inconsistency). Second, we apply nonlinear fitting for the weights assignment of four feature-based methods in Eqs. (4)–(7). In the second stage, to mitigate incompleteness and invalidity, we will try to use weights in $[-1, 1]$, and the sum of all features' weights is not limited to 1. Here, the negative weights mean that in case some invalidity features are considered, we use negative weights to reduce the influence of such invalidity to the final similarity between two concepts.

Finally, to make our methods more realistic, we will explain our methods step by step in the following benchmarks, **RG65** [13], **MC30** [9], **353tc** [1], **Sim666** [4], **Jiang30** [6].

3.1   Low-Frequency Features and Synonym

To construct a feature-based method based on Wikipedia, we first need to extract Wikipedia features for the concepts in different benchmarks. In this paper, we use JWPL[1] (Java Wikipedia Library) to extract Wikipedia features. We also use MySQL to manage data. For the gloss of every concept, we remove the stop words, special characters, punctuation and numbers. This preprocessing is the same as that in [6].

Therefore, by 5 million articles in Wikipedia, for all the concepts in the benchmarks mentioned above (*i.e.*, **RG65**, **MC30**, **353tc**, **Sim666**, **Jiang30**),

---

[1] https://dkpro.github.io/dkpro-jwpl/.

we can extract 12,028 unique words in glosses, 104,963 unique anchors. However, we find that 513 words just appear in ten or less Wikipedia glosses and 1,802 anchors just appear in ten or less Wikipedia articles and. Since there are 5 million articles in Wikipedia and such anchors or words only appeared in a few articles, we call them as the low-frequency features. There is a high possibility that such low-frequency features are coming from mistakes. For instance, there are many terms extracted from gloss just appeared in only one article, such as "medula", "treatmentth" and "absolutein". As a result, such low-frequency features can be considered as a noise which reduces the similarities of concepts.

To address this issue to improve the precision of semantic similarity computation result, in our new method, we first remove the low-frequency features as follows: (a) we will remove the anchors and words that appear no more than 200 times.[2] (b) For categories, we only remove the hidden categories.[3] (c) We do not remove the low-frequency categories since it is reasonable for some categories just appear in only one article.

Hence, many concepts in Wikipedia are ambiguous and will be redirected to the same article. If we compute their similarity by the existing feature-based methods [2,5,6,11,14], their similarity will be the maximum value 1. Besides, the same will happen to polysemic words that have common senses as well. For instance, in [14], they define the similarity of two words (w_1, w_2) as follows.

$$sim(w_1, w_2) = max_{c_1 \in s(w_1), c_2 \in s(w_2)}(sim(c_1, c_2)), \qquad (8)$$

where $s(w)$ denotes a set of concepts that are senses of word w. Therefore, they will get $sim(Football, Soccer) = 1$ in the scope of $[0, 1]$. However, "soccer" means American football and for the rest of the world, "football" means association football. Thus, it is more reasonable to assign $sim(football, soccer) < 1$.

In this paper, both redirected pages and polysemic words that have common senses are called generalized synonyms (synonyms for short). When two synonyms represent different categories of objects, their senses in context will be different. Formally, when Con_1 and Con_2 are synonyms, we have

$$Sim(Con_1, Con_2) = F(B, C) = \begin{cases} B + \frac{R}{n(C)}, & \text{if } n(C) > 0, \\ B, & \text{if } n(C) = 0, \end{cases} \qquad (9)$$

where $n(C)$ represents the number of categories of Con_1 and Con_2. Coefficient "B" ($B \in [0.5, 1]$) is a constant that measures the similarity for every synonym pair and constant "R" measures the degree of influence that the number of categories can have on similarity. Since the influence of the number of categories on similarity can be either positive or negative, we have $R \in [-1, 1]$. Notice that synonyms share the same article in Wikipedia, so Con_1 and Con_2 have the same number of categories.

---

[2] In the experiments, we have tried different thresholds for low-frequency features between 0 and 2000, and the number 200 works better than others.

[3] Hidden categories are used for maintenance of the Wikipedia project which is not part of the encyclopedia. For instance, "1911 Britannica articles needing updates from January 2016" is a hidden category.

The intuition of Eq. (9) is that for the compared concepts which are synonyms, we first give them an initial similarity. Then the more categories they have, the less deviation of the initial similarity they will be. Hence, when R is positive, B is the lower bound of the similarities. Thus, the synonym pairs that have less common categories will be more similar. On the contrary, negative R means B is the upper bound of the similarities. Thus, the synonym pairs that have more common categories will be more similar.

Now, we considering how to give appropriate values for constants B and R in Eq. (9). First, we give a formal definition of discrete spaces as follows:

Definition 1 (Discrete space). *A one dimension discrete space $D = \{a, a + d, a + 2d, a + 3d \cdots a + (n - 1)d, a + nd, b\}$ is defined as $D = [a, b, d]$. Define n dimension discrete space as $D^n = \{(x_1, x_2 \cdots x_n) | x_i \in D, i = 1, 2 \cdots n\}$.*

Then, considering different values of B in discrete space $[0.5, 1, 0.05]$ and R in discrete space $[-1, 1, 0.1]$, we will construct a training process to find best B and R for the experiments. More specially, in a training process, we will try every case of B, R in their corresponding space on the training benchmark and test on other benchmarks, until we find out the values of B and R that can get the best Pearson correlation coefficient on test benchmarks.

Finally, we will give some improvements of the four methods in Eqs. (4)–(7). On the one hand, since for every concept pair that is not synonym, by Eqs. (2) and (3), we have $\Im_X(S) = \Im_{RE}(S) = 0$. In this case, we suggest that the weight of Synonym should be ignored since it will weaken the influence of other features. That is, when we choose the mean function as S_{con} in Eq. (1), we only compute the mean of $\Im(A), \Im(C), \Im(G)$, i.e., define $S_{con} = (\Im(A) + \Im(C) + \Im(G)) \times \frac{1}{3}$. On the other hand, for methods $SimSec$ and $SimFou$ in Eqs. (5) and (7), if we define $\alpha = 0.5$ in default, then all features have the same influence on the semantic similarity of the compared concepts. Thus, we suggest we should try different values in the test benchmarks to find the most appropriate α in discrete space $[0, 1, 0.1]$. The intuitive idea of trying different values for α is that for methods $SimSec$ and $SimFou$, defining $\alpha = 0$ in function $\Im_{RE}(x, y)$ means we only take the particular features of Con_2 into account and ignore the particular features of Con_1. The bigger the α is, the more particular features of Con_1 are for taking into account. But we do not know whose particular features are more credible. Therefore, we try different values of α.

3.2 Weights Assignments with Nonlinear Fitting

In this subsection, we will consider how to measure the weights of features based on their contribution by the nonlinear fitting.

Firstly, for $\Im_X(x, y)$ in Eq. (2), we sort the similarities of four features $\Im(A), \Im(C), \Im(G), \Im(S)$ from small to large, and denote it as $\Im_{X1}, \Im_{X2}, \Im_{X3}, \Im_{X4}$. Similarly, for $\Im_{RE}(x, y)$ in Eq. (3), we can denote the similarities of four features as $\Im_{RE1}, \Im_{RE2}, \Im_{RE3}, \Im_{RE4}$, respectively.

Secondly, we use linear fitting to find best weight $W = (w_1, w_2, w_3, w_4)$ and redefine the four methods in Eqs. (4)–(7) as follows.

$$SimFirFit(Con_1, Con_2) = w_1 * \Im_{X1} + w_2 * \Im_{X2} + w_3 * \Im_{X3} + w_4 * \Im_{X4}, \qquad (10)$$

$$SimSecFit(Con_1, Con_2) = w_1 * \Im_{RE1} + w_2 * \Im_{RE2} + w_3 * \Im_{RE3} + w_4 * \Im_{RE4}. \quad (11)$$

Clearly, we can easily show that the methods in Eqs. (4)–(7) is a special case of Eqs. (10) or (11). For instance, if $W = (\frac{1}{4}, \frac{1}{4}, \frac{1}{4}, \frac{1}{4})$, we have $SimFir$ by Eq. (10) and $SimSec$ by Eq. (11). If $W = (0, 0, 0, 1)$, we have $SimThi$ by Eq. (10). Furthermore, by Eqs. (10) and (11), we can give a formal definition of our method with nonlinear fitting as follows:

Definition 2 (nonlinear fitting method). *Let Con_1 and Con_2 be two concepts defined by four features: Anchor, Category, Gloss, Synonym; $\Im_{X1} < \Im_{X2} < \Im_{X3} < \Im_{X4}$ be the reordered similarities of four features obtained by Eq. (2); $\Im_{RE1} < \Im_{RE2} < \Im_{RE3} < \Im_{RE4}$ be the reordered similarities of four features obtained by Eq. (3); $W = (w_1, w_2, w_3, w_4)$ be the weights set of the features; and $P = (p_1, p_2, p_3, p_4)$ be the exponent of the similarities of four features. Then the similarity between two concepts Con_1 and Con_2 obtained by weighted feature-based methods with nonlinear fitting can be defined as follows:*

$$SimFirNon(Con_1, Con_2) = w_1 * \Im_{X1}^{p1} + w_2 * \Im_{X2}^{p2} + w_3 * \Im_{X3}^{p3} + w_4 * \Im_{X4}^{p4}, \qquad (12)$$

$$SimSecNon(Con_1, Con_2) = w_1 * \Im_{RE1}^{p1} + w_2 * \Im_{RE2}^{p2} + w_3 * \Im_{RE3}^{p3} + w_4 * \Im_{RE4}^{p4}. \quad (13)$$

Thus, by Definition 2, in order to obtain the similarity between two concepts by our new methods, we need to select one benchmark as training data to find the power values set P and the weights set W for methods $SimFitNon$ and $SimSecNon$ in discrete spaces, then test on other benchmarks.

3.3   Training Process of the Parameters

In this subsection, we will show how to use a training process to obtain the power values set P, and the weights set W.

First, when methods $SimFirNon$ and $SimSecNon$ are trained on each benchmark, we denote them as $TestFirTrain$ and $TestSecTrain$. To show the details about training and testing benchmarks, we denote method as $test - benchmark - Fir - train - benchmark$ and $test - benchmark - Sec - train - benchmark$. For instance, method $353tcFirMC30$ is a sub-method of $TestFirTrain$ which means method $SimFitNon$ train on MC30 and test on 353tc. The Pearson correlation coefficient of $TestFirTrain$ and $TestSecTrain$ are defined as the highest Pearson correlation coefficient of all its sub-methods.

In our experiments, we train $SimFirNon$ and $SimSecNon$ in discrete spaces $W \in [-1, 1, 0.02]^4$ and $P \in \{\frac{1}{10}, \frac{1}{9}, \frac{1}{8}, \frac{1}{7}, \frac{1}{6}, \frac{1}{5}, \frac{1}{4}, \frac{1}{3}, \frac{1}{2}, 1\}^4$. And Table 1 shows that the highest Pearson correlation coefficient of method $TestFirTrain$ are 0.726, 0.794, 0.872, 0.871, 0.525 and method $TestSecTrain$ gets 0.738, 0.801, 0.901, 0.880, 0.548, on benchmark 353tc, Jiang30, MC30, RG65, Sim666 respectively. From Table 1 we can get the following statements:

1. We have not listed the methods that train on Sim666, because it does not achieve any good performance on each benchmark. This is because that Sim666 has many antonyms. For instance, the similarity of "South" and "North" is 0.22 (normalized), but our method $SimFirNew$ get 0.731 for them. When $\alpha = 0$, method $SimSecNew$ get 1.0 for them. Antonyms make so many troubles for researchers. This is why all the methods in Table 2 get the worst Pearson correlation coefficient on sim666. It seems to be that Sim666 is not a good data set for training data.
2. Because the concepts in MC30 is a subset of RG65, so we do not train on one of them and test on the other. Similar to 353tc and Sim666.
3. Although benchmark MC30 and Jiang30 both have only 30 concept pairs, training on MC30 can hardly achieve any good performance while training on Jiang30 can get an improvement in each benchmark. This is because Jiang30 is made for computing semantic similarity based on Wikipedia, especially but MC30 is not. Also, there are many concepts in MC30, and other benchmarks are ambiguous in Wikipedia, but all the concept in Jiang30 come from Wikipedia directly.
4. Table 1 shows that our methods can have better performances on each benchmark by the nonlinear fitting. It turns out to be that only Sim666 is not a good data set for training data, and Jiang30 is the best training benchmark. When we train on it, each method can achieve improvement.

4 Evaluations

In this section, we will summarize all of our methods and compare with previous researches on benchmarks 353tc, Jiang30, MC30, RG65 and Sim666.

In order to make it convenient to describe, we denote a tuple (a, b, c, d, e) to describe the best results of all the methods in one paper. For instance, the best results in [14] are (0.508, 0.443, 0.582, 0.824, 0.381) which means among all the methods in [14], the best Pearson correlation coefficient they can get are 0.508, 0.443, 0.582, 0.824, 0.381 on benchmarks 353tc, Jiang30, MC30, RG65 and Sim666, respectively.

Remarks: the Pearson correlation coefficient of the methods in previous researches in Table 2 are not the same as the Pearson correlation coefficient in their original papers. This is because we apply their methods to the same version of Wikipedia data used in our experiments, instead of their original data in their papers.

In this paper, the best results for each benchmarks we can get are (0.738, 0.801, 0.901, 0.880, 0.548) as shown in Table 2. For methods $TestFirTrain$ and $TestSecTrain$, we choose their best Pearson correlation coefficient in Table 1.

Firstly, we compare with eight traditional semantic similarity feature-based methods in [6], i.e., $SimFir \cdots SimEig$. Their best results are (0.622, 0.781, 0.780, 0.826, 0.469). Obviously, in every benchmark, we get a better result, because our methods overcome their limitations. We remove low-frequency features which contain too much noise. We propose a novel way to compute the

Table 1. Pearson correlation coefficient of methods $SimFirNon, SimSecNon$ train on denser spaces: $W \in [-1, 1, 0.02]^4$ and $P \in \{\frac{1}{10}, \frac{1}{9}, \frac{1}{8}, \frac{1}{7}, \frac{1}{6}, \frac{1}{5}, \frac{1}{4}, \frac{1}{3}, \frac{1}{2}, 1\}^4$.

Method	α	POWER	WEIGHT	Pearson
Jiang30Sec353tc	0.2	$(0.125, \frac{1}{9}, 0.5, 1)$	$(0.12, -0.1, 0.68, 0.48)$	0.777
MC30Fir353tc	-	$(0.1, 0.1, 0.5, 0.5)$	$(-0.06, -0.02, 0.34, 0.16)$	0.857
MC30Sec353tc	0.2	$(0.125, \frac{1}{9}, 0.5, 1)$	$(0.12, -0.1, 0.68, 0.48)$	0.864
RG65Fir353tc	-	$(0.1, 0.1, 0.5, 0.5)$	$(-0.06, -0.02, 0.34, 0.16)$	0.871
RG65Sec353tc	0.3	$(0.125, \frac{1}{9}, 0.5, 1)$	$(0.12, -0.1, 0.7, 0.5)$	0.880
Sim666Fir353tc	-	$(0.1, 0.1, 0.5, 0.5)$	$(-0.06, -0.02, 0.34, 0.16)$	0.495
Sim666Sec353tc	0.0	$(0.1, \frac{1}{9}, 0.5, \frac{1}{3})$	$(0.0, 0.04, 0.86, 0.36)$	0.529
353tcFirJiang30	-	$(\frac{1}{9}, 0.1, 0.5, 1)$	$(0.14, -0.16, 0.26, 0.76)$	0.685
353tcSecJiang30	0.3	$(\frac{1}{9}, 0.1, 0.5, 1)$	$(0.06, -0.24, 0.58, 0.76)$	0.714
MC30FirJiang30	-	$(0.1, 0.1, 1, 1)$	$(0.06, -0.04, 0.0, 0.24)$	0.872
MC30SecJiang30	0.1	$(0.1, 0.1, 1, 1)$	$(0.06, -0.04, -0.02, 0.16)$	0.901
RG65FirJiang30	-	$(\frac{1}{9}, 0.1, 0.5, 1)$	$(0.14, -0.16, 0.26, 0.76)$	0.867
RG65SecJiang30	0.5	$(\frac{1}{9}, 0.1, 0.5, 1)$	$(0.14, -0.16, 0.26, 0.56)$	0.880
Sim666FirJiang30	-	$(0.1, 0.1, \frac{1}{7}, \frac{1}{7})$	$(0.1, -0.04, 0.12, 0.3)$	0.521
Sim666SecJiang30	0.0	$(0.1, 0.1, \frac{1}{6}, \frac{1}{6})$	$(0.22, -0.06, 0.12, 0.6)$	0.535
353tcFirMC30	-	$(0.1, \frac{1}{9}, \frac{1}{3}, 0.25)$	$(-0.04, -0.08, 0.64, 0.92)$	0.698
353tcSecMC30	0.7	$(0.1, 0.1, 1, 1)$	$(-0.1, -0.04, 0.94, 0.08)$	0.700
Jiang30FirMC30	-	$(0.1, 0.125, 0.1, 1)$	$(0.04, -0.02, -0.04, 0.16)$	0.794
Jiang30SecMC30	0.0	$(\frac{1}{7}, 0.2, 0.1, 1)$	$(0.18, -0.1, -0.16, 0.46)$	0.797
Sim666FirMC30	-	$(0.1, \frac{1}{9}, \frac{1}{3}, 0.25)$	$(0.0, -0.08, 0.52, 0.98)$	0.509
Sim666SecMC30	0.6	$(0.1, 0.125, 1, \frac{1}{3})$	$(0.18, -0.42, 0.94, 0.76)$	0.469
353tcFirRG65	-	$(1, 1, 0.5, 0.5)$	$(-0.1, 0.02, 0.34, 0.14)$	0.726
353tcSecRG65	0.2	$(0.1, 0.1, 0.5, 0.5)$	$(-0.14, 0.14, 0.98, 0.32)$	0.738
Jiang30SecRG65	0.0	$(\frac{1}{7}, 0.125, 0.5, 1)$	$(0.06, -0.04, 0.06, 0.1)$	0.801
Sim666FirRG65	-	$(0.1, 0.1, 0.25, 0.25)$	$(0.08, 0.12, 0.12, 0.44)$	0.525
Sim666SecRG65	0.2	$(0.1, 0.1, 0.5, 0.5)$	$(-0.14, 0.14, 0.98, 0.32)$	0.548

similarity of a synonym pair. Both negative and positive weights are used to mitigate incompleteness and validity of Wikipedia. Secondly, we compare with two methods $wpath_{IC_{path}}$ and $wpath_{IC_{corpus}}$ in [14] which measure the semantic similarity between concepts in Knowledge Graphs (KGs) such as WordNet and DBpedia. Semantic similarity is measured by combining the shortest path length between concepts and IC based weight of the shortest path. Their best results are $(0.508, 0.443, 0.582, 0.824, 0.381)$. We also get better results in each benchmark. Thirdly, we compare with three methods $NASARI_{embded}$, $NASARI_{lexical}$ and $NASARI_{unified}$ in [2]. It provides a novel multilingual vector representation of

Table 2. Pearson correlation coefficient of all methods.

English Wikipedia

Method	353tc	Jiang30	MC30	RG65	Sim666
TestFirTrain	0.726	0.794	0.872	0.871	0.525
TestSecTrain	0.738	**0.801**	**0.901**	0.880	0.548
SimFir	0.478	0.749	0.716	0.770	0.434
SimSec	0.513	0.757	0.725	0.780	0.453
SimThi	0.567	0.781	0.756	0.808	0.455
SimFou	0.622	0.763	0.770	0.826	0.469
SimFif	0.302	0.305	0.607	0.507	0.172
SimSix	0.305	0.304	0.610	0.510	0.172
SimSev	0.580	0.727	0.780	0.743	0.423
SimEig	0.550	0.713	0.763	0.724	0.416
$wpath_{IC_{corpus}}$	0.483	0.443	0.515	0.784	0.357
$wpath_{IC_{graph}}$	0.508	0.413	0.582	0.824	0.381
$NASARI_{embeded}$	**0.825**	0.722	0.855	0.849	0.512
$NASARI_{lexical}$	0.807	0.724	0.863	0.861	0.557
$NASARI_{unified}$	0.822	0.722	0.842	**0.881**	**0.574**
$Word2Vec$	0.751	-	0.837	0.820	0.511

German Wikipedia

Method	353tc	RG65	Method	353tc	RG65
TestFirTrain	0.517	**0.731**	$SimFou$	0.514	0.590
TestSecTrain	0.529	0.721	$SimFir$	0.369	0.431
$NASARI_{lexical}$	0.658	0.724	$SimSec$	0.415	0.477
$NASARI_{unified}$	**0.673**	0.685	$SimThi$	0.461	0.523
$Word2Vec$	0.657	0.682	$SimFif$	0.578	0.705
$SimSix$	0.569	0.702	$SimSev$	0.544	0.578
$SimEig$	0.526	0.564			

words using structural knowledge from semantic networks with the statistical information derived from text corpora for the effective representation of millions of BabelNet synsets, including nominal WordNet synsets and all Wikipedia articles. Their best results are (0.825, 0.724, 0.863, 0.881, 0.574). We get better results in Jinag30, MC30 and in RG65 they get 0.881, but we get 0.880. Finally, we compare with Word2Vec [8] where words are represented as vectors. A feed-forward neural network is used to learn continuous representations of words. Word2Vec has two architectures Continuous Bag-of-Words (CBOW) and Continuous Skip-gram Model. Their best results are (0.751, -, 0.837, 0.820, 0.511). They get better results in 353tc, but we get better results in MC30, RG65 and Sim666. We do not run their methods in Jiang30, because there are many concepts in Jiang30 that cannot be represented by vectors. For instance, "Nobel_Prize_in_Literature", "Nobel_Peace_Prize", "Summer_Olympic_Games" and "World_championship" are concepts obtained by combined words and representing words by vectors need to split them.

Besides English Wikipedia, we also try German Wikipedia. While German Wikipedia is so small such that many concepts in Jiang30 and Sim666 do not exist the corresponding concept in it. MC30 is a subset of RG65. Therefore, we only try our methods in German Wikipedia in 353tc and RG65.

The lower part of Table 2 shows the Pearson correlation coefficient of our methods (right part) and the methods in precious researches (left part). When train data, discrete spaces are $W \in [-1, 1, 0.02]^4$, $P \in \{\frac{1}{10}, \frac{1}{9}, \frac{1}{8}, \frac{1}{7}, \frac{1}{6}, \frac{1}{5}, \frac{1}{4}, \frac{1}{3}, \frac{1}{2}, 1\}^4$. The best results we can get are (0.529, 0.731). When train data in German Wikipedia, the discrete spaces are the as English Wikipedia. Compared with [2,6,8], they all have better performance on 353tc. On the contrary, we have better performance on RG65. This is because 353tc has nearly 200 concept pairs, but RG65 only has about 60. It is too difficult to get a good result if we train on such a small benchmark and test on a much bigger benchmark.

5   Conclusion

It is hard to deal with the incompleteness, invalidity and inconsistency of the knowledge in Wikipedia because anyone can edit a Wikipedia article at any time. Furthermore, in traditional knowledge and feature-based methods for semantic similarity that without weights, all features are treated equally. Each feature makes the same contribution to similarity. But in the weighted methods, it is a complex task to assign weights to features. To address the above issues, in this paper, for the sake of invalidity, we remove low-frequency features (anchors and terms in glosses) in our experiments. Because of incompleteness, we do not limit the sum of all weights to 1. The inconsistency of knowledge has a great influence on the similarity. So when we apply S_{RE} to our methods, we try different values of α, instead of fixing it as 0.5.

Furthermore, we provide a new way to compute the similarity of synonyms. Many previous methods of semantic similarity take the similarity of all synonyms that have common senses as 1 in the score [0, 1] when they are applied to Wikipedia. But in our novel methods, we give them an initial similarity and adjust it by the number of their categories. Finally, we provide new methods to compute similarity based on nonlinear fitting. We propose a new way to assign weights to features by training data on one benchmark in discrete space to find weights and powers, then test on others. Compared with previous work, our new methods can always get a better Pearson correlation coefficient on some benchmarks. According to our experiments, Jiang30 is the best benchmark for training data. When we train on it, every method has a better performance on other benchmarks. We also try German Wikipedia. But limited to the size of German Wikipedia, many concepts in benchmarks do not have an article in it.

We only try RG65 and 353tc. Training on 353tc has a better performance than previous researches.

In the future, we will try to deal with antonyms. Sim666 is the biggest benchmark among MC30, RG65, Jiang30 and 353tc and training on a bigger data set can always get a better result. But in fact, training on Sim666 is hard to get good results because of antonyms. It is hard to distinguish if a concept pair are antonyms or not by Wikipedia, and they always have many common features. There still lack an efficient way to compute the similarity of two antonyms.

Acknowledgments. The works described in this paper are supported by The National Natural Science Foundation of China under Grant Nos. 61772210 and 61272066; Guangdong Province Universities Pearl River Scholar Funded Scheme (2018); The Project of Science and Technology in Guangzhou in China under Grant No. 201807010043; The key project in universities in Guangdong Province of China under Grant No. 2016KZDXM024.

References

1. Agirre, E., Alfonseca, E., Hall, K., Kravalova, J., Paşca, M., Soroa, A.: A study on similarity and relatedness using distributional and WordNet-based approaches. In: Proceedings of Human Language Technologies, pp. 19–27. Association for Computational Linguistics (2009)
2. Camacho-Collados, J., Pilehvar, M.T., Navigli, R.: Nasari: integrating explicit knowledge and corpus statistics for a multilingual representation of concepts and entities. Artif. Intell. **240**, 36–64 (2016)
3. Choumane, A.: A semantic similarity-based social information retrieval model. Soc. Netw. Anal. Min. **4**(1), 1–6 (2014)
4. Hill, F., Reichart, R., Korhonen, A.: SimLex-999: evaluating semantic models with (genuine) similarity estimation. Comput. Linguist. **41**(4), 665–695 (2015)
5. Jiang, Y., Bai, W., Zhang, X., Hu, J.: Wikipedia-based information content and semantic similarity computation. Inf. Process. Manage. **53**(1), 248–265 (2017)
6. Jiang, Y., Zhang, X., Tang, Y., Nie, R.: Feature-based approaches to semantic similarity assessment of concepts using Wikipedia. Inf. Process. Manage. **51**(3), 215–234 (2015)
7. Meymandpour, R., Davis, J.G.: A semantic similarity measure for linked data: an information content-based approach. Knowl.-Based Syst. **109**, 276–293 (2016)
8. Mikolov, T., Chen, K., Corrado, G., Dean, J.: Efficient estimation of word representations in vector space. Comput. Sci. 1–12 (2013)
9. Miller, G.A., Charles, W.G.: Contextual correlates of semantic similarity. Lang. Cogn. Process. **6**(1), 1–28 (1991)
10. Petrakis, E.G.M., Varelas, G., Hliaoutakis, A., Raftopoulou, P.: X-similarity: computing semantic similarity between concepts from different ontologies. J. Digit. Inf. Manage. **4**(4), 233–237 (2006)
11. Qu, R., Fang, Y., Bai, W., Jiang, Y.: Computing semantic similarity based on novel models of semanticrepresentation using Wikipedia. Inf. Process. Manage. **54**, 1002–1021 (2018)
12. Rodríguez, A., Egenhofer, M.J.: Determining semantic similarity among entity classes from different ontologies. IEEE Trans. Knowl. Data Eng. **15**(2), 442–456 (2003)

13. Rubenstein, H., Goodenough, J.B.: Contextual correlates of synonymy. Commun. Assoc. Comput. Mach. **8**(10), 627–633 (1965)
14. Zhu, G., Iglesias, C.A.: Computing semantic similarity of concepts in knowledge graphs. IEEE Trans. Knowl. Data Eng. **29**(1), 72–85 (2017)

A Two-Stage Model Based on BERT for Short Fake News Detection

Chao Liu[1], Xinghua Wu[1,2], Min Yu[1,2(✉)] (iD), Gang Li[3(✉)] (iD), Jianguo Jiang[1], Weiqing Huang[1], and Xiang Lu[1]

[1] Institute of Information Engineering, Chinese Academy of Sciences, Beijing, China
yumin@iie.ac.cn
[2] School of Cyber Security, University of Chinese Academy of Sciences, Beijing, China
[3] School of Information Technology, Deakin University, Geelong, Australia
gang.li@deakin.edu.au

Abstract. Online social media promotes the development of the news industry and make it easy for everyone to obtain the latest news. Meanwhile, the circumstances get worse because of fake news. Fake news is flooding and become a serious threat which may cause high societal and economic losses, making fake news detection important. Unlike traditional one, news on social media tends to be short and misleading, which is more confusing to identify. On the other hand, fake news may contain parts of the facts and parts of the incorrect contents in one statement, which is not so clear and simple to classify. Hence, we propose a two-stage model to deal with the difficulties. Our model is built on BERT, a pre-trained model with a more powerful feature extractor Transformer instead of CNN or RNN. Besides, some accessible information is used to extend features and calculate attention weights. At last, inspired by fine-grained sentiment analysis, we treat fake news detection as fine-grained multiple-classification task and use two similar sub-models to identify different granularity labels separately. We evaluate our model on a real-world benchmark dataset. The experimental results demonstrate its effectiveness in fine-grained fake news detection and its superior performance to the baselines and other competitive approaches.

Keywords: Fake news detection · Pre-trained model · Attention mechanism · Fine-grained classify

1 Introduction

With the development of the Internet, people get used to checking out the latest news through online social media. Compared with the traditional one, online social media removes the restrictions of centralized publishing and dissemination, so that anyone can share what they see or hear at any time. The benefits are apparent that information can be quickly released or disseminated and is convenient for people to get. On the other hand, due to the lack of review, fake

© Springer Nature Switzerland AG 2019
C. Douligeris et al. (Eds.): KSEM 2019, LNAI 11776, pp. 172–183, 2019.
https://doi.org/10.1007/978-3-030-29563-9_17

news is flooding and become a serious threat which may cause high societal and economic losses.

Under the current circumstances with abundant and fast-flowing news, manual review is no longer effective, which makes automated detection technology based on content understanding increasingly important. Unlike traditional news with rich contents, news in social media like twitter or weibo is always expressed as short comments with limited words. The performance of content-based supervised learning will be seriously affected by fewer features available for extraction. Moreover, different from other detection and classification task, fake news is intentionally written to mislead readers to believe false information. It may contain parts of the facts and parts of the incorrect contents in one statement, which is not as clear and simple as binary-classification. Thus, fake news detection can be regarded as a fine-grained multiple-classification task, making the problem more difficult. In a word, poor features in short statements and misleading with truth and illusion, make automated short fake news detection a big challenge in natural language processing.

In this paper, we focus on fake news detection with short statements. For example, a statement said that "Transgender individuals in the U.S. have a 1-in-12 chance of being murdered", which is short and totally fake. Due to the limited available information, the internal connection should be strengthened and external knowledge should be imported. To address the above challenges, we propose a two-stage model based on BERT [3]. BERT is a pre-trained model using the Transformer encoder, which will help us to model our specific data with trained general data. The Transformer is a advanced architecture using attention mechanism to model language. In our model, we transform BERT through making full use of all hidden states after encoding as parts of features as our primary encoder. Apart from news content itself, there are several categories of extra information such as the speaker's name, job, party affiliation and so on, which can be modeled as features. We will use parts of extra information as inputs and parts of it to calculate weights with attention mechanism. Different from other studies, we regarded fake news detection as a fine-grained multiple-classification tasks. In aspect-based fine-grained sentiment analysis, researchers usually classify aspect first and then analyze sentiment based on classified aspect. Learning from this, we employed a two-stage model to distinguish fine-grained labels for multiple-classification. In summary, the contributions are as follows:

(1) Inspired by aspect-based fine-grained sentiment analysis and considering the potential connection between different labels, we split our fine-grained classification task into two stages, which differentiate respective granularity labels separately at different phases.

(2) We propose a model based on BERT to detect short fake news. Unlike BERT only using first hidden state as the aggregate sequence representation, we utilize all hidden states and apply attention mechanism to calculate weights.

The rest of the paper is organized as follows: Sect. 2 gives a brief overview on the related work. Section 3 describes the proposed approach. The contents of the experiment are given in Sect. 4. Finally, conclusion and future work are presented in Sect. 5.

2   Related Work

2.1   Text Classification and Fake News Detection

Text classification task is one of the most basic tasks in natural language processing. It has gone through changes from rules-based to the statistics-based methods, and now most studies are based on machine learning or deep learning. Fake news detection is one of the subtasks of text classification tasks and can be defined as the task of categorizing news along with a continuum of veracity with an associated measure of certainty [2]. The difficulty comes partly from how to extract effective information from statements which are also difficult for a human to distinguish. In one study, human judges, by a rough measure of comparison, achieved only 50–63% success rates in identifying fake news [11]. Normally, the models constructed on fake news detection can be approximately divided into news content models and social context models [12]. News content models rely on news content features and existing factual sources to classify fake news. Karimi [5] proposes MMDF framework using multi-source including statements, metadata, history, and report. Social context models include related user social engagements in the analysis, capturing this auxiliary information from a variety of perspectives. Qian [10] proposes TCNN-URG to capture semantic information and model users' review. Liu [7] models the propagation path of each news story as a multivariate time series for early detection of fake news on social media. Shu [13] makes use of tri-relationship, the relationship among publishers, news pieces, and users, which has the potential to improve fake news detection.

2.2   Attention Mechanism

Attention mechanism is proposed to weight the dependencies between source and target. Some parts of the input can be more relevant to the output so we should pay more attention to it. Bahdanau [1] firstly introduces the attention mechanism to help memorize long source sentences in neural machine translation and improve the system robustness. Since then, it soon got extended into the computer vision field [19] and people started exploring its variants. Luong [8] proposes two kinds of attention mechanism, global attention and local attention, depending on the size of the attention window. Another variant named inner attention uses the original input instead of encoder ones as the attention input to eliminate the negative influence of RNNs [17]. Recently, self-attention mechanism becomes a hotspot in the field of natural language processing. Google [15] firstly generalizes attention mechanism and proposed the Transformer, which utilizes self-attention and multi-head attention mechanism. Instead of comparing the relevance between input and output, self-attention focus on all tokens in one sentence and reinforce internal connection for helping to encode.

2.3 Pre-trained Model and BERT

Recent years, more works focus on the pre-trained model in NLP. Researchers collect large-scale unlabeled data and train models to extract knowledge from it. After training, other researchers can transfer and fine-tune models with their specific field knowledge [9]. BERT is one of the pre-trained language representation models [3]. Different from the traditional model based on CNNs or RNNs as feature extractors, multi-layer bidirectional Transformer encoder constructs the foundation of BERT. The Transformer encoder is an excellent feature extractor and has advantages in time cost compared with RNN as well as long-term dependency compared with CNN. BERT is pre-trained with two large corpora and outperforms all models in GLUE benchmark when first proposed. After proposing, there are lots of works based on BERT now. Liu [6] combines multi-task networks and BERT, reaching a higher score than BERT. Zhang [20] proposes the first model which applies the BERT into text generation tasks and achieves new state-of-the-art on datasets.

3 Model

The architecture of our proposed BERT-based two-stage model is shown in Fig. 1. In the following subsections, we firstly show the representation of news, then introduce the effect of extra information and how to use it. Finally, we illustrate our two-stage model and its connection.

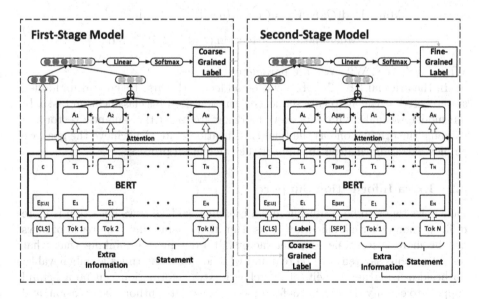

Fig. 1. The architecture of two-stage model.

3.1   News Representation

In our model, BERT is employed as the encoder to represent news. Without CNNs or RNNs, BERT constructs on the Transformer, which has been proved as a more powerful feature extractor. Thanks to pre-trained on large-scale corpora, BERT learns rich knowledge and captures much linguistic meaning to help us train our model. Based on BERT, we fine-tune the model with fake news dataset and the defect of the short news representation will be alleviated to some extent.

Let X = (Tok 1, Tok 2, . . . , Tok N) be a news, where N is the news length and Tok i is the i-th token. Each token will be embedded with token embeddings, segment embeddings, and position embeddings. Token embeddings aim to represent different tokens and segment embeddings differentiate the sentences. While the Transformer is position independent, position embeddings should be applied to obtain position information. After embedding, E = $(E_1, E_2, . . . , E_N)$ replaces tokens as Transformer's input. The Transformer will use self-attention and multi-head attention to encode embedded token to hidden states H = $(T_1, T_2, . . . , T_N)$. Self-Attention mechanism transforms each token to queries, keys, values. The queries, keys and values are packed together into matrices Q, K and V and compute the matrix of outputs as:

$$(Q, K, V) = \text{softmax}\left(\frac{QK^T}{\sqrt{d_k}}\right) V \tag{1}$$

Multi-Head attention learns different connections in one sentence to increase diversities. All heads are connected and decide the final hidden state by:

$$\text{MultiHead}(Q, K, V) = \text{Concat}(\text{head}_1, . . . , \text{head}_h) W^O$$
$$\text{where head}_i = \text{Attention}\left(QW_i^Q, KW_i^K, VW_i^V\right) \tag{2}$$

Where W^O, W^Q, W^K, W^V are parameter matrices.

In the original BERT, [CLS] will be added as the first token and its hidden state is used as the aggregate sequence representation for classification tasks. In our model, we make full use of every hidden state to get the semantic vector and combine the original one as the final classification state. To achieve the goal, we employ extra information to support the calculation process.

3.2   Extra Information Support

Fake news tends to be confusing and misleading, so fake news detection is more difficult than other classification tasks. But at the same time, the truth of news can be more susceptible to other factors. It's our inertia thinking that what honest persons say tends to be real and who lies for many times is unbelievable. So besides using news itself, other related extra information can be a helpful support to classify the truth. As for a piece of news, its author, the occasion, and all related content can be part of the extra information. Moreover, if the authors are public figures, personal information and credit history could be accessible. We can gather all these extra information and make it helpful.

In our model, extra information is divided into two parts. Firstly, news in online social media is short so that it's hard for the model to fit. As mentioned above, extra information can be helpful, so the first part of information is added into the head of the statements to form a longer and more complete news representation. As a result, the Transformer will capture the connection between extra information and statements and make the model more robust. Because of the limitation of vocabulary and representation, some parts of information can't be given directly to BERT but has an essential impact on the results. So as for the second part, we employ it to calculate the attention weights, which decides the usage of all hidden states. The attention can be measured by the relatedness between hidden states H and extra information representation I. The attention weight Ai for each hidden state can be defined as:

$$A_i = \frac{\exp\left(\text{score}\left(H_i, I\right)\right)}{\sum_j \exp\left(\text{score}\left(H_j, I\right)\right)} \tag{3}$$

Where score is score function, which can be defined as:

$$score\left(H_j, I\right) = \tanh\left(W^H\left[H_j : I\right] + B\right) \tag{4}$$

Tanh is a non-linear activation function. W^H is an intermediate matrix. B is the offset. After calculating attention scores, the semantic vector can be gotten by the sum of all hidden states with weights as follows:

$$C' = \sum_j^N A_j H_j \tag{5}$$

At last, we will combine the original classification vector (blue vector shown in Fig. 1) and the new vector (red vector shown in Fig. 1) as the new classification.

$$C = \text{Concat}(C, C') \tag{6}$$

3.3   Two-Stage Model

In many classification tasks, each label is clear and independent. As for fake news detection, categories sometimes could be hard to define. Because fake news is created to be confusing and misleading, one piece of news may include content both in true and false. So in most conditions, fake news detection can't be regarded as a simple binary-classification task. PolitiFact[1], a fact-checking website, rates the degree of claims from "True" for completely accurate statements to "Pants on Fire" for false and ridiculous claims.

As a result, "True" or "False" is not able to cover all situations and more labels should be used for classification, which is more suitable for real conditions. It is known that fine-grained multiple-classification is harder to model than binary-classification, so we need to make more changes to our model. Inspired by

---

[1] http://www.politifact.com/.

aspect-based fine-grained sentiment analysis, classification tasks can be divided into two stages, aspect and sentiment. Aspect and sentiment have specific connections, and the classification results of aspect will affect sentiment classification. Therefore, we subdivide fine-grained labels into primaries and subsidiary categories and propose a two-stage model to differentiate coarse-grained labels and fine-grained labels separately.

As shown in Fig. 1, two stages have a similar architecture. Firstly, we classify all labels into two categories as coarse-grained labels. Then, the numbers of fine-grained labels will be decided by the numbers of the dataset's label. The first-stage model learns to classify coarse-grained label with the above methods. After getting a temporary label, we add it as a part of the input to BERT. Following the same workflow, the second-stage model will construct all inputs and classify fine-grained labels. The final label will be decided by coarse-grained and fine-grained labels.

We employ the cross-entropy loss function to train the model. The loss function is defined as follows:

$$L = -\frac{1}{n} \sum_i^n \sum_j^m y_{ij} \log p_{ij} \tag{7}$$

Where n is the total number of training data; m is the number of labels; y represents the ground-truth while p represents the predicted label.

4   Experiments

4.1   Dataset

There are some collected datasets for fake news detection. Vlachos and Riedel [16] are the first to release a public fake news detection and fact-checking dataset from two fact-checking websites. This dataset only includes 221 statements, which does not permit machine learning based assessments. Wang [18] collected LIAR dataset from PolitiFact, which includes 12.8K short statements labeled for truthfulness, subject, context/venue, speaker, state, party, and prior history with six fine-grained classes, including pants-fire, false, barely-true, half-true, mostly-true and true. Another famous dataset is Fact Extraction and VERification (FEVER) dataset [14], which consists of 185,445 claims with evidence and classified into SUPPORTED, REFUTED or NOTENOUGHINFO. Also, there are many other datasets with more longer statement length [12].

Considering the aim of short fake news detection and multiple-classification, LIAR dataset is chosen for its appropriate statement length (average 17.9 tokens per statement), abundant collected extra information and a well-balanced distribution of fine-grained labels. The statistics of LIAR dataset are shown in Table 1.

Table 1. The LIAR dataset statistics.

Dataset statistics	
Training set size	10,269
Validation set size	1,284
Testing set size	1,283
Avg. statement length (tokens)	17.9

4.2   Settings

Our work is constructed on pre-trained $BERT_{BASE}$ with about 110 million parameters, which is more suitable for individual use comparing with resource dependent $BERT_{LARGE}$. In $BERT_{BASE}$, there are 28,996 tokens in the vocabulary and every token is embedded using WordPiece embeddings. The layer of Transformer encoders and the number of attention heads is set to 12. The hidden size, which denotes the dimension of token representation, is 768. GeLU activation [4] is used in the Transformer rather than the sigmoid, tanh, or standard ReLU. We use Adam with the learning rate of 5e-5. Dropout layers are added to prevent overfitting and the probability of hidden dropout as well as attention dropout is set to 0.1.

During the training procedure, the batch size is set to 32, while during the validation and testing procedure, the batch size is 8. The max input sequence length is 64, aimed to make a balance with batch size. A sequence will be padded or truncated depending on whether it's longer or shorter than 64. The number of train epoch is 3 and every epoch includes 321 steps.

For extra information, the credit histories can be directly used as array and others can be divided into tokens existed in the vocabulary except for the speakers' names. To make use of speakers' names, we embed 2,916 speakers' names into 12-dimensional vectors to represent all. The credit histories and speakers' names are employed to calculate the attention weights and other information is added directly in the head of statements.

LIAR dataset has labeled six fine-grained labels. To maintain the balance of the data, we set pants-fire, false, barely-true to "0" and others as "1" as their coarse-grained labels. As for the fine-grained labels, pants-fire and half-true are set to "−1"; false and mostly-true are set to "0"; barely-true and true are set to "1".

4.3   Result and Analysis

Comparison with Baselines. We compare our proposed model with the following baseline system:

- Basic-SVM. Bag-of-Words, bigrams, and 3-grams are extracted and combined with the history. PCA is used to reduce the dimension. SVM is employed to classify.

- Basic-RandomForests. This baseline is similar to Basic-SVM except using Random Forests as the classifier.
- Basic-NN. One-layer connected neural network is employed as the baseline. The input to NN is the same with the other two classifiers.
- Wang. Wang [18] developed a model based on CNNs and Bi-LSTMs for fake news detection on LIAR dataset.
- BERT and One-Stage Model. BERT [3] can be fine-tuned with LIAR dataset and classify labels. When extra information is used, we update BERT as the one-stage model with extra information and attention mechanism.
- MMFD. Karimi [5] proposed a framework MMFD representing multi-source multi-class Fake news Detection.

Table 2. Result comparison.

Used	Method	Accuracy (%)
Statements	Basic-SVM	20.12
	Basic-RandomForests	23.19
	Basic-NN	21.73
	Wang	27.00
	BERT	29.07
	MMFD	29.06
	Our model	**34.51**
Statements + Information	Basic-SVM	25.07
	Basic-RandomForests	27.63
	Basic-NN	28.16
	Wang	27.40
	One-stage model	30.47
	MMFD	34.77
	Our model	**40.58**

The results compared with baselines is shown in Table 2. We divide the results into two parts based on the usage of different information. The upper part only uses the statements while the lower part uses all information given by LIAR dataset. As we can see, BERT outperforms Basic-NN, Wang's basic CNNs, and Bi-LSTMs, which proves that pre-trained knowledge does a specific help to model short statements. Either with extra information or not, our model has a significant improvement in accuracy compared with other methods. It proves that our architecture is more effective.

Comparing the results of two parts through all methods, it turns out that extra information can be important features for classification. Notably, our model outperforms MMFD which has combined CNNs, LSTMs, and attention mechanism mainly because of our two-stage adoption.

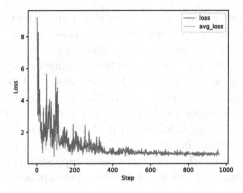

Fig. 2. Loss and average loss during training.

The trend of loss and average loss during training is shown in Fig. 2. The loss value fluctuates up and down but the overall trend is downward, which means our model fits the data. During each epoch, the average loss descends smoothly because of forward and backward propagation. The average loss has a cliff down because the cumulative loss will be clear when it starts a new epoch.

In conclusion, our model outperforms other baselines model and have a certain degree of improvement. To investigate the deep reason for result improvement, we have further ablation studies in the next subsection.

Ablation Study. The ablation study shown in Table 3 gives reasons which might influence the results. One-Stage Model means that information and attention mechanism are all used but only with one stage. It can be described as the left part of Fig. 1 and will classify six fine-grained labels directly. As we can see, one-stage model highest reaches 30.47% accuracy, 10.11% lower than our best two-stage model, which means that two-stage model can capture more features and is useful for fine-grained multiple-classification.

Table 3. Ablation study.

Model		Accuracy (%)	Δ
One-stage model		30.47	−10.11
Two-stage model	Only Statements	34.51	−6.07
	+ Information	39.01	−1.57
	+ Attention	38.55	−2.03
	BEST	40.58	0

As for the two-stage model, we ablate some components to measure the influences. "Only Statements" means that only statements are used and directly fed to two-stage model without extra information and attention mechanism. As expected, without additional components, it reaches the lowest accuracy in the two-stage model, while still outperforms almost all other methods in Table 2. "+ Information" means that parts of extra information are used and inputs are combined with extra information and statements. "+ Attention" means that parts of extra information are used and every hidden state in BERT is calculated compared to extra information with attention mechanism. Δ means the difference comparing to the best model result. Each component has achieved a 4–5% improvement on the original basis. It means that extra information and attention mechanism help to deal with short statements representation and fine-grained classification. Combining all, we reach our best performance.

5   Conclusion and Future Work

In this paper, we focus on fake news detection with short statements. We consider the impacts of a few linguistic features when representing short statements, and propose a two-stage model based on BERT for short fake news detection. Specifically, we add extra information support and transform pre-trained $BERT_{BASE}$ as a foundation through making full use of every hidden state with attention mechanism. Besides, to classify fine-grained labels, we subdivide fine-grained labels into primaries and subsidiary categories and construct two similar sub-model to distinguish labels of different granularities. Coarse-grained labels will help to classify fine-grained labels as inputs of the second-stage model. Because there are more multiple-classification tasks in real life, this way of modeling will have more significance and application prospect. The extensive experiments indicate that our model can effectively distinguish different degrees of fake news. In the future, joint learning can be used for better modeling, which allows two sub-models to influence each other.

Acknowledgment. This work is supported by National Key R&D Program of China (No. 2018YFB0803402), National Natural Science Foundation of China (No. 61402476), the International Cooperation Project of Institute of Information Engineering, Chinese Academy of Sciences under Grant No. Y7Z0511101.

References

1. Bahdanau, D., Cho, K., Bengio, Y.: Neural machine translation by jointly learning to align and translate. arXiv preprint arXiv:1409.0473 (2014)
2. Conroy, N.J., Rubin, V.L., Chen, Y.: Automatic deception detection: methods for finding fake news. In: Proceedings of the 78th ASIS&T Annual Meeting: Information Science with Impact: Research in and for the Community, p. 82. American Society for Information Science (2015)
3. Devlin, J., Chang, M.W., Lee, K., Toutanova, K.: BERT: pre-training of deep bidirectional transformers for language understanding. In: Proceedings of the 2019 Conference of the North American Chapter of the Association for Computational Linguistics: Human Language Technologies (NAACL-HLT) (2019)

4. Hendrycks, D., Gimpel, K.: Bridging nonlinearities and stochastic regularizers with Gaussian error linear units. arXiv preprint arXiv:1606.08415 (2016)
5. Karimi, H., Roy, P., Saba-Sadiya, S., Tang, J.: Multi-source multi-class fake news detection. In: Proceedings of the 27th International Conference on Computational Linguistics (COLING), pp. 1546–1557 (2018)
6. Liu, X., He, P., Chen, W., Gao, J.: Multi-task deep neural networks for natural language understanding. arXiv preprint arXiv:1901.11504 (2019)
7. Liu, Y., Wu, Y.F.B.: Early detection of fake news on social media through propagation path classification with recurrent and convolutional networks. In: Thirty-Second AAAI Conference on Artificial Intelligence (2018)
8. Luong, T., Pham, H., Manning, C.D.: Effective approaches to attention-based neural machine translation. In: Proceedings of the 2015 Conference on Empirical Methods in Natural Language Processing (EMNLP), Lisbon, Portugal, pp. 1412–1421, September 2015
9. Peters, M., et al.: Deep contextualized word representations. In: Proceedings of the 2018 Conference of the North American Chapter of the Association for Computational Linguistics: Human Language Technologies (NAACL-HLT), New Orleans, Louisiana, pp. 2227–2237, June 2018
10. Qian, F., Gong, C., Sharma, K., Liu, Y.: Neural user response generator: fake news detection with collective user intelligence. In: IJCAI, vol. 3834, p. 3840 (2018)
11. Rubin, V.L.: Deception detection and rumor debunking for social media. In: The SAGE Handbook of Social Media Research Methods, p. 342. SAGE (2017)
12. Shu, K., Sliva, A., Wang, S., Tang, J., Liu, H.: Fake news detection on social media: a data mining perspective. ACM SIGKDD Explor. Newslett. **19**(1), 22–36 (2017)
13. Shu, K., Wang, S., Liu, H.: Beyond news contents: the role of social context for fake news detection. In: Proceedings of the Twelfth ACM International Conference on Web Search and Data Mining (WSDM), pp. 312–320. ACM (2019)
14. Thorne, J., Vlachos, A., Christodoulopoulos, C., Mittal, A.: FEVER: a large-scale dataset for fact extraction and verification. In: Proceedings of the 2018 Conference of the North American Chapter of the Association for Computational Linguistics: Human Language Technologies (NAACL-HLT), New Orleans, Louisiana, pp. 809–819, June 2018
15. Vaswani, A., et al.: Attention is all you need. In: Advances in Neural Information Processing Systems (NIPS), pp. 5998–6008 (2017)
16. Vlachos, A., Riedel, S.: Fact checking: task definition and dataset construction. In: Proceedings of the ACL 2014 Workshop on Language Technologies and Computational Social Science, pp. 18–22 (2014)
17. Wang, B., Liu, K., Zhao, J.: Inner attention based recurrent neural networks for answer selection. In: Proceedings of the 54th Annual Meeting of the Association for Computational Linguistics (ACL), vol. 1, pp. 1288–1297 (2016)
18. Wang, W.Y.: "Liar, liar pants on fire": a new benchmark dataset for fake news detection. In: Proceedings of the 55th Annual Meeting of the Association for Computational Linguistics (ACL), pp. 422–426 (2017)
19. Xu, K., et al.: Show, attend and tell: neural image caption generation with visual attention. In: International Conference on Machine Learning (ICML), pp. 2048–2057 (2015)
20. Zhang, H., et al.: Pretraining-based natural language generation for text summarization. arXiv preprint arXiv:1902.09243 (2019)

Research on Resultative/Directional Structures Based on the Corpus of International Chinese Textbooks

Dongdong Guo, Jihua Song[✉], Weiming Peng, and Yinbing Zhang

College of Information Science and Technology, Beijing Normal University,
Beijing 100875, China
{dongdongguo, zhangyinbing}@mail.bnu.edu.cn,
{songjh, pengweiming}@bnu.edu.cn

Abstract. Chinese resultative/directional structures are distinctive from other languages and have distinct uniqueness. The usage of resultative/directional structures is a very common language phenomenon in international Chinese teaching. It is also the key and difficult content of grammar teaching in international Chinese teaching. Studying various structure types and characteristics of resultative/directional structures is a necessary way to master them. Using Chinese information processing technology to study resultative/directional structures in international Chinese teaching, on the one hand, can improve the efficiency and expand the scope of research, make the research of resultative/directional structures more systematic and accurate, and excavate the tacit knowledge and deep value that traditional research methods are not easy to discover; on the other hand, trying to transform the existing achievements of Chinese information processing into the field of international Chinese teaching is conducive to promoting deep integration in the two fields and achieving common and rapid development. This paper first constructs a knowledge base of resultative/directional structure structural modes by annotating the resultative/directional structures in the corpus of a certain scale of international Chinese textbooks. And then the characteristics of resultative/directional structures in the field of international Chinese teaching are analyzed through the constructed structural mode knowledge base. Finally, on the basis of the structural mode knowledge base, the automatic recognition of the resultative/directional structures in the texts of international Chinese textbooks is studied. The results of automatic recognition are satisfactory and it embodies the scientificity, validity and completeness of the structural mode knowledge base.

Keywords: Resultative structures · Directional structures ·
International Chinese textbooks · Structural mode · Knowledge base

1 Introduction

The predicate-complement phrase is a very common and important type of Chinese phrase structure, which consists of the predicate and the complement. According to the meaning of the complement, the complement can be divided into the resultative complement, directional complement, degree complement, modal complement and

© Springer Nature Switzerland AG 2019
C. Douligeris et al. (Eds.): KSEM 2019, LNAI 11776, pp. 184–200, 2019.
https://doi.org/10.1007/978-3-030-29563-9_18

quantity complement. Resultative/directional structures occupy a high proportion of predicate-complement phrases in real language. At the same time, they have become a research hotspot in the fields of Chinese language, language comparison and second language acquisition because they embody many unique characteristics of Chinese.

Resultative/directional structure usage is a very common language phenomenon in international Chinese teaching [1–6]. In Chinese, the resultative/directional structure generally exists in SPRO (Subject + Predicate + Resultative/directional complement + Object), which is different from SPOR in English. Resultative/directional structures are different from other languages in the order of syntactic structure in Chinese, which makes it more difficult for Chinese second language learners to master the usage of these structures. In addition, the semantic limitation of the internal collocation of the resultative/directional structure, the richness and flexibility of the categories and positions of the agentive subjects and the objects, and the possible form of adding "得/不" in the middle make resultative/directional structures the focus and difficult content of grammar teaching in international Chinese teaching. Both the linguistic circle and the field of international Chinese teaching have made abundant research on resultative/directional structures, and many achievements have been made [7–9]. However, there is a lack of related research on resultative/directional structures by using Chinese information processing technology in international Chinese teaching. Using Chinese information processing technology [10, 11] to study resultative/ directional structures in international Chinese teaching, on the one hand, can improve efficiency, make the research more systematic and accurate, and excavate the tacit knowledge and deep value which is not easy to discover in traditional research methods; on the other hand, trying to transform the existing achievements of Chinese information processing into the field of international Chinese teaching is conducive to promoting deep integration in the two fields and achieving common development.

The resultative complement and the directional complement in the resultative/ directional structure are usually acted by verbs or adjectives. There are many kinds of verbs and adjectives as resultative complements. The common verbs are "走(go)", "见 (see)", "懂(understand)", "完(finish)" and so on. Directional verbs act as directional complements, including "上(get on)", "下(go down)", "进(turn into)", "出(get out)", "起 (get up)", "回(go back)", "开(turn on)", "过(get through)", "来(come)" and "去(go)", as well as the compound words composed of them such as "上来(come up)", "下去(go down)", "进来(come in)" and "出去(get out)". Resultative structures have the following basic collocation ways (the "V" means a verb and the "A" means an adjective):

V-V: 拿走(take away), 赶跑(drive away), 听懂(understand), 学会(learn to)
V-A: 长大(grow up), 吃饱(full up), 听清楚(hear clearly), 想明白(puzzle out)
A-V: 急哭(anxious to cry), 累病(tired to sick), 饿晕(hungry to faint), 热醒(heat to wake up)
A-A: 热坏(extremely hot), 饿惨(hungry miserably), 累坏(tired out), 忙坏(busy to the extreme)

Directional structures have the following basic collocation ways:

V-V: 走进(walk into), 举起(hold up), 爬上(climb up), 送回(send back)
A-V: 热起来(heat up), 紧张起来(be keyed up), 慢下来(slow down), 平静下来 (cool down)

Resultative/directional structures show the characteristics and trends of holistic meaning, stable structure and appropriate syllable length, and have distinct modelling characteristics. This paper first constructs a knowledge base of resultative/directional structure structural modes by annotating resultative/directional structures in the corpus of a certain scale of international Chinese textbooks. Then the characteristics of resultative/directional structures in the field of international Chinese teaching are analyzed through the constructed structural mode knowledge base. Finally, on the basis of the structural mode knowledge base, automatic recognition of resultative/directional structures in the corpus of international Chinese textbooks is studied.

2   Construction of the Resultative/Directional Structure Structural Mode Knowledge Base

2.1   Representation of Structural Modes

The predicate-complement phrase with the resultative complement or the directional complement (i.e. the resultative structure or the directional structure) is equivalent to a verb in grammatical function, and can be followed by the tense auxiliary "了" or "过" [12]. In the field of Chinese information processing, a resultative/directional structure is also generally treated as a whole, that is, as a dynamic word [13–18]. Therefore, when describing structural modes of resultative/directional structures, we first determine a whole part of speech for each resultative/directional structure. For the resultative/directional structure whose predicate is a verb, the whole part of speech is expressed by the verb "v". When the predicate part is an adjective, the whole part of speech of the structure is expressed by the adjective "a". In order to effectively reflect and describe the structural features of resultative/directional structures from the two levels of the whole and the internal structure, the following four types of information are used to express knowledge of their structural modes: the whole part of speech of a resultative/directional structure, the part of speech of each internal component, the syllable number of each internal component and structural relationships between the internal components. The structural relationships between the internal components are shown in Table 1.

The knowledge of the resultative/directional structure structural mode is expressed as follows:

- <structural mode> ::= <the whole part of speech of the resultative/directional structure>: <the part of speech of the internal component><the syllable number of the internal component>[<structural relationship symbol><the part of speech of the internal component><the syllable number of the internal component>]+
- <the whole part of speech of the resultative/directional structure> ::= v | a
- <the part of speech of the internal component> ::= n | t | f | m | q | r | v | a | d | p | c | u | e | o | Ug
- <the syllable number of the internal component> ::= <NULL> | 2 | 3 | 4 | ...
- <structural relationship symbol> ::= ← | ¬ | ·· | -

Table 1. Symbols of structural relationships

Relationship	Symbol	Example	Note
述补 (predicate-complement)	←	听←懂 急←哭 举←起 慢←下来	The combination relationship of the predicate and the later resultative complement or directional complement in the resultative/directional structure
述语+ 时态助词 (predicate-tense auxiliary)	¬	写←完¬了 看¬了←下 幸存¬了←下来	The combination relationship of the predicate or complement with the tense auxiliary "了/过"
动词+后缀 (verb-suffix)	··	玩··儿	The combination relationship of verbs and suffixes "儿" and so on
其他 (other)	-	看-得-见 写-不-完	The combination relationship of "得/不" in the possible form of the resultative/directional structure with the predicate and complement

The "n", "t", "f", "m", "q", "r", "v", "a", "d", "p", "c", "u", "e", "o" and "Ug" denote nouns, time words, localizers, numerals, quantifiers, pronouns, verbs, adjectives, adverbs, prepositions, conjunctions, auxiliary words, interjections, onomatopoetic words and affix morphemes (such as the category of the suffix "儿" in "玩儿 (play)") respectively. The syllable number is the default value 1 when it is null.

Table 2. Examples of resultative/directional structure structural modes

Resultative structure	Mode	Directional structure	Mode
拿走	v: v←v	爬上	v: v←v
累病	a: a←v	慢下来	a: a←v2
听得懂	v: v-u-v	上得去	v: v-u-v
吃不饱	v: v-d-v	停不下来	v: v-d-v2
写完了	v: v←v¬u	幸存了下来	v: v2¬u←v2
玩儿尽兴	v: v··Ug←v2	玩儿起来	v: v··Ug←v2

Examples of resultative/directional structure structural modes are shown in Table 2. The structural mode of the directional structure "慢下来(slow down)" is "a: a←v2". In "a: a←v2", the "a" before the colon indicates the whole part of speech is an adjective; the "a" after the colon indicates the part of speech of the internal component "慢(slow)" is an adjective and its syllable number is 1 (the syllable number is the default value 1 when it is null); the "v2" indicates the part of speech of the internal component "下来 (come down)" is a verb and its syllable number is 2; the "←" means the relationship between the internal component "慢(slow)" and the "下来(come down)" is the predicate-complement relationship.

2.2 Annotating of Corpus

The vocabularies included in the Modern Chinese Dictionary (Sixth Edition) are relatively stable [19]. In order to get the information about resultative/directional structure structural modes in the corpus of international Chinese textbooks, we use the vocabularies and parts of speech in the Modern Chinese Dictionary as the basis to annotate the internal components of resultative/directional structures. To analyze structural modes of resultative/directional structures, the internal components of the structures should be separated first. The criterion of segmentation is based on the unity of structure and meaning, until the corresponding sense and part of speech information of each component can be found in the Modern Chinese Dictionary. For example, for the directional structure "想不起来(unable to call to mind)", as the Modern Chinese Dictionary contains "想(call to mind)", "不(not)" and "起来(come true)", so the correct segmentation result should be "想-不-起来".

Undergraduates and postgraduates in the background of linguistics are organized to annotate the resultative/directional structure structural mode in the corpus of international Chinese textbooks (include New Practical Chinese Textbook, Happy Chinese, Great Wall Chinese, Chinese with Me, Mandarin Teaching Toolbox, Contemporary Chinese, Chinese Paradise and other international Chinese textbooks). The annotation work is carried out on a semi-automatic corpus annotation platform which integrates international Chinese textbooks, the knowledge bases of the Modern Chinese Dictionary and Modern Chinese Semantic Dictionary (Peking University), and visual annotation tools. In addition to the internal components of resultative/directional structures and their corresponding parts of speech and other structural mode information in the Modern Chinese Dictionary (the number of syllables of each internal component is automatically acquired by the semi-automatic corpus annotation platform), in order to investigate resultative/directional structures and their characteristics more thoroughly, the corresponding semantic category information of their internal components in the Modern Chinese Semantic Dictionary is also marked. Some examples of specific annotation results are shown in Table 3, where the "category" represents the attribute of the semantic category.

Table 3. Examples of annotating structural modes and other information in the corpus

ID	Example
1	就是这个, 我刚<v mod="v←v"><v category="身体活动">喝</v><v category="变化">完</v></v>一瓶。
2	你不愿意还动那就<a mod="a←v2"><a category="样貌">胖</a><v category="位移">下去</v></a>吧。
3	我<v mod="v-d-a"><v category="信息交流">说</v><d category="否定">不</d><a category="性质">清</a></v>, 真的糊涂了。
4	徐小姐笑称自己的婚礼没伤财, 但可<v mod="v-u-v"><v category="静态关系">算</v><u category="结构助词">得</u><v category="位移">上</v></v>是劳民了。
5	你们把自己愉快的回忆和将来的梦想<v mod="v←v2"><v category="创造">画</v><v category="位移">出来</v></v>吧。

In order to ensure the accuracy and consistency of annotating results, the text of the same paragraph is annotated by two students at least, and annotating results would be audited by an expert. The annotated data which is consistent and approved will be regarded as valid data. If the annotating results are inconsistent or not approved, the annotators and the auditor will be required to discuss and decide the final results.

2.3   Construction of the Knowledge Base

A total of 29465 sentences (498965 words) of corpus data of international Chinese textbooks annotated with the resultative/directional structure structural mode information are obtained in this paper. Use regular expressions to match and extract resultative/directional structures and their structural mode information in the annotated corpus. A regular expression is a formula to match a class of strings in a certain pattern, consisting of a number of ordinary characters and special characters (meta characters). Ordinary characters include small and medium letters, numbers, Chinese characters and punctuations, etc. Meta characters refer to special characters with special meanings. For example, the character "\w" matches letters, numbers or underscores; the character "." can match any single character; the character "+" matches the previous adjacent character or group one or more times; the character "?" is used after "+" to indicate that the matching mode is non-greedy and that the non-greedy mode matches the searched string as little as possible. The rule of resultative/directional structures and their structural mode information in the annotated corpus is clear. Using the regular expression "<\w mod=.+?>.+?</\w></\w>", all the information to be extracted can be accurately matched. According to the statistical analysis of the extracted information, a resultative/directional structure structural mode knowledge base with 28 resultative structure structural modes and 19 directional structure structural modes is established. The structure of the structural mode knowledge base is shown in Table 4, and the 28 resultative structure structural modes and 19 directional structure structural modes are shown in Table 5 and Table 6 respectively (by the order of the frequency of resultative/directional structures corresponding to the structural mode in the corpus from high to low).

Table 4. The structure of the structural mode knowledge base

Field	Illustration
ID	The serial number of the resultative/directional structure structural mode
Mode	The resultative/directional structure structural mode
POS	The whole part of speech of the resultative/directional structure
Syllable	The syllable number of the resultative/directional structure
Frequency	The frequency of resultative/directional structures corresponding to the structural mode in the corpus
Type	The number of the types of resultative/directional structures corresponding to the structural mode in the corpus
Combination	Various combinations of semantic categories corresponding to the structural mode
Detail	Every resultative/directional structure corresponding to the structural mode, its internal component semantic category and the frequency

Table 5. 28 types of resultative structure structural modes

ID	Mode	Example	Frequency	ID	Mode	Example	Frequency
1	v: v←v	吃←完	1461	15	v: v2←a2	打扫←干净	9
2	v: v←a	长←大	389	16	v: v2←a⌐u	商量←好⌐了	6
3	v: v←v⌐u	变←成⌐了	279	17	v: v2-u-v	想象-得-到	5
4	v: v-d-v	找-不-到	233	18	v: v-u-a2	看-得-清楚	4
5	v: v2←v	感觉←到	156	19	v: v←v←v	变←成←为	4
6	v: v←a⌐u	吃←饱⌐了	66	20	v: v-d-v2	听-不-明白	3
7	v: v2←a	准备←好	60	21	v: v←a2⌐u	想←明白⌐了	3
8	v: v-u-v	听-得-懂	44	22	v: v2←v2	赞叹←不已	2
9	v: v←a2	看←清楚	30	23	**v: v‥Ug←v**	玩‥儿←到	2
10	v: v-d-a	记-不-清	27	24	v: v-u-a	说-得-好	2
11	v: v-d-a2	说-不-清楚	22	25	v: v←v2	说←到底	1
12	v: v2-d-v	注意-不-到	19	26	a: a←v	穷←到	1
13	v: v2←v⌐u	培养←成⌐了	17	27	a: a2←v	辛苦←到	1
14	a: a←a	湿←透	13	28	a: a2-d-v	安静-不-了	1

Table 6. 19 types of directional structure structural modes

ID	Mode	Example	Frequency	ID	Mode	Example	Frequency
1	v: v←v	走←进	917	11	a: a←v2	疼←起来	11
2	v: v←v2	站←起来	442	12	v: v2←v⌐u	喜欢←上⌐了	10
3	v: v←v⌐u	留←下⌐了	184	13	v: v-u-v2	爬-得-上去	8
4	v: v2←v2	坚持←下去	85	14	v: v2⌐u←v2	幸存⌐了←下来	5
5	v: v-d-v	回-不-来	84	15	a: a←v	凸←出	2
6	v: v⌐u←v2	走⌐了←进来	62	16	v: v2-u-v	想象-得-出	1
7	v: v2←v	创造←出	57	17	v: v←v2⌐u	走←过来⌐了	1
8	v: v-d-v2	想-不-起来	38	18	a: a2⌐u←v2	平静⌐了←下来	1
9	v: v-u-v	上-得-去	25	19	a: a4←v2	不好意思←起来	1
10	a: a2←v2	紧张←起来	23				

The specific content of the resultative structure structural mode "v: v2←a2" in the knowledge base is shown in Table 7. The "combination" field is the semantic category combinations corresponding to the internal components of the resultative structures with the structure mode of "v: v2←a2". Semantic category compositions define and restrict the internal compositions of resultative/directional structures from the semantic perspective. It is of great value and significance for the in-depth and detailed analysis of resultative/directional structure features and the automatic recognition of resultative/directional structures in text.

Table 7. The resultative structure structural mode "v: v2←a2" in the knowledge base

ID	Mode	POS	Syllable	Frequency	Type	Combination	Detail	
15	v: v2←a2	v	4	9	6	[身体活动][性质]	【打扫[身体活动]干净[性质]】	4
						[心理活动][性质]	【发现[心理活动]及时[性质]】	1
						[位移][境况]	【来去[位移]匆匆[境况]】	1
						[创造][性质]	【清理[身体活动]干净[性质]】	1
						[社会活动][性质]	【表达[创造]清楚[性质]】	1
							【消灭[社会活动]干净[性质]】	1

3 Analysis of Resultative/Directional Structures

3.1 High Frequency Structural Modes

The total number of resultative structures corresponding to the 28 structural modes in the resultative/directional structure structural mode knowledge base is 2860, and the total number of types of resultative structures reaches 1046. Ten structural modes with the highest frequency of corresponding resultative structures in the knowledge base are shown in Table 8. The number of resultative structures corresponding to the ten structural modes accounts for 95.98% of the total number of resultative structures, and the number of the types of resultative structures accounts for 91.78% of the total number of all types. Table 8 shows that the resultative structure of monosyllabic verbs combined with monosyllabic verbs is the most common in international Chinese textbooks. Among them, the combination frequency of monosyllabic verbs and monosyllabic verbs without other components is the highest, reaching 1461 times, accounting for 51.08% of the total resultative structures; the combination frequencies of monosyllabic verbs and monosyllabic verbs with the tense auxiliary "了" or "过"(v: v←v¬u) and the possible form of "不"(v: v-d-v) or "得"(v: v-u-v) in the middle are also high, ranking third, fourth and eighth respectively. The resultative structure of the combination of monosyllabic verbs and monosyllabic adjectives is also very common. The combination of monosyllabic verbs and monosyllabic adjectives with no other components (v: v←a), followed by the tense auxiliary "了" or "过"(v: v←a¬u), and with the negative adverb "不"(v: v-d-a) in the middle ranks second, sixth and tenth respectively.

Table 8. Ten structural modes of resultative structures with the highest frequency

ID	Mode	Frequency	Frequency/Total	Types	Types/Total
1	v: v←v	1461	51.08%	360	34.42%
2	v: v←a	389	13.60%	176	16.83%
3	v: v←v¬u	279	9.76%	118	11.28%
4	v: v-d-v	233	8.15%	90	8.60%
5	v: v2←v	156	5.45%	85	8.13%
6	v: v←a¬u	66	2.31%	50	4.78%
7	v: v2←a	60	2.10%	28	2.68%
8	v: v-u-v	44	1.54%	22	2.10%
9	v: v←a2	30	1.05%	15	1.43%
10	v: v-d-a	27	0.94%	16	1.53%

The total number of directional structures corresponding to the 19 structural modes in the resultative/directional structure structural mode knowledge base is 1957, and the total number of types of directional structures reaches 905. Ten structural modes with the highest frequency of corresponding directional structures in the knowledge base are shown in Table 9. The number of directional structures corresponding to the ten structural modes accounts for 97.96% of the total number of directional structures, and the number of the types of directional structures accounts for 96.91% of the total number of all types. As can be seen from Table 9, the directional structures of monosyllabic verbs combined with monosyllabic directional verbs and disyllabic directional verbs are very common. The combination of monosyllabic verbs and monosyllabic directional verbs with no additional elements(v: v←v), followed by the tense auxiliary "了" or "过"(v: v←v¬u), and with the possible form of "不"(v: v-d-v) or "得"(v: v-u-v) in the middle ranks first, third, fifth and ninth respectively. The combination of monosyllabic verbs and disyllabic directional verbs with no additional elements(v: v←v2), with the tense auxiliary "了" or "过"(v: v¬u←v2) in the middle and with the possible form of "不"(v: v-d-v2) in the middle ranks second, sixth and eighth respectively. The frequency of the directional structure composed of adjectives and directional verbs is low, and the directional structure(a: a2←v2) composed of disyllabic adjectives and disyllabic verbs ranks tenth, with a frequency of 23, accounting for only 1.18% of the total number of directional structures.

Table 9. Ten structural modes of directional structures with the highest frequency

ID	Mode	Frequency	Frequency/Total	Types	Types/Total
1	v: v←v	917	46.86%	344	38.01%
2	v: v←v2	442	22.59%	195	21.55%
3	v: v←v¬u	184	9.40%	89	9.83%
4	v: v2←v2	85	4.34%	67	7.40%
5	v: v-d-v	84	4.29%	49	5.41%
6	v: v¬u←v2	62	3.17%	45	4.97%
7	v: v2←v	57	2.91%	31	3.43%
8	v: v-d-v2	38	1.94%	20	2.21%
9	v: v-u-v	25	1.28%	20	2.21%
10	a: a2←v2	23	1.18%	17	1.88%

3.2   Distribution of Resultative/Directional Complements

In the corpus, 2860 resultative structures (1046 types) contain 2860 resultative complements, including 2223 monosyllabic verbs (64 types), 6 disyllabic verbs (4 types), 563 monosyllabic adjectives (63 types) and 68 disyllabic adjectives (6 types). There are 14 semantic categories of monosyllabic verbs, and the five semantic categories covering the most types of monosyllabic verbs are (1) [变化]([change]), (2) [静态关系]([static relationship]), (3) [其他行为]([other behaviors]), (4) [身体活动]([physical activity]) and (5) [位移]([displacement]). There are four semantic categories of disyllabic verbs, namely, [心理活动]([psychological activity]), [位移]([displacement]), [静态关系]([static relationship]) and [其他行为]([other behaviors]). There are 17 semantic categories of monosyllabic adjectives, and the five semantic categories covering the most types of monosyllabic adjectives are (1) [性质]([property]), (2) [境况] ([situation]), (3) [视感]([vision]), (4) [颜色]([color]) and (5) [品格]([moral character]). There are two semantic categories of disyllabic adjectives, namely, [性质]([property]) and [境况]([situation]). The 10 most frequent monosyllabic verbs and monosyllabic adjectives are shown in Fig. 1 and Fig. 2 respectively. There are only four types of disyllabic verbs in resultative complements, namely, "明白"[心理活动] ("understand"[psychological activity]), "到底"[位移] ("come to an end"[displacement]), "不下"[静态关系] ("unable to stop"[static relationship]) and "不已"[其他行为] ("not stop"[other behaviors]). There are six types of disyllabic adjectives in resultative complements: "清楚"[性质] ("clear"[property]), "干净"[性质] ("clean"[property]), "明白"[性质] ("explicit"[property]), "匆匆"[境况] ("hurried"[situation]), "糊涂"[境况] ("confused" [situation]) and "及时"[性质] ("timely"[property]). In the corpus, 1957 directional structures (905 types) contain 1957 directional complements, including 1280 monosyllabic directional verbs (10 types) and 677 disyllabic directional verbs (14 types). The frequencies of monosyllabic and disyllabic directional verbs are shown in Fig. 3 and Fig. 4 respectively.

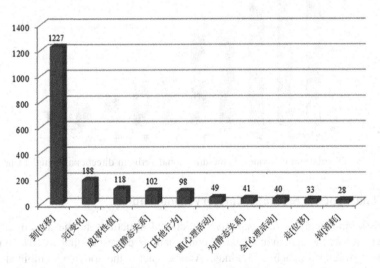

Fig. 1. High frequency monosyllabic verbs in resultative complements

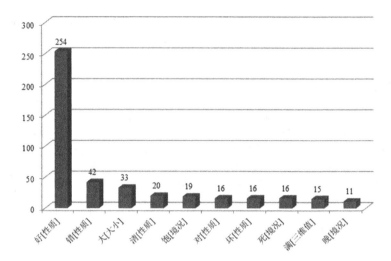

Fig. 2. High frequency monosyllabic adjectives in resultative complements

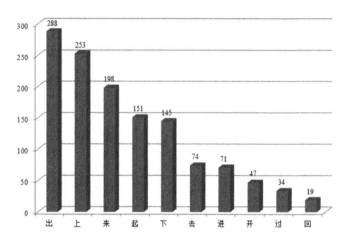

Fig. 3. Distribution of monosyllabic directional verbs in directional complements

3.3   Main Types of Semantic Category Combinations

By statistic and analysis of resultative/directional structures in the structural mode knowledge base, the semantic category combinations corresponding to 1046 types of resultative structures reach 313 kinds. Among them, the top ten combinations of semantic categories covering the most types of resultative structures are: (1) [身体活动][性质]([physical activity] [property]); (2) [身体活动][位移]([physical activity] [displacement]); (3) [身体活动][变化]([physical activity] [change]); (4) [其他行为] [位移]([other behaviors] [displacement]); (5) [变化][位移]([change] [displacement]); (6) [领属转移][位移]([possession transfer] [displacement]); (7) [其他行为][性质] ([other behaviors] [property]); (8) [位移][位移]([displacement] [displacement]); (9) [心

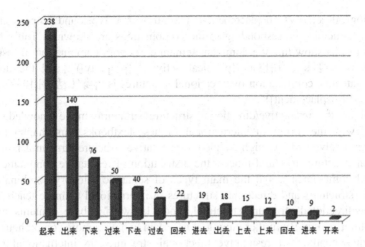

Fig. 4. Distribution of disyllable directional verbs in directional complements

理活动][位移]([psychological activity] [displacement]); (10) [创造][性质]([creation] [property]). The number of types and proportion of the resultative structures corresponding to the combinations are shown in Table 10.

Table 10. Dominant semantic category combinations of resultative structures

ID	Combination	Types	Types/Total	Example
1	[身体活动][性质]	47	4.49%	坐←好
2	[身体活动][位移]	45	4.30%	走←到
3	[身体活动][变化]	36	3.44%	收拾←完
4	[其他行为][位移]	27	2.58%	推迟←到
5	[变化][位移]	23	2.20%	提高←到
6	[领属转移][位移]	23	2.20%	借←走
7	[其他行为][性质]	21	2.01%	搞←清楚
8	[位移][位移]	19	1.82%	上←到
9	[心理活动][位移]	17	1.63%	意识←到
10	[创造][性质]	16	1.53%	写←好

The semantic category combinations corresponding to 905 types of directional structures reach 101 kinds. Among them, the top ten combinations of semantic categories covering the most types of directional structures are: (1) [身体活动][位移] ([physical activity] [displacement]); (2) [位移][位移]([displacement] [displacement]); (3) [其他行为][位移]([other behaviors][displacement]); (4) [变化][位移]([change] [displacement]); (5) [领属转移][位移]([possession transfer] [displacement]); (6) [创造][位移]([creation [displacement]); (7) [接触][位移]([contact [displacement]); (8) [身体活动][位移][时态助词]([physical activity] [displacement] [tense auxiliary]); (9) [信息交流][位移]([information exchange] [displacement]); (10) [心理活动][位移]

([psychological activity] [displacement]). The number of types and proportion of the directional structures corresponding to the combinations are shown in Table 11. The statistical results show that the dominant semantic category combination of resultative structures is "[身体活动][性质]([physical activity] [property])"; and the dominant semantic category combination of directional structures is "[身体活动][位移]([physical activity] [displacement])".

Based on the resultative/directional structure structural mode knowledge base, combined with the corpus of international Chinese textbooks, this chapter makes a preliminary analysis of the high frequency resultative structure structural modes and directional structure structural modes, the distribution of resultative complements and directional complements, and the main types of semantic category combinations of resultative structures and directional structures in international Chinese teaching. The resultative/directional structure structural mode knowledge base contains a lot of valuable information. By further mining, it is certain to have a more comprehensive and deeper understanding of resultative/directional structures in international Chinese teaching.

Table 11. Dominant semantic category combinations of directional structures

ID	Combination	Types	Types/Total	Example
1	[身体活动][位移]	199	21.99%	走←进
2	[位移][位移]	79	8.73%	返←回来
3	[其他行为][位移]	65	7.18%	显露←出来
4	[变化][位移]	52	5.75%	发展←起来
5	[领属转移][位移]	48	5.30%	买←来
6	[创造][位移]	40	4.42%	创造←出
7	[接触][位移]	37	4.09%	拿←出
8	[身体活动][位移][时态助词]	30	3.31%	走←出–了
9	[信息交流][位移]	25	2.76%	谈←起来
10	[心理活动][位移]	25	2.76%	分析←出来

4 Automatic Recognition of Resultative/Directional Structures

The realization of automatic recognition of resultative/directional structures is of great importance to the research and teaching of resultative/directional structures in international Chinese teaching, and it is also an important part of realizing automatic parsing and semantic understanding for international Chinese teaching. In addition, rule-based recognition of resultative/directional structures can be an important complement to statistical-based methods of automatic parsing. It plays an important role in dealing with ambiguities, correcting errors and improving the accuracy of automatic parsing. On the basis of the previous work, this chapter explores automatic recognition of resultative/directional structures in the raw corpus of international Chinese textbooks based on a rule method. In the process of recognition, the information of resultative/directional structure structural modes (including the part of speech of each internal component, the syllable number of each internal component, as well as fixed components such as tense auxiliary words "了" and "过", "得" and "不" in the possible form of resultative complements, directional verbs, etc.) and the "combination" field (providing and restricting the internal combination of resultative/directional structures from the semantic perspective) in the knowledge base are mainly used. In order to objectively reflect the automatic recognition effect of resultative/directional structures, 3 groups of raw corpus of international Chinese textbooks (tens of thousands to hundreds of thousands of Chinese characters in each group) were selected randomly for the experiment.

4.1 Recognition Process

The automatic recognition of resultative structures and directional structures in the raw corpus of international Chinese textbooks is carried out separately. The automatic recognition process is as follows. In the process of automatic recognition, the sequence of resultative structures or directional structures in different structural modes is different.

1. Using the automatic word segmentation tool (with the Modern Chinese Dictionary as the standard vocabulary) [20], the experimental corpus is automatically segmented and tagged with parts of speech to obtain the processed corpus which has been segmented and carries part of speech information.
2. Sort resultative structure (or directional structure) structural modes according to the number of internal components from more to less, the number of syllables of internal components from large to small, and the frequency of corresponding resultative structures (or directional structures) from high to low. For example, there are at most three internal components in the resultative structure structural modes, so the structural mode "v: v-d-a2" with three internal components, four syllables (the largest) and the highest frequency of corresponding resultative structures ranks first in the queue of structural modes.
3. Recognize resultative structures (or directional structures) corresponding to the current resultative structure (or directional structure) structural mode in order. The specific method is to extract the combinations consistent with parts of speech and syllables of the internal components of the current mode from the processed corpus in step 1 as the candidate set of the structure to be identified. Then, through the Modern Chinese Semantic Dictionary, semantic category information is automatically added to all the internal components of each combination in the candidate set. The semantic category combination of each candidate item will be compared with the "combination" field of the current mode in the queue of structural modes. If it exists in the "combination" field, the candidate is qualified and will be included in the resultative structure (or directional structure) set; if it doesn't exist in the "combination" field, the candidate is not qualified. Once identified as resultative structures (or directional structures), the contents are no longer involved in the following recognition operations.

4. Compare automatic recognition results of resultative structures (or directional structures) with the results of manual labeling and auditing, and calculate the accuracy rate, recall rate and F-measure of automatic recognition of resultative structures (or directional structures).

4.2   Recognition Results

According to the above recognition process, the automatic recognition experiment is carried out on 3 groups of randomly selected raw corpus, and the recognition results of resultative structures and directional structures are shown in Table 12 and Table 13 respectively.

Table 12. Recognition results of resultative structures

Raw corpus	Accuracy rate	Recall rate	F-Measure
Group 1	86.92%	80.08%	83.36%
Group 2	82.48%	83.87%	83.17%
Group 3	83.85%	87.57%	85.67%

Table 13. Recognition results of directional structures

Raw corpus	Accuracy rate	Recall rate	F-Measure
Group 1	95.54%	93.46%	94.49%
Group 2	94.32%	94.01%	94.17%
Group 3	94.76%	94.56%	94.66%

According to the experimental results, it can be concluded that the resultative/directional structure structural mode knowledge base has a significant effect on automatic recognition of resultative structures and directional structures. The accuracy and recall rate of automatic recognition of resultative structures and directional structures are both high, and the recognition effect is relatively ideal. The directional complement of a directional structure is very clear and it is a monosyllabic or multisyllabic directional verb. In Chinese, monosyllabic directional verbs and multisyllabic directional verbs are both fixed and few in number, so the accuracy and recall rate of automatic recognition of directional structures are better than resultative structures. The results of automatic recognition are satisfactory and it embodies the scientificity, validity and completeness of the structural mode knowledge base.

4.3   Experimental Analysis

Through analysis of the experimental data, it is found that the rule-based automatic recognition method designed in this paper has some shortcomings and can be improved in the following aspects:

1. Due to the limited size of the corpus of international Chinese textbooks, the acquired resultative/directional structure structural modes can't cover all the classes of resultative/directional structures actually appearing in the texts of international Chinese textbooks, which limits the recall rate of resultative/directional structure recognition. Errors in automatic word segmentation and part of speech tagging also reduce the accuracy and recall rate of resultative/directional structure recognition. In the later stage, it is necessary to further enrich the structural mode knowledge base and improve the accuracy of automatic word segmentation and part of speech tagging.

2. It's difficult to avoid some ambiguities in the process of recognition. The recognition error occurs during the specific recognition process. For example, in the sentence "格林先生不但汉语说得好，而且对中国文化也很有研究(Mr. Green not only speaks Chinese well, but also studies Chinese culture very well)", the "好 (well)" in "说得好(speaks well)" should be used as the modal complement of "说 (speak)", but because its formal structure is identical with the possible form "说得 好(speaks well)" of the resultative structure "说好(speaks well)", it is easy to be classified into the resultative structure set of the structural mode "v: v-u-a". The ambiguities need to be further eliminated by improving and perfecting the recognition conditions and process.

3. The information of resultative/directional structure structural modes and the "combination" field can reflect the structure and semantic features of resultative/directional structures to a certain extent, and can't fully reflect the characteristics of resultative/ directional structures. It is necessary to dig out more effective and quantifiable feature information with the in-depth study of resultative/directional structures.

4. In the process of recognizing resultative structures and directional structures, restrictions and screening conditions are limited. The research resources and achievements in the fields of linguistics, language teaching and Chinese information processing are needed to further enrich the recognition conditions of resultative structures and directional structures.

5 Conclusion

In this paper, we use the method of knowledge engineering to analyze the resultative/ directional structures in the corpus of international Chinese textbooks, and preliminarily build a knowledge base of resultative/directional structure structural modes for international Chinese teaching. Then based on the structural mode knowledge base and the corpus of international Chinese textbooks, the characteristics of the resultative/directional structures in the field of international Chinese teaching are analyzed. Finally, on the basis of the structural mode knowledge base, resultative/directional structures in the corpus of international Chinese textbooks is automatically recognized. This research method can be further extended to the study of other composite structures in the corpus of international Chinese textbooks, so as to better serve international Chinese teaching and information processing for international Chinese teaching.

References

1. Confucius Institute Headquarters (Hanban): HSK Test Syllabus Level 1. People's Education Press, Beijing (2015)
2. Confucius Institute Headquarters (Hanban): HSK Test Syllabus Level 2. People's Education Press, Beijing (2015)
3. Confucius Institute Headquarters (Hanban): HSK Test Syllabus Level 3. People's Education Press, Beijing (2015)
4. Confucius Institute Headquarters (Hanban): HSK Test Syllabus Level 4. People's Education Press, Beijing (2015)
5. Confucius Institute Headquarters (Hanban): HSK Test Syllabus Level 5. People's Education Press, Beijing (2015)
6. Confucius Institute Headquarters (Hanban): HSK Test Syllabus Level 6. People's Education Press, Beijing (2015)
7. Yuan, Y.: On the valence of verb-resultative constructions in Mandarin: toward a top-down and bottom-up analysis. Stud. Chin. Lang. **05**, 399–410+479 (2001)
8. He, M., Lu, S., Zhang, Y.: The typological effect on Chinese resultative construction L2 processing: an eye tracking study. Chin. Teach. World **33**(02), 244–257 (2019)
9. Feng, L., Feng, L.: A study on influential factors of Chinese VR construction understanding as L2. Overseas Chin. Educ. **06**, 40–52 (2018)
10. Yu, S.: An Introduction to Computational Linguistics. Commercial Press, Beijing (2003)
11. Song, J., Yang, E., Wang, Q.: Chinese Information Processing Tutorial. Higher Education Press, Beijing (2011)
12. Zhang, B.: The Modern Chinese Grammar. Commercial Press, Beijing (2010)
13. Peng, W., Song, J., Sui, Z., Guo, D.: Formal schema of diagrammatic Chinese syntactic analysis. In: Lu, Q., Gao, H. (eds.) CLSW 2015. LNCS (LNAI), vol. 9332, pp. 701–710. Springer, Cham (2015). https://doi.org/10.1007/978-3-319-27194-1_68
14. Guo, D., Zhu, S., Peng, W., Song, J., Zhang, Y.: Construction of the dynamic word structural mode knowledge base for the international Chinese teaching. In: Dong, M., Lin, J., Tang, X. (eds.) CLSW 2016. LNCS (LNAI), vol. 10085, pp. 251–260. Springer, Cham (2016). https://doi.org/10.1007/978-3-319-49508-8_24
15. Guo, D., Song, J., Peng, W.: Research on dynamic words and their automatic recognition in Chinese information processing. In: Wu, Y., Hong, J.F., Su, Q. (eds.) CLSW 2017. LNCS (LNAI), vol. 10709, pp. 479–488. Springer, Cham (2018). https://doi.org/10.1007/978-3-319-73573-3_43
16. Guo, D., Song, J., Peng, W., Zhang, Y.: Research on verb reduplication based on the corpus of international Chinese textbooks. In: Hong, J.-F., Su, Q., Wu, J.-S. (eds.) CLSW 2018. LNCS (LNAI), vol. 11173, pp. 707–719. Springer, Cham (2018). https://doi.org/10.1007/978-3-030-04015-4_62
17. Guo, D., Song, J., Peng, W., Zhang, Y.: Analysis of three syllable noun dynamic words based on the corpus of international Chinese textbooks. J. Chin. Inf. Process. **32**(06), 12–18 (2018)
18. Guo, D.: Analyzing on Dynamic Words and Their Structural Modes in Building the Sentence-based Treebank. Beijing Normal University, Beijing (2016)
19. The Dictionary Editing Room in the Linguistics Institute of Chinese Academy of Social Sciences: Modern Chinese Dictionary. Commercial Press, Beijing (2012)
20. Kang, M.: Study of Chinese Word Segmentation System for International Chinese Textbook Analysis. Beijing Normal University, Beijing (2014)

An Automatic Spelling Correction Method for Classical Mongolian

Min Lu, Feilong Bao$^{(\boxtimes)}$, Guanglai Gao, Weihua Wang, and Hui Zhang

College of Computer Science, Inner Mongolia University, Hohhot, China
1427628525@qq.com, csfeilong@imu.edu.cn

Abstract. Classical Mongolian is suffering a serious misspelling matter due to its polyphonic alphabet. One Mongolian glyph can map to different letters, i.e., some letters display the same shape. This special encoding scheme makes the words very easy to be misspelled. About half to three quarters of the words are misspellings in the classical Mongolian text, which is mainly caused by confusion between letters of the same shape. Conventional spelling correction techniques cannot solve such errors with correct shapes well for they mostly focus on errors such as character insertion, deletion and transposition. In this work, we propose the intermediate codes to map the words of the same shape into a single shape-based intermediate representation. According to the corresponding shapes, the hybrid approach is then applied to get the correct spellings by integrating rules and neural representation model (context2vec). The experimental results show that this approach achieves the new state-of-the-art performance. In addition, we also develop an efficient and free Mongolian automatic correction system for the text editors.

Keywords: Classical Mongolian · Spelling errors · Intermediate code · Context2vec · Automatic correction

1 Introduction

Spelling correction is the very first step of a natural language processing (NLP) system to ensure that all of the input text is spelled correctly before feeding them into subsequent steps. In general, a two-step method is utilized to solve this problem: the first step is based on edit distance, which gives some correction candidates for the misspelled input. The second step selects out the most probable output from these candidates. The possibility is usually given by a trained error model, which model the error pattern on the aligned sets of the correct and incorrect word occurred in corpus [8,14], or by a language model which model the k-gram frequency [2,10]. The two models can also be combined to achieve better performance [1].

© Springer Nature Switzerland AG 2019
C. Douligeris et al. (Eds.): KSEM 2019, LNAI 11776, pp. 201–214, 2019.
https://doi.org/10.1007/978-3-030-29563-9_19

In this work, we devote ourselves to the spelling correction problem of Mongolian, specifically the classical Mongolian (ᠮᠣᠩᠭᠣᠯ ᠪᠢᠴᠢᠭ). Mongolian is an alphabetic writing language that can be written in the classical script or the Cyrillic script (**монгол хэл**) which is spelled with Cyrillic letters. The spelling correction problem of Cyrillic Mongolian is relatively simple because it is much like the well-studied English and Russian. Those methods are suitable for solving shape errors which mainly manifest as insertion, deletion and transposition errors. However, the spelling correction problem of classical Mongolian is more challenging. It cannot be solved by the existing method since shape errors in classical Mongolian accounts for a very small proportion of all errors.

The current classical Mongolian encoding scheme uses [3] as the standard code, which is designed to encode every speech sound (nominal characters) with a Unicode code point. This encoding scheme may be suitable for speech transcription but not for printed text. In classical Mongolian, letters have an initial, medial or final presentation form according to their positions within a word. A letter may change its glyph for better visual harmony with the subsequent character, which results in letters with several variant forms according to different contexts. This means a single encoded letter may map to many different glyphs, and a single glyph may map to many different encoded letters, too. For example, a letter "U+1820" maps to "ᠨ", "ᠩ", "ᠠ", "ᠡ" and "ᠲ" according to its contexts. On the other hand, a glyph "ᠣ" maps to letter "U+1832" and letter "U+1833".

The mismatch between encoded letters and glyphs makes classical Mongolian very easy to be misspelled. Numerous words present correct appearance but are typed with incorrect codes in the text since all the text editors care about is the appearance of the input words and nothing else. Accordingly, coding errors in classical Mongolian text are far more serious than that in other languages. For instance, in theory, there are 1,728 different spellings to obtain the same Mongolian word appearance "ᠪᠠᠭᠠᠴᠤᠳ" (meaning: minority), but only one of them is correct. According to the statistic on corpus including 76 million Mongolian words, the word appearance "ᠪᠠᠭᠠᠴᠤᠳ" appears 102,532 times with 291 different spellings, where only 24,708 of them are correctly spelled. It is to say, more than 75% of them are misspellings. Those misspellings with correct shapes are formally known as pronunciation errors which make up a lot more significant share about 95% of the spelling errors.

Our task in this work is to correct the pronunciation error and detect the shape error as well. More specifically, objects to be corrected are structured in monophonic word error, polyphone error and nominal inflectional suffix error. Monophonic word refers to the word whose shape is uniquely mapped to one spelling, while in contrast, polyphone have multiple correct spellings with the same form. Misusing polyphone is contained in real-word error which refers to that the intended word is replaced by another correct spelling with syntax or semantic error. Real-word error [6] generally go unnoticed by most spellcheckers as they deal with words in isolation, accepting them as correct if they are found in the dictionary, and flagging them as errors if they are not. So, as one kind of real-word error, polyphone proofreading is considered the more difficult task. As for nominal inflectional suffix, it attaches to stem through a Narrow Non-Break Space (NNBS) ("U+202F", Latin: "-"). We call it NNBS suffix for short. The correction of the NNBS suffixes is another key object to deal with since they account for almost 20% of the total words in the text.

To solve these encoding scheme misspellings, we involve an intermediate code which is really a glyph code mapping to glyph one-to-one. The proposal successfully avoids the complex algorithm of error detection, candidate generation and ranking process in the conventional correction methods. Then a hybrid approach is applied by integrating rule and context2vec representation model [11] using bidirectional LSTM to obtain the target spellings depending on the intermediate codes. The proposed method yields significant improvements compared to both the state-of-the-art context-free word correction by rules [15] and polyphone correction methods based on traditional k-gram language model [9]. The main contributions are as follows:

1. A rule set is built to convert the Mongolian text encoded with the standard code into its corresponding intermediate representation. The rule set is not really big but very effective.
2. We introduce a well-modeled word and its context representation based on context2vec [11] for polyphone correction. The target spelling is identified by measuring their distances.
3. A Large-scale data source is built, which consists of the corpus and dictionaries of rich coverage.
4. A proofreading free spelling correction system[1] is built based on the proposed method. The system meets the application requirements pretty well.

In the following sections, we introduce the related work firstly, then propose our solution, describe the experiments, and close the paper with a conclusion at last.

2 Related Work

The work in the field of Mongolian spelling correction is not yet mature. The earliest rule-based MHAHP system [5] was just designed to detect errors. [7] extended the rules and summarized the common errors. However, the performance was limited by the complex error types. [15] was the first and only work to use presentation character (glyph code) to represent the word. This research applied finite state automata to establish two kinds of Mongolian lexical analyzer respectively based on presentation character and nominal character. Nominal character automata was applied to detect errors. The other was implemented to correct it. It achieved a remarkable result. However, the conversion to presentation form at the character level cannot handle the errors adequately.

---

[1] http://mc.mglip.com:8080.

In addition, there are also statistical methods similar to English spelling correction. [4] proposed Bayes algorithm taking the alignment sets of correct and incorrect tokens as training corpus. [17] tried to use the hidden Markov model to solve errors at the syllable level. [16] proposed statistical translation framework, which regarded spelling proofreading as the translation from the wrong words to the correct ones. The works mentioned above all focused on the correction of the context-free words. [9] fill the blank in polyphone correction by traditional k-gram language model. Although the statistical-based methods can avoid the complex rules, they are so sensitive to the training corpus. For such an under-resource language as Mongolian, the result is not stable when totally isolated from rules who can handle some errors definitely. As to common spelling errors of correct surface in Mongolian text, candidate generation can be effectively solved by the dictionary lookup procedure if the dictionary is developed to map the presentations of the words to their correct spellings. In this paper, we build this dictionary based on the intermediate codes and also extend the research on the polyphone correction which has not been sufficiently discussed in the most work.

3   Method

The approach corrects the texts in sentences. Firstly, input strings are encoded into their intermediate codes, then undergo dictionary matching to restore the words from the intermediate codes. Monophonic word correction is accomplished in this step first. Then the system finishes NNBS suffix correction based on the suffix concatenation knowledge. Finally, polyphones are identified by measuring the distance between the candidates and their context based on context2vec's [11] representation. The whole process is illustrated in Fig. 1 with an example: "ᠠᠷᠠᠳ ᠲᠦᠮᠡᠨ ᠢᠶᠡᠷ ᠨᠢ ᠲᠡᠳᠡ ᠤᠯᠠᠮ ···" (meaning: They found a livelihood.). For convenience, words are presented with there national Latin transliterations (keyboard corre-spondence).

3.1   Intermediate Code Conversion

As shown in Fig. 1, the code chain produced after the first step of conversion is the intermediate codes. Given the words $\{w_1, w_2, w_3, .., w_m\}$ of the same presen-tation, we want to return the single word spelling W which can represent their surface form. W is called the intermediate code. As a similar shape representa-tion strategy, the intermediate code is an improvement based on the conversion rule [15] which converts the word at the character level. It is to say, the num-bers of characters in a word are the same before and after conversion by [15]. While it cannot handle the errors adequately for some characters are mistakenly typed with a combination of several characters. To make up for the deficiency, we added the correction rule before matching conversion rules, the operation unit of which is not limited to one character. We denote the space of the original Mongolian code as Σ, and the space of the intermediate code as Σ^*. The inter-mediate code conversion is the process to transfer the Mongolian word into the

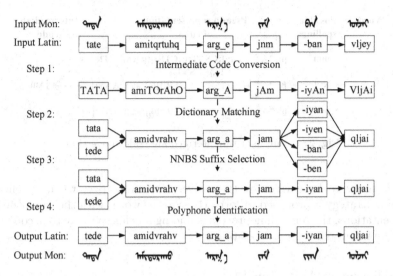

Fig. 1. Example of the correction process. The words marked in red indicate that their corrections are completed. (Color figure online)

intermediate code. I.e., $\Sigma^2 \to \Sigma^{*2}$ by applying a set of rule $\beta \leftarrow \alpha$, where α is the precondition which describes some original code should be converted to β in some context. They are formulated by regular expression based on the position of the characters and the characters on both sides. β is the conversion result. All rules in the rule set are matched to every code in the input text to complete the conversion. We totally summarized 105 rules to convert Mongolian characters into the intermediate representation. Each rule is assigned with the priority. The priorities of the correction rules are higher than that of the conversion rules.

Figure 2 shows a simple case where only one rule is matched. The word "ᠵᠠᠮ" (meaning: road) can be spelled as "jam", "jem" and "jnm". The spellings "jam" and "jem" match the same rule. The matched groups are ("a","e","n"). The replacement is "A". Accordingly, they are all converted to the code "jAm". In the pseudo representation, ":CTR:" represents Mongolian control character[2], ":ANY:" represents any Mongolian letter, ":VOW:" represents any vowel, and ":CSNT:" means any consonant.

The intermediate code representation can greatly reduce the number of words (see the Subsect. 4.1), and the number of the misspelled words are more than the reduced number. Moreover, a very subtle reduction may happen even if the text is full of misspellings. It is caused because that typists made the same mistake when they input the word according to the incorrect principles that

---

[2] Control characters are used in conjunction with Mongolian letters to control the word shapes. They include Mongolian Vowel Separator: "U+180B", three Mongolian Free Variation Selector: "U+180C", "U+180D", "U+180E", Zero Width Non-Joiner: "U+200C", Zero Width Joiner: "U+200D" and Narrow Non-Break Space: "U+202F".

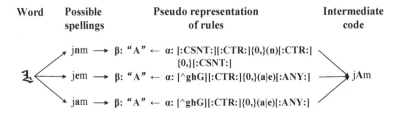

Fig. 2. Example of the intermediate code conversion.

were believed to be correct by themselves. To summarize, when an effective mapping strategy is proposed to correctly map the words with their intermediate representations, the remaining process is finding an effective way to decode them from the intermediate representations.

3.2 Dictionary Matching

Because of Mongolian agglutinative nature, the dictionary resource applied in the work is comprised of the stem and suffix tokens instead of the whole words. We totally constructed the verbal stem dictionary of 47,421 items, the non-verbal stem dictionary of 74,826 items, the verbal suffix dictionary of 151 items and the nominal suffix dictionary of 56 items. Since Mongolian resource is limited, we constructed them by hand. The key of each item is the Mongolian intermediate code, and the value is the correct spelling.

With these dictionaries, we try to find the proper spelling for each intermediate code. Taking the word "ᡡᡁ" showed in Fig. 2 as an example, the target spelling can be obtained directly by dictionary lookup: "jAm" → "jam". The intermediate code which cannot be found in the dictionary is segmented into stem and suffix by morphological rules. There will be character insertion, substitution, and deletion during segmentation and concatenation process. The word will be output as it was and detected as a presentation-error word if the stem is even out of vocabulary.

As for monophonic words, there is just one candidate, which means the correction process is completed in this stage. While for the other two types of words, multiple candidates will be found from the dictionaries.

3.3 NNBS Suffix Selection

The NNBS suffixes will have several spellings in the same semantic group mapped to them after dictionary lookup. Their selection can be addressed by morphological knowledge well. The NNBS suffix can stick to both the Mongolian and non-Mongolian tokens to form new words. We formulated selection rules for both of them. As a non-independent word, its correction totally depends on the feature of the preceding stem. The stem feature set was constructed by the last letter of the stem and its positive-negative feature[3]. The rules for non-Mongolian tokens were built by converting them into Mongolian words in advance. Then feature extraction was applied according to their phonetic transcriptions.

After the feature was successfully extracted, the appropriate one is selected in compliance with the Morphological knowledge.

3.4 Polyphone Identification

As the last step in the procedure, the task is to identify the word out of the polyphone candidates (e.g. "ᠣᠳᠠ": "tede" and "tata") to complete the sentence. The word should be the most meaningful and coherent as the gap-filler. In this work, we apply context2vec [11] to embed entire sentential contexts and target words in the same low-dimensional space using bidirectional LSTM. Then, we choose the word whose target word embedding is the most similar to the embedding of the given context using the target-to-context similarity metric. Context2vec utilizes a full-sentence neural representation of context instead of simply averaging the embeddings of the context words in a window around (CBOW [12]).

Formal specification is as follows: Let lLS be an LSTM reading the words of a given sentence from left to right, and let rLS be a reverse one reading the words from right to left. Given a sentence $w_{1:n}$, the bidirectional LSTM context representation for the target w_i is defined as the following vector concatenation:

$$biLS(w_{1:n}, i) = lLS(l_{1:i-1}) \oplus rLS(r_{n:i+1})$$

where l/r represent distinct left-to-right/right-to-left word embeddings of the sentence words. Next, non-linear function is applied on the concatenation of the left and right context representations:

$$MLP(x) = L_2(ReLU(L_1(x)))$$

where MLP stands for Multi Layer Perceptron, ReLU is the Rectified Linear Unit activation function, and $L_i(x) = W_i x + b_i$ is a fully connected linear operation. Let $c = (w_1, ..., w_{i-1}, -, w_{i+1}, ..., w_n)$ be the sentential context of the word in position i. Context2vec's representation of c is defined as:

$$\vec{c} = MLP(biLS(w_{1:n}, i)).$$

When the embedding of a target word w_i as $\vec{t}$, object function is defined as *word2vec* negative sampling objective function [13]:

$$S = \sum_{t,c} (log\sigma(\vec{t} \cdot \vec{c}) + \sum_{i=1}^{k} log\sigma(-\vec{t} \cdot \vec{c}))$$

where the summation goes over each word token t in the training corpus and its corresponding sentential context c. σ is the sigmoid function and $t_i, ..., t_k$ are the negative samples.

---

[3] If the word contains one of the positive vowels ("a","q","v"), it is regarded as the positive one. Similarly, if it contains a negative vowel, the word is a negative one.

Accordingly, both context and target word representations are studied as same dimensional embeddings. In contrast to *word2vec* and similar word embedding models that use context modeling mostly internally and consider the target word embeddings as their main output, the primary focus of the model is the context representation. The model achieves its objective by assigning similar embeddings to sentential contexts and their associated target words. Further, similar to the case in *word2vec* models, this indirectly results in assigning similar embeddings to target words that are associated with similar sentential contexts, and conversely to sentential contexts that are associated with similar target words.

4   Experiment

As typical two classification problem (whether the word is correctly proofread or not), we evaluate the result by the standard binary classification evaluation metrics of *precision, recall* and *f*-measure. *Precision* (P) means the ratio of correctly proofread items to all proofread items. *Recall* (R) means the ratio of all correctly proofread items to all items that need to be proofread and *f*-measure (F) is the geometric mean of *precision* and *recall*.

The correction performance is evaluated from four aspects: the monophonic word correction, the polyphone correction, the NNBS suffix correction, and the overall performance. We take the [15] as the overall baseline model, and take [9] as the main comparative approach against the proposed polyphone correction method. The experimental results verify the effectiveness of our method. Its performance can meet the needs of practical application well.

4.1   Experimental Data

The corpus in the experiment was collected and collated from the mainstream Mongolian Websites. After filtering too short and too long sentences, we totally selected out 41,416 sentences from the crawled corpus, each of which contained polyphones. The accuracy of the corpus is just 30.27%. It took about 400 h to manually proofread them by several Mongolian native persons. Eventually, the corpus was set up with 41,416 aligned sentences with and without manual correction where there are 5,789,27 words and 24,658 distinct words (vocabulary). The proportion of the monophonic words, the polyphones and the NNBS suffixes are 66.89%, 10.85% and 22.26% in the corpus. The number of distinct token in the original corpus is 44,129, while the number of the intermediate codes is 23,235. It reduces the number by 47.35%. It can be inferred that the number of misspelled words are more than the reduced number.

Test Corpus for Overall Performance. 3600 pairs were extracted from the whole aligned set (41,416 pairs) to evaluate the overall performance. We correct the ones without correction in the sentence pairs by the proposed method taking their corresponding corrected ones as the reference. The proportion of the monophonic words, the polyphones and the NNBS suffixes are 60.89%, 18.55% and 20.56% in the test set. The correction results of them were illustrated in Table 1.

Corpus for Polyphone Identification Model. The corrected ones in the same 3600 pairs were used for testing the polyphone identification model. While the input of the model in the test step did some change by replacing the polyphones by one of their candidates. The selection is randomly assigned. The remaining corrected sentences were used for training the model: 36,000 for the training set and 1,876 for the validating set.

4.2   Results and Analysis

The baseline model [15] also applied the rules and dictionaries to correct the monophonic words and the NNBS suffixes. While the polyphones were corrected according to their prior probabilities. As we can see in Table 1, the proposed approach outperforms the baseline model in all kinds of words. The f-measure of all words is 4.78% higher than the baseline model. The correction of the monophonic words and the NNBS suffixes totally depend on the dictionaries and morphological processing. The f-measure values are respectively 3.20% and 4.30% higher than that of the baseline system. It confirms that our rules and dictionaries are built well.

Table 1. Performance of the baseline model and the proposed approach.

Criteria	Baseline				Proposed			
	Mono	Poly	Suffix	All	Mono	Poly	Suffix	All
P	95.63%	92.30%	97.68%	95.59%	99.76%	93.01%	99.10%	97.89%
R	93.76%	60.86%	92.84%	89.20%	95.74%	94.60%	98.68%	95.51%
F	94.68%	73.36%	95.20 %	92.29%	97.71%	93.80%	99.29%	96.70%

Following sections elaborate the correction performances on three types of words respectively. The reasons for errors failed to be corrected are emphatically introduced and analyzed; Besides, the optimization strategies are put forward at the end of each subsection.

Monophonic Word Correction. Errors failed to be corrected are considered either correction error or missed error. Correction error has a negative impact on the precision and the other does on the recall rate. As to monophonic word, correction error refers to the real-word error. It means that the word is correctly proofread from the point of view of the context-free word, but it has the syntactic and semantic errors in the context. Such issue is not considered in this work. Missed error refers to those words whose shapes (intermediate code) cannot be found in the dictionary. As a result, the word will be printed without any change. As is shown in Table 1, the precision of monophonic words is very high but the recall value is relatively lower. It's because that the correction error is only accounted for 5.05%, while missed error occupies a large proportion by 94.95% in the test sets.

Missed error comes from these three categories (see Table 2): (i) The words out of vocabulary (OOV) including some loanwords and colloquialisms; Table 2 shows that loanword is accounted for the vast majority of the missed error. It occupies 81.24% of missed errors. (ii) Words with incorrect forms; (iii) Intermediate code conversion error. Not all the rules have been contained in the intermediate code conversion rules. Some rules are difficult to represent because of its ambiguity, so there are still the small number of words which failed to be converted to its accurate intermediate code.

Table 2. The proportion of missed errors.

Presentation error	ITMD error	OOV	
		Loan words	Colloquialism
16.89%	1.87%	68.52%	12.72%

How to reduce correction errors, especially missed errors, is the critical task to improve the monophonic correction performance. OOV is the major part to be promoted. We should continue expanding dictionaries while ensuring their accuracy. For correction errors, the real-word error model should be added in the future. In terms of the solution to ambiguity in intermediate conversion rule, statistical methods should be applied after well-considered trade-off between time and efficiency.

NNBS Suffix Correction. The NNBS suffixes appear frequently but they are rare in number (52 items in total). As such, both the intermediate code conversion rules and the selection rules are summarized well. Besides, the typos in front of the NNBS suffixes are possibly but not certainly lead to wrong correction. There is still a possibility of correct correction if the feature needed for the correction is successfully extracted. Indeed, NNBS suffix correction achieved the best results compared with the other two types of words in each criteria whether in baseline model or in our proposed method seen from Table 1.

In addition, we also evaluated the performance of NNBS suffixes when they stick to the Mongolian and non-Mongolian stems (see Table 3). The performance of NNBS suffixes concatenated to non-Mongolian stems is lower relatively. The reason is that (1) Some non-Mongolian stems have not been covered by rules yet; (2) Those stems which have more than one sense cannot be handled by rules. For instance, "A" which can indicate English capital letter and physical unit *ampere* as well. Fortunately, for the proportion of the NNBS suffixes that

Table 3. Evaluation for NNBS suffix correction. "Mon" and "Non-Mon" means the correction performance when the stem is the Mongolian tokens and non-Mongolian tokens respectively. "All" means the overall suffix correction performance.

Criteria	Mon	Non-Mon	All
P	99.92%	92.16%	99.49%
R	99.68%	89.47%	98.68%
F	99.80%	90.16%	99.29%

appear after non-Mongolian stems is very small, the comprehensive result is still quite comfortable.

To further increase the performance of NNBS suffix correction, the feature extraction rules of non-Mongolian stems should be expanded. On the other side, it will certainly benefit if the corrections of the words concatenated by the NNBS suffixes improve further.

Polyphone Identification. The hyperparameters used in the experiments with context2vec are as follows: context word units: 300, LSTM hidden/output units: 600, MLP input units: 1200, MLP hidden units: 1200, sentential context units: 600, target word units: 600, negative samples: 10.

The method [9] applied the statistical k-gram language model to score sentence sequences, each of which was assigned to the different candidates of the polyphones. The one with the highest score was defined as the correct sequence. [9] did some modification on the basis of back-off methods due to unigram's outstanding effect. The conventional back-off method is that if the k-gram has been seen more than t times (t is demarcation value of low-frequency words) in training, the conditional probability of a word given its history is proportional to the maximum likelihood estimate of that k-gram. Otherwise, the conditional probability is set depending on the back-off conditional probability of the prior $(k-1)$ word and the prior probability of the current word. While the modified method directly returns the probability of the lower order phrase if the current phrase was seen less than t times. Taking bigram for example, if the phrase cannot be seen in the trained model, the algorithm will just return the prior probability (unigram) of the current word. Phrases containing polyphones tend to be the stereotyped expression, i.e. one of the candidates cannot make up a new phrase with the context which can be combined with the other one in the candidate group, bigram is therefore strong enough to achieve the best performance in the small data set. In this section, we conduct the unigram, bigram and modified bigram as the comparative methods.

The performance (in F) of unigram, bigram, modified bigram and context2vec's representation model are respectively 92.57%, 87.28%, 93.27% and 93.80%. Overall performance of context2vec is 0.57% higher than modified bigram and 1.33% higher than the unigram model. In addition, we carried out fine-grained experiments by extracting texts with different ratios of high-frequency words to low-frequency words. The correction effect under different distributions is tested as shown in Table 4. The high-frequency word refers to that the correct spelling is the one with the highest prior probability among the candidates of the polyphone, while the low-frequency words mean the ones with lower probabilities. The ratios of high-frequency words to low-frequency words are set as 0, 1:1, 2:1, 3:1 and ∞ respectively. Rate 0 means there is no high-frequency polyphone on the test set and ∞ means the count of the low-frequency word is zero. The numbers of words in the particular distribution from rate 0 to ∞ are as follows: 62, 244, 406, 408 and 8165. The distribution of candidate words varies greatly. The high-frequency candidates make up a very large proportion in the text.

Table 4. Performance (in F) of the polyphone correction on the different distributions.

Methods	0	1:1	2:1	3:1	∞
unigram	2.38%	55.22%	69.14%	73.46%	97.31%
bigram	27.78%	56.00%	58.82%	67.97%	90.89%
modified bigram	27.78%	60.87%	68.67%	67.98%	96.97%
context2vec	**29.41%**	**61.74%**	**71.50%**	**80.00%**	96.90%

Seen from Table 4, context2vec performs well in any distribution, especially for low-frequency words. The result illustrates that the task like sentence completion can benefit from well-studied context representation. Besides, we can see that (1) unigram works actually well. (2) The more high-frequency words in the text, the better the correction results can achieve.

Polyphone correction module can be enhanced further by expanding training data.

5   Conclusion

To address the serious misspelling problem in the classical Mongolian text, this paper proposed the high-quality hybrid approach based on rules and neural models. The intermediate code is a major innovation of success in this paper for avoiding enormous and complicated rules to detect errors in the initial stage of other conventional proofreading systems. In addition, lots of time and efforts were invested to construct both rule base and dictionaries which were served in the rule-based module. Lastly, the polyphone correction based on context2vec's representation also achieves the excellent performance.

The experimental results demonstrate that our method meets the practical demands well. In future work, we will optimize each module under the current architecture. In one hand, we will especially focus on improvement in the correction of OOV by expanding the dictionary and supplementing rules further. On the other hand, correction of polyphones will be improved by expanding the training corpus.

Acknowledgments. This research was supported by the National natural science foundation of China (No. 61563040, No. 61773224) and Natural science foundation of Inner Mongolia (No. 2016ZD06, No. 2018MS06006).

References

1. Brill, E., Moore, R.C.: An improved error model for noisy channel spelling correction. In: Proceedings of the 38th Annual Meeting on Association for Computational Linguistics, pp. 286–293. Association for Computational Linguistics (2000)
2. Choudhury, M., Saraf, R., Jain, V., Mukherjee, A., Sarkar, S., Basu, A.: Investigation and modeling of the structure of texting language. IJDAR **10**(3–4), 157–174 (2007)
3. GB25914-2010: Information technology of traditional Mongolian nominal characters, presentation characters and control characters using the rules. China National Standardization Technical Committee, Beijing (2010)
4. Hao, L., OthonBaatur, Gong, Z., Tuya: Mongolian text automatic proofreading based on Bayes algorithm. J. Inner Mongolia Univ. **41**(4), 440–442 (2010)
5. Hua, S.: Modern Mongolian automatic proofreading system-MHAHP. J. Inner Mongolia Univ. Philos. Soc. Sci. Ed. **4**, 49–53 (1997)
6. Islam, A., Inkpen, D.: Real-word spelling correction using Google Web 1T n-gram with backoff. In: International Conference on Natural Language Processing and Knowledge Engineering (2009)
7. Jiang, B.: Research on rule-based method of Mongolian automatic correction. Ph.D. thesis (2014)
8. Kernighan, M.D., Church, K.W., Gale, W.A.: A spelling correction program based on a noisy channel model. In: Proceedings of the 13th Conference on Computational Linguistics-Volume 2, pp. 205–210. Association for Computational Linguistics (1990)
9. Lu, M., Bao, F., Gao, G.: Language model for Mongolian polyphone proofreading. In: Sun, M., Wang, X., Chang, B., Xiong, D. (eds.) CCL/NLP-NABD 2017. LNCS (LNAI), vol. 10565, pp. 461–471. Springer, Cham (2017). https://doi.org/10.1007/978-3-319-69005-6_38
10. Magdy, W., Darwish, K.: Arabic OCR error correction using character segment correction, language modeling, and shallow morphology. In: Proceedings of the 2006 Conference on Empirical Methods in Natural Language Processing, pp. 408–414. Association for Computational Linguistics (2006)
11. Melamud, O., Goldberger, J., Dagan, I.: context2vec: learning generic context embedding with bidirectional LSTM. In: Proceedings of the 20th SIGNLL Conference on Computational Natural Language Learning, pp. 51–61 (2016)
12. Mikolov, T., Chen, K., Corrado, G., Dean, J.: Efficient estimation of word representations in vector space. arXiv preprint arXiv:1301.3781 (2013)

13. Mikolov, T., Sutskever, I., Chen, K., Corrado, G.S., Dean, J.: Distributed representations of words and phrases and their compositionality. In: Advances in Neural Information Processing Systems, pp. 3111–3119 (2013)
14. Norvig, P.: Natural language corpus data. In: Beautiful Data, pp. 219–242 (2009)
15. Si, L.: Mongolian proofreading algorithm based on non-deterministic finite automata. J. Chin. Inf. Process. **23**(6), 110–116 (2009)
16. Su, C., Hou, H., Yang, P., Yuan, H.: Mongolian automatic spelling proofreading method based on statistical translation framework. J. Chin. Inf. Proces **27**(6), 175–179 (2013)
17. Zhao, J., Oqir, Jirannige, Pu, T., Chen, J.: Design and implementation of Mongolian vocabulary analysis corrector based on statistical language model. In: Proceedings of National Symposium on Information of National Languages and Characters. pp. 158–163 (2007)

Unsupervised Cross-Lingual Sentence Representation Learning via Linguistic Isomorphism

Shuai Wang, Lei Hou$^{(\boxtimes)}$, and Meihan Tong

Tsinghua University, Beijing 100084, China
{Shuai-wa16,tongmh17}@mails.tsinghua.edu.cn,
greener2009@gmail.com, lijuanzi2008@gmail.com

Abstract. Recently, many researches on learning cross-lingual word embeddings without parallel data have achieved success by utilizing word isomorphism among languages. However, unsupervised cross-lingual sentence representation, which aims to learn a unified semantic space without parallel data, has not been well explored. Though many cross-lingual tasks can be solved by learning a unified sentence representation of different languages benefiting from cross-lingual word embeddings, the performance is not competitive with their supervised counterparts. In this paper, we propose a novel framework for unsupervised cross-lingual sentence representation learning by utilizing linguistic isomorphism in both word and sentence level. After generating pseudo-parallel sentence based on the pre-trained cross-lingual word embeddings, the framework iteratively conducts sentence modeling, word embedding tuning and parallel sentences update. Our experiments show that the proposed framework achieves state-of-the-art results in many cross-lingual tasks, as well as improves the quality of cross-lingual word embeddings. The codes and pre-trained encoders will be released upon the paper publishing.

Keywords: Unsupervised learning · Cross-lingual ·
Sentence representation · Language model

1 Introduction

Cross-lingual tasks, such as machine translation [3], cross-lingual sentiment analysis [5], usually learn a mapping between different languages. Such a learning process is supervised in nature and usually requires a large amount of parallel data. However, the cross-lingual parallel corpus is often difficult to obtain, especially for some low-resource languages, and sometimes the labellings are not accurate. Therefore, it is necessary to explore an unsupervised manner to align different languages [1].

Recently, many cross-lingual researches find that the structures of words are similar across different languages [21], showing a possibility to align words without parallel data. For example, the structures are exactly the same between

© Springer Nature Switzerland AG 2019
C. Douligeris et al. (Eds.): KSEM 2019, LNAI 11776, pp. 215–226, 2019.
https://doi.org/10.1007/978-3-030-29563-9_20

English words *man*, *woman*, and *girl* and French words *homme*, *femme*, and *fille*. Ideally the similarity between *man* and *woman* is the same as that of *homme* and *femme*, and so are other parallel words. It is possible to view the two groups of words as two triangles in which vertices and edges represent words and their similarities. Then ideally if the two triangles are aligned, it will be found that the parallel relations between words of different languages as shown in Fig. 1(a). The phenomenon is also called linguistic isomorphism [16]. Based on it, many works have focused on learning cross-lingual mappings of word embeddings across different languages in an unsupervised way, and these approaches can be divided into GAN-based and iteration-based methods. Generative Adversarial Network (GAN)-based methods [7,21] directly align the distributions of word embeddings from different languages as a whole, and iteration-based methods [1, 2] firstly construct initial seeds and iteratively train the linear mappings and update seeds.

Actually, sentences across different languages also exhibit isomorphism. Figure 1(b) illustrates an example. The same isomorphism can also be found among three sentences of different languages. If the sentence isomorphism is utilized, the large number of sentences will provide cross-lingual tasks with strong parallel signals, and the quality of both cross-lingual word and sentence representations can be improved accordingly.

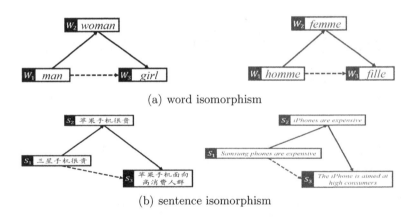

(a) word isomorphism

(b) sentence isomorphism

Fig. 1. Examples of linguistic isomorphism.

In this paper, we expect to exploit the sentence isomorphism to learn unified cross-lingual sentence representations in an unsupervised manner, which will improve the quality of cross-lingual word embeddings and the performance of downstream cross-lingual tasks. However, it is impossible to transplant methods in word level to sentence level because of the following two challenges:

Huge Number of Sentences. The vocabulary size for a monolingual corpus is usually less than 10^6, and after some vocabulary cutoff tricks (removal of meaningless symbols and low-frequency words), it is easy to decrease vocabulary size to at most 10^5. To extract parallel words of two languages, we need to traverse $10^{5 \times 2}$ word pairs, which is feasible under the usage of GPU. However, we have more than 10^7 sentences in our corpus, and they are different from each other. To achieve the parallel sentences, $10^{7 \times 2}$ sentence pairs needed to be traversed, and it also costs far more time to deal with a sentence pair than a word pair. The cost of such methods are unacceptable.

Sentence Representations. It is well acknowledged that words are represented by vectors and they are pre-trained by word2vec [13], GloVe [14], etc., and the cross-lingual mapping is to learn a linear transform [2]. However, there are no such well-acknowledged methods at sentence level. The sentence level information we can leverage includes the co-occurrence of sentences in same language and isomorphism of sentences across different languages. How to utilize this information effectively and efficiently is also a challenging problem.

To address the above issues, we propose a novel framework for unsupervised cross-lingual sentence representation learning. The framework employs an iteration strategy which firstly generates pseudo-parallel sentences by the pre-trained word embeddings, and then iteratively conducts sentence modeling, word embedding tuning and parallel sentences update until meeting the convergence criteria. Specifically, to decrease the number of sentence pairs, we first cluster sentences based on sentence representations (the initial representation is the mean of word vectors), and employ the *cross domain local scaling* technique to generate the initial parallel sentences. For the sentence representation, inspired by [12,13], we formulate it as a binary classification task, i.e., given a sentence, predict its cross-lingual nearby sentences. It can leverage both sentence co-occurrence in a single language and sentence isomorphism across different languages. Besides, we also design a language model to tune the pre-trained word embeddings.

2   Problem Formalization and the Proposed Framework

Preliminaries. We have corpora in two languages l and m, denoted as D^l and D^m. Both corpora consist of a set of documents, and are further split into the sentence sets, i.e., $D^l = \{s_1^l, s_2^l, ..., s_{n_l}^l\}$ and $D^m = \{s_1^m, s_2^m, ..., s_{n_m}^m\}$, where n_l, n_m denote the number of sentences. Note that the sentences come from documents and thus have contextual information. For each sentence $s \in D$, its context is defined as the sentences within a pre-defined window size q in the same document, denoted as $C_q(s)$. And s is represented as a word sequence of length n_s, i.e., $s = \langle w_1, w_2, ..., w_{n_s} \rangle$ (we omit the superscript because the representations are same for both languages). Based on the widely-used word embedding techniques, such as word2vec [13] or GloVe [14], we achieve the pre-trained word embedding matrices V^l and V^m with each column denoting a word embedding.

Definition 1 (Cross-lingual Sentence Representation). *Given the non-parallel corpus D^l and D^m in two different languages, our goal is to build a unified sentence encoder $E(s; V) : s \rightarrow R^d$, which uses word embeddings V*

and maps a sentence s into a low-dimensional real vector with a fixed size d, regardless of languages, satisfying the similarities between vectors revealing the semantic similarities between sentences.

In previous studies, the linguist found the linguistic isomorphism [16] and many recent works [1,2,7,21] used it in unsupervised word representation. In this paper, we verify that this phenomenon also holds in sentence level, and design a novel cross-lingual sentence embedding model accordingly. To support this idea, several cross-lingual parallel sentences are required as seeds, and we will refine and update them based on our learned sentence models. Obviously, it is an iterative framework. Except for the word embedding pre-training, the framework also consists of the following components:

- **Cross-lingual Word Mapping:** To facilitate the following computation, we need to map the word embeddings of the two languages into the same semantic space at first.
- **Parallel Sentences Generation:** At the very first, it generates pseudo-parallel sentences as seeds, denoted as $P = \{(s_{p_1}^l, s_{p_1}^m), (s_{p_2}^l, s_{p_2}^m), ..., (s_{p_n}^l, s_{p_n}^m)\}$, where $s_{p_t}^l$ is the t_{th} parallel sentence in language l, and n is the number of parallel sentences. During the iteration, it updates the parallel sentence pairs according to the learned sentence encoder and word embeddings.
- **Cross-lingual Sentence Modeling:** It leverages the sentence contexts in a single language and sentence isomorphism across languages to build a unified cross-lingual embedding model based on the conventional sentence encoders.
- **Cross-lingual Language Model:** It employs a neural language model to tune the cross-lingual word embeddings.
- **Iterative Strategy:** It iteratively uses the sentence model and the tuned word embeddings in previous two steps to generate more accurate parallel sentences.

Among them, the *cross-lingual word mapping* can be accomplished with an unsupervised algorithm [2]. It learns a mapping matrix for each language, i.e., W_l and W_m, such that $W_l V^l$ and $W_m V^m$ are in the same semantic space. To unify the notations, we concatenate the transformed word embeddings from different languages by column to V, i.e., $V = Concat(W_m V^m, W_l V^l)$. We omit the method details, and interested readers can refer to the original papers.

3   The Proposed Methods

In this section, we present the method details of the key components in our proposed framework.

3.1   Parallel Sentences Generation

Since the following sentence and word models need cross-lingual parallel sentences, it is required to generate initial seed pairs. The seeds could be of low quality, and they will be updated along with the cross-lingual learning. However, the parallel sentences generation is far more difficult than dictionary induction. An alternative way is sampling subsets in both languages and extracting the most similar pairs, but we cannot guarantee that there exist enough similar pairs. To balance the efficiency and coverage, we propose a cluster-based parallel sentences generation method based on pre-mapped word embedding.

Monolingual Sentence Clustering: To cluster sentences, we need their feature representations. Initially, we do not have sentence encoder, so we take the mean of word embeddings as the sentence representation, and cluster sentences of different languages respectively. We do not cluster sentences in both languages together because it generates clusters containing sentences in a single language and might miss many possible sentence pairs. Formally, the corpora $D^l = \{s_i^l\}|_{i=1}^{n_l}$ is clustered into K_l clusters, and the center of the i-th cluster c_i^l, i.e., $center_i^l$, is computed by averaging all its containing sentences. Notations are similar for language m. To avoid extreme big or small clusters (the following computation can be distributed and deployed on GPU servers in a more balanced way), we adopt the same-size K-means variation[1] to complete the clustering.

Cross-Lingual Cluster Alignment: Then we align clusters from different languages based on their centers, and the alignment relations are denoted as a matrix A. Cluster c_i^l is aligned with cluster c_j^m iff $A_{ij} = 1$. A is derived by

$$\arg \min_{ij} A_{ij} \| center_i^l - center_j^m \|. \tag{1}$$

Note that not every cluster finds its alignment especially when the corpus comes from different domains.

Sentence Pairing: Finally, we choose k sentences pairs with the highest similarity, and k is proportional to the total number of sentence pairs in the two languages. The pair selection is conducted only between aligned clusters, thus can significantly reduce the computation complexity. Furthermore, the similarity measure here is not cosine similarity because there is a renowned problem in high dimensional space called *hubness*, which means a single data instance could be the common nearest neighbor of many data instances. Many works have tried to handle the problem, and one of the most effective solutions is Cross-Domain Local Scaling (CDLS) [7]. For two vectors x and y, the similarity metrics is $2cos(x, y) - r_l(x) - r_m(y)$ rather than the simple $cos(x, y)$, where $r_l(x)$ is the mean of cosine similarity k nearest neighbours in source space and $r_m(x)$ is the mean of k nearest neighbours in target space.

After the above process, we obtain the pseudo-parallel sentences P as our seeds.

3.2   Cross-Lingual Sentence Modeling

Given the parallel sentences P and the unified word embeddings V, our goal is to train a unified sentence encoder E to make the paired sentences similar to

---

[1] https://elki-project.github.io/tutorial/same\discretionary-size_k_means.

each other. To utilize context information, the typical task is to, given a sentence, predict its nearby sentences [10,12]. We extend the idea to a cross-lingual setting and design our cross-lingual sentence model as a classification problem that estimates whether a sentence in one language can predict the context in another language. This idea is also consistent with the sentence isomorphism mentioned in the introduction.

Given a cross-lingual sentence pair $(s_{p_i}^l, s_{p_i}^m)$, we replace $s_{p_i}^l$ by $s_{p_i}^m$ in its original context $C_q(s_{p_i}^l)$, and then $s_{p_i}^m$ and $C_q(s_{p_i}^l)$ are concatenated as a positive instance, denoted as CP_i^l. We also randomly sample, as negative instances, some $C_q(s_t^l)$, where $t \neq p_i$ (i.e., they are not parallel) and replace s_t^l by $s_{p_i}^m$. Their contexts are also concatenated with $s_{p_i}^m$, denoted as CN_i^l. It is the same for language m, and then we have a classification dataset

$$T = \{(CP_1^l, 1), ..., (CN_1^l, 0), ..., (CP_1^m, 1), ..., (CN_{p_1}^m, 0), ...\}.$$

Actually it will be better to replace some sentences in the context as well, but under most situation we cannot make sure we can find the parallel counterpart of nearby sentences in P.

To train the model, we design a classifier, denoted as CL, on top of the sentence vectors of these concatenated sentences. Note that CL is a linear classifier because we want to keep most job in sentence encoder E rather than the classifier. The training objective is given by

$$L_s = \sum_{data \in T} L(CL(E(data[0]; V)), data[1]), \tag{2}$$

where L could be 0–1 loss, mean squared error, cross entropy, etc.

3.3 Cross-Lingual Language Model

The above sentence model is constructed from the perspective of sentence co-occurrence, and it does not obviously tune the word embeddings during training. However, the quality of word embeddings influences much on both the sentence encoder and the downstream tasks. To tune the word embeddings, we jointly train another word level language model, and the neural language model has been proven to be an effective way [19].

We employ a masked language model [9,18] here to train a bidirectional language model. This approach just masks some percentage of words in a sentence during the entire process, and they only predict the masked words, which keep a word from seeing itself before prediction. Here masking a word means replacing it by a special token [mask]. For a masked word w_i, the probability of it in position i is also given by $V[w_i]^T o_{i-1}$. The masked language model makes it possible to use bi-directional encoder, like CNN or Transformer. We define $P(T)$ as the collection of positive instances in the dataset T, and our training objective is given by

$$L_w = \sum_{s \in P(D)} \sum_{M(w_i)=1} V[w_i]^T o_i, \tag{3}$$

where $M(w) = 1$ denotes w is masked.

3.4 Iterative Strategy

The seed sentence pairs are extracted only by the word embeddings mapped by an unsupervised method, we do not expect them to be accurate and hence call them pseudo-parallel sentences. Now we have the sentence encoder and tuned word embeddings, so our features are much more precise than the mean of word embeddings and the quality of the parallel sentences could be improved accordingly. The intuitive idea is to repeat the above process, but it has two problems:

- Firstly, it will make the model convergent to local optima very fast. It is similar to the *explore-exploit dilemma* in reinforcement learning, and a similar problem is also proposed and verified in [2].
- Secondly, short sentences (especially single words or digits) tend to have higher cosine similarity. If we always choose sentence pairs with the highest cosine similarity, the set P will finally have many digits or unclear symbols.

For the first problem, we define an increasing probability p such that a sentence can be kept during iteration by the probability (p increases from 0.1 to 1 during training). For the second problem, we design a length-related factor that prefers longer sentences. The final keeping probability for a sentence pair (s_i^l, s_j^m) is computed as

$$p \times \left(1 - \sqrt{\frac{1}{len(s_i^l) + len(s_j^m)}} \right), \tag{4}$$

where $len(\cdot)$ returns the length of the given sentence.

The whole iteration will stop until the loss functions in Eqs. 2 and 3 do not change.

4 Experiments

In this section, we evaluated our proposed method on two pairs of languages, i.e., English-Spanish and English-Chinese.

We use Wikipedia as our training corpus. We replace words with a frequency less than 100. We delete documents with fewer than 8 sentences in Wikipedia. We concatenate all documents sequentially and get the training sentences.

The dimension of the word embeddings is 400. The encoder we adopt is one layer bidirectional GRU with dimension 500 for each direction (i.e., the dimension of sentence representation is 1000). The classifier in cross-lingual sentence modeling is one-layer perceptron with softmax function as activation and cross-entropy as loss function. The optimizer is Adam with learning rate 1e-4 in sentence model and 1e-3 in the language model. The batch size is 512 in the sentence model and 256 in the language model. The norm of gradients is clipped with 1 in both models. The dropout rate is 0.5 in the sentence model, and the masked percentage is 20% in the word model.

The number of clusters in one language is tuned according to the total number of sentences. The calculation and sorting of similarity matrix are implemented under GPU, so the size of clusters should take the efficiency of GPU usage into account. The maximum sentence pairs one GPU can deal is approximately $15,000 \times 15,000$, so the size of clusters is about 15,000. The total number of parallel sentences is 500,000.

4.1   Transfer Tasks

Following settings in monolingual sentence representations [10,12,23], we evaluate our sentence representation on two typical transfer tasks (i.e., text classification, and language understanding), which means we only use the pre-trained encoder as feature extractor, and the parameters in it are fixed.

Settings: The baselines include the sum of cross-lingual word embeddings, mean of cross-lingual word embeddings, LASER [15], and some task-specific methods. The sum or mean of word embeddings is a strong baseline in the monolingual setting. We compare with them to show the performance of our model after incorporating sentence isomorphism. LASER is the state-of-the-art cross-lingual sentence representation which trained on machine translation datasets. It is a supervised method requiring a large scale of parallel data, but it can be used as a general-purpose sentence encoder. We compare with it to show the performance of the proposed method compared with the supervised method. But the pre-trained sentence encoder of LASER does not support Chinese, so we can only compare with it in English-Spanish pair.

Cross-Lingual Text Classification: We use Reuters Corpus, Volume 2 (RCV2) [11] to show the performance of our model in cross-lingual text classification because it contains no cross-lingual parallel signal. The dataset contains news from 1996-08-20 to 1997-08-19 in 13 languages. News from all languages are categorized into 4 topics, and there is no parallel news across different languages. We use three languages here, including English, Chinese, and Spanish. A problem is that the dataset is in corpus level rather than sentence level. Although documents can still be encoded, the proposed method does not focus on long documents. Hence, we only extract the titles of these articles rather than whole documents.

In this task, the sentence representations encoded by our method are fed into a Logistic Regression classifier (LR), and we only tune L2 regularization by the valid set. We train the classifier on one language and test the accuracy on another language (test set and valid set are in the same language, but the language of valid set does not obviously influence the accuracy). The results are reported in Table 1, where en, zh and es represent English, Chinese and Spanish respectively.

From the results, we can see that after incorporating sentence isomorphism, the sentence embeddings are strikingly better than the sum or mean of cross-lingual word vectors, showing the effectiveness of the proposed method. Our model performs well on this dataset because the training objective of our sentence

Table 1. The experiment results

	Cross-lingual text classification				XNLI	
	en-zh	zh-en	en-es	es-en	en-zh	en-es
sum	41.1	55.2	46.3	54.9	49.2	38.4
mean	52.7	52.0	69.4	39.1	47.6	38.4
LASER	-	-	42.0	39.4	-	45.3
MT + BiLSTM-last	-	-	-	-	65.7	67.0
MT + BiLSTM-max	-	-	-	-	67.0	68.8
XCBOW	-	-	-	-	58.8	60.7
Our method	75.7	64.5	75.4	62.3	59.9	48.7

model is also a classification task. The training of our sentence model requires the encoder being capable of capturing the semantic inconsistency in a sentence composed of words from different languages, which is a more difficult problem than the topic classification in this task.

Cross-Lingual Language Understanding: XNLI [8] is a multi-lingual language understanding dataset containing 15 languages. Given two sentences called *Premise* and *Hypothesis*, the task is to predict their relation as one of three labels, i.e., Contradictory, Neutral and Entailment. In this experiment, we use two languages from this dataset, i.e., Chinese and Spanish. Since it only has valid and test set, we use MultiXNLI [20] for training, which is the same with XNLI except it only contains English sentences.

Similar with previous tasks, the features of the sentence pair s_l and s_m are the concatenation of $E(s_l; V)$, $E(s_m; V)$, $|E(s_l; V) - E(s_m; V)|$ and $|E(s_l; V) \cdot E(s_m; V)|$. Following [8], the features are fed into a two-layer feedforward neural network with hidden dimension 128 and dropout rate 0.1. The results are reported in Table 1.

In Table 1, the results of the two task-specific methods and XBOW are reported by the original paper [8]. BiLSTM-last means the representation of sentence is given by the final state of BiLSTM [17], and BiLSTM-max takes the max value over all states [6]. These two methods are task dependent because the parameters in encoder are training according to this task. They first translate valid and test set into English by Machine Translation. XCBOW is just the sum of a cross-lingual word embeddings, and the details of its embeddings can be found in their original paper.

XNLI is a newly constructed baseline to measure the performance of cross-lingual sentence embeddings. It is a difficult task because it requires understanding the logical relations between two sentences. Even many tasks specific sentence embedding methods cannot achieve good performance on this task. From Table 1, we can see that the accuracy of the proposed method is only 10% away from supervised task-specific methods in English-Chinese language pair, showing a good master of the semantics of our sentence encoder.

4.2   Improvement on Word Vectors

The cross-lingual word embeddings are tuned during the training of our sentence model. As mentioned above, after incorporating sentence isomorphism, the quality of cross-lingual word embeddings will also be improved. We test the performance of tuned word embeddings by the dictionary induction task. We search the top 1 nearest neighbor in word embedding space and calculate the accuracy by comparing the results with a bilingual dictionary. We use the English-Spanish dictionary constructed by [2]. The coverage of our word embeddings in the dictionary is 19.13%. We also compare some other unsupervised methods of cross-lingual word embedding mapping. The results in Table 2 shows that the top 1 accuracies are all improved by more than 10%, validating the effectiveness of incorporating sentence isomorphism to leverage the cross-lingual signals in sentence level.

Table 2. Results on English-Spanish bilingual dictionary induction: Before and After gives the Top 1 accuracy before and after our model training

Method	Before	After	Improvement
[21]	45.56	53.17	+16.7%
[7]	47.62	53.01	+11.3%
[2]	49.13	55.44	+12.8%

5   Related Works

Words, especially common ones, are generally isomorphic across different languages, making it possible to learn the mapping without parallel data. After seeing the possibility of aligning words without parallel data, many works have focused on learning cross-lingual word embeddings without parallel data. These methods can be divided into GAN-based methods and iteration-based methods.

GAN-based methods regard word embedding of different languages as different probability distributions, and directly align two distributions as a whole. They hypothesize that once word distributions are aligned, the isomorphism of words will make words of different languages aligned. [4] firstly proposes GAN-based methods on this task, but they fail to produce competitive results. After that, [21] adopt similar architecture but employ some training techniques, such as orthogonal regularization, and they achieve good results on bilingual dictionary induction. [7] refine result word vectors after the above training process. [22] employ Wasserstein-GAN to train the model and minimize earth mover's distance to refine the vectors after training.

Although GAN-based methods work well in their original paper, [2] point out that they lack robustness, i.e., their performance is excellent if they succeed, but they often fail under complicated situations. Once they fail, they cannot produce meaningful results.

Iteration-based methods are more robust by this way. [1] firstly propose the iteration approach to learn across language mapping from a small seed dictionary (as small as 25). They iteratively train the mapping and generate a new dictionary until convergence. After that, [2] create a new fully unsupervised method to generate the initial dictionary and proceed the above iteration. Their experiments show that their approach is competitive and more robust than GAN-based methods.

6   Conclusion

In this paper, we propose a novel framework learning cross-lingual sentence representation in a fully unsupervised manner. The only materials required are raw documents from different languages which are abundant in the big data era. The performance of our sentence encoder is competitive with supervised methods, making it fully possible to achieve good performance on many cross-lingual tasks without parallel annotations.

Acknowledgement. The work is supported by NSFC key project (U1736204, 61533018, 61661146007), Ministry of Education and China Mobile Joint Fund (MCM20170301), and THUNUS NExT Co-Lab.

References

1. Artetxe, M., Labaka, G., Agirre, E.: Learning bilingual word embeddings with (almost) no bilingual data. In: Proceedings of the 55th Annual Meeting of the Association for Computational Linguistics (Volume 1: Long Papers), vol. 1, pp. 451–462 (2017)
2. Artetxe, M., Labaka, G., Agirre, E.: A robust self-learning method for fully unsupervised cross-lingual mappings of word embeddings. arXiv preprint arXiv:1805.06297 (2018)
3. Bahdanau, D., Cho, K., Bengio, Y.: Neural machine translation by jointly learning to align and translate. arXiv preprint arXiv:1409.0473 (2014)
4. Barone, A.V.M.: Towards cross-lingual distributed representations without parallel text trained with adversarial autoencoders. arXiv preprint arXiv:1608.02996 (2016)
5. Chen, Q., Li, W., Lei, Y., Liu, X., He, Y.: Learning to adapt credible knowledge in cross-lingual sentiment analysis. In: Proceedings of the 53rd Annual Meeting of the Association for Computational Linguistics and the 7th International Joint Conference on Natural Language Processing (Volume 1: Long Papers), vol. 1, pp. 419–429 (2015)
6. Collobert, R., Weston, J.: A unified architecture for natural language processing: deep neural networks with multitask learning. In: Proceedings of the 25th International Conference on Machine Learning, pp. 160–167. ACM (2008)
7. Conneau, A., Lample, G., Ranzato, M., Denoyer, L., Jégou, H.: Word translation without parallel data. arXiv preprint arXiv:1710.04087 (2017)

8. Conneau, A., et al.: XNLI: evaluating cross-lingual sentence representations. arXiv preprint arXiv:1809.05053 (2018)

9. Devlin, J., Chang, M.W., Lee, K., Toutanova, K.: BERT: pre-training of deep bidirectional transformers for language understanding. arXiv preprint arXiv:1810.04805 (2018)

10. Kiros, R., et al.: Skip-thought vectors. In: Advances in Neural Information Processing Systems, pp. 3294–3302 (2015)

11. Lewis, D.D., Yang, Y., Rose, T.G., Li, F.: RCV1: a new benchmark collection for text categorization research. J. Mach. Learn. Res. **5**, 361–397 (2004)

12. Logeswaran, L., Lee, H.: An efficient framework for learning sentence representations. arXiv preprint arXiv:1803.02893 (2018)

13. Mikolov, T., Sutskever, I., Chen, K., Corrado, G.S., Dean, J.: Distributed representations of words and phrases and their compositionality. In: Advances in Neural Information Processing Systems, pp. 3111–3119 (2013)

14. Pennington, J., Socher, R., Manning, C.: GloVe: global vectors for word representation. In: Proceedings of the 2014 Conference on Empirical Methods in Natural Language Processing (EMNLP), pp. 1532–1543 (2014)

15. Schwenk, H., Douze, M.: Learning joint multilingual sentence representations with neural machine translation, pp. 157–167 (2017)

16. Storer, T.: Linguistic isomorphisms. Univ. Chicago Press Behalf Philos. Sci. Assoc. **19**(1), 77–85 (1952)

17. Sutskever, I., Vinyals, O., Le, Q.V.: Sequence to sequence learning with neural networks. In: Advances in Neural Information Processing Systems, pp. 3104–3112 (2014)

18. Taylor, W.L.: "Cloze procedure": a new tool for measuring readability. Journal. Bull. **30**(4), 415–433 (1953)

19. Wada, T., Iwata, T.: Unsupervised cross-lingual word embedding by multilingual neural language models. arXiv preprint arXiv:1809.02306 (2018)

20. Williams, A., Nangia, N., Bowman, S.: A broad-coverage challenge corpus for sentence understanding through inference. In: Proceedings of the 2018 Conference of the North American Chapter of the Association for Computational Linguistics: Human Language Technologies, Volume 1 (Long Papers), pp. 1112–1122. Association for Computational Linguistics (2018). http://aclweb.org/anthology/N18-1101

21. Zhang, M., Liu, Y., Luan, H., Sun, M.: Adversarial training for unsupervised bilingual lexicon induction. In: Proceedings of the 55th Annual Meeting of the Association for Computational Linguistics (Volume 1: Long Papers), vol. 1, pp. 1959–1970 (2017)

22. Zhang, M., Liu, Y., Luan, H., Sun, M.: Earth mover's distance minimization for unsupervised bilingual lexicon induction. In: Proceedings of the 2017 Conference on Empirical Methods in Natural Language Processing, pp. 1934–1945 (2017)

23. Zhang, M., Wu, Y., Li, W., Li, W.: Learning universal sentence representations with mean-max attention autoencoder. arXiv preprint arXiv:1809.06590 (2018)

Knowledge Theories and Models

Practical Scheme for Secure Outsourcing of Coppersmith's Algorithm

Jiayang Liu[1] and Jingguo Bi[1,2]([⊠])

[1] Tsinghua University, Beijing 100084, China
liujiaya14@mails.tsinghua.edu.cn
[2] Beijing Research Institute of Telemetry, Beijing 100094, China
bijingguo-001@163.com

Abstract. Coppersmith's Algorithm was proposed by Coppersmith to find all small roots of a univariate polynomial congruence in polynomial time. In practical applications, we are facing a bottleneck of computation with high-dimensional matrix and extra large coefficients. In this case, cloud computing can provide the capability to utilize almost unlimited computational power and storage on cloud servers. In this paper, we investigate secure outsourcing for Coppersmith's Algorithm for the first time. We design a outsource-secure scheme for Coppersmith's Algorithm with extremely high speedup on the client side. The most time-consuming part of algorithm, which is the lattice reduction process, can be outsourced to a malicious cloud. We show that our scheme are correct, secure and have high-efficiency as well as immediate practicability.

Keywords: Cloud computing · Outsource-secure · Lattice · Coppersmith's algorithm · Lattice reduction

1 Introduction

Cloud computing enables convenient and on-demand network access to a shared pool of resources such as computational power and storage. It is becoming mainstream due to the advantages of high computing power, cheap cost of services, high performance, scalability, accessibility as well as availability. The resource-constrained devices can outsource their computation workloads to cloud servers and utilize the unlimited computation resources in a pay-per-use manner. The enterprises and individuals can avoid large capital outlays in hardware/software deployment and maintenance.

In public-key cryptosystems, some types of computations such as exponential operation in a finite group are expensive and almost ubiquitous. In TCC2005, Hohenberger and Lysyanskaya presented two practical outsource-secure schemes

Partially supported by National Natural Science Foundation of China Grants No. 61502269, The National Key Research and Development Program of China No. 2017YFA0303903 and Zhejiang Province Key R & D Project No. 2017C01062.

C. Douligeris et al. (Eds.): KSEM 2019, LNAI 11776, pp. 229–240, 2019.
https://doi.org/10.1007/978-3-030-29563-9_21

for modular exponentiation [1]. Chen et al. in 2014 [2] and Zhou et al. in 2017 [3] presented new algorithms for secure outsourcing of modular exponentiation. In ASIACCS2010, Atallah and Frikken proposed outsource-secure schemes for matrix multiplication [4]. Lei et al. proposed a new efficient scheme in 2014 [5]. In 2015, Lei et al. designed a scheme for matrix determinant computation [6]. Wang et al. in 2013 [7] and Chen et al. in 2015 [8] respectively presented a secure outsourcing algorithm for solving large-scale systems of linear equations. Some other schemes are designed for matrix inverse computation, QR-factorization, linear programming, nonlinear programming and other else computation workloads. The proposed schemes tried to satisfy the goals of correctness, security, robust cheating resistance, and high-efficiency.

Lattices are classical objects of number theory, which are widely used in cryptanalysis and cryptographic design. Lattice reduction is one of the few potentially hard problems used in public-key cryptography. In a seminal work at EUROCRYPT '96, Coppersmith [9] showed how to find all small roots of a univariate polynomial congruence by running LLL algorithm (Lenstra, Lenstra Jr., Lovász [10]), which is a famous algorithm for lattice reduction, on the Coppersmith lattice. Coppersmith's Algorithm has many applications in public-key cryptanalysis and in a few security proofs such as attacks on RSA cryptosystem with short secret exponent, known partial factorization and fixed pattern padding. However, the running time of the algorithm is high-degree polynomial. The bottleneck of the algorithm is an LLL reduction of a high-dimensional matrix with extra-large coefficients. In PKC2014, Bi et al. [11] presented significant speedups over Coppersmith's algorithm. We refer to their framework. In this paper, we investigate secure outsourcing for Coppersmith's algorithm for the first time. We propose a secure outsourcing scheme of Coppersmith's algorithm and keep the original lattice basis secret by concealing the perturbation matrix. In our outsourcing scheme, the clients can outsource their main computation workloads such as LLL-reduction to cloud servers and complete the remaining operations locally e.g. matrix multiplication. We prove the correctness, high-efficiency and resistance to general attacks in this paper.

The main contributions of our paper are summarized as follows:

- We investigate secure outsourcing for Coppersmith's algorithm for the first time.
- We design a scheme to securely outsource LLL-reduction for the Coppersmith lattice.
- We prove the correctness and verifiability of the proposed scheme and analyse its security and efficiency.

We organized the paper as follows. Section 2 shows some backgrounds about model of outsource-secure schemes, lattices and Coppersmith's algorithm. In Sect. 3, we propose our scheme for Coppersmith's algorithm. In Sect. 4, we provide the analyses of correctness, security and efficiency. Finally, we conclude the paper in Sect. 5.

2   Preliminary

2.1   Security Model

A resource-constrained C with limited computational power and storage space intends to outsource an expensive computation task to a cloud server S. However, S is shared and not fully trusted by C. Goldreich et al. introduced the 'honest-but-curious' model (originally called the semi-honest model) in 1987 [12]. Golle and Mironov [13] introduced a 'lazy-but-honest' model for the inversion of one-way function class of outsourcing computations. S may be not only lazy and curious, but also dishonest. It is difficult to design secure and efficient outsourcing algorithms in this case, which is called the malicious cloud model. Hohenberger and Lysyanskaya [1] present a weaker model called 'two untrusted program model' for outsourcing exponentiations modulo a large prime. Canetti et al. [14] introduced the 'refereed delegation of computation model', which can be viewed as an extension of the last one.

In the semi-honest cloud model, the cloud correctly follow the protocol specification. We have to make sure that it is infeasible for S to derive any key information from the outsourced task. In the malicious cloud model, the cloud can arbitrarily deviate from the protocol specification. Therefore, an outsourcing protocol must be able to handle result verification simultaneously. Our protocol should be able to resist a malicious cloud.

Gennaro et al. [15] presented a framework to protect privacy for securely outsourcing computation.

Definition 1 ([15] Securely outsourcing computation scheme). *A securely outsourcing computation scheme consists of a five-tuple:*

1. **KeyGen**$(F, k) \to (PK, SK)$: *Given a security parameter k, the randomized key generation algorithm generates a public key PK that encodes the target function F, and a corresponding secret key SK which is kept private by the client C.*
2. **ProbGen**$_{SK}(x) \to (\sigma_x, \tau_x)$: *The problem generation algorithm uses the secret key SK to encode the function input x as a public value σ_x, which is given to the server S to compute with, and a secret value τ_x, which is kept private by the client C.*
3. **Compute**$_{PK}(\sigma_x) \to \sigma_y$: *Given the public key PK and the encoded input σ_x, the server computes an encoded version σ_y of the output $y = F(x)$.*
4. **Verify**$_{SK}(\sigma_y) \to 1 \cup 0$: *On input the secret key SK, and the encoded value σ_y, the verification algorithm outputs 1 if σ_y is valid; otherwise, outputs 0.*
5. **Solve**$_{SK}(\tau_x, \sigma_y) \to y$: *On input the secret key SK, the secret 'decoding' τ_x, and the encoded value σ_y, the solving algorithm outputs the computation result $y = F(x)$.*

Our outsourcing scheme must be able to work with a cloud server which is assumed to be lazy, curious, and dishonest (fully malicious model). To enable secure and practical outsourcing, we identify the following goals that the scheme should satisfy [5,6]:

- Correctness: If both the cloud server and the client faithfully follow the scheme, the original problem can be fulfilled by the cloud and the correct output can be decrypted and verified successfully by the client.
- Security: The protocol can protect the privacy of the client's data. The cloud cannot get sensitive knowledge of the client's input data and the correct result is also hidden from the cloud, which are respectively called as input privacy and output privacy.
- Efficiency: The local computation done by client should be substantially less than the computation of the original algorithm. The computation burden on the cloud server should be as close as possible to the existing practical algorithms.
- Robust cheating resistance: No false result from a cheating cloud server can pass the verification with a non-negligible probability.

2.2   Lattice

Let $\mathbb{R}^m$ be the m-dimensional Euclidean space. A lattice $\mathcal{L}$ is a discrete subgroup of $\mathbb{R}^m$: there exist $n(\leq m)$ linearly independent vectors $\mathbf{b}_1, \ldots, \mathbf{b}_n \in \mathbb{R}^m$ s.t. $\mathcal{L}$ is the set $\mathcal{L}(\mathbf{b}_1, \ldots, \mathbf{b}_n)$ of all integral linear combinations of $\mathbf{b}_i$,

$$\mathcal{L}(\mathbf{b}_1, \ldots, \mathbf{b}_n) = \left\{ \sum_{i=1}^{n} x_i \mathbf{b}_i : x_i \in \mathbb{Z} \right\}.$$

Then the matrix $\mathbf{B} = (\mathbf{b}_1, \ldots, \mathbf{b}_n)$ is called a *basis* of $\mathcal{L}$ and n is the *rank* (or *dimension*) of $\mathcal{L}$. The (co-)volume of $\mathcal{L}$ is $\mathrm{vol}(\mathcal{L}) = \sqrt{\det(\mathbf{B}^T \mathbf{B})}$ for any basis $\mathbf{B}$ of $\mathcal{L}$, where $\mathbf{B}^T$ denotes $\mathbf{B}$'s transpose. If $\mathbf{B}$ is square, then $\mathrm{vol}(\mathcal{L}) = |\det \mathbf{B}|$, and if $\mathbf{B}$ is further triangular, then $\mathrm{vol}(\mathcal{L})$ is simply the product of the diagonal entries of $\mathbf{B}$ in absolute value.

Definition 2 (Gram-Schmidt orthogonalization). *Let $\mathbf{b}_1, \ldots, \mathbf{b}_n \in \mathbb{R}^m$ be linearly independent vectors. The Gram-Schmidt orthogonalization is the family $(\mathbf{b}_1^*, \ldots, \mathbf{b}_n^*)$ defined recursively as: $\mathbf{b}_1^* = \mathbf{b}_1$ and for $i \geq 2$, $\mathbf{b}_i^*$ is the component of the vector $\mathbf{b}_i$ which is orthogonal to the linear span of $\mathbf{b}_1, \ldots, \mathbf{b}_{i-1}$. Then $\mathbf{b}_i^* = \mathbf{b}_i - \sum_{j=1}^{i-1} \mu_{i,j} \mathbf{b}_j^*$, where $\mu_{i,j} = \frac{\langle \mathbf{b}_i, \mathbf{b}_j^* \rangle}{\|\mathbf{b}_j^*\|^2}$ for $1 \leq j < i \leq n$.*

Definition 3 (Successive minima). *Given a lattice $\mathcal{L}$ with rank n, the i-th minima $\lambda_i(\mathcal{L})$ is the radius of the smallest sphere centered in the origin containing i linearly independent lattice vectors, i.e., $\lambda_i(\mathcal{L}) = \inf\{r : \dim(\mathrm{span}(\mathcal{L} \cap B_n(r))) \geq i\}$, where $B_n(r)$ represents the n-dimension ball centered at the origin with radius r.*

To find a short vector in a given lattice, the first polynomial algorithm is the celebrated LLL algorithm [10]: given a basis $(\mathbf{b}_1, \ldots, \mathbf{b}_n)$ of an integer lattice $L \subseteq \mathbb{Z}^m$, LLL algorithm outputs a non-zero $\mathbf{v} \in L$ s.t. $\|\mathbf{v}\| \leq 2^{\frac{n-1}{2}} \lambda_1$ in time $O(n^5 m b^3)$ (resp. $n^3 m b \widetilde{O}(n) \widetilde{O}(b)$) without (resp. with) fast integer arithmetic, where $b = \max_{1 \leq i \leq n} \log \|\mathbf{b}_i\|$. Strictly speaking, this vector is actually the first vector of the basis outputted by the algorithm. Nguyen and Stehlé [16] introduced the L^2 algorithm, a faster variant of LLL which can output similarly short vectors in time $O(n^4 m(n+b)b)$ without fast integer arithmetic.

Proposition 1. *Let* $(\mathbf{b}_1, \ldots, \mathbf{b}_n)$ *be an LLL-reduced basis of a lattice* $\mathcal{L}$. *Then:*

1. $vol(\mathcal{L}) \leq \prod_{i=1}^{n} \|\mathbf{b}_i\| \leq 2^{\frac{n(n-1)}{4}} vol(\mathcal{L})$.
2. $\|\mathbf{b}_1\| \leq 2^{\frac{n-1}{4}} (vol(\mathcal{L}))^{\frac{1}{n}}$.
3. $\forall 1 \leq i \leq n, \|\mathbf{b}_i\| \leq 2^{\frac{n-1}{2}} \lambda_i(\mathcal{L})$.

A basis $(\mathbf{b}_1, \ldots, \mathbf{b}_n)$ is size-reduced if its Gram-Schmidt orthogonalization satisfies $|\mu_{i,j}| \leq \frac{1}{2}$, for all $1 \leq j < i \leq n$. There is a classical (elementary) algorithm which size-reduces a basis $(\mathbf{b}_1, \ldots, \mathbf{b}_n)$ of an integer lattice $\mathcal{L} \subset \mathbb{Z}^m$ in polynomial time, without ever modifying the Gram-Schmidt vectors $\mathbf{b}_i^*$. This algorithm is included in the original LLL algorithm [10]. In the special case that the input basis is (square) lower-triangular, the running-time of this size-reduction algorithm is $O(n^3 b^2)$ without fast integer arithmetic and $n^3 \widetilde{O}(b)$ with fast integer arithmetic.

2.3   Coppersmith's Algorithm

At EUROCRYPT'96, Coppersmith [9,17] showed how to find efficiently all small roots of polynomial equations (modulo an integer, or over the integers). The simplest result is the following: Given an integer N of unknown factorization and a monic polynomial $f(x) \in \mathbb{Z}[x]$ of degree δ, Coppersmith's lattice-based algorithm finds all integers $x_0 \in \mathbb{Z}$ such that $f(x_0) \equiv 0 \mod N$ and $|x_0| \leq N^{\frac{1}{\delta}}$ in time polynomial in $\log N$ and δ. A useful lemma was presented in [18].

Lemma 1 (Howgrave-Graham [18]). *Let* $h(x) \in \mathbb{Z}[x, y]$ *be a sum of at most* ω *monomials. Let* h *be a positive integer. Assume that* $h(x_0) = 0 \mod N^h$, *where* $|x_0| \leq X$ *and* $\|h(xX)\| < \frac{N^m}{\sqrt{\omega}}$. *Then* $h(x_0) = 0$ *holds over the integers.*

We consider the Coppersmith's matrix $\mathbf{M}$ of dimension $n = h\delta$ whose row vectors are the coefficients of the polynomials $g_{i,j}(xX) = (xX)^j N^{h-1-i} f^i(xX), i = 0, \ldots, h-1, j = 0, \ldots, \delta - 1$. For example, given a univariate equation $f(x) = x^2 + ax + b \mod N$ and $h = 3$, we have the Coppersmith's matrix as below:

$$\begin{pmatrix} N^2 \\ & N^2 X \\ bN & aXN & NX^2 \\ & bNX & aNX^2 & NX^3 \\ b^2 & 2abX & (a^2+2b)X^2 & 2aX^3 & X^4 \\ & b^2 X & 2abX^2 & (a^2+2b)X^3 & 2aX^4 & X^5 \end{pmatrix}$$

In most popular applications, the bit-length of N is at least 1024 bits, from this toy example, we can see that the coefficients of the Coppersmith's matrix are huge in the specific applications. As h increases, these coefficients will become much huger. Thus, the process of LLL reduction will turn to be much slower when one invokes the Coppersmith's method.

Coppersmith's algorithm is presented here (Algorithm 1). The core idea consists in reducing the problem to solving univariate polynomial equations over the integers by transforming modular roots into integral roots.

Algorithm 1. Coppersmith's Algorithm

Input: Two integers $N \geq 1, h \geq 2$, **a univariate degree-**δ **monic polynomial** $f(x) \in \mathbb{Z}[x]$ **with coefficients in** $\{0, \ldots, N-1\}$ **and** $2 < \delta + 1 < \frac{\log N}{2}$.
Output: All $x_0 \in \mathbb{Z}$ **s.t.** $|x_0| \leq N^{\frac{1}{\delta}}$ **and** $f(x_0) \equiv 0 \mod N$.

1. Let $n = h\delta$, $X = \lfloor \frac{1}{\sqrt{2}} N^{\frac{h-1}{n-1}} (n+1)^{-\frac{1}{n-1}} \rfloor$, $t = 0$.
2. while $Xt < N^{\frac{1}{\delta}}$ do
3. $f_t(x) = f(Xt + x)$.
4.   **Build the** $n \times n$ **lower-triangular matrix B whose rows are the coefficients of** $g_{i,j}(xX) = (xX)^j N^{h-1-i} f_t^i(xX + Xt), 0 \leq i < h, 0 \leq j < \delta$.
5.   **Run the** L^2 **algorithm [16] on the matrix B.**
6.   **The first vector of the reduced basis v corresponds to a polynomial of the form** $v(xX)$ **for some** $v(x) \in \mathbb{Z}[x]$.
7.   **Compute all the roots** x_0' **of** $v(x)$ **over** $\mathbb{Z}$.
8.   **Output** $x_0 = x_0' + Xt$ **for each root** x_0' **which satisfies** $f_t(x_0') \equiv 0 \mod N$ **and** $|x_0'| \leq X$.
9. $t \leftarrow t + 1$.
10. **end while**

---

3   Outsourcing Scheme for Coppersmith's Algorithm

Here we present the outsourcing scheme for Coppersmith's Algorithm. Our scheme aims to outsource the main part of computation workloads, which could consist of lattice reduction of Coppersmith's matrix, i.e. lower-triangular matrix over $\mathbb{Z}$ with strictly positive diagonal, and compute all $x_0 \in \mathbb{Z}$ s.t. $|x_0| \leq N^{\frac{1}{\delta}}$ and $f(x_0) \equiv 0 \mod N$ through the output of the cloud server. Set the input of the outsourcing scheme including two integers $N \geq 1, h \geq 2$, a rational $c > 1$, a univariate degree-δ monic polynomial $f(x) \in \mathbb{Z}[x]$ with coefficients in $\{0, \ldots, N-1\}$ and $2 < \delta + 1 < \frac{\log N}{2}$. Bi et al. have presented two speedups over Coppersmith's algorithm for finding small roots of univariate polynomial congruences [11]. We mainly use the technique of combining LLL reduction with rounding.

Theorem 1. *[11] Given as input two integers* $N \geq 1, h \geq 2$, *a rational* $c > 1$, *a univariate degree-*δ *monic polynomial* $f(x) \in \mathbb{Z}[x]$ *with coefficients in* $\{0, \ldots, N-1\}$, *there is an algorithm (presented in [11]), corresponding to* $t < \frac{N^{\frac{1}{\delta}}}{X}$, *outputs all* $x_0 = x_0' + Xt$ *s.t.* $|x_0'| \leq X$ *and* $f(x_0) \equiv 0 \mod N$, *where* $n = h\delta$, $X = \lfloor \frac{N^{\frac{h-1}{n-1}} \kappa^{\frac{-2}{n-1}}}{\sqrt{2} n^{\frac{1}{n-1}}} \rfloor$ *with* $\kappa = n^{\frac{3}{2}} (\frac{3c-2}{2c-2})^{n-1} \lfloor c \rfloor^{-1} + 1$.

According to the above theorem from [11], let $n = h\delta$, $X = \lfloor \frac{N^{\frac{h-1}{n-1}}\kappa^{\frac{-2}{n-1}}}{\sqrt{2n}^{\frac{1}{n-1}}} \rfloor$ with $\kappa = n^{\frac{3}{2}}(\frac{3c-2}{2c-2})^{n-1}\lfloor c \rfloor^{-1} + 1, c = (\frac{3}{2})^n$. Our scheme is given as follows:

Key Generation:

1. While $0 \leq t < \frac{N^{\frac{1}{\delta}}}{X}$, build the $n \times n$ matrix $\mathbf{B}_t$ whose rows are the coefficients of $g_{i,j}(xX) = (xX)^j N^{h-1-i} f^i(xX + Xt), 0 \leq i < h, 0 \leq j < \delta$.
2. For each t, select a random unimodular matrix $\mathbf{D}_t \in \mathbb{Z}^{n \times n}$.
3. Secret key: $\mathbf{B}_t, \mathbf{D}_t$, for $0 \leq t < \frac{N^{\frac{1}{\delta}}}{X}$.

Encryption:

1. Size-reduce $\mathbf{B}_t$ without modifying its diagonal coefficients.
2. Compute the matrix $\tilde{\mathbf{B}}_t = \lfloor \frac{c\mathbf{B}_t}{X^{h\delta-\delta}} \rfloor$ obtained by rounding $\mathbf{B}_t$.
3. Compute the matrix of the new basis $\bar{\mathbf{B}}_t = \mathbf{D}_t \tilde{\mathbf{B}}_t$.

Cloud Computation:

1. Run the L^2 algorithm [16] on the matrix $\bar{\mathbf{B}}_t$.
2. Let $\bar{\mathbf{v}}_t = \mathbf{x}\bar{\mathbf{B}}_t$ be the first vector of the reduced basis obtained.

Result Verification:

1. Check whether $\bar{\mathbf{v}}_t \in \bar{\mathbf{B}}_t$ holds or not.
2. Check whether $\|\bar{\mathbf{v}}_t\| \leq 2^{\frac{n-1}{4}}(\det(\mathcal{L}(\bar{\mathbf{B}}_t)))^{\frac{1}{n}}$.

Decryption:

1. The vector $\mathbf{v}_t = \mathbf{x}\mathbf{D}_t\mathbf{B}_t$ corresponds to a polynomial of the form $v_t(xX)$ for some $v_t(x) \in \mathbb{Z}[x]$.
2. Compute all the roots x_0' of $v_t(x)$ over $\mathbb{Z}$.
3. Output $x_0 = x_0' + Xt$ for each t and each root x_0' which satisfies $f(x_0' + Xt) \equiv 0 \mod N$ and $|x_0'| \leq X$.

4 Analysis

4.1 Correctness and Verifiability Guarantee

The correctness of our scheme is guaranteed by Theorem 1 and the following theorem cited from [11].

Theorem 2. *[11] There is an algorithm which, given as input an integer N of unknown factorization and a monic polynomial $f(x) \in \mathbb{Z}[x]$ of degree δ and coefficients in $0, \ldots, N-1$, outputs all integers $x_0 \in \mathbb{Z}$ such that $f(x_0) \equiv 0 \mod N$ and $|x_0| \leq N^{\frac{1}{\delta}}$ in time $O(\log^7 N)$ without fast integer arithmetic using the L^2 algorithm [16], or $O(\log^{6+\varepsilon} N)$ for any $\varepsilon > 0$ using fast integer arithmetic and the L^1 algorithm [19].*

Considering the proof of the above theorem, we remain to prove that $\mathbf{xDB}$ is kept short enough when $\mathbf{xD\tilde{B}}$ is a short vector. Let $\|\mathbf{B}\|_2 = \max\limits_{\|\mathbf{x}\| \neq 0} \frac{\|\mathbf{xB}\|}{\|\mathbf{x}\|} \leq \sqrt{n} \max\limits_{1 \leq j \leq n} \sum\limits_{i=1}^{m} |b_{i,j}|$.

Lemma 2. *Let $\mathbf{B} = (b_{i,j})$ be an $n \times n$ lower-triangular matrix over $\mathbb{Z}$ with strictly positive diagonal. Let $c > 1$. If $\tilde{\mathbf{B}} = \lfloor \frac{c\mathbf{B}}{\min\limits_{i=1}^{n} b_{i,i}} \rfloor$ and $\mathbf{xD\tilde{B}}$ is the first vector of an LLL-reduced basis of $\mathbf{D\tilde{B}}$, then*

$$0 < \|\mathbf{xDB}\| < (n\|\tilde{\mathbf{B}}^{-1}\|_2 + 1)2^{\frac{n-1}{4}} \det(\mathbf{B})^{\frac{1}{n}}.$$

Proof. Let $\alpha = \frac{\min\limits_{i=1}^{n} b_{i,i}}{c}$. Define $\mathbf{C} = \alpha\tilde{\mathbf{B}}$, then we have $0 \leq b_{i,j} - c_{i,j} < \alpha$, $\|\mathbf{B} - \mathbf{C}\|_2 < n\alpha$. Considering that $\|\mathbf{D}\| = 1$, we can estimate that

$$\|\mathbf{xDB}\| \leq \|\mathbf{xD(B - C)}\| + \|\mathbf{xDC}\|$$
$$\leq \|\mathbf{x}\| \times \|\mathbf{D}\| \times \|\mathbf{B} - \mathbf{C}\|_2 + \alpha\|\mathbf{xD\tilde{B}}\|$$
$$< n\alpha\|\mathbf{x}\| + \alpha\|\mathbf{xD\tilde{B}}\|.$$

Let $\bar{\mathbf{v}} = \mathbf{xD\tilde{B}}$. We have $\|\mathbf{x}\| \leq \|\bar{\mathbf{v}}\|\|\tilde{\mathbf{B}}^{-1}\|_2$. Since $\bar{\mathbf{v}}$ is the first vector of an LLL-reduced basis of $\mathbf{D\tilde{B}}$, we have

$$\alpha\|\bar{\mathbf{v}}\| \leq \alpha 2^{\frac{n-1}{4}} \det(\tilde{\mathbf{B}})^{\frac{1}{n}}$$
$$= 2^{\frac{n-1}{4}} \det(\mathbf{C})^{\frac{1}{n}}$$
$$\leq 2^{\frac{n-1}{4}} \det(\mathbf{B})^{\frac{1}{n}}.$$

Then

$$\|\mathbf{xDB}\| < n\alpha\|\mathbf{x}\| + \alpha\|\mathbf{xD\tilde{B}}\|$$
$$< (n\|\tilde{\mathbf{B}}^{-1}\|_2 + 1)\alpha\|\bar{\mathbf{v}}\|$$
$$\leq (n\|\tilde{\mathbf{B}}^{-1}\|_2 + 1)2^{\frac{n-1}{4}} \det(\mathbf{B})^{\frac{1}{n}}.$$

Combing with Lemma 2 and the following lemma, we can prove the correctness of our scheme. That is, Theorems 1 and 2 still hold under our design conditions.

Lemma 3. *[11] Let $\mathbf{B} = (b_{i,j})$ be an $n \times n$ size-reduced lower-triangular matrix over $\mathbb{Z}$ with strictly positive diagonal. Let $c > 1$. If $\tilde{\mathbf{B}} = \lfloor \frac{c\mathbf{B}}{\min\limits_{i=1}^{n} b_{i,i}} \rfloor$, then*

$$\|\tilde{\mathbf{B}}^{-1}\|_2 \leq \frac{\sqrt{n}(\frac{3c-2}{2c-2})^{n-1}}{\lfloor c \rfloor}.$$

We must guarantee that the decryption process will always yield the correct result after a successful verification and hence the proposed scheme is correct. The client must verify the correct result from the cloud server. If the output $\bar{\mathbf{v}}_t \notin \bar{\mathbf{B}}_t$, the client definitely get a false result. To guarantee the success of decryption and compute the right root x'_0 which satisfies $f(x'_0 + Xt) \equiv 0 \mod N$ and $|x'_0| \leq X$, the client must verify that $\bar{\mathbf{v}}_t$ is short enough. Further more, we can know that for each $\bar{\mathbf{v}}_t \in \bar{\mathbf{B}}_t$,

$$\|\bar{\mathbf{v}}_t\| \leq 2^{\frac{n-1}{4}} (\det(\mathcal{L}(\bar{\mathbf{B}}_t)))^{\frac{1}{n}}$$

is one of the necessary conditions for the correctness of Lemma 2. The other properties of LLL-reduced basis are not utilized during the proof of Lemma 2 and Theorems 1 and 2. Actually, we even don't need to prove that the vector $\bar{\mathbf{v}}_t$ which we receive from the cloud is the first vector of an LLL-reduced basis of $\mathbf{D}\tilde{\mathbf{B}}$. We can check whether the vector $\bar{\mathbf{v}}_t$ satisfies that $\|\bar{\mathbf{v}}_t\| \leq 2^{\frac{n-1}{4}} (\det(\mathcal{L}(\bar{\mathbf{B}}_t)))^{\frac{1}{n}}$. According to 1 and 2 and step 6–8 of Algorithm 1, verifying the correctness of the norm size of $\bar{\mathbf{v}}_t$ can guarantee that we can find all the small roots of the target polynomial equation. The computation of verification mainly consists of the cost of matrix determinant computation, which is $O(\log^3 N)$ with classical algorithm.

4.2 Security Analysis

The proposed scheme can protect input privacy if the cloud cannot recover the original matrix $\mathbf{B}_t$ from the encrypted matrix $\tilde{\mathbf{B}}_t$. $\mathbf{B}_t$ is encrypted by rounding. It is hard to recover $\mathbf{B}_t$ by $\tilde{\mathbf{B}}_t$ through the following equation.

$$\tilde{\mathbf{B}}_t = \lfloor \frac{c\mathbf{B}_t}{X^{h\delta-\delta}} \rfloor. \tag{1}$$

A direct attack is exhaustive search for the least significant bits. We multiply $\tilde{\mathbf{B}}_t$ by a random unimodular matrix to hide the most significant bits of $\mathbf{B}_t$. This process don't change the basis of the lattice and it is harder to recover $\mathbf{B}_t$ from $\bar{\mathbf{B}}_t$. The cloud server only gets $\bar{\mathbf{B}}_t$ for $0 \leq t < \frac{N^{\frac{1}{3}}}{X}$ throughout the whole process. $\bar{\mathbf{B}}_t$ has a completely different basis from $\mathbf{B}_t$ and the most significant bits of the matrix elements can be hidden after multiplying by a perturbation matrix $\mathbf{D}_t$. Without the parameter of rounding $\frac{c}{X^{h\delta-\delta}}$ and the perturbation matrix $\mathbf{D}_t$, it is believed that $\mathbf{B}_t$ can not be recovered by trivial means.

The proposed scheme can protect output privacy if the cloud cannot recover the target vector $\mathbf{v}_t$ and the small roots of polynomial equations. Though the cloud server gains an equation that $\bar{\mathbf{v}}_t = \mathbf{x}\bar{\mathbf{B}}_t$, $\mathbf{v}_t$ cannot be recovered without the original matrix $\mathbf{B}_t$ and the perturbation matrix $\mathbf{D}_t$. No useful information for small roots can be obtained from $\bar{\mathbf{v}}_t$. The original polynomial equations and its small roots are kept from revealing.

According to the above analysis, input privacy and output privacy of our scheme is protected. The security level of our scheme is strong enough in practice and our scheme is feasible.

4.3 Efficiency Analysis

Now we consider the cost of our scheme on cloud side and on local side. J. Bi et al. proved that the complexity upper-bound of their algorithm is $O(\log^7 N)$. We outsource the main part of the original algorithm, which is the L^2 algorithm, to the cloud server. The cost on cloud side is just $O(\log^7 N)$. On local side, the theoretical number of t is at most $O(\frac{N^{\frac{1}{\delta}}}{X})$, which can be known to be $O(1)$. We have $h = O(\frac{\log N}{\delta})$. So $n = O(\log N)$, the bit-size of $\mathbf{B}_t$'s entries is $O(\frac{\log^2 N}{\delta})$ and the bit-size of $\bar{\mathbf{B}}_t$'s entries is $O(\log N)$. Consider the running-time of this size-reduction algorithm, the local computational complexity is upper bounded by $O(\frac{\log^5 N}{\delta})$. The efficiency of our outsourcing scheme is significant.

We now assess the practical efficiency of the outsourcing scheme with experiments. In our experiments, we use Shoups NTL library and use Inter(R) Xeon(R) CPU E5620@2.40 GHz with 4 cores in the whole process both on the client side and the cloud side. Experiment results are presented in Table 1. We list the computation time on client side and cloud side separately.

The asymmetric speedup (AS), which is defined as $time_{\text{orginal}}/time_{\text{client}}$, exhibits the client efficiency gained by outsourcing and represents the savings of the computing resources. Considering the framework of J. Bi's speedups over Coppersmith's algorithm [11], for the sake of convenience, we can take $time_{\text{orginal}} = time_{\text{client}} + time_{\text{cloud}}$ because the only extra cost is the generation of $\mathbf{D}_t$. To limit the difference in the bit lengths of matrix elements between $\bar{\mathbf{B}}_t$ and $\tilde{\mathbf{B}}_t$, we take $\mathbf{D}_t$ as an upper triangular matrix, where its diagonal elements are ± 1 and the upper bound of the bit lengths of nonzero elements is 4. The value $time_{\text{orginal}}/time_{\text{client}}$ theoretically should be much greater than 1. Our results show that the performance of our scheme is significantly effective.

The cloud efficiency (CE), which is defined as $time_{\text{cloud}}/time_{\text{orginal}}$, represents the overall computation cost on cloud introduced by solving encrypted lattice reduction problem. It is desirable that the value $time_{\text{cloud}}/time_{\text{orginal}}$ is close to 1. In most cases, the values are a little bigger than 1 because the schemes need some extra operations to keep security. The experiment results of our scheme are even smaller than 1. It means that our scheme do not contain too many superfluous processes because the original algorithm is single threaded for a fixed t.

We can claim that the proposed scheme will not introduce a substantial amount of computation overhead. The experimental data confirms that secure-outsource scheme for Coppersmith's algorithm in cloud computing is economically feasible.

Table 1. Experiment results for scheme 1

Size of N	h	Size of X	Cloud (sec)	Client (sec)	AS	CE
1024	8	310	23.9	0.36	67.4	0.985
1024	10	316	103.1	0.64	162.1	0.994
1024	12	320	346.6	1.54	226.1	0.996
1536	8	466	63.7	0.59	109.0	0.991
1536	10	475	283.2	1.36	209.2	0.995
1536	12	481	921.7	2.68	344.9	0.997
2048	8	622	135.3	0.88	154.8	0.994
2048	10	634	572.6	1.49	385.3	0.997
2560	8	778	229.2	1.21	190.4	0.995
2560	10	793	1029.9	2.83	364.9	0.997

5 Conclusion

In this paper, we present a new outsource-secure scheme for Coppersmith's Algorithm. We have shown that the proposed scheme simultaneously fulfills goals of correctness, robust cheating resistance, high-efficiency and security. The clients can outsource their main computation workloads such as LLL-reduction to cloud servers and only perform a small part of calculations e.g. matrix multiplication locally. It is hoped that the outsource-secure scheme can shed light in designing other secure outsourcing schemes for cryptography and may be profitable by means of providing large-scale scientific computation services for many potential clients.

References

1. Hohenberger, S., Lysyanskaya, A.: How to securely outsource cryptographic computations. In: Kilian, J. (ed.) TCC 2005. LNCS, vol. 3378, pp. 264–282. Springer, Heidelberg (2005). https://doi.org/10.1007/978-3-540-30576-7_15
2. Chen, X., Li, J., Ma, J., Tang, Q., Lou, W.: New algorithms for secure outsourcing of modular exponentiations. IEEE Trans. Parallel Distrib. Syst. **25**(9), 2386–2396 (2014)
3. Zhou, K., Afifi, M.H., Ren, J.: ExpSOS: secure and verifiable outsourcing of exponentiation operations for mobile cloud computing. IEEE Trans. Inf. Forensics Secur. **12**(11), 2518–2531 (2017)
4. Atallah, M.J., Frikken, K.B.: Securely outsourcing linear algebra computations. In: Proceedings of the 5th ACM Symposium on Information, Computer and Communications Security, ASIACCS 2010, Beijing, China, 13–16 April 2010, pp. 48–59 (2010)
5. Lei, X., Liao, X., Huang, T., Heriniaina, F.: Achieving security, robust cheating resistance, and high-efficiency for outsourcing large matrix multiplication computation to a malicious cloud. Inf. Sci. **280**, 205–217 (2014)

6. Lei, X., Liao, X., Huang, T., Li, H.: Cloud computing service: the case of large matrix determinant computation. IEEE Trans. Serv. Comput. **8**(5), 688–700 (2015)

7. Wang, C., Ren, K., Wang, J., Wang, Q.: Harnessing the cloud for securely outsourcing large-scale systems of linear equations. IEEE Trans. Parallel Distrib. Syst. **24**(6), 1172–1181 (2013)

8. Chen, X., Huang, X., Li, J., Ma, J., Lou, W., Wong, D.S.: New algorithms for secure outsourcing of large-scale systems of linear equations. IEEE Trans. Inf. Forensics Secur. **10**(1), 69–78 (2015)

9. Coppersmith, D.: Finding a small root of a univariate modular equation. In: Maurer, U. (ed.) EUROCRYPT 1996. LNCS, vol. 1070, pp. 155–165. Springer, Heidelberg (1996). https://doi.org/10.1007/3-540-68339-9_14

10. Lenstra, A.K., Lenstra Jr., H.W., Lovász, L.: Factoring polynomials with rational coefficients. Mathematische Annalen **261**(4), 515–534 (1982)

11. Bi, J., Coron, J.-S., Faugère, J.-C., Nguyen, P.Q., Renault, G., Zeitoun, R.: Rounding and chaining LLL: finding faster small roots of univariate polynomial congruences. In: Krawczyk, H. (ed.) PKC 2014. LNCS, vol. 8383, pp. 185–202. Springer, Heidelberg (2014). https://doi.org/10.1007/978-3-642-54631-0_11

12. Goldreich, O., Micali, S., Wigderson, A.: How to play any mental game or a completeness theorem for protocols with honest majority. In: Proceedings of the 19th Annual ACM Symposium on Theory of Computing, New York, New York, USA, pp. 218–229 (1987)

13. Golle, P., Mironov, I.: Uncheatable distributed computations. In: Naccache, D. (ed.) CT-RSA 2001. LNCS, vol. 2020, pp. 425–440. Springer, Heidelberg (2001). https://doi.org/10.1007/3-540-45353-9_31

14. Canetti, R., Riva, R., Rothblum, G.N.: Practical delegation of computation using multiple servers. In: Proceedings of the 18th ACM Conference on Computer and Communications Security, CCS 2011, Chicago, Illinois, USA, 17–21 October 2011, pp. 445–454 (2011)

15. Gennaro, R., Gentry, C., Parno, B.: Non-interactive verifiable computing: outsourcing computation to untrusted workers. In: Rabin, T. (ed.) CRYPTO 2010. LNCS, vol. 6223, pp. 465–482. Springer, Heidelberg (2010). https://doi.org/10.1007/978-3-642-14623-7_25

16. Nguyen, P.Q., Stehlé, D.: An LLL algorithm with quadratic complexity. SIAM J. Comput. **39**(3), 874–903 (2009)

17. Coppersmith, D.: Finding a small root of a bivariate integer equation; factoring with high bits known. In: Maurer, U. (ed.) EUROCRYPT 1996. LNCS, vol. 1070, pp. 178–189. Springer, Heidelberg (1996). https://doi.org/10.1007/3-540-68339-9_16

18. Howgrave-Graham, N.: Finding small roots of univariate modular equations revisited. In: Darnell, M. (ed.) Cryptography and Coding 1997. LNCS, vol. 1355, pp. 131–142. Springer, Heidelberg (1997). https://doi.org/10.1007/BFb0024458

19. Novocin, A., Stehlé, D., Villard, G.: An LLL-reduction algorithm with quasi-linear time complexity: extended abstract. In: Proceedings of the 43rd ACM Symposium on Theory of Computing, STOC 2011, San Jose, CA, USA, 6–8 June 2011, pp. 403–412 (2011)

A Novel Genetic Algorithm Approach to Improving Error Correction Output Coding

Yu-Ping Zhang and Kun-Hong Liu[(✉)]

School of Software, Xiamen University, No. 422, Siming South Road,
Siming District, Xiamen, Fujian, China
24320152202862@stu.xmu.edu.cn, lkhqz@xmu.edu.cn

Abstract. This paper proposes a genetic algorithm (GA) for error correcting output codes (ECOC). In our GA framework, the individual structure represents a solution for the multiclass problem, consisting of a codematrix and filtered feature subsets. Besides, the selection of base classifier is injected to form the second type of individual structure. A novel mutation operator is proposed to produce ECOC-compatible children in the evolutionary process, along with a set of legality checking schemes guaranteeing the legality of individuals. In addition, a local improvement function is implemented to optimize individuals, with the goal of further promoting their fitness value. To verify the performances of our algorithm, experiments are carried out with deploying some state-of-art ECOC algorithms. Results show that our GA with two different individual structures may perform diversely, but they can both lead to better results compared with other algorithms in most cases. Besides, the base learner selection embedded in GA leads to higher performance across different data sets.

Keywords: Genetic algorithm (GA) · Error correcting output coding (ECOC) · Legality checking · Multiclass classification

1 Introduction

Error Correction Output Coding (ECOC) is a divide-and-conquer strategy for the multiclass classification problem, and it has been applied to various fields successfully, such as face recognition [1] and action recognition [2].

An ECOC algorithm converts a multiclass classification problem into multiple two-class problems, with the class decomposition scheme represented by a codematrix T. The codematrix production process is referred as the encoding stage. In T, each column represents a partition strategy, and each row represents a class. So for a N class problem with M dichotomizers deployed, the size of T is $N \times M$. In the testing stage, the outputs of M dichotomizers for an unknown sample S_0 are compared with each row in T, and S_0 is assigned to the class represented by the row obtaining the highest similarity. In a typical ternary T, classes are relabeled as $+1/-1/0$. The classes with $+1/-1$ will be assigned to the positive/negative group; and the remaining classes labelled as 0 are to be ignored in the training process.

T is key to an ECOC algorithm, so many encoding algorithms have been put forward. For example, Sun designed an ECOC algorithm based on data complexity

© Springer Nature Switzerland AG 2019
C. Douligeris et al. (Eds.): KSEM 2019, LNAI 11776, pp. 241–249, 2019.
https://doi.org/10.1007/978-3-030-29563-9_22

theory [3], which searches class partition schemes with the goal of minimizing data complexity index between two groups. Zhou used Fisher criterion to produce novel codematrices, and enhanced the generalization ability of the codematrix by adding columns to deal with hard classes [4]. Genetic Algorithm (GA) was proposed to find optimal solutions by mimicking the mechanism of nature choice and heredity, and it has been proved to be successful at tackling the optimization problem in various research fields. And some GA based ECOC algorithms had been proposed by optimizing a random initialized T in the evolutionary process, aiming to reduce the number of dichotomizes without deteriorating generalization ability. [5] proposed a GA to optimize sparse random codematrices, the length of which are limited within [30, 50] and [$\log_2 N$, N] respectively. While Bautista [6] proposed Minimal ECOC using a standard GA, and they obtained optimal codematrices with limiting the maximum size to [$\log_2 N$] without losing discriminative. These works reveal that GA provides fast search ability and obtain optimal ECOC coding matrices.

In this paper, we propose a novel GA to improve ECOC. An individual is designed to match a class partitioning scheme in an optimal feature subspace. Besides, another type of individual structure is proposed by appending the classifier selection unit. A crossover and mutation operator is designed to operate on individuals at the level of binary class problems. In this way, the contribution of a column to a codematrix is evaluated as a unit.

The structure of this paper is organized as follows: Sect. 2 introduces the framework of our GA, with details about GA operators and the local improvement algorithm. In Sect. 3, experiments are carried out to compare our algorithm with seven ECOC algorithms based on UCI data sets, along with some discussions. And Sect. 4 concludes this paper.

2   The Design of GA Based ECOC

2.1   The Individual Structure

This paper proposes a GA based ECOC algorithm by presenting a codematrix T as an individual. Each individual consists of a set of segments, each of which standing for a binary class problem. Assume there are N classes along with m features in a data set. Each segment may include some units, as illustrated in Fig. 1. (1) The class reassignment unit. This unit represents a column in the coding matrix, made up by N ternary bits. Each bit takes value of $\{+1, -1, 0\}$, where $+1/-1$ represents to assign a class to the positive/negative group, and 0 indicates the ignored classes. (2) The feature subset unit. It uses the m bits binary codes to match m features, setting each bit to +1 or 0 to indicate the corresponding feature is or isn't selected. (3) The base leaner unit. If there are k types of classifiers as candidates, this bit takes value in the range of [1, k], so as to indicate the index of selected classifier.

There are two types of individuals in our algorithm: the first type is formed by segments consisting of the first two units (GA-1); the second type contains three units (GA-2). So the difference between them is the use of homogenous or heterogeneous classifiers. For an individual consist of M segments, the length of an individual is

$(m + N) \times M$ for GA-1, and $(m + N + 1) \times M$ for GA-2. While the size of T for them are both $N \times M$. It should be noted that the first unit and second unit employ the binary and ternary scheme respectively, while the third part use an integer coding scheme to select learners. So our GA is not a standard GA due to its mixture of coding schemes. At the same time, the length of individual isn't fixed in the evolutionary process, so we do not need to pre-set the ensemble scale. The varying lengths of individuals' allows GA to optimize the ensemble with high performance and compact size simultaneously.

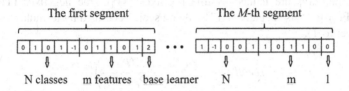

Fig. 1. The design of the chromosome of GA.

2.2 Legality Check

Each codematrix should satisfy the constraints described by formula (1–5). Here $c_{i,j}$ represents the code of i-th row and j-th column in T, and c_i denotes the codes in i-th row. Formula (1) indicates that each row should contain at least a '+1' or a '−1' at least, otherwise the samples in the corresponding class are always ignored in the training process. Formula (2) shows that each column should contain both '+1' and '−1', so that each dichotomizer can receive proper training samples. Formula (3) and (4) reveal that there should not be two identical columns and rows. Besides, there should not be converse relationship between any column pair, as shown in formula (5). All these conditions should be satisfied at the same time for each valid codematrix [7]. When a transformed coding matrix fail to meet these constrains, our mutation operator will work to correct it.

$$\sum\nolimits_{j=1}^{M} abs(c_{i,j}) \neq 0, \forall i \in [1, N] \tag{1}$$

$$\sum\nolimits_{i=1}^{N} abs(c_{i,j}) \neq abs\left(\sum\nolimits_{i=1}^{n} c_{i,j}\right), \forall j \in [1, M] \tag{2}$$

$$\sum\nolimits_{i=1}^{N} abs(c_{(i,j)} - c_{(i,l)}) \neq 0, \forall j, l \in [1, M], j \neq l \tag{3}$$

$$\sum\nolimits_{j=1}^{M} abs(c_{i,j} - c_{l,j}) \neq 0, \forall i, l \in [1, N], i \neq l \tag{4}$$

$$\sum\nolimits_{i=1}^{N} abs(c_{i,j} + c_{i,l}) \neq 0, \forall j, l \in [1, M], j \neq l \tag{5}$$

For the first unit of each segment, the number of selected features should be larger than 0. The minimum number of feature size is set as $\lceil m/5 \rceil$ in this study, because the extreme small feature size can't offer enough information for accurate classification.

2.3   Individual Evaluation

Our fitness function consists of two parts. Fscore is used as the first part of fitness value, because it measures the balance among multiple classes (denoted by f_1). Assume for the i-th class, measures are named as true positives (TP$_i$), true negatives (TN$_i$), false positives (FP$_i$) and false negatives (FN$_i$), then Fscore is defined by formula (6)–(8) (β is generally set to 1).

$$recall = avg\left(\sum\nolimits_{i=1}^{n} \frac{TP_i}{TP_i + FN_i}\right) \tag{6}$$

$$precision = avg\left(\sum\nolimits_{i=1}^{n} \frac{TP_i}{TP_i + FP_i}\right) \tag{7}$$

$$Fscore = avg\left(\sum\nolimits_{i=1}^{n} \frac{(\beta^2 + 1) * precision_i * recall_i}{\beta^2 * precision_i + recall_i}\right) \tag{8}$$

$$D_{HM} = \sum\nolimits_{i=1}^{N} abs(c_i - c_j), i \neq j, \forall j \in [1, N] \tag{9}$$

For each T, the sum of Hamming distance of each row pair D_{HM} (given by formula (9)) reveals its quality. Usually a larger distance provides higher probability to correct wrong decisions in the decoding process, so D_{HM} is used as the second fitness value, denoted by f_2. In our GA, for two individuals, the one with a larger f_1 score gets a higher rank. For those with the same f_1 score, their f_2 scores are compared, and the one with larger f_2 score gets higher rank. If individuals get the same f_1 and f_2 scores, the one requiring fewer columns receives a higher rank.

2.4   Crossover and Mutation Operators

The crossover operator picks up a pair of individuals as parents by the roulette wheel scheme. That is, the probability of selecting an individual is proportional to its f_1 score, and a higher f_1 score provides a larger probability. The crossover operator exchanges the worst segments between each parent pair. The quality of a segment s_i is evaluated by its Fscore value, and the segments with poor performance would be of less value to the corresponding multiclass classification task, but the worst segment s_i in an individual I_1 may benefit another individual I_2. And it is a very small probability that s_i give equal or even worse contribution to I_2 than the worst segment in I_2. So the exchange of segments tends to improve the performances of their parents'.

But it is still possible that an individuals' performance becomes lower after crossover, so a new mutation operator is proposed to handle such situation. This mutation operator checks a segment at a time, providing each segment a chance to be mutated. If segment s_i in I_1 gets lower f_1 score than a threshold, a high mutation rate r_{mh} is assigned to the individual; otherwise a lower rate r_{ml} is set to s_i.

Once the mutation operator works, it mutates a segment by randomly selecting a bit in each unit in sequence. In the first unit of s_i, the operator changes a bit according to the rules: (1) $-1 \rightarrow +1$; (2) $+1 \rightarrow -1$; (3) $0 \rightarrow +1/-1$. For the second unit, the operator inverts a bit to change the selection status of the corresponding feature. In the third unit, this operator revises the index of classifier.

3   Experiments and Results

3.1   Experiments Settings

In experiments, ten UCI data sets are deployed [8], and Table 1 gives their details. All data sets are divided into training set, validation set and test set by the proportion of 2:1:1. Base learners are trained based on training data sets, and their fitness indices are evaluated on the validation set. Test sets are used as unknown data, and the Fscore indices on test sets are reported for performance comparisons.

Table 1. Experimental UCI data set description

Data	Number of class	Number of samples	Number of features
abalone	3	4177	8
cmc	3	1473	9
derma	6	366	34
glass	6	214	10
iris	3	150	4
wine	3	178	13
mfeatpix	10	1000	240
mfeatzer	10	1000	47
sat	6	3217	36
waveforms	3	2500	40

Seven ECOC algorithms are used for performance comparisons: One VS One (OVO), One VS All (OVA), Dense Random (DR), Sparse Random (SR) [9], A-ECOC [10], D-ECOC [11], ECOC-ONE [12]. Three classifiers, decision tree (DT), GAUS-SINBN (GBN) and KNN, are deployed as base learners with default settings, provided by Scikit-learn toolbox [13].

In our GA framework, the population size is 20, and the maximum generation is 100. r_{mh} and r_{ml} are set as 0.2 and 0.1 respectively. The size of T takes value within the range $[N-1, 2 \times N]$. The settings for GA-1 and GA-2 are the same except that GA-1 uses a same type of classifier in each run, and GA-2 tries to find an optimal classifier for each column among the three types of classifiers. So the third unit of each segment takes value in the set $\{1, 2, 3\}$ for GA-2. In experiments, GA runs ten times with different seeds, and the best result of each run is recorded. Then the average and the best of these ten best results are used for comparisons with other algorithms. The best average results are marked as underline, and the best of best results are marked with bold font.

3.2 Results Comparisons

Figure 2 compares the best results of GA-1 and other algorithms. It is obvious that GA-1 outperforms other algorithms in most cases, as GA-1 losses only in one case with GBN and KNN respectively.

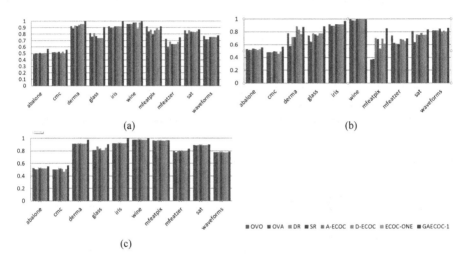

(a)   (b)

(c)

Fig. 2. Results using different ECOC algorithms with: (a) DT; (b) GBN; (C) KNN.

Table 2. Results comparison of GA-1 and GA-2

Data	Average of best results				GA-2	Best of best results				GA-2
	GA-1					GA-1				
	DT	GBN	KNN	Mix_Avg		DT	GBN	KNN	Mix_Avg	
abalone	0.540	<u>0.544</u>	0.539	0.541	0.540	**0.570**	0.554	0.555	0.560	0.561
cmc	0.544	<u>0.550</u>	0.531	0.542	0.537	0.556	0.566	0.569	0.564	**0.577**
derma	<u>0.946</u>	0.753	0.952	0.884	0.912	**1.000**	0.878	0.978	0.952	0.978
glass	0.788	0.803	<u>0.816</u>	0.802	0.800	0.907	0.889	0.907	0.901	**0.925**
iris	0.959	0.955	0.947	0.954	<u>0.960</u>	**1.000**	0.974	**1.000**	0.991	**1.000**
wine	0.963	0.977	0.978	0.973	<u>0.979</u>	**1.000**	**1.000**	**1.000**	**1.000**	**1.000**
mfeatpix	0.892	0.820	<u>0.963</u>	0.892	0.941	0.92	0.854	**0.966**	0.913	0.956
mfeatzer	0.698	0.662	<u>0.830</u>	0.730	0.772	0.75	0.698	**0.836**	0.761	0.802
sat	0.847	0.815	<u>0.895</u>	0.852	0.891	0.871	0.835	0.900	0.869	**0.904**
waveforms	0.756	<u>0.847</u>	0.776	0.793	0.833	0.780	**0.860**	0.789	0.810	0.848
Avg	0.793	0.773	<u>0.823</u>	0.796	0.817	0.835	0.811	0.850	0.832	**0.855**

It should be noted that on the same data set, the changes of performance of seven ECOC algorithms are not predictable. In some data sets, these algorithms may achieve similar performances. However, in extreme cases, the difference between their minimum and maximum Fscore indices may be surprisingly high. For example, it is found that for the mfeatpix data, such a difference reaches 33% when comparing OVO and DR. And none of these algorithms can always win. In contrast, our GA-1 achieves good and stable performances with three different types of classifiers.

Because GA-2 consists of heterogeneous learners, and none of other algorithms has such a character, it is only compared with GA-1, as listed in Table 2. The average and best results of GA-1 are shown, and the columns titled with **Mix_Avg** refers to the average of three base learners' results. In the comparisons of the best results, GA-2 achieves the highest scores 5 times and obtains the highest average best results. While the performance of GA-1 changes greatly with diverse learners, and only with KNN can it obtain the highest scores 4 times. However, its average of average results of reaches 0.823, which is the highest average performance in all cases. The average results of GA-2 are much better than those of GA-1 with different classifiers, proving that it provides an excellent capability in searching optimal classifiers.

In short, although GA-1 is already an effective algorithm compared with other ECOC algorithms, further experiments show that GA-2 outperforms GA-1 in considering the best results. Even though GA-2 cannot always achieve the best average performance, it is more reliable in dealing with diverse data sets. So GA-2 is an effective solution for diverse data sets with combining heterogeneous learners.

3.3 Analysis of Codematrices

Figure 3 shows the relationships between properties of codematrices and their performances on validation set by comparing the number of columns, Hamming distances and the Fscore indices. All indices are mapped to the interval of [0, 1] based on the min-max normalization scheme, so as to get intuitive comparisons. The x-axis represents the number of generations. As Fscore value (first priority) plays a key role in determining the fitness value of individuals, columns would be added if necessary. So in Fig. 3, the number of columns turns to increase in the evolutionary process, along with the decrease of distances between the row pairs unavoidably. The upper bound of the number of column is set as $2 \times N$. The superiority of our algorithm lies in that it achieves the balance between the ensemble size and the performance.

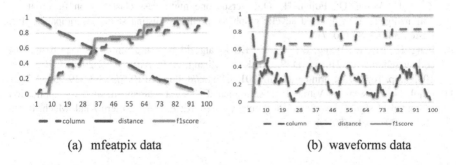

(a) mfeatpix data   (b) waveforms data

Fig. 3. The change of coding matrices and the corresponding performances.

4 Conclusions

In this paper, we propose a genetic algorithm (GA) based framework for error correcting output codes (ECOC). Two individual structures are designed, along with a crossover and a mutation operators for guiding the evolutionary process. Besides, a local improvement strategy is used to accelerate the evolutionary process. Experimental results show that compared with seven well known ECOC algorithms, our algorithm can produce robust results in considering both the average and the best of results. The results also confirm that our algorithm can reach excellent trade-off between the ensemble scale and performance, with the aid of the fitness function. In addition, two individual structures result in diverse performances, and by integrating the classifier selection in the individual structure, GA can produce more stable and accurate results.

Acknowledgment. This work is supported by National Natural Science Foundation of China (No. 61772023), and Natural Science Foundation of Fujian Province (No. 2016J01320).

References

1. Nazari, S., Moin, M., Rashidy Kanan, H.: Securing templates in a face recognition system using error-correcting output code and chaos theory. Comput. Electr. Eng. **72**, 644–659 (2018)
2. Qin, J., et al.: Zero-shot action recognition with error-correcting output codes. In: IEEE Conference on Computer Vision and Pattern Recognition (CVPR), pp. 1042–1051 (2017)
3. Sun, M., Liu, K., Hong, Q., Wang, B.: A new ECOC algorithm for multiclass microarray data classification. In: Presented at the 24th International Conference on Pattern Recognition Beijing, China, 20–24 August 2018
4. Zhou, J., Yang, Y., Zhang, M., Xing, H.: Constructing ECOC based on confusion matrix for multiclass learning problems. Sci. China **59**(1), 1–14 (2016)
5. Lorena, A.C., Carvalho, A.C.: Evolutionary design of multiclass support vector machines. J. Intell. Fuzzy Syst. **18**(5), 445–454 (2007)
6. Bautista, M.A., Escalera, S., Baro, X., Radeva, P., Vitria, J., Pujol, O.: Minimal design of error-correcting output codes. Pattern Recogn. Lett. **33**(6), 693–702 (2012)
7. Simeone, P., Marrocco, C., Tortorella, F.: Design of reject rules for ECOC classification systems. Pattern Recogn. **45**(2), 863–875 (2012)
8. Dua, D., Karra Taniskidou, E.: UCI machine learning repository. University of California, School of Information and Computer Science, Irvine (2017). http://archive.ics.uci.edu/ml
9. Zhou, L., Wang, Q., Fujita, H.: One versus one multi-class classification fusion using optimizing decision directed acyclic graph for predicting listing status of companies. Inf. Fusion **36**, 80–89 (2017)
10. Feng, K., Liu, K., Wang, B.: A novel ECOC algorithm with centroid distance based soft coding scheme. In: Huang, D.-S., Jo, K.-H., Zhang, X.-L. (eds.) ICIC 2018. LNCS, vol. 10955, pp. 165–173. Springer, Cham (2018). https://doi.org/10.1007/978-3-319-95933-7_21
11. Pujol, O., Radeva, P., Vitrià, J.: Discriminant ECOC: a heuristic method for application dependent design of error correcting output codes. IEEE Trans. Pattern Anal. Mach. Intell. **28**(6), 1007–1012 (2006)

12. Escalera, S., Pujol, O.: ECOC-ONE: a novel coding and decoding strategy. In: International Conference on Pattern Recognition, pp. 578–581 (2006)
13. Pedregosa, F., et al.: Scikit-learn: machine learning in Python. J. Mach. Learn. Res. **12**, 2825–2830 (2011)

A New Monarch Butterfly Optimization Algorithm with SA Strategy

Xitong Wang[1,2], Xin Tian[3], and Yonggang Zhang[1,2(✉)]

[1] College of Computer Science and Technology,
Jilin University, Changchun 130012, China
zhangyg@jlu.edu.cn
[2] Key Laboratory of Symbolic Computation and Knowledge Engineering,
Ministry of Education, Jilin University, Changchun 130012, China
[3] The Second Hospital of Jilin University, Changchun 130041, China

Abstract. Monarch butterfly optimization (MBO) is a newly proposed meta-heuristic algorithm for solving optimization problems. It has been proved experimentally that MBO is superior to the other five state-of-the-art meta-heuristic algorithms on most test problems. This paper presents a new improved MBO algorithm with Simulated Annealing (SA) strategy, in which the SA strategy is involved into the migration operator and butterfly adjusting operator. So the newly proposed algorithm SAMBO not only accepts all the butterfly individuals whose fitness are better than their parents' but also randomly selects some individuals that are worse than their parents to disturbance the convergence of algorithm. In the final, the experiments are carried out on 14 famous continuous nonlinear functions; the results demonstrate that SAMBO algorithm is significantly better than the original MBO algorithm on most test functions.

Keywords: Monarch butterfly optimization · Simulated annealing · Benchmark problems · Neighborhood search

1 Introduction

Recently, more and more nature-inspired algorithms [1] have been proposed and generally applied in numerous applications, such as path planning [2], machine learning [3], knapsack problem [4], fault diagnosis [5, 6] and directing orbits of chaotic system[7]. Swarm intelligence (SI) [8] is a current artificial intelligence method related to the design and application of multi-agent systems. Particle swarm optimization (PSO) [9–11], animal migration optimization (AMO) [12], artificial fish swarm algorithm [13] and monarch butterfly optimization (MBO) [14] belong to this category.

Neighborhood search (NS) [15] is an incomplete and perturbed search method. This approach starts with the candidate solution, iteratively looking for a better alternative in its neighborhood. Neighborhood search have been applied triumphantly in many combinatorial optimization problems, such as bin-packing [16] and scheduling [17]. Several popular NS methods appear such as hill climbing (HC) [18], steepest descent (SD) [19], simulating annealing (SA) [20], and tabu search (TS) [21, 22].

© Springer Nature Switzerland AG 2019
C. Douligeris et al. (Eds.): KSEM 2019, LNAI 11776, pp. 250–258, 2019.
https://doi.org/10.1007/978-3-030-29563-9_23

This paper presents an improved version of MBO, called SAMBO. In SAMBO, simulated annealing is involved to escape from the optimal and augment the diversity of individual. Towards proving the advantage of SAMBO, a series of experiences are performed on 14 test instances. The results indicate that SAMBO perform better than basic MBO in finding the optimal solution on almost all the benchmarks.

Section 2 reviews MBO algorithm and Sect. 2.3 introduces simulating annealing. Section 3 discusses how to incorporate the simulating annealing strategy into MBO algorithm. Section 4 shows the comparison of MBO and SAMBO through testing on 14 benchmark problems. Finally, Sect. 5 outlines the summary of algorithm and the plan for the future work.

2 Monarch Butterfly Optimization

Inspired by the migration behavior of monarch butterfly individuals in the nature, Wang et al. put forward monarch butterfly optimization (MBO) [14] recently. The migration of monarch butterfly could be reduced to the following regulations [14]:

(1) The butterflies which are on Land1 and Land2 make up the whole species group.
(2) Every progeny is just produced by the individuals in Land1 or Land2.
(3) The scale of the butterfly species group remains the same.
(4) There is elitist strategy that the individual with the best fitness is preserved.

Accordingly, the position of butterflies in Land1 and Land2 are renovated by migration operator and butterfly adjusting operator respectively. It is repeated until stop condition is satisfied.

2.1 Migration Operator

All the butterflies in Land1 are updated by migration operator. The process can be marked out below [14]:

$$x_{i,k}^{t+1} = x_{r_1,k}^{t} \tag{1}$$

p presents the ratio of butterfly individuals in Land 1. While $r \leq p$, $x_{i,k}^{t+1}$ is updated by Eq. (1). r is computed as

$$r = rand * peri \tag{2}$$

When $r > p$, $x_{i,k}^{t+1}$ is updated by

$$x_{i,k}^{t+1} = x_{r_2,k}^{t} \tag{3}$$

2.2 Butterfly Adjusting Operator

For all the elements of monarch butterfly j in Land2, the process can be marked out below [14]: if $rand \leq p$,

$$x_{j,k}^{t+1} = x_{best,k}^{t} \tag{4}$$

If $rand > p$, it could be generated as

$$x_{j,k}^{t+1} = x_{r_3,k}^{t} \tag{5}$$

With this addition, if $rand > BAR$, it is generated as [14]:

$$x_{j,k}^{t+1} = x_{j,k}^{t+1} + \alpha \times (dx_k - 0.5) \tag{6}$$

where BAR presents butterfly adjusting rate. dx could be computed as shown in Eq. (7). α indicates the weighting factor as below in Eq. (8).

$$dx = Levy(x_j^t) \tag{7}$$

$$\alpha = S_{max}/t^2 \tag{8}$$

Through comparing with other five state-of-the-art algorithms on thirty-eight benchmark problems, experiment results indicate that MBO exceeds five other meta-heuristic methods in most instances.

2.3 Simulated Annealing

In the neighborhood search algorithms, simulated annealing plays an important role. We plan to use simulated annealing to improve MBO performance. The main idea of simulated annealing is summarized as follow. To avoid local optimum, Simulated annealing accepts a worsening move $m \in N(s)$ at certain probability which depends on $\Delta_f(s, m)$. The probability of electing a move m is calculated as [23]:

$$P(m|s, temp) = \begin{cases} e^{-\Delta_f(s,m)/temp} & if \ \Delta_f(s, m) > 0 \\ 1 & otherwise \end{cases} \tag{9}$$

To command the frequency of accepting worse moves, a parameter $temp$ (temperature) is presented and updated continually in terms of a cooling schedule as Eq. (10) where $0 < \lambda < 1$. Then, r' is a random number in (0,1). If $r' < P(m|s,temp)$, the move m is adopted. If not, the move is refused.

$$temp = \lambda \cdot temp \tag{10}$$

We control the stop condition through the iteration generation of monarch butterfly in algorithm.

3 SAMBO Algorithm

Though MBO has revealed its advantage on some benchmark problems, it may fail to obtain the optimal property on average value. So we present SAMBO by incorporating simulated annealing to enhance the property of algorithm.

The butterflies in Land1 and in Land2 are updated according to Eqs. (1)–(3) and Eqs. (4)–(8) respectively. If the newly generated individual is better than its parent, it will be accepted. Otherwise P(m|s,temp) can be formulated by Eq. (9). If random number r' is less than P(m|s,temp), the generated individuals could also be accepted. Besides, the algorithm will refuse new generated individuals. There are three parameters, when incorporating simulated annealing, initial temperature and cooling rate that have great influence on the experimental results.

On the basis of above analysis, the updated migration operator and updated butterfly adjusting operator are shown in Figs. 1 and 2.

---

(1) **for** i =1 to *NP1* (all the individuals in Land1) **do**
(2) **for** k=1 to dim (all the elements of ith butterfly) **do**
(3) Generate $x_{i,k}^{t+1}$ by Eqs.(1) and Eq.(3).
(4) **end for** k
(5) Evaluate the fitness $f(x_i^{t+1})$ of x_i^{t+1}.
(6) **if** $f(x_i^{t+1}) < f(x_i^t)$
(7) $x_{i,new}^{t+1} = x_i^{t+1}$
(8) **end if**
(9) Generate a random number r' in (0,1).
(10) Calculate P(m|s,temp) as Eq.(9).
(11) **if** $r' <$ P(m|s,temp)
(12) $x_{i,new}^{t+1} = x_i^{t+1}$
(13) **else**
(14) $x_{i,new}^{t+1} = x_i^t$
(15) **end if**
(16) **end for** i

Fig. 1. Pseudo code of renewed migration operator

The main frame of SAMBO could be described in Fig. 3.

(1) **for** j=1 to *NP2* (all the individuals in Land2) **do**
(2)   Calculate the walk step dx by Eq.(7).
(3)   Calculate the weighting factor by Eq.(8).
(4)   **for** k=1 to *dim*(all the elements of jth butterfly) **do**
(5)   Generate $x_{j,k}^{t+1}$ by Eqs.(4) - Eq.(6).
(6)   **end for** k
(7)   Evaluate the fitness $f(x_j^{t+1})$of x_j^{t+1}.
(8)   **if** $f\left(x_j^{t+1}\right) < f(x_j^t)$
(9) $x_{j,new}^{t+1} = x_j^{t+1}$
(10) **end if**
(11) Generate a random number r' in (0,1).
(12) Calculate $P(m|s,temp)$ as Eq.(9).
(13) **if** $r' < P(m|s,temp)$
(14) $x_{j,new}^{t+1} = x_j^{t+1}$
(15) **else**
(16) $x_{j,new}^{t+1} = x_j^t$
(17) **end if**
(18) **end for** j

Fig. 2. Pseudo code of renewed butterfly adjusting operator

Algorithm SAMBO
(1) **Step1:Initialization.**Initialize the population *NP* of all the monarch butterflies, initial temperature $t_0$and cooling rate λ .Set the generation counter t=1,the maximum generation *MaxGen*, the population *NP1* of butterflies in Land1,and the population *NP2* of butterflies in Land2.
(2) **Step2:Fitness evaluation.** Evaluate each individual.
(3) **Step3:While** $t < MaxGen$ **do**
(4)   Sort the butterfly population according to their evaluation.
(5)   Divide all the butterfly individuals into Land1 and Land2.
(6)   **for** i =1 to *NP1* **do**
(7)   Generate $x_{i,new}^{t+1}$ as Fig.2.
(8)   **end for** i
(9)   **for** j=1 to *NP2* **do**
(10)   Generate $x_{j,new}^{t+1}$ as Fig.3.
(11)   **end for** j
(12)   Combine new updated Land1 with Land2 to generate a new population.
(13)   Evaluate each butterfly individual.
(14)   *temp=temp*λ .
(15) $t=t$+1.
(16) **Step4:end while**

Fig. 3. Pseudo code of SAMBO algorithm

4 Experiments and Analysis

In this section, in order to investigate the advantage of SAMBO, fourteen benchmark functions which are shown in Table 1 are adopted to evaluate the algorithm improved above. In addition, all the tests are implemented under the same conditions: MATLAB R2014b on Win7 64-bit Intel i7-3770 processor, 8 GB RAM.

The same parameters of MBO method and SAMBO method are set as [14]. The number of iteration is taken as stop condition and set to 50.

Table 1. Benchmark functions.

No.	Name	No.	Name
F01	Ackley	F08	Rosenbrock
F02	Fletcher	F09	Generalized Schwefel2.26
F03	Griewank	F10	Schwefel 1.2
F04	Penalty1	F11	Schwefel 2.22
F05	Penalty2	F12	Schwefel 2.21
F06	Quartic	F13	Sphere
F07	Rastrigin	F14	Step

All of three parameters above mentioned need to be tuned. Simulated annealing is introduced at 10, 15, 20 generation respectively, the initial temperature is set to 200, 500 and 1000 respectively, and the cooling rate is set to 0.9, 0.95, and 0.99 respectively. We run 27 kinds of the combination on each function. In order to reduce the effect of random number, each experiment runs two hundred times independently. Each value recorded in tables is the average value of two hundred experiments, and the optimum of best and mean solution for each function is bold.

A. $D = 20$

The dimension of benchmark functions is set to 20. Table 2 shows the experiment results obtained by MBO and SAMBO.

Table 2. Best and mean function values obtained by MBO and SAMBO ($D = 20$).

No.	MBO		SAMBO	
	Best	Mean	Best	Mean
F01	11.7705	12.6519	**10.6003**	**11.3043**
F02	0.3735e+06	1.1873e+06	**2.2333e+05**	**2.3636e+05**
F03	96.1304	136.2024	**76.3990**	**99.2212**
F04	2.1934e+07	4.9713e+07	**7.8373e+06**	**8.0896e+06**
F05	0.6782e+08	1.4290e+08	**1.7739e+07**	**1.8635e+07**
F06	10.5719	44.5388	**7.1984**	**11.9005**
F07	88.2089	114.7303	**74.4715**	**79.6291**
F08	747.4	2668.4	**328.9859**	**360.3084**

(continued)

Table 2. (*continued*)

No.	MBO		SAMBO	
	Best	Mean	Best	Mean
F09	3.5192e+03	4.2384e+03	**2.8417e+03**	**2.8529e+03**
F10	0.1028e+05	4.9686e+05	**7.2452e+03**	**7.4306e+03**
F11	**24.9725**	1.3684e+12	25.0488	**34.6025**
F12	35.3581	35.4068	**29.8312**	**29.8628**
F13	23.2107	**23.2107**	**21.9257**	34.6831
F14	1.0e+04*1.0641	1.0e+04*1.5337	**1.0e+03*7.2464**	**1.0e+03*7.3133**

There is no ambiguity in concluding that SAMBO could find the better value of most functions than MBO except the best value of F11 and mean value of F13. For F10 and F11, the solutions found by SAMBO are better than those obtained by MBO about 67 times and 4×10^{10} times, respectively. For F04, F05 and F08, the result that MBO obtains is larger than those which found by SAMBO about 6 times, 7.7 times and 7.4 times, respectively.

B. *D = 40*

The dimension of benchmark functions is set to 40. Table 3 shows the experiment results obtained by MBO and SAMBO.

Table 3. Best and mean function values obtained by MBO and SAMBO (D = 40).

No.	MBO		SAMBO	
	Best	Mean	Best	Mean
F01	14.8501	15.5245	**13.6714**	**14.3519**
F02	2.9336e+06	5.7194e+06	**1.5742e+06**	**1.7756e+06**
F03	324.6347	474.6744	**257.0004**	**279.0702**
F04	1.3332e+08	2.5998e+08	**5.8350e+07**	**6.5413e+07**
F05	2.6344e+08	4.9240e+08	**1.3252e+08**	**1.4393e+08**
F06	80.2079	264.8352	**71.8131**	**80.5933**
F07	294.9648	384.7409	**245.2640**	**257.0589**
F08	3.2633e+03	7.3208e+03	**1.4958e+03**	**1.7963e+03**
F09	8.2927e+03	9.6962e+03	**7.3367e+03**	**7.4462e+03**
F10	4.5868e+04	4.5824e+06	**2.8705e+04**	**3.1838e+04**
F11	91.1913	1.1171e+28	**75.6560**	**94.5078**
F12	**36.6260**	**36.6846**	36.6973	36.7500
F13	101.3803	158.6964	**82.0935**	**103.3361**
F14	3.3558e+04	4.9196e+04	**2.1735e+04**	**2.2891e+04**

It can be obviously observed that SAMBO outperforms MBO on most test functions (except F12). For F10 and F11, the solutions obtained by MBO is about 144 times and 1.2 × 1026 times larger than that of SAMBO, respectively. And for F04 and F08, the average values acquired by SAMBO are 4 times smaller than that of MBO. Then for F02, F05 and F06, the solution which MBO obtains are more than 3 times of that of SAMBO. While for F03 and F14, the results obtained by SAMBO are about 2 times smaller than that of MBO.

C. *D = 80*

The dimension of benchmark functions is set to 80. This time we only choose five test functions (F02, F04, F05, F08 and F10), because the advantage of SAMBO could be seen clearly. Table 4 shows the experiment results acquired by MBO and SAMBO. There is no ambiguity in concluding that SAMBO outperforms MBO.

Table 4. Best and mean function values obtained by MBO and SAMBO (D = 80)

No.	MBO		SAMBO	
	Best	Mean	Best	Mean
F02	1.8289e+07	2.7423e+07	**1.0179e+07**	**1.1553e+07**
F04	4.0641e+08	8.0260e+08	**2.7744e+08**	**3.2124e+08**
F05	1.0348e+09	2.0543e+09	**5.5375e+08**	**6.1619e+08**
F08	1.1140e+04	2.4538e+04	**5.8067e+03**	**6.6961e+03**
F10	2.1304e+05	4.1116e+07	**1.0909e+05**	**1.3203e+05**

5 Conclusions and Future Work

In this paper, a novel version of MBO with simulated annealing called SAMBO is proposed. In SAMBO, except that the updated butterflies whose fitness are better than their parents are accepted, the algorithm also adopts the worsening new individuals with a certain probability. This can churn search space to seek the better solution. The experiment results demonstrate that SAMBO can find better solutions than MBO especially on average value on most functions. In future, we could study a self-adapting way to solve how to tune parameters.

Acknowledgments. This work is supported by the National Natural Science Foundation of China (61373052), the Project of Jilin Provincial Science and Technology Development (20170414004GH).

References

1. Yang, X.S.: Nature-Inspired Optimization Algorithms. Elsevier, Amsterdam (2014). ISBN: 978-0-12-416743-8
2. Wang, G., Guo, L., Duan, H., Liu, L., Wang, H., Shao, M.: Pathplanning for uninhabited combat aerial vehicle using hybrid metaheuristic DE/BBO algorithm. Adv. Sci. Eng. Med. **4**(6), 550–564 (2012)
3. Zhou, Z.: Machine Learning. Tsinghua University Press, Beijing (2016)
4. Feng, Y., Wang, G.G., Deb, S., Lu, M., Zhao, X.J.: Solving 0-1 knapsack problem by a novel binary monarch butterfly optimization. Neural Comput. Appl. **28**(7), 1619–1634 (2017). https://doi.org/10.1007/s00521-015-2135-1
5. Duan, H., Luo, Q.: New progresses in swarm intelligence-based computation. Int. J. Bio-Inspired Comput. **7**(1), 26–35 (2015)
6. Gao, X.Z., Ovaska, S.J., Wang, X., Chow, M.Y.: A neural networks-based negative selection algorithm in fault diagnosis. Neural Comput. Appl. **17**(1), 91–98 (2007)
7. Cui, Z., Fan, S., Zeng, J., Shi, Z.: APOA with parabola model for directing orbits of chaotic systems. Int. J. Bio-Inspired Comput. **5**(1), 67–72 (2013)
8. Cui, Z., Gao, X.: Theory and applications of swarm intelligence. Neural Comput. Appl. **21**(2), 205–206 (2012)
9. Zhao, X.: A perturbed particle swarm algorithm for numerical optimization. Appl. Soft Comput. **10**(1), 119–124 (2010)
10. Kennedy, J., Eberhart, R.: Particle swarm optimization. In: Proceedings of the IEEE International Conference on Neural Networks, Perth, Australia, pp. 1942–1948 (1995)
11. Mirjalili, S., Wang, G.-G., Coelho, L.S.: Binary optimization using hybrid particle swarm optimization and gravitational search algorithm. Neural Comput. Appl. **25**(6), 1423–1435 (2014)
12. Li, X., Zhang, J., Yin, M.: Animal migration optimization: an optimization algorithm inspired by animal migration behavior. Neural Comput. Appl. **24**(7–8), 1867–1877 (2014)
13. Zainal, N., Zain, A.M., Sharif, S.: Overview of artificial fish swarm algorithm and its applications in industrial problems. Appl. Mech. Mater. **815**, 253–257 (2015)
14. Wang, G.G, Deb, S, Cui, Z.: Monarch butterfly optimization. Neural Comput. Appl., 1–20 (2015)
15. Ahuja, R.K., Orlin, J.B., Sharma, D.: Very large-scale neighborhood search. Int. Trans. Oper. Res. **7**(4-5), 301–317 (2000)
16. Ceschia, S., Schaerf, A., Stützle, T.: Local search techniques for a routing-packing problem. Comput. Ind. Eng. **66**(4), 1138–1149 (2013)
17. Ceschia, S., Schaerf, A.: Local search and lower bounds for the patient admission scheduling problem. Comput. Oper. Res. **38**(10), 1452–1463 (2011)
18. Sha, Z.-C., Huang, Z.-T., Zhou, Y.-Y., Wang, F.-H.: Blind spreading sequence estimation based on hill-climbing algorithm. In: Proceedings of 2012 IEEE 11th International Conference on Signal Processing (ICSP 2012) Renovate (2012)
19. Meza, J.C.: Steepest descent. Wiley Interdisc. Rev. Comput. Stat. **2**(6), 719–722 (2010)
20. Kirkpatrick, S., Gelatt, C.D., Vecchi, M.P.: Optimization by simulated annealing. Science **220**(4598), 671–680 (1983)
21. Glover, F.: Tabu search - part I. ORSA J. Comput. **1**(3), 190–306 (1989)
22. Glover, F.: Tabu search - part II. ORSA J. Comput. **2**(1), 4–32 (1990)
23. Urli, T.: Hybrid meta-heuristics for combinatorial optimization. Ph.D. Thesis, Università degli Studi di Udine, Udine, Italy (2014)

Reasoning of Causal Direction in Linear Model Based on Spearman's Rank Correlation Coefficient

Boxu Zhao[✉] [ID] and Guiming Luo

School of Software, Tsinghua University, Beijing, China
boxu.zhao@foxmail.com, gluo@mail.tsinghua.edu.cn

Abstract. Currently, the mining of causality has drawn enormous attention in artificial intelligence. The paper mainly focuses on the causal direction inference problem from an observational sample of the joint distribution in a linear model where the data contain less asymmetric information compared to nonlinear situation. The paper studies the linear additive noise model and analyses the inferring conditions for linear causal direction inference. This paper proposes the copula for modeling dependence and presents a new causal inference method based on Spearman's rank correlation coefficient. The performance of the proposed method is verified through the experiments and analysis on both simulated data and real-world data.

Keywords: Causal inference ·
Spearman's rank correlation coefficient · Linear additive noise model

1 Introduction

The strong AI suggests that it is possible to create intelligent machines that can truly analyse and solve problems [14], and such machines can be considered self-conscious. Data science algorithms usually focus more on correlation, but correlation does not always help people make a right decision in many scenarios [8]. So it is necessary to thoroughly study and explore causal relations in the data analysis. At present, discovering causality from observational data is also a research focus in many fields [18].

In this paper, the causal direction inference algorithm based on Spearman's rank correlation coefficient for linear system is developed. This algorithm uses a copula to model the dependence and estimate Spearman's rank correlation coefficient between the variables. To the best of our knowledge, we are the first to propose such a causal inference method. We perform an analysis on the method and show that the causal direction can be identified by our method under proper assumptions. This method outperforms the existing methods for linear causal direction inference and show good performance on linear data.

In the following sections, the lecture review will be given in Sect. 2. Section 3 analyses causal inference condition in the linear system. Besides, the process

© Springer Nature Switzerland AG 2019
C. Douligeris et al. (Eds.): KSEM 2019, LNAI 11776, pp. 259–270, 2019.
https://doi.org/10.1007/978-3-030-29563-9_24

of the proposed method is given in Sect. 4. Section 5 show the experiments and analysis and Sect. 6 concludes the whole paper.

2   Related Work

In causal inference, a directional relation usually exists between two variables and this relation often cannot be established in the opposite direction [12]. We usually use the asymmetry between cause and effect to judge the causal direction [1]. When solving causal inference problem in linear systems [16], the asymmetry information contained in the variables tends to be less than the nonlinearity. However, linear methods tend to give better results, considering that a very large sample size and high time cost is usually required to build a nonlinear model [7]. A few methods have been proposed to solve the linear causal problem in recent years.

Shimizu et al. [15] proposed a linear non-Gaussian acyclic model to discover causal structure for continuous data based on the independent component analysis. Hyttinen et al. [4] described a procedure to identify linear models containing cycles and latent variables, gave the proof of the necessary and sufficient conditions for causal identifiability and proposed a complete search algorithm. Zhang and Luo [19] calculated the entropy of the observed data by estimating the equivalent generalized Gaussian distribution parameters and proposed a causal inference method based on unit entropy. Rothenhäusler et al. [13] proposed a fast inference method in linear structural equation models with hidden variables under additive interventions. They also gave identifiability conditions for the causal parameter and derive asymptotic confidence intervals in the low-dimensional setting.

3   Causal Inference Condition Description

Suppose X and Y are random variables on the real set $\mathbb{R}$, a linear additive noise model is shown as

$$Y = a_1 X + E_1, \quad E_1 \perp X \tag{1}$$

$$X = a_2 Y + E_2, \quad E_2 \perp Y \tag{2}$$

where Eqs. (1) and (2) respectively indicate causal direction are $X \rightarrow Y$ and $Y \rightarrow X$. When the models in both directions are simultaneously true, we call the model reversible. However, we usually assume that the model is irreversible.

For $X \rightarrow Y$, the model contains two known variables X and Y and two unknown quantities a_1 and E_1. For $Y \rightarrow X$, the two unknown quantities are a_2 and E_2. To judge the direction, we generally assume that the model can not be established in both directions. The first step is to find specific a_1, E_1, a_2, E_2 so that the cause variable and the noise variable are as independent as possible. The second step is to judge the causal direction based on the independence degree between the noise and the cause.

Different input variables, noise variables and linear coefficients result in different outputs. (In Eq. (1), X and Y are also called input and output, respectively.) Usually we can infer the causal direction based on the fit degree between data and model. However, it may not be easy to find the model asymmetry due to the particularity of the data distribution. This section mainly discusses the causal inference condition of linear additive noise model.

In general, the real number a must be unique if $Y = aX + E$ and $X \perp E$ are simultaneously established. Then, we can find the only possible a_1, E_1 or a_2, E_2 to establish the model in one direction. When the causal direction is $X \rightarrow Y$, we think that a_1, E_1 and X together result in an effect variable Y. Next, what we need to do is compare dependence between input and noise in both directions. Now we assume that the direction of the causal model is $X \rightarrow Y$. There is a noise variable E_1, so that $Y = a_1X + E_1$ is true and X and E_1 are independent.

3.1   X and E_1 Are Independent and Are both Gaussian Distribution

Now we have a continuous two-dimensional random variable (X, Y) and a sample $\{(x_i, y_i)|i = 1, ..., n\}$ generated by the variable. We can sort the $\{x_i|i = 1, ..., n\}$ in ascending order and obtain the data sequence $(x_1', ..., x_n')$, where $x_1' \leq x_2' \leq ... \leq x_n'$. If x_i is located at the kth position of the data sequence, we denote it as $xp_i = k$. yp_i is defined in the same way as xp_i. Then, the Spearman rank correlation coefficient is defined as [3]:

$$r_s(X, Y) = \frac{\sum_{i=1}^n (xp_i - \overline{xp})(yp_i - \overline{yp})}{\sqrt{\sum_{i=1}^n (xp_i - \overline{xp})^2 \sum_{i=1}^n (yp_i - \overline{yp})^2}}. \tag{3}$$

With the continuous random variables U and V, we discuss the statistical features of the Spearman's rank correlation coefficient $r_s(U, V)$ when the two-dimensional joint distribution $f_{U,V}(U, V)$ is the Gaussian. Let (U, V) generate the sample $\{(u_i, v_i)|i = 1, ..., n\}$. The correlation coefficient of the joint distribution is ρ, and up_i and vp_i represent the order of u_i and v_i, respectively. We can let

$$Sum = \sum_{i=1}^n (up_i - 1)(vp_i - 1) \tag{4}$$

Then,

$$r_s(U, V) = \frac{Sum - \frac{1}{4}n^2(n-1)^2}{\frac{1}{12}n(n^2 - 1)} \tag{5}$$

To calculate $E(r_s)$ we need to know $E(Sum)$, and

$$Sum = \sum_{i=1}^n \sum_{j=1}^n \sum_{k=1}^n L(u_i - u_j)L(v_i - v_j) \tag{6}$$

Terms are 0 in Sum when $i = j = k$, and we further discuss in two cases.

(1) When i, j, and k are different from each other, $(u_i - u_j, v_i - v_j)$ is a two-dimensional normal distribution with correlation coefficient $\rho/2$. $E\{L(u_i - u_j)L(v_i - v_k)\}$ is the probability that both values are greater than 0, which is the integral of the probability distribution in the first quadrant. This integral result is $[1 - arccos(\rho/2)/\pi]/2$ and that such items have a total of $n(n-1)(n-2)$ items.

(2) When two of i, j and k are equal but the third is not, the correlation coefficient of $u_i - u_j$ and $v_i - v_j$ is ρ. The expected value for each item is $(1 - arccos(\rho)/\pi)/2$ and such items have a total of $n(n-1)$.

Consequently, we can obtain

$$E(Sum) = \frac{1}{2}n(n-1)(n-2)[1 - \frac{1}{\pi}arccos(\frac{1}{2}\rho)] + \frac{1}{2}n(n-1)[1 - \frac{1}{\pi}arccos(\rho)] \quad (7)$$

According to Eq. (5), we can obtain

$$E(r_s) = \frac{6}{\pi}[\frac{n-2}{n+1}arcsin(\frac{1}{2}\rho) + \frac{1}{n+1}arcsin(\rho)] \quad (8)$$

When $\rho = 0$ and $\rho = 1$, it is equal to 0 and 1, respectively. When n is large enough and ρ is small enough, we can obtain

$$r_s = \frac{6}{\pi}arcsin(\frac{1}{2}\rho) \quad (9)$$

Let $U = Y$, $V = E_2$. Because X and E_1 are independent Gaussian distributions, and U and V can be obtained by the linear sum of X and Y, (U,V) is also a two-dimensional Gaussian distribution. Since Pearson correlation coefficient

$$r_p(U,V) = \frac{COV(U,V)}{\sqrt{D(U)D(V)}} = \frac{COV(a_1X + E_1, \frac{1}{1+a_1^2}X - \frac{a_1}{1+a_1^2}E_1)}{\sqrt{D(U)D(V)}} = 0 \quad (10)$$

and $\rho = r_p$, we have

$$r_s(U,V) = 0 \quad (11)$$

The above results show that when X and E_1 are Gaussian distributions, it is difficult to obtain the dependence by using the Spearman rank correlation coefficient. So it is difficult to judge the causal direction.

3.2 X and E_1 Are Independent and Are Not both Gaussian Distributions

When X and E_1 are independent and are not both Gaussian, the variables Y and E_2 are not Gaussian. It is not possible to statistically conclude that the Spearman's rank correlation coefficient of Y and E_2 is zero. However, we conclude that the Spearman's rank correlation coefficient of the two variables is equal to the Pearson correlation coefficient of the copula variable. To illustrate this situation, we first introduce the concept of a copula in this situation.

Copula. A copula [2] is a multivariate probability distribution function with a uniform marginal distribution function. It allows the problem of estimating the multidimensional distribution to be decomposed into estimations of the individuals' marginal distributions and joint dependence. To further illustrate the concept of a copula, we introduce Sklar's theorem [17].

Theorem 1 (Sklar's theorem). *H represents an n-dimensional probability distribution function. The marginal distribution of H is $F_1, F_2, ..., F_n$. For all $\mathbf{x} \in \mathbb{R}^n$, there is an n-dimensional copula function $\mathcal{C}$:*

$$H(x_1, ..., x_n) = \mathcal{C}(F_1(x_1), ..., F_n(x_n)) \tag{12}$$

If $F_1(x_i)$ are continuous, $\mathcal{C}$ is unique. Otherwise $\mathcal{C}$ can be uniquely determined by the Cartesian product of the distribution function value set $Range(F_1) \times Range(F_2) \times ... \times Range(F_n)$. Conversely, if $\mathcal{C}$ is an n-dimension copula and F_i is a distribution function, then the function H defined above is an n-dimensional distribution function, and the marginal distribution is $F_1, F_2, ..., F_n$.

A corollary to Sklar's Theorem is that if the multivariate distribution has a probability density function h, we can derive

$$h(x_1, ..., x_n) = c(F_1(x_1), ..., F_n(x_n)) \cdot f_1(x_1) \cdot f_2(x_2) \cdot ... \cdot f_n(x_n) \tag{13}$$

where c is the probability density of the copula function. From Sklar's Theorem and its corollary, the marginal distribution and multivariate dependence structures can be separated and the dependence structure can be represented by a copula.

Copula Representation of the Spearman's Rank Correlation Coefficient. A copula provides a natural way to study and measure the dependence between random variables. Linear correlation is most commonly used as an indicator of relevance in practice because it is easy to calculate and is a natural scalar measure of multivariate normal distribution. However, that is not the case in most random variables, where using linear correlation may be misleading. Therefore, linear correlation should not be considered a measure of relevance of the specification. We focus on the copula-based Spearman's rank correlation coefficient.

Let (X_1, Y_1), (X_2, Y_2) and (X_3, Y_3) be random vectors that are independently distributed with (X, Y). The Spearman's rank correlation coefficient can be also defined as follows:

$$r_s(X, Y) = 3(P\{(X_1 - X_2)(Y_1 - Y_2) > 0\} - P\{(X_1 - X_2)(Y_1 - Y_3) < 0\}) \tag{14}$$

Let (x_1, y_1) and (x_2, y_2) be two observations of the continuous random vector (X, Y). When $(x_1 - x_2)(y_1 - y_2) > 0$, (x_1, y_1) and (x_2, y_2) are consistent. Otherwise, they are inconsistent. To illustrate the copula representation of the Spearman's rank correlation coefficient, we introduce the following theorem. This theorem and related information can be found in the paper [11].

Theorem 2. *Let (X_1, Y_1) and (X_2, Y_2) be two independent continuous random variables whose joint distribution functions are F_1 and F_2. X_1 and X_2 have a common marginal distribution of G, Y_1 and Y_2 have a common marginal distribution of H. Let C_1 and C_2 denote copula functions of (X_1, Y_1) and (X_2, Y_2), respectively. If Q indicates the difference between the probability of the consistency and inconsistency between (X_1, Y_1) and (X_2, Y_2):*

$$Q = P\{(X_1 - X_2)(Y_1 - Y_2) > 0\} - P\{(X_1 - X_2)(Y_1 - Y_2) < 0\} \tag{15}$$

then

$$Q = 4 \iint_{[0,1]^2} C_2(u, v) dC_1(u, v) - 1 \tag{16}$$

If (X, Y) is a two-dimensional continuous random variable, its copula function is represented by $\mathcal{C}$. $X \sim G$, $Y \sim H$, $U = G(X)$, $V = H(Y)$. Based on the above theorem, the Spearman's rank correlation coefficient between X and Y can be expressed as follows:

$$r_s(X, Y) = 12 \iint_{[0,1]^2} uv dC(u, v) - 3 \tag{17}$$

Since the variables U and V are evenly distributed over $[0, 1]$, then

$$var(U) = var(Y) = 1/12 \tag{18}$$

Therefore,

$$r_s(X, Y) = 3Q = 12 \iint_{[0,1]^2} uv dC(u, v) - 3 = 12E(UV) - 3$$

$$= \frac{E(UV) - 1/4}{1/12} = \frac{Cov(U, V)}{\sqrt{var(U)}\sqrt{var(V)}} = corr(U, V) \tag{19}$$

4   Method Design and Description

Assuming that the causality is linear, the first step in causal inference is to estimate the coefficients $\hat{a}_1$ and $\hat{a}_2$ based on the sample data. The second step is to estimate the noise variables $\hat{E}_1$ and $\hat{E}_2$ by the observed variables and coefficients. Then, the dependence of the noise variable and the hypothetical cause variable is calculated based on the estimation. Finally, the dependence is calculated based on the estimated result of the copula function, and the causal direction is identified.

4.1   Copula Construction by Observations

From Sklar's theorem, we can find that the copula function can describe the dependence structure of the multidimensional joint distribution. That means the copula function separates the dependence structure from the marginal distribution. We obtain $\{\mathbf{X}^t | t = 1, ..., N\}$ as a random sample from the distribution F. $\{\mathbf{U}^t | t = 1, ..., N\}$ is the sample of F corresponding to the copula function $\mathcal{C}$. The construction of $\mathcal{C}$ depends on $\{\mathbf{U}^t | t = 1, ..., N\}$ instead of the original sample point $\{\mathbf{X}^t | t = 1, ..., N\}$.

$\mathbf{U}^t$ is called an observation, but $\mathbf{U}^t$ cannot be obtained directly and usually be replaced by its estimation $\hat{\mathbf{U}}^t$, called a pseudo-observation. $\mathbf{X}^t = (X_1^t, X_2^t)$, $\mathbf{U}^t = (U_1^t, U_2^t)$. The marginal distribution estimation is usually also expressed as follows [6]:

$$\hat{F}_i(x) = \frac{1}{N} \sum_{t=1}^{N} \mathbf{1}(X_i^t \le x). \tag{20}$$

Typically, we do not know the a priori marginal distribution of the observational variables. The above formula evenly distributes the original sample observational data into the unit cube, resulting in a nearly uniform distribution of F_i. To avoid extreme values of copula density on the $[0, 1]^2$ boundary, the above equation is often scaled to obtain $\hat{U}_i^t$, where

$$\hat{U}_i^t = \frac{N}{N+1} \hat{F}_i(X_i^t) \tag{21}$$

The above equation can be regarded as the empirical formula for calculating the marginal probability given by $U_i^t = F_i(X_i^t)$, and $\hat{U}_i^t$ can be used as the estimated copula function.

4.2 Linear System Causal Inference Method

For any observational data X and Y, both a and E can be found that fit $Y = aX + E$. In addition, an a' and an E' for $X = a'Y + E'$ can also be found. Unlike

---

Algorithm 1. Causal inference algorithm based on Spearman's rank correlation coefficient (SCCI)

Input: Observations X_1, X_2.
Output: *Direction.*
1: $\hat{a}_1 = COV(X_1, X_2)/D(X_1)$, $\hat{a}_2 = COV(X_1, X_2)/D(X_2)$.
2: $\hat{E}_1 = X_2 - \hat{a}_1 X_1$, $\hat{E}_2 = X_1 - \hat{a}_2 X_2$.
3: Estimate the pseudo-observations of $U_1 = (X_1, \hat{E}_1)$ and $U_2 = (X_2, \hat{E}_2)$.
4: Calculate the Spearman's rank correlation coefficients D_1 for X_1 and $\hat{E}_1$, D_2 for X_2 and $\hat{E}_2$.
5: **if** $D_2 > D_1$ **then**
6:      *Direction* $: X_1 \to X_2$.
7: **else if** $D_1 > D_2$ **then**
8:      *Direction* $: X_2 \to X_1$.
9: **else**
10:      *Direction* $:$ *unknown*.
11: **end if**

---

the irreversible and asymmetrical characteristics of most nonlinear functions, a linear function is usually reversible, so the causal direction cannot be judged by the asymmetry of the linear function. Therefore, the dependence between variables needs to be considered. By comparing the dependence between X_i and E_i, the causal direction between the observational variables can be inferred.

If $D_1 < D_2$, the assumed "cause variable" and the noise variable are more independent in the direction $X_1 \rightarrow X_2$, and we accept the assumption of $X_1 \rightarrow X_2$. Conversely, the inferred causal direction is the opposite of the first hypothesis.

5   Experiment and Analysis

In this section, we do the experiments under different conditions, including the different distributions of the cause variable X and noise E and different signal-to-noise ratio (SNR) γ. We observe the trends and effects of the algorithm through multiple sets of comparison experiments. We compare the proposed algorithm with the IGCI method [5] and the UECI method [19]. The results of the various algorithms will be influenced by the factors listed above.

First, we introduce a generalized Gaussian distribution (GGD) in order to generate the experimental data for the simulation [10]. A generalized Gaussian distribution is a family of continuous symmetric distribution functions that integrate multiple distributions. The distribution function can be expressed as follows:

$$f(x) = \frac{s}{2\sigma \Gamma(1/s)} \, e^{-(|x-\mu|/\sigma)^s} \tag{22}$$

5.1   The Effect of Variable Distribution

We first study the effect of the distribution function on the experimental results. In the first set of experiments, the noise variable and the input variable satisfy generalized Gaussian distributions of the same parameters. These GGDs correspond to different s values. For the convenience, the distribution takes $\mu = 0$ and $\sigma = 1$, which means that the distribution function is symmetric about the y-axis and has unit variance. The signal-to-noise ratio is $\gamma = 1$ and the observation sample data amount is $N = 1000$. The generalized Gaussian distribution has a large variation in the distribution function curve when $s \in (0, 4]$ and the curve changes gradually when $s > 4$. So we select a dense point sample in $(0, 4]$ and do a set of experiments every 0.1. We take a more sparse point sample in the interval $[4, 10]$ and perform a set of experiments every 1. Each set of experiments were performed 100 times. The experimental data for each of the 100 executions was independently generated under the same parameters. The y-axis in Fig. 1 represents the accuracy of causal analysis, and the curves fitted by data points of different colors correspond to the overall performances of the three causal inference methods.

The experimental results in Fig. 1 show that when the parameter s of the GGDs is near 2, the accuracy of the three causal inference methods is approximately 50% at the global level. At this point, the effects of the three methods are basically the same as the random guess method, which verifies the case in the Gaussian distribution. Because the linear sum (or difference) of the Gaussian distribution is still a Gaussian distribution, the cause and effect cannot be inferred by the asymmetric nature of the distribution. However, when s is far from 2, the inferring accuracies of the three methods show a gradual upward trend. Note that the UECI method has poor performance at $s < 0.6$ exhibiting some drawbacks.

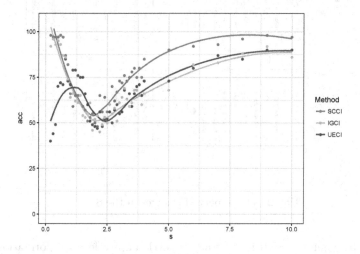

Fig. 1. The impact of changes in s

5.2   Signal-to-Noise Ratio γ

The signal-to-noise ratio (SNR) is usually used to indicate the ratio of useful information to irrelevant information in the process of information transmission. In the experiments, we ensure that the other conditions remain the same. The input variable satisfies a generalized Gaussian distribution, and the noise variable is the standard normal distribution. The experiments were conducted in 6 groups and s varied among $\{0.5, 1.0, 1.5, 2.0, 2.5, 3.0\}$. In each group, the SNR γ was adjusted so that $\gamma = [0.5, 1, 1.5, 2, 2.5, 3]$, respectively. A set of experiments was conducted for each different γ, and the accuracy of three methods was compared as shown in Fig. 2.

The inferring accuracy usually increases as the SNR increases, which is consistent with the definition of SNR. In other words, when the SNR is higher, the useful information in the observational data exceeds the irrelevant information. Then, the interference from noise is small, and the inferring results are better.

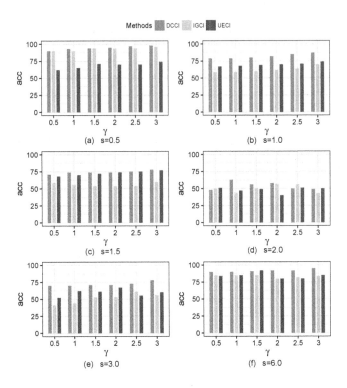

Fig. 2. The impact of changes in the SNR γ

Conversely, when the SNR is low, the proportion of irrelevant information in the observational data is large, and the noise influences the inference greatly, which increases the uncertainty of causal inference and reduces the inferring accuracy. Thus, the performance is not as good as when the SNR is high. However, there are some exceptions. When the value of s is approximately 2, none of the three algorithms obtains high accuracy because the generalized Gaussian distribution is equivalent to the normal distribution, making linear causal inference difficult. There is no apparent correlation between the inferring accuracy and the SNR in this situation. From (a) to (f), the inferring accuracy has an overall trend of decreasing initially, followed by an increasing and there is a significant "depression" near $s = 2$, which reflects the influence of distribution function.

5.3   Experiments on a Real Dataset

In this section, we study the inference results of the proposed algorithm on a real data set. The proposed algorithm is primarily applicable to cases in which the variable relation is linear or nearly linear, while the relation of most variables in the real world is nonlinear. However, this fact does not mean that the simple linear model has no value. When the direct calculation method is used to obtain the dependence between the variables, some intermediate calculation steps can be reduced, which speeds up the algorithm and improves its runtime performance.

In the experiments, we used the CEP dataset[1] which consists of different "causal pairs" [9]. Each data item consists of a pair of statistically related random variables, one of which is the cause and the other is the effect. It is an extension of the classical causal data set formed in the Pot-Luck competition[2]. These data pairs are a good reflection of the causal inference problems faced in an actual work situation and can be used as an benchmark data set. Comparing the performances of different algorithms on this data set, we obtain the results shown in Table 1.

Table 1. Experiment on real-world data

Method	Accuracy (%)	Error
SCCI	82	±3
IGCI	71	±5
UECI	73	±3

6   Conclusion

Identifying causal direction between variables is an important but challenging problem in artificial intelligence. In the paper, we studies the linear causal inference problem for continuous data based on dependence calculation to obtain the correct direction. First, we introduce the linear additive noise causal model and the variable dependence calculation method of continuous variables. Then, we do some theoretical analysis and demonstrate the causal inference conditions in the linear case. With the Spearman's rank correlation coefficient calculated by copula model, this paper develops an effective causal direction inference method for linear data. Experimental results on both simulated data and real data verify our theoretical results and support the validity of the proposed method. However, this study does not give a quantitative measure of the causality, therefore significance testing will be conducted in the future work.

Acknowledgments. The research reported here was supported by the National Natural Science Foundation of China under contract number NSFC61572279.

References

1. Bontempi, G., Flauder, M.: From dependency to causality: a machine learning approach. J. Mach. Learn. Res. **16**(1), 2437–2457 (2015)

---

[1] http://webdav.tuebingen.mpg.de/cause-effect/.
[2] http://www.causality.inf.ethz.ch/cause-effect.php.

2. Durante, F., Sempi, C.: Principles of Copula Theory. Chapman and Hall/CRC, Boca Raton (2015)
3. Hauke, J., Kossowski, T.: Comparison of values of Pearson's and Spearman's correlation coefficients on the same sets of data. Quaestiones Geographicae **30**(2), 87–93 (2011)
4. Hyttinen, A., Eberhardt, F., Hoyer, P.O.: Learning linear cyclic causal models with latent variables. J. Mach. Learn. Res. **13**(1), 3387–3439 (2012)
5. Janzing, D., Steudel, B., Shajarisales, N., Schölkopf, B.: Justifying information-geometric causal inference. In: Vovk, V., Papadopoulos, H., Gammerman, A. (eds.) Measures of Complexity, pp. 253–265. Springer, Cham (2015). https://doi.org/10.1007/978-3-319-21852-6_18
6. Laux, P., Vogl, S., Qiu, W., Knoche, H.R., Kunstmann, H.: Copula-based statistical refinement of precipitation in RCM simulations over complex terrain. Hydrol. Earth Syst. Sci. **15**(7), 2401–2419 (2011)
7. Lopez-Paz, D., Muandet, K., Schölkopf, B., Tolstikhin, I.: Towards a learning theory of cause-effect inference. In: International Conference on Machine Learning, pp. 1452–1461 (2015)
8. Marwala, T.: Causality, Correlation and Artificial Intelligence for Rational Decision Making. World Scientific, Singapore (2015)
9. Mooij, J.M., Peters, J., Janzing, D., Zscheischler, J., Schölkopf, B.: Distinguishing cause from effect using observational data: methods and benchmarks. J. Mach. Learn. Res. **17**(1), 1103–1204 (2016)
10. Nadarajah, S., Kotz, S.: On the generation of Gaussian noise. IEEE Trans. Signal Process. **55**(3), 1172–1172 (2007)
11. Nelsen, R.B.: An introduction to copulas. Springer Series in Statistics, 2nd edn. Springer, New York (2007). https://doi.org/10.1007/0-387-28678-0
12. Peters, J., Janzing, D., Schölkopf, B.: Elements of Causal Inference: Foundations and Learning Algorithms. MIT Press, Cambridge (2017)
13. Rothenhäusler, D., Bühlmann, P., Meinshausen, N., et al.: Causal dantzig: fast inference in linear structural equation models with hidden variables under additive interventions. Ann. Stat. **47**(3), 1688–1722 (2019)
14. Russell, S.J., Norvig, P.: Artificial Intelligence: A Modern Approach. Pearson Education Limited, Malaysia (2016)
15. Shimizu, S., Hoyer, P.O., Hyvärinen, A., Kerminen, A.: A linear non-Gaussian acyclic model for causal discovery. J. Mach. Learn. Res. **7**, 2003–2030 (2006)
16. Shimizu, S., Hyvarinen, A., Kano, Y., Hoyer, P.O.: Discovery of non-Gaussian linear causal models using ICA. arXiv preprint arXiv:1207.1413 (2012)
17. Úbeda-Flores, M., Fernández-Sánchez, J.: Sklar's theorem: the cornerstone of the Theory of Copulas. Copulas and Dependence Models with Applications, pp. 241–258. Springer, Cham (2017). https://doi.org/10.1007/978-3-319-64221-5_15
18. Zhang, Y., Cen, Y., Luo, G.: Causal direction inference for air pollutants data. Comput. Electr. Eng. **68**, 404–411 (2018)
19. Zhang, Y., Luo, G.: An entropy based method for causal discovery in linear acyclic model. In: Lee, M., Hirose, A., Hou, Z.-G., Kil, R.M. (eds.) ICONIP 2013. LNCS, vol. 8227, pp. 250–256. Springer, Heidelberg (2013). https://doi.org/10.1007/978-3-642-42042-9_32

Urban Traffic Flow Prediction Using a Gradient-Boosted Method Considering Dynamic Spatio-Temporal Correlations

Jie Yang[1] , Linjiang Zheng[1(✉)] , and Dihua Sun[2]

[1] College of Computer Science, Chongqing University, Chongqing, China
zlj_cqu@cqu.edu.cn
[2] College of Automation, Chongqing University, Chongqing, China

Abstract. Traffic flow prediction at the city scale is an important topic useful to many transportation operations and urban applications. However, this is a very challenging problem, affected by multiple complex factors, such as the spatial correlation between different locations and temporal correlation among different time intervals. Considering spatio-temporal correlations, we propose a novel short-term traffic flow prediction model, which combining a gradient–boosted regression tree model and principal component analysis, and we name our model as DSTGBRT. First, we analyze the spatio-temporal correlations among different locations, using Pearson correlation coefficient. Second, we combine Pearson correlation coefficient and historical traffic flow data to construct feature vector and get original training data. Third, to eliminate the linear correlation between features, we use principal component analysis to construct new feature vector and get new training data. In the experiments, compared with traditional spatio-temporal gradient–boosted regression tree model named as STGBRT, the results demonstrate that our proposed DSTGBRT can do a timely and adaptive prediction even in the rush hour when the traffic conditions change rapidly. At the same time, it outperforms the existing methods.

Keywords: Traffic flow prediction · Spatio-temporal correlation ·
Gradient–boosted regression tree model · Principal component analysis

1 Introduction

The vehicles bring convenience to the citizens. But at the same time, their continual growth inevitably leads to problems, such as environmental pollution, waste of resources and traffic congestion. How to effectively relieve urban traffic congestion bottleneck has become a major issue faced by most of big cities. Accurate estimation of the traffic state can provide guiding advice for citizens' travel and traffic regulation. For example, the information of short-term traffic flow prediction can be provided to drivers in real time to give them realistic estimation of travel state, expected delays and alternative routes to their destinations. The transportation system is a complex system involved with human, vehicle and road [1]. It is nonlinear and has a high degree of uncertainty. Therefore, The short-term traffic flow prediction is more easily affected by random factors. It is more difficult for short-term traffic flow to predict with higher

© Springer Nature Switzerland AG 2019
C. Douligeris et al. (Eds.): KSEM 2019, LNAI 11776, pp. 271–283, 2019.
https://doi.org/10.1007/978-3-030-29563-9_25

accuracy. With the development of research for this topic, several traffic flow predicting methods have been proposed, such as statistical and regression methods, traffic flow theory methods, historical average methods, and so on. The models based on machine learning widely used in the transportation field, including neural network models, support vector machines and boosting. Among the models and methods, the Autoregressive Integrated Moving Average (ARIMA) model has gradually become the benchmark for evaluating new development prediction models [2]. This model has a good predictive effect when the traffic flow changes regularly by time. In [3], the ARIMA model is used to predict traffic accidents, and proves that it has high prediction accuracy through experiments, which provides guidance for the government and transportation departments to prevent traffic accidents. In [4], the support vector machine method is used to predict short-term traffic speed and verify its effectiveness. In [5], Random Forest (RF) model is used to predict short-term traffic flow and proves its effectiveness. In [6], the gradient-boosted regression tree is used to train historical travel time data and predict it, comparing it with other integrated methods to prove the applicability of the method in highway travel time prediction. In [7], considering the spatio-temporal correlation, it is proved that the gradient-boosted regression tree has higher prediction accuracy in the prediction of travel time of urban sections. In Reference [8], the gradient-boosted regression tree is used to predict the passenger flow of the short-term subway, considering the influence of a series of factors such as the passenger flow of the bus station adjacent to the subway.

Although the above method has been improved in prediction accuracy, there are still some shortcomings in the spatio-temporal correlation analysis. To this end, this paper proposes a short-term traffic flow prediction model based on gradient-boosted regression tree and principal component analysis. The difference from the literatures [7, 8] is that this paper proposes a method to construct feature vector considering spatio-temporal correlations among target road cross-section and its adjacent road cross-section in road network. In order to eliminate the linear correlation between features, we use Principal Component Analysis (PCA) to reduce the dimensionality of original feature vector and then we get new feature vector. The experiment was carried out using Electronic Registration Identification of the Motor Vehicle (ERI) data. The difference between the predicted and observed values is converted into the mean absolute percentage error (MAPE), and the model is compared with the results of ARIMA model and the traditional Spatio-temporal Gradient–boosted Regression Tree model [8]. The comparison results show that our proposed DSTGBRT outperforms the existing methods, which verifies the effectiveness of our model in short-term traffic flow prediction.

2   Methodology

Gradient–boosted Regression Tree (GBRT) is different from traditional Boosting. The core of GBRT is that each calculation is to reduce the previous residual. And in order to reduce these residuals, you can create a new model in the direction of the residual reduction of the gradient. The specific process of GBRT model is as follows: Assuming that the data set is $D = \{(x_1, y_1), (x_2, y_2), \ldots, (x_N, y_N)\}$ and the loss function is $L(y, f(x))$. Assuming that the number of leaves for each tree is J, the space of the m-th tree can be divided into J disjoint subspaces, such as R_{1m}, $R_{2m}, \ldots$, R_{jm} and the predicted value for subspace R_{im}, is the constant b_{im}. Therefore, the regression tree can be expressed by Eqs. (1) and (2):

$$g_m(x) = \sum_{i=1}^{j} (b_{jm}I), x \in R_{jm} \tag{1}$$

$$I(x \in R_{jm}) = \begin{cases} 1, & x \in R_{jm}; \\ 0, & \text{otherwise.} \end{cases} \tag{2}$$

The following is the model training step.

Input: data set $D = \{(x_1, y_1), (x_2, y_2), \ldots, (x_N, y_N)\}$, learning rate lr, number of trees M.

Output: model $f_M(x)$

Step 1: initialization

$$f_0(x) = \arg\min_{\rho} \sum_{i=1}^{n} L(y_i, \rho) \tag{3}$$

Step 2: Iteratively generate M regression trees. For $m = 1$ to M, m denotes the index of the tree.

For all samples N, for $i = 1$ to N, Calculating the negative gradient value of the loss function and use it as an estimate of the residual r_{im}.

$$r_{im} = -\left[\frac{\partial L(y_i, f_{m-1}(x_i))}{\partial f_{m-1}(x_i)}\right]_{f(x)=f_{m-1}(x)} \tag{4}$$

A training set $D_m = \{(x_1, r_{1m}), (x_2, r_{2m}), \ldots, (x_N, r_{Nm})\}$ is generated for the residual generated in the previous step, and a regression tree $g_m(x)$ is generated for the new training set D_m, and the output is divided into J disjoint regions $R_{1m}, R_{2m}, \ldots, R_{jm}$, according to the input of the m-th regression tree, and the step size of the gradient is calculated.

$$\rho_m = \arg\min_{\rho} \sum_{i=1}^{n} L(y_i, f_{m-1}(x_i) + \rho g_m(x_i)) \tag{5}$$

Step 3: Update the model

$$f_m(x) = f_{m-1}(x) + lr \times \rho_m g_m(x) \tag{6}$$

Step 4: Output the model $f_M(x)$

3   Road Cross-section Flow Analysis

In this section, we will firstly introduce the data resource, and then introduce the fundamental concept of our work. Our purpose is to provide the near future traffic states for citizens in time. We will achieve this purpose by proposing an accurate short-term traffic flow prediction algorithm by fully mining the traffic information from time, day and location.

ERI is based on RFID. RFID is a non-contact information transmission technology using radio frequency signal through spatial coupling (alternating magnetic field or electromagnetic field), and automatically identify the object through the information transmitted. It has many advantages, such as long recognition distance, high recognition accuracy, more information stored, fast reading speed and so on. The characters make it very suitable for urban traffic information collection. All vehicles in Chongqing are equipped with electronic license plates. The reader mounted on the road will identify each passing car. Figure 1 shows the real scene of an ERI use.

Fig. 1. ERI reader mounted on a road cross-section

3.1   Definitions

Defination 1 ERI Record: Every piece of ERI data is a triad like<*EID, CID, PAS-STIME*>. The *EID* is the electronic license plate number of the passing through vehicle, and the *CID* is the road cross-section id that the vehicle passes, and the *PASSTIME* is the time when the vehicle passes the current road cross-section.

Defination 2 ERI Flow: Assume the time interval is Tc, which is in minutes. Then one day can be divided into $24 \times 60/Tc$ equal length time segments. The traffic flow dataset can be obtained by group counting the records of ERI dataset according to *CID* and *PASSTIME*. Every piece of traffic flow dataset is a four-tuple like <*CID, date,*

T_Stamp, L>. The *CID* is the road cross-section id, and the *date* is the date value, and *T_Stamp* is the time segment index, and *L* is the traffic flow value.

Defination 3 Road Network: $G(E, V)$ is a directed graph, V is the set of road cross-section, and E is the set of road segment. If $\exists v_1, v_2 \in V$, and in the physical space, there are some vehicles passed through v_1 and then v_2, then there exists a directed edge e_{12} from v_1 to v_2. In previous research, we studied the trajectories of all the vehicles in Chongqing during the week. And then we have established a road network based on trajectories and collection points.

Defination 4 Road Cross-section Coefficient: $\rho_{x,y,\tau}$ is the Pearson correlation coefficient between the flow of current time segment on road cross-section x and the flow of previous τ-th time segment on road cross-section y. It presents the correlation between y and x with different time interval.

3.2   Spatial and Temporal Correlation Verification

Many indices have been designed to quantitatively measure the correlations among spatio-temporal data, and most of these indices are based on Pearson's coefficient [10]. In statistics, the Pearson correlation coefficient (referred to as PCC) is a measure of the linear correlation between two variables X and Y, and takes a value between −1 and +1. If the value is 1, it indicates a perfect positive correlation, while 0 indicates no correlation and −1 indicates perfect negative correlation. The Pearson's correlation coefficient is defined as follows:

$$\rho_{X,Y} = \frac{E[(X - \mu_X)(Y - \mu_Y)]}{\sigma_X \sigma_Y} \tag{7}$$

Where μ_X and μ_Y are the averages of variables X and Y, respectively. Similarly, σ_X and σ_Y are the corresponding standard deviations of variables X and Y. The spatial correlation coefficient between a target point and an adjacent point can be calculated according to Eq. (7).

Temporal Correlation
The accessed data were aggregated over 15-min. time intervals because of the scarcity of ERI data. Therefore, one day was divided into 96 time segments. As shown in Table 1, there is a certain correlation among the flow of current segment and the flow of the four most recent segments. All of their PCC are higher than 0.6. Meanwhile, in the statistical analysis, if the correlation coefficient is higher than 0.6, it can be considered that there is a high degree of correlation. Therefore, the flow of 4 most recent segments are used as the feature vector.

Spatial Correlation
In temporal correlation, we verify the temporal correlation of the flow. In the next, the upstream road section flow sequence and downstream flow sequence are divided into five groups in the same way as the temporal correlation verification. Table 2 reveals the spatial correlation between Caiyuanba Yangtze River Bridge and its upstream road cross-section and Table 3 reveals the spatial correlation between Caiyuanba Yangtze

River Bridge and its downstream road cross-section. Therefore, the 3 most recent flows of upstream road cross-section and the 2 most recent flows of downstream road cross-section are used as the feature vector considering the PCC of spatial correlation.

Table 1. Temporal autocorrelation

	L1	L2	L3	L4	L5	L6	L7	L8	L9	L10
L1	1	0.94	0.86	0.72	0.62	0.50	0.40	0.36	0.29	0.24
L2	0.94	1	0.95	0.85	0.71	0.61	0.53	0.47	0.41	0.36
L3	0.85	0.95	1	0.95	0.83	0.73	0.63	0.57	0.50	0.44
L4	0.72	0.85	0.95	1	0.94	0.85	0.74	0.66	0.59	0.53
L5	0.57	0.70	0.83	0.94	1	0.95	0.86	0.76	0.67	0.61
L6	0.50	0.61	0.73	0.85	0.95	1	0.95	0.86	0.76	0.68
L7	0.40	0.53	0.63	0.74	0.86	0.95	1	0.95	0.87	0.77
L8	0.36	0.47	0.57	0.66	0.76	0.86	0.95	1	0.95	0.87
L9	0.29	0.41	0.50	0.59	0.67	0.76	0.87	0.95	1	0.95
L10	0.24	0.36	0.44	0.53	0.61	0.68	0.77	0.87	0.95	1

Table 2. Spatial correlation of upstream road cross-section

T	T + 1	T + 2	T + 3	T + 4	T + 5
0.98	0.91	0.74	0.59	0.47	0.41

Table 3. Spatial correlation of downstream road cross-section

T	T + 1	T + 2	T + 3	T + 4	T + 5
0.78	0.69	0.54	0.49	0.38	0.28

3.3   Spatio-Temporal Correlation Feature Extraction

In short-term traffic flow prediction, the accuracy of prediction is affected by the extraction of feature vectors. However, there are many variables related to short-term traffic flow, so choosing the appropriate variables to construct feature vector is the most critical step in predicting. This paper verifies the spatio-temporal correlation of traffic flow in detail in Sect. 3.2. On this basis, we construct the feature vector by collecting the historical traffic flow of target and collecting the historical traffic flow of the upstream and downstream road cross-section as key variables.

We have defined the road network G, in which we can find adjacent road cross-section of every target road cross-section. Furthermore, the adjacent road cross-section can be divided into upstream road cross-section V_u and downstream road cross-section V_d. And $|V_u| = M$, $|V_d| = N$. According to the temporal-spatial correlation analysis, we extract the feature vector f_v for road cross-section v which is a $5 + 5M + 3N$ dimensional vector showed according to Eq. (8).

$$
\begin{aligned}
f_v = <&T\_stamp,\ l_1,\ l_2,\ l_3,\ l_4,\ \Delta l_1,\ \Delta l_2,\ \Delta l_3,\ lu_{m1,1} \times \rho_{v,m1,1},\ lu_{m1,2} \times \rho_{v,m1,2},\ lu_{m1,3} \times \rho_{v,m1,3}, \\
&lu_{m2,1} \times \rho_{v,m2,1},\ lu_{m2,2} \times \rho_{v,m2,2},\ lu_{m2,3} \times \rho_{v,m2,3}, \ldots,\ lu_{M,1} \times \rho_{v,M,1},\ lu_{M,2} \times \rho_{v,M,2},\ lu_{M,3} \times \rho_{v,M,3}, \\
&\Delta lu_{m1,1}/lu_{m1,2},\ \Delta lu_{m1,2}/lu_{m1,3},\ \Delta lu_{m2,1}/lu_{m2,2},\ \Delta lu_{m2,2}/lu_{m2,3}, \ldots,\ \Delta lu_{M,1}/lu_{M,2},\ \Delta lu_{M,2}/lu_{m2,3}, \\
&ld_{n1,1} \times \rho_{v,n1,1},\ ld_{n1,2} \times \rho_{v,n1,2},\ ld_{n2,1} \times \rho_{v,n2,1},\ ld_{n2,2} \times \rho_{v,n2,2}, \ldots,\ ld_{N,1} \times \rho_{v,N,1},\ ld_{N,2} \times \rho_{v,N,2}, \\
&\Delta ld_{n1}/ld_{n1,2},\ \Delta ld_{n2}/ld_{n2,2}, \ldots,\ \Delta ld_N/ld_{N,2} >
\end{aligned}
$$

$$(8)$$

T_stamp is the index of time segment. l_1, l_2, l_3, l_4 are the four most recent historical flow values of target road cross-section and Δl_1, Δl_2, Δl_3 are the growth rate of flow between two consecutive time segments, as calculated according to Eqs. (9), (10) and (11). $lu_{1,1}$, $lu_{1,2}$, $lu_{1,3}$, $lu_{2,1}$, $lu_{2,2}$, $lu_{2,3}$, ..., $lu_{m,1}$, $lu_{m,2}$, $lu_{m,3}$ are the three most recent historical flow values of each M upstream road cross-section, and $\Delta lu_{1,1}$, $\Delta lu_{1,2}$, $\Delta lu_{2,2}$, ... $\Delta lu_{m,1}$, $\Delta lu_{m,2}$, are the growth rate of flow between two consecutive time segments of each M upstream road cross-section, as calculated according to Eq. (12) and (13). $ld_{1,1}$, $ld_{1,2}$, $ld_{2,1}$, $ld_{2,2}$, ..., $ld_{n,1}$, $ld_{n,2}$ are the two most recent historical flow values of each N downstream road cross-section, and Δld_1, Δld_2, ..., Δld_n are the growth rate of flow between two consecutive time segments of each N downstream road cross-section, as calculated according to Eq. (14).

$$\Delta l_1 = l_1 - l_2 \tag{9}$$

$$\Delta l_2 = l_2 - l_3 \tag{10}$$

$$\Delta l_3 = l_3 - l_4 \tag{11}$$

$$\Delta lu_{m,1} = lu_{m,1} - lu_{m,2} \tag{12}$$

$$\Delta lu_{m,2} = lu_{m,2} - lu_{m,3} \tag{13}$$

$$\Delta ld_n = ld_{n,1} - ld_{n,2} \tag{14}$$

We extract the features vector of target road cross-section, and get the original training data set C. But the dimension of it is very big. The bigger the dimension is, the more time for model training will be used. Since the target point is far from some adjacent points, the impact among them is small. Meanwhile, there is some useless information in training data. So we use PCA to reduce the dimension of feature vector, which contributes to reduce the time for model training. We reserve principal components whose contribution rate is 95%. By dealing C with PCA, we can get training data D with low dimension, transformation matrix U and mean vector u. For one piece of original test data x, whoes format is the same as the data in C, we can transform its format as data in D by Eq. (15).

$$x' = U^T(x - u) \tag{15}$$

4 Experiment

In order to verify the feasibility of our prediction algorithm, we chose four places for experiment. They are Gaojia Garden Bridge, Mingjia Road, Xiaoshizi and Hongqihegou. Gaojia Garden Bridge is an important bridge in Chongqing. Minjia Road is a crossroads in the Nan'an District of Chongqing. Xiaoshizi and Hongqihegou are two important rail transit hubs in Chongqing. Firstly, we adjust some important parameters of the model, and analyze the impact of different parameter combinations on predictive performance. And then we analyze the model performance for the four places. Finally, we compare our model with some classical predicting models.

4.1 Parameter Adjustment

To obtain the optimal model, understanding the influence of different parameter combinations on the model performance is critical. This section shows how performance varies from different choices of parameters. The parameters include the number of trees N and the learning rate lr. We fitted the DSTGBRT using different numbers of trees (1–2000) and various learning rates (0.01–0.5) to training data. To evaluate the performance of a DSTGBRT model that combines various parameters, we introduced the mean absolute percentage error (MAPE) as an indicator. The definition of the MAPE is as Eq. (16).

$$MAPE = 100\% \times \frac{1}{n}\sum_{i=1}^{n} \frac{|l_{pv,i} - l_{true,i}|}{l_{true,i}} \tag{16}$$

Where $l_{pv,i}$ denotes the flow prediction for a point at some future time and $l_{true,i}$ is the true flow.

Figure 2 demonstrate the influence of various parameters including the number of trees (N) and the learning rate (lr) on the flow prediction errors using the MAPE. Theoretically, higher prediction accuracy can be achieved by increasing the number of trees in the model. When there are too many trees, overfitting may occur. MAPE decreases as the number of regression trees increases, up to a certain value. The slopes of the plotted curves vary with different learning rates lr. The curve for $lr = 0.01$ has the smallest slope. It reaches a minimum, with $N = 500$. The curves corresponding to higher learning rates decline more quickly and quickly reach the minimum MAPE using basic trees.

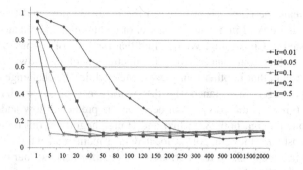

Fig. 2. The relationship between MAPE and number of trees with different learning rate

4.2 Prediction Result

To verify the feasibility of our model for predicting traffic flow, we obtained ERI data in Chongqing from 1 March 2016 to 31 March 2016. The data on 25 March 2016 was used as test data, and the rest data is training data. Our model predicts flow of one segment (that is 15 min) after the present time. Figures 3, 4, 5 and 6 reveals the comparison of the predicted flow and true flow. In these figures, the abscissa is the index of time segment and the ordinate is the flow.

Figure 3 reveals the comparison between the true flow and the predicted flow of the Gaojia Garden Bridge. Overall, the performance of this model is better than that in Caiyuanba Yangtze River Bridge with the PAME is 4.8%. There are many vehicles passing through in rush hour and the performance of the model is always good even though when there are fewer vehicles in the early hours of the morning.

Figure 4 reveals the comparison between the predicted flow and true flow of the Mingjia Road. Different from the bridge, Minjia Road is a crossroads and vehicles will pass in four directions. We found that there is a large fluctuation in flow during the day, with a range from 20 to 680 throughout the day. Overall, the performance of this model is very good with the MAPE is 5.2%. There are two peak values in the morning and in the afternoon.

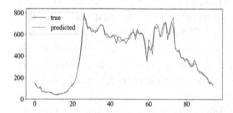

Fig. 3. Comparisons between predicted value and expected value of Gaojia Garden Bridge with MAPE 4.8%

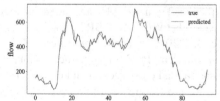

Fig. 4. Comparisons between predicted value and expected value of Mingjia Road with MAPE 5.2%

Figure 5 reveals the comparison between the predicted flow and true flow of the Xiaoshizi which is Located in Yuzhong District of Chongqing and Yuzhong District is the most congested in Chongqing. We can find that the flow of Xiaoshizi is obviously less than that in other four places. And the fluctuation of the flow in one hour is obviously bigger than that in other four places. Meanwhile, the challenge of predicting its flow is much bigger. Simultaneously, the performance of our model is not good enough. Figure 6 reveals the comparison between the predicted flow and true flow of the Hongqihegou. Though both Xiaoshizi and Hongqihegou are rail transit hubs, different from Xiaoshizi, Hongqihegou is located in a main road whose road width is wider than road in Xiaoshizi. So it is normal that the performance of our model is better than that is used in Xiaoshizi.

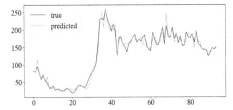 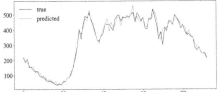

Fig. 5. Comparisons between predicted value and expected value of Xiaoshizi with MAPE 7.81%

Fig. 6. Comparisons between predicted value and expected value of Hongqihegou with MAPE 6.12%

4.3   Model Comparison

To test the performance of DSTGBRT, we compared the predictive performance of DSTGBRT with that of the ARIMA and Spatio-temporal Gradient-boosted Regression Tree (STGBRT) method in terms of their absolute percentage errors (MAPE). The ARIMA model is a generalization of the autoregressive moving average (ARMA) model and is one of the most widely recognized methods for traffic parameter forecasting. ARIMA is applied in cases where data show evidence of non-stationarity. It converts non-stationary time series to stationary time series. The model is constructed using the dependent variable, its lag value, and the present value of the random error; predictions from ARIMA are based on regression of current and past data. The difference between STGBRT method and DSTGBRT is the feature vector. The DSTGBRT proposed by us considers all of the adjacent road cross-section and their different PCC to construct feature vector, but STGBRT just considers one upstream road cross-section and one downstream road cross-section and the PCC is not used for the feature vector.

To compare these three methods for predicting traffic flow, we obtained ERI data in Chongqing from 1 March 2016 to 31 March 2016. The data on 25 March 2016 was used as test data to compare the prediction performance among the three models (DSTGBRT, STGBRT and ARIMA). The prediction accuracy of these three models was compared based on their predicting one segment (that is 15 min) after the present time. For ARIMA and STGBRT, we tested different combinations of variables during the training process and selected the parameters that achieved the minimum MAPE values. The line charts in Figs. 7, 8, 9, 10 illustrate the variation among predictions from the three models, respectively. The black line in the two figures represents the true traffic flow, while the red line represents prediction results from the ARIMA model, the green line represents the prediction from STGBRT and the purple line represents the prediction results from the DSTGBRT model. As shown, the DSTGBRT model fit the true traffic flow most closely. ARIMA provided the least favorable match to the true traffic flow among the three models. Under the same conditions, the predictions of DSTGBRT outperform in our experiments. Figure 11 shows a comparison of the MAPE values for the performance of these three models for predictions in different places. As illustrated in Fig. 11, the prediction results of DSTGBRT outperformed those of the other two models in Gaojia Garden. The MAPE for DSTGBRT (4.8%) was superior to the MAPE values for STGBRT and ARIMA, which were 9.1% and 16.7%, respectively.

Fig. 7. Comparisons of prediction for one day in Gaojia Garden Bridge (Color figure online)

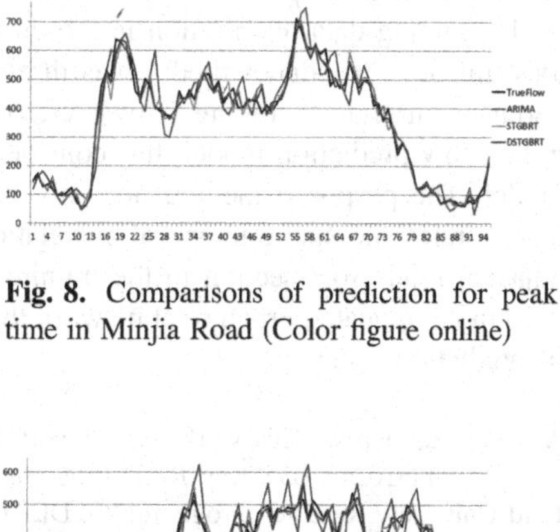

Fig. 8. Comparisons of prediction for peak time in Minjia Road (Color figure online)

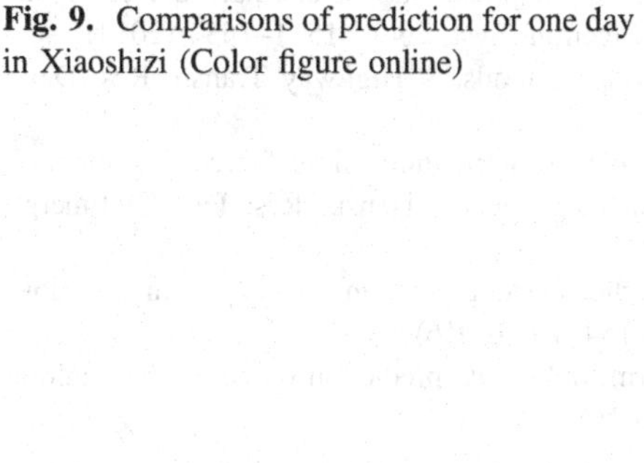

Fig. 9. Comparisons of prediction for one day in Xiaoshizi (Color figure online)

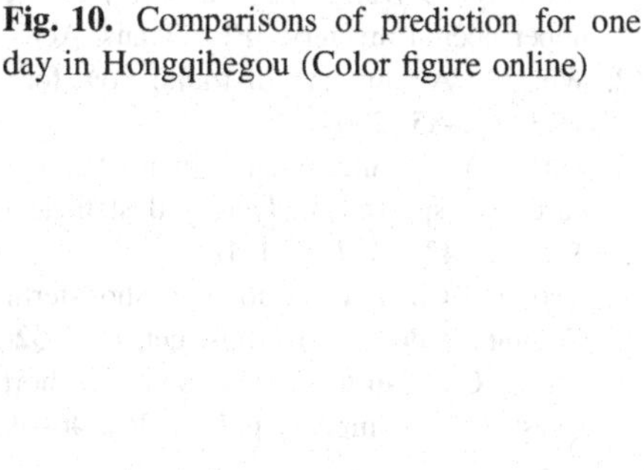

Fig. 10. Comparisons of prediction for one day in Hongqihegou (Color figure online)

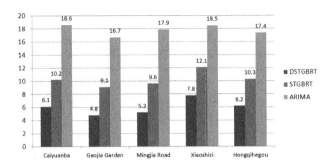

Fig. 11. Comparisons of MAPEs

5 Discussion and Conclusions

Our DSTGBRT model has characteristics that make it different from traditional ensemble methods, such as the random forest and bagged trees approaches, as well as classical statistical approaches. And it grows trees sequentially by adjusting the weight of the training data distribution in the direction of "steepest descent" to minimize the loss function. It reduces model bias through forward stepwise modeling and reduces variance through averaging. However, our proposed method, the DSTGBRT-based traffic flow prediction model, has considerable advantages over the traditional GBRT model. The proposed method not only uses the "steepest descent" method but also incorporates the spatio-temporal correlation between a target road cross-section and adjacent road cross-section in the training data. Thus, it delivers higher performance used in complicated urban road network than the ARIMA or STGBRT models in terms of prediction accuracy.

Acknowledgments. This work was supported by the National Key R&D Program of China (No. 2017YFC0212103), Key R&D Program of Chongqing (No. cstc2018jszx-cyztzxX0019), Ford University Research Program (No. DEPT2018-J030.1).

References

1. Chen, S.Y., Wang, Y., Wu, C.C.: Real-time causal processing of anomaly detection for hyperspectral imagery. IEEE Trans. Aerosp. Electron. Syst. **50**(2), 1511–1534 (2014)
2. Wei, G.: A summary of traffic flow forecasting methods. J. Highway Transp. Res. Dev. **21**(3), 82–85 (2004)
3. Zhang, Y., Zhang, Y., Haghani, A.: A hybrid short-term traffic flow forecasting method based on spectral analysis and statistical volatility model. Transp. Res. Part C: Emerg. Technol. **43**, 65–78 (2014)
4. Yao, B., Chen, C., Cao, Q.: Short-term traffic speed prediction for an urban corridor. Comput.-Aided Civil Infrastruct. Eng. **32**(2), 154–169 (2016)
5. Zheng, C., Xianfu, C.: The model of short term traffic flow prediction based on the random forest. Microcomput. Appl. **35**(10), 46–49 (2016)

6. Zhang, Y., Haghani, A.: A gradient boosting method to improve travel time prediction. Transportation Research Part C: Emerging Technologies **58**, 308–324 (2015)
7. Faming, Z.: Urban link travel time prediction based on a gradient boosting method considering spatiotemporal correlations. ISPRS Int. J. Geo-Inf. **5**(11), 201–229 (2016)
8. Ding, C., Wang, D., Ma, X.: Predicting short-term subway ridership and prioritizing its influential factors using gradient boosting decision trees. Sustainability **8**(11), 1100–1115 (2016)
9. Polikar, R.: Ensemble based systems in decision making. IEEE Circuits Syst. Mag. **6**(3), 21–45 (2006)
10. Soper, H.E., Young, A.W., Cave, B.M., Lee, A., Pearson, K.: On the distribution of the correlation coefficient in small samples. Appendix II to the papers of Student. Biometrika **11**, 328–413 (1917)
11. Liu, Y., Kang, C., Gao, S., Xiao, Y., Tian, Y.: Understanding intra-urban trip patterns from taxi trajectory data. J. Geogr. Syst. **14**, 463–483 (2012)
12. Liu, X., Gong, L., Gong, Y., Liu, Y.: Revealing travel patterns and city structure with taxi trip data. J. Transp. Geogr. **43**, 78–90 (2013)
13. Zhang, F., Zhu, X., Guo, W., Ye, X., Hu, T., Huang, L.: Analyzing urban human mobility patterns through a thematic model at a finer scale. ISPRS Int. J, Geo-Inf (2016)

A Trust Network Model Based on Hesitant Fuzzy Linguistic Term Sets

Jieyu Zhan[1], Yuncheng Jiang[1(✉)], Wenjun Ma[1], Xudong Luo[2], and Weiru Liu[3]

[1] School of Computer Science, South China Normal University, Guangzhou, China
ycjiang@scnu.edu.cn
[2] Department of Information and Management Science, Guangxi Normal University, Guilin, China
[3] School of Computer Science, Electrical and Electronic Engineering, and Engineering Maths, University of Bristol, Bristol, UK

Abstract. Trust evaluation in a network is important in many areas, such as group decision-making and recommendation in e-commerce. Hence, researchers have proposed various trust network models, in which each agent rates the trustworthiness of others. Most of the existing work require the agents to provide accurate degrees of trust and distrust in advance. However, humans usually hesitate to choose one among several values to assess the trust in another person and tend to express the trust through linguistic descriptions. Hence, this paper proposes a novel trust network model that takes linguistic expression of trust into consideration. More specifically, we structure trust scores based on hesitant fuzzy linguistic term sets and give a comparison method. Moreover, we propose a trust propagation method based on the concept of computing with words to deal with trust relationships between indirectly connected agents, and such a method satisfies some intuitive properties of trust propagation. Finally, we confirm the advantages of our model by comparing it with related work.

Keywords: Trust network · Trust propagation ·
Hesitant fuzzy linguistic term sets · Concatenation operator ·
Aggregation operator

1 Introduction

Trust between people is one of the most important factors that influence people's decision making. For example, in the group decision-making problem, the trust relationships between experts can be considered as a reliable source about the importance of the experts [3,6,13,14]. Also, in e-commerce, consumers often know very little about providers of goods or services, but they can choose providers through the recommendations of the people who they trust [7]. Trust relationships in offline communities are often based on face-to-face social experiences. However, the evaluation of trust between users in online social communities should be done through an efficient computational model because of the

© Springer Nature Switzerland AG 2019
C. Douligeris et al. (Eds.): KSEM 2019, LNAI 11776, pp. 284–297, 2019.
https://doi.org/10.1007/978-3-030-29563-9_26

lack of direct communication between users [9]. Therefore, various trust network models in which each agent rates the trustworthiness of others have been proposed to describe the trust relationships between users [1,4,11].

One of the main issues in the study of trust networks is how to assess the degree to which one agent trusts in another [10]. In most studies, trust is often expressed by accurate numerical values. Nevertheless, these representations cannot reflect well the uncertainty of trust. On the one hand, in real life, because of the different ways of obtaining information, a person may hesitate to choose one among several values to assess the trust in another person. On the other hand, people are more likely to use linguistic descriptions to express their trust. Hence, the uncertainty of assessing trust is also expressed as the ambiguity of language [8]. However, the current representations of trust are often quantitative, which are not always the case in real life. Since online social networks are usually larger than offline social circles, it is difficult for an agent to establish direct trust with some agents. More often, trust relationships between two agents are indirect. Hence, how to infer the trust relationship among indirectly connected agents is an important problem that needs to be solved. However, most of the current trust propagation methods are limited to the quantitative trust score expression, rather than vague linguistic descriptions ones [2,10,14].

To tackle the above problems, this paper firstly will propose a novel trust model that takes linguistic expression of trust into consideration. Then, after introducing the concept of hesitant fuzzy linguistic term set (HFLTS) based trust model, we will propose a new method to compare different trust scores based on HFLTS. Further, we will propose a trust propagation mechanism to evaluate trust between two indirectly connected agents.

The main contributions of this paper can be summarized as follows. (1) We propose a trust model based on hesitant fuzzy linguistic term set to better reflect the uncertainty and ambiguity of trust. (2) For indirectly connected agents in trust networks, we propose a trust propagation method based on computing with word methodology to deal with new expression of trust.

The rest of this paper is organised as follows. Firstly we recap the basic concepts and notations about hesitant fuzzy linguistic term sets. Then we propose trust score based on HFLTS and their comparison. Next we present two operators in trust propagation mechanism and reveal some properties of the operators. Finally we discuss the related work and draw our conclusion of the paper.

2   Preliminaries

Human usually use linguistic terms for modeling performance evaluations, such as the word *low, medium, high* and so on. The linguistic term set (LTS) can be defined as an ordered structure providing the term set that is distributed on a scale on which a total order is defined [15]. Taking a linguistic term set with seven terms, S, as an example, it could be given as follows:

$$S = \{s_0(\text{nothing}), s_1(\text{very low}), s_2(\text{low}), s_3(\text{medium}), s_4(\text{high}), s_5(\text{very high}), s_6(\text{perfect})\}.$$

And the following additional characteristics should be satisfied:

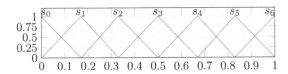

Fig. 1. Membership functions of linguistic terms

(a) negation operator: $\text{neg}(s_i) = s_j$ so that $j = g - i$ ($g + 1$ is the granularity of the term set);
(b) maximisation operator: $\max(s_i, s_j) = s_i$ if $s_i \geq s_j$; and
(c) minimisation operator: $\min(s_i, s_j) = s_i$ if $s_i \leq s_j$.

In this paper, we assign each linguistic term s_i with a triangular membership function as its semantics, which can be represented as $s_i = (a, b, c)$ (a, b and c are parameters of the membership function), because this type of membership function can not only express the ambiguity of linguistic terms, but also reduce the complexity of later calculation about computing with word. More specifically, their semantics can be graphically represented by Fig. 1, where $s_0 = (0, 0, 0.17)$, $s_1 = (0, 0.17, 0.33)$, $s_2 = (0.17, 0.33, 0.5)$, $s_3 = (0.33, 0.5, 0.67)$, $s_4 = (0.5, 0.67, 0.83)$, $s_5 = (0.67, 0.83, 1)$, and $s_6 = (0.83, 1, 1)$.

A linguistic variable represents a variable whose values are words or sentences. For example, *age* is a linguistic variable if its values are linguistic, such as *young*, *not young* and so on [16], and we can also regard *trust* as a linguistic variable. However, in some situation, people may hesitate to choose one among several values to assign to linguistic variable. To this end, the concept of *hesitant fuzzy linguistic term sets* (HFLTSs) is introduced as follows [8]:

Definition 1. *Let S be a linguistic term set, $S = \{s_0, \ldots, s_g\}$, an HFLTS, denoted as h_S, is an ordered finite subset of the consecutive linguistic terms of S. The set of all HFLTSs based on the S is denoted by H_S.*

Example 1. Let $S = \{s_0(\text{nothing}), s_1(\text{very low}), s_2(\text{low}), s_3(\text{medium}), s_4(\text{high}), s_5(\text{very high}), s_6(\text{perfect})\}$ be a linguistic term set, then $h_S^1 = \{s_1(\text{very low}), s_2(\text{low}), s_3(\text{medium})\}$ and $h_S^2 = \{s_3(\text{medium}), s_4(\text{high}), s_5(\text{very high})\}$ are both HFLTSs.

As the expression of HFLTS is still not natural enough, a context-free grammar approach is proposed to generate linguistic term sets [8].

Definition 2. *Let* $G_H = (V_N, V_T, I, P)$ *be a context-free grammar, and* $S = \{s_0, \ldots, s_g\}$ *be a linguistic term set. The elements of* G_H *are defined as follows:*

- $V_N = \{<primary\ term>, <composite\ term>, <unary\ relation>, <binary\ relation>, <conjunction>\};$
- $V_T = \{lower\ than,\ greater\ than,\ at\ least,\ at\ most,\ between,\ and,\ s_0, s_1, \ldots, s_g\};$
- $I \in V_N;$
- $P = \{I ::= <primary\ term> \mid <composite\ term>$
  $<composite\ term> ::= <unary\ relation> <primary\ term> \mid <binary\ relation>$
  $<primary\ term> <conjunction> <primary\ term>$
  $<primary\ term> ::= s_0 | s_1 | \ldots | s_g$
  $<unary\ relation> ::= lower\ than | greater\ than | at\ least | at\ most$
  $<binary\ relation> ::= between$
  $<conjunction> ::= and\},$

where the brackets enclose optional elements and the symbol | indicates alternative elements.

Example 2. Let S be the same as that in Example 1. The following linguistic information (denoted as ll) can be obtained by the context-free grammar G_H, such as $ll_1 =$ very low, $ll_2 =$ lower than medium, $ll_3 =$ between low and high.

The following definition [8] transforms the linguistic expressions produced by G_H into HFLTSs.

Definition 3. *Let* S_{ll} *be the set of linguistic expressions* ll *produced by* G_H, H_S *be the set of HFLTSs,* $E_{G_H} : S_{ll} \to H_S$ *be a function that transforms linguistic expressions into HFLTSs, the linguistic expressions* $ll \in S_{ll}$ *are transformed into HFLTSs in different ways according to their meanings:*

- $E_{G_H}(s_i) = \{s_i \mid s_i \in S\};$
- $E_{G_H}(less\ than\ s_i) = \{s_j \mid s_j \in S\ and\ s_j < s_i\};$
- $E_{G_H}(greater\ than\ s_i) = \{s_j \mid s_j \in S\ and\ s_j > s_i\};$
- $E_{G_H}(at\ least\ s_i) = \{s_j \mid s_j \in S\ and\ s_j \geq s_i\};$
- $E_{G_H}(at\ most\ s_i) = \{s_j \mid s_j \in S\ and\ s_j \leq s_i\};$
- $E_{G_H}(between\ s_i\ and\ s_j) = \{s_k \mid s_k \in S\ and\ s_i \leq s_k \leq s_j\}.$

Next, we recall the concept of uninorm operator.

Definition 4. *A binary operator* $\uplus: [0,1] \times [0,1] \to [0,1]$ *is a uninorm operator that satisfies increasing, associative and commutative properties, and there exists* $\tau \in [0,1]$, *s.t.*

$$\forall a \in [0,1], a \uplus \tau = a, \tag{1}$$

where τ *is said to be the unit element of a uninorm.*

3 Trust and Distrust Modeling in Trust Networks

In this section, we will discuss how to model the trust and distrust degree in trust network, and how to compare different trust scores based on HFLTS.

3.1 Trust and Distrust Assessment

Definition 5. *A trust network is a 3-tuple (A, E, R), where*

- *A is the set of agents in the network;*
- *E is the set of trust connections (x, y), where agents x, y ∈ A; and*
- *R is a function E → T, where R(x, y) is called the trust score of agent x in agent y and T is the set of trust scores.*

A trust network assigns scores for pairs of agents reflecting the opinions of agents about each other. In order to be close to the use of natural language, we use linguistic expressions to represent trust scores.

Definition 6. *Given S_t as a linguistic term set of trust and S_d as a linguistic term set of distrust, a trust score defined in Definition 5 is a pair (t, d), where*

- *$t \in S_{ll_t}$ is a trust degree, where S_{ll_t} is the set of linguistic expressions of trust produced by G_H with S_t.*
- *$d \in S_{ll_d}$ is a distrust degree, where S_{ll_d} is the set of linguistic expressions of distrust produced by G_H with S_d.*

Example 3. Let x and y be two directly connected agents in the trust network,

$$S_t = \{s_0(\text{no trust}), s_1(\text{very low trust}), s_2(\text{low trust}), s_3(\text{medium trust}),$$
$$s_4(\text{high trust}), s_5(\text{very high trust}), s_6(\text{complete trust})\} \text{ and}$$
$$S_d = \{s_0'(\text{no distrust}), s_1'(\text{very low distrust}), s_2'(\text{low distrust}), s_3'(\text{medium distrust}),$$
$$s_4'(\text{high distrust}), s_5'(\text{very high distrust}), s_6'(\text{complete distrust})\}$$

be a linguistic term set of trust and a linguistic term set of distrust, respectively, then the trust relationship between x and y can be represented as follows:

- $R(x, y) = $ (greater than medium trust, low distrust), and
- $R(y, x) = $ (low trust, at least high distrust).

According to Definition 3, the trust scores in Example 3 can be transformed into the following expressions:

- $R(x, y) = $ ({high trust,very high trust, complete trust}, {low distrust}), and
- $R(y, x) = $ ({low trust}, {high distrust, very high distrust, complete distrust}).

3.2 Comparison of Trust Score

For an agent in the network, how to select a more trusted agent in the same network is one of the most important issues. Hence we present a method for comparison. Since the two components of trust score, trust degree and distrust degree, can be transforms into HFLTS in our model, we use h_{S_t} and h_{S_d} to represent the trust degree and distrust degree, respectively. Such two dimensions should be considered when comparing trust scores. The intuition is that the higher the trust degree and the lower the distrust degree, the higher trust scores for another agent. Since both trust and distrust degrees are represented by HFLTSs, we first need a method of comparing HFLTSs. Formally, we have:

Definition 7. *Given two HFLTSs h_S^1 and h_S^2, the dominance degree of h_S^1 to h_S^2 is defined as follows:*

$$D(h_S^1, h_S^2) = \sum_{s_i^1 \in h_S^1} \|\{s_i^2 \in h_S^2\} \mid s_i^1 \geq s_i^2\|, \tag{2}$$

where $\|S\|$ is the cardinality of set S.

The above definition means when the elements in the both HFLTSs are compared in pairs, the number of undominanted pairs is used as the dominance degree of one set to the other.

We present a method for comparison as follows:

Definition 8. *Given $R(x,y) = (h_{S_t}^1, h_{S_d}^1)$, and $R(x,z) = (h_{S_t}^2, h_{S_d}^2)$, $R(x,y) \geq R(x,z)$ if $D(h_{S_t}^1, h_{S_t}^2) \geq D(h_{S_t}^2, h_{S_t}^1)$ and $D(h_{S_d}^2, h_{S_d}^1) \geq D(h_{S_d}^1, h_{S_d}^2)$.*

The above definition means that for two trust scores, if one's trust degree is not lower than the other's and the distrust degree is not higher than the other's, then this trust score is not lower than the other trust score. Next we reveal some properties of this method. Firstly, we introduce the concepts of upper bound and lower bound of HFLTS.

Definition 9. *The upper bound h_{S+} and lower bound h_{S-} of the HFLTS h_S are defined as follows:*

- $h_{S+} = \max(s_i) = s_j, \forall s_i \in h_S, s_i \leq s_j$;
- $h_{S-} = \min(s_i) = s_j, \forall s_i \in h_S, s_i \geq s_j$.

The following theorem states that when all the linguistic terms of trust degree in a trust score are not lower than any linguistic terms of the other's and all the linguistic terms of distrust degree are not higher than any linguistic terms of the other's, then the trust score is definitely not lower than the other one.

Theorem 1 (Complete Domination). *Given $R(x,y) = (h_{S_t}^1, h_{S_d}^1)$, and $R(x,z) = (h_{S_t}^2, h_{S_d}^2)$, if $h_{S_t}^1 \geq h_{S_t}^2$ and $h_{S_d}^1 \leq h_{S_d}^2$, then $R(x,y) \geq R(x,z)$.*

Proof. Because $h_{S_t}^1 \geq h_{S_t}^2$ and $h_{S_d}^1 \leq h_{S_d}^2$, then $\forall(s_i^1, s_j^1) \in h_{S_t}^1 \times h_{S_d}^1, \forall(s_i^2, s_j^2) \in h_{S_t}^2 \times h_{S_d}^2, s_i^1 \geq s_i^2$ and $s_j^1 \leq s_j^2$. By formula (2), we have:

$$D(h_{S_t}^1, h_{S_t}^2) = \sum_{s_i^1 \in h_{S_t}^1} \|\{s_i^2 \in h_{S_t}^2\} \mid s_i^1 \geq s_i^2\| = \|h_{S_t}^1\| \cdot \|h_{S_t}^2\|,$$

$$D(h_{S_t}^2, h_{S_t}^1) = \begin{cases} 1 & \text{if } h_{S_t}^1 = h_{S_t}^2, \\ 0 & \text{otherwise.} \end{cases}$$

Hence, $D(h_{S_t}^1, h_{S_t}^2) \geq D(h_{S_t}^2, h_{S_t}^1)$. Similarly, we have

$$D(h_{S_d}^2, h_{S_d}^1) = \|h_{S_d}^1\| \cdot \|h_{S_d}^2\|,$$

$$D(h_{S_d}^1, h_{S_d}^2) = \begin{cases} 1 & \text{if } h_{S_d^+}^1 = h_{S_d^-}^2, \\ 0 & \text{otherwise.} \end{cases}$$

Hence, $D(h_{S_d}^2, h_{S_d}^1) \geq D(h_{S_d}^1, h_{S_d}^2)$. According to Definition 8, we have $R(x,y) \geq R(x,z)$. □

The following theorem reveals the monotonicity of trust score.

Theorem 2 (Monotonicity). *Given* $S_t = \{s_0^1, \ldots, s_{N-1}^1\}, S_d = \{s_0^2, \ldots, s_{M-1}^2\}, R(x,y) = (h_{S_t}, h_{S_d})$, *where*

$$h_{S_t} = \{s_k^1, s_{k+1}^1, \ldots, s_{k+n-1}^1\}, 0 \leq k \leq N - n,$$
$$h_{S_d} = \{s_g^2, s_{g+1}^2, \ldots, s_{g+m-1}^2\}, 0 \leq g \leq M - m,$$

where N, M, n *and* m *are the cardinality of* S_t, S_d, h_{S_t} *and* h_{S_d}, *respectively. Let* $R^1(x,y) = (h_{S_t}', h_{S_d})$, $R^2(x,y) = (h_{S_t}, h_{S_d}')$, $R^3(x,y) = (h_{S_t}'', h_{S_d})$, $R^4(x,y) = (h_{S_t}, h_{S_d}'')$, *in which*

$$h_{S_t}' = \{s_k^1, s_{k+1}^1, \ldots, s_{k+n}^1 \mid k + n \leq N - 1\},$$
$$h_{S_d}' = \{s_{g-1}^2, s_g^2, \ldots, s_{g+m-1}^2 \mid g - 1 \geq 0\},$$
$$h_{S_t}'' = \{s_{k-1}^1, s_k^1, \ldots, s_{k+n-1}^1 \mid k - 1 \geq 0\},$$
$$h_{S_d}'' = \{s_g^2, s_{g+1}^2, \ldots, s_{g+m}^2 \mid g + m \leq M - 1\},$$

then (1) $R^1(x,y) \geq R(x,y)$, *(2)* $R^2(x,y) \geq R(x,y)$, *(3)* $R(x,y) \geq R^3(x,y)$, *and (4)* $R(x,y) \geq R^4(x,y)$.

Proof. (1) Because $\forall s_i^2 \in h_{S_t}, s_{k+n}^1 > s_i^2$, we have

$$D(h_{S_t}', h_{S_t})$$
$$= D(h_{S_t}, h_{S_t}) + \|\{s_j^2 \in h_{S_d}\} \mid s_{k+n}^1 \geq s_j^2\|$$
$$= D(h_{S_t}, h_{S_t}) + \|h_{S_t}\|,$$

and

$$D(h_{S_t}, h_{S_t}') = D(h_{S_t}, h_{S_t}).$$

Hence, $D(h_{S_t}', h_{S_t}) \geq D(h_{S_t}, h_{S_t}')$. Because $D(h_{S_d}, h_{S_d}) \geq D(h_{S_d}, h_{S_d})$, by Definition 8, we have $R^1(x,y) \geq R(x,y)$. Similarly, the other situations (2), (3) and (4) can be proved. □

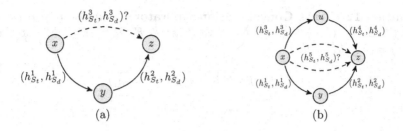

Fig. 2. Trust propagation in a trust network

4   Trust Propagation Method

In this section, we propose a trust propagation method that can be used in HFLTS based trust model. It consists of two important components: one is used to propagate the trust score along a path in the trust network that connects two indirectly connected agents with trusted third agents (see Fig. 2(a)); and the other one is used to aggregate the assessments in different trust paths, because there may be multiple paths to access the same indirectly connected agent (see Fig. 2(b)). Hence, we define two operators: concatenation operator $\otimes$ and aggregation operator $\oplus$, to solve the above problems, respectively. Finally, we evaluate the trust propagation method and reveal some properties of the operators.

4.1   Concatenation Operator

Definition 10. *Given two triangular membership functions of linguistic terms $s_1 = (a_1, b_1, c_1)$ and $s_2 = (a_2, b_2, c_2)$, the aggregation of s_1 and s_2, denoted as s_3 in a linguistic term set S, is defined as $s_3 = app_S(s_3{}')$, where*

$$s_3{}' = s_1 \diamond s_2 = (a_1 \cdot a_2, b_1 \cdot b_2, c_1 \cdot c_2), \tag{3}$$

and $app_S(s_i)$ is a linguistic approximation process, which is used to select a linguistic term $s^\star$ in S that has minimum distance to s_i, i.e., $\forall s_j \in S, d(s^\star, s_i) \leq d(s_j, s_i)$, where $d()$ is the distance between two membership functions.

We adopt Euclidean distance in this paper, which is defined as follows:

Definition 11. *Give $s_i = (a_i, b_i, c_i)$ and $s_j = (a_j, b_j, c_j)$,*

$$d(s_j, s_i) = \sqrt{p_1(a_i - a_j)^2 + p_2(b_i - b_j)^2 + p_3(c_i - c_j)^2}, \tag{4}$$

where p_i ($i \in \{1, 2, 3\}$) measures the representativeness of parameters of membership functions. We set $p_1 = 0.1$, $p_2 = 0.8$ and $p_3 = 0.1$, because for a triangular membership function $s = (a, b, c)$, b is the most representative component.

Definition 12 (Trust Concatenation Operator). *Suppose in a trust network (A, E, R), $(x, y), (y, z) \in E$, while $(x, z) \notin E$, $R(x, y) = (h^1_{S_t}, h^1_{S_d})$ and $R(y, z) = (h^2_{S_t}, h^2_{S_d})$, then*

$$(h^3_{S_t}, h^3_{S_d}) = (h^1_{S_t}, h^1_{S_d}) \otimes (h^2_{S_t}, h^2_{S_d})$$

where

$$h^3_{S_t^+} = apps_t(h^1_{S_t^+} \diamond h^2_{S_t^+}), h^3_{S_t^-} = apps_t(h^1_{S_t^-} \diamond h^2_{S_t^-}),$$
$$h^3_{S_d^+} = apps_d(h^1_{S_t^+} \diamond h^2_{S_d^+}), h^3_{S_d^-} = apps_d(h^1_{S_t^-} \diamond h^2_{S_d^-}),$$

with $\otimes$ is a concatenation operator.

Example 4. Given the semantics of linguistic term sets of trust and distrust, S_t and S_d as in Example 3 with membership functions as in Fig. 1, and a trust network as shown in Fig. 2(a), in which agents x and y are connected, y and z are connected, while x and z are indirectly connected, $R(x, y) = (h^1_{S_t}, h^1_{S_d}), R(y, z) = (h^2_{S_t}, h^2_{S_d})$, where $h^1_{S_t} = \{s_4, s_5\}$, $h^1_{S_d} = \{s'_0, s'_1\}$, $h^2_{S_t} = \{s_5\}$, and $h^2_{S_d} = \{s'_2, s'_3\}$, we can evaluate the trust of x in z based on concatenation operator $\otimes$.

Now we see how to calculate the trust score $R(x, y) = (h^3_{S_t}, h^3_{S_d})$. Specifically, we should calculate the upper bounds and lower bounds of $h^3_{S_t}$ and $h^3_{S_d}$, respectively. We take $h^3_{S_t^+}$ as an example. By formula (3), we have

$$h^{3'}_{S_t^+} = h^1_{S_t^+} \diamond h^2_{S_t^+} = s_5 \diamond s_5 = (0.67 \cdot 0.67, 0.83 \cdot 0.83, 1 \cdot 1) = (0.4489, 0.6889, 1).$$

By formula (4), we have

$$d(s_6, h^{3'}_{S_t^+}) = \sqrt{0.1(0.83 - 0.4489)^2 + 0.8(1 - 0.6889)^2 + 0.1(1 - 1)^2} = 0.3032.$$

Similarly, we can obtain

$$d(s_5, h^{3'}_{S_t^+}) = 0.1443, d(s_4, h^{3'}_{S_t^+}) = 0.0586, d(s_3, h^{3'}_{S_t^+}) = 0.2021,$$
$$d(s_2, h^{3'}_{S_t^+}) = 0.3685, d(s_1, h^{3'}_{S_t^+}) = 0.5296, d(s_0, h^{3'}_{S_t^+}) = 0.6846.$$

Hence, $h^3_{S_t^+} = apps_t(h^{3'}_{S_t^+}) = s_4$. Similarly, we can obtain $h^3_{S_t^-} = apps_t(s_4 \diamond s_5) = s_3$, $h^3_{S_d^+} = apps_d(s_5 \diamond s'_3) = s'_3$, and $h^3_{S_d^-} = apps_d(s_4 \diamond s'_2) = s'_1$, then $R(x, z) = (\{s_3, s_4\}, \{s'_1, s'_2, s'_3\})$.

From the results we can see that compared with the trust degrees and distrust degrees of x in y and y in z, those of x in z decrease slightly. This is similar to our intuition that as agents' distance increases, the degree of trust will decrease.

4.2   Aggregation Operator

There may be more than one path to propagate trust scores from an agent to an indirectly connected agent in a trust network. Therefore, we need a method that aggregates the trust scores passed through different trust paths to have an overall understanding of the unknown agent.

When aggregating different trust scores, it is necessary to conform to such intuitions: when an agent obtains high degrees of trust through different trust paths, its trust in the unknown agent should be strengthened; when the results obtained are low degrees of trust, its trust in the unknown agent should be weakened; and when the results obtained are in conflict, the aggregated one is a compromise. Hence, when aggregating several triangular membership functions of linguistic terms in the aggregation phase, we employ a uninorm operator to aggregate the parameters of membership functions. Formally, we have:

Definition 13. *Given n triangular membership functions of linguistic terms $s_i = (a_i, b_i, c_i), i \in \{1, \ldots, n\}$, the aggregation of these linguistic terms, denoted as s in a linguistic term set S, is defined as $s = apps_S(s')$, where*

$$s' = \blacktriangle_{i=1}^{n} s^i = (a_1 \uplus_1 a_2 \uplus_1 \cdots \uplus_1 a_n, b_1 \uplus_2 b_2 \uplus_2 \cdots \uplus_2 b_n, c_1 \uplus_3 c_2 \uplus_3 \cdots \uplus_3 c_n), \quad (5)$$

where $\uplus_i$ is give by:

$$x \uplus_i y = \begin{cases} 0.5 & \text{if } (x,y) = (1,0) \text{ or } (x,y) = (0,1), \\ \frac{(1-\tau_i)xy}{(1-\tau_i)xy + \tau_i(1-x)(1-y)} & \text{otherwise,} \end{cases}$$

and $apps_S(s_i)$ is the same as that in Definition 10.

Definition 14 (Trust Aggregation Operator). *Suppose in a trust network (A, E, R), $(x, y) \notin E$, while there are n paths to propagate trust from x to y, and the propagation results are $R^{path_i}(x, y) = (h_{S_t}^{path_i}, h_{S_d}^{path_i}), i \in \{1, \ldots, n\}$, the aggregation of trust scores along all paths, denoted as $R(x, y) = (h_{S_t}, h_{S_d})$, is given by:*

$$(h_{S_t}, h_{S_d}) = \otimes_{i=1}^{n}(h_{S_t}^{path_i}, h_{S_d}^{path_i})$$

where

$$h_{S_t^+} = apps_{S_t}(\blacktriangle_{i=1}^{n} h_{S_t^+}^{path_i}), h_{S_t^-} = apps_{S_t}(\blacktriangle_{i=1}^{n} h_{S_t^-}^{path_i}),$$
$$h_{S_d^+} = apps_{S_d}(\blacktriangle_{i=1}^{n} h_{S_d^+}^{path_i}), h_{S_d^-} = apps_{S_d}(\blacktriangle_{i=1}^{n} h_{S_d^-}^{path_i})$$

with $\oplus$ is a aggregation operator.

Example 5. Given the semantics of linguistic term sets of trust and distrust, S_t and S_d as in Example 3 with membership functions as in Fig. 1, and a trust network (A, E, R) as shown in Fig. 2(b), in which $(x, y), (y, z), (x, u), (u, z) \in E$, while $(x, z) \notin E$, and $\tau_1 = 0.33, \tau_2 = 0.5, \tau_3 = 0.67$, let $R(x, y) = (h_{S_t}^1, h_{S_d}^1)$, $R(y, z) = (h_{S_t}^2, h_{S_d}^2)$, $R(x, u) = (h_{S_t}^3, h_{S_d}^3)$, $R(u, z) = (h_{S_t}^4, h_{S_d}^4)$, where $h_{S_t}^1 = \{s_4, s_5\}$, $h_{S_d}^1 = \{s_0', s_1'\}$, $h_{S_t}^2 = \{s_5\}$, $h_{S_d}^2 = \{s_2', s_3'\}$, $h_{S_t}^3 = \{s_6\}$, $h_{S_d}^3 = \{s_0', s_1'\}$, $h_{S_t}^4 = \{s_5, s_6\}$, and $h_{S_d}^4 = \{s_1'\}$. Then we can evaluate the trust score of x in z based on both concatenation operator $\otimes$ and aggregation operator $\oplus$.

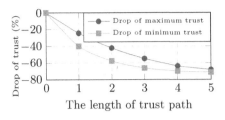
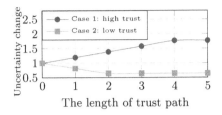

Fig. 3. Drop of trust   **Fig. 4.** Uncertainty change of trust degree

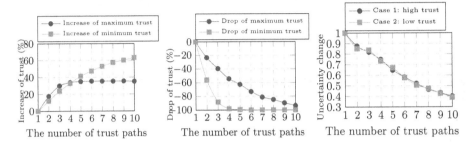

Fig. 5. Increase of trust   **Fig. 6.** Drop of trust   **Fig. 7.** Uncertainty change

Now we see how to calculate $R(x,z) = (h_{S_t}^5, h_{S_d}^5)$. Firstly, we find that there are two trust propagation paths from x to y, that is, "$path_1 : x \to y \to z$" and "$path_2 : x \to u \to z$". Hence, we should first calculate the trust scores along different trust propagation paths separately. According to Definition 12, we have

$$R^{path_1}(x,z) = (h_{S_t}^{path_1}, h_{S_d}^{path_1}) = (\{s_3, s_4\}, \{s_1', s_2', s_3'\}),$$
$$R^{path_2}(x,z) = (h_{S_t}^{path_2}, h_{S_d}^{path_2}) = (\{s_5, s_6\}, \{s_1'\}).$$

Secondly, we aggregate the above trust scores along different paths into $R(x,z)$ by Definition 14. We take $h_{S_t^+}^3$ as an example. By formula (5), we have

$$h_{S_t^+}^{5'} = h_{S_t^+}^{path_1} \blacktriangle h_{S_t^+}^{path_2} = s_4 \blacktriangle s_6 = (0.5 \uplus_1 0.83, 0.67 \uplus_2 1, 0.83 \uplus_3 1) = (0.9084, 1, 1).$$

By formula (4), we obtain $d(s_6, h_{S_t^+}^{5'}) = 0.0248$, $d(s_5, h_{S_t^+}^{5'}) = 0.1697$, $d(s_4, h_{S_t^+}^{5'}) = 0.3266, d(s_3, h_{S_t^+}^{5'}) = 0.4943, d(s_2, h_{S_t^+}^{5'}) = 0.6623, d(s_1, h_{S_t^+}^{5'}) = 0.8237, d(s_0, h_{S_t^+}^{5'}) = 0.9754$. Hence, $h_{S_t^+}^5 = apps_{S_t}(h_{S_t^+}^{5'}) = s_6$. Similarly, we can obtain

$$h_{9_t^-}^5 = apps_{S_t}(s_3 \blacktriangle s_5) = s_5, h_{S_t^+}^5 = apps_{S_d}(s_3' \blacktriangle s_1') = s_1', h_{S_t^-}^5 = apps_{S_d}(s_1' \blacktriangle s_1') = s_0'.$$

Hence, $R(x,z) = (\{s_5, s_6\}, \{s_0', s_1'\})$. This result is in line with intuition that when the information obtained through two paths are both relatively high trust and low distrust, the aggregated result should strengthen the original degrees.

4.3   Evaluation

This section conducts two experiments to reveal some insight into our method.

The first experiment is conducted to see how the operator influences the trust degree and uncertainty of trust degree when the length of trust path changes. We randomly generate an HFLTS based trust degree from the semantics of linguistic term sets of trust S_t as in Example 3 with membership functions as in Fig. 1. We suppose the agents have the same trust degree along a trust path with n agents ($n-1$ is the length of trust path). We use the ratio of original trust degree and final one to represent changes of trust and use the number of elements in an HFLTS based trust degree to represent the uncertainty of trust degree. We run the calculation of propagation results 1,000 times under the above setting. From Fig. 3, we can that see no matter what the original trust degree is, both the maximum and minimum trust degrees drop when the length of trust path increases. However, there are two different trends of uncertainty changes. Figure 4 shows that if the trust in propagation is high, then the uncertainty will increase, because the trust degree is weakening in the process of propagation. However, if the trust in propagation is low, the uncertainty of trust degree decreases in the process of propagation and the trust degree will reach a low level quickly.

We carry out the second experiment to see how the aggregation operator influences the trust degree and uncertainty of trust degree as the number of trust paths changes. We randomly generate n (in-between 1 and 10) HFLTS based trust degrees from the semantics of linguistic term sets of trust $\{s_3, s_4, s_5\}$ and $\{s_1, s_2, s_3\}$, respectively. We aggregate the n trust degrees along different paths and run the calculation 1,000 times under the above setting. Figure 5 shows that when the trust degree of each trust path is relatively high, the trust degree of aggregation will be enhanced, especially when the aggregation route increases, the enhancement effect will be more obvious. However, Fig. 6 shows that when trust degree of each trust path is relatively low, the aggregation results will gradually weaken with the increase of the number of paths. Different from the concatenation operator, in Fig. 7 we can see the uncertainty of aggregated results decreases with the increase of the number of trust paths if all the trust degrees on different trust paths are relatively high or all of them are relatively low.

From the above analysis, we can see that the operators play different roles in trust propagation, and each of them satisfies some intuitive properties of propagation. Therefore, the HFLTS based trust model is not only closer to human users in expression, but also can maintain intuitive trust propagation properties.

5   Related Work

Majd and Balakrishnan [7] propose a trust model, which considers reliability, similarity, satisfaction and trust transitivity. In the trust transitivity step, they also employ the concatenation operator and aggregation operator proposed by [12] to identify the trust value of each suggested recommender. Their model focuses on how to choose more reliable recommender based on identified components, while in our model, we pay more attention to characterising the trust model that is more similar to humans' expression and the trust propagation mechanism based on this kind of model.

Wu et al. [14] propose a trust network model for determining the importance value assigned to the experts in group decision making problem. They investigate a uninorm propagation operator to propagate both trust and distrust information and prevents the loss of trust information. Later, Wu et al. [13] propose a visual interaction consensus model for social network group decision making based on this trust propagation method. We also employ uninorm operator in trust propagation process. However, we use it to aggregate the trust scores passed through different trust paths, and the aggregation operator is used in qualitative trust model, in which the trust scores are represented by linguistic expressions. Moreover, their propagation method only considers the shortest trust path and neglects the others, while ours consider all paths when aggregating trust scores.

The methods of fuzzy logic have been used in some trust network models. For example, Kant and Bharadwaj [5] propose a fuzzy computation based trust model, which is employed in recommender systems to deal with the cold start problem. They also use linguistic expressions to represent trust and distrust concepts and propose relevant propagation and aggregation operators. However, in their model, only one linguistic expression can be assigned to trust and distrust degrees, while our model employ hesitant fuzzy linguistic term sets to reflect that a person may hesitate to choose one among several values to assess the trust.

6   Conclusion

This paper studied how to evaluate trust scores in trust network with linguistic expressions. Firstly, we proposed the representation of trust score based on HFLTS to reflect humans' hesitation and developed a novel method of comparison between trust scores. Secondly, we introduced concatenation operator and aggregation operator to deal with the problem of evaluating trust between indirectly connected agents. Finally, we showed that the operators meet the intuitions of trust propagation. In the future, one of the most interesting thing is to employ the HFLTS based trust model to construct a recommendation system in e-commerce that can improve the accuracy of recommendations.

Acknowledgments. The works described in this paper are supported by the National Natural Science Foundation of China under Grant Nos. 61772210, 61272066 and 61806080; Guangdong Province Universities Pearl River Scholar Funded Scheme (2018); the Project of Science and Technology in Guangzhou in China under Grant No. 201807010043; the key project in universities in Guangdong Province of China under Grant No. 2016KZDXM024; the Doctoral Start-up Project of Natural Science Foundation of Guangdong Province in China under Grant No. 2018A030310529; the Project of Department of Education of Guangdong Province in China under Grant No. 2017KQNCX048; China Postdoctoral Science Foundation under Grant No. 2018M643115; and Humanities and Social Sciences Foundation of Ministry of Education of China (No. 18YJC72040002).

References

1. Agreste, S., De Meo, P., Ferrara, E., Piccolo, S., Provetti, A.: Trust networks: topology, dynamics, and measurements. IEEE Internet Comput. **19**(6), 26–35 (2015)
2. Ghavipour, M., Meybodi, M.R.: Trust propagation algorithm based on learning automata for inferring local trust in online social networks. Knowl.-Based Syst. **143**, 307–316 (2018)
3. Herrera-Viedma, E., Cabrerizo, F.J., Kacprzyk, J., Pedrycz, W.: A review of soft consensus models in a fuzzy environment. Inf. Fusion **17**, 4–13 (2014)
4. Jøsang, A., Hayward, R., Pope, S.: Trust network analysis with subjective logic. In: Proceedings of the 29th Australasian Computer Science Conference, pp. 85–94 (2006)
5. Kant, V., Bharadwaj, K.K.: Fuzzy computational models of trust and distrust for enhanced recommendations. Int. J. Intell. Syst. **28**(4), 332–365 (2013)
6. Liu, Y., Liang, C., Chiclana, F., Wu, J.: A trust induced recommendation mechanism for reaching consensus in group decision making. Knowl.-Based Syst. **119**, 221–231 (2017)
7. Majd, E., Balakrishnan, V.: A trust model for recommender agent systems. Soft. Comput. **21**(2), 417–433 (2017)
8. Rodriguez, R.M., Martinez, L., Herrera, F.: Hesitant fuzzy linguistic term sets for decision making. IEEE Trans. Fuzzy Syst. **20**(1), 109–119 (2012)
9. Ruan, Y., Durresi, A.: A survey of trust management systems for online social communities-trust modeling, trust inference and attacks. Knowl.-Based Syst. **106**, 150–163 (2016)
10. Verbiest, N., Cornelis, C., Victor, P., Herrera-Viedma, E.: Trust and distrust aggregation enhanced with path length incorporation. Fuzzy Sets Syst. **202**, 61–74 (2012)
11. Wang, Y., Vassileva, J.: Bayesian network-based trust model. In: Proceedings of the IEEE/WIC International Conference on Web Intelligence, pp. 372–378 (2003)
12. Wang, Y., Singh, M.P.: Trust representation and aggregation in a distributed agent system. In: Proceedings of the 21st AAAI Conference on Artificial Intelligence, pp. 1425–1430 (2006)
13. Wu, J., Chiclana, F., Fujita, H., Herrera-Viedma, E.: A visual interaction consensus model for social network group decision making with trust propagation. Knowl.-Based Syst. **122**, 39–50 (2017)
14. Wu, J., Xiong, R., Chiclana, F.: Uninorm trust propagation and aggregation methods for group decision making in social network with four tuple information. Knowl.-Based Syst. **96**, 29–39 (2016)
15. Yager, R.R.: An approach to ordinal decision making. Int. J. Approximate Reasoning **12**(3–4), 237–261 (1995)
16. Zadeh, L.A.: The concept of a linguistic variable and its application to approximate reasoning-I. Inf. Sci. **8**(3), 199–249 (1975)

An Improved Discretization-Based Feature Selection via Particle Swarm Optimization

Jiping Lin, Yu Zhou$^{(\boxtimes)}$, and Junhao Kang

Shenzhen University, Shenzhen 518060, China
lin_ji_ping@163.com, zhouyu_1022@126.com,
1800271054@email.szu.edu.cn

Abstract. Feature selection (FS) aims to remove the redundant or irrelevant features of the data, which plays a very important role in data mining and machine learning tasks. Recent studies focus on integrating the data discretization technique into the FS process to help achieve superior performances in classification. In this paper, we proposed an improved discretization-based FS method via particle swarm optimization to obtain a higher classification accuracy with a smaller size of feature subset. In our approach, we use a novel encoding and decoding way for particle swarm optimization (PSO) which can efficiently select multiple cut-points for discretization. In addition, a new updating strategy and a local search procedure is proposed to strengthen the searching ability and avoid being trapped into local optimal. Experimental results on benchmark datasets demonstrate the efficacy of our proposed methods both in the classification accuracy and the feature subset size.

Keywords: Feature selection · Discretization ·
Particle swarm optimization

1 Introduction

Current machine learning algorithms often need to handle high-dimensional data of different areas. The 'high-dimension' means a huge number of features while having only a few samples, which often brings the difficulty in establishing the model, for example in classification or regression task. However, it is often the case that a great number of features are irrelevant and redundant, which might negatively affect the performances of training models. Too many features may result in overfitting phenomenon, which will seriously decrease the test accuracy [20].

Although the cutting-edge techniques, such as deep learning, have the ability to automatically learn the features with a much smaller size, the availability of a small number of samples can not guarantee a good enough model to well fit the task. Therefore, FS [13] is focused to reduce the number of features while maximizing the performances of the training model. With FS, irrelevant and redundant features, known as noise [18] are identified and discarded. In this way, the algorithms not only need a significantly less amount of space and time but also avoid suffering from overfitting.

© Springer Nature Switzerland AG 2019
C. Douligeris et al. (Eds.): KSEM 2019, LNAI 11776, pp. 298–310, 2019.
https://doi.org/10.1007/978-3-030-29563-9_27

FS is essentially a combinatorial optimization problem which is hard to solve by some traditional approaches, such as sequential search [9–11,17], especially for some high-dimensional cases. Recent studies focus on applying evolutionary computation (EC) approaches to solve FS due to the merits of population-based search. A detailed survey can be found in [23], among which particle swarm optimization (PSO) [7] is most widely used due to its simplicity and fast convergence.

The encoding (representation) of particle in PSO is very critical to describe the solution space. A proper representation not only well defines the characteristics of the problem, but also facilitates the search procedure. Binary PSO (BPSO) [3,22] considers binary value of each feature indicating whether selecting it or not. However, these binary encoding often generates many locally optimal solutions, resulting in a large feature size. Although some heuristic search methods, such as Tabu search [4,6] are applied to cooperate with BPSO to decrease features effectively. The performances in classification are still limited.

Recently, the discretization technique is involved in FS to get a novel encoding for PSO. In [19], after a cut-point table for feature discretization is obtained, the index of selected cut-point for each feature is encoded as each dimension of the particles. With this type, the search scope of solutions are greatly reduced. In [12], different from the previous work, the number of selected cut-points for each feature is encoded in PSO and a random selection of cut-points is applied based on the characteristics of the dataset. In comparison to [19], although using multiple cut-points for discretization is able to achieve better performances, the searching space is still too large, resulting in lower efficiency.

In this paper, we propose an improved discretization-based FS method. Firstly, to shrink the number of features and the scope of solution space, a filtering approach, ReliefF [15,18] and minimum description length principle (MDLP) [2] are applied to pre-select the features. Then, based on the reduced feature set, a ranked cut-point table is obtained, in which the priority of the cut-points for each feature is calculated based on the information gain. In PSO, by considering the ranking of cut-points, a novel particle encoding and decoding way are developed, which can effectively identifying the number and indexes of the selected features simultaneously. In each iteration of PSO, a particle updating procedure is applied to avoid being trapped into local optimal and a local search procedure is applied to properly strengthen the searching scope of particles. Experimental studies are carried out which demonstrates that the proposed approach can efficiently remove the irrelevant features while maintaining competitive results of classification accuracy compared with some state-of-the-art methods.

2 Related Works

2.1 ReliefF Algorithm

ReliefF [18], a filter algorithm, can pre-select the features by evaluating their importance. By assigning weight to each feature according to the basis that a good feature has eigenvalues in the nearest point neighbor close to similar samples but far from dissimilar samples, the algorithm could hence initialize ordered features. Theoretically, a greater weight indicates a greater classifying-ability and vice versa. The subset of features could be screened by setting a threshold of the weights. The formula (1) updates the weights for feature F:

$$W(F) = W(F) - \sum_{i=1}^{k} \frac{diff(F, R, H_j)}{mk}$$

$$+ \sum_{C \neq class(R)} \frac{[\frac{p(C)}{1-p(Class(R))} \sum_{j=1}^{k} diff(F, R, H_j(C))]}{mk} \tag{1}$$

where R suggests a random sample selected from the dataset for training purpose, H and M represent the closest neighbor of the same class of sample R and that of the different class of sample R, respectively. m represents the size of random samples selected, and $diff()$, as shown in (2), is used to provide the difference between those two samples while normalizing the variable. where the $p()$ function gives the probability of the attribute of that class and k suggests the number of samples for each class.

$$diff(F, R_1, R_2) = \begin{cases} \dfrac{|R_1[F] - R_2[F]|}{\max(F) - \min(F)} & if\ F\ is\ continuous \\ 0 & if\ F\ is\ discrete\ and\ R_1[F] = R_2[F] \\ 1 & if\ F\ is\ discrete\ and\ R_1[F] \neq R_2[F] \end{cases} \tag{2}$$

By considering the probability of different classes and finding out the average k-nearest neighbor [5] differences between samples in the same classes and between those from different classes, ReliefF can effectively reduce the noise and deal with multi-class classification problems.

2.2   Cut-Points Generated by MDLP

In [19], MDLP is applied to obtain the cut-points for each feature independently in terms of the information gain (IG) that the cut-point brings to the current interval it lies in. All the generated cut-points should satisfy the MDLP criterion shown in (4).

$$IG(C, F; S) = E(S) - \frac{|S_1|}{S}E(S_1) - \frac{|S_2|}{S}E(S_2). \tag{3}$$

The cut-point C is accepted when the cost classes of the instances in the interval produced by C together with the cost of creating cut-point C is smaller than the total information gain according to Eq. (3) [24]. F stands for individual feature, and S_1, S_2 are the subsets of S after partitions.

$$IG(C, F; S) > \frac{log_2|S_1| - 1}{|S|} + \frac{\delta(C, F; S)}{|S|} \tag{4}$$

$$\delta(C, F; S) = log_2(3^{k_S} - 2) - [k_S E(S) - k_{S_1} E(S_1) - k_{S_2} E(S_2)] \tag{5}$$

MDLP could also treat noise and irrelevant data by calculating whether its information gain is larger than the cost of creating C, where $|S|$ is the size of S; $E(S)$ is the entropy of S; and k_S is the class number shown in S. More details about discretization can refer to [8].

3   Proposed IDFS-PSO

The overview algorithmic framework of our proposed IDFS-PSO is presented in Fig. 1, where the proposed encoding and decoding process of PSO in FS and the local search procedure are applied to obtain better feature subset in terms of both the classification accuracy and the number of the selected features.

Fig. 1. Overview framework of IDFS-SPO

3.1   Feature Pre-selection

In order to reduce the size of the features, we apply ReliefF algorithm to obtain the nonzero weights filtered by a threshold, where the relevant features can be identified. Then, we choose the significant features which own at least one cut-point based on information gain (IG) via MDLP. At last, the intersection of relevant features and significant features are obtained as the pre-selected feature subset. In this way, the dimension of the search spaces will be narrowed down. Thus, the initial cut-point table by MDLP is obtained in Fig. 2, where a reduced number of features with their cut-points are recorded accordingly.

Initial Cut-point Table

	Cut point 1	Cut point 2	Cut point 3	Cut point 4
Feature 1	2.62	4.75	6.11	8.35
Feature 3	4.72	9.05		
Feature 16	5.72			
...				
Feature N	1.97	2.43	4.67	

Fig. 2. Initial cut-point table

3.2   Encoding and Decoding of the Particles

In our problem, we sort the indexes of the pre-select features in an ascending order. For each particle, the number of selected cut-points of each pre-select feature is stored.

It is noted that only determining the number of selected features is not sufficient to apply the discretization. Based on the generation scheme of the cut-points by MDLP, it is observed that the cut-points are obtained recursively, which means that the firstly obtained cut-point has the largest contribution in dividing the values into two separate parts. With the recursion moving on, the sub-parts are then determined whether it should be split or not judged by the IG. To model the relationship between these cut-points of any feature, we apply the binary tree, of which the nodes store the cut-points generated by MDLP. Since it is expected that the cut-points with larger contribution in separating the values be preferred, the cut-points are ranked by the levels of the binary tree (the root node rank first, then the children of the root node and so on). For the cut-points lying in the same level of the tree, we compare the priority P_{z_s} defined in (6).

$$P_{z_s} = IG(z_s)/MDLP(L_s^{z_s}) \quad z \in z_l \tag{6}$$

where z_l denotes the cut-points in level l of the tree ($l = 1$ for root node), z_s represents any cut-point in z_l for feature s, $IG(z_s)$ is the information gain introduced by the evaluated cut-point and MDLP ($L_s^{z_s}$) denotes the MDLP of the partition L_s from the cut-point in level $l - 1$, where the cut-point z_s lies.

The cut-point with a larger priority is ranked before the lower one. So, a tree-based cut-point storage based on ranking is applied to each feature. Therefore, we can obtain a ranked cut-point table for the pre-selected features in Fig. 3. For each particle, when the number of selected features for feature s, M_s is indicated, the first M_s cut-points in the ranked cut-point table are chosen for the discretization. Specifically, for feature s, if M_s is equal to 0 or bigger than the number of cut-points, the feature will be discarded. Therefore, we are able to decode the particle representation and implement the cut-point selection process.

3.3 Discretized Samples Based on the Selected Cut-Points

After determining the cut-points for each feature, we can obtain the discretized training samples which is more convenient for classification task. The discretization rule is stated as follows:

(1) The values of feature s across all the samples are sorted in an ascending order.
(2) Suppose M_s selected cut-points that divides the feature s into $M_s + 1$ segments.
(3) Any value of s that falls into the range of the first segment are recorded as 1 and so forth for the values in the rest segments.

3.4 Fitness Function

We adopt the fitness function proposed in [19], which considers both the balanced accuracy [16] and distances [1] between instances of the same and different classes.

$$fitness = (k * balanced\_accuracy + (1 - k) * distance) \tag{7}$$

$$balanced\_accuracy = \frac{1}{n} \sum_{i=1}^{n} \frac{TP_i}{|S_i|} \tag{8}$$

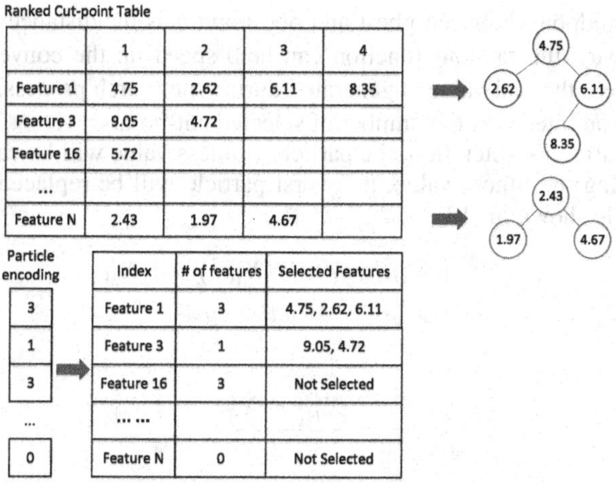

Ranked Cut-point Table

	1	2	3	4
Feature 1	4.75	2.62	6.11	8.35
Feature 3	9.05	4.72		
Feature 16	5.72			
...				
Feature N	2.43	1.97	4.67	

Particle encoding		Index	# of features	Selected Features
3		Feature 1	3	4.75, 2.62, 6.11
1		Feature 3	1	9.05, 4.72
3		Feature 16	3	Not Selected
...		... ...		
0		Feature N	0	Not Selected

Fig. 3. Binary tree based cut-point storage

$$distance = \frac{1}{1 + exp^{-5(D_B - D_W)}} \tag{9}$$

$$D_B = \frac{1}{|S|} \sum_{i=1}^{|S|} \min_{\{j|j \neq i, class(V_i) \neq class(V_j)\}} Dis(V_i, V, j) \tag{10}$$

$$D_W = \frac{1}{|S|} \sum_{i=1}^{|S|} \min_{\{j|j \neq i, class(V_i) = class(V_j)\}} Dis(V_i, V, j) \tag{11}$$

where $Dis(V_i, V_j)$ represents the Hamming distance between two vectors V_i and V_j. The differences between instances from different classes, D_B, is maximized while the differences between the instances from the same class, D_W, is minimized. n represents the total number of classes, TP_i represents the number of correctly classified samples of class i, and $|S_i|$ represents the number of samples in class i.

3.5 The Updating Operators

In our method, we apply the Bare-bone PSO (BBPSO) [14], in which the magnitude of each particles is determined by the position of gbest and pbest. The position of each particle is updated by adopting a Normal distribution $N(\mu, \sigma)$ with mean, μ, and standard deviation, σ, as follows:

$$x_{id}^{t+1} = \begin{cases} N(\mu, \sigma), if \ random() < 0.5 \\ p_{id}^t \quad otherwise \end{cases} \tag{12}$$

where μ is the midpoint between gbest and pbest and σ is the distance between these points. In this way, the random function can help speed up the convergence. When BBPSO is applied, the real value is generated during the search process. So, we round the real value to an integer as the number of selected cut-points.

In addition, after each iteration, the particle's fitness value will be calculated using Eq. (7). By sorting the fitness value, the worst particle will be replaced by the newly generated particle shown in (13)

$$X_W^{t+1} = \begin{cases} N(\mu_B, \lambda_B) & f(X_W^{t+1}) > f(X_W^t) \\ X_W^t & otherwise \end{cases} \tag{13}$$

$$\mu_B = \frac{X_{B_1}^t + X_{B_2}^t}{2} \tag{14}$$

$$\lambda_B = |X_{B_1}^t - X_{B_2}^t| \tag{15}$$

where X_{B_1}, X_{B_2}, X_W represents two best particles and the worst particle, respectively. The new particle is created by an Gaussian Distribution $N(\mu_B, \lambda_B)$ according to (13), (14) and (15). In (13), the fitness of the newly generated particle is compared with the current worst one and will replace it if the fitness value is improved. Therefore, the best features will be retained and duplicated after each iteration, which helps reduce the noisy features and expedite the convergence of the particles. In this way, the classification is able to gain a higher overall accuracy.

3.6   The Local Search Procedure

Local search is usually applied to explore more solutions by alternating some solutions in its neighborhood. In some discrete problems, the neighborhood of a solution is often defined as changing one element of the solution. In our problem, taking the feature s for example, we have the ranked cut-points $C_s^1, C_s^2, \ldots, C_s^{N_s}$. When the number of selected cut-points M_s is smaller than the number of cut-points, N_s, we apply the local search by randomly replacing one selected cut-point by the cut-point $C_s^{M_s+1}$.

4   Experimental Results and Analysis

4.1   Experimental Settings

To demonstrate the superiority of our IDFS-PSO on high dimensional data, ten gene expression benchmark datasets shown in Table 1 are used to test the performances of different algorithms. In our settings, the population size is set to 1/20 times of the number of features of each dataset with a restriction of 300. The number of iterations is set to 70. When the value of gbest does not improve in ten consecutive iterations, the algorithm is stopped. The weight threshold of ReliefF is set to 0.35. The value k in K-NN is chosen to be 1 to accelerate the classification. For the compared methods, the parameters are set to when their best performances can be achieved.

Table 1. Datasets

Dataset	#Features	#Instances	#Classes
SRBCT	2,308	83	4
DLBCL	5,469	77	2
9Tumor	5,726	60	9
Leukemia 1	5,327	72	3
Brain Tumor 1	5,920	90	5
Leukemia 2	11,225	72	3
Brain Tumor 2	10,367	50	4
Prostate	10,509	102	2
Lung Cancer	12,600	203	5
11Tumor	12,533	174	11

4.2 Statistical Results and Analysis

In this section, we compare our proposed IDFS-PSO with several state-of-the-art methods, including the full size feature by KNN denoted as Full, the classic PSO-FS algorithm [19], EPSO [21] and PPSO in [19] and APPSO [12]. The average accuracy for the algorithm is collected after running 30 times.

As shown in Table 2, for all of the datasets, the average number of features selected by IDFS-PSO, EPSO, PPSO and APPSO are significantly less than those of Full and PSO-FS and the accuracy on testing data is significantly better. The results indicates that the introduction of discretization into the PSO search helps to improve the classification performances greatly.

In comparison to EPSO, PPSO and APPSO, our proposed approach also show its advantages on 9 out of 10 datasets in terms of the feature subset size. When evaluating the classification accuracy, IDFS-PSO outperform EPSO, PPSO and APPSO on 9, 8 and 9 out of 10 dataset, respectively. In most of the cases, IDFS-PSO and APPSO have similar advantages over EPSO and PPSO. The reason may lie in the fact that both of the algorithms use multiple cut-points during the discretization process in contrast to one cut-point in EPSO and PPSO. So, more discriminative information is explored so as to improve the classifying performance.

It is also noted that IDFS-PSO perform slightly better than APPSO both in feature size and test accuracy. Although they use the similar encoding method in PSO, our proposed method considers the ranking of selected cut-points other than randomly selecting in APPSO. Therefore, more accurate identification of the cut-points are implemented which helps to improve the performances in a certain scale.

Table 2. Experimental results

Dataset	Method	#Features	Size	Accuracy
SRBCT	Full	2308	2308.0	87.08
	PSO-FS		150.0	91.31
	EPSO		137.3	96.89
	PPSO		108.5	95.78
	APPSO		24.8	**99.59**
	IDFS-PSO		**23.6**	99.52
DLBCL	Full	5469	5469.0	83.00
	PSO-FS		101.8	80.03
	EPSO		42.8	85.18
	PPSO		44.0	86.22
	APPSO		19.1	94.71
	IDFS-PSO		**17.8**	**94.95**
Prostate	Full	10509	10509.0	85.33
	PSO-FS		777.4	85.20
	EPSO		54.9	83.74
	PPSO		65.6	91.82
	APPSO		37.6	91.22
	IDFS-PSO		**31.7**	**91.48**
Leukemia 1	Full	5327	5327.0	79.72
	PSO-FS		150.0	81.60
	EPSO		135.9	93.37
	PPSO		80.4	94.37
	APPSO		**22.3**	94.50
	IDFS-PSO		23.8	**94.83**
Leukemia 2	Full	11225	11225.0	89.44
	PSO-FS		150.0	86.11
	EPSO		139.9	89.93
	PPSO		86.7	**96.74**
	APPSO		35.8	95.72
	IDFS-PSO		**33.2**	95.96
9Tumor	Full	5726	5726.0	36.67
	PSO-FS		955.0	45.95
	EPSO		138.5	58.22
	PPSO		118.1	**59.28**
	APPSO		39.5	42.23
	IDFS-PSO		**34.5**	51.28

(countinued)

Table 2. (*countinued*)

Dataset	Method	#Features	Size	Accuracy
11Tumor	Full	12533	12533.0	71.42
	PSO-FS		1638.8	82.62
	EPSO		**149.9**	79.29
	PPSO		167.0	76.83
	APPSO		325.8	87.46
	IDFS-PSO		170.6	**88.16**
Brain Tumor 1	Full	5920	5920.0	72.08
	PSO-FS		317.3	71.00
	EPSO		150.7	72.79
	PPSO		73.4	74.40
	APPSO		**41.3**	87.92
	IDFS-PSO		41.6	**88.27**
Brain Tumor 2	Full	10367	10367.0	62.50
	PSO-FS		417.9	69.11
	EPSO		152.8	70.76
	PPSO		66.7	68.75
	APPSO		39.4	70.62
	IDFS-PSO		**35.8**	**70.93**
Lung cancer	Full	12600	12600.0	78.05
	PSO-FS		686.2	81.72
	EPSO		150.8	80.60
	PPSO		203.0	79.38
	APPSO		157.8	92.58
	IDFS-PSO		**145.8**	**92.89**

4.3 Effectiveness of the Local Search

To evaluate the performances of local search in IDFS-PSO, we conduct the comparison between the algorithm with (denoted by w) and without (denoted by w/o) local search on ten datasets. The comparison results are presented in Table 3.

It it observed that the algorithm with local search is able to achieve better performances in most of the test data. The local search is able to explore more possible cut-points combination, so better PSO solutions can be found.

Table 3. Comparison results

Dataset	#Features (w)	#Features (w/o)	Accuracy (w)	Accuracy (w/o)
SRBCT	**23.6**	23.9	**99.52**	99.35
DLBCL	**17.8**	18.2	**94.95**	94.87
9Tumor	**31.7**	32.6	**91.48**	90.76
Leukemia 1	**23.8**	24.3	**94.83**	94.80
Brain Tumor 1	**33.2**	34.1	95.96	**96.14**
Leukemia 2	**34.5**	34.9	51.28	**52.78**
Brain Tumor 2	**170.6**	173.8	**88.16**	88.13
Prostate	**41.6**	42.5	88.27	**88.45**
Lung Cancer	**35.8**	37.2	**70.93**	70.55
11Tumor	**145.8**	148.9	**92.89**	92.57

4.4 Computational Time

We have measured the time for running the PPSO, APPSO and our proposed method in Table 4, since all these three approaches are based on offline cut-point table. Although EPSO has proven its advantages in computational time, the accuracy is limited compared to these three methods. The computational time is denoted by the time cost of the PSO search procedure. Overall, IDFS-PSO has less computational time than PPSO and APPSO. Intuitively, IDFS-PSO and APPSO select more cut-points during the update process. However, pre-selecting a number of features in the first stage helps in an increase of the convergence speed in the discretization-based FS. So, they need less time to run. The reason why IDFS-PSO spends less time than APPSO is that the speed of finding the good cut-points in IDFS-PSO is quite fast based on the ranking rather than a random selection often with a number of trials.

Table 4. Running time (s)

Dataset	PPSO	APPSO	IDFS-PSO
SRBCT	220.5	197.8	**174.5**
DLBCL	226.9	185.6	**162.6**
9Tumor	324.7	244.6	**218.1**
Leukemia 1	379.6	350.4	**315.2**
Brain Tumor 1	327.8	317.2	**290.5**
Leukemia 2	236.4	225.3	**194.6**
Brain Tumor 2	176.2	167.9	**158.8**
Prostate	305.2	210.2	**202.3**
Lung Cancer	1186.9	598.5	**533.8**
11Tumor	785.8	497.7	**462.7**

5 Conclusion

In this paper, a new approach is proposed where the feature is pre-processed using both the ReliefF algorithm and MDLP to find their intersecting cut points. This approach further narrows down the dimension of the features before the particle swarm begins to converge. Then, a new updating strategy and a local search procedure is proposed. Experimental results on ten benchmark datasets shows that IDFS-PSO selects significantly less amount of features while keeping the competitive accuracy compared with some state-of-the-art methods.

Acknowledgment. This work is supported in part by the Natural Science Foundation of China under Grant 61702336, in part by Shenzhen Emerging Industries of the Strategic Basic Research Project JCYJ20170302154254147, and in part by Natural Science Foundation of SZU (grant No. 2018068).

References

1. Al-Sahaf, H., Zhang, M., Johnston, M., Verma, B.: Image descriptor: a genetic programming approach to multiclass texture classification. In: 2015 IEEE Congress on Evolutionary Computation (CEC), pp. 2460–2467. IEEE (2015)
2. Barron, A., Rissanen, J., Yu, B.: The minimum description length principle in coding and modeling. IEEE Trans. Inf. Theory **44**(6), 2743–2760 (1998)
3. Chuang, L.Y., Chang, H.W., Tu, C.J., Yang, C.H.: Improved binary pso for feature selection using gene expression data. Comput. Biol. Chem. **32**(1), 29–38 (2008). https://doi.org/10.1016/j.compbiolchem.2007.09.005. http://www.sciencedirect.com/science/article/pii/S1476927107001181
4. Chuang, L.Y., Yang, C.H., Yang, C.H.: Tabu search and binary particle swarmoptimization for feature selection using microarray data. J. Comput. Biol. **16**(12), 1689–1703 (2009). https://doi.org/10.1089/cmb.2007.0211. pMID: 20047491
5. Cover, T., Hart, P.: Nearest neighbor pattern classification. IEEE Trans. Inf. Theory **13**(1), 21–27 (1967)
6. Dara, S., Banka, H.: A binary PSO feature selection algorithm for gene expression data. In: 2014 International Conference on Advances in Communication and Computing Technologies (ICACACT 2014), pp. 1–6, August 2014. https://doi.org/10.1109/EIC.2015.7230734
7. Eberhart, R., Kennedy, J.: A new optimizer using particle swarm theory. In: 1995 Proceedings of the Sixth International Symposium on Micro Machine and Human Science, MHS 1995, pp. 39–43. IEEE (1995)
8. Fayyad, U., Irani, K.: Multi-interval discretization of continuous-valued attributes for classification learning. In: IJCAI (1993)
9. Gasca, E., Sánchez, J.S., Alonso, R.: Eliminating redundancy and irrelevance using a new MLP-based feature selection method. Pattern Recogn. **39**(2), 313–315 (2006)
10. Guan, S.U., Liu, J., Qi, Y.: An incremental approach to contribution-based feature selection. J. Intell. Syst. **13**(1), 15–42 (2004)
11. Hsu, C.N., Huang, H.J., Dietrich, S.: The annigma-wrapper approach to fast feature selection for neural nets. IEEE Trans. Syst. Man Cybern. Part B (Cybern.) **32**(2), 207–212 (2002)
12. Huang, X., Chi, Y., Zhou, Y.: Feature selection of high dimensional data by adaptive potential particle swarm optimization. In: 2019 IEEE Congress on Evolutionary Computation (CEC), June 2019

13. Jović, A., Brkić, K., Bogunović, N.: A review of feature selection methods with applications. In: 2015 38th International Convention on Information and Communication Technology, Electronics and Microelectronics (MIPRO), pp. 1200–1205 May 2015. https://doi.org/10.1109/MIPRO.2015.7160458

14. Kennedy, J.: Bare bones particle swarms. In: 2003 Swarm Intelligence Symposium. SIS 2003. Proceedings of the 2003 IEEE, pp. 80–87. IEEE (2003)

15. Liu, M., Xu, L., Yi, J., Huang, J.: A feature gene selection method based on reliefF and PSO. In: 2018 10th International Conference on Measuring Technology and Mechatronics Automation (ICMTMA), pp. 298–301. IEEE (2018)

16. Patterson, G., Zhang, M.: Fitness functions in genetic programming for classification with unbalanced data. In: Orgun, M.A., Thornton, J. (eds.) AI 2007. LNCS (LNAI), vol. 4830, pp. 769–775. Springer, Heidelberg (2007). https://doi.org/10.1007/978-3-540-76928-6_90

17. Reunanen, J.: Overfitting in making comparisons between variable selection methods. J. Mach. Learn. Res. 3(3), 1371–1382 (2003)

18. Reyes, O., Morell, C., Ventura, S.: Scalable extensions of the reliefFalgorithm for weighting and selecting features on the multi-label learningcontext. Neurocomputing 161, 168–182 (2015). https://doi.org/10.1016/j.neucom.2015.02.045. http://www.sciencedirect.com/science/article/pii/S0925231215001940

19. Tran, B., Xue, B., Zhang, M.: A new representation in PSO for discretization-based feature selection. IEEE Trans. Cybern. 48(6), 1733–1746 (2018). https://doi.org/10.1109/TCYB.2017.2714145

20. Tran, B., Xue, B., Zhang, M.: Improved PSO for feature selection on high-dimensional datasets. In: Dick, G., et al. (eds.) SEAL 2014. LNCS, vol. 8886, pp. 503–515. Springer, Cham (2014). https://doi.org/10.1007/978-3-319-13563-2_43

21. Tran, B., Xue, B., Zhang, M.: Bare-bone particle swarm optimisation for simultaneously discretising and selecting features for high-dimensional classification. In: Squillero, G., Burelli, P. (eds.) EvoApplications 2016. LNCS, vol. 9597, pp. 701–718. Springer, Cham (2016). https://doi.org/10.1007/978-3-319-31204-0_45

22. Vieira, S.M., Mendonça, L.F., Farinha, G.J., Sousa, J.M.: Modified binary pso for feature selection using SVM applied to mortality prediction of septicpatients. Appl. Soft Comput. 13(8), 3494–3504 (2013). https://doi.org/10.1016/j.asoc.2013.03.021. http://www.sciencedirect.com/science/article/pii/S1568494613001361

23. Xue, B., Zhang, M., Browne, W.N., Yao, X.: A survey on evolutionary computation approaches to feature selection. IEEE Trans. Evol. Comput. 20(4), 606–626 (2016). https://doi.org/10.1109/TEVC.2015.2504420

24. Xue, B., Cervante, L., Shang, L., Browne, W.N., Zhang, M.: A multi-objective particle swarm optimisation for filter-based feature selection in classification problems. Connect. Sci. 24(2–3), 91–116 (2012)

Network Knowledge Representation and Learning

Feature-Aware Attentive Convolutional Neural Network for Sequence Processing

Jingchao Dai[ID], Kaiqi Yuan[ID], Yuexiang Xie, and Ying Shen[✉][ID]

School of Electronics and Computer Engineering,
Peking University Shenzhen Graduate School, Shenzhen, China
{daijingchao,kqyuan,xieyx}@pku.edu.cn, shenying@pkusz.edu.cn

Abstract. Sequence processing has attracted increasing attention recently due to its broad range of applications. The development of deep neural network has made great progress in research. However, the domain features used and their interactions that play crucial roles in feature learning are still under-explored. In this paper, we propose a feature-aware **Seq**uence **A**ttentive Convolutional **N**eural **N**etwork (SeqANN) that interactively learns the sequence representations by harnessing the sequence global and local information as well as the expressive domain knowledge. In specific, we develop a one-channel Convolutional Neural NetWork (CNN) and a multi-channel CNN to learn the information of global sequence and local sequence, respectively. In addition, a feature-aware attention mechanism is designed to learn the interactions between features and adaptively determine the significant parts of local representations based on the sequence representations of domain features. SeqANN is evaluated on a widely-used biomedical dataset: RBP-24. Experiment results demonstrate that SeqANN has robust superiority over competitors and achieves competitive performance.

Keywords: Sequence processing · Attention mechanism ·
Convolution neural network

1 Introduction

Sequence data processing which aims to process ordered lists of events has received significant attention in the past few years. In sequence data processing, events can be represented as symbol values, numeric real values, real-value vectors, and complex data types [16,17]. A board range of applications can be benefited from sequence processing such as the heart disease detection via the observed time series of heart rates [21], the illegal money laundering detection via the analysis of the transaction information of bank accounts, and the anomalous intrusion detection via the monitor of the order of user activity access on UNIX system [2,9].

Supported by the National Natural Science Foundation of China (No. 61602013), and the Shenzhen Fundamental Research Project (No. JCYJ20170818091546869).

© Springer Nature Switzerland AG 2019
C. Douligeris et al. (Eds.): KSEM 2019, LNAI 11776, pp. 313–325, 2019.
https://doi.org/10.1007/978-3-030-29563-9_28

In this study, we study the process of RNA sequencing which is composed of four nucleotides A, G, C, U (such as ACCCUCCA), so as to detect RNA-binding proteins that play key roles in many biological processes in genomic analysis research [6].

Compared with traditional text processing, sequence processing has two major challenges. (1) There is a problem of performing sequence learning with explicit feature sparseness and high dimension. (2) The interactions between different features derived from sequence and external knowledge bases have received little attention in existing sequence learning methods.

To address the problems above, we propose a feature-aware sequence attentive neural network for the dimensionality reduction and sequence interactive denoising, so as to improve the sequence processing. In specific, we first train a global single-channel CNN and a local multi-channel CNN in parallel to learn the global/local sequence representations respectively. In addition, domain features in the context of the application of sequences as well as the feature-driven attention are considered. In the biomedical domain, using various domain features (e.g., Kmer is a feature of RNA sequence) and exploring their interaction via attention mechanism can improve the informative knowledge acquisition from long and sparse sequences. Finally, we evaluate our model using publicly large-scaled dataset: RBP24. The experimental results show that our model outperforms other existing methods in terms of prediction accuracy.

The main contributions of this work can be summarized as follows:

(1) We propose a novel sequence processing model, Sequence Attentive CNN (SeqANN), which leverages the global information, local information and domain features in the application field. Compared with previous works, the model combines more information.
(2) We design a feature-aware attention mechanism to learn the interactions between features and adaptively determine the significant parts of local representations based on the sequence representations of domain features.
(3) Experiment results show that compared with the existing methods, SeqANN consistently outperforms the state-of-art methods.

2   Related Work

In this section, we discuss previous works which are related to our method and analyze their differences.

2.1   Sequence Processing

Traditional sequence processing methods [8,21] mainly include three types of approaches, i.e., feature classification, distance classification, and statistical method. Feature classification methods transform the sequence into feature vectors by feature selection and then classified by traditional classification methods. Distance classification methods are performed by defining and calculating the distance function of the similarity between sequences. Statistical methods are classified based on statistical models such as Hidden Markov Model. Recently with the rapid development of deep learning, neural networks have been applied to various sequence processing tasks [18]. In genomic research, convolutional neural networks (CNNs) [7] based methods outperforms other traditional methods for predicting protein-binding RNAs/DNAs [5,14,22]. Pan [13] presents a computational model iDeepE by combing global and local information. In addition, DeepSea trains a CNN model to predict the chromatin effects of sequence changing [24]. On the tasks of time series classification, a deep learning framework for multivariate time series classification is proposed by Zheng [23]. After that, Cui [3] presents an end-to-end convolutional neural network model which incorporates feature extraction and classification in a single framework. Nan [12] formulates Recurrent neural network (RNN) encoders using a multilayer conditional sequence encoder that reads in one token at a time. In this way, it can focus on the key parts of the input as needed. But the methods above ignore domain features of the sequences, especially the interactions among different features.

2.2   Attention Mechanism

Attention mechanism [20] is designed to alleviate the limitation of traditional encoder-decoder structure, which is first proposed in the field of visual images. Google studies the image classification by using attention mechanism in RNN model [11]. Subsequently, Bahdanau applies the attention mechanism in the field of natural language processing [1], which simultaneously translates and aligns the text in the tasks of machine translation. After that, Paulus [15] presents a new training method in abstractive summarization. Recently, attention mechanism plays an important role in sequence learning tasks. Tian [19] proposes an attention aware bidirectional GRU framework to classify the sentiment polarity from the aspects of sentential-sequence modeling and word-feature seizing. We can reweight the value of the source data by adding attention mechanism to the encoder or change the weight of the target data by adding attention mechanism to the decoder, which can effectively improve the system performance of the sequence in the natural way of the sequences. In this paper, we utilize attention mechanism to focus on the most important and relevant parts of the domain features and sequences to improve the performance and effect of the model.

3   Methodology

Given a sequence, our model aims to process and classify the sequence. Concretely, we firstly employ a single-channel CNN to learn the global representations (Sect. 3.1). Then a multi-channel CNN is designed to learn the local features in the sequence (Sect. 3.2). Afterwards, we introduce the self-attention mechanism to learn domain features. Meanwhile, we present a feature-aware attention mechanism to adaptively decide the important information of local representations based on the domain feature representations of sequences (Sect. 3.3).

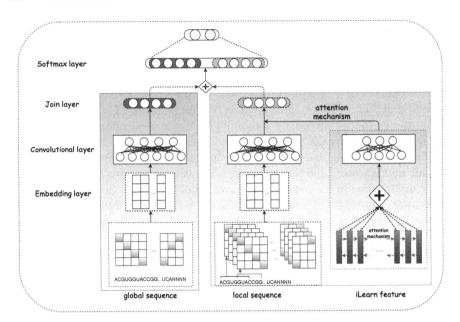

Fig. 1. The overall architecture of SeqANN. Red and green parts denote global and local sequences respectively. Blue part denotes the domain features of sequence in the application field. (Color figure online)

Finally, there is a join layer before the final binary classification to integrate all information. Figure 1 illustrates the overall architecture of SeqANN.

3.1 Representation Learning of Global Sequence

In the representation learning of global sequence, the CNN model captures information from the whole sequences. Considering that the length of sequences varies greatly while CNN model requires input with a fixed length, we need to preprocess the sequences. To ensure that the length of the input sequence is equal, we pad all sequences into the maximum length which is predefined by calculating the longest sequence in the whole dataset. Since the sequence is composed of characters, we convert it into a one-hot encoding matrix.

The detailed architecture of our model is illustrated in Fig. 2. Concretely, we employ two convolutional layers, two pooling layers, a Rectified Linear Units layer (ReLU) and a dropout layer. Convolutional and pooling layers are designed alternately to connect to extract features of different layers. The convolutional layer is employed to extract different non-linear features of the input sequence. The convolution outputs the pointwise product between input one-hot matrix and filters. The first layer of convolutional layer may only extract some low-level features. The second layer can iteratively extract more complex features from low-level features. The step of convolutional layer is formatted as follows:

$$conv(S): x_i = \sum_{j=1}^{k}\sum_{l=1}^{n} Si + j, l \tag{1}$$

$$ReLU = \begin{cases} 0 & if\ x < 0 \\ x & else \end{cases} \tag{2}$$

where S is the input one-hot matrix of sequence s, k is the kernel size, i is the index in a sequence, n is the kinds of characters, l is the index corresponding to the character in the matrix. The outputs x_i denotes the feature maps. The max pooling operation is applied to further extract features and reduce the vector dimensionality and training parameters by selecting the maximum value over a window. Moreover, in order to prevent over-fitting, dropout technology is introduced in convolution layer. When updating the weight of neurons in the network, some neurons are selected randomly without updating, which weakens the joint adaptability between neurons and enhances the generalization ability. The model uses ReLU as the activation function. ReLU can not only mine features better in sparse data, but also avoid the problem of gradient disappearance.

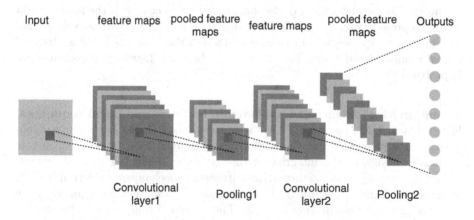

Fig. 2. The detailed structure of CNN model

3.2   Representation Learning of Local Sequence

The representation of local sequence is designed to learn the local structure context. In order to take the local sequences into account, we first decompose the RNA sequence with length L into several subsequences with window size W, and consider each subsequence as a channel. These subsequences overlap with each other in superposition length S. Accordingly, the number of subsequences is

$(L-W)/(W-S)$. In addition, we calculate the maximum number of channels C according to the predefined longest sequence in the training set. If the number of channels of a sequence is less than C, it will extend the channels derived from the sequence with meaningless characters to C. Finally, we encode the subsequences into a one-hot matrix and the multi-channel CNN of local sequences is performed by inputting them into CNN as Fig. 2.

3.3   Feature-Aware Attention Mechanism

Attention Mechanism Among Domain Features. Considering that there are some important interactions among the domain features, we extract the feature and adopt the self-attention mechanism to enable the features to be aware of informative knowledge and hidden relationships. As shown in the right panel of Fig. 1.

$$w_i = \frac{exp(f_i))}{\sum_{i=1}^{n} exp(f_i)} \tag{3}$$

$$F = softmax \sum_{i=1}^{n} w_i f_i \tag{4}$$

where n is the number of kinds of features, f_i scores the correlation between the features, w_i is the new weight of the domain feature vector. F is the final domain feature representation vector. The softmax function, also known as softargmax or normalized exponential function, is a function that takes as input a vector of K real numbers, and normalizes it into a probability distribution consisting of K probabilities.

Attention Mechanism Between Domain Features and Local Sequences. For the local CNN, we convert the sequence into multiple overlapping fixed-length subsequences. Since the sliding window separation of the sequence is artificially designed, the integrity of the sequence is affected to some extent. Therefore, we design a feature-driven attention mechanism to determine the influence of domain features on local sequence information for improving the entire sequence representation learning. The specific formulas are as follows:

$$a_i = \frac{exp(e_i)}{\sum_{i=1} exp(e_i)} \tag{5}$$

where e_i scores the correlation between the local sequence and the domain features, a_i is the new weight of the local sequence vector.

3.4   Joint Learning Method

Finally, in order to make our model more robust and accurate, the global and local model is integrated by a join layer which concatenates the global sequence vector and the local sequence vector. The outputs of the two fully connected layer then go through a softmax layer for binary classification.

$$y = softmax(W_y x + b_y) \tag{6}$$

where each dimension of y denotes the normalized probability of a certain classification, i.e., positive or negative, in accordance with the fully connected layer, W_y and b_y are trainable weight and bias, d is the projection matrix. The softmax function has the same meaning as Eq. 4.

4   Experiments

4.1   Datasets

We evaluate our model on a real-world widely-used dataset: RBP-24, which is a subsequence-level dataset used for modeling binding preferences of RNA-binding proteins. The training and testing datasets are available via the GraphProt website[1]. There are 21 RBPs and 24 experiments in the dataset. For each sequence, it has positive sites and negative sites. For each experiment, the positive sites are the subsequences anchored at the peak center derived from CLIP-seq processed in doRiNA [6], while the negative sequence sites are the regions with no supportive evidence of being binding sites. The number of positive and negative samples is balanced.

4.2   Implementation Details

Data Processing

Sequence Encoding. After preprocessing the sequences as stated in Sect. 3, we convert the sequences into one-hot matrix [4]. Given the sequence $s = (s_1, s_2, ...s_n)$, where n is the length of the sequence and k is the kernel size. Then the one-hot matrix $\mathbf{M}$ is given by:

$$M_{i,r} = \begin{cases} 1 & if \ s_{i-k+1} \ in \ (A, C, G, U) \\ 0.25 & if \ s_{i-k+1} = N \ or \ i > n - k \\ 0 & otherwise \end{cases} \tag{7}$$

where i is the index of the sequence, r is the index corresponding to the order A, C, G, U. For the padded Ns, it is assumed that they are random distributions of four existing characters, which means that the probability of any nucleotide is equal. Therefore, we use [0.25,0.25.0.25.0.25] to represent them.

---

[1] http://www.bioinf.unifreiburg.de/Software/GraphProt.

iLearn Features. As for the domain features, we employ iLearn[2] which is a versatile Python-based toolkit to analyze the structures and functions of the biological sequences. We obtain 12 types of biological features, including Kmer, RCKmer, NAC, DNC, TNC, ANF, ENAC, binary, CKSNAP, NCP, EIIP, and PseEIIP. Then we fill the feature vector to the same maximum length with the meaningless value "−1". Moreover, we pad the features into four dimensions as the global and local sequences are both four-dimensional vectors to ensure the data consistency.

Parameters Configuration. As for the global CNNs, the maximum length of sequence L is set as the rule that L is longer than 90% of sequences in the training set and the left 10% sequences are truncated to length L. As for the local CNNs, the window size W and shift size S are selected by grid search. In this way, L, W, S are set to be 501, 101, and 20 respectively in RBP-24. The dropout rate is set to be 0.25. We train our models in batches with size of 100 and epoch size of 50. Adam is used to minimize binary cross-entropy loss. The number of filters is set to 16. The initial weights and bias use default setting in Pytorch. For the baseline models, we follow exactly the same parameter setting as those in their original papers.

4.3   Baseline Methods

iDeepE [13] is a computational method to predict RNA-protein binding sites from RNA sequences by combining global and local convolutional neural networks (CNNs).

CNN-LSTM-E [13] is a computational method which adds a two-layer bidirectional Long Short-Term Memory (LSTM) before the fully connected layers based iDeepE.

GraphProt [10] is a computational framework for learning sequence- and structure-binding preferences of RNA-binding proteins (RBPs) from high-throughput experimental data.

Deepnet-rbp [22] is a deep learning framework for modeling structural binding preferences and predicting binding sites of RBPs, which takes (predicted) RNA tertiary structural information into account.

4.4   Results

The experimental results on RBP-24 are summarized in Table 1. We compare our results with the recent work reported in literature as we mentioned in Sect. 4.3. And we measure AUC on each protein as our evaluating indicator. There is multiple analysis as follows:

---

[2] http://ilearn.erc.monash.edu/.

(1) SeqANN yields the best average AUC across 24 experiments and the best AUC on 18 experiments. The results of SeqANN significantly outperform other methods, which demonstrates the effectiveness of incorporating biological features, local structure context and attention mechanism.
(2) It is observed that SeqANN performs worse on RBPs such as ALKBH5. The reason is that CNN-based models need large-scale data to fit. Similarly, ResNet, which is a complex neural network, has limited performance due to insufficient datasets.

Table 1. The performance (AUC) of SeqANN and other baseline methods on RBP-24

RBP	SeqANN	iDeepE	CNN-LSTM-E	GraphProt	Deepnet-rbp
ALKBH5	0.700	0.682	0.653	0.680	**0.714**
C17ORF85	**0.836**	0.830	0.822	0.800	0.820
C22ORF28	**0.838**	0.837	0.801	0.751	0.792
CAPRIN1	**0.905**	0.893	0.871	0.855	0.834
Ago2	**0.872**	0.868	0.851	0.765	0.809
ELAVL1H	**0.980**	0.979	0.975	0.955	0.966
SFRS1	**0.949**	0.946	0.929	0.898	0.931
HNRNPC	**0.981**	0.976	0.973	0.952	0.962
TDP43	**0.946**	0.945	0.928	0.874	0.876
TIA1	**0.942**	0.937	0.911	0.861	0.891
TIAL1	**0.934**	0.934	0.901	0.833	0.870
Ago1-4	**0.920**	0.915	0.873	0.895	0.881
ELAVL1B	**0.978**	0.971	0.963	0.935	0.961
ELAVL1A	**0.974**	0.964	0.962	0.959	0.966
EWSR1	**0.973**	0.969	0.965	0.935	0.966
FUS	**0.985**	0.985	0.980	0.968	0.980
ELAVL1C	0.990	0.988	0.986	0.991	**0.994**
IGF2BP1-3	**0.954**	0.947	0.940	0.889	0.879
MOV10	**0.928**	0.916	0.899	0.863	0.854
PUM2	0.969	0.967	0.963	0.954	**0.971**
QKI	0.974	0.970	0.966	0.957	**0.983**
TAF15	0.980	0.976	0.974	0.970	**0.983**
PTB	0.949	0.944	0.929	0.937	**0.983**
ZC3H7B	**0.908**	0.907	0.879	0.820	0.796
Mean	**0.932**	0.927	0.912	0.887	0.902

In order to analyze the effectiveness of different factors of SeqANN, we also report the ablations test in terms of discarding global CNN (w/o global), local CNN (w/o local) and feature-aware attention mechanism (w/o attention), respectively. The comparison results are shown in Table 2. Generally, these three parts all contribute to the performance of the model. The global information plays the greatest role in improving the performance of the whole model. In addition, as we expected, the introduction of the biological feature-aware attention mechanism provides supplementary information, which properly improves the accuracy of the model. It proves that our method of introducing feature-aware mechanism can improve the performance compared with those without feature-aware methods.

Table 2. The performance (AUC) of ablations test on RBP-24

RBP	SeqANN	w/o global	w/o local	w/o attention
ALKBH5	**0.700**	0.636	0.699	0.682
C17ORF85	**0.836**	0.808	0.810	0.830
C22ORF28	**0.838**	0.807	0.808	0.837
CAPRIN1	**0.905**	0.859	0.888	0.893
Ago2	**0.872**	0.853	0.843	0.868
ELAVL1H	**0.980**	0.965	0.977	0.979
SFRS1	**0.949**	0.916	0.936	0.946
HNRNPC	**0.981**	0.971	0.976	0.976
TDP43	**0.946**	0.929	0.932	0.945
TIA1	**0.942**	0.924	0.927	0.937
TIAL1	**0.934**	0.926	0.914	0.934
Ago1-4	**0.920**	0.907	0.899	0.915
ELAVL1B	**0.978**	0.974	0.968	0.971
ELAVL1A	**0.974**	0.960	0.970	0.964
EWSR1	**0.973**	0.958	0.967	0.969
FUS	**0.985**	0.979	0.979	0.985
ELAVL1C	**0.990**	0.986	0.989	0.988
IGF2BP1-3	**0.954**	0.913	0.936	0.947
MOV10	**0.928**	0.900	0.905	0.916
PUM2	**0.969**	0.955	0.961	0.967
QKI	**0.974**	0.969	0.966	0.970
TAF15	**0.980**	0.974	0.970	0.976
PTB	**0.949**	0.940	0.937	0.944
ZC3H7B	**0.908**	0.901	0.877	0.907
Mean	**0.932**	0.913	0.918	0.927

To evaluate the performance of the model more intuitively and comprehensively, we draw ROC curves on two datasets: CLIPSEQ_SFRS1 and

PARCLIP_EWSR1. As shown in Fig. 3, we can intuitively observe that the area of SeqANN is larger than the baseline models. Furthermore, we also show the training loss on CLIPSEQ_SFRS1 with the number of epochs in Fig. 4. The result shows that our model converges with lower training loss than the other models.

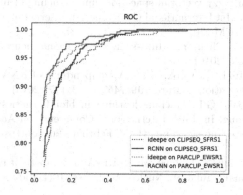

Fig. 3. The ROC curve on CLIPSEQ_SFRS1 and PARCLIP_EWSR1.

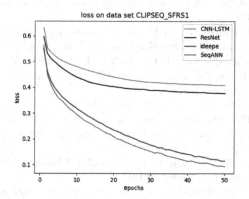

Fig. 4. The training loss on CLIPSEQ_SFRS1

5   Conclusion

In this paper, we propose a feature-aware attentive neural network for sequence processing, which effectively incorporates the global information, local information and domain features. It is proved that the attention mechanism can be more effective to notice the crucial information between the sequences and the domain features. The experimental results on the real-world widely-used dataset demonstrate the superiority of our proposed method on sequence processing.

References

1. Bahdanau, D., Cho, K., Bengio, Y.: Neural machine translation by jointly learning to align and translate. Computer Science (2014)
2. Colloc, J., Yameogo, R.A., Summons, P.F., Shen, Y., Park, M., Aronson, J.E.: Epice an emotion fuzzy vectorial space for time modeling in medical decision. In: Proceedings of the 1st International Conference on Internet of Things and Machine Learning, p. 29. ACM (2017)
3. Cui, Z., Chen, W., Chen, Y.: Multi-scale convolutional neural networks for time series classification (2016)
4. Debashish, R., Hilal, K., Cook, K.B.: A compendium of RNA-binding motifs for decoding gene regulation. Nature **499**(7457), 172–177 (2015)
5. Dixit, P., Prajapati, G.I.: Machine learning in bioinformatics: a novel approach for DNA sequencing. In: Fifth International Conference on Advanced Computing Communication Technologies, pp. 41–47, February 2015. https://doi.org/10.1109/ACCT.2015.73
6. Gerd, A., Mackowiak, S.D., Jens, M.: doRiNA: a database of RNA interactions in post-transcriptional regulation. Nucleic Acids Res. **40**(Database issue), D180–D186 (2012)
7. Lecun, Y., Bottou, L., Bengio, Y., Haffner, P.: Gradient-based learning applied to document recognition. Proc. IEEE **86**(11), 2278–2324 (1998). https://doi.org/10.1109/5.726791
8. Lei, K., et al.: Cooperative denoising for distantly supervised relation extraction. In: Proceedings of the 27th International Conference on Computational Linguistics, pp. 426–436 (2018)
9. Leontjeva, A., Conforti, R., Di Francescomarino, C., Dumas, M., Maggi, F.M.: Complex symbolic sequence encodings for predictive monitoring of business processes. In: Motahari-Nezhad, H.R., Recker, J., Weidlich, M. (eds.) BPM 2015. LNCS, vol. 9253, pp. 297–313. Springer, Cham (2015). https://doi.org/10.1007/978-3-319-23063-4_21
10. Maticzka, D., Lange, S.J., Costa, F., Backofen, R.: GraphProt: modeling binding preferences of RNA-binding proteins. Genome Biol. **15**(1), R17 (2014)
11. Mnih, V., Heess, N., Graves, A., Kavukcuoglu, K.: Recurrent models of visual attention **3** (2014)
12. Nan, R.K., Zolna, K., Sordoni, A., Lin, Z., Pal, C.: Focused hierarchical RNNs for conditional sequence processing (2018)
13. Pan, X., Shen, H.B.: Predicting RNA-protein binding sites and motifs through combining local and global deep convolutional neural networks. Bioinformatics (2018)
14. Pan, X., Fan, Y.X., Yan, J., Shen, H.B.: IPMiner: hidden ncRNA-protein interaction sequential pattern mining with stacked autoencoder for accurate computational prediction. BMC Genomics **17**(1), 582 (2016)
15. Paulus, R., Xiong, C., Socher, R.: A deep reinforced model for abstractive summarization (2017)
16. Shen, Y., et al.: Drug2Vec: knowledge-aware feature-driven method for drug representation learning. In: IEEE International Conference on Bioinformatics and Biomedicine (BIBM), pp. 757–800. IEEE (2018)
17. Shen, Y., et al.: KMR: knowledge-oriented medicine representation learning for drug-drug interaction and similarity computation. J. Cheminformatics **11**(1), 22 (2019)

18. Sutskever, I., Vinyals, O., Le, Q.V.: Sequence to sequence learning with neural networks (2014)
19. Tian, Z., Rong, W., Shi, L., Liu, J., Xiong, Z.: Attention aware bidirectional gated recurrent unit based framework for sentiment analysis. In: Liu, W., Giunchiglia, F., Yang, B. (eds.) KSEM 2018. LNCS (LNAI), vol. 11061, pp. 67–78. Springer, Cham (2018). https://doi.org/10.1007/978-3-319-99365-2_6
20. Vaswani, A., et al.: Attention is all you need (2017)
21. Xing, Z., Pei, J., Keogh, E.J.: A brief survey on sequence classification. ACM SIGKDD Explor. Newsl. **12**(1), 40–48 (2010)
22. Zhang, S., et al.: A deep learning framework for modeling structural features of RNA-binding protein targets. Nucleic Acids Res. **44**(4), e32 (2015)
23. Zheng, Y., Liu, Q., Chen, E., Ge, Y., Zhao, J.L.: Time series classification using multi-channels deep convolutional neural networks. In: Li, F., Li, G., Hwang, S., Yao, B., Zhang, Z. (eds.) WAIM 2014. LNCS, vol. 8485, pp. 298–310. Springer, Cham (2014). https://doi.org/10.1007/978-3-319-08010-9_33
24. Zhou, J., Troyanskaya, O.G.: Predicting effects of noncoding variants with deep learning-based sequence model. Nat. Methods **12**(10), 931–934 (2015)

Exploiting Tri-types of Information for Attributed Network Embedding

Cheng Zhang[1,2,3], Le Zhang[1,2,3], Xiaobo Guo[1,2,3], and Ying Qi[3(✉)]

[1] School of Cyber Security, University of Chinese Academy of Sciences,
Beijing, China
[2] State Key Laboratory of Information Security, Chinese Academy of Sciences,
Beijing, China
[3] Institute of Information Engineering, Chinese Academy of Sciences, Beijing, China
{zhangcheng,zhangle,guoxiaobo,qiying}@iie.ac.cn

Abstract. With a surge of network data, attributed networks are widely applied for various applications. Recently, how to embed an attributed network into a low-dimensional representation space has gained a lot of attention. Noting that nodes in attributed networks not only have structural information, but also often contain attribute and label information. Actually, these types of information could help to learn effective node representations since they can strengthen the similarities of nodes. However, most existing embedding methods consider either network structure only or both of the structural and attribute information, ignoring node labels. They merely produce suboptimal results as these methods fail to leverage all of these information. To address this issue, we propose a novel method called EANE that is Exploiting tri-types of information (*i.e.*, network structure, node attributes and labels) for learning an effective Attributed Network Embedding. Specifically, EANE consists of three modules that separately encode these three information while preserving their correlations. Experimental results on three real-world datasets show that EANE outperforms the state-or-art embedding algorithms.

Keywords: Network embedding · Attributed networks · Autoencoder

1 Introduction

In the era of big data, attributed networks are ubiquitous in various applications, such as social media and academic networks. Different from plain networks, nodes in attributed networks often contain both topological structure and attribute information, and maybe have label information [6,13]. Mining useful information from such network data is beneficial for many network related applications. Most of these tasks require to how effectively represent the network data. Centered around this goal, network embedding aims to map nodes of a network into low-dimensional representation space while preserving the inherent properties of the original network [3,23]. Afterwards, the learned representations can be directly

© Springer Nature Switzerland AG 2019
C. Douligeris et al. (Eds.): KSEM 2019, LNAI 11776, pp. 326–338, 2019.
https://doi.org/10.1007/978-3-030-29563-9_29

applied to subsequent network analysis tasks, such as node classification [17,22], community detection [2,20] and anomaly detection [9,26].

It is worth noting that attributed networks often contain three types of information, such as network structure, node attributes and node labels [3,23]. These information have inherent correlations [13,25], which systematically reflect the structure proximity, attribute affinity and label similarity of nodes. Typically, nodes with similar attributes tend to be connected together, then they usually have similar labels and belong to the same group [10,11]. In real-world social networks such as Facebook and Weibo, labels often denote groups or communities. Due to users having similar interests or properties, they frequently interact with each other, and join the specific groups, then contain the same labels [6,23]. Hence, all of these information could strengthen the similarities of nodes, and thus they are potentially helpful in learning effective node representations. However, most existing network embedding methods consider either network structure only [14,18] or both of the structural and attribute information [22,25], but ignore label information. These methods merely produce suboptimal representations as they fail to collectively utilize these three information [3,23].

In order to obtain better node representations, we try to collectively leverage three types of information including network structure, node attribute and label information, while capturing their intrinsic relationships. Nevertheless, it is a difficult task because there exists several main challenges. Firstly, since node attributes are usually sparse and high dimensional [6,22], it is difficult to reduce the dimensionality of node attributes while preserving useful attribute information. Secondly, the heterogeneity of these three information imposes a great challenge to seamlessly integrate them into a unified representation space [4,7]. If these heterogeneous information are simply concatenated together, we cannot capture their mutual relationships, thus only get the suboptimal results [22,23]. Thirdly, how to effectively explore the inherent correlations among these types of information for finding an optimal network embedding is a hard task.

To address the above challenges, we propose a novel method called EANE that collectively leverages tri-types of information, *i.e.*, network structure, node attributes and node labels, for learning an Effective Attributed Network Embedding. Specifically, the proposed method consists of three modules. Firstly, EANE designs an autoencoder module to map node attributes into a low-dimensional representation space, while getting useful information from node attributes. Secondly, to capture the structural proximity between nodes, EANE employs the skip-gram module to predict the contexts by giving a current node's generated representation. Meanwhile, to strength the label similarities of nodes, EANE adopts the canonical multilayer perceptron (MLP) module to predict the node label by input its representation. Finally, we introduce a joint framework to iteratively optimize these modules so that these types of information map into a unified space while simultaneously preserving their intrinsic correlations. In summary, our main contributions are as follows:

– We propose the EANE algorithm to jointly exploit three types of information (*i.e.*, network structure, node attributes and labels) for learning an effective attributed network embedding, and use the autoencode, skip-gram and MLP modules to encode these three information accordingly.

- We develop a joint framework that effectively integrates these three information into a unified representation space while maximizing their mutual interactions to generate optimal node representations.
- We conduct experiments on three real-world network datasets through node classification and link prediction, and empirically evaluate the effectiveness of our proposed model EANE.

2   Related Works

Network embedding algorithms have received increasing attention. Among them, DeepWalk [14] adopts truncated random walks to capture the structural proximity between nodes, and then applies the skip-gram model [12] to get node representations; Node2Vec [5] performs the breadth-first (BFS) and depth-first (DFS) search strategy to effectively explore the structural information, then uses skip-gram to generate the network embedding; LINE [16] explicitly defines two objective functions to describe the first-order and second-order proximity respectively, and optimize these two functions to learn node representations; GraRep [1] exploits k-th proximities among nodes for finding node representations. With the development of deep learning techniques, SDNE [18] firstly employs the deep autoencoder model to capture the non-linear structural information to obtain the network embedding. However, the above methods have only focused on utilizing network structure for the embedding learned, but ignored other valuable information in attributed networks, thus produce suboptimal representations.

In order to obtain better node representations, several related efforts attempt to jointly exploit three information sources, such as network structure, node attribute and label information. They believe that these three sources exist mutual correlations that could enhance the similarities of nodes [3,23]. Through capturing their interplays, these methods enable the aforementioned three information to complement with each other, thus find a better attributed network embedding [22,25]. For instance, PTE [15] utilizes label information and different levels of word co-occurrence information to generate predictive text representations; TriDNR [13] leverages three parties of information including node link, node content and node labels (if available) for generating node representations; LANE [6] investigates the potential of integrating labels with network structure and node attributes into an embedding representation, while preserving their correlations; SEANO [9] takes the input from the aggregation of current node attributes and its average neighborhood attributes to smooth the negative effect of outliers in the representation learning process.

3   Problem Statement

In this section, we firstly introduce some notations used in this paper, then describe our problem. Given $G = (\mathcal{V}, \mathcal{E}, \mathbf{X}, \mathbf{Y})$ is an attributed network, where $\mathcal{V}$

is the set of $|\mathcal{V}|$ nodes, and $\mathcal{E}$ is the set of edges. Matrix $\mathbf{X} \in \mathbb{R}^{|\mathcal{V}| \times m}$ collects all node attribute information, and its row x_i denotes the m-dimensional attribute vector of a node v_i. Let $\mathbf{Y} \in \mathbb{R}^{|\mathcal{V}_L| \times H}$ be a label matrix that describes the set of $|\mathcal{V}_L|$ labeled nodes in G, where H is the number of label categories. Each element $y_i^h = 1$ in Y represents a node v_i associated with a label l_h, otherwise $y_i^h = 0$. Accordingly, there are $|\mathcal{V}_U|$ unlabeled nodes in an attributed network G, and we have $|\mathcal{V}| = |\mathcal{V}_L| + |\mathcal{V}_U|$.

Our problem is to represent each node $v_i \in \mathcal{V}$ as a low-dimensional vector space $\phi_i \in \mathbb{R}^d$, where $d \ll |\mathcal{V}|$. The learned node representations effectively incorporate three types of information (*i.e.*, network structure, node attributes and node labels) together while preserving their correlations among these three information. After that, the learned node representations are taken as the input to subsequent analysis tasks such as node classification and link prediction.

4   Methodological

In this part, we propose the EANE model that collectively exploits three types of information, such as network structure, node attributes and labels, for generating an optimal representation of each node in a network G.

The overall architecture of the model EANE is shown in Fig. 1. The core idea of EANE is that node attribute information is closely correlated to both of the network structure and label information [11,24]. Specifically, nodes with similar attributes often have structural proximities, then they also tend to share similar labels. Therefore, these three types of information are potentially helpful in learning better node representations as they could strengthen the similarities of nodes. Motivated by this fact, we propose to study how network structure, node attributes and labels can be jointly incorporated into EANE. Next, we introduce the proposed model EANE in detail.

4.1   The Autoencoder Module

Since node attributes are often very noise and high dimensional, it is important to distill useful features from the attribute information. As shown in [25,26], we also design an autoencoder module to model node attributes. And it consists of two parts: the encoder and the decoder. Especially, the encoder part projects a node v_i with attributes x_i into a low-dimensional hidden representation that preserves valuable information in node attributes and reduces the attribute dimension. Then the decoder part reconstructs the input attributes from the hidden representation. And therefore, the hidden representation for each layer is formulated as:

$$y_i^{(1)} = \sigma \left(W^{(1)} \cdot x_i + b^{(1)} \right)$$
$$y_i^{(k)} = \sigma \left(W^{(k)} \cdot y_i^{(k-1)} + b^{(k)} \right), k = 2, \ldots, K \tag{1}$$

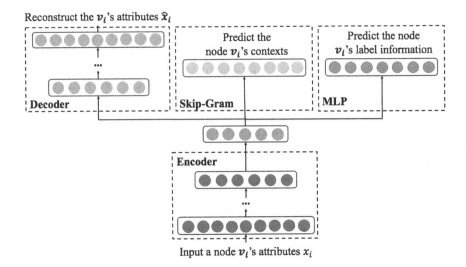

Fig. 1. Our proposed model EANE designs three modules, including the autoencoder, skip-gram, and canonical multilayer perceptron (MLP), to model three types of information (*i.e.*, network structure, node attributes and labels). Specifically, autoencoder projects the input node v_i's attributes x_i into a low-dimensional representation space, then reconstructs the target attributes $\hat{x}_i$ from this space. Besides, the learned representations are fed into the skip-gram and MLP modules to predict the contexts C_i of a node v_i and its label information y_i, respectively. Through jointly optimizing these three modules, EANE generates desirable node representations while preserving the mutual correlations among these three types of information in an attributed network.

where K denotes the number of layers for the encoder and decoder, $\sigma(\cdot)$ defines the activation functions, such as ReLU. $W^{(k)}$ and $b^{(k)}$ are the transformation matrix and bias vector in the k-th layer, separately. The goal of the autoencoder is to minimize the reconstruction error of the input and output. And its process is written as:

$$\mathcal{L}_{ae} = \sum_{i=1}^{|\mathcal{V}|} \|\hat{x}_i - x_i\|_2^2 \qquad (2)$$

Here $\hat{x}_i$ is the reconstruction output of decoder. Through making the input node attributes and reconstruction targets as similar as possible, we get the low-dimensional representation $f(x_i)$ in the hidden layers. Similar to [9,25], to have better training performance, the regularization of parameters $W^{(k)}$ and $\hat{W}^{(k)}$ should be imposed on the Eq. (2). Then the loss function is rewritten as:

$$\mathcal{L}_{ae} = \sum_{i=1}^{|\mathcal{V}|} \|\hat{x}_i - x_i\|_2^2 + \frac{\beta}{2} \sum_{k=1}^{K} \left(\left\| W^{(k)} \right\|_F^2 + \left\| \hat{W}^{(k)} \right\|_F^2 \right) \qquad (3)$$

The function $\|\cdot\|_F^2$ is the ℓ_2 norm and β is the regularizer coefficient.

4.2   The Skip-Gram Module

Note that recent works are widely used the skip-gram model to encode network structure [5,14]. They assume that nodes with similar contexts tend to have similar representation. Actually, node attributes are closely related with the network structure. It's obvious that nodes in an attributed network are closely connected with each other because they share similar attributes [10,11]. Therefore, the attribute information could strengthen the similarities of nodes, which may help to get better node representations [22,25]. Motived by this fact, we propose to incorporate node attribute information with network structure together. Specifically, the objective function minimizes the following log probability of skip-gram model by giving current node x_i with its learned representation $f(x_i)$.

$$\mathcal{L}_{sg} = -\sum_{i=1}^{|\mathcal{V}|} \sum_{v_j \in C_i} \log \Pr(v_j|x_i) \tag{4}$$

where $v_j \in \{v_{i-t}, \ldots, v_{i+t}\} \setminus v_i$ is the node context in the generated random walk and t is the window size. And the conditional probability of $\Pr(v_j|x_i)$ is the likelihood of the current node context by giving its attributes. Therefore, the probability is formulated as:

$$\Pr(v_j|x_i) = \frac{\exp\left(\mathbf{v}_j^T \cdot f(x_i)\right)}{\sum_{s=1}^{|\mathcal{V}|} \exp\left(\mathbf{v}_s^T \cdot f(x_i)\right)} \tag{5}$$

Here $f(\cdot)$ is the encoder component, which transforms the input attribute information x_i into a low-dimensional representation. And $\mathbf{v}_j$ is the corresponding representations when node v_j is the context for the node v_i. Nothing that if we directly calculate the Eq. (5), it's rather expensive because we require to iterate through all the nodes in a network. To speed up the training process, we adopt the negative sampling strategy proposed in [12] that samples multiple negative contexts according to some noisy distributions. And thus, how well a node $v_i \in \mathcal{V}$ generates its context $v_j \in C_i$ is measured by the following objective:

$$\mathcal{L}_{sg} = \log \sigma\left(\mathbf{v}_j^T \cdot f(x_i)\right) + \sum_{n=1}^{|neg|} \mathbb{E}_{v_n \sim P_n(v)} \log \sigma\left(-\mathbf{v}_n^T \cdot f(x_i)\right) \tag{6}$$

Here $\sigma(x) = 1/(1 + \exp(-x))$ is the sigmoid function. In total, there are $|neg|$ negative samples. As suggested in [22,25], we randomly sample the negative context v_n according to the probability $P_n(v) \propto d_v^{3/4}$, where d_v is the degree of node v. Therefore, for all node $v_i \in \mathcal{V}$, the objective function is rewritten as:

$$\mathcal{L}_{sg} = -\sum_{i=1}^{|\mathcal{V}|} \sum_{v_j \in C_i} \left[\log \sigma\left(\mathbf{v}_j^T f(x_i)\right) + \sum_{n=1}^{|neg|} \mathbb{E}_{v_n \sim P_n(v)} \log \sigma\left(-\mathbf{v}_n^T f(x_i)\right) \right] \tag{7}$$

After optimizing the Eq. (7), useful node attribute information consistent with network structure can be preserved in the representation space.

4.3   The MLP Module

As mentioned above, the node label information also has an intrinsic relationship with node connectivity and attribute information. When nodes have similar labels, they also have structural proximity and attribute affinity that could potentially reinforce the similarities of nodes in a network. Based on that, the model EANE should exploit node label information and integrate it with node attributes together. Similar to [9,21], we also introduce a canonical multilayer perceptron (MLP) module to predict a current node's label by input its learned representation. And thus, its loss function is written as:

$$\mathcal{L}_{la} = - \sum_{i \in \mathcal{V}_L} \log \Pr\left(y_i | f\left(x_i\right)\right) \tag{8}$$

where $\Pr\left(y_i | f\left(x_i\right)\right)$ is the possibility of a node v_i's target label y_i and it is formally defined as follows:

$$\Pr\left(y_i | f\left(x_i\right)\right) = \frac{\exp\left(f\left(x_i\right) \cdot W_{y_i}^{(S)}\right)}{\sum_{y_j \in \mathcal{Y}} \exp\left(f\left(x_i\right) \cdot W_{y_j}^{(S)}\right)} \tag{9}$$

Here, $\mathcal{Y}$ denotes the set of possible node labels in G and $W^{(s)}$ is the weight matrix of the softmax layer used in MLP module. When optimizing Eq. (8), node attribute and label information will jointly affect the learned node representation, which makes them compensate with each other.

4.4   Joint Optimization Framework

Three types of information including network structure, node attributes and labels, are leveraged for generating effective representation of an attributed network. Especially, these three information have intrinsic correlations that could potentially strengthen the similarities of nodes in the network, and thus may lead to producing better node representations. Inspired by [6,23,25], we also construct a joint optimization framework to effectively map these three information into a unified representation while maximizing their mutual relations. And we combine the loss function $\mathcal{L}_{ae}$, $\mathcal{L}_{sg}$ and $\mathcal{L}_{la}$ defined in Eqs. (3), (7) and (8) as the final loss function:

$$\mathcal{L} = \mathcal{L}_{ae} + \alpha \mathcal{L}_{sg} + \mathcal{L}_{la} \tag{10}$$

where α is the hyper parameter to smooth the loss of skip-gram module.

Similar to [9,25], we also use the stochastic gradient algorithm to minimize $\mathcal{L}$ on Eq. (10). Since $\mathcal{L}$ composes of three modules, we iteratively optimize these components to integrate the aforementioned three information into an unified representation space. And we develop a joint optimization framework, which is summarized in Algorithm 1. Firstly, as the encoder part of the autoencoder module, the function $f\left(\cdot\right)$ transforms the node v_i's attribute information x_i into

---

Algorithm 1. A joint Optimization Framework for EANE

Input: an attributed network $G = (\mathcal{V}, \mathcal{E}, \mathbf{X}, \mathbf{Y})$, window size t, walks per node γ, walk
  length l, the dimension d of the learned node representation, trade-off parameter
  α, regularization coefficient β.

Output: node representation $\Phi(v) \in \mathbb{R}^{|\mathcal{V}| \times d}$ for each node $v \in \mathcal{V}$.

 1: Perform random walks from each node by starting γ times with walk length l
 2: Construct node contexts C for each node, and sample its negative contexts
 3: Random initialization for all parameters in the model EANE.
 4: **while** not converged **do**
 5:     Sample a mini-batch of nodes with its contexts and negative samples.
 6:     Calculate the gradient of $\nabla \mathcal{L}_{ae}$ based on Equation (3);
 7:     Update the autoencoder module parameters.
 8:     Calculate the gradient of $\nabla \mathcal{L}_{sg}$ based on Equation (7);
 9:     Update the skip-gram module parameters.
10:     Calculate the gradient of $\nabla \mathcal{L}_{la}$ based on Equation (8);
11:     Update the MLP module parameters.
12: **end while**
13: Generate the representation $\Phi(v)$ for each node $v \in \mathcal{V}$ based on Equation (1).

---

a low-dimensional embedding space $\phi_i^{(K)}$, where generates the node representation. Then, in order to effectively encode the structural and label information, EANE predicts the current node's contexts and labels by giving its learned representation, respectively. By iteratively optimizing these modules until their converges, we respectively update parameters of the model EANE in line 7, 9 and 11. Finally, these types of information are seamlessly encoded into a joint representation space $\phi_i^{(k)}$. Consequently, the interplays among these three types of information enable them to complement with each other towards learning a desirable representation for the attributed network G.

5 Experiments

In this section, we conduct node classification and link prediction tasks on three real-world network datasets to verify the effectiveness of the proposed EANE.

5.1 Experimental Setup

Datasets. In our experiments, we adopt three real-world attributed networks including Cora[1], Citeseer and Pubmed[2]. These network datasets are also used in previous work [7,9,25]. Among them, nodes denote papers and edges describe the citation relations between papers. The attributes of each node are the bag-of-words representations of the corresponding paper. And each node in these datasets only has one of the class labels. A summary of these three datasets is listed in Table 1.

---

[1] https://snap.stanford.edu/data/.
[2] http://linqs.cs.umd.edu/projects/projects/lbc.

Table 1. The statistics of three real-world attributed networks.

Datasets	#of Nodes	#of Edges	#of Attributes	#of Labels
Cora	2,708	5,429	1,433	7
Citeseer	3,327	4,732	3,703	6
Pubmed	19,717	44,328	500	3

Baselines. To verify the performance of our proposed model EANE, we compare it with the following five baseline methods.

- **DeepWalk** [14] performs the truncated random walks on the plain network to generate node sequences, then feeds these sequences to the Skip-Gram model [12] to learn the node representations.
- **LINE** [16] exploits the first-order and second-order proximity between nodes, separately. After learning two types of representations, it concatenates them together to form the final node representations.
- **SDNE** [18] uses multiple layers of non-linear functions to capture the highly non-linear network structure to generate the node representations.
- **LANE** [6] utilizes three kinds of information from node structure, attributes, and labels for learning the representation for each node in a network.
- **SEANO** [9] takes advantage of the deep model to obtain the node embeddings that simultaneously preserve the topological proximity, attribute affinity and label information similarity.

In Particular, the first three baselines only exploit the network structure for getting node representations, and the remaining two methods jointly leverage network structure, node attributes and labels to learn the embedding representation of an attributed network.

Experiment Settings. For all baselines, we use the implementation released by the original authors, and set default parameters according to their report. To be fair comparison, the dimension d of the learned representations is set as 128 for all algorithms. For EANE, we set window size t as 10, walk length l as 80, walks per node γ as 5, and negative samples as 5. Furthermore, the architecture of our approach for different datasets is shown in Table 2.

Table 2. Detailed neural network layers structure information.

Datasets	Number of neurons in each layer
Cora	1,433→1,000→500→128→500→1,000→1,433
Citeseer	3,703→1,000→500→128→500→1,000→3,703
Pubmed	500→200→128→200→500

5.2   Node Classification

In this subsection, we perform node classification task to evaluate the quality of node representations learned by different methods. To be specific, we randomly select 30% labeled nodes as the training set, and the remaining nodes are treated as testing. Note that the label information within labeled nodes is used for training the model EANE. After obtaining node representations, we use them to train a SVM classifier, then the classifier is to predict the testing set, thus the prediction results are measured in terms of both Macro-F1 and Micro-F1 values. And we repeat this process 10 times, and report average results. The detailed experimental results are listed in Table 3.

Table 3. Node classification results on Cora, Citeseer and Pubmed datasets. We use **blue** to highlight the best results.

Datasets	Cora		Citeseer		Pubmed	
Evaluation	Micro_F1	Macro_F1	Micro_F1	Macro_F1	Micro_F1	Macro_F1
DeepWalk	0.648	0.602	0.587	0.534	0.809	0.795
LINE	0.612	0.572	0.546	0.512	0.766	0.749
SDNE	0.623	0.591	0.571	0.528	0.699	0.677
LANE	0.631	0.608	0.578	0.541	0.784	0.765
SEANO	0.713	0.706	0.719	0.671	0.842	0.828
EANE	**0.778**	**0.756**	**0.738**	**0.694**	**0.886**	**0.862**

We observe from Table 3 that EANE always achieves the best performance on all three datasets. This fact shows that EANE jointly utilizes the autoencoder, skip-gram and MLP modules to effectively model three types of information (*i.e.*, network structure, node attribute and label information), then properly captures their correlations, thus gains better performance. Besides, structure-only methods such as DeepWalk, LINE and SDNE achieve weak classification result because the topological structure could not provide valuable information for learning effective node representations. And SEANO aggregates node link, attribute and label information into a joint representation space. However, it leverages the label information to eliminate network outliers, thus fails to integrate these three information into the representation space. Accordingly, SEANO learns the suboptimal node embeddings.

5.3   Link Prediction

In this part, we conduct link prediction task on only two Cora and Citeseer datasets to evaluate the quality of network embedding generated by various models. All node labels are used in this task. Similar to [5,25], we randomly hide 30% of existing links as positive instances, and generate an equal number of non-existing links as negative instances. Then we use the remaining network links to train different models. Subsequently, we obtain node representations, which will be applied to predict positive links. Based on the cosine similarity function, we rank both positive and negative instances. Finally, we employ the AUC values as metrics, where a higher value means a better performance, to evaluate the ranking list. And we present the experimental results in Fig. 2.

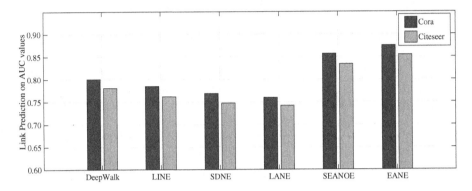

Fig. 2. Link prediction results on the two real-world datasets. The y-axis describes the AUC value of each method while the x-axis shows the name of these methods.

We draw from Fig. 2 that EANE consistently obtains the best AUC results on the two datasets. Specifically, at the Cora dataset, EANE gains about 3% improvement over SEANO who is the best performance approach. We argue that a major reason is because EANE jointly captures the structural proximity, attribute affinity and label similarity of nodes, thus produces better prediction results. As for Deepwalk, LINE and SDNE, they only utilize network structure for learning an embedding representation for a plain network. Consequently, they barely distill very limited information for link prediction. Although SEANO takes three types of information (*i.e.*, network structure, node attributes and labels) into consideration, it merely uses node labels to smooth the adverse effects of network outliers, then ignores their mutual relations, thus leads to weak prediction results.

6 Conclusion and Future Work

In this paper, we propose a novel method called EANE that jointly exploits three types of information *i.e.*, network structure, node attributes and node labels, for learning an Effective Attributed Network Embedding. In particular, EANE designs three modules to encode these three information separately. In detail, the autoencoder module obtains the node representation by encoding node attributes. Then the skip-gram and MLP modules predict the current node labels and its contexts by giving the learned representations. To learn the optimal node representations, we introduce a joint optimization framework and iteratively optimize these three modules. Experimental results on several real-world datasets demonstrate that the proposed EANE outperforms the state-of-the-art embedding approaches. As future work, we plan to extend EANE to other types of networks, such as dynamic attributed networks [8] and heterogeneous information networks [19].

Acknowledgments. This work is supported by National Key R&D Plan of China (Grant Nos. 2016QY02D0400), and National Natural Science Foundation of China (Grant Nos. U163620068).

References

1. Cao, S., Lu, W., Xu, Q.: GraRep: learning graph representations with global structural information. In Proceedings of CIKM, pp. 891–900 (2015)
2. Cavallari, S., Zheng, V.W., Cai, H., Chang, K.C.-C., Cambria, E.: Learning community embedding with community detection and node embedding on graphs. In Proceedings of CIKM, pp. 377–386 (2017)
3. Cui, P., Wang, X., Pei, J., Zhu, W.: A survey on network embedding. IEEE Trans. Knowl. Data Eng. (2018)
4. Gao, H., Huang, H.: Deep attributed network embedding. In: Proceedings of IJCAI, pp. 3364–3370 (2018)
5. Grover, A., Leskovec, J.: node2vec: scalable feature learning for networks. In: Proceedings of SIGKDD, pp. 855–864 (2016)
6. Huang, X., Li, J., Hu, X.: Label informed attributed network embedding. In: Proceedings of WSDM, pp. 731–739 (2017)
7. Kipf, T.N., Welling, M.: Semi-supervised classification with graph convolutional networks. In: Proceedings of ICLR (2017)
8. Li, J., Dani, H., Hu, X., Tang, J., Chang, Y., Liu, H.: Attributed network embedding for learning in a dynamic environment. In: Proceedings of CIKM, pp. 387–396 (2017)
9. Liang, J., Jacobs, P., Sun, J., Parthasarathy, S.: Semi-supervised embedding in attributed networks with outliers. In: Proceedings of SDM, pp. 153–161 (2018)
10. Marsden, P.V., Friedkin, N.E.: Network studies of social influence. Sociol. Methods Res. **22**(1), 127–151 (1993)
11. McPherson, M., Smith-Lovin, L., Cook, J.M.: Birds of a feather: homophily in social networks. Annu. Rev. Sociol. **27**(1), 415–444 (2001)
12. Mikolov, T., Sutskever, I., Chen, K., Corrado, G.S., Dean, J.: Distributed representations of words and phrases and their compositionality. In: Proceedings of NPIS, pp. 3111–3119 (2013)
13. Pan, S., Wu, J., Zhu, X., Zhang, C., Wang, Y.: Tri-party deep network representation. In: Proceedings of IJCAI, pp. 1895–1901 (2016)
14. Perozzi, B., Al-Rfou, R., Skiena, S.: DeepWalk: online learning of social representations. In: Proceeding of SIGKDD, pp. 701–710 (2014)
15. Tang, J., Qu, M., Mei, Q.: PTE: predictive text embedding through large-scale heterogeneous text networks. In: Proceedings of SIGKDD, pp. 1165–1174 (2015)
16. Tang, J., Qu, M., Wang, M., Zhang, M., Yan, J., Mei, Q.: LINE: large-scale information network embedding. In: Proceedings of WWW, pp. 1067–1077 (2015)

17. Tu, C., Zhang, W., Liu, Z., Sun, M.: Max-margin DeepWalk: discriminative learning of network representation. In: Proceedings of IJCAI, pp. 3889–3895 (2016)
18. Wang, D., Cui, P., Zhu, W.: Structural deep network embedding. In: Proceedings of SIGKDD, pp. 1225–1234 (2016)
19. Xiao, W., et al.: Heterogeneous graph attention network. In: Proceedings of WWW (2019)
20. Yang, J., McAuley, J., Leskovec, J.: Community detection in networks with node attributes. In: Proceedings of ICDM, pp. 1151–1156 (2013)
21. Yang, Z., Cohen, W.W., Salakhutdinov, R.R.: Revisiting semi-supervised learning with graph embeddings. In: Proceedings of ICML (2016)
22. Zhang, D., Yin, J., Zhu, X., Zhang, C.: User profile preserving social network embedding. In: Proceedings of IJCAI, pp. 3378–3384 (2017)
23. Zhang, D., Yin, J., Zhu, X., Zhang, C.: Network representation learning: a survey. IEEE Trans. Big Data (2018)
24. Zhang, L., Li, X., Shen, J., Wang, X.: Structure, attribute and homophily preserved social network embedding. In: Proceedings of ICONIP, pp. 118–130 (2018)
25. Zhang, Z., et al.: ANRL: attributed network representation learning via deep neural networks. In: Proceedings of IJCAI, pp. 3155–3161 (2018)
26. Zhou, C., Paffenroth, R.C.: Anomaly detection with robust deep autoencoders. In: Proceedings of SIGKDD, pp. 665–674 (2017)

Answer-Focused and Position-Aware Neural Network for Transfer Learning in Question Generation

Kangli Zi[1,2(✉)], Xingwu Sun[3], Yanan Cao[4], Shi Wang[1],
Xiaoming Feng[5], Zhaobo Ma[5], and Cungen Cao[1]

[1] Key Laboratory of Intelligent Information Processing,
Institute of Computer Technology, Chinese Academy of Sciences, Beijing, China
zikangli@126.com, {wangshi,cgcao}@ict.ac.cn
[2] University of Chinese Academy of Sciences, Beijing, China
[3] Meituan AI Lab, Beijing, China
sunxingwu01@gmail.com
[4] Institute of Information Engineering,
Chinese Academy of Sciences, Beijing, China
caoyanan@iie.ac.cn
[5] Beijing Qihu Keji Co. Ltd., Beijing, China
{fengxiaoming,mazhaobo}@360.cn

Abstract. Question generation aims to generate natural questions conditioned on answer and the corresponding context pairs, which has the potential value of developing annotated data sets for natural language processing (NLP) researches in education, reading comprehension and question answering. In this paper, focusing on the problem that scarce labeled data of different domains may constrain researchers training their models using supervised or semi-supervised approaches to obtain more semantically similar questions in those areas, we present two transfer learning techniques to further improve a well-performed hybrid question generation model trained on one domain and adapted to another domain. The hybrid question generation model uses an answer-focused and position-aware neural network to improve the model's ability on source domain data, while the utilization of transfer learning approaches can further enhance the performance of the hybrid model on target domain data. We conduct experiments on two data sets and a significant improvement in the model performance is observed which confirms our hypothesis that a preferable neural network model trained on one domain, attached with transfer learning approaches can further promote the performance on another domain.

Keywords: Natural Language Processing · Question generation · Transfer learning

1 Introduction

Question generation (QG) which is also known as question expansion, is one of the core problems for Natural Language Processing (NLP) that has been attracting increasing interest in recent years. The intention of question generation is to

© Springer Nature Switzerland AG 2019
C. Douligeris et al. (Eds.): KSEM 2019, LNAI 11776, pp. 339–352, 2019.
https://doi.org/10.1007/978-3-030-29563-9_30

reformulate a natural language question into similar meaning questions, based on the meaning of a given sentence or paragraph [1]. In addition to its applications in machine comprehension, such as the applications based on QG and question answering (QA) for generating reading comprehension materials for education, QG systems have been widely used as components to improve QA systems, such as in a clinical tool for evaluating or assisting mental health [2, 3], or in a chatbot or intelligent customer service system which can initiate a conversation or request users' feedback [4].

Nowadays, although the rise of large-scale human-annotated datasets with high-quality has motivated the development of models such as deep neural networks, the data collection of different domains is still scarce and time-consuming. As a result, that limited question-answer corpora available, especially in less common domains, constrains researchers training their models using supervised or semi-supervised approaches on labeled data to obtain more semantically similar questions in those areas. Therefore, studies on transferring QG systems trained on source domains to other domains of datasets can provide an aid in the development of annotated datasets for natural language processing research in QA and reading comprehension areas [5–8]. Nevertheless, directly adopting a QG model trained on one domain to paraphrase questions from another domain may suffer domain maladjustment and performance degradation.

In this research, we address this problem by proposing an answer-focused and position-aware neural QG model, then exam it to be trained on Stanford Question Answering Dataset (SQuAD) which consists of more than 100,000 question-answer pairs on Wikipedia [7], and apply transfer learning techniques to tune the proposed hybrid model on the Microsoft MAchine Reading COmprehension (MS MARCO) dataset which comprises anonymized real-life questions sampled from Bing's search query logs, human rewritten answers and paragraphs extracted from web documents which involve enough necessary information in response to answers [8]. By using the entire pretrained hybrid model and transfer learning techniques, we are able to outperform a distinct baseline of applying a well-performing QG model trained on SQuAD to MARCO dataset, and we also achieve a valid improvement on the baseline of Sun et al. (2018) and a baseline model which directly been trained and evaluated on the MARCO dataset [9].

2 Related Work

2.1 Question Generation

Since the work of Rus et al. [10] the task of QG has attracted interest from the natural language generation (NLG) community, and researches on QG can be classified into two categories: rule-based and neural network-based approaches. Generally, the earlier works which tackle the QG task with rule-based approaches or slot-filling with question templates [11–16] often heavily rely on rules or templates that are expensive to maintain manually [9], with consequences in not making full use of the semantic information of words apart from their syntactic role [5], and they lack of diversity. Moreover, the categories of question types they can deal with are limited, and they often involve pipelines of independent components that are hard to tune and measure the final performance [17].

In recent years, to address those issues of rule-based approaches, neural network-based approaches are proposed to deal with the task of QG. Those neural network models are typically data driven, trained on question-answer pairs, and employ question generation in an end-to-end trainable framework [18]. Serban et al. [5] firstly apply an encoder-decoder framework with attention mechanism to generate factoid questions from FreeBase. Yuan et al. [19] improved the model performance with a similar network architecture through policy gradient techniques. As the answer is a span from the sentence/text words, Zhou et al. [20] and See et al. [21] enrich their pointer-generator models with features of answer position and rich lexical features, and incorporate attention mechanism and copy mechanism.

In addition to researches on improving the performance of QG models, several neural network models with a QG component have already been widely used for the improvement of machine translation, reading comprehension and QA models [6, 22–24].

2.2 Transfer Learning

The motivation of studying transfer learning is the fact that human can accumulate knowledge and reuse learned information to figure out better solutions or to deal with new problems. Besides, researches on transfer learning have attracted attention since 1995 [25] and have been successfully applied to several domain tasks, such as multi-task learning [26], machine translation [27], object recognition [28] and visual or textual question answering [29–31]. In transfer learning, major research fields include determining what knowledge to be transferred, which indicates that some knowledge may be common and can be shared among different domains, confirming the feasibility of applying transfer learning techniques on the upcoming task, and utilizing appropriate algorithms to the task.

The recent achievements in neural QG and QA lead to numerous datasets, such as the SQuAD [7] and the MARCO [8] dataset. However, the availability of larger datasets in less common domains is still insufficient. Moreover, the sparsity of training data may result in that when machine learning approaches are directly applied to deal with the tasks, e.g. reading comprehension and natural language generation on a specific domain, the neural networks often suffer from the problem of poor performance or over-fitting [31].

In this paper, we address this problem in QG task through an answer-focused and position-aware neural network model which can generate questions over paragraphs and answers on a target domain by fine-tuning this hybrid model pretrained on the original source domain (Fig 1).

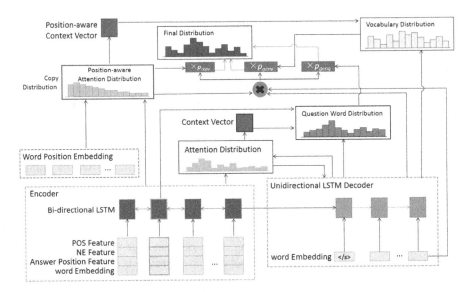

Fig. 1. Diagram of our hybrid model for question generation. The question word distribution is calculated by non-position-aware context vector joint with answer embedding while the copy distribution and vocabulary distribution are generated from position-aware context vector. The final distribution is calculated via a weighted sum of the three probability distributions.

3 Our Models

This paper involves two tasks, pre-training a hybrid QG model for generating questions on the source domain data and utilizing transfer learning approaches to the hybrid QG model. The first task of question generation takes as input a tokenized context sentence p in sequence, and outputs a question sentence q which could be answered by corresponding answer a from the source domain. The second task is to transfer the hybrid QG model that is already trained in the source domain s over another target domain t.

3.1 Our Hybrid Question Generation Model

Our hybrid question generation model is an encoder-decoder neural network model[1] which absorbed the idea of Pointer Network [32] that uses an attention-based pointer-generator architecture [21] and enhanced the model with rich features proposed by Zhou et al. [20] in the embedding layer of the encoder, such as named entity, part-of-speech and answer position.

Encoder. The encoder is a bi-directional LSTM architecture which takes the joint feature embeddings of word, answer position (the BIO scheme) and lexical features (name entity, part-of-speech) as input $(w_1, w_2, \ldots, w_{T_x})$ with $w_i \in R^{d_w + d_a + d_n + d_p}$, where T_x is the sentence length, w_i is the joint embeddings of various features of each

---

[1] More details can be found in (Sun et al.) [9].

word and d_w, d_a, d_n, d_p is the corresponding dimension of word embedding, answer position embedding, name entity embedding and part-of-speech embedding respectively.

Decoder. The decoder is a uni-directional LSTM which reads an input word embedding w_t, the previous attention-blended context vector c_{t-1} which generated via attention mechanism (Bahdanau et al.) [33] and its previous hidden state s_{t-1} to update its current hidden state $s_t \in R^{d_h}$ at each decoding step t.

Specifically, in the decoding stage, we divide the final predictor for calculating the generation probability from a given vocabulary into three sub-predictors, one for producing question word distribution from a specific vocabulary of question words which be called the answer-focused model where the answer embedding used in this model is the encoded hidden state at the answer start position, and the other two which additionally absorbed word position features into predictions and be called the position-aware predictor and the copy mechanism respectively, remain in predicting the vocabulary distribution of words and directly copy text words from context sentence. Moreover, we apply the position-aware attention distribution as the copy probability.

So far, there are two types of context vector calculated by two types of attention distribution: position-aware and non-position-aware attention distribution. At last, the final probability distribution for one word is calculated via a weighted sum of the three predictors' probability distributions. The whole hybrid model is trained according to the negative log likelihood of all target words probability $P(w^*)$.

3.2 Training by Transfer Learning Approaches

After training our hybrid QG model on source domain of SQuAD dataset, we simulate training our hybrid question generation model on the target domain of MARCO dataset by applying transfer learning approaches. First, we pretrain the hybrid model on the source domain and training the whole network in an end-to-end fashion.

Second, referring to the method of data-regularization [34], we tune all trainable parameters on the synthetic data of mini-batches from domain s and t. For each k batches from the source domain s, we randomly sample 1 batch of $\{p_t, q_t, a_t\}_{i=1}^{batch\_size}$ triples from the target domain dataset t where k is a hyper-parameter. The fine-tuning train procedure is illustrated in Table 1, the Algorithm 1.

At last, considering the synthetic data are usually noisy, which may affect the performance of question generation, we apply checkpoint averaging method [35, 36] to improve the stability of our hybrid model and deal with the problem of over-fitting. The algorithm of checkpoint averaging method is illustrated in Table 2, the Algorithm 2. In our experiment, we set $\gamma = 8$ and $\beta = 5$ for the reasons that the results on test dataset of target domain t at those eight of saved checkpoints are comparably better than the others and selecting 5 checkpoints from those eight of saved checkpoints shows better results than selecting more of them.

At test time, we feed context-answer pairs $\{p_t^*, a_t^*\}_{i=1}^m$ from the target domain t into our fine-tuned hybrid QG model to get a sentence of generated question q_{QG} for each pair, and measure the performance by evaluation metrics.

Table 1. The fine-tuning train procedure

Algorithm 1: Fine-tuning Train Procedure
Input: $\{p_s, q_s, a_s\}_{i=1}^n$ triples from source domain s; pretrained QA model on s; $\{p_t, q_t, a_t\}_{i=1}^L$ triples from target domain t.   Output: generative question sentences on target domain t.
i. Train the hybrid QG model on source data.   ii. Generate samples of batches of $\{p_t, q_t, a_t\}_{i=1}^{batch\_size}$ triples from domain t jointly with mini-batches of $\{p_s', q_s', a_s'\}_{i=1}^{batch\_size}$ triples from source domain s;   iii. Use the synthetic data to fine-tune the hybrid QG model on domain t. For each batch sampled from the target domain t, sample k batches from the source domain s.

Table 2. The checkpoint averaging method

Algorithm 2: Checkpoint Averaging Method
i. Pretrain the hybrid QG model on the synthetic data, save model checkpoints every α seconds and get a list of checkpoint IDs $C = \{C_1, C_2, C_3, ..., C_n\}$, corresponding models $M = \{M_1, M_2, M_3, ..., M_n\}$ as well as evaluated scores $S = \{S_1, S_2, S_3, ..., S_n\}$ on the development set, where each model M_i contains a set of parameters W_i with size of $|W|$;   ii. Sort the scores S in descending order, and get $C_d = \{C_{(1)}, C_{(2)}, C_{(3)}, ..., C_{(n)}\}$, $S_d = \{S_{(1)}, S_{(2)}, S_{(3)}, ..., S_{(N)}\}$ and $M_d = \{M_{(1)}, M_{(2)}, M_{(3)}, ..., M_{(n)}\}$ where $C_j = C_{(i)}$, $M_j = M_{(i)}$ and $S_j = S_{(i)}$.   iii. Select β models used for parameters' averaging: evaluate at most γ saved models before and after the top one model $M_{(1)}$ on the test dataset, then sort the γ models by their scores in descending order, and select the top β models.   iv. Return model $M_{average}$ with parameters $W_{average} = \frac{1}{|W|}\sum_{i=1}^{|W|} W_{(i)}$.

4 Experiments

4.1 Experiment Settings

Baseline Model. Our baseline model is also an attention-based pointer-generator model (See et al.) [21] enhanced with features proposed by Zhou et al. [20]. The encoder architecture in the baseline model is the same to our hybrid model, but there are only two predictors in the decoder which determine when to predict a word from a given vocabulary or to copy the word from the original context. Besides, both predictors adopt the non-position-aware context vector into calculating probabilities.

Dataset. In this experiment, we pretrain the hybrid QG model on SQuAD, fine-tune and test it on MARCO dataset. The SQuAD and MARCO datasets are two commonly used datasets which originally developed for the reading comprehension task. In SQuAD, we randomly split the development set into two parts for development set and test set, and there are 86,635, 8,965 and 8,964 question-answer pairs in the training, development and test sets, while the MARCO dataset consists of 74,097, 4,539 and 4,539 question-answer pairs in the training, development and test sets. Besides, we directly use the extracted features shared by Zhou et al. [20] for SQuAD data[2] while utilizing the Stanford CoreNLP[3] to extract lexical features from MARCO data.

Implementation Details and Evaluation Metrics. We set the input sentence into cutoff length of 100 words, and initialize word embeddings with 300 dimensions pre-trained Glove word vectors[4] [37]. The vocabulary contains the most frequent 20,000 words in each training set while there are 20 words in the vocabulary of question words. The embeddings of the answer position feature and lexical features of the encoder are randomly initialized as 32 dimensions. The dimension of hidden state of both the encoder and decoder is 512. The relative distance between answers and other tokens in context sentence ranges from 0 to 80, and its embedding size is 16. Besides, we use dropout [38] and maxout [39] to address over-fitting problem and further tune the word embeddings in the training stage while the former is only applied in the encoder with a dropout rate of 0.5. The optimization algorithm is Adagrad [40] with a learning rate of 0.15, the initial accumulator value is 0.1 and the batch size is 64. We also use gradient clipping with a maximum gradient norm of 2. Every eight minutes, we save a copy of the whole model. Besides, to fine-tune the baseline model and hybrid model, we set $k = 2$ to generate the synthetic data from SQuAD and MARCO dataset, and in developing time on the synthetic data, we evaluate $\gamma = 8$ fine-tuned models on the total test set in MARCO dataset, and eventually apply checkpoint averaging approach on the top $\beta = 5$ models respectively. We report the BLEU score [41] as our main evaluation metric of the baseline model and the hybrid question generation model.

4.2 Experimental Results

Models

   i. Baseline: It is a sequence-to-sequence model which has added feature embeddings into the embedding layer, and been trained on SQuAD.

  ii. Baseline+Fine-tuning: we fine-tune the baseline model by applying the Algorithm 1 with the synthetic data of SQuAD and MARCO training set.

 iii. Baseline+Fine-tuning+Checkpoint-averaging: we apply the Algorithm 2 to the fine-tuned baseline model.

---

[2] https://res.qyzhou.me/redistribute.zip.

[3] https://nlp.stanford.edu/software/.

[4] https://nlp.stanford.edu/data/glove.6B.zip.

iv. Hybrid model: It is our answer-focused and position-aware model trained on SQuAD, which contains the same encoder as the baseline model, but comprises three predictors in the decoder as introduced in Sect. 3.1.

v. Hybrid+Fine-tuning: In accordance with the synthetic data of fine-tuned baseline model and the Algorithm 1, we fine-tune the hybrid model.

vi. Hybrid+fine-tuning+Checkpoint-averaging: we utilize the Algorithm 2 on the fine-tuned hybrid mode

Table 3. The main experimental results of baseline model and hybrid model on MARCO. The subscripts of D, F-K2, F-K2-CA refers to apply the baseline and hybrid model directly onto the MARCO test dataset, fine-tune the model with k = 2, use checkpoint averaging approach to the fine-tuned model with k = 2 respectively.

DataSet	MARCO			
Model	BLEU1	BLEU2	BLEU3	BLEU4
Baseline Model (Sun et al. 2018)	44.45	31.85	23.32	17.90
Baseline Model$_D$	39.02	21.76	13.45	8.85
Baseline Model$_{F-K2}$	53.61	35.96	25.94	19.49
Baseline Model$_{F-K2-CA}$	**54.85**	**37.89**	**27.40**	**20.60**
Hybrid Model (Sun et al. 2018)	48.24	35.95	25.79	19.45
Hybrid Model$_D$	38.67	22.17	14.05	9.33
Hybrid Model$_{F-K2}$	54.24	36.88	26.71	20.07
Hybrid Model$_{F-K2-CA}$	**54.39**	**37.37**	**27.29**	**20.76**

Main Results. We report the main results on the MARCO test set (Table 3), with observations as follows:

i. Comparing with applying the baseline model and our hybrid model trained on the MARCO training dataset to generate questions on MARCO test dataset, in which the Sun et al. [9] gets BLEU4 of 17.90 and 19.45 respectively, we find that both of the baseline model and our hybrid model trained just on SQuAD training dataset suffer from performance degrade by directly applying each of them to the MARCO test dataset, which get BLEU4 of 8.85 and 9.33 respectively.

ii. After we fine-tune the baseline model and our hybrid model on the synthetic data of SQuAD and MARCO training dataset, and evaluate each of them to the MARCO test dataset, we get remarkable improvement of BLEU4 score of 19.49 and 20.07, which both outperform the result of the hybrid model that directly trained on MARCO dataset [9]. This verifies the knowledge gained from the source SQuAD, which contributes to question generation on target MARCO dataset.

iii. Even though the fine-tuned baseline model and fine-tuned hybrid model get better performance than the results reported by Sun et al. [9], the checkpoint averaging approach shows its ability in slightly promoting the fine-tuned results by 1.11 and 0.70 respectively.

iv. Besides, the BLEU4 results shows the performance of our hybrid model are better than the baseline model in all cases which indicate that the hybrid model is more effective in the task of question generation and transfer learning.

4.3   Ablation Studies

To better understand how various settings in our training procedure impact overall performance, we conduct the following ablation studies.

Model Fine-tuning. In order to see how the constitution of synthetic data set during fine-tuning training procedure affects models' performance on test dataset of MARCO, we construct $k = \{0, 2, 4\}$ mini-batches from SQuAD training dataset jointly with every synthetic mini-batch from MARCO training dataset to fine-tune the baseline model and our hybrid model respectively. We report the results in Table 4, and we find each of the three models gets good results that even outperform the result of original model trained directly on MARCO dataset [9]. Besides, as the proportion of data from MARCO increases, the performance has continuously been improved, which confirms the hypothesis that knowledge has domain-particularity, and the common knowledge gained from the SQuAD could assist the model for better performance on the MARCO dataset.

Nevertheless, since large quantity of high quality annotated data from different domains are still insufficient, our batching scheme could provide a simple way to train models for supervised or semi-supervised tasks.

Table 4. The results of fine-tuned baseline and hybrid model when set $k = \{0, 2, 4\}$. The subscripts of F-K4, F-K2, F-K0 indicate applying fine-tuning train method to these model with $k = \{0, 2, 4\}$ in turn.

DataSet		MARCO			
Model	Fine-tuning Setting	BLEU1	BLEU2	BLEU3	BLEU4
BaselineModel$_{F-K4}$	K = 4	54.28	36.46	26.09	19.52
Hybrid Model$_{F-K4}$		53.25	36.04	26.09	19.62
BaselineModel$_{F-K2}$	K = 2	53.22	35.77	25.81	19.57
Hybrid Model$_{F-K2}$		54.24	36.87	26.71	20.07
Baseline Model$_{F-k0}$	K = 0	54.65	37.17	26.69	19.89
Hybrid Model$_{F-K0}$		54.37	37.03	26.74	20.11

Checkpoint Averaging. Since the synthetic data may be noisy, and regularization approach, such as dropout, can not overcome over-fitting problem, we apply checkpoint averaging approach to the fine-tuned baseline model and our hybrid model. We set $\gamma = 8$ and $\beta = 5$. Besides, all checkpoints selected are saved in 1 h intervals. Seen from the results in Table 5, when we set k from 4 to 2, the performance of our fine-tuned baseline and hybrid model on BLEU4 get better, while when we set $k = 0$ which refers to not mixing SQuAD data into synthetic data, we notice that the models' performances slightly drop which makes us assume that when facing the whole MARCO dataset, the model trained just on SQuAD need to smooth the noisy and keep balance between each of the knowledge in both data, so the results would not be better than the situation of $k = 2$. In spite of this phenomenon, compared with the fine-tuned baseline model and our hybrid model, this approach–checkpoint averaging still helps the performances on BLEU4 by increasing about 0.39 points when we set $k = 0$ in these two models, 0.73 and 0.99 points when we set $k = 4$, and 1.03 and 0.69 points when we

Table 5. The results of applying checkpoint averaging algorithm to the fine-tuned baseline and hybrid model with $k = \{0, 2, 4\}$ respectively. The subscripts of F-K4-CA, F-K2-CA, F-K0-CA refers to utilizing the fine-tuning approach with three settings of k and checkpoint averaging approach to the baseline and hybrid model.

DataSet		MARCO			
Model	Checkpoint Averaging	BLEU1	BLEU2	BLEU3	BLEU4
BaselineModel$_{F\text{-}K4\text{-}CA}$	$\gamma = 8$ and $\beta = 5$	54.60	37.11	26.82	20.25
Hybrid Model$_{F\text{-}K4\text{-}CA}$		54.71	37.49	27.29	20.61
BaselineModel$_{F\text{-}K2\text{-}CA}$		54.85	37.89	27.40	20.60
Hybrid Model$_{F\text{-}K2\text{-}CA}$		**54.39**	**37.37**	**27.29**	**20.76**
Baseline Model$_{F\text{-}k0\text{-}CA}$		55.00	37.70	27.11	20.28
Hybrid Model$_{F\text{-}K0\text{-}CA}$		54.63	37.45	27.18	20.50

set $k = 2$ in turn. All of these improvements gained also testify the comment of Chen et al. [35] and Popel et al. [36] that the checkpoint averaging could further reduce over-fitting and take advantage of local optima.

Error Analysis. In this section, we provide some instances in MARCO test dataset jointly with the questions generated by the baseline and our hybrid model in the situations of (1) directly apply those two models, (2) fine-tuned with $k = 2$ and (3) utilizing checkpoint averaging in the fine-tuned models, and analyze them to help guide further research in this task.

The first example is listed in Table 6, and we notice that the word "glyceryl" together with "trinitrate" are out-of-vocabulary (OOV) words, and may influence the models to generate words from the context. As a result, the baseline model and its fine-tuned model use the UNK tag instead, and after checkpoint averaging, the fine-tuned baseline model picks up an irrelevant word "angina" to fill in the blank. In the meanwhile, the copy mechanism in the hybrid model could select the right OOV words to generate the question.

Although the fine-tuned hybrid model, after been applied the checkpoint averaging approach, appears to have the better result, the critical word "spray" is still missed, which indicates that the model still doesn't totally digest the knowledge that the phrase "glyceryl trinitrate spray" should be taken as a whole.

In Table 7, we list another example. In this case, the answer span is an explanation of the reason which confuses models to trigger the wrong question word "what" instead of the word "why", while the key context phrase "because of" is far from the answer. Except for this factor and OOV words that may cause the generation of mismatched question words, some cases are due to the semantic ambiguity. In the meantime, language diversity results in synonyms and expressions such as "where ... located" and "what continent ...", "what kind of ..." and "what type of ...", etc. which are semantically similar and should not be regarded as wrong results.

Table 6. One instance from MARCO dataset and corresponding generated questions by different settings of the baseline model and our hybrid model. It shows the influence of OOV words in contexts to the generators.

Context: You may use **glyceryl trinitrate spray to relieve the pain of an angina attack as soon as it has started or to prevent it starting by using immediately before events which may set off your angina, for instance physical effort, emotional stress or exposure to cold**	
Answer: Glyceryl trinitrate spray to relieve the pain of an angina attack as soon as it has started or to prevent it starting by using immediately before events which may set off your angina, for instance physical effort, emotional stress or exposure to cold	
Reference: What is glyceryl trinitrate spray used for?	
Directly apply:	**Baseline model:** What is the purpose of [UNK]?
	Hybrid model: What is the purpose of glyceryl spray?
Fine-tuning with k = 2:	**Baseline model:** How to relieve [UNK] trinitrate spray?
	Hybrid model: How to relieve trinitrate trinitrate?
Checkpoint averaging:	**Baseline model:** How to prevent angina trinitrate?
	Hybrid model: What does glyceryl trinitrate do?

Table 7. Another instance from MARCO test dataset and its generated questions in several models. The results indicate the question words may not only be connected with the answer span, but also be relevant to the content sometimes.

Context: Linen is a natural fibre, made from the stalk of a flax plant. It is regarded in Europe as the best quality fabric. Europeans have long favoured linen for their sheeting because of its amazing properties. **It softens the more it is used and washed, is extremely durable and lasts decades when cared for correctly**	
Answer: It softens the more it is used and washed, is extremely durable and lasts decades when cared for correctly	
Reference: Why is linen used?	
Directly apply:	**Baseline model:** What is the purpose of linen?
	Hybrid model: Why is linen regarded in Europe?
Fine-tuning with k = 2:	**Baseline model:** What is linen used for?
	Hybrid model: What is linen used for?
Checkpoint averaging:	**Baseline model:** What is linen used for?
	Hybrid model: What is linen used for?

5 Conclusion

In this paper, to support tackling the problem of insufficient annotated datasets for NLP researches, and to verify the transfer learning in aiding a pre-trained well-performance neural network trained on one domain to adapt to another domain, we apply two transfer learning approaches – fine-tuning and checkpoint averaging, to an answer-focused and position-aware neural network model compared with the original hybrid model and a baseline model. With our transfer learning techniques, our fine-tuned hybrid QG model trained on the source domain dataset significantly outperform the state-of-art systems (the Sun et al. [9] and the baseline model) on the target domain dataset. After utilizing a simple checkpoint averaging algorithm, we have made an extra slight improvement with the fine-tuned baseline model and our fine-tuned hybrid model. But for all this, our hybrid model still excels at the task of question generation and transfer learning. Besides, we provide ablation studies and error analysis which can contribute to further research in this task.

Acknowledgments. This work is supported by the "National Key R&D Program of China" (grant no. 2017YFC1700300).

References

1. Allam, A.M.N., Haggag, M.H.: The question answering systems: a survey. Int. J. Res. Rev. Inf. Sci. (IJRRIS) **2**(3), 211–221 (2012)
2. Weizenbaum, J.: ELIZA—a computer program for the study of natural language communication between man and machine. Commun. ACM **9**(1), 36–45 (1966)
3. Colby, K.M., Weber, S., Hilf, F.D.: Artificial paranoia. Artif. Intell. **2**(1), 1–25 (1971). https://doi.org/10.1016/0004-3702(71)90002-6
4. Mostafazadeh, N., Misra, I., Devlin, J., Mitchell, M., He, X., Vanderwende, L.: Generating natural questions about an image. In: Proceedings of the 54th Annual Meeting of the Association for Computational Linguistics, vol. 1, pp. 1802–1813. Association for Computational Linguistics, Berlin (2016)
5. Serban, I.V., et al.: Generating factoid questions with recurrent neural networks: the 30m factoid question-answer corpus. In: ACL (2016)
6. Duan, N., Tang, D.Y., Chen, P., Zhou, M.: Question generation for question answering. In: Proceedings of the 2017 Conference on Empirical Methods in Natural Language Processing, pp. 866–874 (2017)
7. Rajpurkar, P., Zhang, J., Lopyrev, K., Liang, P.: SQuAD: 100,000+ questions for machine comprehension of text. In: Proceedings of the 2016 Conference on Empirical Methods in Natural Language Processing (EMNLP), pp. 2383–2392. Association for Computational Linguistics, Austin, Texas (2016)
8. Nguyen, T., et al.: MS MARCO: a human generated machine reading comprehension dataset. arXiv preprint arXiv:1611.09268 (2016)
9. Sun, X.W., Liu, J., Lyu, Y., He, W., Ma, Y.J., Wang, S.: Answer-focused and position-aware neural question generation. In: Proceedings of the 2018 Conference on Empirical Methods in Natural Language Processing, pp. 3930–3939 (2018)
10. Rus, V., Wyse, B., Piwek, P., Lintean, M., Stoyanchev, S., Moldovan, C.: The first question generation shared task evaluation challenge. In: Proceedings of the 6th International Natural Language Generation Conference, pp. 251–257. Association for Computational Linguistics, Stroudsburg (2010)
11. Chen, W., Aist, G., Mostow, J.: Generating questions automatically from informational text. In: Proceedings of the 2nd Workshop on Question Generation (AIED 2009), pp. 17–24 (2009)

12. Ali, H., Chali, Y., Hasan, S.A.: Automation of question generation from sentences. In: Proceedings of QG2010: The Third Workshop on Question Generation, pp. 58–67 (2010)
13. Mannem, P., Prasad, R., Joshi, A.: Question generation from paragraphs at UPenn: QGSTEC system description. In: Proceedings of QG2010: The Third Workshop on Question Generation, pp. 84–91 (2010)
14. Curto, S., Mendes, A.C., Coheur, L.: Question generation based on lexico-syntactic patterns learned from the web. Dialogue Discourse 3(2), 147–175 (2012)
15. Lindberg, D., Popowich, F., Nesbit, J., Winne, P.: Generating natural language questions to support learning on-line. In: Proceedings of the 14th European Workshop on Natural Language Generation, pp. 105–114 (2013)
16. Labutov, I., Basu, S., Vanderwende, L.: Deep questions without deep understanding. In: Proceedings of the 53rd Annual Meeting of the Association for Computational Linguistics and the 7th International Joint Conference on Natural Language Processing, vol. 1, pp. 889–898 (2015)
17. Wang, T., Yuan, X., Trischler, A.: A joint model for question answering and question generation. arXiv preprint arXiv:1706.01450 (2017)
18. Dong, L., Mallinson, J., Reddy, S., Lapata, M.: Learning to paraphrase for question answering. arXiv preprint arXiv:1708.06022 (2017)
19. Yuan, X., et al.: Machine comprehension by text-to-text neural question generation. arXiv preprint arXiv:1705.02012 (2017)
20. Zhou, Q., Yang, N., Wei, F., Tan, C., Bao, H., Zhou, M.: Neural question generation from text: a preliminary study. In: Huang, X., Jiang, J., Zhao, D., Feng, Y., Hong, Yu. (eds.) NLPCC 2017. LNCS (LNAI), vol. 10619, pp. 662–671. Springer, Cham (2018). https://doi.org/10.1007/978-3-319-73618-1_56
21. See, A., Liu, P.J., Manning, C.D.: Get to the point: Summarization with pointer-generator networks. arXiv preprint arXiv:1704.04368 (2017)
22. Sutskever, I., Vinyals, O., Le, Q.V.: Sequence to sequence learning with neural networks. In: Advances in Neural Information Processing Systems, pp. 3104–3112 (2014)
23. Du, X., Shao, J., Cardie, C.: Learning to ask: neural question generation for reading comprehension. arXiv preprint arXiv:1705.00106 (2017)
24. Tang, D., Duan, N., Qin, T., Yan, Z., Zhou, M.: Question answering and question generation as dual tasks. arXiv preprint arXiv:1706.02027 (2017)
25. Pan, S.J., Yang, Q.: A survey on transfer learning. IEEE Trans. Knowl. Data Eng. 22(10), 1345–1359 (2010)
26. Argyriou, A., Evgeniou, T., Pontil, M.: Multi-task feature learning. In: Advances in Neural Information Processing Systems, pp. 41–48 (2007)
27. Zoph, B., Yuret, D., May, J., Knight, K.: Transfer learning for low-resource neural machine translation. arXiv preprint arXiv:1604.02201 (2016)
28. Russakovsky, O., Deng, J., Su, H., Krause, J., Satheesh, S., Ma, S., et al.: Imagenet large scale visual recognition challenge. Int. J. Comput. Vis. 115(3), 211–252 (2015)
29. Zhou, B., Tian, Y., Sukhbaatar, S., Szlam, A., Fergus, R.: Simple baseline for visual question answering. arXiv preprint arXiv:1512.02167 (2015)
30. Yang, Z., He, X., Gao, J., Deng, L., Smola, A.: Stacked attention networks for image question answering. In: Proceedings of the IEEE Conference on Computer Vision and Pattern Recognition, pp. 21–29 (2016)
31. Konrád, J.: Transfer learning for question answering on SQuAD. http://radio.feld.cvut.cz/conf/poster/proceedings/Poster_2018/Section_IC/IC_031_Konrad.pdf. Accessed 30 May 2019
32. Vinyals, O., Fortunato, M., Jaitly, N.: Pointer networks. In: Advances in Neural Information Processing Systems, pp. 2692–2700 (2015)

33. Bahdanau, D., Cho, K., Bengio, Y.: Neural machine translation by jointly learning to align and translate. Computer Science (2014)

34. Golub, D., Huang, P.S., He, X., Deng, L.: Two-stage synthesis networks for transfer learning in machine comprehension. arXiv preprint arXiv:1706.09789 (2017)

35. Chen, H., Lundberg, S., Lee, S.I.: Checkpoint ensembles: ensemble methods from a single training process. arXiv preprint arXiv:1710.03282 (2017)

36. Popel, M., Bojar, O.: Training Tips for the Transformer Model. Prague Bull. Math. Linguist. **110**(1), 43–70 (2018)

37. Pennington, J., Socher, R., Manning, C.: Glove: global vectors for word representation. In Proceedings of the 2014 Conference on Empirical Methods in Natural Language Processing (EMNLP), pp. 1532–1543 (2014)

38. Srivastava, N., Hinton, G., Krizhevsky, A., Sutskever, I., Salakhutdinov, R.: Dropout: a simple way to prevent neural networks from overfitting. J. Mach. Learn. Res. **15**(1), 1929–1958 (2014)

39. Goodfellow, I.J., Warde-Farley, D., Mirza, M., Courville, A., Bengio, Y.: Maxout networks. arXiv preprint arXiv:1302.4389 (2013)

40. Duchi, J., Hazan, E., Singer, Y.: Adaptive subgradient methods for online learning and stochastic optimization. J. Mach. Learn. Res. **12**(Jul), 2121–2159 (2011)

41. Papineni, K., Roukos, S., Ward, T., Zhu, W.J.: BLEU: a method for automatic evaluation of machine translation. In: Proceedings of the 40th Annual Meeting on Association for Computational Linguistics, pp. 311–318. Association for Computational Linguistics (2002)

Syntax-Aware Sentence Matching
with Graph Convolutional Networks

Yangfan Lei[1,2], Yue Hu[1,2(✉)], Xiangpeng Wei[1,2], Luxi Xing[1,2],
and Quanchao Liu[1,2]

[1] Institute of Information Engineering, Chinese Academy of Science, Beijing, China
{leiyangfan,huyue}@iie.ac.cn
[2] School of Cyber Security, University of Chinese Academy of Science, Beijing, China

Abstract. Natural language sentence matching, as a fundamental technology for a variety of tasks, plays a key role in many natural language processing systems. In this article, we propose a new method which incorporates syntactic structure into "matching-aggregation" framework for sentence matching tasks. Our approach can be used in "matching-aggregation" framework efficiently. Concretely speaking, we introduce a multi-channel-GCN layer, which takes both words and the syntactic dependency trees of sentence pair as input to incorporate syntax information to the matching process. We also use a gating mechanism to dynamically combine the raw contextual representation of a sentence with the syntactic representation of the sentence to relieve the noise caused by the potential wrong dependency parsing result. Experimental results on standard benchmark datasets demonstrate that our model makes a substantial improvement over the baseline.

Keywords: Sentence matching · Dependency parsing ·
Graph convolutional network

1 Introduction

Natural language sentence matching is a task which tries to identify the relationship between two sentences. The type of relationship is determined by specific tasks. For a paraphrase identification task, the relationship means the semantic similarity between two sentences. In a natural language inference task, relationship refers to whether a hypothesis sentence can be inferred from a premise sentence. Sentence matching technology has a wide application in many natural language processing systems. For example, the Customer Service System can judge the similarity of the sentences asked by the users, and merge the questions that can be answered with the same answer, thereby reducing the number of requests, and saving a lot of cost for the enterprise. The question and answer website (e.g., Quora) need to merge similar questions to avoid repeating questions so that it can increase the quality of community responses and enhance

© Springer Nature Switzerland AG 2019
C. Douligeris et al. (Eds.): KSEM 2019, LNAI 11776, pp. 353–364, 2019.
https://doi.org/10.1007/978-3-030-29563-9_31

the user experience. Therefore, solving sentence matching problem has both academic and industrial significance.

The models basing on deep neural network have recently shown impressive results in sentence matching tasks. These models can be divided into two frameworks on the whole. The first framework directly encodes sentences into fixed-dimensional vectors in the same embedding space without any interaction information of smaller units of two sentences [3,25]. The second framework takes more consideration of word-level interaction information which called "matching-aggregation" framework [17,20]. In the matching step, smaller units (such as words or contextual vectors) of the two sentences are firstly matched, while in the aggregation step the matching results are aggregated into a vector to make the final decision.

When natural language is understood by human beings, its sentence's structure is not linear. Instead, it has a graph structure. Although the text is written in a linear structure, we subconsciously acquire the relationship between different parts of the sentence during the reading process. Recently, there are several efforts in incorporating syntactic information into the sentence matching task. Chen et al. [4] encodes syntactic parse trees of a premise and hypothesis through tree-LSTM [26] to make natural language inference, which got a state of art results in natural language inference task. Bowman et al. [3] proposes a model which can parsing the sentence and encoding it simultaneously. The model can perform the batch operation while achieving an improvement in accuracy, which is significantly faster than tree-structured models. The above methods successfully improve the accuracy of the model, but there is space to be improved from the point of model efficiency. The method adopted by Bowman et al. [3] needs to represent the syntax tree as a shift-reduce sequence, increasing the length of the sequence, which leads to the increase of computing time. And this method cannot be directly used in the "matching-aggregation" framework. At the same time, the above models are based on the LSTM structure, which limits the parallelism of the models.

In order to solve the above problems, we use the graph convolutional network (GCN) [6] to replace tree-LSTM. It has two distinctive advantages: (i) Each word in the sentence corresponds to a node in the graph without additional nodes, making it possible to combine with other sentence matching architecture; (ii) GCN is convenient for batched computation and can be calculated in parallel to achieve much higher efficiencies. Meanwhile, considering the noise caused by the incorrect output of syntactic parser, we proposed the so called multi-channel-GCN method. We use GCN with edge gate to encode syntactic information [14]. Meanwhile, we use a gating method to dynamically combine the raw contextual representation of a sentence with the syntactic representation of the sentence in order to relieve the damage of the mistakes of dependency parsing.

Our main contributions can be summarized as follows: (i) we propose a method which utilizes syntactic message to complete sentence matching tasks. Our method can be used in "matching-aggregation" framework with a more efficient way. (ii) To the best of our knowledge, this is the first time that utilizing

GCNs to encode syntactic information into sentence matching tasks. (iii) Our experiment results demonstrate the validity of incorporating dependency syntax information in sentence matching task with our multi-channel-GCN layer.

2   Background

2.1   Graph Convolutional Network

In this section we will describe GCNs of Kipf *et al.* [13]. You can see more GCN architectures from Gilmer *et al.* [7].

GCN is a neural network designed to encode graph information. Traditional neural networks architectures such as RNN and CNN can't deal with data with graph structure. GCN encodes graph information of a node by calculating a real-valued vector with the neighborhood of this node. Every node can get information from its direct neighbor through a one-layer GCN. When multiple GCN layers are stacked, a wider range of nodes can be considered. For example, in the second layer, one node can get information from its neighbors belong to the first layer. Meanwhile, the nodes at the first layer already include information from their neighbors. In a word, a GCN with k layers can make the nodes receive information from neighbors at most k hops away.

2.2   Syntactic GCNs

The parse tree of a sentence is a special graph. It's a directed graph with various types of edges. Marcheggiani *et al.* [14] put forward syntactic GCNs on the basis of general GCN. The directed graph can be processed with this architecture, and edge labels play an important role. The syntactic GCNs mainly includes three modifications: directionality, labels, edge-wise gating. We will briefly describe these modifications.

Directionality. We have a weight matrix W for each GCN layer. In order to model the direction of parser tree, W_{in} and W_{out} are used for incoming and outgoing edges, respectively. Where W_{in} is a weight matrix used for edges which back to the current node and W_{out} is used for the reverse direction. In the context of Dependency Parsing tree, outgoing edges are used for head-to-dependent connections, and incoming edges are used for dependent-to-head connections. The new representations can be computed as follows:

$$h_v^{j+1} = \rho \left(\sum_{u \in N(v)} W_{dir(u,v)}^j h_u^j + b_{dir(u,v)}^j \right) \tag{1}$$

Where $dir(u, v)$ is an operation that gets the direction of the edge between node u and node v. For example, we will choose W_{in} for edge v-to-u, W_{out} for edge u-to-v, and W_{self} for edge u-to-u. And the same is true for bias b; ρ is an activation function.

Labels. The labels in the dependency tree are the relation of two words, which is crucial to the representation of sentence information for sentence representation. *et al.* [14] makes a small modification to make GCN sensitive to labels by adding more weight matrix:

$$h_v^{j+1} = \rho \left(\sum_{u \in N(v)} W_{label(u,v)}^j h_u^j + b_{label(u,v)}^j \right) \tag{2}$$

Where $label(u, v)$ is used to get the label type and direction type of node u and v. In order to avoid over-parametrization, the $label(u, v)$ operation is only used at bias terms, in other words: $W_{label(u,v)} = W_{dir(u,v)}$.

Edge Gating. Now, the result of automatically predicted syntactic structures is unsatisfactory. To ignore potentially erroneous syntactic edges, and allow flexible selection of graph information, Marcheggiani *et al.* [14] proposes a gate method for calculation along edges. For each edge, a scalar gate is calculated as follows:

$$g_{u,v}^j = \sigma \left(h_u^j \cdot W_{dir(u,v)}^j + b_{label(u,v)}^j \right) \tag{3}$$

Where σ is the logistic sigmoid function, and $w \in R^d$ and $b \in R$ are learned parameters. Then, the computation of node representation becomes:

$$h_v^{j+1} = \rho \left(\sum_{u \in N(v)} g_{u,v}^j (W_{dir(u,v)}^j h_u^j + b_{label(u,r)}^j) \right) \tag{4}$$

3   Our Approach

In this work, we propose a new method which utilizes syntactic message to complete sentence matching tasks. The output of syntactic GCNs can be regarded as a structural representation of a sentence. We will proceed the discussion under the hypothesis: using a structural sentence representation when doing a match operation will gain more meaningful information. We adopt syntax trees of sentences as model input and take the GCN to encode syntax information. We employ BiMPM [21] as our base model, and change the representation layer and aggregation layer to use the syntactic signal. In this section, we review the BiMPM model and introduce our extension, i.e., the multi-channel GCN layer. We demonstrate the architecture of our model in Fig. 1. The whole model consists of six layers.

3.1   Word Representation Layer

Just as in the base model, the output of this layer is a sequence of words, and each word is represented as a d-dimensional vector. The vector is composed of

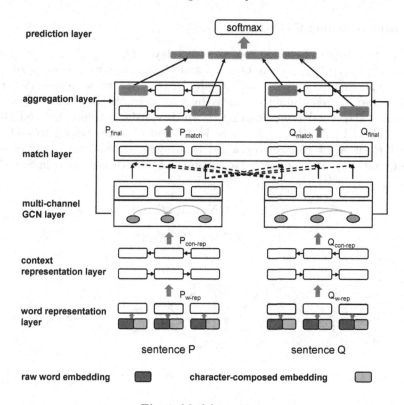

Fig. 1. Model overview.

two parts. The first part is a word embedding, and the second part is a character-composed embedding. The word embedding is a fixed vector for each individual word, which is pre-trained with GloVe [15]. The character-composed embedding is calculated by feeding character sequence within a word into a Long Short-Term Memory Network (LSTM) [10]. We concatenate the word embedding and character-composed embedding as the final output. For sentence matching task, we have two sentences P and Q. The output of word representation layer is $P_{w\text{-}rep}[p^1_{w\text{-}rep}, \ldots, p^M_{w\text{-}rep}]$ and $Q_{w\text{-}rep}[q^1_{w\text{-}rep}, \ldots, q^N_{w\text{-}rep}]$. Here M and N are the lengths of two sentences.

3.2 Context Representation Layer

Again as in the base model, this layer aims to incorporate contextual information into the representation of two sentences. We utilize two bi-directional LSTM to encode two sentences, respectively. This layer uses the output from the previous layer as input, and output a contextual representation of sentence.

3.3   Multi-channel GCN Layer

Consider the output of context representation layer, $Q_{con\text{-}rep}[q^1_{con}, \ldots, q^M_{con}]$ and $P_{con\text{-}rep}[P^1_{con}, \ldots, Q^N_{con}]$: Where $Q_{con\text{-}rep}$ and $P_{con\text{-}rep}$ are two sequences of contextual embeddings, and M and N are lengths of two sentences. We calculate syntax representation of words by two steps. Let us choose Q as an example, a structural representation of words can be obtained by feed GCN with graph $G(V_q, E_q, Q_{con\text{-}rep})$, where V_q is a set of words belong to sentence Q, and E_q is a set of edges obtained from syntactic analysis result of sentence Q. GCN_{syn} is a syntactic GCNs operation which is defined in Sect. 2.2. $(Q_{gcn}[q^1_{gcn}, \ldots, q^M_{gcn}], P_{gcn}[p^1_{gcn}, \ldots, p^N_{gcn}])$:

$$Q_{gcn} = GCN_{syn}(V_q, E_q, Q) \tag{5}$$

$$P_{gcn} = GCN_{syn}(V_p, E_p, P) \tag{6}$$

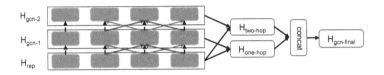

Fig. 2. Multi-channel 2-layer-GCN architecture.

Considering the accuracy of the current result of dependency parsing, the input of the model will produce a lot of noise. Like the gate method used in LSTM, we use a gate to determine how much information is available for each dimension. The raw contextual embeddings and syntactic embeddings can be viewed as signals from a different channel. Take the k-th word of sentence Q as an example:

$$g^k_q = \sigma(W_{word}q^k_{con} + W_{gcn}q^k_{gcn}) \tag{7}$$

$$q^k_{final} = g_q \cdot q^k_{con} + (1 - g_q) \cdot q^k_{gcn} \tag{8}$$

Where $q^k_{con} \in R^d$ is the contextual embedding of k-th word of sentence Q and $q^k_{gcn} \in R^d$ is the syntactic embedding of this word. $W_{word} \in R^{d*d}$ and $W_{gcn} \in R^{d*d}$ are weight matrixes. σ is the sigmoid function. We take $Q_{gcn\text{-}final}[q^1_{final}, \ldots, q^M_{final}]$ as the final output of multi-channel GCN layer. As shown in Fig. 2, we stack more than one GCN layers, in order to get the representation of the sentence from different perspectives. In this figure, $H_{rep} \in R^{L*d}$ is the contextual embeddings of words, $H_{gcn\text{-}1} \in R^{L*d}$ is the output of the first GCN layer and $H_{gcn\text{-}2} \in R^{L*d}$ is the output of second GCN layer. We can get $H_{one\text{-}hop}$ by taking H_{rep} and $H_{gcn\text{-}1}$ as input and use the multichannel operation which we mentioned earlier. Again, we can get $H_{two\text{-}hop}$ with H_{rep} and $H_{gcn\text{-}2}$. In order to get the final output of multi-channel GCN layer, we concatenate $H_{one\text{-}hop}$ and $H_{two\text{-}hop}$ as the representation of a sentence.

3.4   Matching Layer

As in BiMPM, the goal of this layer is to match two sentences from various aspects and various granularity. We match the two sentences P and Q in two directions: match each time-step of P against all time-steps of Q, and match each time-step of Q against all time-steps of P. Four matching strategies are proposed to compare each time-step of one sentence against all time-steps of the other sentence. We will introduce two of these strategies, and you can see more details from Wang et al. [21]:

Attentive-Matching. Attention mechanism is proved to be effective in lots of NLP task [1,9,16]. The attention mechanism is in the form of attentive-matching in BiMPM model. We first calculate the cosine similarities between $P_{gcn-rep}$ and $Q_{gcn-rep}$ to get the weight of h_j^q or h_i^p. Then an attentive vector is calculated with $P_{gcn-rep}$ and $Q_{gcn-rep}$ with this weight:

$$\overrightarrow{\alpha}_{i,j} = \cos(\overrightarrow{h}_i^p, \overrightarrow{h}_j^q) \tag{9}$$

$$\overleftarrow{\alpha}_{i,j} = \cos(\overleftarrow{h}_i^p, \overleftarrow{h}_j^q) \tag{10}$$

$$\overrightarrow{\alpha}_i^{mean} = \frac{\sum_{j=1}^N \overrightarrow{\alpha}_{i,j} \cdot \overrightarrow{h}_j^q}{\sum_{j=1}^N \overrightarrow{\alpha}_{i,j}} \tag{11}$$

$$\overleftarrow{\alpha}_i^{mean} = \frac{\sum_{j=1}^N \overleftarrow{\alpha}_{i,j} \cdot \overleftarrow{h}_j^q}{\sum_{j=1}^N \overleftarrow{\alpha}_{i,j}} \tag{12}$$

Where f_m is a matching method to calculate the similarity of two vectors, which called multi-perspective matching, and it has proven to be effective in sentence match task.

Max-Attentive-Matching. Instead of taking the weighted sum of all the contextual embeddings as the attentive vector, this strategy chooses the one with the highest cosine similarity as the attentive vector.

The output of match layer is P_{match} (Q_{match}), which composed by the outputs of four matching strategies.

3.5   Aggregation Layer

This layer is used to aggregate two sequences of matching vectors to a fixed-length matching vector. We utilize a BiLSTM as aggregation layer and collect the last time-step vectors as output. We use a similarity output of raw match layer and a multi-channel GCN layer output as the input of aggregation layer together. The new input of aggregation layer will be:

$$Q_{in-ag} = concat(Q_{match}, Q_{gcn-final}) \tag{13}$$

$$P_{in-ag} = concat(P_{match}, P_{gcn-final}) \tag{14}$$

3.6   Prediction Layer

As in BiMPM, we use a simple two-layer feed-forward neural network and a softmax layer as prediction layer. The number of nodes in the softmax layer depends on the specific task. The output of this layer is a distribution $Pr(y|P, Q)$ on all the possible labels.

4   Experiments and Results

In order to quantitatively analyze the performance of the proposed model, we conduct experiments on two tasks with three datasets, and analyze the accuracy on these datasets. These three datasets belong to two tasks: paraphrase identification and natural language inference. In the following, we will first describe these tasks and the corresponding datasets separately, and then show the detail of our experimental results.

4.1   Tasks and Datasets

Paraphrase Identification. The paraphrase identification task can be treated as a binary classification problem, and the goal is to judge whether two sentences are paraphrases or not according to their similarity. To prove the validity of our model in this task, we use a widely used dataset: "Quora Question Pairs" (QUORA) [11] dataset.

The QUORA dataset consists of 400,000 question pairs, and each question pair is annotated with a binary value indicating whether the two questions are paraphrase of each other. We use the validation and test set as BiMPM, which randomly select 5,000 paraphrases and 5,000 non-paraphrases as the validation set, and sample another 5,000 paraphrases and 5,000 non-paraphrases as the test set. We keep the remaining instances as the training set.

Natural Language Inference. Natural language inference is a task which attends over the premise conditioned on the hypothesis. The input is a pair of sentences, and one is hypothesis and another is premise. We use two widely used datasets for this task: SNLI and MultiNLI.

SNLI is a natural language inference dataset [2]. The original data set contains 570,152 sentence pairs, each labeled with one of the following relationships: entailment, contradiction, neutral and -, where - indicates a lack of human annotation. In the end, we have 549,367 pairs for training, 9,842 pairs as the development set and 9,824 pairs as the test set.

The Multi-Genre Natural Language Inference (MultiNLI) corpus is a crowd-sourced collection of 433k sentence pairs annotated with textual entailment information [24]. We use 392,703 pairs for training, 10,000 matched pairs as the development set and 10,000 mismatched pairs as the test set.

4.2   Experiment Setting

In order to compare with the baseline, we use the same setting as BiMPM. We initialize word embeddings in the word representation layer with the 300-dimensional GloVe word vectors pre-trained from the 840B Common Crawl corpus [15]. For the out-of-vocabulary words, we initialize the word embeddings with uniform distribution. For the character-composed embeddings, we initialize each character as a 20-dimensional vector, and compose each word into a 40-dimensional vector with a LSTM layer. We set the hidden size as 100 for all Bi-LSTM layers, and set the size as 50 for attention layer. We use the ADAM optimizer [12] to update parameters. We set the learning rate as 0.0005. During training, we do not update the pre-trained word embeddings. We get the dependency trees for all sentences by Stanford Parser[1]. For all the experiments, we pick the model which works the best on the development set, and then evaluate it on the test set.

4.3   Result on Paraphrase Identification

We compare our model with several baselines shown in Table 1. "Siamese-LSTM" and "Siamese-CNN" [22] are two simple models which encode two input sentences into sentence vectors with LSTM and CNN, respectively. Then the cosine similarity was used to make the classification. "Multi-Perspective-CNN" and "Multi-Perspective-LSTM" improve them by replacing the cos similarity with Wang et al. [21]'s multi-perspective cosine matching function. L.D.C is proposed by Wang et al. [23], which belong to the "matching-aggregation" framework. The results of the above models are reported in Wang et al. [21]. DIIN and MwAN are proposed by Gong et al. [8] and Tan et al. [17]. These two models acquire the state-of-the-art performance on several tasks. BiMPM [21] is our base model and get 88.17% on the test set. Our model outperforms all baselines with 90.1% accuracy on the development set and 89.53% accuracy on the test set.

Table 1. Performance of paraphrase identification on the QUORA dataset.

Model	Dev	Test
Siamess-CNN	–	79.6
Multi-Perspective-CNN	–	81.38
Siamese-LSTM	–	82.58
Multi-Perspective-LSTM	–	83.21
L.D.C	–	85.55
BiMPM	88.69	88.17
DIIN	89.44	89.06
MwAN	89.60	89.12
OurModel	**90.07**	**89.53**

---

[1] https://nlp.stanford.edu/software/lex-parser.shtml.

4.4   Result on Natural Language Inference

We show our results of natural language inference in Table 2. For SNLI dataset, we use five baseline models. As our base model, BiMPM obtains the accuracy of 86.9 on the test set. Our model has improved by 0.5% compared to the BiMPM model. For MultiNLI dataset, the results of CBOW, BiLSTM and ESIM were reported at Williams *et al.* [24], and trained with both SNLI and MultiNLI train sets. We train the BiMPM model and our model with MultiNll train set only, and report our results. We get 77.8% accuracy on the match set and 77.0% accuracy on the mismatch set.

Table 2. Performance on the SNLI dataset and MultiNLI dataset.

snli		MultiNLI		
Model	Accuracy	Model	Match	Mismatched
[Bowman et al. 2015] [2]	77.6	CBOW	65.2	64.6
[Vendrov et al. 2015] [18]	81.4	BiLSTM	67.5	67.1
SPINN [3]	82.6	ESIM	72.4	71.9
[Wang and Jiang 2015] [19]	86.1	BiMPM	77.0	76.7
[Cheng et al. 2016] [5]	86.3	–	–	–
BiMPM	86.9	–	–	–
OurModel	**87.4**	**Our**	**77.8**	**77.0**

4.5   Effect of GCN Layers

We evaluate the effectiveness of the number of GCN layers. We hypothesize that different level of information can be obtained with syntactic GCN by choosing the number of layers. To test this hypothesis, we choose QUORA as our dataset, and use max attentive match function as our match strategy. The accuracy of development set is shown in Table 3. We get 88.5% on the development set with a BiMPM model. When a one-layer multi-channel-GCN layer is used, we get an improvement of 0.9%. Adding an additional layer gives improvements of 0.3%.

Table 3. Results for QUORA dataset with different number of GCN layers.

Model	Accuracy
$GCN_{layers=0}$ (BiMPM)	88.5
$GCN_{layers=1}$	89.4
$GCN_{layers=2}$	**89.7**
$GCN_{layers=3}$	89.3

However, there is a decline of 0.4% when the number of GCN layer increased to 3. We think GCN with two hops can effectively capture the syntactic information, while GCN with three hops brings more noise to the model, making a worse result.

5 Conclusions and Future Work

In this work, we propose a multi-channel GCN layer to incorporate the information of dependency parsing to the "matching-aggregation" framework. Our multi-channel GCN layer takes the contextual embeddings of words together with the dependency tree as input and output a set of embeddings which is used in matching layer. Experimental results on standard benchmark datasets show that our model obtains significant improvement compared with the base model.

Future work will be carried out in the following aspects: firstly, we will apply our multi-channel GCN layer to more models to prove the robustness of our method; secondly, we will evaluate the effect of different dependency parser, which has different quality; finally, the more effective word embedding will be used to find out whether our method will improve the performance even when the parse information is added to an already very strong system.

References

1. Bahdanau, D., Cho, K., Bengio, Y.: Neural machine translation by jointly learning to align and translate. In: 3rd International Conference on Learning Representations (2015)
2. Bowman, S.R., Angeli, G., Potts, C., Manning, C.D.: A large annotated corpus for learning natural language inference. In: Proceedings of the 2015 Conference on Empirical Methods in Natural Language Processing, pp. 632–642 (2015)
3. Bowman, S.R., Gupta, R., Gauthier, J., Manning, C.D., Rastogi, A., Potts, C.: A fast unified model for parsing and sentence understanding. In: 54th Annual Meeting of the Association for Computational Linguistics, pp. 1466–1477 (2016)
4. Chen, Q., Zhu, X., Ling, Z.H., Wei, S., Jiang, H., Inkpen, D.: Enhanced LSTM for natural language inference. In: Proceedings of the 55th Annual Meeting of the Association for Computational Linguistics (Volume 1: Long Papers), pp. 1657–1668 (2017)
5. Cheng, J., Dong, L., Lapata, M.: Long short-term memory-networks for machine reading. In: Proceedings of the 2016 Conference on Empirical Methods in Natural Language Processing, pp. 551–561 (2016)
6. Duvenaud, D.K., et al.: Convolutional networks on graphs for learning molecular fingerprints. In: Advances in Neural Information Processing Systems, pp. 2224–2232 (2015)
7. Gilmer, J., Schoenholz, S.S., Riley, P.F., Vinyals, O., Dahl, G.E.: Neural message passing for quantum chemistry. In: Proceedings of the 34th International Conference on Machine Learning, vol. 70. pp. 1263–1272 (2017)
8. Gong, Y., Luo, H., Zhang, J.: Natural language inference over interaction space. In: 6th International Conference on Learning Representations (2018)

9. Hermann, K.M., et al.: Teaching machines to read and comprehend. In: Advances in Neural Information Processing Systems, pp. 1693–1701 (2015)

10. Hochreiter, S., Schmidhuber, J.: Long short-term memory. Neural Comput. **9**(8), 1735–1780 (1997)

11. Iyer, S., Dandekar, N., Csernai, K.: First quora dataset release: question pairs. data. quora.com (2017)

12. Kingma, D.P., Ba, J.: Adam: a method for stochastic optimization. arXiv preprint arXiv:1412.6980 (2014)

13. Kipf, T.N., Welling, M.: Semi-supervised classification with graph convolutional networks. In: 5th International Conference on Learning Representations (2017)

14. Marcheggiani, D., Titov, I.: Encoding sentences with graph convolutional networks for semantic role labeling. In: Proceedings of the 2017 Conference on Empirical Methods in Natural Language Processing, pp. 1506–1515 (2017)

15. Pennington, J., Socher, R., Manning, C.: Glove: global vectors for word representation. In: Proceedings of the 2014 Conference on Empirical Methods in Natural Language Processing (EMNLP), pp. 1532–1543 (2014)

16. Rush, A.M., Chopra, S., Weston, J.: A neural attention model for abstractive sentence summarization. In: Proceedings of the 2015 Conference on Empirical Methods in Natural Language Processing, pp. 379–389 (2015)

17. Tan, C., Wei, F., Wang, W., Lv, W., Zhou, M.: Multiway attention networks for modeling sentence pairs. In: Proceedings of the 27th International Joint Conference on Artificial Intelligence, pp. 4411–4417 (2018)

18. Vendrov, I., Kiros, R., Fidler, S., Urtasun, R.: Order-embeddings of images and language. In: 4th International Conference on Learning Representations (2016)

19. Wang, S., Jiang, J.: Learning natural language inference with LSTM. In: North American Chapter of the Association for Computational Linguistics, pp. 1442–1451 (2016)

20. Wang, S., Jiang, J.: A compare-aggregate model for matching text sequences. In: 5th International Conference on Learning Representations (2017)

21. Wang, Z., Hamza, W., Florian, R.: Bilateral multi-perspective matching for natural language sentences. In: Proceedings of the 26th International Joint Conference on Artificial Intelligence, pp. 4144–4150 (2017)

22. Wang, Z., Mi, H., Ittycheriah, A.: Semi-supervised clustering for short text via deep representation learning. In: Proceedings of The 20th SIGNLL Conference on Computational Natural Language Learning, pp. 31–39 (2016)

23. Wang, Z., Mi, H., Ittycheriah, A.: Sentence similarity learning by lexical decomposition and composition. In: Proceedings of COLING 2016, the 26th International Conference on Computational Linguistics: Technical Papers, pp. 1340–1349 (2016)

24. Williams, A., Nangia, N., Bowman, S.: A broad-coverage challenge corpus for sentence understanding through inference. In: Proceedings of the 2018 Conference of the North American Chapter of the Association for Computational Linguistics: Human Language Technologies, Volume 1 (Long Papers), pp. 1112–1122 (2018)

25. Yu, L., Hermann, K.M., Blunsom, P., Pulman, S.: Deep learning for answer sentence selection. In: Neural Information Processing Systems (2014)

26. Zhu, X., Sobihani, P., Guo, H.: Long short-term memory over recursive structures. In: International Conference on Machine Learning, pp. 1604–1612 (2015)

Music Genre Classification via Sequential Wavelet Scattering Feature Learning

Evren Kanalici[1,2] and Gokhan Bilgin[1,2(✉)]

[1] Department of Computer Engineering, Yildiz Technical University (YTU),
34220 Istanbul, Turkey
evren.kanalici.501@std.yildiz.edu.tr, gbilgin@yildiz.edu.tr
[2] Signal and Image Processing Lab. (SIMPLAB) at YTU, 34220 Istanbul, Turkey

Abstract. Various content-based high-level descriptors are used for musical similarity, classification and recommendation tasks. Our study uses wavelet scattering coefficients as features providing both translation-invariant representation and transient characterizations of audio signal to predict musical genre. Extracted features are fed to sequential architectures to model temporal dependencies of musical piece more efficiently. Competitive classification results are obtained against hand-engineered feature based frameworks with proposed technique.

Keywords: Wavelet transform · Wavelet scattering ·
Recurrent neural networks · LSTM · Genre classification · MIR

1 Introduction

Wavelet approach is spreading in research of music information retrieval (MIR), which deals with real-world audio signals including everyday consumed multimedia content. Indexing multimedia data for retrieval tasks, retrieval by example, digital watermarking, similarity and recommender systems are one of few concrete examples of MIR and music genre classification in particular is an open search problem aiming to provide automated genre-classification for musical audio signals. Wavelet transform, being linked with the human auditory perception brought new perspective to these research fields and its capability of fast computation [12] made it practical in digital world.

This work presents our approach for music genre classification problem. We use wavelet scattering framework for audio descriptors. Scattering wavelet transform (SWT), introduced by Mallat [11], provides stable, translation-invariant decomposition. Derived decomposition coefficients as time-series features are fed to sequential learning architectures, including long short-term memory (LSTM) networks [5], to model temporal dependencies of musical piece. LSTMs were developed to deal with the exploding and vanishing gradient problems that can be encountered when training traditional recurrent neural network (RNN) models.

C. Douligeris et al. (Eds.): KSEM 2019, LNAI 11776, pp. 365–372, 2019.
https://doi.org/10.1007/978-3-030-29563-9_32

2   Methodology

Our approach can be formulated as a classification problem from sequential input data. For a given sequence of time-series features $x = \{x_t\}$ our task is to derive a predictive model that is capable to perform assignment of a label from known classes;

$$x = x_1, ..., x_T; \quad x \in R^N$$
$$\mathbf{C} = c_1, ..., c_M \tag{1}$$
$$\hat{y} = f(x)$$

where sequence-length (T) may be varied but dimension of features (N) and number of class labels (M) should be fixed. Each x_t is a feature vector regarding to the attributes at time-step t. $\hat{y}$ represents the prediction for input x, hence classification problem is that minimizing the error between prediction and true labels $\mathbf{C}$. For f, as a predictor, and for x time-based sequential features we investigate Sequential Network Models and Wavelet Scattering respectively.

2.1   Wavelet Scattering

A wavelet transform W is convolutions with wavelet functions (Eq. 2). Since wavelets are localized in time they are not invariant to translation in spatial domain.

$$Wx(t) = \{x \star \phi(t), x \star \psi_\lambda(t)\}_\lambda$$
$$\psi_\lambda(t) = 2^{-jQ}\psi(2^{-jQ}t); \qquad \lambda = 2^{-jQ} \tag{2}$$

Scattering wavelet transform (SWT) is translation-invariant signal decomposition implemented as similar to convolutional networks whose filters are not learned, but fixed being wavelet filters. SWT is presented by Mallat [11], which is computed through a cascade of wavelet decompositions iteratively. The output is time-averaged coefficients of modulus. SWT provides signal invariants i.e. translation-invariance, stability to time-warping deformations (Eq. 3) and inverse transform without losing information.

$$\|\Phi x - \Phi(x_\tau)\| < C \sup_t |\nabla\tau(t)| . \|x\| \tag{3}$$

To have informative invariant which is not zero it has to have non-linearity. Coarsely, the basic idea of SWT is based on applying a non-linear map i.e. modulus operator M that is translation-invariant and commutes with diffeomorphism (Eq. 4) and $\mathbf{L}^2$ stable to additive perturbation since its contractive (Eq. 5).

$$\int M(x \star \phi_\lambda)(t)dt \tag{4}$$

$$\|Mh\| = \|h\|$$
$$\|Mg - Mh\| \le \|g - h\| \tag{5}$$
$$\Rightarrow M(h)(t) = |h(t)| = \sqrt{|h(t_r)|^2 + |h(t_i)|^2}$$

A modulus computes a smooth lower frequency envelop for complex waveforms. The integral of modulus is $\mathbf{L}^1$ norm which is stable invariant (Eq. 6).

$$\int |x \star \phi_\lambda(t)| dt = \|x \star \phi_\lambda\|_1 \tag{6}$$

The wavelet power spectrum is given (Eq. 7)

$$|W|x(t, \lambda) = (x \star \phi, |x \star \psi_\lambda|) \tag{7}$$

whereas modulus discards the phase information, it retains sufficient information for signal reconstruction since wavelet transform is redundant thanks to over-sampling. Mel-spectrograms are obtained by low-pass filtering $|W|x(t, \lambda)$, which corresponds to low-frequency component of second wavelet transform (Eq. 8);

$$|W||x \star \psi_{\lambda_1}| = (|x \star \psi_{\lambda_1}| \star \phi, ||x \star \psi_{\lambda_1}| \star \psi_{\lambda_2}|) \tag{8}$$

In Eq. 8 averaging by scaling function $|x \star \phi_\lambda| \star \phi$ removes high frequencies. By applying the same time-window averaging, information in the higher-order components can be recovered in a stable and time-shift invariant manner;

$$\forall \lambda_1, \lambda_2; \quad ||x \star \psi_{\lambda_1}| \star \psi_{\lambda_2}| \star \phi \tag{9}$$

By using Eq. 9 in a cascaded fashion, windowed scattering for any path of scales $p = (\lambda_1, ..., \lambda_m)$ of order m is given in Eq. 10. All the output coefficients at each layer will be averaged by the scaling function ϕ. Also, the energy of the decomposition goes to zero as the depth m increases.

$$S[p]x(t) = ||x \star \psi_{\lambda_1}| \star \psi_{\lambda_2}|...| \star \psi_{\lambda_m}| \star \phi(t)$$
$$\{S[p]x\}_{p \in P} \tag{10}$$

Substantially, 1st layer outputs of SWT decomposition $S[\lambda_1]x$ gives mel-frequency cepstral coefficients (MFCC) values, which is well-known representation for music and speech related information retrieval tasks [1]. Cited work also explores the similarities between SWT and convolutional networks [8].

Figure 1 shows wavelet scattering framework with 2 filter banks. Wavelets are in form of modulated Gaussian by sine and cosine wave as a complex waveform. In Fig. 1(a) it can be seen that the scaling filter is localized in *invariance-scale* (0.5 s) by design. Also the time support of the coarsest-scale wavelet is bounded by the invariance-scale of the wavelet scattering. Whereas second order filter bank wavelets are more localized in time with shorter support in Fig. 1(b).

2.2 Sequential Network Models

2.3 Recurrent Neural Network

A recurrent neural network (RNN) is a type of artificial neural network, where its recurrent loop can be unfolded as a directed graph between cells along a temporal

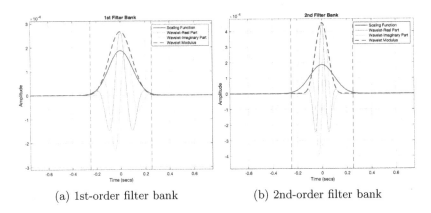

(a) 1st-order filter bank   (b) 2nd-order filter bank

Fig. 1. Scattering wavelets with 2 filter banks

sequence. RNN cells or steps apply same transformation to every element of a sequence and hold an internal memory that summarize the history of the sequence it has seen.

Directed connection allows network to exhibit temporal dynamic behavior. RNNs can use their internal state (memory) to process sequential input data series by using a conceptual delay blocks which make them distinct from feed-forward neural networks.

For a given sequence of input vectors $x = x_1, ..., x_T$, an L-layer classical RNN computes, at layer l and time-step t;

$$h_t^1 = W x_t \tag{11}$$

$$h_t^l = tanh(W_{hh}^l h_{t-1}^l + W_{xh}^l h_t^{l-1})$$
$$y_t = W_{hy} h_t^L \tag{12}$$

where h_t^l is the hidden unit at the layer l and t-th time-step, and W, W_{hh}, W_{xh}, W_{hy} are the weights of the model.

Considering a multi-class classifications problem, softmax activation (softmax classifier) is used to train sequential input of the same class in one-vs-rest scheme of C classes;

$$\tilde{y} = softmax(y_T^L)$$
$$\hat{y} = \underset{c \in C}{argmax}(\tilde{y})_c \tag{13}$$

2.4 Long Short-Term Memory Network

Classical RNNs suffer from vanishing gradients over long-term dependencies [3]. Long Short-Term Memory Networks (LSTMs) [5] on the other hand are capable of learning long-term dependencies by allowing gradients to flow unchanged. A common architecture of LSTM unit is composed of a cell, containing three gates/regulators: input gate, an output gate and a forget gate. The gates regulate the flow of information in and out of the particular LSTM unit and they are responsible to protect and control the cell state.

For a given sequence of input vectors $x = x_1, ..., x_T$, an L-layer LSTM with forget gate computes, at layer l and time-step t;

$$h_t^1 = x_t \tag{14}$$

$$\begin{bmatrix} i \\ f \\ o \\ \tilde{C} \end{bmatrix} = \begin{bmatrix} sigm \\ sigm \\ sigm \\ tanh \end{bmatrix} W^l \begin{bmatrix} h_t^{l-1} \\ h_{t-1}^l \end{bmatrix}$$

$$\tag{15}$$

$$C_t^l = f \odot C_{t-1}^l + i \odot \tilde{C}_t^l$$
$$h_t^l = o \odot tanh(C_t^l)$$
$$y_t = W_{hy} h_t^L$$

where $\odot$ is hadamard product for point-wise multiplication. Variables i, f, o are the same dimensional input gate, forget gate, output gate of the LSMT unit and $\tilde{C}, C$ correspond to block gate, and candidate context respectively at the l-th layer and t-th time-step. For classification problems, the prediction is made by calculating $\hat{y}$ as in Eq. 13.

3   Results

3.1   Experiments

In our experiments we use well-known GTZAN Genre Collection data set [15]. The data consist of excerpts from 10 musical genres (rock, blues, classical, country, disco, hip-hop, jazz, metal, pop, reggae), containing 100 example per each genre. Each example is about 30 s of data with sampling rate Fs = 22050 Hz. RMS normalization is applied for each audio data before SWT decomposition.

Shown as the optimal settings in [1], 2-depth SWT decomposition is preferred. For filter bank Q-factors, $(Q1, Q2) = (8, 1)$ configuration is used, considered as $Q1 = 8$ having enough frequency resolution to separate harmonic structures.

An example of 6-seconds long audio clip shown in Fig. 2(a). Also zeroth-order SWT decomposition coefficients are plotted. Note that, the scaling function ϕ (behaving as the averaging operator), the large values of coefficients reflects the energy concentration of audio signal. In Fig. 2(b) and (c), scattering coefficients of 2-level filter banks are shown. Where 1st level wavelet decomposition captures the pitch information (a), transient attributes are more apparent in 2nd level as expected (b).

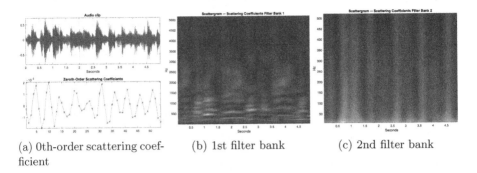

(a) 0th-order scattering coefficient   (b) 1st filter bank   (c) 2nd filter bank

Fig. 2. zeroth-order scattering coefficients (a) Scattergram - 2-level filter banks (b), (c).

We use 6-seconds long segments for each audio file in GTZAN data set for our sequential time-series features x (having 1000 audio-files $\times$ (30/6) s = 5000 features). Dataset is split in order of $(0.7, 0.1, 0.2)$ for training, validation and test purposes. Various invariance-scale (2^J-samples), time-window (N-samples) and first filter-bank q-factor (Q) parameter configuration is possible in wavelet scattering for our specific task, but we found best invariance-scale is $2^J = 2^{12}$ (i.e. $2^{12}/Fs = 190$ ms.) by grid search[1]. Giving time-series features as $x = x_1, ..., x_T; x \in R^{545}, T = 32$.

After feature extraction step, different network architectures are fit for given recurrent models. Majority voting is used for predicted results. We used Pytorch [13] for our network models and scikit-learn [14] for baseline tests. Baseline comparisons and analysis of classification results are given in next section.

3.2   Analysis

We designed our recurrent network architectures similar to Irvin et al. [7]. As summarized in same the work, few notable results in literature for genre classification on GTZAN data set is given in Table 1. The best result is in bold, which uses aggregated ensemble learner Adaboost features from segmented audio. All the listed works use analogous cross-validation methods to calculate reported accuracies.

Also, we tested our feature extraction output with various internal baseline classifiers. Table 2 shows test accuracies of optimal baselines. The best baseline classification result is shown as bold type in Table 2. Linear SVM and Logistic regression classifiers perform well enough over our feature set and deliver very close scores to external baselines.

In Table 3, we present our experimental test results for recurrent networks. For single and two-layers networks, recurrent unit dimensions are optimized by

---

[1] We used various combinations of wavelet scattering parameters of N: transform support length of input signal length, 2^J: maximum log-scale of the scattering transform and Q: The number of first-order wavelets per octave for; $N \in [2^{15}, 2^{16}, 2^{17}]$, $J \in [2^{10}, 2^{11}, 2^{12}]$ and $Q \in [8, 10, 12]$.

Table 1. Examples of external baselines on the GTZAN [15] dataset [7]

Model	Test Acc. (%)
Bergstra et al. [4]	**82.5**
Li et al. [9]	78.5
Lidy et al. [10]	76.8
Benetos et al. [2]	75
Holzapfel et al. [6]	74
Tzanetakis et al. [16]	61

Table 2. Baseline classifiers test accuracy

Classifier	Test Acc. (%)
LR	77.00
kNN	71.65
SVC-rbf	67.23
SVC-poly1	62.35
lin-SVC1	**77.88**
lin-SVC2	77.77
DT	44.00
RF	47.88
AdaBoost	16.23
MLP1	75.35
MLP2	73.73
NB	49.27
QDA	51.31

grid search (with cell dimensions = {60, 125, 250, 500, 1000}, drop-out probabilities = {0.1, 0.2, 0.4}, batch-sizes = {64, 128}) and the best results are shown. Recurrent networks, LSTMs in particular, deliver higher accuracies from our baseline results as excepted, that is highly correlated temporal dependencies of musical data is well modeled with sequential models. Note that the performance of simple RNN models are below LSTM networks due to possible realisation of vanishing gradients over long time-series sequences. The accuracy of best LSMT model, given bold, also out-performs cited baselines.

Table 3. Summary of experimental results

Model	Test Acc. (%)
RNN: 1-Layer, 60-dim. cell	77
RNN 2-Layer, 60-dim. cell	75.5
LSTM 1-Layer, 250-dim. cell	82.1
LSTM 2-Layer, 120-dim. cell	**85.7**

4   Conclusion

In this paper, we demonstrated that audio segments can be described as robust features for music genre classification by wavelet scattering transform and combined with sequential network models this framework delivers very high accuracy results. We noted external baseline results for genre classification and indeed our best model out-performs all the given baselines without any hand-crafted features. Hyper-parameter optimization and impact of audio pre-processing should be analyzed further and we plan to take forward these topics in our future works.

References

1. Andén, J., Mallat, S.: Deep scattering spectrum. IEEE Trans. Signal Process. **62**(16), 4114–4128 (2014)
2. Benetos, E., Kotropoulos, C.: A tensor-based approach for automatic music genre classification. In: 2008 16th European Signal Processing Conference, pp. 1–4. IEEE (2008)
3. Bengio, Y., Simard, P., Frasconi, P., et al.: Learning long-term dependencies with gradient descent is difficult. IEEE Trans. Neural Netw. **5**(2), 157–166 (1994)
4. Bergstra, J., Casagrande, N., Erhan, D., Eck, D., Kégl, B.: Aggregate features and ada boost for music classification. Mach. Learn. **65**(2–3), 473–484 (2006)
5. Hochreiter, S., Schmidhuber, J.: Long short-term memory. Neural Comput. **9**(8), 1735–1780 (1997)
6. Holzapfel, A., Stylianou, Y.: Musical genre classification using nonnegative matrix factorization-based features. IEEE Trans. Audio Speech Lang. Process. **16**(2), 424–434 (2008)
7. Irvin, J., Chartock, E., Hollander, N.: Recurrent neural networks with attention for genre classification (2016)
8. LeCun, Y., Kavukcuoglu, K., Farabet, C.: Convolutional networks and applications in vision. In: Proceedings of IEEE International Symposium on Circuits and Systems, pp. 253–256. IEEE (2010)
9. Li, T., Ogihara, M., Li, Q.: A comparative study on content-based music genre classification. In: Proceedings of the 26th Annual International ACM SIGIR Conference on Research and Development in Information Retrieval, pp. 282–289. ACM (2003)
10. Lidy, T., Rauber, A., Pertusa, A., Quereda, J.M.I.: Improving genre classification by combination of audio and symbolic descriptors using a transcription systems. In: International Society for Music Information Retrieval Conference, ISMIR 2007, pp. 61–66 (2007)
11. Mallat, S.: Group invariant scattering. Commun. Pure Appl. Math. **65**(10), 1331–1398 (2012)
12. Mallat, S.G.: A theory for multiresolution signal decomposition: the wavelet representation. IEEE Trans. Pattern Anal. Mach. Intell. **11**(7), 674–693 (1989)
13. Paszke, A., et al.: Automatic differentiation in PyTorch. In: Neural Information Processing Systems Workshop (2017)
14. Pedregosa, F., et al.: Scikit-learn: machine learning in Python. J. Mach. Learn. Res. **12**, 2825–2830 (2011)
15. Tzanetakis, G., Cook, P.: Gtzan genre collection (2002). http://marsyas.info/downloads/datasets.html
16. Tzanetakis, G., Cook, P.: Musical genre classification of audio signals. IEEE Trans. Speech Audio Process. **10**(5), 293–302 (2002)

Efficient Network Representations Learning: An Edge-Centric Perspective

Shichao Liu[1], Shuangfei Zhai[2], Lida Zhu[1(✉)],
Fuxi Zhu[3], Zhongfei (Mark) Zhang[2], and Wen Zhang[1]

[1] College of Informatics, Huazhong Agricultural University, Wuhan, China
scliu@mail.hzau.edu.cn, zhulida@hotmail.com
[2] Department of Computer Science, Binghamton University, Binghamton, USA
[3] AI Application Research Center, Wuhan College, Wuhan, China

Abstract. Learning succinct/effective representations is of essential importance to network modeling. Network embedding is a popular approach to this end, which maps each vertex of a network to a fixed-length, low-dimensional vector. Previous efforts on network embedding mainly fall into two categories: (1) link based and (2) link + node feature based. In this paper, we provide an edge-centric view where features are associated with edges, in addition to the network structure. The edge-centric view provides a fine-grained characterization of a network, where the dynamic interactions between vertices are considered instead of the static property of vertices. Methodology-wise, we propose an efficient network representations learning approach called the NEEF (network embedding with edge features) model. In particular, the NEEF model seamlessly incorporates the edge features when considering the proximity of a pair of vertices. The model is then trained to maximize the occurrence probability of the neighboring vertices conditioned on the edge features. In our experiments, we show that many of the real-world networks can be abstracted as network with edge features, among which we choose the DBLP coauthor network, the Reddit review network, and the Enron email network for evaluations. Experimental results show that our proposed NEEF model outperforms the other state-of-the-art baselines on tasks such as classification and clustering. We also visualize the learned representations, and show intuitive interpretations of the NEEF model.

Keywords: Network embedding · Representations learning · Edge feature

1 Introduction

Proper representations are the key to the success of most machine learning and data mining algorithms. For network modeling and analysis, low dimensional embedding approaches have become popular in recent years [7,18,22]. Each vertex of the graph is represented as a fixed-length vector, where vertices with similar semantics are assigned with similar embeddings w.r.t. a certain metric

© Springer Nature Switzerland AG 2019
C. Douligeris et al. (Eds.): KSEM 2019, LNAI 11776, pp. 373–388, 2019.
https://doi.org/10.1007/978-3-030-29563-9_33

(e.g., Euclidean distance). Such low-dimensional vector representations naturally encodes the structure of a network can be easily fed into machine learning models in a various range of network analysis tasks, such as classification, link prediction and visualization.

A large body of works on network embedding falls into the category where only linkage information is used [5,13,18,22]. DeepWalk [18] samples the graph structure into a stream of random walks, with which a Skip-gram model [16] is trained to predict the path of the random walk. LINE [22] defines a loss function to capture both 1-step and 2-step local structure information, and further extends to k-step by GraRep [5]. These models have enriched the "context" of each vertex by introducing k-step relational information, but link sparsity problem still exists in many real networks. For example, two users who have similar attributes (e.g., interests, behaviors) are not well handled if they do not share similar local structure.

One of the techniques to overcome the aforementioned problem is to fuse the vertex information (vertex features) with linkage information for representations learning [10,26]. The assumption is that vertices should have similar representations if they reside in the same local community and/or have similar features. In such a way, learning can still proceed even for vertices around which network connection is sparse.

The two lines of work share the similarity in that they both take a vertex-centric view of a network, and edges are treated as either binary (existence or not) or scalar variables (weighted edges). In this work, we study a different scenario where edge features exist, in addition to the network structure, and we call this type of networks edge-centric networks. This view can be regarded as a generalization of edge-weighted networks where the weights are not constrained to be scalars, but rather vectors. Also, it relates to vertex-feature networks in that it can be reduced from an edge-feature network, but aggregating the features associated with all the edges of a vertex. However, the edge-centric view provides a much fine-grained characterization of the network, and we show that edge-feature networks are abundant in real world, such as email network, collaboration network and online forum network.

In this paper, we propose NEEF, a novel network embedding model by incorporating linkage structure and edge features to represent edge-centric graphs. Firstly, NEEF samples the input network using truncated random walks; Such an initialization is easy to parallelize and we can just update the learned model for new coming walks without global computation. For weighted graphs, the probability that each vertex walks to its neighbors is proportional to the weight of edges between the vertex and its neighbors. Our model is then trained to maximize the occurrence probability of each pair of vertices that appear within a window w conditioned on its associated edge features. After training, edge features are eventually projected into the learned representations of vertices.

To summarize, our main contributions are described below:

- We introduce NEEF, the efficient model for network representations learning with edge features, which provide a new insight for learning low-dimensional vectors of vertices and model the linkage structure and edge features in a seamless way.

- We extensively evaluate our model on several tasks on three real-world networks with edge features; Experimental results show that the NEEF model outperforms the state-of-art methods in most cases, even training with less labeled data.
- We conduct case studies on DBLP coauthor network, the results show that NEEF can learn fine-grained representations of vertices, where the value of each dimensionality is meaningful for its associated features; Moreover, NEEF generates more meaningful layout of the DBLP coauthor network than Deep-Walk and TADW.

2 Related Work

Classical approaches to network embedding or dimension reduction have been proposed in the last decades [3,8,20]. Surveys on network embedding have been proposed to describe the problems, methods and applications recent two years [4, 11,14]. Considering the efficiency to handle large-scale networks, we summarize the most recent work and group them into three categories:

2.1 Representations Learning only Using Linkage Information

There are several recent network embedding models based on the network structure without additional information. Factorization based methods represent the connections between nodes in the form of a matrix and factorize this matrix to obtain the embedding. Graph Factorization [1] is a matrix factorization approach for learning low-dimensional vectors, which is optimized by using stochastic gradient descent. HOPE [17] preserves higher proximity by minimizing the similarity matrix and use generalized Singular Value Decomposition to obtain the embedding efficiently.

DeepWalk [18] first introduces the word embedding model [16] to network representations learning task; A truncated random walk approach is used to transform the graph into several linear vertex sequences. Acting like a depth-first search strategy, the random walk approach brings the indirect neighbors to enrich the "context" of each vertex; The drawback of the depth-first search strategy is that it may bring vertices that are long away. Node2vec [13] presents a bias random walk to explore neighborhoods incorporating breadth-first search and depth-first search strategies to sample the network, which provides a flexible control over low-dimensional space through tunable parameters. LINE [22] defines objective functions to preserve both the 1-step and 2-step relational information and optimizes the objective functions through an edge-sampling algorithm; The model is scalable to very large, arbitrary types of networks. Learning network representations with global structural information, GraRep [5] defines different objective functions for capturing the different k-step relational information; The model optimizes each objective functions with matrix factorization techniques and finally integrates the learned representations from k-step relational information to a global representations of network.

There are several deep learning based methods applied to network embedding. SDNE [25] utilizes deep autoencoders to preserve the first and second order network proximities. DNGR [6] combines random surfing with deep autoencoder, the random surfing model is used to capture higher order proximities of network. These two methods take as input the global neighborhood of each node, which leads to the expensive computation for large sparse graphs.

2.2 Representations Learning with Node Features

Previous approaches incorporate textual information and linkage information to learn network representations, where features extracted from the textual information are associated with vertices. Author2vec [10] combines paper content and coauthor link information for learning author representation model contains two components: Content-Info model and Link-Info model, which share the author embedding for training. Authors who have similar paper content and share similar structures are closer in the learned low-dimensional vector space. TADW [26] first proves that DeepWalk is equivalent to matrix factorization and incorporates text features into network representations learning using matrix factorization. Experimental results show that TADW achieves better performance than the naive combination of DeepWalk and text features.

2.3 Representations Learning with Edge Features

There are several related researches on network representations learning using edge features. ELAINE [12] uses a coupled deep variational autoencoder to capture highly non-linear nature of interactions between nodes and an edge attribute decoder to reconstruct the edge labels. Tang et al. [23] propose the methods for extracting latent social dimensions from community detection models. The latent social dimensions can be transformed to the low-dimension vectors of the network. To capture the structural proximities and edge features, our proposed NEEF model provides a remarkable view for network embedding with edge features which is not considered by the previous work. we describe the NEEF model in the following section.

3   NEEF: Network Embedding with Edge Features

3.1   Problem Definition

We formally define the problem of network embedding with edge features as follows:

Definition 1 *(Network Embedding with Edge Features): Given a network $G = (V, E, F)$, where $V = \{v_1, v_2, ..., v_n\}$ is the set of vertices; $E = \{e_{uv}\}$ is the set of edges and $F = \{f_{uv} \in R^k | (u, v) \in E\}$ is the feature set corresponding to E; k is the dimensionality of the feature set. The goal of network embedding with edge features aims to learn a low-dimensional space R^d of each vertex where both linkage structure E and its associated edge features F are captured.*

Note that the embedding size $d \ll |V|$ and the feature set F is prepared from the edge-centric view of the input network.

3.2 Feature Construction

We first extract edge features F from the content information of edges which are usually represented by Bag-of-words or TF-IDF. The high dimensionality k of F equals to the size of the content vocabulary, which leads to expensive computation and storage cost. Consequently, we reduce the extracted feature $F \in R^k$ to R^d space ($d \ll k$) using non-negative matrix factorization, where d is the embedding size of the network. On the other hand, F is very sparse in general. To enrich the feature set, we introduce the triangular effect as below:

Definition 2 *(Triangular Effect): Given a network $G = (V, E, F)$, if edge $(i, l) \in E$ and edge $(l, j) \in E$, we assume that the latent feature f'_{ij} is obtained from a triangular effect $(i \rhd l \rhd j)$ even if edge $(i, j) \notin E$.*

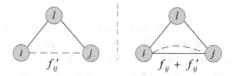

Fig. 1. Examples of the triangular effect.

Figure 1 shows two examples of the triangular effect. The latent feature f'_{ij} can be considered as the effect of similar behavior between vertex i and j. As shown in the right part of Fig. 1, If vertex i and j have links, the latent feature f'_{ij} adds to the existing edge feature f_{ij} directly. Mathematically, the latent feature f'_{ij} forms as follows:

$$f'_{ij} = \sum_{l \in N(i) \cap N(j)} \sqrt{f_{il} \circ f_{lj}}, \tag{1}$$

where $\circ$ denotes the element-wise product between vectors due to the former non-negative feature reduction; $N(\cdot)$ is a function which returns the neighbors of an input vertex. Without loss of generality, we assume that the latent features between vertices with no links follow a uniform distribution. If all the edge features follow a uniform distribution, our proposed NEEF model reduces to DeepWalk.

3.3 NEEF Model Description

Here, we present the NEEF model to learn representations of networks with edge features. The main idea is that vertices with similar network structures and similar behaviors over edge features are closer in the learned vector space.

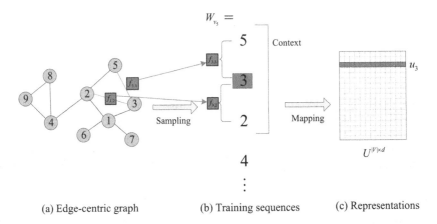

(a) Edge-centric graph   (b) Training sequences   (c) Representations

Fig. 2. Overview of NEEF. We first sample the edge-centric graph into several random walks; The representation u_3 of vertex v_3 is updated to maximize the probability of v_3 co-occurring with its context $\{v_2, v_5\}$ conditioned on the edge features $\{f_{3,2}, f_{3,5}\}$ when window $w = 1$.

NEEF first generates several random walks to sample the input graph uniformly, which is introduced in DeepWalk. For a weighted graph, staring by a vertex v_i, we sample the walks proportionally to the weight of the edge associated to v_i. Such walks can be seen as the input corpus of language models [16].

In this paper, we improve the Skip-gram model to train the walks with enriched features; Different with DeepWalk, our model maximizes the co-occurrence probability of each pair of vertices that appear within a window w conditioned on the edge features (see Fig. 2). We form the objective function as follows:

$$Pr(v_j|v_i; F) = \frac{\exp((\vec{c_j} \circ f_{ij})^T \cdot (\vec{u_i} \circ f_{ij}))}{\sum_{l \in V} \exp((\vec{c_l} \circ f_{il})^T \cdot (\vec{u_i} \circ f_{il}))}, \tag{2}$$

where $\circ$ denotes the element-wise product between vectors, that means for each training pairs, the vertex vectors are firstly projected into the edge feature space; $\vec{u_i}$ is the representation of vertex v_i; $\vec{c_j}$ is the representation of vertex v_j when it is treated as the "context" of v_i; $f_{ij} \in F$ means the feature of edge e_{ij} derived from feature construction. Different from the Skip-gram model, we naturally project the edge features into the representations of vertices, which provides a new insight for learning representations of network with features. We describe the NEEF model in Algorithm 1.

3.4   Optimization

To avoid the expensive computation of normalization factor in objective function (2), we employ the negative sampling method introduced in [16]. For each edge

Algorithm 1. NEEF Model

Input: Graph $G(V, E, F)$
    window size w
    learning rate α
Output: representations of vertices $\overrightarrow{u} \in R^{|V| \times d}$
 1: Initialization: sample $\overrightarrow{u}$ from $R^{|V| \times d}$ randomly
 2: **for each** $v_l \in V$ **do**
 3:    Generate random walks W_{v_l}
 4:    **for each** $v_i \in W_{v_l}$ **do**
 5:        **for each** $v_j \in W_{v_l}[i - w : i + w]$ **do**
 6:            $J(\overrightarrow{u}) = -\log \Pr(v_j | v_i; F)$
 7:            $\overrightarrow{u} = \overrightarrow{u} - \alpha * \frac{\partial J}{\partial \overrightarrow{u}}$
 8:    **end for**
 9: **end for**
10: **end for**

(i, j), the loss function is specified as follows:

$$
J(\overrightarrow{u}) = -\log \sigma((\overrightarrow{c_j} \circ f_{ij})^T \cdot (\overrightarrow{u_i} \circ f_{ij}))
$$
$$
- \sum_{i=1}^{K} E_{c_v \sim P_n(v)}[\log \sigma((\overrightarrow{c_v} \circ f_{iv})^T \cdot (\overrightarrow{u_i} \circ f_{iv}))] \,,
\tag{3}
$$

where $\sigma(\cdot)$ is the sigmoid function that is defined as $\sigma(x) = 1/(1 + \exp(-x))$; K is the number of negative samples; $E_{c_v \sim P_n(v)}[\cdot]$ means the expectation when negative instance c_v follows the distribution $P_n(v)$. As suggested in [16], we set $P_n(v) \propto d_v^{0.75}$, where d_v is the frequency count of vertex v in the sampling walks.

We adopt a scalable technique, called asynchronous stochastic gradient algorithm (ASGD) [19] to optimize the loss function (3). ASGD is proved efficient for parallel optimization by the previous models [18,22].

4 Experiment Design

In this section, we describe the datasets and baseline methods briefly.

4.1 Datasets

Many real-world networks can be described as edge-centric networks where features are associated with edges. Here, we present three edge-centric networks for evaluation.

- DBLP Coauthor Network: This data set contains three fields of top conferences from 2001 to 2011, where KDD, ICDM, ICDE, VLDB, SIGMOD are grouped as "DM&DB"; AAAI, IJCAI, ICML, NIPS are grouped as "AI&ML"; CVPR, ICCV, ECCV are grouped as "CV&PR". The short paper titles are extracted as the edge content. We describe the edge features by a vector of 1518 dimensions. Authors who published less than 5 papers during the 11 years are not considered. Therefore, there are overall 3,136 authors and 28,964 relationships.

– Reddit Review Network: This data set contains user interactions of three sub-forums (Movies, Politics, Science) in *Reddit*. Vertices represent forum users and edges represent interactions among users. We extract the reviews between users as the edge content. Each edge is described by a vector of 9224 dimensions. Users who submitted less than 5 reviews are not considered. Therefore, there are overall 4,759 authors and 35,598 relationships.

– Enron Email Network: The data set contains 1700 email messages labeled by 53 categories. Vertices represent email senders and receivers while edges represent communications between email users. The email messages are processed as the edge features by a vector of 13608 dimensions. Users who have less than 5 communications are removed. Therefore, there are overall 306 users and 4,923 relationships.

4.2   Baseline Methods

We choose several representative models of each category as baselines, which are described as below:

– NMF [27]: This method generates overlapping modules using a non-negative matrix factorization approach, which can be used to learn a R^d representation by social dimensions learning [23].
– EdgeCluster [24]: This method extracts sparse social dimensions from an edge-centric clustering scheme, which is scalable for large networks.
– Modularity [23]: This method generates a R^d representation from top-d eigenvectors of modularity matrix.
– DeepWalk [18]: DeepWalk is a method for learning representations of social networks only considering linkage information.
– CESNA [28]: This method extracts community memberships from linkage structure and node features. Similar to NMF [27], the latent social dimensions can be learned from this model.
– TADW [26]: TADW incorporates text features into network representations learning by proving that DeepWalk is equivalent to matrix factorization. Features are associated to vertices in this model.

4.3   Parameter Settings

For all data sets, edge features are described by $R^{|E| \times d}$, where d is the size of learned representations. We prepare node features from vertex-centric view for CESNA and TADW. The learning rate is initially set as 0.025 and the number of negative sample is 5. For DeepWalk and NEEF models, a weighted random walk is used to sample the network structure. We set walks per vertex $\gamma = 40$, walk length $T = 40$ and window size $w = 10$. The learned representations are L2 normalized for TADW model.

Table 1. Classification results on DBLP Coauthor Network.

Metric	Type	Algorithm	10%	20%	30%	40%	50%	60%	70%	80%	90%
Micro-F1	Link only	NMF	76.23	79.85	81.28	82.53	82.83	83.39	83.41	83.56	84.30
		EdgeCluster	80.00	82.61	83.61	84.22	84.47	84.53	84.65	84.84	85.04
		Modularity	73.43	81.94	85.26	86.65	87.40	87.97	88.05	88.23	88.77
		DeepWalk	86.56	87.39	87.81	88.00	88.16	88.33	88.35	88.47	88.44
	Link + Node feature	CESNA	76.68	80.64	82.34	83.32	84.03	84.41	84.67	84.80	84.97
		TADW($d = 200$)	87.08	88.53	89.08	89.50	89.68	**90.02**	90.16	90.43	90.53
		TADW($d = 128$)	86.79	88.13	88.68	89.02	89.29	89.46	89.54	89.72	89.82
	Link + Edge feature	NEEF($d = 200$)	**87.88**	**88.78**	**89.09**	**89.52**	**89.70**	89.80	**90.39**	**90.94**	**91.52**
		NEEF($d = 128$)	86.80	88.01	88.53	89.12	89.43	89.66	89.79	90.10	90.54
Macro-F1	Link only	NMF	76.23	79.82	81.24	82.48	82.77	83.33	83.36	83.48	84.26
		EdgeCluster	79.99	82.58	83.59	84.20	84.45	84.52	84.63	84.80	85.03
		Modularity	73.41	81.88	85.19	86.59	87.34	87.91	88.01	88.17	88.73
		DeepWalk	86.51	87.37	87.79	87.99	88.15	88.32	88.35	88.46	88.41
	Link + Node feature	CESNA	76.65	80.60	82.29	83.27	83.98	84.36	84.62	84.77	84.95
		TADW($d = 200$)	86.87	88.35	88.93	89.35	89.65	**89.88**	90.03	90.30	90.42
		TADW($d = 128$)	86.57	87.94	88.51	88.86	89.14	89.32	89.40	89.59	89.70
	Link + Edge feature	NEEF($d = 200$)	**87.87**	**88.77**	**89.07**	**89.51**	**89.67**	89.76	**90.33**	**90.84**	**91.40**
		NEEF($d = 128$)	86.68	87.81	88.32	88.59	88.89	89.24	89.49	89.52	90.05

4.4 Evaluation Metrics

In this paper, we conduct several experiments between the NEEF model and baselines on classification and clustering tasks. For classification, we use one-vs-rest linear SVM implemented by LibLinear [9] and the classification metrics F1 score. For each training ratio, we randomly select the vertices as training data for 10 times and report the average performance.

$$F1 = \frac{2 \times precision \times recall}{precision + recall}, \qquad (4)$$

For clustering, we use and accuracy (AC) score normalized mutual information (NMI) score [21] to evaluate the performance, where AC means the size of the best matched cluster divided by the size of total vertices.

$$NMI(X;Y) = \frac{2\sum_{x,y} p(x,y) log \frac{p(x,y)}{p(x)p(y)}}{-\sum_x p(x) log p(x) - \sum_y p(y) log p(y)}, \qquad (5)$$

where X(Y) is a division of the network, $p(\cdot)$ is the probability distribution function.

5 Experiment Results

In this section, we present the performance among NEEF and baselines on different data sets.

Table 2. Classification results on Reddit Review Network.

Metric	Type	Algorithm	10%	20%	30%	40%	50%	60%	70%	80%	90%
Micro-F1	Link only	NMF	77.29	75.86	76.58	77.04	77.25	77.56	77.68	77.47	77.72
		EdgeCluster	46.62	48.19	48.77	49.02	49.18	49.52	49.65	49.61	49.74
		Modularity	42.65	45.12	46.45	47.64	48.34	48.84	49.40	49.47	49.66
		DeepWalk	97.48	97.62	97.72	97.79	97.82	97.87	97.80	97.83	97.88
	Link + Node feature	CESNA	84.31	86.79	87.97	88.60	88.98	89.28	89.33	89.37	89.42
		TADW($d = 200$)	91.95	92.45	92.73	92.91	92.97	93.16	93.12	93.17	93.40
		TADW($d = 128$)	91.7	92.42	92.85	93.11	93.24	93.38	93.49	93.51	93.79
	Link + Edge feature	NEEF($d = 200$)	**97.69**	**97.79**	**97.90**	**97.94**	**97.96**	**98.07**	**98.03**	**98.00**	**98.04**
		NEEF($d = 128$)	97.68	97.78	97.83	97.85	97.88	97.96	97.94	97.96	97.97
Macro-F1	Link only	NMF	73.01	75.03	75.91	76.46	76.74	77.08	77.22	77.05	77.32
		EdgeCluster	30.42	32.71	33.71	34.21	34.54	34.99	35.27	35.51	35.73
		Modularity	35.62	37.18	38.46	39.28	39.53	40.15	40.50	40.50	40.40
		DeepWalk	97.21	97.37	97.47	97.55	97.59	97.64	97.55	97.59	97.65
	Link + Node feature	CESNA	82.74	85.52	86.81	87.52	87.93	88.24	88.30	88.36	88.47
		TADW($d = 200$)	91.38	91.95	92.24	92.45	92.52	92.72	92.66	92.73	92.97
		TADW($d = 128$)	91.08	91.90	92.36	92.65	92.80	92.93	93.03	93.07	93.37
	Link + Edge feature	NEEF($d = 200$)	**97.45**	**97.57**	**97.69**	**97.74**	**97.76**	**97.87**	**97.83**	**97.80**	**97.96**
		NEEF($d = 128$)	97.45	97.57	97.63	97.65	97.68	97.77	97.74	97.77	97.79

Table 3. Classification results on Enron Email Network.

Metric	Type	Algorithm	10%	20%	30%	40%	50%	60%	70%	80%	90%
Micro-F1	Link only	NMF	72.97	74.87	75.51	75.98	76.65	76.94	77.28	77.73	78.07
		EdgeCluster	74.18	75.39	76.41	77.24	77.83	78.26	78.69	79.15	79.31
		Modularity	68.63	66.84	65.53	64.52	64.04	63.28	63.52	63.32	63.27
		DeepWalk	78.43	80.55	81.73	82.58	83.11	83.76	84.15	84.27	84.34
	Link + Node feature	CESNA	73.71	75.66	76.72	77.30	77.82	78.14	78.58	79.04	79.32
		TADW($d = 200$)	78.43	80.92	82.04	82.92	83.38	84.02	84.20	84.32	84.42
		TADW($d = 128$)	79.21	81.28	82.16	82.91	83.36	83.82	84.07	84.32	84.34
	Link + Edge feature	NEEF($d = 200$)	79.26	81.52	82.34	83.19	83.41	83.94	84.16	84.21	84.25
		NEEF($d = 128$)	**79.41**	**81.58**	**82.46**	**83.28**	**83.63**	**84.26**	**84.42**	**84.47**	**84.50**
Macro-F1	Link only	NMF	50.56	53.50	54.07	54.49	55.6	55.43	56.01	54.87	51.82
		EdgeCluster	50.78	52.22	53.07	53.65	53.89	54.23	54.79	54.67	51.08
		Modularity	47.54	48.06	47.40	47.09	46.28	45.55	45.51	44.93	41.89
		DeepWalk	56.12	58.38	**60.52**	60.75	61.91	62.52	**62.42**	60.64	58.97
	Link + Node feature	CESNA	50.82	53.33	54.54	55.11	56.15	56.67	57.24	56.89	53.48
		TADW($d = 200$)	54.85	57.87	59.70	60.25	61.40	62.45	62.10	60.32	59.08
		TADW($d = 128$)	55.38	57.99	59.80	60.06	61.05	61.54	61.17	59.13	57.88
	Link + Edge feature	NEEF($d = 200$)	56.36	58.78	60.01	60.83	61.28	62.21	61.66	60.36	59.50
		NEEF($d = 128$)	**56.45**	**58.93**	60.39	**61.19**	**62.00**	**62.73**	62.21	**61.04**	**59.65**

5.1 Classification

Tables 1, 2 and 3 describe the classification results by different training ratios
on three datasets. We set dimensionality $d = 200$ for NMF, EdgeCluster, Modularity and DeepWalk. The best performance is highlighted in bold for each
column. Based on DeepWalk, TADW gets better performance than DeepWalk
on DBLP coauthor network and Enron email network by incorporating node
features. However, the poor performance in Reddit review network of TADW
shows that vertex-centric view is not always suitable for these specific networks.

NEEF can well deal with the network with edge features from edge-centric view and consistently outperforms all the other baselines in most cases. It is worth mentioning that DeepWalk and our NEEF models achieve more than 97% of F1 score on Reddit review network, the reason may be that the three classes of Reddit review network are well separated after data preprocessing.

5.2   Clustering

In this experiment, we first compare NEEF with baselines by clustering the learned embedding via k-means algorithm [2]. For clustering task, we choose dimensionality $d = 128$ for NMF, EdgeCluster, Modularity and DeepWalk, since increasing the dimensionality d does not improve the performance. Due to too much overlaps between clusters in Enron email network, we just report the clustering results on DBLP coauthor network and Reddit review network. As shown in Tables 4 and 5, NEEF outperforms the other baselines on both DBLP coauthor network and Reddit review network.

Table 4. Clustering results on DBLP Coauthor Network.

Type	Algorithm	NMI	AC
Link only	NMF	12.65	52.17
	EdgeCluster	7.08	47.54
	Modularity	14.08	48.34
	DeepWalk	56.30	85.84
Link + Node feature	CESNA($d = 200$)	15.65	50.13
	CESNA($d = 128$)	14.76	51.98
	TADW($d = 200$)	57.67	86.22
	TADW($d = 128$)	56.34	85.68
Link + Edge feature	NEEF($d = 200$)	57.65	85.75
	NEEF($d = 128$)	**58.03**	**86.61**

5.3   Parameter Sensitivity

In this experiment, we evaluate the performance of our model on different dimensionalities d.

Figure 3 (top three sub figures) show Micro-F1 scores of different training ratios over different dimensionalities on three datasets. NEEF achieves the best performance on DBLP coauthor network and Reddit review network when dimensionality d is close to 200 and on Enron Email network, the dimensionality d is close to 128. Note that the optimal dimensionality d of our model is independent on the training ratios for these three datasets. In addition, We investigate the clustering results over different dimensionalities on three networks. As

Table 5. Clustering results on Reddit Review Network.

Type	Algorithm	NMI	AC
Link only	NMF	28.59	60.12
	EdgeCluster	-	-
	Modularity	11.43	40.03
	DeepWalk	86.86	97.00
Link + Node feature	CESNA($d = 200$)	54.13	72.41
	CESNA($d = 128$)	53.01	81.51
	TADW($d = 128$)	66.88	89.49
	TADW($d = 64$)	52.04	77.45
Link + Edge feature	NEEF($d = 200$)	88.14	97.46
	NEEF($d = 128$)	**88.41**	**97.58**

shown in Fig. 3 (bottom three sub figures), NEEF gets the best performance when dimensionality $d = 128$ for DBLP coauthor network and Reddit review network while dimensionality $d = 200$ for Enron email network.

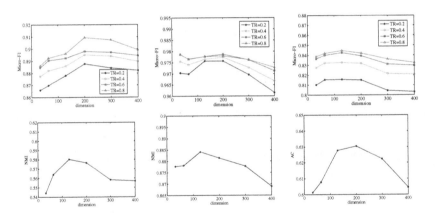

Fig. 3. Parameter sensitivity over dimension d.

5.4 Case Study

To better understand the learned representations of NEEF model, we present two case studies on DBLP coauthor network.

Visualization. We map the learned representations to a 2-dimensional space with the standard $t-SNE$ tool [15], where authors within a group share the same

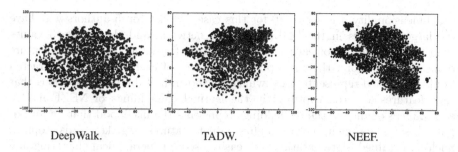

| DeepWalk. | TADW. | NEEF. |

Fig. 4. Visualization of DBLP coauthor network. Red: "CV&PR", blue: "AI&ML", and green: "DM&DB". (Color figure online)

Table 6. Features extracted from learned embeddings.

Authors	Top 15 most frequent keywords
Jiawei Han	Information approach web knowledge query rank system index constraint top-k user local aggregation similarity source
Philip S. Yu	Mining network system stream graph information pattern approach content large similar frequent itemset rule association
Shuicheng Yan	Image recognition face robust object classification feature representation sparse label visual segment context local action video
Thomas S. Huang	Image recognition face computer retrieval classification 3d information content local system representation application sparse robust
Bernhard Schölkopf	Learn kernel machine model linear metric classification regression feature function predict statistical latent markov supervised

color. Authors from the same research domain are closer in the low-dimensional space. As shown in Fig. 4, NEEF and TADW perform better than DeepWalk by considering both linkage information and content information, while the group boundaries from NEEF are clearer than those from TADW. The result proves that NEEF can capture the dynamic interactions between vertices, which leads to a better performance than the other baselines. We also find an interesting point that some authors from "AI&ML" domain are mislabeled in "CV&PR" and "DM&DB", that may because these authors always collaborate cross domains. Such interaction patterns are well captured by NEEF.

Fine-Grained Representations. NEEF projects the edge features into the representations of vertices, where the value of each dimensionality represents the author's preference to associated latent topics; These topics are derived from feature reduction through non-negative matrix factorization. For simplification, the dimensionality d is set to 20 for this case. We list top 5 authors who have the largest degrees in the DBLP coauthor network, and choose top 3 values from the embeddings of each author indicating the latent topics after feature reduction. Therefore, the corresponding features of each author are extracted from the learned representations, which are shown in Table 6. It is obvious that edge features are well captured in the learned embeddings of NEEF model, each dimensionality of the embeddings represents the likelihood that an author publishes papers on its corresponding latent features (e.g. keywords, topics). Such fine-grained representations are easily used for hierarchical clustering and link prediction on the specific topics.

6   Conclusion

In this paper, we presented NEEF, a novel model to learn network embedding with edge features. Our model naturally projects the edge features into the learned representations, the value of each dimensionality is meaningful for its associated features. Such a fined-grained representation is significant for many network mining tasks. Experimental results on classification, clustering and visualization show that our model achieves the best performance than the baselines. There are several promising directions for future work, such as predicting missing edges, extending the model to dynamic and heterogeneous networks and exploring the application scenarios.

Acknowledgements. This paper is supported by the Fundamental Research Funds for the Central Universities under Grant No. 2662019QD011.

References

1. Ahmed, A., Shervashidze, N., Narayanamurthy, S., Josifovski, V., Smola, A.J.: Distributed large-scale natural graph factorization. In: Proceedings of the 22nd International Conference on World Wide Web, pp. 37–48. International World Wide Web Conferences Steering Committee (2013)
2. Arthur, D., Vassilvitskii, S.: k-means++: the advantages of careful seeding. In: Proceedings of the Eighteenth Annual ACM-SIAM Symposium on Discrete Algorithms, pp. 1027–1035. Society for Industrial and Applied Mathematics (2007)
3. Belkin, M., Niyogi, P.: Laplacian eigenmaps and spectral techniques for embedding and clustering. In: NIPS, vol. 14, pp. 585–591 (2001)
4. Cai, H., Zheng, V.W., Chang, K.C.C.: A comprehensive survey of graph embedding: problems, techniques, and applications. IEEE Trans. Knowl. Data Eng. **30**(9), 1616–1637 (2018)
5. Cao, S., Lu, W., Xu, Q.: GraRep: learning graph representations with global structural information. In: Proceedings of the 24th ACM International on Conference on Information and Knowledge Management, pp. 891–900. ACM (2015)
6. Cao, S., Lu, W., Xu, Q.: Deep neural networks for learning graph representations. In: Thirtieth AAAI Conference on Artificial Intelligence (2016)

7. Chang, S., Han, W., Tang, J., Qi, G.J., Aggarwal, C.C., Huang, T.S.: Heterogeneous network embedding via deep architectures. In: Proceedings of the 21st ACM SIGKDD International Conference on Knowledge Discovery and Data Mining, pp. 119–128. ACM (2015)

8. Cox, T.F., Cox, M.A.: Multidimensional Scaling. CRC Press, Boca Raton (2000)

9. Fan, R.E., Chang, K.W., Hsieh, C.J., Wang, X.R., Lin, C.J.: Liblinear: a library for large linear classification. J. Mach. Learn. Res. **9**, 1871–1874 (2008)

10. Ganguly, S., Gupta, M., Varma, V., Pudi, V., et al.: Author2Vec: learning author representations by combining content and link information. In: Proceedings of the 25th International Conference Companion on World Wide Web, pp. 49–50. International World Wide Web Conferences Steering Committee (2016)

11. Goyal, P., Ferrara, E.: Graph embedding techniques, applications, and performance: a survey. Knowl. Based Syst. **151**, 78–94 (2018)

12. Goyal, P., Hosseinmardi, H., Ferrara, E., Galstyan, A.: Capturing edge attributes via network embedding. IEEE Trans. Comput. Soc. Syst. **5**(4), 907–917 (2018)

13. Grover, A., Leskovec, J.: node2vec: scalable feature learning for networks

14. Hamilton, W.L., Ying, R., Leskovec, J.: Representation learning on graphs: methods and applications arXiv preprint: arXiv:1709.05584 (2017)

15. Van der Maaten, L., Hinton, G.: Visualizing data using t-SNE. J. Mach. Learn. Res. **9**(2579–2605), 85 (2008)

16. Mikolov, T., Sutskever, I., Chen, K., Corrado, G.S., Dean, J.: Distributed representations of words and phrases and their compositionality. In: Advances in Neural Information Processing Systems, pp. 3111–3119 (2013)

17. Ou, M., Cui, P., Pei, J., Zhang, Z., Zhu, W.: Asymmetric transitivity preserving graph embedding. In: Proceedings of the 22nd ACM SIGKDD International Conference on Knowledge Discovery and Data Mining, pp. 1105–1114. ACM (2016)

18. Perozzi, B., Al-Rfou, R., Skiena, S.: DeepWalk: online learning of social representations. In: Proceedings of the 20th ACM SIGKDD International Conference on Knowledge Discovery and Data Mining, pp. 701–710. ACM (2014)

19. Recht, B., Re, C., Wright, S., Niu, F.: Hogwild: a lock-free approach to parallelizing stochastic gradient descent. In: Advances in Neural Information Processing Systems, pp. 693–701 (2011)

20. Roweis, S.T., Saul, L.K.: Nonlinear dimensionality reduction by locally linear embedding. Science **290**(5500), 2323–2326 (2000)

21. Strehl, A., Ghosh, J., Mooney, R.: Impact of similarity measures on web-page clustering. In: Workshop on Artificial Intelligence for Web Search (AAAI 2000), pp. 58–64 (2000)

22. Tang, J., Qu, M., Wang, M., Zhang, M., Yan, J., Mei, Q.: Line: large-scale information network embedding. In: Proceedings of the 24th International Conference on World Wide Web, pp. 1067–1077. International World Wide Web Conferences Steering Committee (2015)

23. Tang, L., Liu, H.: Relational learning via latent social dimensions. In: Proceedings of the 15th ACM SIGKDD International Conference on Knowledge Discovery and Data Mining, pp. 817–826. ACM (2009)

24. Tang, L., Liu, H.: Scalable learning of collective behavior based on sparse social dimensions. In: Proceedings of the 18th ACM Conference on Information and Knowledge Management, pp. 1107–1116. ACM (2009)

25. Wang, D., Cui, P., Zhu, W.: Structural deep network embedding. In: Proceedings of the 22nd ACM SIGKDD International Conference on Knowledge Discovery and Data Mining, pp. 1225–1234. ACM (2016)

26. Yang, C., Liu, Z., Zhao, D., Sun, M., Chang, E.Y.: Network representation learning with rich text information. In: Proceedings of the 24th International Joint Conference on Artificial Intelligence, Buenos Aires, Argentina, pp. 2111–2117 (2015)
27. Yang, J., Leskovec, J.: Overlapping community detection at scale: a nonnegative matrix factorization approach. In: Proceedings of the sixth ACM International Conference on Web Search and Data Mining, pp. 587–596. ACM (2013)
28. Yang, J., McAuley, J., Leskovec, J.: Community detection in networks with node attributes. In: 2013 IEEE 13th International Conference on Data Mining (ICDM), pp. 1151–1156. IEEE (2013)

Representation Learning in Academic Network Based on Research Interest and Meta-path

Wei Zhang[1,2,3], Ying Liang[1,2(✉)], and Xiangxiang Dong[1,2,3]

[1] Institute of Computing Technology,
Chinese Academy of Sciences, Beijing, China
{zhangwei17s,liangy,dongxiangxiang}@ict.ac.cn
[2] Beijing Key Laboratory of Mobile Computing and New Devices,
Beijing, China
[3] University of Chinese Academy of Sciences, Beijing, China

Abstract. Network representation learning can transform nodes into a low-dimensional vector representation, which has been widely used in recent years. As a heterogeneous information network, the academic network contains more information than the homogeneous information network, which attracts many scholars to do research. Most of the existing algorithms cannot make full use of the attribute or text information of nodes, which contains more information than structural features. To solve this problem, we propose a network representation learning algorithm based on research interest and meta-path. Firstly, the author's research interest are extracted from their published papers, and then the random walk based on meta-path is used. The author node is transformed into several research interest nodes by mapping function, and the skip-gram model is used to train and get the vector representation of the nodes. Experiments show that our model outperforms traditional learning models in several heterogeneous network analysis tasks, such as node classification and similarity search. The obtained research interest representation can help solve the cold start problem of authors in the academic network.

Keywords: Representation learning · Academic network · Research interest · Meta-path

1 Introduction

Network data is different from relational data. It is larger and more sparsely distributed, which makes it difficult to apply traditional algorithms to the network data on a large scale. Network embedding, also known as network representation learning [1, 2], aims to learn the low-dimensional dense vector representation of a network. The result can be easily used in deep learning algorithms, and has a wide range of applications in community discovery [3] and recommendation systems [4]. According to the type of network nodes, it can be divided into homogeneous network and heterogeneous network. All nodes in the homogeneous network are of the same type and the information conveyed is very limited. However, heterogeneous information networks, such as academic networks, have different types of nodes in the network, and correspondingly,

© Springer Nature Switzerland AG 2019
C. Douligeris et al. (Eds.): KSEM 2019, LNAI 11776, pp. 389–399, 2019.
https://doi.org/10.1007/978-3-030-29563-9_34

the types of edges thereof are different. The algorithms traditionally used for homogeneous networks cannot completely capture the rich semantic information in heterogeneous networks.

Academic network refers to a network composed of authors, papers, conferences, etc., which is a special form of the heterogeneous network. At present, the research based on academic network mainly has the following difficulties:

(1) Heterogeneity: The semantics of directly connected nodes will be different. The authors and the papers are creation relationships, and the papers and conferences are published relationships. Nodes that are not directly connected may have relation. For example, authors can build collaborative relationships by writing papers together. Papers and papers are co-published in conference proceedings. There are a large number of such relationships in the academic network.

(2) Rich in attributes: Different nodes in the academic network have different attributes. For example, the paper nodes have the title and abstract information, while authors may have influence attributes, such as h-index and p-index. The existence of these information greatly enriches the meaning of the network, making the academic network not just a complex network structure, but an information network like a knowledge database [5].

(3) Cold start problem [6]: The existing network representation learning algorithms mostly cannot handle nodes that are not in the network, and its output is a vector representation corresponding to a number of fixed nodes in the network. For any given author who is not in the academic network, the traditional models have to retrain to get its representation.

In order to solve the above problems, this paper proposes a novel academic network representation learning algorithm. The algorithm first extracts the research interests of each author from the academic network, and establishes the mapping relationship between author nodes and research interests. Then we use a meta-path-based random walk strategy to obtain a series of meaningful multi-type node sequences, and the author nodes in the original sequence are replaced by the mapping relationship. Finally, the skip-gram model is used for training the sequences, thereby the vector representations of the nodes and the research interests are obtained.

The main contributions of this paper are as follows:

(1) Proposes a network representation learning method combining research interest and meta-path. The method captures the structural information and text information in the academic network at the same time, so that the obtained nodes contain more abundant semantic information.

(2) Cold start problem of author nodes can be solved by using the representation of research interests. The corresponding research interests can be extracted from the papers published by the author. Then the vector representation of the author can be obtained according to the research interests.

2 Related Work

In recent years, the network representation learning has received the attention of scholars and witnessed great progress. The most basic form of a network is the adjacency matrix, which can be factorized by matrix decomposition to get the node vector. This method is mathematically explainable but limited by the magnitude of the network and the sparseness of network data, and it is not easy to be extended to large-scale data.

Influenced by the word embedding model word2vec [7, 8] in the field of natural language processing, Perozzi et al. [9] verified that the node frequencies in the walk sequence are in accordance with the power law distribution and proposed a method using random walk and skip-gram model. Grover [10] proposed node2vec, which introduced the breadth-first search and depth-first search into the random walk process by introducing two parameters p and q. Tang [11] proposed a representation learning algorithm LINE that can be used for large-scale networks, making the model have a training goal by introducing the concept of first-order and second-order proximity.

Heterogeneous networks, especially the diversity of the academic network, have attracted a large number of scholars to conduct a lot of research. Sun [12] proposed a method for performing Top-K similarity search in heterogeneous information networks using symmetric meta-paths. The meta-path is an important concept in a heterogeneous network, which implies the interrelationship between different types of nodes. Dong [13] proposed a random walk algorithm based on the meta-path, using the preset meta-path to guide the random walk process and using skip-gram for training.

The attribute information of the nodes and edges is more abundant than the structural information, which can describe some characteristics of the network more accurately. The CANE model [14] is a kind of network representation learning considering context sensitivity. With deep network representation, the association information between different nodes is integrated into CNN, and the obtained vector quality is better than when just capturing structural information. The CENE model [15] treats text content as a special type of node, using node-to-node links, node-to-text links for representation learning, minimizing both types of loss.

3 Methodology

3.1 Problem Definitions

We define some concepts and our problem in this chapter.

Definition I. *Network.* A network is a directed graph $G = (V, E, T_v, \tau)$, where $V = \{v_1, v_2, \ldots v_n\}$ indicates the set of nodes, $E = \{e_{i,j}\}_{1 \leq i,j \leq n}$ indicates the set of edges connecting each of v_i and v_j, T_v represents the set of types to which the node belongs. $\tau : V \rightarrow T_v$ is a type mapping function for nodes, each node v_i can be mapped to a single node type in T_v, i.e. $\tau(v_i) \in T_v$. There are three types of nodes in the original network in this paper, including A for authors, P for papers and C for conferences. The network in this paper is called as an academic network, which is a heterogeneous network, because there's more than one type of node, i.e. $|T_v| > 1$.

Definition II. *Meta-path.* In a heterogeneous network, a meta-path ρ is defined as a sequence of edges and nodes connecting two nodes v_k and v_l: $\rho = v_k \xrightarrow{e_{k,k+1}} v_{k+1} \rightarrow \ldots \xrightarrow{e_{l-1,l}} v_l$. Starting from different nodes, we can generate a variety of instances of meta-path ρ in the heterogeneous network.

Definition III. *Author Interest.* Define the mapping function $\varphi(v_i) = \{I_1, \ldots, I_K\}$, indicating author node v_i has a total of K interests, where I_i is the i-th research interest.

Considering research interests as nodes, we can construct an undirected edge for each author and his or her K research interests, as shown in Fig. 1.

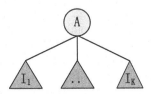

Fig. 1. Author interest mapping example

Definition IV. *Academic Network Representation Learning.* Given the academic network $G = (V, E, T_v, \tau)$. The goal of academic network representation learning is to learn a mapping function $\phi(V) : V \rightarrow \Re^d$, which maps each node to a d dimensional vector, where $d \ll |V|$. The vectors can further be used in several downstream machine learning tasks.

3.2 Research Interest Extraction

The papers in the academic network contain a lot of important text information, including title, abstract and full-text. The text information conveys richer information than the network structure and determines certain attributes of other nodes in the network. For an author, the research interests and productivity are directly determined by the paper he published. For a journal, its impact factor depends on the quality of the papers published in the previous years. So it is necessary to integrate textual information into the node vector representation.

The extraction process is shown in Table 1. Given the authors, the papers and their relationship, the algorithm can process and extract research interest information for each author.

The n-gram is a very important concept in natural language processing. Its basic idea is to use a window of size N to slide through the text content to obtain a series of sequences of length N. Similarly, a research interest may contain multi-words, so we conducted an interest extraction of n-gram research. By extracting the research interests of the papers in Aminer [16] dataset, the top frequent uni-gram and bi-gram interest are shown in Fig. 2.

Table 1. Research interest extract algorithm

Algorithm 1. Research Interest Extraction
Input: Authors, Papers, Author-paper relation
Output: Author Interest Mapping
Step1. Select an author, get all papers he published
Step2. Join all titles of the selected papers into one long text
Step3. Clean the text by:
Transform to lower case
Removing special characters
Removing stop words
Step4. Perform Stemming and Lemmatization

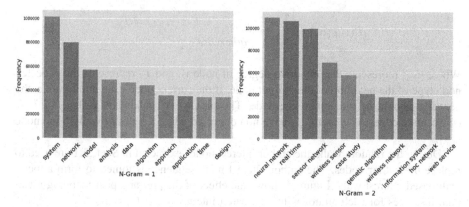

Fig. 2. Top 10 frequent n-gram interest in Aminer academic network

The extracted research interests are regarded as nodes in the network. Each author node establishes a connection with its corresponding interest node. An example of a mapped academic network is shown in Fig. 3.

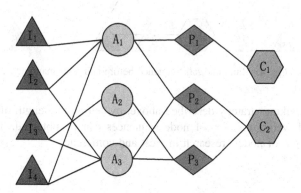

Fig. 3. An example of the academic network with research interest

The author A_1 has published a paper P_1 at conference C_1, so this author has interest I_1 that is not shared with other authors. And the three authors have published two papers P_2 and P_3 through various partnerships. Thus they also have intersections in research interests.

3.3 Meta-path Based Interest Random Walk

The meta-path is an important piece of information in the academic network, and it is necessary to make full use of the meta-path information. In this paper, the author's research interest is combined with the meta-path information to form a random walk of research interest based on the meta-path. The original meta-path used in this paper is ACA (i.e. Author-Conference-Author). Whether an author node and a conference node are connected depends on whether the author has published any papers at the conference. If the current node is located at v_t, then the probability of the next node v_{t+1} is:

$$P(v_{t+1}|v_t) = \begin{cases} \frac{1}{|N_{v_t}|} & e_{v_t,v_{t+1}} \in E, \tau(v_{t+1}) = T_d \\ 0 & otherwise \end{cases} \qquad (1)$$

Where $|N_{v_t}|$ represents the outbound degree of node v_t, and T_d represents the expected node type of the next hop of the current node. If the current node is an author node, the next hop should be the conference node. The strategy of walking will always follow consecutive edges. If v_t and v_{t+1} have no connected edge, it will not walk to the node v_{t+1}.

During the random walk, the author interest nodes extracted in Sect. 3.1 are used to replace the author nodes. The author interest node sequence is joined to form a meta-path-based interest walk. Figure 4 shows the effect of the pre- and post-mapping meta-path instances for each author with 2 research interest nodes (K = 2).

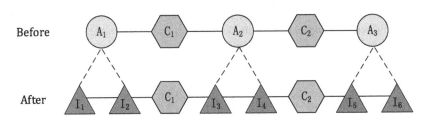

Fig. 4. Random walk sequence before and after mapping

After the walking strategy described above, by setting the length of the walk and the number of walks, a series of node sequences can be obtained. The sequences include two types of nodes: research interest and conference.

3.4   Skip-Gram and Optimization

The Skip Gram model in natural language processing is widely used to model the co-occurrence relationship between vocabularies. This paper also uses this model to model the co-occurrence relationship between nodes. The skip-gram model achieves node modeling by maximizing the co-occurrence probability of nodes within a certain size of window:

$$\text{maximize} \sum_{v_o \in V} \sum_{v_c \in N_{v_c}^w} \log p(v_c|v_o) \tag{2}$$

Where $p(v_c|v_o)$ denotes the probability of node v_c appearing around the central node v_o. Node set $N_{v_c}^w$ represent the context node of node v_c within the window size of w. V represents all the nodes that appear in the walk sequence, similar to the vocabulary in language modelling. The model needs to maximize the sum of the probabilities of all nodes co-occurring using softmax.

Inspired by the technology in word2vec, negative sampling can be used instead of the softmax process described above:

$$\log \sigma(\phi(v_c) \cdot \phi(v_o)) + \sum_{s=1}^{Samples} v_s {\sim} P(v_c)[\log(1 - \sigma(\phi(v_s) \cdot \phi(v_o)))] \tag{3}$$

Where $\phi(v_t)$ is the vector of node v_t, $P(v_c)$ represents the nodes sampled that don't co-occur in the window of central node v_o, and σ is the sigmoid function. The formula aims to maximize the possibility of the positive pair, and minimize the co-occurrence of negative pairs. In this paper, the number of negative samples is set to 5.

4   Experiment

4.1   Dataset and Models

In this paper, the public data set Aminer [16] is used to verify the correctness of the algorithm and model. These data are available on the Aminer official website, including data on authors, papers, conferences, and relationship data on author-paper, paper-conference. The network contains 1,693,531 authors, 3,194,405 papers, and 3,883 conferences. Each paper in the data contains the title to be extracted as interests.

This paper uses several models to verify the advancement of the algorithm, including:

(1) **DeepWalk:** DeepWalk is a classic network representation learning algorithm that obtains a sequence of nodes through random walks and optimizes modeling using hierarchical softmax.
(2) **node2vec:** Node2vec introduces two hyper-parameters p and q based on Deep-Walk to complete the probability walk. In this paper, both p and q are set to 0.5.
(3) **LINE:** LINE uses the first-order and second-order proximity to model the similarity relationship between connected nodes and the same neighbor nodes.

(4) **metapath2vec:** Metapath2vec extends the DeepWalk walk mode in a heterogeneous information network, also use skip-gram to model the co-occurrence relationship between nodes.

4.2   Multi-class Node Classification

4.2.1   Classification Performance

In this experiment, all models have a number of 10 walks and a walk length of 80. The data consists of 8 research areas, which is divided into training and testing set, then multi-classification is applied by using the Logistic Regression of the OnevsRest strategy. By using the stratified sampling strategy, the labels in the training set and testing set are identical to the original dataset. The proportion of the training set is controlled to increase from 10% to 90%. The performance is evaluated with the Micro-F1 values, shown in Table 2.

Table 2. Micro-F1 value of multi-class conference node classification

Model	10%	20%	30%	40%	50%	60%	70%	80%	90%
DeepWalk	0.7892	0.8346	0.8862	0.9113	0.9149	0.9037	0.9225	0.9481	0.9143
node2vec	0.7008	0.7869	0.8500	0.8575	0.8761	0.8648	0.8775	0.9111	0.8786
LINE	0.8858	0.9246	0.9389	0.9400	0.9393	0.9381	0.9300	0.9604	0.9471
metapath2vec	0.8200	0.9318	0.9319	0.9275	0.9433	0.9426	0.9475	0.9630	0.9357
This paper	**0.8573**	**0.9346**	**0.9384**	**0.9527**	**0.9525**	**0.9590**	**0.9730**	**0.9680**	**0.9692**

It can be seen from Table 2 that the model performs better than the comparison models at different training ratios. This paper directly models the co-occurrence relationship between research interests and conferences, so as to better distinguish the research areas of the conference and improve classification performance. Compared with traditional methods, the method proposed in this paper has a 1%–10% increase in Micro-F1 values, which proves that more information about the academic network is captured and embedded into the vectors.

4.2.2   Parameter Sensitivity

We conduct a sensitivity analysis on several hyper-parameters in our representation learning model. The parameter K is the number of author interest used in the random walk mapping process, while n-gram means the n-gram research interest.

Figure 5 shows their influence on Micro-F1 values in conference classification. We can see that the number of 2 and 3 interests actually produces better conference embedding. Because when parameter K is too large, it is hard for skip-gram to model the co-occurrence of two similar conferences. Figure on the right shows our algorithm is not so sensitive to n-gram setting. Different n-gram setting tends to give similar trends and results.

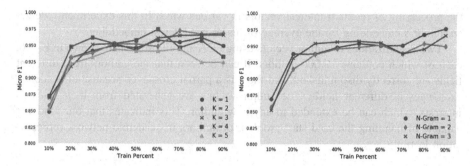

Fig. 5. Parameter sensitivity on research interest parameter K and n-gram

4.3 Similarity Search

In network representation learning, similar nodes have similar representation in the vector space. We choose some of the conferences as a sample, and perform unsupervised algorithm KNN [17] on the sample. The top 5 most similar conferences according to different conferences are listed in Table 3.

Table 3. Similarity search results for the conferences

Top	STOC	CVPR	WWW	ICSC	IPDPS
0	STOC	CVPR	WWW	ICSC	IPDPS
1	FOCS	ECCV	WSDM	Natural Language Engineering	Parallel Distribute Computing
2	SODA	CVPR Workshops	CIKM	Computational Linguistics	Future Generation Comp. Syst.
3	SIAM	ICCV	SIGMOD	Language Resources and Evaluation	HPCA
4	STACS	IJCV	ACM TIST	Interacting with Computers	Euro Sys

For example, IPDPS is a conference on distributed computing, so the top similar conferences don't contain any well-known machine learning conferences. The conferences similar to CVPR are all related to computer vision, which means the vector representation successfully capture the conference interests and topics.

4.4 Cold Start for Authors

Cold start problem of authors can be solved in this paper. Traditional models fail to handle new authors because they are overly dependent on nodes' structural features. However, it is text features like research interest that can generalize to a changing network, which describe an author without relying on network structure.

For an author who has published any papers, we can extract research interest from the title of papers he has published. The vector of the author can be obtained through the processing of research interest vectors in various ways. In this experiment, we get an author's embedding by the average of his or her interest embedding.

Two visualizations of author vectors using PCA algorithm [18] are shown in Fig. 6, each of which contains 10,000 authors. It can be seen that the authors from different fields are correctly distinguished, and there is a partial crossover because of academic exchanges in different fields. The author vectors are generated from their research interests, which can be extended to any new author. This indicates that our model is capable of handling the cold start problem of authors in academic network representation learning.

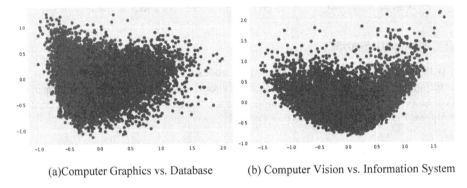

    (a)Computer Graphics vs. Database   (b) Computer Vision vs. Information System

Fig. 6. Visualization of authors in different research fields

5   Conclusion

This paper proposes an academic network representation learning algorithm based on meta-path and research interest. The algorithm uses both academic network structure and text information to obtain the author's research interest and vector representation of the conference. By using multiple research interests to represent an author, the cold start problem of authors can be solved. Experiments on real-world dataset show that our model performs better than other models, which indicate research interest plays an import role in academic network representation learning.

Our future work focuses on leveraging attributes and textual information in heterogeneous networks. Except for extracting features from neighbor nodes and use mapping function, some deep network architecture may be used. We want to explore more effective models and embed sematic information in node representations.

Acknowledgments. The work in this paper is supported by the National Key Research and Development Plan (2018YFB1004700, 2016YFB0800403).

References

1. Zhang, D., Yin, J., Zhu, X., et al.: Network representation learning: a survey. IEEE Trans. Big Data, 1 (2018)
2. Cui, P., Wang, X., Pei, J., et al.: A survey on network embedding. IEEE Trans. Knowl. Data Eng. **PP**(99), 1 (2017)
3. Wang, X., Cui, P., Wang, J., et al.: Community preserving network embedding. In: Thirty-First AAAI Conference on Artificial Intelligence (2017)
4. Zhang, F., Yuan, N.J., Lian, D., et al.: Collaborative knowledge base embedding for recommender systems. In: Proceedings of the 22nd ACM SIGKDD International Conference on Knowledge Discovery and Data Mining, pp. 353–362. ACM (2016)
5. Liu, C., Bai, B., Skogerbø, G., et al.: NONCODE: an integrated knowledge database of noncoding RNAs. Nucleic Acids Res. **33**(Database issue), D112–D115 (2005)
6. Bobadilla, J., Ortega, F., Hernando, A., et al.: A collaborative filtering approach to mitigate the new user cold start problem. Knowl. Based Syst. **26**, 225–238 (2012)
7. Mikolov, T., Chen, K., Corrado, G., et al.: Efficient estimation of word representations in vector space (2013). arXiv preprint: arXiv:1301.3781
8. Le, Q., Mikolov, T.: Distributed representations of sentences and documents. In: International Conference on Machine Learning, pp. 1188–1196 (2014)
9. Perozzi, B., Al-Rfou, R., Skiena, S.: DeepWalk: online learning of social representations. In: Proceedings of the 20th ACM SIGKDD International Conference on Knowledge Discovery and Data Mining, pp. 701–710. ACM (2014)
10. Grover, A., Leskovec, J.: node2vec: Scalable feature learning for networks. In: ACM SIGKDD International Conference on Knowledge Discovery and Data Mining (2016)
11. Tang, J., Qu, M., Wang, M., et al.: LINE: large-scale information network embedding (2015)
12. Sun, Y., Han, J., Yan, X., et al.: PathSim: meta path-based top-k similarity search in heterogeneous information networks. Proc. VLDB Endow. **4**(11), 992–1003 (2011)
13. Dong, Y., Chawla, N.V., Swami, A.: metapath2vec: Scalable representation learning for heterogeneous networks. In: Proceedings of the 23rd ACM SIGKDD International Conference on Knowledge Discovery and Data Mining, pp. 135–144. ACM (2017)
14. Tu, C., Liu, H., Liu, Z., et al.: Cane: context-aware network embedding for relation modeling. In: Proceedings of the 55th Annual Meeting of the Association for Computational Linguistics. Long Papers, vol. 1, pp. 1722–1731 (2017)
15. Sun, X., Guo, J., Ding, X., et al.: A general framework for content-enhanced network representation learning (2016). arXiv preprint arXiv:1610.02906
16. Tang, J., Zhang, J., Yao, L., et al.: ArnetMiner: extraction and mining of academic social networks. In: Proceedings of the 14th ACM SIGKDD International Conference on Knowledge Discovery and Data Mining, pp. 990–998. ACM (2008)
17. Roussopoulos, N., Kelley, S., Vincent, F.: Nearest neighbor queries. ACM SIGMOD Rec. **24**(2), 71–79 (1995)
18. Jolliffe, I.T., Cadima, J.: Principal component analysis: a review and recent developments. Philos. Trans. R. Soc. A Math. Phys. Eng. Sci. **374**(2065), 20150202 (2016)

Knowledge-Aware Self-Attention Networks for Document Grounded Dialogue Generation

Xiangru Tang[1,2] and Po Hu[1,2(✉)]

[1] School of Computer Science, Central China Normal University, Wuhan, China
xrtang@mails.ccnu.edu.cn, phu@mail.ccnu.edu.cn
[2] Hubei Provincial Key Laboratory of Artificial Intelligence and Smart Learning,
Central China Normal University, Wuhan, China

Abstract. Dialogue systems have attracted more and more attention. Different from traditional open-domain conversational systems, document grounded dialogue generation aims to ground the semantics in a specified document and leverage contextual cues from dialogue history to generate on-topic and coherent responses, which is a renewed and challenging task. Some prior studies via neural sequence-to-sequence models have been conducted. However, they often treat the dialogue history and the given document independently while fail to model contextual dependence between them. To understand the dialogue better and respond more appropriately and informatively, we present a novel knowledge-aware self-attention approach for document grounded dialogue, called DIALOGTRANSFORMER. DIALOGTRANSFORMER can fully leverage the semantic knowledge from both the dialogue history and the given document to joint improve the content quality of generated responses. We conduct extensive experiments on the CMU-DoG benchmark dataset and the experimental results show that our approach outperforms several state-of-the-art models, which can generate more appropriate and informative responses.

Keywords: Document grounded dialogue generation ·
Self attention networks · Knowledge-aware approach

1 Introduction

Dialogue generation is a rising topic in recent years that is attracting increasing attention from academia and industries. Recent breakthrough in deep learning has accelerated the progress of this field. And the generative dialog model has been widely adopted for two types of generation tasks: (1) task-oriented dialog system: it is application-specific dialog generator which aims to provide hotel booking or technical support service. (2) non-task-oriented dialog system (also known as chat bots): it does not have a clear goal yet to react to both user's engagement and dialog generation by some conversational strategies.

© Springer Nature Switzerland AG 2019
C. Douligeris et al. (Eds.): KSEM 2019, LNAI 11776, pp. 400–411, 2019.
https://doi.org/10.1007/978-3-030-29563-9_35

However, existing generative models did not achieve satisfactory results, because the generative model still faces some challenges. For instance, it is difficult to integrate multi-source knowledge, which may cause generating universal and nonsense responses. In other words, it often fail to generate meaningful, diverse on-topic responses. In this case, a new task called document grounded conversation [1] was presented. Document grounded conversation expects the agent to smoothly interleave between task-related text flow and casual chat in a document grounded situation. Specially, this task requires two agents chatting around a topic with more lasting turns. CMU-DoG is a document grounded conversation dataset which is open available[1].

Recently, neural sequence-to-sequence method (SEQ2SEQ) has become the mainstream because of its capability to capture semantic and syntactic relations. SEQ2SEQ method with attention mechanism [2, 3] represents the state-of-the-art neural network model for dialog generation. However, SEQ2SEQ method tends to generate dull responses [11], which carry little information. In addition, standard SEQ2SEQ models often treat the dialogue history and the given document independently. As a consequence, they often ignore contextual dependence between them. For these reasons, standard encoder has a poor capacity to generate informative and interesting response and may quickly lead current dialogue to an end. It will severely hurt the user experience in real application.

In this work, we devise a novel Knowledge-Aware Self-Attention Networks, called DIALOGTRANSFORMER. It utilizes self-attention mechanism as an encoder to facilitate the fusion of dialogue history and unstructured document knowledge. We also improve the performance and efficiency of our model by enhancing the architecture with incremental-based encoder and then combining with extraction-based approach, which called DIALOGTRANSFORMER-PLUS and DIALOGTRANSFORMERX. DIALOGTRANSFORMER-PLUS uses multi-head attention encoding to represent dialogue history and knowledge at the same time, and DIALOGTRANSFORMERX draw lessons from extraction-based model, both of them leverage multi-source knowledge more efficiently. The experimental results on the CMU-DoG dataset demonstrate that DIALOGTRANSFORMER is effective in document grounded dialogue task. And DIALOGTRANSFORMER can generate more appropriate and informative responses, compared to several baselines such as the hierarchical recurrent encoder-decoder (HRED) [5].

In summary, the major contributions of this paper are highlighted as follows:

(a) We devise Knowledge-Aware Self-Attention Networks with multi-head attention for document grounded dialogue system to generate the responses grounded on a given document. Our proposed DIALOGTRANSFORMER incorporates the given document and dialogue history in the encoding step to force the multi-head attentions to concentrate on both sources.

(b) We further introduce two improved methods called DIALOGTRANSFORMER-PLUS and DIALOGTRANSFORMERX, which leverage external knowledge more efficiently. The experimental results on the CMU-DoG dataset show

---

[1] https://github.com/festvox/datasets-CMU_DoG.

that our model outperforms several state-of-the-art baselines. And the results verify the effectiveness of our methods, in terms of both automatic evaluation and human judgement.

2   Related Work

With the increasing of dialog-related data, there are growing interests on research about conversational response retrieval. They usually select the appropriate response from a known set based on similarity metrics [6,7]. But retrieval methods face difficulties of gathering high-quality data and fusing knowledge. Along with the development of neural networks [8,9], some researchers view the response generation problem as a translation task. Based on the work of [4] that directly applies SEQ2SEQ architecture for dialogue generation, [10] introduce the global and local scheme with attention signal into the response generation. And [12] takes contextual information into account to generate context-sensitive responses. Hierarchical recurrent encoder-decoder [5,17] aims to generate coherent and meaningful responses, by modeling the utterances and interactive structure of the dialogue. However, only query and contextual information are inclined to produce high-frequency but less informative responses.

By utilizing some explicit factors, several works incorporate topics [18], external knowledge, emotional content, and responding mechanism to generate diverse and interesting responses. [27] uses LDA model to extract topics from the context, then adds these with SEQ2SEQ framework. [13] and [14] explore the influence of the affective information in response generation with AFFECT-LM and emotional memory. Considerable efforts have been made to study these explicit factors. But we propose to adopt a straightforward solution by using external knowledge like CMU-DoG dataset [1]. Followed by [16], which adopts a joint attention mechanism to encode dialogue history and knowledge. We extend it by adopting a similar attention mechanism to model contextual dependency between dialogue history and external knowledge. Specifically, self-attention architectures [22] is leveraged as encoder to get hidden representation in this study.

Thus, knowledge-grounded dialogue model attracts increasing attention in recent years [23,24]. Some researchers make investigations in task-oriented conversation, by using a set of external world facts to generate the output response about a specific task [19,26]. Some researchers focus on large scale commonsense knowledge bases [21,25] via finding the relevant assertions in the common sense knowledge base [20]. However, unlike those models, we use multi-head attention [22] architecture as incremental encoder [28]. Our approach encodes previous dialogue and knowledge representation jointly. In this way, our hierarchical and incremental structure can capture the corresponding information between knowledge and dialogue history.

3   Task Definition

The task is to generate a dialogue response with the given dialogue context and document. Consequently, the probability of generating a dialogue response r^{k+1} can be formulated as:

$$P(r^{k+1}|R^{\leq k}, D^{\leq k+1}; \theta) = \prod_{m=1}^{M} (R^{\leq k}, D^{\leq k+1}, r^{k+1}_{<m}; \theta) \qquad (1)$$

We use r^{k+1} to indicate the dialogue response, and the previous k dialogue utterances $R^{\leq k}$ and their unstructured external knowledge $d^{\leq k}$ are combined as model input. Besides, the response's related external knowledge d^{k+1} is another input. While the kth dialogue utterance contains M words $r^k = r^k_1, ..., r^k_M$, and the unstructured external knowledge related to the kth utterance contains N words $d^k = d^k_1, ..., d^k_N$.

4   The Proposed Model

In this work, we develop several knowledge-aware self-attention networks for document grounded dialogue generation, which are all based on Transformer [22]. SEQ2SEQ is not so effective to encode long context. Our devised DIALOGTRANS-FORMER can jointly encode knowledge and dialogue context. Therefore, it captures related information and can generates on-topic and coherent responses.

Furthermore, two improved models are devised to incorporate knowledge more effectively. (a) DIALOGTRANSFORMER-PLUS utilizes a three-stage method, (b) DIALOGTRANSFORMERX leverages a copying mechanism to generate OOV words. The models are trained on the given documents and multi-turn dialogues using the cross entropy loss.

4.1   DialogTransformer

The disadvantage of the standard RNN model is that it is hard be parallelized, in order to solve this problem, Transformer [22] was proposed. Most notably, Transformer completely discards the architecture of RNN and CNN. Transformer has emerged as the dominant SEQ2SEQ paradigm for two reasons. Firstly, it could be trained fast for its parallelizable structure, while standard RNN model is computationally time consuming, due to its recurrent structure. Secondly, it naturally constructs the long-term dependence via attention mechanism. It implies that Transformer architecture learns non-local dependencies between tokens regardless of the distance between them. More specifically, the encoder in Transformer is made up of 6 Encoders (N = 6 in our work), and the decoder is made up in the same way.

$$\text{Attention}(Q, K, V) = \text{Softmax}(\frac{QK^T}{\sqrt{d_k}})V. \qquad (2)$$

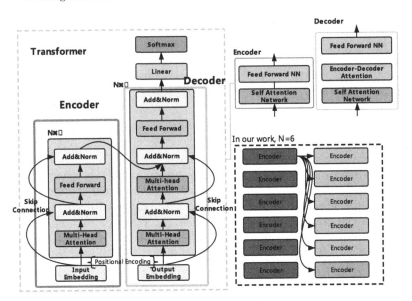

Fig. 1. It shows the construction of Multi-Head Self-Attention mechanism and how it works

where Q indicates the query, K indicates the key and V indicates the value. The dimension of K is d_k.

The Transformer model consists of three different attentions: (a) the encoder self-attention, while query, key and value are encoded representations; (b) the decoder self-attention, while query, key and value are historical decoded representations; and (c) the encoder-decoder attention (see Fig. 1 for an illustration of Transformer architecture). For each part, it stacks 6 identical layers of multi-head attention:

$$\text{MultiHead}(Q, K, V) = [\text{H}_1, \dots, \text{H}_n] W^O$$
$$\text{H}_i = \text{Attention}(QW_i^Q, KW_i^K, VW_i^V) \tag{3}$$

where W_i^Q, W_i^K, W_i^V and W^O are learnable parameters.

Our model can be divided into two parts, i.e., knowledge memory and response generation, illustrated by the flow-process diagram in Fig. 2. We adopt two separative Transformer encoder for each of these two parts.

Knowledge Memory: The aim of this part is to create a representation about the external knowledge. Before the encoding step, the multi-source knowledge will be concatenated. This includes basic key-value knowledge, review knowledge and textual knowledge.

Response Generation: On the one hand, dialogue history is encoded with a hierarchical Transformer encoder. On the other hand, we adopt attentive pooling operation to select which knowledge should be used to generate the dialogue response. More specifically, the attentive pooling operation is a kind of

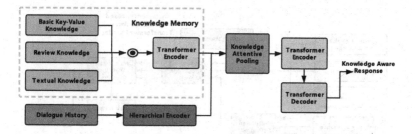

Fig. 2. The structure of DIALOGTRANSFORMER. It can be divided into two parts which are knowledge memory and response generation.

dot-product attention. And finally, a decoder is leveraged to generate the knowledge-aware response. Our model aims to minimize the negative log-likelihood of the response.

4.2   DialogTransformer-Plus

In fact, dialogue history and external knowledge are so relevant that they should not be encoded individually. Consequently, we devise an incremental-based knowledge aware Transformer encoder, called DIALOGTRANSFORMER-PLUS to represent dialogue utterances and unstructured external knowledge in the meantime. In such a manner, this incremental-based attention can establish a combined encoding from the utterance vectors and the knowledge vectors.

As shown in Fig. 3, more specifically, incremental-based encoder utilizes a three-stage multi-head attention mechanism to incorporate dialogue history and knowledge representation. Overall, the Transformer equipped with an incremental-based structure can encode dialogue effectively. And the multi-head attention mechanism can use multi-source knowledge effectively. When encoding the current sentence X_i, it obtains a context vector which is an attentive read of the preceding sentence X_{i-1}. In this manner, the relationship between the words in adjacent sentences can be captured implicitly. This encoding process of DialogTransformer-Plus can be divided into three stages as follows.

At each step, number n indicates the layer, Out^k is the output of the k layer, and $Know^k$ indicates unstructured knowledge. The Multi-Head Attention is being calculated three times in the three stages:

$$ST^n = \textbf{MultiHead}(Out^{n-1}, Out^{n-1}, Out^{n-1}) \tag{4}$$

$$ND^n = \textbf{MultiHead}(Know^k, Know^k, ST^n) \tag{5}$$

$$RD^n = \textbf{MultiHead}(Dia^{k-1}, Dia^{k-1}, ND^n) \tag{6}$$

while Dia^{k-1} indicates the last dialogue utterance. On the whole, the output representation for the kth layer is:

$$\textbf{Incremental-encoder}^n = \textbf{Feedforward}(RD^n) \tag{7}$$

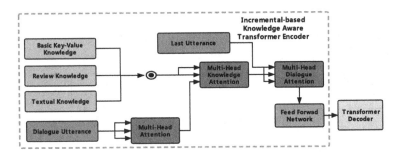

Fig. 3. The structure of DIALOGTRANSFORMER-PLUS. It utilizes a three-stage multi-head attention mechanism to incorporate dialogue utterances and knowledge representation

4.3   DialogTransformerX

Our DIALOGTRANSFORMER will still suffer the OOV problem, which means that lots of important words will fail to be generated because of their low-frequency. Thus, we adopt a modified version of Pointer-Generator Network [15], which can copy original words to avoid OOV problem. At each decoding step, the model can either sample a word from its vocabulary, or copy a word directly from the source passage. The main difference is that our DIALOGTRANSFORMERX copies a word from dialogue utterance or textual knowledge, but original Pointer-Generator Network only copies from document for abstractive summarization.

This is enabled by the attention mechanism, which includes a distribution a_i over all encoding steps, and a context vector c_t that is the weighted sum of encoder's hidden states. However, our model fits three kinds of distribution: dialogue attention distribution, knowledge attention distribution and generation distribution. They are combined as a final output distribution. Thus, the combination of three kinds of distribution signifies that the decoder will calculate three kinds of action probabilities.

The model is depicted in Fig. 4. In this study, dialogue attention distribution and knowledge attention distribution can be calculated as follows:

$$\alpha_{dialogue-attn} = Softmax(v_L^D * tahn(W_p^D \cdot h_D^i + W_D^m \cdot h_t^S + b^D)) \tag{8}$$

$$\alpha_{knowledge-attn} = Softmax(v_L^K * tahn(W_q^K \cdot h_K^j + W_K^n \cdot h_t^S + b^K)) \tag{9}$$

Finally, we calculate the probability with feedforward network and softmax layer:

$$P = \sum_{mode=1}^{3} (Softmax(Feedforward(\sum_{i=1}^{I} \alpha_{dialogue-attn} \cdot h_D^i \oplus \sum_{j=1}^{P}$$
$$\alpha_{knowledge-attn} \cdot h_K^j \oplus h_t^S \oplus x_t))) \cdot \sum_{mode=1}^{3} \alpha^{mode} \tag{10}$$

while v_L^D, W_p^D, h_D^i, W_D^m, b^D, v_L^K, W_q^K, h_K^j, W_K^n, b^K are learnable parameters and h_t^S indicates the hidden state of an output response at time step t. And

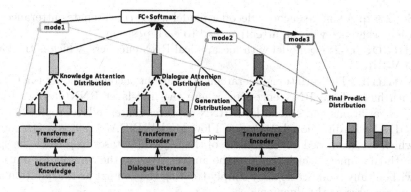

Fig. 4. The structure of DIALOGTRANSFORMERX. There are three modes: (1) Generating a word, (2) Copying a word from dialogue utterance, (3) Copying a word from unstructured external knowledge.

α^{mode} is a attention weights to compute word occurring probability in dialogue or knowledge.

5 Experimental Evaluation

5.1 Dataset

In this study, we use CMU-DoG as the document grounded dialog generation dataset for our experiments. In CMU-DoG, dialogues are about the contents of a specified document. In this dataset, the specified documents are Wikipedia articles about popular movies. The dataset contains 4112 conversations with an average of 21.43 turns per conversation. It is therefore worth noting that we only use dialogue that rating >1. See the Table 1 for more details.

5.2 Baselines

Five baseline methods are used in the comparison, including standard SEQ2SEQ [4], HRED [5], V-HRED [17], BiDAF [29] and standard Transformer.

Table 1. Statistics of CMU-DoG dataset

CMU-DoG	Training data	Validation data	Testing data
max turns	97	63	60
min turns	11	15	13
user1 saw	520	38	80
user2 saw	574	31	122
both saw	1125	88	200
rating >1	2219	157	402
utterance num	60562	4141	10727

1. **Seq2Seq:** A simple encoder-decoder model which concatenates utterances to a long sentence with an attentive read to each position.
2. **HRED:** SEQ2SEQ model with hierarchical RNN encoders, which is the basis of V-HRED.
3. **V-HRED:** The variational hierarchical recurrent encoder-decoder is a CVAE with hierarchical RNN encoders, where the first-layer RNN encodes token level variations and second-layer RNN captures sentence-level topic shifts.
4. **BiDAF:** Bi-directional Attention Flow Model (BiDAF) [29] is a QA model which was proposed in the context of the SQuAD dataset to predict the span in the document which contains the answer. We use their model for our task without any modifications by simply treating the context as the question and the resource as the document.
5. **Standard Transformer:** It is the traditional Transformer [22], which has not been modified.

5.3   Evaluation Metrics

We use both quantitative metrics and human judgements to evaluate the proposed models.

Automatic Evaluation: To automatically evaluate the fluency of the models, we use perplexity, which is generally used in statistical language modeling. BLEU is widely accepted evaluation methods in translation based on n-gram matching. Perplexity (PPL) measures how well the model predicts a response. A lower perplexity score indicates better generation performance.

Table 2. Evaluation results.

Model	PPL-T	BLEU (%)	Fluency	Knowledge capacity
SEQ2SEQ	79.1	0.89	2.33	2.43
vHRED	74.3	1.22	2.51	2.65
BiDAF	82.6	1.31	1.91	3.54
HRED w/ knowledge	84.8	1.24	2.43	2.85
HRED w/o knowledge	79.5	0.71	2.49	1.52
Transformer w/ knowledge	80.7	1.13	2.87	3.13
Transformer w/o knowledge	71.2	0.62	2.61	1.65
DIALOGTRANSFORMER	**50.3**	1.28	3.07	3.83
DIALOGTRANSFORMER-PLUS	53.2	**1.41**	3.15	3.92
DIALOGTRANSFORMERX	57.8	1.38	**3.23**	**3.96**

Human Judgment: In addition to automatic evaluation, we further recruited human annotators to judge the quality of the generated responses of different models. Volunteers were asked to rate the response on a scale of 1 to 5 on the following metrics: (a) Fluency (b) Knowledge Capacity of the generated response. Volunteers were asked to rate the response on a scale of 1 to 5. And 1 is the worst.

5.4 Implementation Details

In our model, the vocabulary size is 27316. We used a pre-trained 300 dimensional GloVe embedding. We utilized AdaGrad optimizer, and our batch size is 50, with learning rate 0.15 and gradient clipping 2. We trained our model in about 60 epochs and keep the best model on the validation set. For encoding step, Our self-attention structure has 6 heads. For decoding step, we adopt beam search with a beam size of 5 and select the top-1 generated reply for an evaluation. For the coefficient of a penalty term, we take the hyper-parameters which achieve the best performance on the validation set. Thus, we use a small grid search and choose λ as 0.95 and γ as 0.05. We employ a beam search of 5 to select our best response. Our knowledge-aware self-attention structure is implemented and available for download at GitHub[2].

5.5 Results and Analysis

The more precise quantitative evaluation results are summarized in Table 2. First of all, it can be seen that the knowledge is of great importance. And our proposed models all significantly outperform baselines. Due to space limitations, the case study is omitted. From comparison, we can see that for DIALOGTRANS-FORMER, document knowledge not only helps form the structure of responses, but also acts as "building blocks" and carrying responses with richer information. Furthermore, DIALOGTRANSFORMER-PLUS and DIALOGTRANSFORMERX can provide rich prior knowledge during generation step, which help to form a more on-topic and coherent response. For example, some detailed facts such as number and movie name can be generated by them, while this is rare for those baselines. On the other hand, although responses from SEQ2SEQ and HRED also bring some message because of high frequency, they carry little information and easily lead the dialogue to an end.

By the way, we do not adopt some previous work [14,16] as baselines because of the major difference between these data-aware tasks. Comparing with them directly makes little sense. The final results also illustrate that our incremental-based knowledge aware self-attention structure can deal with long context well, with a variant to address the OOV problem.

6 Conclusion

We propose a novel knowledge-aware self-attention approach for document grounded dialogue generation. Our approach fully leverage the semantics from

---

[2] https://github.com/tangxiangru/KAT.

conversational context as well as the given document to joint generate informative and coherent responses. The experiments on the CMU-DoG dataset show that our proposed model outperforms several state-of-the-art baselines. Our future work includes extending the knowledge from commonsense knowledge graph, and exploiting a better mechanism with reinforcement learning.

Acknowledgement. This work was supported by the National Natural Science Foundation of China (No. 61402191), the Fundamental Research Funds for the Central Universities (No. CCNU18TS044), and the Thirteen Five-year Research Planning Project of National Language Committee (No. WT135-11).

References

1. Zhou, K., Prabhumoye, S., Black, A.W.: A dataset for document grounded conversations (2018). arXiv preprint: arXiv:1809.07358
2. Cho, K., et al.: Learning phrase representations using RNN encoder-decoder for statistical machine translation (2014). arXiv preprint: arXiv:1406.1078
3. Cho, K., Courville, A., Bengio, Y.: Describing multimedia content using attention-based encoder-decoder networks. IEEE Trans. Multimed. **17**(11), 1875–1886 (2015)
4. Vinyals, O., Le, Q.: A neural conversational model (2015). arXiv preprint: arXiv:1506.05869
5. Serban, I.V., Sordoni, A., Bengio, Y., Courville, A., Pineau, J.: Building end-to-end dialogue systems using generative hierarchical neural network models. In: Thirtieth AAAI Conference on Artificial Intelligence, March 2016
6. Zhou, X., et al.: Multi-view response selection for human-computer conversation. In: Proceedings of the 2016 Conference on Empirical Methods in Natural Language Processing, pp. 372–381 (2016)
7. Chaudhuri, D., Kristiadi, A., Lehmann, J., Fischer, A.: Improving response selection in multi-turn dialogue systems (2018). arXiv preprint: arXiv:1809.03194
8. Serban, I.V., Lowe, R., Henderson, P., Charlin, L., Pineau, J.: A survey of available corpora for building data-driven dialogue systems (2015). arXiv preprint: arXiv:1512.05742
9. Chen, H., Liu, X., Yin, D., Tang, J.: A survey on dialogue systems: recent advances and new frontiers. ACM SIGKDD Explor. Newsl. **19**(2), 25–35 (2017)
10. Shang, L., Lu, Z., Li, H.: Neural responding machine for short-text conversation (2015). arXiv preprint: arXiv:1503.02364
11. Li, J., Galley, M., Brockett, C., Gao, J., Dolan, B.: A diversity-promoting objective function for neural conversation models (2015). arXiv preprint: arXiv:1510.03055
12. Sordoni, A., et al.: A neural network approach to context-sensitive generation of conversational responses (2015). arXiv preprint: arXiv:1506.06714
13. Ghosh, S., Chollet, M., Laksana, E., Morency, L.P., Scherer, S.: Affect-LM: a neural language model for customizable affective text generation (2017). arXiv preprint: arXiv:1704.06851
14. Zhou, H., Huang, M., Zhang, T., Zhu, X., Liu, B.: Emotional chatting machine: emotional conversation generation with internal and external memory. In: Thirty-Second AAAI Conference on Artificial Intelligence, April 2018
15. See, A., Liu, P.J., Manning, C.D.: Get to the point: summarization with pointer-generator networks (2017). arXiv preprint: arXiv:1704.04368

16. Dinan, E., Roller, S., Shuster, K., Fan, A., Auli, M., Weston, J.: Wizard of wikipedia: knowledge-powered conversational agents (2018). arXiv preprint: arXiv:1811.01241
17. Serban, I.V., et al.: A hierarchical latent variable encoder-decoder model for generating dialogues. In: Thirty-First AAAI Conference on Artificial Intelligence, February 2017
18. Xing, C., et al.: Topic aware neural response generation. In: Thirty-First AAAI Conference on Artificial Intelligence, February 2017
19. Ghazvininejad, M., et al.: A knowledge-grounded neural conversation model. In: Thirty-Second AAAI Conference on Artificial Intelligence, April 2018
20. Young, T., Cambria, E., Chaturvedi, I., Zhou, H., Biswas, S., Huang, M.: Augmenting end-to-end dialogue systems with commonsense knowledge. In: Thirty-Second AAAI Conference on Artificial Intelligence, April 2018
21. Zhou, H., Young, T., Huang, M., Zhao, H., Xu, J., Zhu, X.: Commonsense knowledge aware conversation generation with graph attention. In: IJCAI, pp. 4623–4629, July 2018
22. Vaswani, A., et al.: Attention is all you need. In: Advances in Neural Information Processing Systems, pp. 5998–6008 (2017)
23. Liu, S., Chen, H., Ren, Z., Feng, Y., Liu, Q., Yin, D.: Knowledge diffusion for neural dialogue generation. In: Proceedings of the 56th Annual Meeting of the Association for Computational Linguistics. Long Papers, vol. 1, pp. 1489–1498, July 2018
24. Sun, M., Li, X., Li, P.: Logician and orator: learning from the duality between language and knowledge in open domain. In: Proceedings of the 2018 Conference on Empirical Methods in Natural Language Processing, pp. 2119–2130 (2018)
25. Mihaylov, T., Frank, A.: Knowledgeable reader: enhancing cloze-style reading comprehension with external commonsense knowledge (2018). arXiv preprint: arXiv:1805.07858
26. Madotto, A., Wu, C.S., Fung, P.: Mem2Seq: effectively incorporating knowledge bases into end-to-end task-oriented dialog systems (2018). arXiv preprint: arXiv:1804.08217
27. Chen, Q., Zhu, X., Ling, Z.H., Inkpen, D., Wei, S.: Neural natural language inference models enhanced with external knowledge (2017). arXiv preprint: arXiv:1711.04289
28. Guan, J., Wang, Y., Huang, M.: Story ending generation with incremental encoding and commonsense knowledge (2018). arXiv preprint: arXiv:1808.10113
29. Seo, M., Kembhavi, A., Farhadi, A., Hajishirzi, H.: Bidirectional attention flow for machine comprehension (2016). arXiv preprint: arXiv:1611.01603

A Multi-View Spatial-Temporal Network for Vehicle Refueling Demand Inference

Bo Ma[1,2,3] , Yating Yang[1,2,3(✉)], Guangyi Zhang[1], Fan Zhao[1,3],
and Yi Wang[1,3]

[1] The Xinjiang Technical Institute of Physics and Chemistry,
Chinese Academy of Sciences, Urumqi 830011, Xinjiang, China
yangyt@ms.xjb.ac.cn
[2] University of the Chinese Academy of Sciences, Beijing 100049, China
[3] XinJiang Laboratory of Minority Speech and Language Information
Processing, Urumqi 830011, Xinjiang, China

Abstract. Petroleum station location selection is an important component to enabling public service in a smart city. While refueling data from petroleum stations is collected, vehicle refueling demand inference involves many other external features, such as POIs, road networks, and meteorological data. Traditional location selection approaches mostly rely on discrete features, which fail to model the complex non-linear spatial-temporal relations. We leverage both the information from petroleum stations and urban data that are closely related to refueling demand inference and design an end-to-end structure based on unique properties of spatio-temporal data. More specifically, we employ feedforward FC layers and LSTMs for modeling spatial and temporal features as well as capturing deep feature interactions. Experiments on real-world vehicle refueling dataset demonstrate the effectiveness of our approach over the state-of-the-art methods.

Keywords: Spatio-temporal data · Deep learning · Vehicle refueling ·
Demand inference · Location selection

1 Introduction

As a public infrastructure, the location selection of petroleum stations has an impact on the city's transportation and residents' daily lives. Much effort needs to be considered from inception till materialized for investing in a new place for a brick and mortar kind of establishment. Factors affecting the locational decision making includes external & internal environment, locational management activities and their portfolios [1]. Take petroleum station location selection for instance: Where should a new petroleum station be located? Is it near the main road or a residential area? What are the important aspects in the surrounding area that need to be observed in order to assure that it will maximize the convenience for the residents? These are part of the questions that need to be considered when choosing the location for new petroleum stations.

© Springer Nature Switzerland AG 2019
C. Douligeris et al. (Eds.): KSEM 2019, LNAI 11776, pp. 412–423, 2019.
https://doi.org/10.1007/978-3-030-29563-9_36

With the enhancement of urban perception, the collection and acquisition of spatio-temporal data has been greatly improved, which makes it becoming a valuable resource for spatio-temporal big data analytics. At the same time, the inherent heterogeneity and complicated relationships of spatio-temporal data also brings great challenges to traditional location selection (site selection) approaches. This research will leverage the availability of urban spatio-temporal data by exploiting the petroleum station internal characteristics and the external features (e.g., petroleum station data, POIs, road networks, and meteorological data) within the nearby area, and the main challenges come from the following three aspects:

(1) Different from facility location selection or business retail site selection, the location of petroleum stations could be any point on the map.
(2) The heterogeneity and geographical distribution of refueling data make it hard for applying traditional location selection (site selection) approaches.
(3) Traditional location selection approaches cannot handle urban spatio-temporal data in one framework simultaneously.

We address the aforementioned problems by introducing a multi-view spatial-temporal network. The complex nonlinear relations of both spatio features and temporal features are captured by harnessing the power of multi-view joint model. The biggest contribution of this paper is that we explore the use of multi-view network for modeling heterogeneous data (e.g., petroleum station data, POIs, road networks, and meteorological data) in a unified way. Experiments on real-world vehicle refueling dataset and the results demonstrate the superiority of our approach in demand inference performance.

The remainder of this paper is organized as follows: Sect. 2 summarizes the related work in different research fields and makes a comparison with our proposed approach. Section 3 describes some preliminaries and definitions of vehicle refueling demand inference problem. Section 4 introduces our proposed multi-view spatial-temporal network. Section 5 reports the experimental results to compare our approach's performance with some state-of-the-art algorithm. Finally, Sect. 6 concludes the paper.

2 Related Work

Our work involves two research areas: location selection and spatio-temporal data analytics.

The previous work on selecting locations are mainly using the traditional qualitative approach of interviewing, observation and survey [2]. The newer approaches of location analytics are using rich social media data such as Facebook [3] and Foursquare [4]. Another online resource is using the search query data from Baidu Maps [5]. Huang et al. [6] proposed an outdoor advertising display location selection using mobile phone data, Specifically, a continuous space maximal coverage model, the MCLP-complementary coverage (MCLP-CC), was utilized to search for the optimal locations for a given category of advertisements. Zhong et al. [7] solved electric vehicle charging station site selection problem by using an intuitionistic fuzzy projection-based approach. The above approaches take location selection task as a multi-criteria decision-making problem, which are not suitable for processing urban spatio-temporal data.

Traditional methods trade time series data and spatial data separately. Representatively, autoregressive integrated moving average (ARIMA) and its variants have been widely used in traffic prediction problem [8–10]. Recent advances in deep learning have shown superior performance on traditionally challenging tasks such as image vision and natural language processing fields [11]. This breakthrough inspires researchers to explore deep learning techniques on spatio-temporal analytics problems. Zhang et al. [12] proposed a deep spatio-temporal residual networks for citywide crowd flows prediction, by designing an end-to-end structure of ST-ResNet, they employed the residual neural network framework to model the temporal closeness, period, and trend properties of crowd traffic. Cheng et al. [13] proposed a neural attention model for urban air quality inference, they leveraged both the information from monitoring stations and urban data that are closely related to air quality, including POIs, road networks and meteorology, and proved that external information do has a positive impact on air quality inference. Yao et al. [14] explored taxi demand prediction problem by proposing a Deep Multi-View Spatial-Temporal Network (DMVST-Net) framework to model spatial and temporal relations simultaneously. Wang et al. [15] presented dynamic spatio-temporal graph-based CNNs (DST-GCNNs) by learning expressive features to represent spatio-temporal structures and predict future traffic from historical traffic flow. These attempts show superior performance compared with previous approaches based on traditional time series prediction methods. However, vehicle refueling demand inference for petroleum station is a brand new application area, and there is little research literature related to it.

In summary, the biggest difference of our proposed approach compared with the above literature is that we consider spatial relation, temporal sequential relation and external features in a joint deep learning framework.

3 Preliminaries

In this section, we first make some definitions of the vehicle refueling demand inference problem. We define the set of non-overlapping locations $L = \{l_1, l_2, \cdots, l_N\}$ as rectangle partition of a city followed previous studies [12, 14, 15], and the time intervals as $I = \{I_0, I_1, \cdots, I_T\}$. 1 h is set as the length of time interval. Given the set of locations L and time intervals T, we further make the following definitions.

Definition 1 (Vehicle Refueling Data): When a driver drives to the petroleum station to fill up a car, a refueling record is generated. For a specific petroleum station, its refueling data is measured by the total refueling volume during time interval t.

Definition 2 (POI): A point of interest (POI) represents a specific location, with name, category, coordinates and several auxiliary attributes. We denote by D_p the set of all POIs in a city.

Definition 3 (Road Network): A road network D_r consists of a set of linked road segments in a city. Each road segment includes features such as the numbers of roads, viaducts, intersections, overpasses, lanes, and streets.

Definition 4 (Meteorological Data): A meteorology dataset D_m includes district-level meteorological records of a city. Let D_m^t denote the real-time meteorological information like weather, temperature, pressure, humidity during time period t.

Definition 5 (Refueling Demand): The refueling demand is defined as the refueling volume of a particular petroleum station per time point. For simplicity, we use the index of time intervals t representing I_t, and the index of locations i representing l_i for rest of the paper.

Problem Statement: The demand inference problem aims to predict the demand at time interval $t + 1$ for not only existing petroleum stations but also for any other locations of the city, given the data until time interval t. In addition to historical temporal demand data, we also incorporate external features such as POI features, road features, meteorological features, and distance between petroleum stations as defined above. Consider a particular petroleum station, given its refueling data $D_s = \{D_s^t\}_{t=1}^{T}$, POI data D_p, road network D_r, and meteorology dataset $D_m = \{D_m^t\}_{t=1}^{T}$. We aim to inference vehicle refueling volume for any location l during time interval t.

In this paper, we aim to infer vehicle refueling demand based on the above heterogeneous data.

4 Proposed Multi-View Spatial-Temporal Network

4.1 Feature Extraction

We first introduce the features used in this paper. We focus on estimating vehicle refueling volume for location l with features within l's affecting regions. By default, the certain distance d is set to 2 km.

Meteorological Features X^m. Refueling status of petroleum stations is easily influenced by meteorological factors. We consider four meteorological features: weather, temperature, pressure, humidity in this paper. Among these features, weather is categorical with 12 categories, while the others are numerical. We adopt one-hot encoding to represent weather features. For numerical ones, we normalize their values to be in the range of [0, 1]. Features are extracted for each region periodically (e.g., every 1 h). X^{mt} denotes the set of meteorological features during time period t.

Road Network Features X^r. The conditions of road networks also affect the refueling status of petroleum stations. Seven features of road networks are considered: road sections, viaducts, intersections, overpasses, roads, lanes, and streets. To capture the intensiveness of road networks, we measure the number of the above features per category within a region.

POI Features X^p. Intuitively, regions having many residential areas and CBDs tend to have a higher demand for vehicle refueling. As POIs well capture the characteristics of locations, POI data is utilized for vehicle refueling demand inference. We consider a set

C^p of 13 POI categories (restaurant, hospital, sightseeing, park, carnie, supermarket, library, school, company, bus stop, subway station, residential area, and hotel) and compute the number of each POI category within a region as one feature. Let $X^p = \left\{ x_c^p \right\}_{c \in C^p}$ denote the POI features extracted for a location l.

Self Features X^d and X^a. For each petroleum station s, meteorological, road network, POI features X_s^m, X_s^r, and X_s^p are extracted from data within s's affecting region (2 km). We also consider two self-related features: X_s^d and X_s^v. X_s^d records the distance and direction of s to other petroleum stations (target location). And X_s^v contains a sequence of observed refueling volume values in s during time period t.

4.2   Proposed Multi-View Network

In this section, we provide details for our proposed multi-view spatio-temporal network. Figure 1 shows the architecture of our proposed model, which consists of two views: spatio view and temporal view.

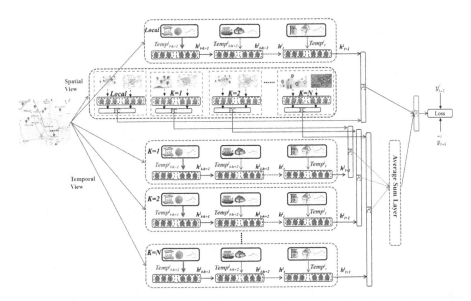

Fig. 1. The architecture of our proposed multi-view spatio-temporal network.

Spatial View

For non-sequential features related to spatially nearby regions $X_s^r \cup X_s^p \cup X_s^d$, we simply apply an individual stack of the fully connected (FC) layers (**basic FC layer**) to learn high-order interactions from each feature group.

$$
z_*^m = \begin{cases} \phi \left(W_*^{(m)} \cdot \left(X_*^p \oplus X_*^r \oplus X_*^d \right) + b_*^{(m)} \right), m = 1 \\ \phi \left(W_*^{(m)} \cdot z_*^{m-1} + b_*^{(m)} \right), 1 \leq m \leq L \end{cases}
\tag{1}
$$

Where * denotes l for local features or s for station-oriented features, and L is the number of FC layer. ϕ is the activation function, i.e., ReLU.

Temporal View

In our case, we adopt recurrent neural networks (RNN) to encode sequential features. Sequential features often exhibit long periodicity, however, traditional RNN can hardly capture long-term dependencies because of gradient vanishing and exploding problems [16]. Hence Long Short-Term Memory (LSTM) [17] is employed to encode our sequential features $X_s^m \cup X_s^v$.

LSTM learns sequential correlations stably by maintaining a memory cell c_t in time interval t, which can be regarded as an accumulation of previous sequential information. Each memory cell is associated with input gate i, forget gate f and output gate o to control the flow of sequential information. In our study, consider sequences $\{X^m\}_{t=1}^T$ of meteorological features and $\{X^v\}_{t=1}^T$ of refueling volume features. The LSTM maps the input sequences to an output sequence as follows:

$$i^t = \sigma\left(W_{ix} \cdot (X^{mt} \oplus X^{vt}) + W_{ih} \cdot h^{t-1} + W_{ic} \odot c^{t-1} + b_i\right) \tag{2}$$

$$f^t = \sigma\left(W_{fx} \cdot (X^{mt} \oplus X^{vt}) + W_{fh} \cdot h^{t-1} + W_{fc} \odot c^{t-1} + b_f\right) \tag{3}$$

$$c^t = f^t \odot c^{t-1} + i^t \odot \tanh\left(W_{cx} \cdot (X^{mt} \oplus X^{vt}) + W_{ch} \cdot h^{t-1} + b_c\right) \tag{4}$$

$$o^t = \sigma\left(W_{ox} \cdot (X^{mt} \oplus X^{vt}) + W_{oh} \cdot h^{t-1} + W_{oc} \odot c^{t-1} + b_o\right) \tag{5}$$

$$h^t = o^t \odot \tanh(c^t) \tag{6}$$

Where $X^{mt} \oplus X^{vt}$ and h^t are the concatenation sequential input element and the corresponding memory cell output activation vector at time t. The W terms denote weight matrices, and b terms are bias vectors. $\odot$ denotes the Hadamard product and σ represents the sigmoid function.

Putting Together

Another FC layer (**fusion FC layer**) on top of the basic FC and LSTM layers is added to capture interactions among sequential and non-sequential features.

$$z_*^n = \begin{cases} \phi\left(W_*^{(n)} \cdot \left(z_*^{(L)} \oplus h_*^T\right) + b_*^{(n)}\right), n = L+1 \\ \phi\left(W_*^{(n)} \cdot z_*^{n-1} + b_*^{(n)}\right), L+2 \le n \le L+L' \end{cases} \tag{7}$$

As mentioned above, * denotes l or s, and L' represents the number of high level FC layer.

To combine the latent features for location l and the average sum high-level features $\{z_s^{(L+L')}\}_{s \in S}$, a hidden concatenation layer is added to learn high-order interactions:

$$z_f = \phi\left(W_f \cdot \left(z_l^{(L+L')} \oplus \left\{z_s^{(L+L')}\right\}_{s \in S}\right) + b_f\right) \tag{8}$$

At last, the output vector of the fusion layer z_f is transformed to the final inference score:

$$\widehat{y} = w_i^T \cdot z_f + b_i \tag{9}$$

Where w_i and b_i are the weight vector and bias scalar parameters.
In our case, Dropout and L_2 regularization are adopted for loss function to prevent possible overfitting problem.

$$\mathcal{L}(\theta) = \sum_{i=1}^{N} \left(y_{t+1}^i - \widehat{y}_{t+1}^i \right)^2 + c \|W\|^2 \tag{10}$$

Algorithm 1 outlines our proposed Multi-View Network training process as follows.

Algorithm 1: Training Pipeline of Our Proposed Multi-View Network

Input: Meteorological features X^m;
  Road Network features X^r;
  POI features X^p;
  Self features X^d and X^a

Output: Learned Multi-View Network

1. $\mathcal{D} \leftarrow \phi$

// construct spatial views

2. for *local station l and K (1 ≤ K ≤ N)nearby stations* **do**

3.   apply stacked FC layers to learn high-order interactions from $X_*^r \cup X_*^p \cup X_*^d$ by Eq. (1)

4. end

// construct temporal views

5. for $1 \le t \le T$ **do**

6.   **for** *local station l and K (1 ≤ K ≤ N)nearby stations* **do**

7.   apply LSTMs to generate outputs h_{t+1}^* by Eq. (2-6)

8.   **end**

// putting spatial views and temporal views together

9.   combine the latent features for location l and the average sum high-level features for time t by Eq. (7-8)

10.   put an training instance into $\mathcal{D}$

11. end

12. initialize all learnable parameters θ in the Multi-View Network

13. repeat

14.   randomly select a batch of instances $\mathcal{D}_b$ from $\mathcal{D}$

15.   find θ by minimizing the objective Eq. (10) with $\mathcal{D}_b$

16. until *stopping criteria is met*

---

5 Experiments

5.1 Experimental Settings

DataSet Description
In this paper, we use a large-scale vehicle refueling dataset collected from petroleum stations along with the related heterogeneous data in Urumqi, China.

(1) Vehicle refueling data: The vehicle refueling data was collected by 161 petroleum stations from 2019/01/25 to 2019/03/26, the stream data is real-time and we cut them by time interval of 1 h.
(2) Meteorological data: The meteorological data was downloaded from meteomanz.com and consists of hour-level meteorological records. Weather, temperature, pressure, and humidity are adopted as the meteorological features.
(3) POI data and road Network data: We downloaded POIs and road networks in Urumqi from Baidu Map APIs and obtain 194,020 POIs and 32,873 road marks.
(4) Distance and direction data: We choose the size of affected area for location l as 2 km × 2 km, the distance and direction of each petroleum station in this area are recorded.

Preprocessing and Parameters
Input values were normalized to [0, 1] by Min-Max normalization on the training set. And all experiments were run on a linux server with four NVIDEA TESLA K80 GPUs.

The number of neurons of the basic FC layer (Inside spatial view, $L = 1$) was set to 100 per layer, and LSTMs inside temporal view were set to two layers with 300 memory cells per layer. Then the number of neurons of the fusion FC layers ($L' = 2$) combining the output of spatial view and temporal view were set to 200 per layer.

Evaluation Metric
We use mean average percentage error (MAPE) and rooted mean square error (RMSE) to evaluate the performance of our proposed framework, which are defined as follows:

$$MAPE = \frac{1}{N} \sum_{i=1}^{N} \frac{\left| \widehat{y}_{t+1}^{i} - y_{t+1}^{i} \right|}{y_{t+1}^{i}} \tag{11}$$

$$RMSE = \sqrt{\frac{1}{N} \sum_{i=1}^{N} \left(\widehat{y}_{t+1}^{i} - y_{t+1}^{i} \right)^2} \tag{12}$$

Where N is total number of the test samples, $\widehat{y}_{t+1}^{i}$ and y_{t+1}^{i} mean the inference value and real value for time interval $t + 1$.

Methods for Comparison
We compare our proposed framework with the following two methods.

- Long Short-Term Memory (LSTM): LSTM is an artificial recurrent neural network architecture used in the field of deep learning, its networks are well-suited to classifying, processing and making predictions based on time series data.
- Bidirectional LSTM (Bi-LSTM) [18]: Bi-LSTM models sequences along both forward and backward directions and are generally known to perform better because it captures a richer representation of the data.

5.2   Experimental Results

Table 1 gives the comparison between our network and aforementioned baselines on both MAPE and RMSE metrics. From Table 1 we can observe that our network achieves the lowest MAPE (41.99%) and the lowest RMSE (0.0963) among all the methods, which is 79.78% (MAPE) and 8.62% (RMSE) relative improvement over the best performance among baseline methods.

Table 1. Comparison with different baselines.

Method	MAPE	RMSE
LSTM	76.32%	0.1052
Bi-LSTM	75.49%	0.1046
Proposed network	41.99%	0.0963

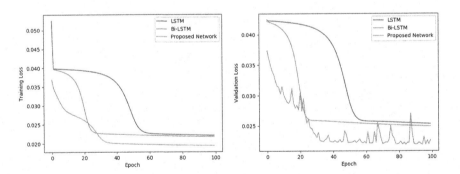

Fig. 2. Training Loss and Validation Loss of baselines and our proposed network.

From Fig. 2 we can see that the loss curve of our proposed network converges faster than LSTM and Bi-LSTM on both training dataset and validation dataset. Figure 3 shows the convergence curve of LSTM, Bi-LSTM and our proposed network, we can also observe that our approach achieves the fastest convergence rate and the lowest RMSE.

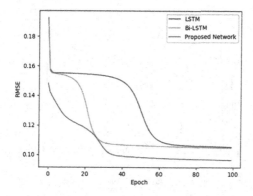

Fig. 3. RMSE of baselines and our proposed network.

Figure 4 shows MAPE of baselines and our proposed network on seven different weeks, and our proposed network significantly outperforms the other two methods in six weeks of seven. When we remove the external features such as POIs, road networks, and meteorological features, our network will degenerate into LSTMs. And the comparisons of the above experimental results indicate that external features do have positive impacts on vehicle refueling demand inference.

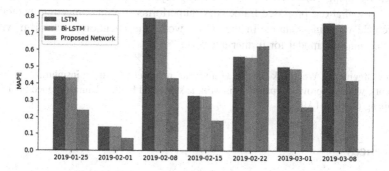

Fig. 4. MAPE of baselines and our proposed network on different weeks.

Figure 5 visually shows the comparison of ground truth refueling volume with predictions of above mentioned three methods. From Fig. 5 we can observe that our approach does not achieve significantly better results than the other two methods on the prediction curve, which indicates that there is still room for improvement.

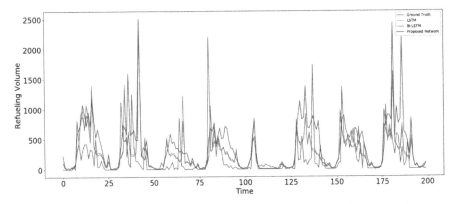

Fig. 5. The comparison of ground truth refueling volume with predictions of different methods.

6 Conclusion

In this paper, a multi-view spatial-temporal network for vehicle refueling demand inference is proposed in order to choose the optimal location for new petroleum stations. Our approach integrates heterogeneous urban data and extracts important self-features by combining spatial view and temporal view. We model static and sequential features by using stacked FC layers, LSTM layers respectively. The experimental results show that our proposed framework outperforms several competing methods on real vehicle refueling dataset. In the future work, the attention mechanism will be integrated into the model for further attempts.

Acknowledgement. We thank all the anonymous reviewers for their insightful and helpful comments, which improve the paper. This work is supported by the Natural Science Foundation of Xinjiang (2019D01A92).

References

1. Hernandez, T., Bennison, D.: The art and science of retail location decisions. Int. J. Retail Distrib. Manag. **28**(8), 357–367 (2000)
2. Waxman, L.: The coffee shop: social and physical factors influencing place attachment. J. Inter. Des. **31**(3), 35–53 (2006)
3. Lin, J., Oentaryo, R., Lim, E.P., Vu, C., Vu, A., Kwee, A.: Where is the goldmine? Finding promising business locations through Facebook data analytics. In: Proceedings of the 27th ACM Conference on Hypertext and Social Media, pp. 93–102. ACM, New York (2016)
4. Karamshuk, D., Noulas, A., Scellato, S., Nicosia, V., Mascolo, C.: Geo-spotting: mining online location-based services for optimal retail store placement. In: Proceedings of the 19th ACM SIGKDD International Conference on Knowledge Discovery and Data Mining, pp. 793–801. ACM, New York (2013)
5. Xu, M., Wang, T., Wu, Z., Zhou, J., Li, J., Wu, H.: Store location selection via mining search query logs of Baidu maps (2016). arXiv:1606.03662

6. Huang, M., Fang, Z., Xiong, S., Zhang, T.: Interest-driven outdoor advertising display location selection using mobile phone data. J. IEEE Access **7**, 30878–30889 (2019)
7. Zhong, L., Wu, Z.: Site selection of public fast electric vehicle charging station by using an intuitionistic fuzzy projection-based approach. In: Proceedings of International Conference on Management Science and Engineering, pp. 1688–1696 (2017)
8. Li, X., et al.: Prediction of urban human mobility using large-scale taxi traces and its applications. J. Front. Comput. Sci. **6**(1), 111–121 (2012)
9. Moreira-Matias, L., Gama, J., Ferreira, M., Mendes-Moreira, J., Damas, L.: Predicting taxi-passenger demand using streaming data. J. IEEE Trans. Intell. Transp. Syst. **14**(3), 1393–1402 (2013)
10. Shekhar, S., Williams, B.M.: Adaptive seasonal time series models for forecasting short-term traffic flow. J. Transp. Res. Rec. **2024**, 116–125 (2008)
11. LeCun, Y., Bengio, Y., Hinton, G.: Deep learning. J. Nat. **521**(7553), 436–444 (2015)
12. Zhang, J., Zheng, Y., Qi, D.: Deep spatio-temporal residual networks for citywide crowd flows prediction. In: Proceedings of the 31st AAAI Conference on Artificial Intelligence, pp. 1655–1661 (2017)
13. Cheng, W., Shen, Y., Zhu, Y., Huang, L.: A neural attention model for urban air quality inference: learning the weights of monitoring stations. In: Proceedings of the 32nd AAAI Conference on Artificial Intelligence, pp. 2151–2158 (2018)
14. Yao, H., et al.: Deep multi-view spatial-temporal network for taxi demand prediction. In: Proceedings of the 32nd AAAI Conference on Artificial Intelligence, pp. 2588–2595 (2018)
15. Wang, M., Lai, B., Jin, Z., Gong, X., Huang, J., Hua, X.: Dynamic spatio-temporal graph-based CNNs for traffic prediction (2018). arXiv:1812.02019
16. Graves, A.: Generating sequences with recurrent neural networks (2013). arXiv:1308.0850
17. Hochreiter, S., Schmidhuber, J.: Long short-term memory. J. Neural Comput. **9**(8), 1735–1780 (1997)
18. Huang, Z., Xu, W., Yu, K.: Bidirectional LSTM-CRF models for sequence tagging (2015). arXiv:1508.01991

Correction to: A Distributed Topic Model for Large-Scale Streaming Text

Yicong Li(iD), Dawei Feng, Menglong Lu, and Dongsheng Li

Correction to:
Chapter "A Distributed Topic Model for Large-Scale Streaming Text" in: C. Douligeris et al. (Eds.): *Knowledge Science, Engineering and Management*, **LNAI 11776,**
https://doi.org/10.1007/978-3-030-29563-9_4

The book was inadvertently published with an uncorrected version. The following corrections should have been carried out before publication:

1. Page 42: Sentence "By computing the natural gradient, corpus-level parameters are updated according to Eq. (Error! Reference source not found)–Eq. (17)." Correctly it should read "By computing the natural gradient, corpus-level parameters are updated according to Eqs. (17)–(19)."
2. Page 48: Reference [18] was inserted in the list of references but not cited in the text. It should be added in the text. The wrong sentence was on page 44 reading: "PubMed [17] is with regard to medicine papers containing 21,148,298 documents, and a vocabulary size of 196,425." Correctly it should read: "PubMed [18] is with regard to medicine papers containing 21,148,298 documents, and a vocabulary size of 196,425."
3. Page 48: The references [19, 20] were inserted in the list but not cited in the text and should have been deleted. References [21, 22] in the reference list and the corresponding citations of them in the text have been adjusted.

The updated version of this chapter can be found at
https://doi.org/10.1007/978-3-030-29563-9_4

© Springer Nature Switzerland AG 2019
C. Douligeris et al. (Eds.): KSEM 2019, LNAI 11776, p. C1, 2019.
https://doi.org/10.1007/978-3-030-29563-9_37

Author Index

Printed in the United States
By Bookmasters